GERHARD VON RAD

GENESIS

THE OLD TESTAMENT LIBRARY

GERHARD VON RAD

GENESIS

A Commentary

REVISED EDITION

The Westminster Press
Philadelphia

Second printing, 1974

Original translation by John H. Marks from the German *Das erste Buch Mose, Genesis* (Das Alte Testament Deutsch 2–4) published by Vandenhoeck & Ruprecht, Göttingen. Text revised on the basis of the ninth German edition, 1972.

Published by The Westminster Press®
Philadelphia, Pennsylvania

PRINTED IN THE UNITED STATES OF AMERICA

Library of Congress Cataloging in Publication Data

Rad, Gerhard von, 1901–1971.
Genesis: a commentary.

(The Old Testament library)
Translation of Das erste Buch Mose: Genesis, v. 2–4 of Das Alte Testament deutsch. Text revised on the basis of the 9th German ed., 1972.
Bibliography: p.
1. Bible. O. T. Genesis—Commentaries. I. Bible. O. T. Genesis. English. Revised standard. 1973. II. Title. III. Series.
BS1235.3.R3213 1973 222′.11′07 72–6413
ISBN 0–664–20957–2

CONTENTS

Abbreviations 8

Publisher's Note 9

Foreword to the First Edition 11

I. Introduction 13

1. Genesis as part of the Hexateuch 13
2. The three narrative sources 24
3. The theological problem of the Yahwist 29
4. Hermeneutical problems of the Genesis narratives 31

II. The Biblical Primeval History 45

1. The creation of the world. Chs. 1.1 to 2.4a (P) 46
2. Genealogical table of the patriarchs from Adam to Noah. Ch. 5 67
3. The Yahwistic story of Paradise. Ch. 2.4b–25 73
4. The story of the Fall. Ch. 3 86
5. The story of Cain and Abel. Ch. 4.1–16 102
6. The genealogy of the Kenites. Ch. 4.17–26 109
7. The angel marriages. Ch. 6.1–4 113
8. The prologue to the Flood. Ch. 6.5–8 116
9. The Flood (J) 118
10. The epilogue to the Flood. Ch. 8.21–22 121
11. The Flood (P) 125
12. God's covenant with Noah. Ch. 9.1–17 130
13. Noah's curse and blessing. Ch. 9.18–29 134
14. The table of nations (P) 139
15. Fragments of the Yahwistic table of nations 145
16. The story of the Tower of Babel and the confusion of language. Ch. 11.1–9 147
17. The fathers from Shem to Abraham. (P) Ch. 11.10–27, 31–32 155
18. Abraham's origin and call. (J) Chs. 11.28–30; 12.1–3 158
19. Abraham's departure. (J) Ch. 12.4–9 161

III. The Biblical Patriarchal History 164

1. Abraham and Sarah in Egypt. Chs. 12.10 to 13.1 167
2. The separation from Lot. Ch. 13.2–18 170

3. Abraham's victory over the eastern kings and his encounter with Melchizedek. Ch. 14 174
4. God's promise and covenant with Abraham. Ch. 15 181
5. Hagar. Ishmael's birth. Ch. 16 190
6. God's covenant with Abraham. Institution of circumcision. Ch. 17.1–14 197
7. The promise of a son. Ch. 17.15–27 202
8. God's visit with Abraham. Ch. 18.1–16 203
9. God's soliloquy. Ch. 18.17–19 209
10. Abraham's dialogue with God. Ch. 18.20–33 210
11. Sodom's destruction. Lot's deliverance. Ch. 19.1–29 215
12. Lot's daughters. Ch. 19.30–38 222
13. Abraham and Sarah in Gerar. Ch. 20 225
14. Isaac's birth. Ishmael's expulsion. Ch. 21.1–21 230
15. Abraham and Abimelech of Gerar. Ch. 21.22–34 235
16. The great temptation. Ch. 22.1–19 237
17. Nahor's descendants. Ch. 22.20–24 245
18. Sarah's death and the purchase of the burial plot. Ch. 23 245
19. The matchmaking. Ch. 24 250
20. Keturah's sons. Abraham's death. Ishmael's descendants. Ch. 25.1–18 260
21. The birth of Esau and Jacob. The sale of the birthright. Ch. 25.19–34 264
22. Isaac stories. Ch. 26 268
23. The cunning acquisition of the blessing. Ch. 27.1–45 274
24. Jacob's departure for Aram. Chs. 27.46 to 28.9 281
25. Jacob's dream in Bethel. Ch. 28.10–22 282
26. Jacob's arrival at Laban's house. Ch. 29.1–14 287
27. Jacob's marriage to Leah and Rachel. Ch. 29.15–30 289
28. The birth and naming of Jacob's children. Chs. 29.31 to 30.24 292
29. Jacob's wealth. Ch. 30.25–43 297
30. Jacob's flight; his contract with Laban. Ch. 31 303
31. The angels of Mahanaim. Ch. 32.1–2 313
32. Jacob's preparations to meet Esau. Ch. 32.3–21 316
33. Jacob's struggle at Penuel. Ch. 32.22–32 319
34. Jacob's meeting with Esau. Ch. 33 326
35. The rape of Dinah. Ch. 34 329
36. Jacob's return to Bethel. Ch. 35.1–8, 14–15 335
37. God's appearance at Bethel. Ch. 35.9–13 338
38. Benjamin's birth, Jacob's sons, Isaac's death. Ch. 35.16–29 339
39. Edomite lists. Chs. 36.1 to 37.1 342
40. The story of Joseph 347
    a. Joseph's dreams and sale into Egypt. Ch. 37.2–36 348

41. Judah and Tamar. Ch. 38 355
b. Joseph's temptation. Ch. 39 362
c. The interpretations of the dreams in prison. Ch. 40 368
d. The interpretation of Pharaoh's dream. Joseph's elevation to power. Ch. 41 372
e. The brothers' first journey to Egypt. Ch. 42 379
f. The brothers' second journey to Egypt. Ch. 43 384
g. The final test of the brothers. Ch. 44 389
h. The recognition. Ch. 45 395
i. Jacob's removal to Egypt. Ch. 46 400
k. Jacob before Pharaoh. Joseph's agrarian policy. Ch. 47.1–27 404
l. The blessing of Ephraim and Manasseh. Chs. 47.28 to 48.22 411
m. Jacob's blessing. Ch. 49.1–28a 419
n. Jacob's death and burial. Joseph's forgiveness. Chs. 49.28b to 50.26 428

ABBREVIATIONS

ANET	James B. Pritchard, *Ancient Near Eastern Texts Relating to the Old Testament*. Princeton University Press, 2d ed., 1955
AOT	*Altorientalische Texte*, ed. Hugo Gressmann. Walter de Gruyter & Company, Berlin & Leipzig, 2d ed., 1926
AOB	*Altorientalische Bilder*, ed. Hugo Gressmann. Walter de Gruyter & Company, 2d ed., 1927
ATD	*Das Alte Testament Deutsch*, V. Herntrich and A. Weiser, eds. Vandenhoeck & Ruprecht, Göttingen
BH	*Biblia Hebraica*, 3d ed. by Rud. Kittel, ed. by A. Alt and O. Eissfeldt. Priv. Württ. Bibelanstalt, Stuttgart, 1945
BL	Hans Bauer-Pontus Leander, *Historische Grammatik der hebräischen Sprache des Alten Testamentes*. M. Niemeyer, Halle, 1922
Del.	Franz Delitzsch, *Neuer Commentar über die Genesis*. Dörffling und Franke, Leipzig, 1887
Di.	August Dillmann, *Die Genesis*. S. Hirzel, Leipzig, 1892
Fr.	Hellmut Frey, *Das Buch der Anfänge*. Calwer Vereinsbh., Stuttgart, 1935
G.A.	Eduard Meyer, *Geschichte des Altertums*, 2d ed. J. G. Cotta Nachf., Stuttgart, 1909
Gu.	Hermann Gunkel, *Genesis, übersetzt und erklärt*, 5th ed. Vandenhoeck & Ruprecht, Göttingen, 1922
Jac.	Benno Jacob, *Das erste Buch der Tora, Genesis*. Berlin, 1934
JBL	*Journal of Biblical Literature*
L	Luther's translation of the Bible
LXX	Greek translation of the Old Testament (Septuagint)
MT	Masoretic Text, Hebrew Bible
Pr.	Otto Procksch, *Die Genesis*, 3d ed. A. Deichert, Leipzig, 1924
RSV	Revised Standard Version
SVT	Supplements to *Vetus Testamentum*
WA	Weimar Edition of Luther's works
ZAW	*Zeitschrift für die Alttestamentliche Wissenschaft*
ZDMG	*Zeitschrift der Deutschen Morgenländischen Gesellschaft*
Zi.	Walther Zimmerli, *1. Mos. 1–11* (Prophezei). Zwingli-Verlag, Zürich, 1943

PUBLISHER'S NOTE

THE LAST WORK undertaken by Professor von Rad before his death in the autumn of 1971 was a revision of his commentary on Genesis, the first part of which originally appeared in German as long ago as 1949. He completed the work personally, but the degree of revision he felt to be necessary varied through the book. The Introduction has been very extensively rewritten, and the early chapters of the commentary have been reworked equally thoroughly. In the later part of the book, however, alterations become much less frequent, apart from a new postscript to the Joseph story, and many of them concern little more than points of style.

The German text was revised in the context of a resetting of the whole commentary in a new format, where minor alterations caused no problem. These alterations do, however, cause difficulties for the English edition. It would have been possible to follow the German revision entirely, but to have reset the whole of the text would have been very costly indeed and would have increased the price of what has become a classic textbook beyond all reason. We have therefore compromised. The first part of the book has been reset, but Part III, from Genesis 12 onwards, has only been altered to the extent possible in a photographic reproduction of the text. We believe that in this way we have incorporated Professor von Rad's last thoughts in substance, if not to the final detail.

As in earlier editions, the biblical text used is that of the Revised Standard Version. It will be clear where von Rad's proposed translation, printed in the German text of his commentary, differs materially. Italic type has been used to distinguish the Priestly document (P) from the earlier strata of Genesis.

March 1972

FOREWORD TO THE FIRST EDITION

THE FOLLOWING COMMENTARY, like every other, results from a very definite phase of our scientific knowledge with all its limits and privileges. An obligatory examination of the very different hexateuchal sources is one of the points at which our exposition reveals the time of its writing. Precisely this commentary may make one perceive that source analysis is not the final conclusion of wisdom; but once we know about the differences in the sources we can no longer have the whole without knowing the exact nature of its parts. This book, therefore, often speaks about the "Yahwist," about "saga," etc. A great deal of effort has been expended to give the reader as clear an idea as possible of the kind of literature with which he is dealing in each instance. If he learns, for instance, that a text must be considered a narrative saga or that it is sacred Priestly doctrine, then this knowledge about the specific character of the literature will have its imperceptible effect on the understanding of the heart of the matter.

This interest in literary criticism may seem antiquated from a certain theological viewpoint, but the author is prepared on the opposite side for objection at a point where he is especially sure of himself, namely, the reproof that he has "overinterpreted" the texts and "gone beyond" their content. Now, strangely enough, we know a great deal about the meaning of the ancient traditions in their *pre*literary form, but we are largely unable to fix their substance *after* they became literature. We must reckon with a high degree of spiritualization and rearranging of the ancient structure of meaning, a fact that the complicated combination of the ancient materials into large theological compositions makes clear. The fear of acknowledging a sublime spirituality (*Geistigkeit*) "already" in the early royal period is, in our opinion, misplaced scientific method. "The spirit was already complete at an early period." (J. Burckhardt.)

Since the plan of the entire series was that the exposition should be readable for nontheologians, limits were set to the discussion of individual problems, namely, those of philological and archaeological nature. The theologian, especially the student, must by all means consult in addition a more exhaustive scientific commentary.

GERHARD VON RAD

Göttingen, February, 1949

INTRODUCTION

1. GENESIS AS PART OF THE HEXATEUCH

GENESIS IS NOT AN INDEPENDENT BOOK that can be interpreted by itself. On the contrary, the books Genesis to Joshua (Hexateuch) in their present form constitute an immense connected narrative. It matters little whether one is more interested in the great individual narrative sources that make up the book or in the composition as a whole which arose when a final redactor skillfully combined these individual sources. In either case, whereever he begins, the reader must keep in mind the narrative as a whole and the contexts into which all the individual parts fit and from which they are to be understood. The present, pronounced division of this originally unified material into the books of Genesis, Exodus, Leviticus, etc., is merely a subsequent partition of the massive material into single intelligible sections; one must not lose sight of the great unit of which these are only parts.

A work of such dimension and with such remarkable content—it takes us from Creation to the entrance of the tribes into Canaan—must be investigated carefully with regard to its purpose and theological character. Much has already been done with respect to its literary characteristics, and today we understand tolerably the nature and origin of many individual bits of material. But there has been much too little inquiry into what the Hexateuch is as a whole, what its basic theme really is, and therefore the exposition of Genesis has often been somewhat atomistic. Little, if any, attention has been paid to the fact that this book is significantly related to those events reported in the later books of the Hexateuch.

The basic theme of the Hexateuch may be stated as follows: God, the Creator of the world, called the patriarchs and promised them the Land of Canaan. When Israel became numerous in Egypt, God led the people through the wilderness with wonderful demonstrations of grace; then after their lengthy wandering he gave them under Joshua the Promised Land. If we compare this table of contents with the Hexateuch itself, we are struck with the incongruity between the theme and its actual development, with this colossal massing and arranging of the most varied kinds of material around so simple a basic design. From this observation we draw an immediately illuminating conclusion: this way of structuring the material for so simple a theme must represent a final conception, the last and last possible. This baroque fashioning of the basic theme into such gigantic proportions, when considered from the viewpoint of the history of literature, cannot have been a first conception, not even one that blossomed into classic maturity and balance. Rather, it is a final conception that has burgeoned from earlier stages to the limits of the possible and readable.

If we examine the Old Testament with the question of the theme of the Hexateuch in mind, our attention is drawn to a whole series of shorter or longer texts. For example, the prayer to be spoken when the first fruits were delivered to the sanctuary is especially ancient:

> A wandering Aramean was my father; and he went down into Egypt and sojourned there, few in number; and there he became a nation, great, mighty, and populous. And the Egyptians treated us harshly, and afflicted us, and laid upon us hard bondage. Then we cried to the Lord the God of our fathers, and the Lord heard our voice, and saw our affliction, our toil, and our oppression; and the Lord brought us out of Egypt with a mighty hand and an outstretched arm, with great terror, with signs and wonders; and he brought us into this place and gave us this land, a land flowing with milk and honey.—Deut. 26.5–9.

There can be no doubt that this is how men really spoke in ancient times, and we see that within the cultic framework it was customary, among other things, to recite a short form of the sacred history as a confession. For what we find here is a kind of credo, not a personal prayer of thanksgiving. There is no divinely addressed Thou. Rather, the speaker recapitulates the great, sacred facts that constitute the community. He abstains from all individual concerns and in this moment identifies himself completely with the community; that is, he makes a confession of faith.

A similar summary of the sacred history in a creed occurs in Deut.

6.20–24. The text, which is now completely imbedded in the great paraenetic context, is easily recognizable as having been originally independent, with regard both to form and to content.

> When your son asks you in time to come, "What is the meaning of the testimonies and the statutes and the ordinances which the Lord our God has commanded you?", then you shall say to your son, "We were Pharaoh's slaves in Egypt; and the Lord brought us out of Egypt with a mighty hand; and the Lord showed signs and wonders, great and grievous, against Egypt and against Pharaoh and all his household, before our eyes; and he brought us out from there, that he might bring us in and give us the land which he swore to give to our fathers. And the Lord commanded us to do all these statutes, to fear the Lord our God, for our good always, that he might preserve us alive, as at this day."

We may add still a third example, the speech of Joshua before the assembly at Shechem. It is somewhat more extensive because of a few embellishments, but there can be no doubt that basically this historical review is not a distinct literary creation. Here too, apparently, an essentially fixed form is used, a form with which one can take only minor liberties.

> Thus says the Lord, the God of Israel, "Your fathers lived of old beyond the Euphrates, Terah, the father of Abraham and of Nahor; and they served other gods. Then I took your father Abraham from beyond the River and led him through all the land of Canaan, and made his offspring many. I gave him Isaac; and to Isaac I gave Jacob and Esau. And I gave Esau the hill country of Seir to possess, but Jacob and his children went down to Egypt. And I sent Moses and Aaron, and I plagued Egypt with what I did in the midst of it; and afterwards I brought you out. Then I brought your fathers out of Egypt, and you came to the sea; and the Egyptians pursued your fathers with chariots and horsemen to the Red Sea. And when they cried to the Lord, he put darkness between you and the Egyptians, and made the sea come upon them and cover them; and your eyes saw what I did to Egypt; and you lived in the wilderness a long time. Then I brought you to the land of the Amorites, who lived on the other side of the Jordan; they fought with you, and I gave them into your hand, and you took possession of their land, and I destroyed them before you. Then Balak the son of Zippor, king of Moab, arose and fought against Israel; and he sent and invited Balaam the son of Beor to curse you, but I would not listen to Balaam; therefore he blessed you; so I delivered you out of his hand. And you went over the Jordan and came to Jericho, and the men of Jericho fought against you, and also the Amorites, the Perizzites, the Canaanites, the Hittites, the Girgashites, the Hivites, and the Jebusites; and I gave them into your hand. And I sent the hornet before you, which drove them out before you, the two kings of the Amorites; it was not by

your sword or by your bow. I gave you a land on which you had not labored, and cities which you had not built, and you dwell therein; you eat the fruit of vineyards and oliveyards which you did not plant."—Josh. 24.2–13.

None of the three passages mentioned above contains even a parenthetical recollection of anything historical; rather, each one is considered a recitation, elevated in form and in direct discourse. Obviously they are constructed according to a scheme, i.e., they follow a canonical pattern of the sacred history, long established in all its essentials. Though this virtually creed-like recitation of the sacred facts may appear far removed from our Hexateuch in its final form, still the uniformity here and there in thought and theme is often surprising. At bottom there is one and the same extremely simple train of thought, and Josh. 24.2–13 can be characterized as a "Hexateuch" *in nuce*. If one now surveys the beginning and end of the process, one gains some notion of the persevering power of the essential content of Old Testament faith. For no matter how numerous the additions to it are or how intensive its revision is, still there is always a fixed datum, a basic apprehension of faith, beyond which the Hexateuch in its final form did not and would not go.

The text Deut., ch. 26, bears clear signs of a later revision. So it is hard to say when such historical summaries arose and came into use. In our view there is no difficulty in supposing that they existed as early as the time of the Judges. At the other extreme it would be impossible to take these historical summaries to be later résumés of the great historical outlines of the Hexateuch. Were that the case they would inevitably have a different appearance. This applies above all to the absence of the Sinai event, which must be discussed immediately.

The Yahwist, however, wrote in a period quite different from that of the Deuteronomist. No very great span of years lay between him and the time of the old Israelite amphictyony (we have reason to assume that he wrote at the time of Solomon or a little later), but even so, much had changed culturally and cultically between the time of the amphictyony and his own day.

For a thorough understanding of the first books of the Bible it is crucial that this notation "J" lose its schematic character and that we come to a realistic view about the formation of the literary tradition. For it was the Yahwist who, so far as we can see, gave to the entire Hexateuch its form and compass. The Yahwist marks that decisive line of demarcation in the history of culture which we can observe for so many peoples: he was the collector of the countless old traditions which until then had circulated freely among the people. With him began the writing down of those poetic or cultic narratives which previously had circulated orally and without context among the people. It seems probable that this process was not one in which a great literary work issued at a stroke. Perhaps the Yahwist followed earlier works about which, of course, we know nothing. Such a collecting and refashioning of old material cannot, of course, be ascribed to the initiative of the Yahwist alone; the time must have been ripe for it. Indeed, what is most important is that the presuppositions for this collecting and refashioning must have been present in the ancient material itself. The majority of these old narratives were aetiologies, i.e., their purpose was to explain some facts in tribal history, about a place, or in the cult. Previously the validity of these traditions and the interest in them had been regionally limited to that area in which the question was alive and to which the existing aetiological narrative would give the answer. This is especially easy to comprehend in the case of cult legends.

The old cultic traditions in particular were previously unthinkable outside the sacred framework. Only in the course of the cultic act could one meet and experience them. These sacred traditions were not some kind of ornamental addition to the cult; rather, they were its inmost nerve, by which it lived and from which proceeded the content and form of the festivals.* What a profound change occurred when materials from the most dissimilar cult centers became unified and even substantially altered by a superimposed plan, when, in a word, they became available as literature! For that to happen it was necessary, as we have said, for the presuppositions to be present in the material itself. A slackening (harmful to the cult!) must already have occurred in the connection between the materials and their hereditary cultic points of reference. At the time of the first kings a crisis

*By cult legend or *hieros logos* we mean a sacred story that tells of a god's appearance and revelation at a place which for that reason became a cultic center. Such traditions were, of course, carefully cultivated at the shrines and passed on, for from them alone derived the legitimacy of a cult center. Everything depended upon this legitimacy. Men did not believe it necessary to pray and offer sacrifice everywhere, of course, but only where God had already revealed himself and where he had prescribed the manner for prayer. (The narrative in Gen., ch. 18, was once the cult legend of Mamre, that in ch. 28, the cult legend of Bethel. See further Judg. 6; 13; II Sam., ch. 24; etc.) The great festivals too were based on a sacred story; by it they were justified and shaped, often to the extent of becoming part of the cult drama.

seems to have occurred in the genuine, naïve, ancient cult; its spiritual fundamentals began to change, and in this process those traditions were gradually liberated from their imprisonment in the hereditary sphere of the sacred cult.

This was the great crisis that went hand in hand with the formation of the Israelite state. Connected with the crisis was the decline of the ancient Israelite tribal unity, which took place toward the end of the period of the Judges, and the crisis reached its first high point in the enlightenment of the Solomonic era. No matter where one dates the Yahwist, when he is judged by the age of the traditions on which he worked he signifies a *late* phase. One must realize, therefore, that becoming literature meant in a sense an end for this material, which until then had already had a varied history behind it.*

*It is well to consider what in all probability would have happened to these traditions if they had not been united in a fixed literary form. Without doubt the fact that some traditions were detached from the cultic sphere meant that their content was heavily spiritualized. Nor will it be denied that this liberation from a musty and materialistic cult was a fortunate occurrence, which opened up the possibility of unsuspected development of the subject of this material. But by the same token, the traditions would be more and more subject to inner dissipation. Every such spiritualization is at the same time a dangerous process of dissolution working at the marrow of the material, for every spiritualization is also a rationalization. One no longer finds oneself before the material in the naïve attitude of reverential acceptance, but rather, one begins to stand over it and to interpret and reform it according to one's own reason. Take an example in which this process can be well observed, the Manna story (Ex., ch. 16). The older Manna story (especially vs. 4–5, 13b–15, 27–30) is meant to be understood quite objectively and is full of historical difficulties. The version of the Priestly document is quite different (vs. 2–3, 6–13a, 16–26). The event is apparently described concretely, yet in such a way that no reader is detained by the external details, but rather its secret spiritual meaning becomes clear as day. A miracle, limited in space and time, becomes something universal, almost timelessly valid. Here no storyteller is speaking, but rather a man who is theologian through and through, who has clothed his reflections in the very transparent garb of a historical narrative. But the Deuteronomist has taken a great step even beyond this position.

> "And he humbled you and let you hunger and fed you with manna, which you did not know, nor did your fathers know; that he might make you know that man does not live by bread alone, but that man lives by everything that proceeds out of the mouth of the Lord."—Deut. 8.3.

Where the Priestly document externally preserved the old form of the report throughout—the spiritualization existed only in a certain transparency of the narrative—the Deuteronomist gave up the old meaning altogether. He speaks only indirectly of actual eating to still hunger and substitutes for it feeding on God's word. Bluntly he tells what spiritual meaning actually lay behind the material event at that time. Here too it must be said that the old, simple story has been beautifully and significantly enlarged by that spiritualization; but one cannot deny it was providential that free reign for such progressive spiritualization and religious

But at the same time it meant the beginning of a much longer history! Above all, there occurs at this stage a profound inner shift in the meaning of those narratives. One need only ask how much of the old meaning is still left when a cult legend is deprived of its cultic aetiological point! The same can be said of the old ethnological tribal sagas, which at that time were also bound to a limited area. When they were uprooted they were open to every kind of spiritualized literary application. For what is the content of Gen., ch. 18, if the narrative no longer serves to legitimize the cultic center of Mamre? What is the content of ch. 22 if the narrative no longer legitimizes the abolition of child sacrifice? What is the meaning of ch. 28 if the narrative no longer legitimizes the sacredness of Bethel and its customs? What is the meaning of ch. 16—to take an ethnological saga—if the narrative no longer answers the question of the origin and way of life of the Ishmaelites? (The Yahwist himself probably no longer had any interest in the aetiological question because the Ishmaelites at his time no longer existed as a tribe.) These questions indicate one of the most important tasks that face anyone who interprets the stories in Genesis today. In many narratives he can ascertain with a probability verging on certainty the meaning and purpose which the material once had in an earlier, pre-literary phase. But he must not forget that the narrative has changed by virtue of the context in which the Yahwist has put it. Sometimes he must reckon with profound changes, since when the old aetiological focus of a story is diffused, its whole structure can collapse. Thus once again we face the question of the meaning of the whole of the Yahwist's work.

Suppose we visualize the matter roughly. On the one hand he had one of those summaries of salvation history (from the patriarchs to the conquest). On the other hand he had a very great number of loose compositions, of which a few perhaps had already coalesced into smaller compositions. Most of them, however, were certainly short and without context. The astonishing creative accomplishment was that by means of the simple plan of that credo of sacred history he was successful in forging the immense mass of narrative detail into a

---

transformation was not given to all traditions of the Hexateuch. One can only surmise that process of dissolution which was arrested when the traditions were written down. This much in any case can be observed: when the material was written down, it became fixed at a phase of its development in which a certain religious transformation had already occurred, but when, notwithstanding, the historical element was preserved undissipated and with the full import of uniqueness.

supporting and unifying basic tradition, and indeed in such a way that the simple and manifest thought of that credo remained dominant and almost unchanged in its theological outline. It is scarcely possible to determine all the single traditions which the Yahwist incorporated into his work. Perhaps he had earlier models to follow. However, his inclusion of traditions that could not immediately be incorporated into the old pattern is of theological interest. The result of such inclusions and additions was naturally an over-extension of the old plan and a theological diffusion of its original basis. This is particularly striking at three main points: (*a*) the incorporation of the Sinai tradition, (*b*) the extension of the patriarchal tradition, and (*c*) the inclusion of the primeval history.

A. THE INCORPORATION OF THE SINAI TRADITION

If one looks over the data of the sacred history in the short compositions introduced above, one is struck by the complete absence of any mention of the Sinai episode. In Josh., ch. 24 especially, it seems that the greatest event of the desert wandering could well have been mentioned alongside many less important recollections, if its mention were at all demanded by the canonical tradition. The conjecture that this plan of the old tradition about the conquest did not originally contain the Sinai event first becomes a certainty when we examine the free modifications of the credo in poetry (Ps. 78; 105; 135; 136; Ex., ch. 15), and secondly when we notice the remarkable position of the Sinai pericope in its present context. The Sinai tradition, too, probably owes its form (as the exposition of Exodus will show) to a cult festival, but in the history of the cult as in the history of the tradition it must be separated from our conquest tradition. Remarkably, this material, which is without doubt particularly old, had its own history.* The Yahwist (and perhaps even his predecessor) was the first to unite these widely separated traditions and to incorporate the Sinai tradition into the conquest tradition. Most important, however, is the great theological enlargement that was accomplished by the union of both traditions. The conquest tradition in our credo is a witness to God's gracious leading; it is sacred history. The Sinai tradition celebrates God's coming to his people, and at its center is the demand of Yahweh's lawful will, the revelation of the great sovereign right of God over Israel. Without question the simple,

* M. Noth, *Überlieferungsgeschichte des Pentateuch*, [3]1963, pp. 63 ff.

soteriological motif of the credo receives powerful support from the Sinai tradition. In the union of these traditions the two basic elements of all biblical proclamation are outlined: law and gospel.

B. THE EXTENSION OF THE PATRIARCHAL TRADITION

The summaries made only brief mention of the patriarchal period (Deut. 26.5; Josh. 24.2; I Sam. 12.8). In our Genesis the narrative material extends over thirty-eight chapters. How can we analyse such extremely complex material? There is now no fundamental dispute that it is to be assigned to the three source documents J, E, and P, and there is even agreement over detail. But it is equally certain that the narratives incorporated into the source documents already have a long history behind them. So where do they come from, and what is the nature of the information that they give about Abraham, Isaac, and Jacob? If we examine the geographical area within which they move, the "local points of reference" of the narrative material, we find that they are spread over Palestine in a remarkable way. With their connections with Shechem (Gen. 33.18 f.), Bethel (Gen. 28.11 ff.; 35.3 ff.) and Penuel (Gen. 32.22 ff.), the Jacob stories are clearly rooted in central Palestine, whereas the Isaac stories never leave the area of Beersheba in the extreme south (Gen. 26). The Abraham stories cannot all be located so clearly, but they too surely belong in the south (Mamre, Gen. 18). The only explanation of this remarkable position is that as the semi-nomadic ancestors of what later became Israel gradually settled in Palestine, they transferred the traditions which they had brought with them to the sanctuaries there. This transplantation of their traditions to ancient Palestinian sanctuaries meant that their religion, which was probably a cult of an ancestral God,* was mixed with ancient Canaanite traditions. So while we may not doubt that as "recipients of revelation" and "founders of cults" (A. Alt), Abraham, Isaac, and Jacob were historical personalities, it is no longer possible to use the narrative material for biographical accounts. It has passed through too many hands. The narratives offer little more than a few indications of the characteristic cultural situation that governed the living conditions of these clans. Nor do they offer any point of reference for even an approximate dating of the patriarchs. The living conditions of these semi-nomadic groups remained the same for hundreds of years, and they never made history.

*A. Alt, "The God of the Fathers" (1929), in: *Essays on Old Testament History and Religion*, 1966.

If one assumes (with J. Bright) that they lived early in the second millennium, then something like nine hundred years lay between them and the narratives of the Yahwist!

So it is the Yahwist who tells us of the experiences of the ancestors of Israel. But he does not think in terms of interpreting the old traditions (as a modern historian would do) completely from the conceptions of the "religion of the fathers" held at that early period. Rather, quite "anachronistically," he incorporated them into the view which he and his time had of the action of Yahweh toward men, and thus almost made them his contemporaries.

To weld the very varied and often unwieldy material of the patriarchal narratives into a great narrative complex required a thoroughgoing redactional technique. These many individual narratives, together with the larger units that had already been formed, the so-called "saga clusters" (e.g. the Lot–Sodom and the Jacob–Laban complexes), did not come together of their own accord to form a continuous narrative that was also governed by a particular theological theme. The internal connection between individual narratives can be seen above all in the way in which they are now all subordinated to the theme of the "promise to the patriarchs": especially the promise of land, but also the promise of descendants. In some cases this promise was already rooted in the narrative material before it was taken over (Gen. 15.18; 26.4, 24), but elsewhere we can see that it was only woven into the narrative later, by the Yahwist (e.g., Gen. 18.13; 22.17; 50.24). At least the promise of land is an element which goes back to the time of the "religion of the fathers". This earliest promise in the patriarchal sagas was, of course, at that time an immediate one. It promised possession of cultivated land to those semi-nomadic "patriarchs" who were then living. Thus originally it did not reckon at all with an imminent abandonment of the land and a second conquest (under Joshua). But because of the inclusion of this patriarchal tradition in the great salvation-historical scheme of historical summaries, that first ancient promise appears strangely broken. Now the reader must understand the promise mediately, because it now refers to the conquest under Joshua. Thus the relation of the patriarchs to the land in which they live appears as something temporary; indeed, the entire patriarchal period thus becomes theologically a peculiar intermediate state, a wandering from promise to fulfillment which gives to all events the character of temporariness and at the same time mysterious portent. The

Hexateuch was already laid out by the Yahwist around the great theological pragmatic plan: patriarchal period and promise, conquest and fulfillment. Even the covenant with Abraham, as an element of tradition, probably belongs to that ancient religion of the fathers (cf. below on Gen. 15.17 ff.). Now, however, it is obviously related to the covenant at Sinai. The relation of the patriarchs not only to the land, but especially to God, is temporary; it finds its fulfillment in God's revelation at Sinai and in the sequestering of the people who had descended by God's will from the patriarchs.

Finally, the content of the patriarchal narratives was broadened because all events of the patriarchal period were connected with *all* Israel by being oriented toward the conquest under Joshua. If one remembers that the old cultic traditions of the pre-Mosaic period always belonged only to a very small cultic community and that formerly the numerous aetiological narratives likewise had only a limited regional validity, then one will comprehend the full importance of that broadening and orientation toward the Israel of the twelve tribes.

The Yahwist worked to join the traditional material together in yet another way, by the occasional insertion of "interludes". These are sections which, as can be seen relatively easily, do not go back to ancient tradition but represent short bridges between early narrative material (thus e.g., Gen. 6.5–8; 12.1–9; 18.17–33). These "interludes" are characterized by a higher degree of theological reflection, and for that very reason they are particularly important to us for determining the religious ideas of the Yahwist himself, which otherwise we can discover only in an indirect way.

C. THE INCLUSION OF PRIMEVAL HISTORY

By including a primeval history (chs. 2.4b to 12.3) the Yahwist shows the greatest independence of that sacred tradition which otherwise supports him. The tradition of the conquest began with the patriarchal stories, and never did it contain anything of the primeval history, creation, etc. But where it left the Yahwist in the lurch he was quite self-reliant and free to unfold his own conceptions. Strict proof that the Yahwist had no precursor in that theological union of primeval history and sacred history is, of course, not available. On the other hand, there are no indications that the Yahwist was here following a received tradition. This view is thus unique, and one may still be able to sense the boldness of the first draft in this loosest part of the whole composition.

The primeval history, which the Yahwist constructed from elements of very different kinds, proclaims first of all with impressive one-sidedness that all corruption, all confusion in the world, comes from sin; but it also testifies that the continually widening cleft between God and man is matched by a secret increasing power of grace. The stories of the Fall, of Cain, and of Noah show God's forgiving and supporting act of salvation. Only in the story of the Tower of Babel, when the nations are scattered and the unity of mankind is lost, does the judgment of God seem to be the last word. But here primeval history dovetails with sacred history: Abraham is called from the multitude of nations, "that in him all generations of the earth should be blessed." Thus the insertion of sacred history gives the answer to the unsolved question of primeval history, the question about the relation of God to all peoples. This entry of sacred history in ch. 12.1–3 is thus not only the conclusion to primeval history but the actual key to it. In this close union of primeval history and sacred history the Yahwist does justice to the meaning and purpose of the conditions of salvation which Yahweh has granted to Israel. He gives the aetiology of all aetiologies in the Old Testament and becomes at this point a true prohet, for he proclaims the distant goal of the sacred history effected by God in Israel to be the bridging of the cleft between God and all mankind; and he announces it neither as being rationally grounded nor as being already comprehensible in its details. The promise in Gen. 12.1 ff. contains three promises of blessing: (1) Abraham will be blessed and become a great nation, (2) Yahweh will give the land to Abraham's seed (v. 7), (3) in Abraham all nations of the earth will be blessed (v. 3). The first two promises were already known to the Yahwist from the tradition of the patriarchal sagas, the third, however, obviously arose from none of the older traditions but directly from the authority of his prophetic inspiration (commentary on chs. 11.28–30; 12.1–3).

2. THE THREE NARRATIVE SOURCES

The preceding discussion presupposes the recognition of a fact that has become accepted in contemporary Old Testament science after almost 200 years of research: The books Genesis to Joshua consist of several continuous source documents that were woven together more or less skillfully by a redactor. The oldest source documents are known as "Yahwist" (J) and "Elohist" (E) because of their distinctive use of the name for God. The Yahwist may be dated ca. 950, the Elohist perhaps one or two centuries later. Deuteronomy (D) is literarily distinct; we have it in the book of Deuteronomy, but Deuteronomistic additions and revisions occur also in the Book of Joshua. The latest source is the Priestly document (P); its actual composition (without the later additions, of course) falls in the postexilic period, ca. 538–450.

The importance of these dates must not be overestimated, both because they are in every instance only guesses and, above all, because they refer only to the completed literary composition. The question of the age of a single tradition within any one of the source documents is an entirely different matter. The youngest document (P), for example, contains an abundance of ancient and very ancient material.

This is not the place for even a partially exhaustive characterization of the descriptive method of the sources. We shall be content with a few indications. As regards the creative genius of the *Yahwist's narrative* there is only admiration. Someone has justly called the artistic mastery in this narrative one of the greatest accomplishments of all times in the history of thought. Wonderful clarity and utter simplicity characterize the representation of the individual scenes. The meagerness of his resources is truly amazing, and yet this narrator's view encompasses the whole of human life with all its heights and depths. With unrivalled objectivity he has made man the subject of his presentation—both the riddles and conflicts of his visible acts and ways of behaving as well as the mistakes and muddles in the secret of his heart. He among the biblical writers is the great psychologist. However, he is concerned, not with man who with his desires and despair believes himself to be alone in the world, but rather with man to whom the living God has been revealed and who therefore has become the object of divine address, a divine act, and therefore a divine judgment and divine salvation. Thus in the primeval history he subjects the great problems of humanity to the light of revelation: creation and nature, sin and suffering, man and wife, fraternal quarrels, international confusion, etc. But above all, he investigates God's activities in the beginnings of Israel, both their visible wonders and their hidden mysteries. He sees the complete mystery of the election of the Old Testament community, and in Gen. 12.3 he answers the riddle of this divine act with prophetic authority. "Yahweh is the

God of the world, his presence is felt everywhere with profound reverence." (Pr.) Yet precisely the Yahwistic narrative is full of the boldest anthropomorphisms. Yahweh walks in the garden in the cool of the evening; he himself closes the ark; he descends to inspect the Tower of Babel, etc. This is anything but the bluntness and naïveté of an archaic narrator. It is, rather, the candor and lack of hesitation which is only the mark of a lofty and mature way of thinking. This glasslike, transparent, and fragile way of thinking in the Yahwistic narratives makes of every exposition, which inevitably coarsens the original text, a difficult and almost insoluble task.

The work of the *Elohist* probably arose one or two centuries later. Soon, it was closely intertwined with the work of the Yahwist by a redactor. Even so, it differs rather distinctly from the work of the Yahwist. As a whole, it does not attain the splendor and brilliant perfection of the Yahwistic account. The fabric is much less finely woven. Thus, for example, the spectacular aspect of the miracles is much more strongly emphasized. The work does not require the same degree of reflection from its readers and expositors; it is more "popular", i.e., it has taken over the old sacred folk tradition with less modification and spiritualization. This accounts for the fact that the Elohist cannot create so many great, overlapping contextual units. (Compare the singleness of purpose in the Yahwistic stories of Abraham or Jacob!) His dependence on popular tradition is especially recognizable in the total plan. The Elohist begins with Abraham and therefore does not have a primeval history. Thus he stands closer than the Yahwist to the old canonical form of the sacred history. The Yahwist, by including the primeval history, deviated from the old tradition more than the Elohist, who felt more bound to the old form of the credo, which had been hammered into the religious consciousness of the people by the tradition of centuries.

This description would be false, however, if the fact were not mentioned at once that the Elohist has clear statements of theological reflection which go beyond what is simply popular. In many places one can recognize almost a systematic theological revision of the old traditions. We will mention only two peculiarities of the Elohist: (1) The immediacy of God with man, his appearances, his movement on earth is severely limited. The angel of Yahweh calls down from heaven, and is therefore no longer thought of as walking on earth (Gen. 21.17; 22.11, 15). Related to this removal of God from men and from anything earthly is the great significance given to dreams. They are now the spiritual plane on which God's revelation meets men. The more neutral sphere of the dream is to some extent the third place where God meets man. But even here man is given no direct access to God's revelation, for man cannot simply interpret the dream except through the power of special inspiration which comes from God (Gen. 40.8; 41.15 f.).

(2) This loss of immediacy with God and his revealed word in the Elohistic work is matched by the great significance that is given to the prophet and his office. The prophet is the properly qualified mediator between God and men; he is the one who receives God's revelation, and he is the one who brings the concerns of men in supplication before God (Gen. 20.7, 17; Ex. 15.20; 20.19; Num., ch. 11; 12.6 ff.; 21.7). The Elohist's concern for the prophet and his tasks is so strong that much can be said for the conjecture that the entire work arose in old prophetic circles. Our exposition, however, does not conceive as its task a thorough elaboration of this narrative in its original form. The interweaving with the Yahwistic narrative is so thorough that any separation can be made only with great damage to the text. Attention will be given in every instance to the theological distinctiveness of the Elohistic tradition.*

The *Priestly narrative* is quite different from the sources characterized above. Its text can be recognized even by laymen because of its striking peculiarities with regard to form and content. One may not consider this document a narrative at all. It is really a Priestly document, i.e., it contains *doctrine* throughout. It is the result of intensive, theologically ordering thought. Consequently the manner of presentation is quite different. The language is succinct and ponderous, pedantic and lacking artistry. Only at the points of primary interest does the usual, excessively terse diction become relaxed and more detailed in an effort to paraphrase the matter conceptually (e.g., Gen., chs. 1; 9; 17). If in the Yahwist we found a narration of overpowering simplicity without anything doctrinal (in the narrower sense of the word), in the Priestly document we find a minimum of vivid narration and artistic movement. In this respect the writing is divested of every impressive ornament. To be sure, the greatness of the work lies precisely in that renunciation, for this sober objectivity is in reality the deepest concern, the most intense concentration on what is revealed by God. Here everything is written after reflection;

*On the Elohist, see H.-W. Wolff, "Zur Thematik der elohistischen Fragmente im Pentateuch," *Evangelische Theologie* 1969, 59 ff.

nothing is without theological relevance, for in this work we have the essence of the theological labor of many generations of priests. No effort is given to depicting man as the recipient of revelation or to the circumstances, the conflicts, the spiritual or social uncertainties attending that experience. The figures of the Priestly account are in this respect completely colorless and shadowy. The whole interest is focused exclusively on what comes from God, his words, judgments, commands, and regulations. Thus it describes a course of history only with respect to God's revealed judgments and regulations, with respect to divine regulations which with increasing number establish and assure the salvation of God's people. It presents history, not of men, but of divine regulations on earth, in so far as one can speak of history in this way. The "composition" of such a work with its infinitely slow growth of such sacred traditions cannot be determined in terms of a year or a century. Even though it may really have received its final form only in the postexilic period, still, along with later material and material that has been considerably revised theologically, it also preserves very ancient matter in almost unchanged archaic garb.

The interweaving by the redactor of this document with the previously united Yahwist and Elohist documents ("the Jehovist") could not, of course, be done organically. The Priestly texts are as a rule simply recorded, each in its place, in the composition of the Hexateuch. In Genesis, apart from minor insertions from the Priestly document, the redactor found himself forced to unite the tradition of P and J to *one* text only in the story of the Flood.

The Hexateuch in its present form arose by means of redactors who heard the peculiar testimony of faith of each document and considered it binding. There is no doubt that the present Hexateuch in its final form makes great demands on the understanding of every reader. Many ages, many men, many traditions and theologies, have constructed this massive work. Only the one who does not look superficially at the Hexateuch but reads it with a knowledge of its deep dimension will arrive at true understanding. Such a one will know that revelations and religious experiences of many ages are speaking from it. *For no stage in this work's long period of growth is really obsolete; something of each phase has been conserved and passed on as enduring until the Hexateuch attained its final form.*

3. THE THEOLOGICAL PROBLEM OF THE YAHWIST

One further question most be answered if one is to understand the Yahwistic (and also Elohistic) work. A great number of old cultic traditions are included in the Yahwist's work, materials that were created, formed, and preserved by the cult through long periods of time. But now this cultic attachment and orientation, without which these materials were at one time unthinkable, has been absolutely stripped away, as we saw; it is as though they had changed into a chrysalis and now emerged in new, free form. They all have risen high above their sacred, native soil, and now, having grown independent, they move in a partially or even completely "cult-less" atmosphere. The Yahwist's distinctively spiritual method, which, by the way, is almost without parallel in Old Testament religious history, seems to us like a cool breath from the freethinking era of Solomon. The question now is whether this process by which the traditions outgrew their origins was a necessary secularization, or whether the loss that these traditions suffered by being separated from the cult was compensated for by a new but different kind of theological attachment. A witness in the theological sense of the word arises only in relation to a preceding divine act of revelation; and it is really quite unthinkable that the Yahwist spoke to his people without such a backing for his words.

It is surely not unprofitable to inquire after the divine fact which formed the background against which the Yahwist plotted his entire work. *Ancient* Israel considered God's speaking and acting for man's salvation as confined to the sacred institutions, particularly to the narrower cultic sphere of sacrifice and divine decision mediated by the priest. But men also experienced God's gracious, saving act in the wider cultic sphere, in the holy war, the *charisma* of a qualified leader, the "terror of God" which fell upon the enemy without human agency, or in other miracles that occurred because of the presence of the sacred Ark. The Yahwist, however, considers God's activity in a fundamentally different way. He does not challenge the possibilities with which his forebears reckoned, but he goes far beyond these notions of faith. He sees God's leading in the facts of history as well as in the quiet course of a human life, in the sacred things, but not less in the profane, in great miracles as well as in the innermost secrets of the human heart. (In the story of Jacob and Joseph we are brought close to the thought that God works even in and through man's sin!) In a word, the chief importance of God's activity suddenly lies outside the sacred institutions. It is thereby perhaps more concealed from the natural eye because the entire profane sphere is also the domain of God's activity; but it is nevertheless looked at more inclusively, not intermittently, but much more continually. The Yahwist presents one story of divine guidance and disposition; God's providence is revealed in all areas of life, the public as well as the private.

This view, which did not consider God's activity as confined to the old sanctified sacred institutions but which ventured to discover it retrospectively in the tortured paths of political as well as personal fortune, was something new when compared to the old conception of the patriarchal cult. But it is in fact connected very closely with the great historical events of the Davidic period especially. The ancient sacred union of tribes (in the period of the Judges) had dissolved, and national life had begun to shed its old forms and to become profane. By the time of Saul the national mind had already become emancipated from the old cultic regulations, and this process certainly made further progress under the much more systematically constructed state apparatus of David, with its newly organized court and military life. Ordinary life in its details became more autonomous and demanding. At all events, the period had ended when sacred regulations on principle took precedence over all other legitimacies of life. Had Israel thus slipped from the hand of its ancient God, the God of the patriarchs and of Moses? Had she thus departed from the domain of his salvation and his leading? That was the great question.

The reader will not find it hard to read the answer from the Yahwist's work. This narrative displays boundless confidence in the nearness of Yahweh, in the immediacy of his rule and in the possibility of speaking of all this, in the simplest possible terms, in the new religious language. Of course, to discover the whole range of the Yahwist's thought it is necessary to add to his stories of the patriarchs the narratives about Moses, the event on Sinai and the wandering in the wilderness, as they are contained in Exodus and Numbers. It then becomes quite clear that the old times, including the period of the Judges, lie far behind him. It can, however, be ascertained that the historical situation presupposed by the Yahwist's work must have arisen in the period immediately following the formation of the state. It is striking that the tribes have given up their political independence, but that we can discover no reference to the deep division of Israel into two kingdoms.*

More important than the political changes that can be inferred is, however, the change in religious conceptions which have become more "modern" than those of the archaic period of the Judges. Behind the work of the Yahwist stands a new experience of God. Throughout this work, which is still a unique history of miraculous and hidden guidance and divine providence, one feels able to trace the freshness of the joy of a new discovery. These remarks have to be made to warn the reader of these stories against deceiving himself by his familiarity with them, and to urge him to understand their revolutionary contemporary character against their special background.

4. HERMENEUTICAL PROBLEMS OF THE GENESIS NARRATIVES

At first, knowledge of the long process to which individual traditions were subjected before they received their final and present form in our book of Genesis makes the work of the exegete difficult. Above all, there are two groups of hermeneutic questions that we must wrestle to answer. For a long time Old Testament science has called these traditions "sagas." Thus one of the first tasks of the exegete is to give an exact account of this term, the possibility and the limits of its use. A second task arises from the fact that the narratives, which formerly began in isolation, are now related to a large overarching context and obviously must be interpreted within this context, from the particular spot that has been assigned to them within the whole. Finally, as a result of putting together the source documents, there have arisen relationships and theological interplay between the individual texts which demand discussion. In connection with this last problem the question about the historicity (*Geschichtlichkeit*) of these narratives (in their present form) must be raised anew and answered.

It is to the undying credit of H. Gunkel that in his great commentary on Genesis he separated the original narrative units from the larger whole and analyzed them with a distinctive aesthetic *charisma*. These individual traditions were of very different kinds. As we have seen, a number of them were cultic aetiological narratives. Others arose from the need to explain the origin of certain curiosities in the relationship of the tribes and the nations to one another; these

*More details in H. W. Wolff, "Das Kerygma des Jahwisten," *Gesammelte Studien zum AT*, 1964, 345 ff.

are traditions with an ethnological aetiology. Some narratives are like rather short novellistic poems. Indeed, one may not refuse on principle to accept an originally vacillating character of one or another narrative in its oldest form—we are speaking now of the oldest *pre*literary form of these single traditions! But that these very old traditions are for the most part *sagas* is a fact, the background of which we can investigate no further. What does this fact, which today is neither new nor scientifically disputed, and yet concerning which so much lack of clarity still prevails, mean for the exegete?

Suspicion of saga begins as a rule with doubt concerning its "historical" content. It is considered a product of poetic fantasy, and as such it has at best a broken relation to historical reality, or none at all. Consciously or unconsciously this depreciation proceeds from a one-sided overestimation of historical writing, which records exactly and trustworthily everything the saga mentions unclearly and often with distortion.* This way of judging—one could call it historical materialism—contains an extremely crass misunderstanding of the essence of saga; it was, however, by and large a characteristic of the nineteenth century, which was otherwise so well schooled in historical perception.†

No, the saga is the result of a kind of intellectual activity quite different from that of history (*Historie*), and it is advisable to compare history (*Historie*) with sagas as little as possible. To be sure, there exists one point in common—and it was the cause of all fatal comparisons: both are concerned with history (*Geschichte*). That is true of the biblical saga even when it is concerned with apparently unhistorical material. Whatever saga we examine, we find with respect to its simplest and most original purpose that it narrates an actual event that occurred once for all in the realm of history. It is therefore to be taken quite seriously (as distinct, for example, from fairy tales, which serve primarily to entertain)—it is to be "believed."‡ In all that follows, therefore, let us hold fast to this: by no means is saga

*"The form which we have provisionally called history (*Historie*) acts as an enemy of the saga; it threatens it, it waylays it, it slanders it and perverts the words in its mouth. That which was positive in the saga becomes negative in history. That which was truth becomes falsehood. The tyranny of history is in fact able to assert of the saga that it simply does not exist but is only a kind of timid preparation for history itself." (A. Jolles, *Einfache Formen*², 1956, 64.)

†Thus even in Grimm's dictionary this term "saga" is defined as information about events in the past which lack historical verification.

‡A. W. Schlegel, *Sämtliche Werke* XII, 1847, 387; K. Wehrhan, *Sachwörterbuch der Deutschkunde*, 2, 1930, s.v. "Sage."

merely the product of free-ranging fantasy; it, too, conjures up history. It is the form favoured by a people for depicting its early history. Of course it does not feel bound by the modern demand for exactness. The saga* comes from a quite different period of the people. Its roots are in a form of society preceding that of the state, which means that it lives and grows at a time when the power of rational and logical, historical perception is not yet fully liberated, at a time, however, when the powers of instinctive, intuitively interpretative, one could almost say mantic, understanding dominate all the more freely. In its sagas a people is concerned with itself and the realities in which it finds itself. It is, however, a view and interpretation not only of that which once was but of a past event that is secretly present and decisive for the present. Thus, just as for an individual certain events or decisions of the past determine his whole life, so in the life of tribes and peoples past events have a direct influence on the present and mold it. It is the saga, much more than historical writing, that knows this secret contemporary character of apparently past events; it can let things become contemporary in such a way that everyone detects their importance, while the same events would probably have been overlooked by historical writing (if it can be thought to have existed at the time). For there is another history that a people makes besides the externals of wars, victories, migrations, and political catastrophes. It is an inner history, one that takes place on a different level, a story of inner events, experiences, and singular guidance, of working and becoming mature in life's mysteries; and for Israel that meant a history with God. One can see that the subject-matter of saga is quite special; above all, the way in which it describes and re-presents the past has unmistakable characteristics. For example, it is simply a fact—to begin with something general—that the sagas about the patriarchs, in spite of their complexity, preserve a mood, a spiritually religious atmosphere, if one may put it this way, that was obviously a characteristic of the pre-Mosaic period. And one can say that the prerogative of the saga over all "more exact" traditions is just to preserve these imponderable, intimate experiences from a people's youth. Thus occasionally the things of which the saga takes possession are trifling. And yet, even then it is often concerned with facts and events of much greater inner significance than many things that history (*Historie*) puts down, because they have a longer aftereffect

*For the saga in ancient Israel, now see K. Koch, *The Growth of the Biblical Tradition*, 1969, §12.

and therefore remain decisive for the existence of posterity. There is often an entire world of events—actual, experienced events!—enclosed in a single saga. The saga, therefore, has a much higher degree of density than has history (*Historie*).

This is also expressed in the style. Through centuries of being told and heard, that primitive art, which can speak simply of small as well as quite important things without diminishing their substance, grew equal to the task of describing all human experience. Indeed, this art was the first to appear as the only monumental form appropriate for such content. The biblical traditions are characterized by a thoroughgoing economy of expression on the emotional side. What men thought or felt, what moved them, is subordinate to the objective events. When the narrator does say something about the fright or anxiety that took hold of a man (Gen. 15.12; 32.7), his remark seems all the more primitive precisely because of its rareness.

Anyone who wants to understand such sagas correctly must acquire a broader and more profound conception of "history" (*Geschichte*) than what is often accepted today. At the beginning, the saga in most cases certainly contained a "historical" fact as its actual crystallizing point. But in addition it reflects a historical experience on the relevant community which extends into the present time of the narrator. This second constructional element is, as a rule, the stronger, often dominating to such an extent that it can expand and elevate the material to a historical type behind which the original historical fact more and more disappears. In other cases the degree of inner revision and fashioning of the material by those who came later is much smaller, as for example in the tradition of God's covenant with Abraham (Gen. 15.7 ff.), a cult saga that in all essential points was obviously left in its archaic form.

Despite the great differences in style and theme which distinguish the individual stories of Abraham, Isaac, and Jacob from each other, they have one common factor: with the exception of Gen. 14 they all move in the same social and political sphere, that of the independent family.* The family in which so many astounding things happen, the family which has to sustain such severe tensions, is not one partial sphere of communal human life here, set over against other forms. Rather, it is the total sphere of all human communal life; it is the framework of all human activity, politics and economics as

*C. Westermann, "Arten der Erzählung in der Genesis", *Forschung am Alten Testament*, 1964, 35–39.

well as religion. In this sphere, events like the birth of a child or a quarrel have a special importance which is only attached to them here. The way in which the narrative material is thus rooted in the family or the clan is a sign of its antiquity. Of course, both its form and its content changed a great deal as it was handed down. Thus one may reckon correctly with subsequent expansion of old traditions by means of material, even by means of fairy-tale motifs.* This does not endanger the "historicity" of the saga in any way, in so far as with the help of such means it elucidates real events and experiences; for the saga cannot report in abstract formulas, but its manner of communicating is highly figurative. History has therefore not directly merged with saga, so to speak, but rather its form has been changed by long thought and is reflected somewhat brokenly in single images. This peculiar process of symbolization attempts primarily to demonstrate, through the experiences of a single individual, historical facts that originally belonged completely to the group. In Abraham and Jacob, Israel saw, increasingly, simply the need and the promise of its own existence before God. That does not mean, of course, that these figures and the traditions about them are nothing more than subsequent projections of popular faith back into the primeval period. It means, rather, that this material did not lie in the archives untouched but was molded and substantially enlarged by being handed down for centuries. Certainly one would understand the saga of Jacob's nocturnal struggle at the Jabbok, for example, only superficially, and would miss its primary meaning, if one were to suppose that its concern were exhausted in describing the details of an event of the distant past as objectively as possible. No! The saga Gen. 32.22 ff. in its present form, in the garb and style of a narrative of bygone events, tells of things that at the same time are thoroughly present. Israel recognized something of her own relation to God in what Jacob experienced at that time. Thus the saga has a wonderful transparence of its own, and only in this character has it become the witness of a past, and at the same time completely contemporary, act of God.

In ancient Israel the principal power in the forming of saga was faith. In any case, we do not have a single saga that has not received from faith its decisive stamp and orientation. In every instance the degree of this revision, stamp, and orientation is completely different.

*O. Eissfeldt, "Stammessage und Novelle in den Geschichten von Jakob und seinen Söhnen," in: *Eucharisterion für H. Gunkel*, 1, 1923, 56 ff.

There are sagas—especially those which formerly were cult sagas—which through many generations, from their beginning until their mature final form, were under the formative influence of faith. Other material existed popularly for a long time in more worldly narratives (perhaps even of doubtful value!) before it was incorporated into the religious realm. One must not think, however, that this religious requisition, even if it changed the content of the saga only at a relatively late period, was therefore only superficial and did not touch its essential content. The opposite is true. The later the version of a saga, the more theologically reflective and less naïve it is. Even if this transformation altered the external form of the text only slightly, even if it is true that on occasion only the name of Yahweh was subsequently added, that change is nevertheless radical, for this inserted name, Yahweh, is something very presumptuous.* When this ancient material was related to Yahweh, when Yahweh loomed above the previous substance of the saga, which was perhaps profane, this meant a complete abrogation of its ancient immanental meaning and a new illumination of all parts of the narrated material. Thus we must reckon with the fact that certain individual characteristics, formerly belonging to the insignificant accessories, have now become extremely significant. This requisition of ancient saga by theological reflection mirrors nothing other than what all Israel experienced by the revelation of Yahweh: the requisition of all areas of life, of all profane spheres, by God's exacting and promising will.

To bring out the point, one might even say that the patriarchal narratives deal more with God than with men. Men are not important in themselves, but only as the objects of divine planning and action. Above all, one must ask where and in what sense Abraham, Jacob, or Joseph are meant by the narrator to be understood as models, by virtue of their own actions or of divine providence. In some cases —e.g., Gen. 13; 15.6; 22.1 ff.—that is probably indeed the case. Such narratives are meant to encourage imitation, "discipleship." But they are in the minority. The figures of the patriarchs are presented with a matter-of-fact realism which by no means suppresses those things that move and concern mankind, and on some occasions weakness and failure are brought out with unrelieved harshness. One need only think of the three variations on the narrative of the

*"One need delete only the name of Yahweh to remove almost all the varnish with which Israel covered the strange pictures." H. Gressmann, ZAW, 1910, 24 f.

"endangering of the ancestress" (Gen. 12.10 ff.; 20.1 ff.; 26.7 ff.).* The patriarchal narratives are remarkably free of that urge to transfigure and idealize the figures of earlier times, which plays such a great role in popular literature. The patriarchal narratives do not fall short of the rest of the Old Testament in drawing a picture of man which Israel only found through a long conversation with Yahweh. It is the picture of a man who is directed to hear the divine address and who is sheltered by the guidance of this God.

Of course, one can now ask whether the designation "saga" is still appropriate for this material which is so permeated through and through by faith. It is certainly misleading if we apply it to the present forms of the Old Testament traditions, for from a literary point of view we have here narratives which have reached a high degree of artistry and which venture to depict God's ways in sacred history by means of constantly new pictures.

The measure of freedom that J, E, or P could exercise in their literary modification of the available material was scarcely great. In any case this freedom was much more limited than any modern Western author would be permitted to claim for himself. The Yahwist, in shaping the individual narrative, probably did not go beyond some trimming of the archaic profiles and making definite fine accents. He could naturally act much more freely when joining originally independent narratives. And even if some attempts at uniting various traditions into a small unit in a few cases have been made, nevertheless the actual composition of the narratives in Genesis is without question his work. And the important thing is this: the individuality of the Yahwist, his basic theological conceptions, are much less apparent within the individual narratives than in the character of the composition as a whole. The Yahwist's theology of history is essentially expressed in the way he has linked together the materials, connected and harmonized them with one another. This theological conception of the Yahwist is important for the exegete

*Delitzsch says of the Tamar story (Gen., ch. 38): "Thus . . . the beginnings of the tribe of Judah were shaped by the remarkable interaction of human sin and divine guidance. . . . How simple are the images of Israel's ancestors! They have almost more shadow than light. National ambition did not add to them or change them. No trace of an idealizing myth is noticeable. The nobleness of these figures consists in the fact that they conquer in the strength of the grace granted to them, and when defeated, they arise again and again. Their mistakes are the foils of their greatness for sacred history. By the yardstick of the Old Testament even Tamar, with all her going astray, is a saint because of her wisdom, her tenderness, her nobility." (451 f.)

because it became the canon to a certain extent for the interpretation of the other source narratives and thereby also became definitive for the final form of Genesis.

The way the Yahwist, from the most varied kinds of building material, formed in the primeval history (chs. 2 to 11) a story of mankind's increasing alienation from God has already been indicated (in the section "The Inclusion of the Primeval History"). He obviously set as the theme of the Abraham narratives the postponement of the promise. The outstanding characteristic of the Yahwistic (also of the Elohistic) narratives in contrast to the Priestly document is that they summarize with particular minuteness of detail the subjective situation of the one who receives the promise. They note the characteristic conflicts, temptations, and errors into which the patriarchs fell precisely in receiving the promise, both because of its increasing expression and because of its delay.

Compare the narratives of ch. 12.10 ff. (Sarah in Egypt) and ch. 16 (Hagar)! In ch. 12.10 ff. immediately after receiving the great, divine promise—enhanced meanwhile by the promise of land in v. 7—Abraham is beset with great difficulties (famine in the Promised Land!). He acts as though God's promise could not be relied upon at all, that is, in complete unbelief. God saves her who is to be the mother of Israel and carries forward his promise over all the chasms of despair regarding the heir of promise. This narrative, which recurs in three forms in Genesis (chs. 20; 26), obviously was especially important to the ancients. It shows something of the confusion and perplexity that the divine promise evoked in men, but more than that, it shows the faithfulness of Yahweh, who stands by his plan of salvation which is often betrayed by men. In ch. 16, judging by human standards, the possibility of receiving the heir of promise from Sarah is past. This dilemma causes those concerned to take matters into their own hands, and men try to force the fulfillment of the promise because they do not trust God for it. But this Ishmael, begotten in defiance and lack of faith, cannot be the child of promise. God will be with him indeed, but he will be a brute (!) fighting against everyone and everyone against him. With respect to the psychology of faith, both narratives illustrate Abraham's extremely different reactions to the promise. Two basic attitudes appear as almost typical: (1) disregard for, and (2) arbitrary wresting of, the divine offer. In both cases a difficulty that has emerged over the bearer of the promise gives rise to an action which works against Yahweh's plan. This conviction of a historical plan conceived by Yahweh and the assurance with which this plan is contrasted with human action is very reminiscent of the authority of the prophets, who in other circumstances claimed to know the long-term divine plan for history. The necessity for psychological uniformity in the human portrait that was being sketched was foreign to these narrators.

Naturally one cannot expect complete thematic consistency in a composition that joins together the most varied preformed materials. Occasionally the narratives are even unyielding toward one another. In the stories of Laban, for instance, one cannot help feeling that the individual traditions to which the Yahwist was bound by the history of tradition had resisted thematic permeation more than others because of their specific weight and particular character. And yet the plan for a thematic synopsis of the whole cannot be misunderstood. The Jacob story in its "Jehovistic" form is like a bridge supported from within by two pillars: by the Bethel story (ch. 28) on the one hand and the Peniel story (ch. 32.22 ff.) on the other. And, what is more, the paradox of the divine act in each of the two incidents is extremely harsh. Where Jacob has experienced bankruptcy, where everything seems done for, blessing turned to curse, there God gives him the promise. And where the narrative shows him prosperous, where he thinks he has only to survive a quarrel with Esau, there God falls on him like a nocturnal ghost. And here again the point is the blessing! (v. 26.) Obviously these striking narrative sections are meant to indicate the leading theological ideas and cause the reader to read the entire story of Jacob with respect to the inscrutability and freedom of God's ways.

Any scholarly commentary must attempt to understand the narrative material of Genesis primarily in the way in which it was understood in the context of the great narrative works J, E, and P, that is, as it was understood in Israel between the ninth and the fifth centuries B.C. This is difficult, because the narrators do not interpret the events directly, but are quite restrained in their judgments. They do not hand over an explanation to the reader, but take him through the events without assessing men's actions and experiences, evidently on the presupposition that these events are able to speak for themselves to the reader or hearer. For this reason, the interpreter has to give up from the start any search for one meaning which is the only meaning that the narrator can have intended. He will have to concede that it could have prompted the reflections of the reader in more than one direction. Equally, however, the exegete must reserve for himself the right to reject interpretations which are inappropriate to the narrative or to the understanding of the reader. If he is to keep on the right lines, he needs to read the material very carefully. The interpreter will find great help in the leading ideas which permeate the narratives, for example the theme of promise, which was discussed above (pp. 22f.). Whatever happened to the patriarchs was part of the divine plan for history, which was directed beyond the life of these men toward a still distant goal.

If the reader of today raises the question of the "historicity" of the events, he must first realize that the ancient narrators were simply not aware of this question that so often troubles modern man. Still less did they see an "either-or" here. So we must attempt to answer the question in an indirect way, i.e., in terms of the very nature of these stories. What we have said so far has already suggested one thing: the old, naïve idea of the historicity of these narratives as being biographically reliable stories from the life of the patriarchs must be abandoned. If the narratives of Gen., chs. 18; 22; 28; 32 were once very early Palestinian cult legends (and therefore pre-Israelite and pre-Canaanite), and if the tradition of the patriarchs was only interwoven with these narratives after the Israelite incursion, we can no longer accept them as documents from the life of the patriarchs. The same is true of most of the patriarchal narratives. (This is not to deny that individual elements—now bound up with these narratives—in fact go back to the "patriarchal period"; but that does not alter the general picture.) The stories are about the past, indeed the distant past, but the God who directs events and speaks to the patriarchs is Yahweh, who was as yet unknown to the pre-Mosaic ancestors of Israel (Exod., 3.13 ff.; 6.6). Similarly, the religious field of tension in which the faith of an Abraham had to make its choice between temptation and faith, is much less that of the ancestors of Israel than that of the narrators and their time. They were not concerned to revive a long past religious situation. On the contrary, these narratives express everything that Israel had learnt from her association with Yahweh right down to the narrator's own time. By the medium of these sagas, the narrators express many of the essentials of what Israel had learnt in her history with Yahweh. In this sense the narratives are deeply rooted in history. So it is no longer possible to discover what historical event lies behind the narrative of the jeopardizing of Sarah; we must, in fact, assume that the transfer of the material to Abraham and Sarah was only made subsequently (see the expositions on chs. 12; 20; 26). Therefore one could say pointedly that this narrative is not "historical"; but the experience that God miraculously preserves the promise beyond human failure was eminently historical (*geschichtlich*) for the community. These narratives have a very high degree of compactness because they compress experiences that faith brought to the community slowly, perhaps over centuries. And this is primarily what gives the narratives their proper characteristic witness. So much is clear: if the historicity of the patriarchal narratives now rests essentially upon the community's experiences of faith, then that fact has far-reaching consequences for exegesis. No one will deny that dangers threaten this kind of exegesis. Even though we stand for a high degree of spiritualizing—in our opinion the subtle spirituality of these narratives has been greatly underestimated even in their first literary version—nevertheless, this way of exegesis threatens to evaporate into purely allegorical interpretation, a tendency that must nevertheless be resisted. One needs to understand that the communal theological element of which we are speaking may never be declared the sole content of the narrative. It is indeed an important component that again and again must be freshly considered; but with it in individual traditions there have been preserved characteristics of a more ancient, indeed, most ancient, meaning, which the exegete may not overlook. Therefore, it is impossible even for the most carefully thought out hermeneutical rule to mark the middle course which will preserve in these narratives their characteristic uniqueness for sacred history. Under no circumstances may the narratives be deprived of this imponderable element of historical moment.

The long process of tradition which many narratives have undergone has left a number of traces behind in them. Usually it is a matter of some inner unevennesses or dislocations in the structure of a particular narrative. These are nowhere so obvious as in the narrative of Jacob's struggle in Gen. 32.10 ff., where in one and the same story quite different conceptions of the event have been preserved side by side (see the commentary). The question of the nature of the narrative material at a pre-literary stage has been discussed most perceptively by H. Gunkel in his great commentary. It is still largely open, even today, as in the meantime the way of posing the problems it raises has shifted, and Gunkel's explanations are no longer always adequate. Occasionally the question must be posed in an entirely new way. However, one should not investigate the earlier history of the material with the expectation of finding what is really "authentic" at the lowest level attainable, of coming upon the historical tracks of the patriarchs themselves. Quite apart from the fact that this will very rarely be the case, the narrative never for a moment leaves us in doubt that it does not share this interest in its earliest level. Consequently, I feel that it is particularly important today that we should turn once again to exegesis of the texts in their present form, that is, that we should take up the question of the meaning that was gradually attached to them, not least through their incorporation into a great narrative complex with its specific themes.* Is there unanimity among exegetes about the meaning of the narrative of the "sacrifice of Isaac" in its present literary (*not* its preliterary) form? Furthermore, the exegete must take into account the fact that the sources are no longer separate from each other, but have been combined together. Must one not say that the two creation stories are in many respects open to each other? In the exposition it will be pointed out that the Yahwist has an intimate world constructed around man (the garden, the trees, the animals, the wife), while P paces the great cosmos in all dimensions before he treats the creation of man. Genesis, ch. 2, complements ch. 1 by its witness to God's providential, almost fatherly, act toward man, etc. Futhermore, the story of the Fall can no longer be expounded without reference to the "very good" in ch. 1.31. And for the patriarchal stories it must at least be kept in mind that the God of Abraham, Isaac, and Jacob is also the Yahweh who grants forgiveness in the cultic sacrifice in the Tabernacle. True, in Genesis, the redactor has in many instances given precedence to the Yahwistic-Elohistic tradition over the Priestly document. But in the book of Exodus the situation is reversed, and since Genesis and Exodus are not two separate "books," that must be considered in the exegesis.

Franz Rosenzweig once remarked wittily that the sign "R" (for the redactor of the Hexateuch documents, so lowly esteemed in Protestant research) should be interpreted as Rabbenu, "our master," because basically we are dependent only on him, on his great work of compilation and his theology, and we receive the Hexateuch at all only from his hands.† From the standpoint of Judaism, that is consistent. But for us, in respect to hermeneutics, even the redactor is not

*See now H. W. Wolff, "Kerygma", cited p. 31 above.

†M. Buber and Franz Rosenzweig, *Die Schrift und ihre Verdeutschung*, 1936, 322.

"our master." We receive the Old Testament from the hands of Jesus Christ, and therefore all exegesis of the Old Testament depends on whom one thinks Jesus Christ to be. If one sees in him the bringer of a new religion, then one will consistently examine the chief figures of the patriarchal narratives for their inward religious disposition and by, say, drawing religious "pictures from life" will bring into the foreground what comes close to Christianity or even corresponds with it. But this "pious" view is unsatisfactory because the principal subject of the account in the Genesis stories is not the religious characteristics of the patriarchs at all. Any mention of them is almost an aside. Often the details have to be drawn from the reader's imagination. The real subject of the account is everywhere a quite definite act of Yahweh, into which the patriarchs are drawn, often with quite perplexing results. So the first interest of the reader must be in what circumstances and in what way Yahweh's guidance is given, and what consequences result from it. In all the variety of the story, can we perhaps recognize some things that are typical of the action of God towards men? Then we must go on to raise the chief question: can we not recognize a common link even between the revelation of God in the old covenant and that in the new, a "type"? The patriarchal narratives include experiences which Israel had of a God who revealed himself and at the same time on occasions hid himself more deeply. In this very respect we can see a continuity between the Old Testament and the New. In the patriarchal narratives, which know so well how God can conceal himself, we see a revelation of God which precedes his manifestation in Jesus Christ. What we are told here of the trials of a God who hides himself and whose promise is delayed, and yet of his comfort and support, can readily be read into God's revelation of himself in Jesus Christ.

THE BIBLICAL PRIMEVAL HISTORY

THE CREATION STORY IN THE PRIESTLY NARRATIVE

WE NOTED THAT THE THEME of the ancient credo (Deut. 26.5 ff.)—the story of the patriarchs, the departure from and the re-entry into Canaan—is also the theme of the Hexateuch, where the material is massively expanded and thoroughly permeated theologically. As befits its format and importance, the entire work is supported by the Priestly and Yahwistic primeval history as by two mighty theological pillars. The immense theological development of the tradition about the patriarchs and Moses made necessary a foundation different from what the ancient credo could give. The basis and origin of sacred history was now traced to the creation of the world, and all prior phases in the history of the divine work of salvation were formulated in precise theological terms. The form of this theological preface in the Priestly document is characteristically distinct from that of the Yahwist. Wherever the separation of the two strands by literary criticism is recognized at all there is absolute unanimity of opinion.

Before we begin detailed exposition, we emphasize once more that the biblical primeval history, especially the testimony regarding creation, is not an independent unit within the context of the Hexateuch. The position of the creation story at the beginning of our Bible has often led to misunderstanding, as though the "doctrine" of creation were a central subject of Old Testament faith. That is not the case.* Neither here nor in Deutero-Isaiah is the witness to creation given

*G. von Rad, "The Theological Problem of the Old Testament Doctrine of Creation," *The Problem of the Hexateuch and Other Essays*, 131 ff.

for its own sake. Faith in creation is neither the basis nor the goal of the declarations in Gen., chs. 1 and 2. Rather, the position of both the Yahwist and the Priestly document is basically faith in salvation and election. They undergird this faith by the testimony that this Yahweh, who made a covenant with Abraham and at Sinai, is also the creator of the world. Therefore with all its astonishing concentration on the individual objects of its faith in creation, this preface has only an ancillary function. It points the course that God took with the world until he called Abraham and formed the community; and it does this in such a way that Israel looked back in faith from her own election to the creation of the world, and from there drew the line to herself from the outermost limit of the protological to the center of the soteriological.

1. THE CREATION OF THE WORLD. (P) Chs. 1.1 to 2.4a

1 1 *In the beginning God created the heavens and the earth.* 2 *The earth was with-*
out form and void, and darkness was upon the face of the deep; and the Spirit of
God was moving over the face of the waters.

3 *And God said, "Let there be light"; and there was light.* 4 *And God saw that*
the light was good; and God separated the light from the darkness. 5 *God called the*
light Day, and the darkness he called Night. And there was evening and there was
morning, one day.

6 *And God said, "Let there be a firmament in the midst of the waters, and let it*
separate the waters from the waters." 7 *And God made the firmament and separated*
the waters which were under the firmament from the waters which were above the
firmament. And it was so. 8 *And God called the firmament Heaven. And there was*
evening and there was morning, a second day.

9 *And God said, "Let the waters under the heavens be gathered together into one*
place, and let the dry land appear." And it was so. 10 *God called the dry land*
Earth, and the waters that were gathered together he called Seas. And God saw
that it was good. 11 *And God said, "Let the earth put forth vegetation, plants*
yielding seed, and fruit trees bearing fruit in which is their seed, each according to
its kind, upon the earth." And it was so. 12 *The earth brought forth vegetation,*
plants yielding seed according to their own kinds, and trees bearing fruit in which
is their seed, each according to its kind. And God saw that it was good. 13 *And*
there was evening and there was morning, a third day.

14 *And God said, "Let there be lights in the firmament of the heavens to*
separate the day from the night; and let them be for signs and for seasons and for
days and years, 15 *and let them be lights in the firmament of the heavens to give light*
upon the earth." And it was so. 16 *And God made the two great lights, the greater*
light to rule the day, and the lesser light to rule the night; he made the stars also.
17 *And God set them in the firmament of the heavens to give light upon the earth,*
18 *to rule over the day and over the night, and to separate the light from the darkness.*
And God saw that it was good. 19 *And there was evening and there was morning,*
a fourth day.

20 *And God said, "Let the waters bring forth swarms of living creatures, and*
let birds fly above the earth across the firmament of the heavens." 21 *So God*
created the great sea monsters and every living creature that moves, with which
the waters swarm, according to their kinds, and every winged bird according to its
kind. And God saw that it was good. 22 *And God blessed them, saying, "Be fruitful*
and multiply and fill the waters in the seas, and let birds multiply on the earth."
23 *And there was evening, and there was morning, a fifth day.*
24 *And God said, "Let the earth bring forth living creatures according to their*
kinds: cattle and creeping things and beasts of the earth according to their kinds."
And it was so. 25 *And God made the beasts of the earth according to their kinds and*
the cattle according to their kinds, and everything that creeps upon the ground
according to its kind. And God saw that it was good.
26 *Then God said, "Let us make man in our image, after our likeness; and let*
them have dominion over the fish of the sea and over the birds of the air, and
over the cattle, and over all the earth, and over every creeping thing that creeps upon
the earth." 27 *So God created man in his own image, in the image of God he created*
him; male and female he created them. 28 *And God blessed them, and God said to*
them, "Be fruitful and multiply, and fill the earth and subdue it; and have dominion
over the fish of the sea and over the birds of the air and over every living thing that
moves upon the earth." 29 *And God said, "Behold, I have given you every plant*
yielding seed which is upon the face of all the earth, and every tree with seed in its
fruit; you shall have them for food. 30 *And to every beast of the earth, and to every*
bird of the air, and to everything that creeps on the earth, everything that has the
breath of life, I have given every green plant for food." And it was so. 31 *And God*
saw everything that he had made, and behold, it was very good. And there was
evening and there was morning, a sixth day.
2 1 *Thus the heavens and the earth were finished, and all the host of them.* 2 *And*
on the seventh day God finished his work which he had done, and he rested on the
seventh day from all his work which he had done. 3 *So God blessed the seventh day*
and hallowed it, because on it God rested from all his work which he had done in
creation.
4a *These are the generations of the heavens and the earth when they were*
created.

Anyone who expounds Gen., ch. 1, must understand one thing: this chapter is Priestly doctrine—indeed, it contains the essence of Priestly knowledge in a most concentrated form. It was not "written" once upon a time; but, rather, it is doctrine that has been carefully enriched over centuries by very slow growth. Nothing is here by chance; everything must be considered carefully, deliberately, and precisely. It is false, therefore, to reckon here even occasionally with archaic and half-mythological rudiments, which one considers venerable, to be sure, but theologically and conceptually less binding. What is said here is intended to hold true entirely and exactly as it stands. There is no trace of the hymnic element in the language, nor is anything said that needs to be understood symbolically or whose deeper meaning has to be deciphered. The exposition must painstakingly free this compact and rather esoteric doctrine sentence by sentence, indeed, word by word. These sentences cannot be easily overinterpreted theologically! Indeed, to us the danger appears greater that the expositor will fall short of discovering the concentrated doctrinal content. Today's reader, preoccupied with the problem of faith and knowledge, must be careful not to read such tensions into the text. Without doubt, there is to be found here a great deal of the knowledge of the origin of the world that had been worked out and taught at the time, and as knowledge it is largely obsolete today. But this knowledge does not come under discussion here for its own sake; it is there, rather, as an aid towards making detailed statements about God's creation. Faith and the scientific picture of the world are so closely integrated here that the very material of knowledge of the world makes it possible to speak of God! So what is said here is not of interest only to palaeontologists. When Israel talked of the creation and ordering of the cosmos, she was discussing matters that were topical for the man living here and now. The exegete must look everywhere for this theological topicality—and not just in v. 27—if he is to do justice to the content of this chapter.

The sequence of particular declarations in vs. 1–3 comprises in its details a theological wealth of reference whose fullness is scarcely to be comprehended. We do not follow the old conjecture that v. 1 is not to be understood as an independent sentence but as the introductory clause to v. 2 or even to v. 3 ("at the beginning when God created heaven and earth . . ."). Syntactically perhaps both translations are possible, but not theologically. One must not deprive the declaration in v. 1 of the character of a theological principle. If one considers vs. 1–2 or 1–3 as the syntactical unit, then the word about chaos would stand logically and temporally before the word about creation. To be sure, the notion of a created chaos is itself a contradiction; nevertheless, one must remember that the text touches on things which in any case lie beyond human imagination. That does not mean, however, that one must renounce establishing quite definite and unrelinquishable theologumena. The first is that God, in the freedom of his will, creatively established for "heaven and earth," i.e., for absolutely everything, a beginning of its subsequent existence. The second is expressed in v. 2, for unless one speaks of chaos, creation cannot be sufficiently considered at all. To express divine creation, the Hebrew language already had a verb, which, as the Phoenician shows, could designate artistic creation. But the Old Testament usage rejects even this comparison. The verb was retained exclusively to designate the divine creative activity. This effective theological constraint which extends even into the language is significant (cf. *sālaḥ*, "to forgive," alluding only to divine forgiving). It means a creative activity, which on principle is without analogy. It is correct to say that the verb *bārā'*, "create," contains the idea both of complete effortlessness and *creatio ex nihilo*, since it is never connected with any statement of the material. The hidden grandeur of this statement is that God is the Lord of the world. But not only in the sense that he subjected a pre-existing chaos to his ordering will! It is amazing to see how sharply little Israel demarcated herself from an apparently overpowering environment of cosmological and theogonic myths. Here the subject is not a primeval mystery of procreation from which the divinity arose, nor of a "creative" struggle of mythically personified powers from which the cosmos arose, but rather the one who is neither warrior nor procreator, who alone is worthy of the predicate, Creator.

[1–2] One may understand v. 1 as the summary statement of everything that is unfolded step by step in the following verses. The first of these theological specifications is the statement about the chaotic original condition of the earth. The Priestly document gropes into this difficult subject with the aid of a number of terms that were familiar to priestly-cosmological thought. "Tohuwabohu" means the formless; the primeval waters over which darkness was superimposed characterizes the chaos materially as a watery primeval element, but at the same time gives a dimensional association: *t^ehōm* ("sea of chaos") is the cosmic abyss (Jac.). This damp primeval element, however, was agitated by a divine storm (cf. Dan. 7.2). The much disputed *m^eraḥepet* (L: *schwebte*, "hovered") is not to be translated by "brood," but, according to Deut. 32.11 and Jer. 23.9, the verb appears to have the meaning of "vibrate," "tremble," "move," "stir." This is supported by Dan. 7.2, which is to be referred to for interpretation. *Rūaḥ 'elōhīm* ("Spirit of God") is better translated "storm of God," i.e., terrible storm (cf. "mountain of God," "lands of God," "silver of God," meaning simply the superlative, in J. M. P. Smith, *Old Testament Essays*, 1927, 166 f.). The declaration, then, belongs completely to the description of chaos and does not yet lead into the creative activity; in fact this "spirit of God" takes no more active part in creation. The Old Testament nowhere knows of such a cosmological significance for the concept of the spirit of God.

There has been an increasing disinclination to interpret the concepts contained in v. 2 in terms of the mythological conceptions of neighbouring religions. The Hebrew word for "primeval flood" (*tᵉhōm*) probably has a linguistic affinity with Tiamat, the Babylonian dragon of chaos. A more direct connection, amounting to a "borrowing," cannot be assumed. Nor can it be assumed that the Hebrew *bōhū* goes back to the Phoenician mother-goddess Baau. *Bōhū* is a noun (always connected with *tōhū*) which means emptiness, desolation. *Tōhū* is connected more with the concept of the wilderness or even with the wilderness itself (Deut. 32.10; Ps. 107.40, etc.). So it is inappropriate to suppose, as has long been the case, that P had to resort to strange and semi-mythical conceptions to elucidate the primal state of chaos. The concepts used in v. 2 are cosmological keywords which were the indispensable requisites of Priestly learning. The relationship of Gen. 1 to Babylonian mythology now looks quite different from the way it did to the generation of the "Babel-Bibel" conflict at the beginning of the century.

A comparison with the Ras Shamra mythology leads to essentially the same result. The poets and prophets, it is true, are less troubled about borrowing common Oriental ideas (cf. Ps. 104.5–9; 89.10 f.; 74.12–17; Isa. 51.9 ff.; Ezek. 32.2–8). When one considers the other subjects of Old Testament religious faith, the contents of this verse are in another respect unusually daring, for they reach almost speculatively behind creation, i.e., behind what lies palpably before man's eyes, and they make that peculiar intermediate state between nothingness and creation, i.e., the chaos, the subject of a theological declaration.

It has always been seen that v. 2 is not an advance over the concise statement of v. 1, but is almost a step backward. Earlier theologians sought to explain this break by means of an immense speculation, the so-called hypothesis of restitution.* The assumption, however, of a cosmic Luciferlike plunge of the creation from its initial splendor is linguistically and objectively quite impossible. But the unevenness may be explained from the fact that v. 2, along with v. 1, which is obviously the dominant verse, has to preserve a special concern of faith. Thus this second verse speaks not only of a reality that once

*Cf. its classic treatment in Franz Delitzsch, *System der biblischen Psychologie*², 1861, 60 ff.

existed in a preprimeval period but also of a possibility that always exists. Man has always suspected that behind all creation lies the abyss of formlessness; that all creation is always ready to sink into the abyss of the formless; that the chaos, therefore, signifies simply the threat to everything created. This suspicion has been a constant temptation for his faith. Faith in creation must stand this test. Verse 2 teaches one to understand the marvel of creation, therefore, from the viewpoint of its negation; thus it speaks first of the formless and the abysmal out of which God's will lifted creation and above which it holds it unceasingly. For the cosmos stands permanently in need of this supporting Creator's will. We see here that the theological thought of ch. 1 moves not so much between the poles of nothingness and creation as between the poles of chaos and cosmos. It would be false to say, however, that the idea of the *creatio ex nihilo* was not present here at all (v. 1 stands with good reason before v. 2!), but the actual concern of this entire report of creation is to give prominence, form, and order to the creation out of chaos (cf. the fundamental idea of "separating").

[3–5] After the theologically important digression of v. 2, the text again turns at v. 3 to positive declarations about God's creative activity. It ventures to unfold the gradual evolution of creation and thus makes possible the orderly presentation of individual fundamental elements of the Old Testament belief in creation. It is therefore an expression of ultimate cosmological knowledge for P to begin the series of creative acts with light streaming into chaos. Light, as the "sublimest element" (Jac.), "the finest of all elementary powers" (Di.), is the first-born of creation. Without light there is no creation; only light reveals the contours of the creature blurred in darkness. The Oriental did not consider the remarkable separation of light and stars as something that could not be performed, because he did not think of light and darkness exclusively in connection with the heavenly bodies (Job 38.19–20). Immediately and without resistance light fills the world, which was flooded by chaos. In contrast to a few freer poetic declarations (Ps. 104.2), here the creatureliness even of light is emphasized. It is not somehow an overflow of the essence of deity, but rather an object, even though preferential, of God's creation.

The idea of creation by the word preserves first of all the most radical essential distinction between Creator and creature. Creation cannot be even remotely considered an emanation from God; it is not somehow an overflow or reflection of his being, i.e., of his divine nature, but is rather a product of his personal will.* The only continuity between God and his work is the Word (Bonhoeffer).

This creative word is different from any human word; it is not "empty" (Gen. 32.47; Isa. 55.11), but powerful and of the highest creative potency. In the second place, therefore, this conception contains the knowledge that the world wholly belongs to God: it is the creation of his will, and he is its Lord. (Just as ch. 1 understands nature as created by God's word, so the Old Testament knows history also as created by God's word. See Isa. 9.7; 55.10 ff.; Jer. 23.29, but also I Kings 2.27, etc.) With regard to the history of religions, one cannot deny that there is a connection between this idea and belief in magic. (The god Marduk, for example, in the Babylonian epic of creation also displays his power before the gods through effective magical words; AOT, 117; ANET, 66.) But it is also clear that in Israel the idea was purified theologically of every vestige of magical thinking through centuries of Priestly tradition. This is an illustration of the fact that in the history of religion some terms and ideas evidently related to one another occasionally have nothing more in common than a certain formal similarity. To the previous statements about creation (essential distinction from God, belonging to God) must now be added as the third a declaration of value: the creature brought into existence is *ṭōb* ("good"). The word contains less an aesthetic judgment than the designation of purpose and correspondence. (It corresponds, therefore, though with much more restraint to the content of Ps. 104.31; Ps. 104 tells not so much of the beauty as of the marvelous purpose and order of creation.)

But one important work is yet outstanding. The light has poured in and has removed chaos to a gloomy condition of twilight—we must imagine the creative acts quite realistically! Now from what has flowed together God separates the elements of light and darkness as day and night. Both are thus creatively quite unlike. While the day is light from the first created original light, night consists in nothing more than that darkness of chaos which was eliminated, now limited, to be sure, by wholesome order. Every night, when the created world of forms flows together into formlessness, chaos regains a certain power over what has been created. (Many of our evening hymns know how to express impressively the creaturely feeling of dread

*Here therefore "the divine creator of the world" is not "exalted above creation merely as a natural power, as in the case of other creation stories, and thereby included within the realm of nature" (Hönigswald).

toward the night.) And every morning "with the light which springs from the heights to unite the dusky shadows" (Hölderlin), something of God's first creation is repeated. Related to this unlike gradation in creation is the fact that only the light receives the predicate "good." The ultimate enunciation of this orderly cosmic arrangement and wholesome stabilization is the divine naming of the present darkness as night and the present light as day. "The name, given by God, is an expression of essence and a seal of the way it will look henceforth" (Del.). Thus the accent lies, not on the verbal naming, but on the "calling into and fixing of the existence of creation" (Di.). The precise translation, therefore, is "And God *appointed* the light as day . . ." (Jac.). But in the ancient Oriental view the act of giving a name meant, above all, the exercise of a sovereign right (cf. II Kings 23.34; 24.17). Thus the naming of this and all subsequent creative works once more expresses graphically God's claim of lordship over the creatures. The day here appears to be reckoned from morning to morning, in strange contrast to its reckoning in the cultic law.

[6–8] The second day brings the creation of the firmament, which the ancients imagined as a gigantic hemispherical and ponderous bell (Ps. 19.2; Job 37.18). *Rāqīaʿ* means that which is firmly hammered, stamped (a word of the same root in Phoenician means "tin dish"!). The meaning of the verb *rqʿ* concerns the hammering of the vault of heaven into firmness (Isa. 42.5; Ps. 136.6). The Vulgate translates *rāqīaʿ* with *firmamentum*, and that remains the best rendering. This heavenly bell, which is brought into the waters of chaos, forms first of all a separating wall between the waters beneath and above. The so-called formula of approbation ("good") is here intentionally omitted, since this work of creation is not concluded until the third day.

A conspicuous fact about the process of creation is that along with the creative word there is also talk of God's immediate "making." This decisive terminological unevenness, which persists clearly throughout the chapter, is the trace of two different conceptions in the report of creation. The first, doubtless the older, moves within the simple framework of an immediate, imaginative creating ("then God made," vs. 7, 16 f., 21, 25); the other speaks of the creation by means of the commanding word. Whether these two conceptions can also be textually separated or whether they stand out from each other only in their content is a secondary question. More important is the fact that the younger has not displaced the older, that rather both voices in the present text receive their due: the older, which tries to preserve the direct, effectively applied creative working of God in the world (the world came directly from God's hands which fashioned it),and the younger, which, without removing this testimony, speaks of the absolute distance between Creator and creature.

[9–10] The third day includes first of all the completion of what was begun on the second. The water still under the heavenly dome is drained off and given a place befitting creation, which we now call the ocean. This restriction of the waters now brings to light, beneath the firmament, the dry ground, which was imagined as a disk resting upon primeval waters and washed on all sides by the ocean. At this point the world in its basic characteristics is roughly finished. Above the firmament are the waters of the heavenly ocean whose blue color we see from below. From it fall rains upon the earth (cf., however, Gen. 7.11); under the firmament is the earth disk surrounded by oceans and miraculously held above waters (Ps. 24.2; 136.6; Ex. 20.4). It would be wrong, however, when speaking of the "waters" and the "ocean," to think too rationalistically only about man's physical and geographical world. The origin of the ocean from the dimension of the chaotic is clear enough. The cosmos, therefore, is surrounded entirely and thus threatened on all sides, above, and below, by cosmic spaces, which, to be sure, can no longer be called directly chaotic, but which still permanently preserve something hostile to God and creation. It is a miracle that God's will for order has set for them a salutary boundary. The Priestly impassive language should not be allowed to gloss over the burning interest of this creative act either. Poets and prophets speak differently of the same things. The waters fled before God and his reprimand; he set bounds for them which they may not transgress (Ps. 104.7–9; Jer. 5.22); the power of chaos is watched over by God (Job 7.12); indeed, it is bound (Prayer of Manasseh 3). Should it want to arise, God would still it (Ps. 89.10; Job 26.12), etc. Here again the naming! In distinguishing things according to their nature, God therewith also distinguishes terms and names; the human name-giving is, as it were, only a distance echo of this divine naming (Del.) (cf. for this thought Gen. 2.19 f.).

[11–13] The second work of this day is the world of plants as the lowest level of organic life. Here one can ask if a Hebrew would also rank the plants in this way. They obviously do not have *nepeš* ("life") like the animals. This creature too is called into existence by God's creative word, but here an expression unused until now attracts attention. The addressed subject is the earth, summoned and empowered to maternal participation in this creative act. Here ancient thoughts about the mother earth may in fact be prominent. And yet the concern is certainly not with ideas that were unassimilated and rather unwillingly handed down by tradition, but rather with something carefully considered: the mediate relation existing between God and the plant world is not to be overlooked. The life of plants as such has its immediacy to the earth and her creative power; it springs from her and returns to her. The "greenness" is here divided into two chief kinds (the passage beginning with *'ēśeb* ("herb") in v. 11 must be taken appositionally): herbs, which yield seed directly, and trees, which yield fruit in which their seed is contained. Here too in briefest terms a broad area of creation is conceptually outlined: the vital seed, which is thrown off the plant; the fruitfulness of the maternal earth; and behind and beyond everything, God's creative word of command. One is reminded unmistakably of the term *natura*; the term, however, is bounded by the term *creatura*.

[14–19] Fourth day: creation of the stars. The entire passage vs. 14–19 has a strongly antimythical feeling. The stars are considered as creatures and as dependent on God's ordering creative will. The expression "lights" or "lamps" is meant to be prosaic and degrading. These created objects are expressly not named "sun" and "moon" so that every tempting association may be evaded; for the common Semitic word for "sun" was also a divine name. P speaks of the appropriate purpose of the stars with distinctly reasoned coolness and broad ceremoniousness. Their "ruling" is in reality the most sensible service to which as created objects they are commissioned by their creator's will. In the passage about the creation of plants the marked lack of purpose was striking; there was no trace of any ancillary relationship or alliance between this entire domain and the world of man or beast. Here, however, the relationship is unmistakably clear, in spite of the fact that beasts and men have not yet been created. This is connected with the diligence with which every form of independent godlike astral power here is disputed. To comprehend the significance of these statements, one must remember that they were formulated in a cultural and religious atmosphere that was saturated with all kinds of astrological false belief. All ancient Oriental (not Old Testament!) thinking with regard to time was determined by the cyclical course of the stars. Man's world, down to each individual destiny, was determined by the working of the powers of the stars. The restraining power necessary to deny them divine veneration is shown on the one hand by the solemn warning of the Deuteronomist (Deut. 4.19; cf. Jer. 10.2; Job 31.26 f.), and on the other by the severe incursion of the cult of the stars at the later period of the monarchy into the center, so to speak, of the practice of faith (II Kings 23.11 f.). Only the prophet could bring himself to mock at this reversion: Isa. 47.13. "Signs" in Gen. 1.14 are perhaps the sights in the heavenly vault which were not normal, as eclipses of the sun; in any case they were fixed astral points for regulating cult and work. Evidently the stars are not creators of light, but only mediating bearers of a light that was there without them and before them.

[20–23] Now the world is ready as a dwelling place for living creatures. All the conditions for life have been given; therefore, on the fifth day begins the creation of living creatures. The report first names the inhabitants of the created spheres far from man, the water and the air. In theological formulation the report emphasizes very strongly what is new and unprecedented on this day of creation: the creation of living beings. (According to ancient Hebrew thought, plants did not share in life.) The verb *bārā'* ("create") to designate special and exclusive divine creativity is used here again deliberately. Significantly it is used first (if we disregard the summary v. 1) for the creation of living creatures (v. 21). Compared with creation by word, *bārā'* ("create") points without doubt to a direct relationship between creature and creator. Life came into being not only by a word of command, but it derives from a more direct creative act of God. Moreover, this newly created life is also the object of the divine blessing, i.e., these living creatures are the recipients of a life-giving, divine power by virtue of which they themselves are capable of passing on the life they have received by means of their own procreation. The first living creatures that the report names are the mythical beings who live at the extreme limits of the created realms known to man, removed completely from human understanding and human use, but precisely therefore an object of special divine pleasure (Ps. 104.26; Job 40.15 ff.; 41.1 ff.). In the sequence of animals created, the fish and the fowl follow next. The progression from the almost mythical sea monsters to the smaller and more harmless animals contains a significant theological statement: nothing in this realm, which, as we saw, is close nevertheless to the dimension of chaos, is outside the creative will of God. Outside God there is nothing to fear; even this creature is good in God's sight!

[24–25] The creation of the land animals, the first work of the sixth day, concludes the work of the fifth day. Here again, as in the creation of the plants, a creative participation of the maternal earth is mentioned. The beast is referred altogether to the earth for the foundation of its life, and from this created bond it receives life and death. The absence here of divine blessing is intentional. Only indirectly do the animals receive the power of procreation from God; they receive it directly from the earth, the creative potency of which is acknowledged throughout.* Water, by creation, stands lower in rank than the earth; it could not be summoned by God to creative participation (but cf. LXX!). The land animals are classified into three groups: (1) wild animals (beasts of prey, but also our "game"), (2) cattle, and (3) all small beasts (reptiles, etc.). In sharp contrast to this bond of animal world with earth, the text in what follows speaks of the creation of man, who now comes from above, from God, in absolute immediacy.

[26–28] The creation of man is introduced more impressively than any preceding work by the announcement of a divine resolution: "Let us make man." God participates more intimately and intensively in this than in the earlier works of creation. The use of the verb *bārā'* in v. 27 receives its fullest significance for that divine creativity which is absolutely without analogy. It occurs three times in the one verse to make clear that here the high point and goal has been reached toward which all God's creativity from v. 1 on was directed. Concerning the disputed "us" in v. 26, see below. The Hebrew word *'ādām* ("man") is a collective and is therefore never used in the plural; it means literally "mankind" (L. Köhler). Luther instinctively translated the word very well with "*Menschen.*"

The declaration about man in God's image depends on two substantives in v. 26, which cannot be expounded with complete unambiguity because of their shades of meaning and the prepositions preceding them ("in our . . . according to our"). *Ṣelem* ("image") means predominantly an actual plastic work, a duplicate, sometimes an idol (I Sam. 6.5; Num. 33.52; II Kings 11.18; a painting, Ezek. 23.14); only on occasion does it mean a duplicate in the diminished sense of a semblance when compared with the original (Ps. 39.6). *D^emūt* ("likeness") is a verbal abstraction and means predominantly

*J. Hempel, *Das Ethos des A.T.*, 1938, 174.

something abstract: "appearance," "similarity," "analogy" (Ezek. 1.5, 10, 26, 28, but also "the copy" II Kings 16.10). There is no particular significance in the change of prepositions ("in" our image, "according to" our likeness). In 5.3 they are exchanged without any difference in meaning. The essential word for the idea of God's image is obviously *ṣelem* ("image"), which appears without *d*ᵉ*mūt* ("likeness") in the solemn v. 27; likewise in ch. 9.6. We learn from a number of ancient Oriental myths that a god makes a man (or a god) in his likeness. It is also particularly significant that in ancient Egypt the Pharaoh was regarded as "the image of God living on earth."* Our text may not simply be detached from its broader connection with such evidently common Oriental ideas. This basic word *ṣelem* ("image") is more closely explained and made precise by *d*ᵉ*mūt* ("similarity"), with the simple meaning that this image is to correspond to the original image, that it is to resemble it. The interpretations, therefore, are to be rejected which proceed from an anthropology strange to the Old Testament and one-sidedly limit God's image to man's spiritual nature, relating it to man's "dignity," his "personality" or "ability for moral decision," etc. The marvel of man's bodily appearance is not at all to be expected from the realm of God's image. This was the original notion, and we have no reason to suppose that it completely gave way, in P's theological reflection, to a spiritualizing and intellectualizing tendency. Therefore, one will do well to split the physical from the spiritual as little as possible: the whole man is created in God's image. Even later times did not exclude corporeality, as is clear from a tradition referred to by Ezekiel, according to which the first man was perfect in beauty (*k*ᵉ*lîl yōpî*), Ezek. 28.12. Psalm 8 also points decisively to the physical, with obvious reference to Gen. 1.26 ff. It is the only text after Gen. 1.26 ff. that makes a declaration about God's image in man. Psalm 8 also gives us an important complement to the idea. In it Yahweh is addressed; nevertheless, man is said to be made a little lower than "Elohim." This means that God's image does not refer directly to Yahweh but to the "angels." So also in v. 26. The extraordinary plural ("Let us") prevents one from referring God's image too directly to God the Lord. God includes himself among the heavenly beings and thereby conceals himself in this multiplicity. That, in our opinion, is the only possible explanation for this striking stylistic form. Proof for the correctness of this interpretation appears in Gen. 3.22,

*W. H. Schmidt, *Die Schöpfungsgeschichte der Priesterschrift*[2], 1967, 137.

where the plural again occurs just as abruptly and yet obviously for the same reason.

The notion that Yahweh is surrounded by heavenly beings is in itself quite common to the Old Testament (I Kings 22.19 f.; Job, ch. 1; Isa., ch. 6); but one must explain why it seems so abrupt here. The declaration about God's image is indeed highly exalted, but it also remains intentionally in a certain state of suspense. In Old Testament terms, the meaning of vs. 26 f. is that man is created by God in the form of and similar to Elohim. If one wants to determine the content of this statement more closely, one must ask how ancient Israel thought in detail of this Elohim. Here two predicates are important: "wise" (II Sam. 14.17, 20) and "good" (I Sam. 29.9). (Both assertions, as unreflected popular sayings, reveal the universal, almost proverbial, character of this notion.) It is necessary, however, to be careful not to see something additional in this image of God in man. It is not limited to any part of man. Man is like God in the way in which he is called into existence, in the totality of his being. And here, finally, in this supreme mystery of the whole work of creation, the language of P takes on a solemn tone (v. 27). Of course, even here P limits itself to fixing the matter. It refrains from any reflection of this "gracious act of God who, in his sovereign freedom, has willed out of all creation to have man alone as his real counterpart with whom he will speak and have communion."* Without question, in the broader background of this Priestly statement about God's image in man there is the notion of Yahweh's human form. But did the great prophets speak any differently of God? (Amos 4.13; 9.1; Isa. 6.1; etc.) One thinks especially of the appearance of the "glory of Yahweh" in Ezek. 1.26. The equally subtle and careful statement in Ezekiel ("a likeness as it were of a human form," *d^{e}mūt k^{e}mar'ē 'ādām*) seems exactly the prelude to Gen. 1.26.†

When, however, one has traced in a general way the distribution of weight in the Priestly account of man's creation, one will admit that the text speaks less of the nature of God's image than of its purpose. There is less said about the gift itself than about the task. This then is sketched most explicitly: domination in the world, especially over the animals. This commission to rule is not considered as belonging to the definition of God's image; but it is its consequence, i.e., that for which man is capable because of it. The close relation of

*F. Horst, *Gottes Recht*, 1961, 230.

†P. Humbert, *Etudes sur le récit du Paradis et la chute dans la Genèse*, 1940, 172.

the term for God's image with that for the commission to exercise dominion emerges quite clearly when we have understood *ṣelem* as a plastic image. Just as powerful earthly kings, to indicate their claim to dominion, erect an image of themselves in the provinces of their empire where they do not personally appear, so man is placed upon earth in God's image as God's sovereign emblem. He is really only God's representative, summoned to maintain and enforce God's claim to dominion over the earth. The decisive thing about man's similarity to God, therefore, is his function in the non-human world.* The expressions for the exercise of this dominion are remarkably strong: *rādā*, "tread," "trample" (e.g., the wine press); similarly *kābaš*, "stamp." Thus man's creation has a retroactive significance for all nonhuman creatures; it gives them a new relation to God. The creature, in addition to having been created by God, receives through man a responsibility to God; in any case, because of man's dominion it receives once again the dignity belonging to a special domain of God's sovereignty.

Sexual distinction is also created. The plural in v. 27 ("he created them") is intentionally contrasted with the singular ("him") and prevents one from assuming the creation of an originally androgynous man. By God's will, man was not created alone but designated for the "thou" of the other sex. The idea of man, according to P, finds its full meaning not in the male alone but in man and woman (Pr.). "That is the immense double statement, of a lapidary simplicity, so simple indeed that we hardly realize that with it a vast world of myth and Gnostic speculation, of cynicism and asceticism, of the deification of sexuality and fear of sex completely disappears." (E. Brunner, *Man in Revolt*, 346.) Man also receives from God's hand the blessing that enables him to propagate and increase. Thus everything about man points to God. With regard to the origin of both his nature and his destiny, man is completely referred to and understood from God. One must observe, however, that man's procreative ability is not here understood as an emanation or manifestation of his creation in God's image. Heathen myths had many ways to express the mystery of procreation, the *hieros gamos* of the divinity. Especially in the Canaanite cult this divine event was orgiastically celebrated sexually in the form of sacred prostitution. Thereby the way seemed open for man to share in the divine world. Thence one can understand the designation of this Canaanite cult as "harlotry" (Hos., chs. 1 to 3;

*W. Caspari, "Imago Divina," in: *Festschrift für R. Seeberg*, 1929, 208.

Jer. 3.1 ff.). It is noteworthy that procreative ability is removed from God's image and shifted to a special word of blessing (Zi.).

[29–30] For nourishment, man is given every kind of vegetable food; the animals are given only the herb of the field. That is the only suggestion of the paradisiacal peace in the creation as it came God-willed from God's hand. Thus, on the other hand, our report of creation places man in striking proximity to the animals. Just as he was created with them on the same day, so he is referred with them to the same table for his bodily needs (K. Barth). Killing and slaughtering did not come into the world, therefore, by God's design and command. Here too the text speaks not only of prehistoric things but of a particular matter, without which the testimony of faith in creation would not be complete. No shedding of blood within the animal kingdom, and no murderous action by man! This word of God, therefore, also means a limitation in the human right of dominion. The age of Noah knows other orders of life (Gen. 9.2).

[31] Verse 31 contains the concluding formula of approval for the entire work of creation. This formula "Behold, it was very good" is of great importance within the terse and unsuperlative language of P. It could also be correctly translated "completely perfect" (Pr.), and rightly refers more to the wonderful purposefulness and harmony than to the beauty of the entire cosmos. This statement, expressed and written in a world full of innumerable troubles, preserves an inalienable concern of faith: no evil was laid upon the world by God's hand; neither was his omnipotence limited by any kind of opposing power whatever. When faith speaks of creation, and in so doing directs its eye toward God, then it can only say that God created the world perfect. This statement, however, cannot be readily understood; if it were, the cosmos in its created splendor would have to be thoroughly intelligible and clear as crystal to men. The question of its riddles and troubles is now answered, after the redactor's theological coupling of the documentary sources, by the Yahwistic chapter of the Fall, with its strong aetiological orientation.

[2.1–3] The declarations about a Sabbath at creation contain one of the most remarkable and daring testimonies in the entire Priestly document. In reading these statements, which move, to be sure, at that extreme limit of the protological, one must once again remember especially that they too derive completely from Israel's position before God as it was constituted by the covenantal relation. But what sense can there be in mentioning one further matter *above* and *beyond* the creation of the entire cosmos and all living creatures? And this matter is obviously of such significance that it is ranked above all the rest, and forms the final conclusion to the whole. The Babylonian creation epic also contains a concluding act following the work of creation; it is the public glorification of the god Marduk, in the assembly of the gods, as the chief gods name his fifty names and extol him. How different, how much more profound, is the impressive rest of Israel's God! This rest is in every respect a new thing along with the process of creation, not simply the negative sign of its end; it is anything but an appendix. Furthermore, it is significant that God "completed" his work on the seventh day (and not, as seems more logical, on the sixth—so the LXX!). This "completion" and this rest must be considered as a matter for itself. One should be careful about speaking of the "institution of the Sabbath," as is often done. Of that nothing at all is said here. The Sabbath as a cultic institution is quite outside the purview. The text speaks, rather, of a rest that existed before man and still exists without man's perceiving it. The declaration mounts, as it were, to the place of God himself and testifies that with the living God there is rest. But this word about rest is not at all speculative; it speaks of one facet of God which is turned to the world. Its first testimony is negative, but important enough: that the world is no longer in process of being created. It was not and is not incomplete, but it has been "completed" by God. Even more, that God has "blessed," "sanctified" ("to sanctify" means to separate exclusively for God), this rest, means that P does not consider it as something for God alone but as a concern of the world, almost as a third something that exists between God and the world. The way is being prepared, therefore, for an exalted, saving good. Nothing of that is apparent to man. How could "the" man be informed of this mystery? But once a community and a tabernacle are present, they will be bound to observe this rest of God (Ex. 31.12 ff.). Further, we must remember that these statements received their final form at the time of the exile, a time when Israel perceived in the Sabbath (and in circumcision) the real sign of the covenant that expressed compactly the entire difference distinguishing them from the heathen world (cf. Ezek. 20.12, 20 ff.; 22.8, 26; Isa. 56.2, 4, 6; 58.13). Thus at creation God prepared what will benefit man in this life, what in fact will be necessary for him, yes, that which one day will receive him eschatologically in eternity. This last, to be sure, lies beyond the theological purview of the Priestly theology! The Sabbath at creation, as the last of the creative days, is not limited; the concluding formula ("and it was evening and it was morning . . .") is lacking, and that too, like everything else in this chapter, is intentional. Thus Gen. 2.1 ff. speaks about the preparation of an exalted saving good for the world and man, of a rest "before which millennia pass away as a thunderstorm" (Novalis). It is as tangibly "existent" protologically as it is expected eschatologically in Hebrews (Heb., ch. 4).

These declarations conclude the Priestly account of the creation of heaven and earth with their hosts. The use of the word *ṣābā'* ("host") to include all the elements and living creatures that fill the cosmos (Ps. 103.21) is unusual. Perhaps it is a technical term in the Priestly classification. (Compare Num. 4.3; 8.24.) But perhaps the writer was thinking of the chief beings who, according to the ancient Israelite view, surround God's domain and occasionally mediate between him and man (I Kings 22.19; Josh. 5.14; etc.). **[2.4a]** The statement in ch. 2.4a is difficult. The formula is common in Genesis as a title (chs. 5.1; 6.9; 10.1; 11.10, 27; 25.12, 19; 36.1, 9; 37.2). Here, however, the passage cannot be a title; the formula is Priestly. Another difficulty arises from the use of the word *tōlᵉdōt* in this verse, for the word means "family tree," "genealogy," literally, "generations." We assume that the formula, which represents a kind of chapter division in the Priestly document, was subsequently added to the chapter on creation because of the need for system. It then was used in this story with the figurative sense of "story of origin." Since, however, the beginning of the chapter was canonically fixed, the interpolator had to be satisfied with adding the statement as a concluding word. For a further discussion of the problem, which is eonnected with the origin of the entire Priestly document, see the commentary at ch. 5.1.

NOTES ON THE PRIESTLY ACCOUNT OF CREATION

The text about God's creation of the world has no author in our sense of the word. In essence it is not myth and not saga, but Priestly doctrine, i.e., ancient, sacred knowledge, preserved and handed on by many generations of priests, repeatedly pondered, taught, reformed and expanded most carefully and compactly by new reflections and experiences of faith. To write out these thirty-five verses, Israel's faith required centuries of carefully collected reflection. Such cosmological and theological knowledge, even that in the "table of nations," Gen., ch. 10, was nourished in ancient Israel at the sanctuaries. The final form of the material as we have it may date from the exile, but its roots and beginnings certainly lie hidden in the bosom of the oldest Yahweh community.

Various irregularities in the material make it clear that this process of transmission went hand in hand with a more and more radical purification and distillation of all mythical and speculative elements, an amazing theological accomplishment! This account of creation is unique in this respect among the cosmogonies of other religions. This process of inner purification is also evident in the language. Language and expression are concentrated to the utmost on the purely theological; not a word is poetic flourish (Jac.), there is "no effort of fancy to describe the process more closely."* Psalm 104 and other texts† show us that Israel also knew how to speak in a different, more lively, way about God's creation. But the atmosphere of Gen., ch. 1, is not primarily one of reverence, awe, or gratitude, but one of theological reflection. The sober monotony of the account, precisely because of this radical renunciation, emphasizes what faith is capable of declaring objectively. But just this renunciation also mediates aesthetically the impression of restrained power and lapidary greatness.

The long road in the history of tradition which lies behind the present form of this account of creation is in many respects recognizable. The exposition has dealt with the tension between creation by act and creation by word. Even though we have to admit a more mature theological appreciation in the latter, still the later version did not consider giving up the older, which presented the relation of the creator to the material as unmediated. Only the harmony of both declarations gives the full witness. Another form of work on the old material can be seen from the inconsistency between works and days of creation. The third and sixth day each have two created works; the creation of the firmament cuts across the second and the third day. The order of the works, therefore, must at one time have been different, and a reconstruction is possible. For us it is important to recognize that it was because of the seven-day scheme that some violence was done to the old material. There must be here an important concern of faith which would force on the ancient material an element that until then was so strange to it; the inclusion of the events of creation within the course of a series of days provides the last possible delimitation to

*J. Wellhausen, *Prolegomena to the History of Ancient Israel*, r.p. 1957, 299.
†Ps. 74.12 ff.; 89.10 ff.; Isa. 51.9 f.

every kind of mythical thinking. The events that are recorded happened once for all and their results are irrevocably permanent. The seven days are unquestionably to be understood as actual days and as a unique, unrepeatable lapse of time in this world. "Creation as God's work inaugurates time and thus the temporality and finiteness of the world" (E. Osterloh). Genesis, ch. 1, begins the *work of history*, which continues to the revelation at Sinai and the tribal conquest. The author does not speculatively develop a cosmogonic drama, whose acts he can follow with interest as though from a detached point of observation. Rather, his point of reference is wholly within time and within creation, to the coming into being of which he attests; and when he speaks of this coming into being he at no point goes beyond what faith can experience and express in this life. We must realize that we have an account of creation in which the subject of creation appears only to the extent that faith can know it as a creative will directed earthward, that for the rest, however, as befits its nature, it has no mythological character. Likewise P resists the temptation of an actual description of the acts of creation. One can speak, therefore, only in a very limited sense of a dependence of this account of creation on extra-Israelite myths. Doubtless there are some conceptions which obviously were common to ancient Oriental, cosmological thought; but even they are so theologically filtered in P that scarcely more than the word itself is left in common. Considering P's superior spiritual maturity, we may be certain that terms which did not correspond to his ideas of faith could be effortlessly avoided or recoined. Genesis, ch. 1, does not know the struggle of two personified cosmic primordial principles; not even a trace of one hostile to God can be detected! Chaos has no power of its own; one cannot speak of it at all as though it existed for itself alone, but it exists for faith only with reference to God's creative will, which is superior to it.

In the North-Canaanite Ras Shamra texts (from the second half of the second century), no creation myth proper has been found. But the account of the struggles of their gods over creation gives us some idea of the religious environment with which Israel had to fight. One cannot marvel enough at the power which made it possible for Israel to break away from this world of ideas and speak about the relationship of God to the world in quite a different way.

One further note must be made to the inner construction of the whole: the statement in v. 1 embraces the content of the entire chapter. All subsequent statements, which in a certain sense are only unfoldings of this programmatic statement, move basically along the line that is given in the first verse of the chapter: everything was created by God, there is no creative power apart from him. Along with this line (let us call it horizontal), which goes from the beginning to the end of the creation account, there is also an ascending line, a clear sequence of stages in the relationship of the creatures to the Creator; for not all have the same immediacy to God. Farthest from God is *chaos*, which can scarcely be formulated theologically. *Night* is created, to be sure, but not on the same level with the day at all, for it is the darkness of chaos driven into cosmic order. The *plants* have direct relationship only to the fruitful earth and derive only mediately from God, since God made the earth "fruitful with his Word" (Calvin). The *animals*, however, are higher. With them begins the actual use of the verb *bārā'* ("to create"). A clear distinction is made, however, between water animals and land animals. The former, corresponding to the greater distance that exists between God and the waters, originate from the creative command; the latter originate from the earth, which is empowered to participate in creation. Most important, however, is the word of blessing addressed to the creature, which empowers the animals to propagation. (Why this word of blessing is missing in the case of the land animals was explained above. Perhaps, however, the word of v. 22 ought to apply to the land animals as well.) At the very end of this succession is *man*, and he is quite directly responsible to God! The world is oriented toward man, and in him it has its purest direct relation to God. The simplest consequence of this statement is that man, therefore, cannot seek his direct relation to God in the world, in the realm of nature. It is significant that the concept of the creative *natura* occurs only in passing and with severe restriction (v. 11 and v. 24); dominating throughout is the concept of the *creatura*.

One should not deny that P makes his great declarations of faith in the form of, and in closest connection with, the sacred "natural science" of his time. However, things are not so simple that we can leave aside as theologically negligible everything in this creation story that can be attributed to an ancient view of the world. This would be to condense the content of Gen., ch. 1, to the statement that God created the world. Such a condensation, however, would do scant justice to Israel's centuries-long concern to define the relationship of God to the world in a way which has found detailed expression in this chapter. We have seen how, even within Gen. 1, in the course of time the conceptions have found more appropriate expression (for example, in respect of creation by action and creation by word). We can derive far more theological significance from this chapter than the statement that God created the world. Israel did not simply borrow a neutral picture of the world from the ancient Orient and limit itself to inscribing v. 1 above it. Precisely because it was bound to its faith in Yahweh, it could no longer speak in mythological terms of struggles between the gods or divinize the mysteries of the creative earth (v. 24!); it had to recreate its picture of the world from the beginning. From the standpoint of modern science this picture may seem antiquated, but the exegete must not ignore the immense theological content which Israel gave to this chapter.

We will follow first of all the Priestly tradition as far as Noah; then we will be able to present the equally compact narrative of the Yahwist in its original form as far as Noah.

2. GENEALOGICAL TABLE OF THE PATRIARCHS FROM ADAM TO NOAH. Ch. 5

5 1 *This is the book of the generations of Adam. When God created man, he made*
him in the likeness of God. 2 *Male and female he created them, and he blessed them*
and named them Man when they were created. 3 *When Adam had lived a hundred*
and thirty years, he became the father of a son in his own likeness, after his image,
and named him Seth. 4 *The days of Adam after he became the father of Seth were*
eight hundred years; and he had other sons and daughters. 5 *Thus all the days that*
Adam lived were nine hundred and thirty years; and he died.

6 *When Seth had lived a hundred and five years, he became the father of Enosh.*
7 *Seth lived after the birth of Enosh eight hundred and seven years, and had other*
sons and daughters. 8 *Thus all the days of Seth were nine hundred and twelve years;*
and he died.

9 *When Enosh had lived ninety years, he became the father of Kenan.* 10 *Enosh*
lived after the birth of Kenan eight hundred and fifteen years, and had other sons
and daughters. 11 *Thus all the days of Enosh were nine hundred and five years;*
and he died.

12 *When Kenan had lived seventy years, he became the father of Mahalalel.*
13 *Kenan lived after the birth of Mahalalel eight hundred and forty years, and*
had other sons and daughters. 14 *Thus all the days of Kenan were nine hundred and*
ten years; and he died.

15 *When Mahalalel had lived sixty-five years, he became the father of Jared.*
16 *Mahalalel lived after the birth of Jared eight hundred and thirty years, and had*
other sons and daughters. 17 *Thus all the days of Mahalalel were eight hundred*
and ninety-five years; and he died.

18 *When Jared had lived a hundred and sixty-two years he became the father of*
Enoch. 19 *Jared lived after the birth of Enoch eight hundred years, and had other*

sons and daughters. [20]*Thus all the days of Jared were nine hundred and sixty-two*
years; and he died.
21 *When Enoch had lived sixty-five years, he became the father of Methuselah.*
[22]*Enoch walked with God after the birth of Methuselah three hundred years, and*
had other sons and daughters. [23]*Thus all the days of Enoch were three hundred*
and sixty-five years. [24]*Enoch walked with God; and he was not, for God took him.*
25 *When Methuselah had lived a hundred and eighty-seven years, he became*
the father of Lamech. [26]*Methuselah lived after the birth of Lamech seven hundred*
and eighty-two years, and had other sons and daughters. [27]*Thus all the days of*
Methuselah were nine hundred and sixty-nine years; and he died.
28 *When Lamech had lived a hundred and eighty-two years, he became the*
father of a son, [29]and called his name Noah, saying, "Out of the ground
which the LORD has cursed this one shall bring us relief from our work
and from the toil of our hands." [30]*Lamech lived after the birth of Noah five*
hundred and ninety-five years, and had other sons and daughters. [31]*Thus all the*
days of Lamech were seven hundred and seventy-seven years; and he died.
32 *After Noah was five hundred years old, Noah became the father of Shem,*
Ham, and Japheth.

A new chapter of the primeval history begins here. The section is from the Priestly document and was formerly the direct continuation of chs. 1 to 2.4a. Now nothing more is said about the creation of the world and the blessing of man, but, rather, Noah and men of his time become the subject of the account. First there is an introduction to Noah. It must be observed that this is not merely a secondary transition, but is, rather, an independent subject of the narrative with a time span of quite definite duration. Above all else, one must observe the effort of ch. 5 to arrange the ages of man and of the world theologically. Old Testament faith in Yahweh is conspicuous by its distinctive thinking about time (in contrast to the mythical, cyclical thinking of ancient Oriental religions!). It knows of God's dealings with man and with his people Israel, of events that are unique and unrepeatable. This demarcation of sacred historical epochs is a striking characteristic of the Priestly narrative.

The outline of this post-Adamic era consists of a ten-membered genealogical table with exact figures for age, begetting of the first-born, etc. The final link of the chain is open; the details about Noah are incomplete because the document will be concerned in detail with him and his age. (The formal closing of the last link occurs only after the Flood story, ch. 9.29.)

Interest is immediately attracted, of course, to the numbers. It is quite probable that the number of years given in ch. 5 has some mysterious proportional relation to other dates in the biblical sacred history (construction of the Tabernacle? conquest? building of the Temple?); but a satisfactory key to the theological meaning of that assumed system has not yet been found. It is to be supposed that the numbers in the table of Semites (ch. 11.10 ff.) are harmonized with those from our list into a system. If one adds the time spans of both lists and reckons to them the dates of chs. 21.5; 25.26; 47.9; and Ex. 12.40, the result is the year 2666 for the exodus from Egypt. That would be two thirds of a world era of four thousand years. But in addition to our Masoretic, canonical text, the conspicuously differing dates of the Septuagint and the Samaritan Pentateuch must be examined. A number of more recent exegetes have considered the figures of the latter as more original, while early church exegesis accepted the data of the Septuagint. But one must also reckon with the possibility that subsequently the various texts were thoroughly corrected with reference to one another, For Methuselah, that is certain. According to Codex A, he must have outlived the Flood by fourteen years, which gave the early church cause for continued discussion. Codex D (among others) accepted the birth date of the MT and thereby lowered the year of the Flood.

So far as the life span is concerned one must renounce apologetic efforts (most striking is the late age for begetting!); the author here shares generally accepted ancient ideas about the longevity of the ancestral fathers. (A corresponding Babylonian list of kings—see pp. 71, 145 f.—gives regnal years in tens of thousands.) Nevertheless, in the strange form of this period we must perceive an important statement of faith; namely, a witness to the great vitality of the first men in procreation (and with it a quiet judgment about our present natural condition in life!). We must remember that the Priestly document had no story of the Fall which spoke theologically of the disorders and degeneracy in man's creaturely condition and which formed thereby a transition to man's state at the time of Noah. Here we have something more or less equivalent to that story. Therefore we must understand man's slowly diminishing life span (most consistent in the Samaritan system) as a gradual deterioration of his original, wonderful vitality, a deterioration corresponding to his increasing distance from his starting point at creation. P reckons the life span of the fathers from Adam to Noah as seven hundred to one thousand years, from Noah to Abraham as two hundred to six hundred years, for the patriarchs one hundred to two hundred years, and for the present seventy to eighty years. Thus Gen., ch. 5, describes something like a "transitional period, during which death caused by sin only slowly broke the powerful physical resistance of primitive human nature" (Del.). To be sure, the Priestly document does not speak of the cause, but only of the fact of this decline; this corresponds to its way of concentrating on the attestation of the objective orders established by God. Accordingly, to discover man's humanity and his *need* for salvation, we turn to the Yahwist.

[1–3] The long genealogy begins: "This is the book of the genealogy of Adam." The title, "This is the genealogy of . . ." occurs at the beginning of eleven sections that contain lists, whose literary relation to the Priestly document has often been discussed.* There can be no doubt that the statement: "This is the book of the genealogies . . ." designates the beginning of an actual book. We have to imagine the following literary process: there was once a "toledoth book," consisting only of genealogies, lists, and, at the most, quite brief theological remarks. Its ancient title is preserved for us in ch. 5.1. This book formed the oldest foundation of the Priestly document, from which it slowly grew by purposeful expansion to include the most varied sacred traditions. The especially significant account of creation had, of course, to be placed before the beginning of the book (which began with Adam); and it too received the statement demanded by the system, *'ēlleh tōlᵉdōt* ("these are the generations . . .") (ch. 2.4a). It is secondary to the old toledoth book, as also its use of "heaven and earth" forces the original meaning of the term *tōlᵉdōt*, "generations," "register of generations." Today one can translate the word *tōlᵉdōt* in ch. 2.4a only in the very extended sense of "history of the origin."

Details. The list begins with a somewhat circumstantial recapitulation of the important theological data in the creation of man. Yet it appears that the tradition of ch. 5.1–3 is somewhat independent of ch. 1. Above all, *'ādām* ("man") is here used as a proper name ("Adam"), which was true neither in ch. 1 nor in chs. 2; 3. Further, the note that God himself so named his creature has no equivalent in ch. 1.26 ff. The statement about God's image in the first man, moreover, is theologically expanded in the remark that Adam begat a son, Seth, corresponding to his image and his likeness. God's image was therefore peculiar not only to the first man, but was inherited in successive generations. Only through this expansion is the actuality

*Gen. 5.1; 6.9; 10.1; 11.10, 27; 25.12, 19; 36.1, 9; 37.2; Num. 3.1. G. von Rad, *Die Priesterschrift im Hexateuch*, 1934, 33 ff.

of this testimony guaranteed to the reader, for without this addition the reference to a primeval man in God's image would be a meaningless mythologumenon.

The names in the Priestly Sethite genealogy correspond remarkably to those in the Yahwistic table of Kenites (ch. 4.17 ff.). It is obviously one and the same list, which with minor orthographic changes and a modification in the sequence was used here and there in various traditional contexts. There are also connections between this list and one with ten Babylonian primeval kings, who are said to have ruled until the Flood (AOT², 147 ff.; ANET, 265). The relationship, however, is not so close as was thought at an earlier stage (cf. Zimmern in ZDMG, 1924, 19 ff.). Nevertheless, the Babylonian tradition relates that the seventh king was actually carried off to the gods and shared in their secrets (like Enoch); and in that list the tenth king is also the hero of the Flood. It is important, however, to see how differently that ancient tradition of human beginnings was framed in Israel. One does not read the names of primeval kings, i.e., of mythical representatives of a polis, but rather of patriarchs, i.e., representatives of a unified, prenational humanity. In Israel men did not succumb to the temptation to make a particular polis-religion absolute by dating it back and mythically deriving it from the creation itself (see pp. 145 f.).

[22–24] The genealogy of Enoch is a special and mysterious statement because of its conciseness. "Enoch walked with God," and after he had lived 365 years "he was not, for God took him." It is important to see how the Priestly account, which is so unusually bridled theologically, can also handle those things which really lie at the outermost edge of the mystery between God and man. It speaks of a living communion with God, which lies beyond our imagination, for it recognizes a walk *with* God only for members of antediluvian humanity (cf. Gen. 6.9; Abraham walked *before* God, ch. 17.1). There is here no trace of that eager interest of later writers in Enoch, in the "miracle of knowledge of God" (Ecclus. 44.16), or in the great initiate into the mysteries of God. Only the reality of so intimate an association with God, and the reality of a removal into otherworldly spheres of existence is recorded. And that, for humanity after the Flood, is to be sure a meaningful sign of the freedom of divine election and of a power that is not restrained even at the precinct of death. The verb *lāqaḥ* (subject: God; object: a man) is a theological term for translation into otherworldly spheres of existence (II Kings

2.10; Ps. 49.15). The passage, to be sure, gives the impression of being only a brief reference to a much more extensive tradition; it is an open question, therefore, whether much of the apocalyptic Enoch tradition is not really very old and precedes in time (not follows) the Priestly narrative. The origin and meaning of the name Methu*salem* [cf. Vulgate] is obscure; it was already in use in the early church.

[29] If the story of Enoch radiates, so to speak, the light of a past aeon and thereby points backward more than forward, then the statement of Lamech concerning the comfort of Noah in v. 29 is directed completely forward to the future. It is a statement based on long experience of earthly sorrow; it is important, however, as one of the first witnesses to man's hope for divine comfort. The question about what the comfort of Noah is cannot be answered from the context. Is it an allusion to that sacrifice which came with Noah between God and man and to the stabilizing of the natural orders by the divine word of grace (ch. 8.20 ff.)? Or does it allude to the first planting of the vine (ch. 9.20 ff.)? We must return to this statement, which because of its reference to ch. 3 originally belonged to the Yahwistic-Sethite genealogy. (See at ch. 9.18 ff.)

The long lives ascribed to the patriarchs cause remarkable synchronisms and duplications. Adam lived to see the birth of Lamech, the ninth member of the genealogy; Seth lived to see the translation of Enoch and died shortly before the birth of Noah. Lamech was the first to see a dead man—Adam; Noah outlived Abraham's grandfather, Nahor, and died in Abraham's sixtieth year. Shem, Noah's son, even outlived Abraham. He was still alive when Esau and Jacob were born! Delitzsch's question about whether the dates were really given in the knowledge of such consequences must be answered in the affirmative, in view of the painful deliberateness of the Priestly statements.

> It was really a golden age, in comparison with which our own can scarcely be called filth, for nine patriarchs lived at the same time with all their descendants. . . . This is the greatest glory of the first world, that in it at one time were people who were so much more pious, wise, and holy. For we ought not to think that they were simple, ordinary people; on the contrary, they were the greatest heroes. . . . At the Judgment Day we will see their majesty and be amazed when we see their wonderful story and acts too. . . . But no one ought to think, therefore, that they lived without the greatest misfortune, cross and temptation. Such things will all become clear and apparent at the Judgment Day. (Luther, WA, XLII, 245 ff.)

In the Priestly tradition the story of the Flood follows immediately after the genealogical tree of Seth. We will take up the thread of P again on p. 125.

3. THE YAHWISTIC STORY OF PARADISE. Ch. 2.4b–25

2 4bIn the day that the LORD God made the earth and the heavens,
5when no plant of the field was yet in the earth and no herb of the field
had yet sprung up—for the LORD God had not caused it to rain upon
the earth, and there was no man to till the ground; 6but a mist went up
from the earth and watered the whole face of the ground—7then the
LORD God formed man of dust from the ground, and breathed into his
nostrils the breath of life; and man became a living being. 8And the
LORD God planted a garden in Eden, in the east; and there he put the
man whom he had formed. 9And out of the ground the LORD God made
to grow every tree that is pleasant to the sight and good for food, the
tree of life also in the midst of the garden, and the tree of the knowledge
of good and evil.
10 A river flowed out of Eden to water the garden, and there it
divided and became four rivers. 11The name of the first is Pishon; it is
the one which flows around the whole of Havilah, where there is
gold; 12and the gold of that land is good; bdellium and onyx stone are
there. 13The name of the second river is Gihon; it is the one which flows
around the whole land of Cush. 14And the name of the third river is
Hiddekel, which flows east of Assyria. And the fourth river is the Euphrates.
15 The LORD God took the man and put him in the garden of Eden
to till it and keep it. 16And the LORD God commanded the man, saying,
"You may freely eat of every tree of the garden; 17but of the tree of the
knowledge of good and evil you shall not eat, for in the day that you eat
of it you shall die."
18 Then the LORD God said, "It is not good that the man should be
alone; I will make him a helper fit for him." 19So out of the ground the
LORD God formed every beast of the field and every bird of the air, and
brought them to the man to see what he would call them; and whatever
the man called every living creature, that was its name. 20The man gave
names to all cattle, and to the birds of the air, and to every beast of the
field; but for the man there was not found a helper fit for him. 21So the
LORD God caused a deep sleep to fall upon the man, and while he slept
took one of his ribs and closed up its place with flesh; 22and the rib
which the LORD God had taken from the man he made into a woman
and brought her to the man. 23Then the man said,

"This at last is bone of my bones
and flesh of my flesh;
she shall be called Woman,
because she was taken out of Man."

[24]Therefore a man leaves his father and his mother and cleaves to his wife, and they become one flesh. [25]And the man and his wife were both naked, and were not ashamed.

Ever since the advent of critical science in theology, the story of Paradise and the Fall has repeatedly been the subject for thorough analysis. The results of this research, recorded in many monographs and articles, were complex, to be sure, and often mutually contradictory; but they agreed, nevertheless, on one point: that they vigorously contradicted the traditional exposition of the church. Above all, there were an increasing number of irregularities, doublets, and clear breaks in the progression of the narrative which struck the critical exegetes, and raised serious doubts about the unity and inner compactness of the text. So first the attempt was made to master the difficulties by means of simple source analysis. Its mildest form was the assumption of a primary strand that was subsequently expanded by glosses and other additions (Budde). Those analyses, which, especially in the variants to the story of the tree of life, seemed to reveal an earlier independent parallel narrative, went even farther (Gu.; Pr.). H. Schmidt went farthest by working out three narratives, the chief features of which he felt he could also distinguish literarily from one another.* A fact, however, which has meanwhile become more and more recognized is that the possibilities for solving the difficulties of chs. 2 and 3 by means of pure literary dissection are limited and probably exhausted. A more penetrating investigation has brought another point of view to prominence, namely, the assumption of various narrative contexts, which were attracted to one another and united long *before* the present literary form took shape. The irregularities and flaws in the narrative, therefore, may not be explained simply by literary analysis, because they did not originate by way of literary combination, but rather through a growth of various ancient traditions long before their literary fixation by the Yahwist. Once one has seen that such old stories in the process of oral tradition are constantly in motion, so to speak, because of a shift in the inner motivation or because of the attachment of related narrative material, one will readily admit that in these or other ways "gaps and contradictions occur which are not cause for denying the unity and organic growth of the narratives" (J. Begrich, ZAW, 1932, 99).

*H. Schmidt, *Die Erzählung vom Paradies und Sündenfall*, 1931; similarly J. Meinhold, *Festschrift für Budde*, 122 ff.

Literary criticism must go hand in hand with criticism of the subject matter. It is clear that this recognition makes the outlook for a reconstruction of the original texts much less favorable. But this is not the primary task of exegesis, all the less so since recently a more synthetic, unified approach has been gaining ground (cf. especially P. Humbert, *Études sur le récit du Paradis et la chute dans la Genèse*, 1940). No matter how much a knowledge of the previous stages of the present text can preserve us from false exposition, still there is no question that the narrative of chs. 2 f., in spite of certain tensions and irregularities, is not a rubble heap of individual recensions but is to be understood as a whole with a consistent train of thought. Above all else, the exegete must come to terms with this existing complex unity.

The text of chs. 2 f. presents a *narrative*. It is not doctrine (at least not in direct sense), but rather it tells a story, a part of a traveled road that cannot be traversed again. One must therefore bear in mind that here a factual report is meant to be given about facts which everyone knows and whose reality no one can question. They concern the field upon which the story of man with God is played; and the means of presentation, which serve to make the process more tangible, are correspondingly different from those applied by the historian. We read a narrative that proceeds amidst the simplest and clearest imagery; but that, of course, does not mean it does not intend throughout to report actuality. The story certainly also contains a didactic element, but much less directly than does ch. 1; it is concealed in the facts that are placed before the reader. And here is the source of so many false expositions. The narrative demands that we follow the way it goes precisely. It raises many more questions than it answers about "the" original state and "the" Fall. In theological thought and even more in popular, conceptions about just these subjects had grown all too stable. Furthermore, one must remember that also nonbiblical mythical ideas about the blessedness of man's original state have merged unnoticeably with Christian thought. The exegete must free himself of all these burdens. There is perhaps no other biblical text which is so inflexible with regard to this confused mass of stalled questions and whose witness proceeds from a road as narrow as a razor's edge. One misses the road completely if one does not entrust oneself to it completely.

[4b–7] The narrative begins with a somewhat difficult sentence (vs. 4b–7), which, however, is neither damaged nor a torso at all. Rather, here is something almost like a traditional stylistic form (cf.

the Babylonian creation epic or the Wessobrunner prayer!).* In any case it is natural for naïve ancient thought to transmit a concept of the world's primitive state by way of the barest outline. Both the time given in v. 4b and the description by means of five identically subordinate conditional statements are quite general. Neither the modest prairie brush nor the more pretentious cultivated herb could live, for neither was there rain from above nor cultivating work of man upon the earth. For moisture there was only the ground water (?) rising from the waters beneath the earth. Here clearly, in contrast to P, the indifference in narration is striking. The creation of the actual cosmic system is loosely referred to only in an introductory clause.

Where does the main clause begin? In v. 6 (beginning of the first moisture) or in v. 7 (statements of fact—first action)? The latter is both syntactically and materially the more likely. The decision is rendered difficult by the obscurity of the word *'ēd* ("mist"). According to Job 36.27 the meaning may be "mist," "vapor." If the meaning is given from the Akkadian, it would be "surging of waves." The LXX understood the word as meaning "spring." We follow Albright's explanation (JBL, 1938, 231). Evidently the *'ēd* rises up out of the earth. The meaning is that only ground water arose. Verse 6 is thus a sort of intermediary sentence which follows the negative details and precedes the positive ones. In contrast to Gen. 1.1 ff., one cannot speak here of the creation of a world-structure which was described extensively in the Priestly source. The creation of the world is mentioned in vs. 4–6 only in the sense of a *terminus a quo*. This narrative is concerned with man, his creation, and the care God devoted to him. The setting outlined by the Yahwist in the general introductory statement concerns the much narrower realm of the *earth*. Whereas in ch. 1 creation moves from the chaos to the cosmos of the entire world, our account of creation sketches the original state as a desert in contrast to the sown. It is man's world, the world of his life (the sown, the garden, the animals, the woman), which God in what follows establishes *around man*; and this forms the primary theme of the entire narrative, *'ādām 'ᵃdāmā* (man—earth). The cosmological ideas from which our Yahwistic account of creation proceeds are thus very unlike those which we met in P and must stem from a quite different circle of life and tradition. Water is here the assisting element of creation. In P and in some psalms (see above) it was the

*One of the oldest poems of German literature, the first lines of which contain an account of creation.

enemy of creation. In this world, which is regarded quite anthropocentrically, man is the first creature. "In chapter 1 man is the pinnacle of a pyramid, in chapter 2 the center of a circle" (Jac.). The weighty main clause of the long sentence is therefore v. 7; after the statements of condition it introduces the first action, the creation of man. God "forms" him from the ground; the bond of life between man and earth given by creation is expressed with particular cogency by the use of the Hebrew words *'ādām* and *'ªdāmā*. (The word "dust" has perhaps been introduced here from ch. 3.19b for the sake of consistency.) This man, however, formed from the earth, becomes a living creature only when inspired with the divine breath of life. *Nᵉšāmā* corresponds to our "breath." This divine vital power is personified, individualized, but only by its entry into the material body; and only this breath when united with the body makes man a "living creature." Thus v. 7 is a *locus classicus* of Old Testament anthropology. It distinguishes not body and "soul" but more realistically body and life. The divine breath of life which unites with the material body makes man a "living soul" both from the physical as well as from the psychical side. This life springs directly from God, as directly as the lifeless human body received breath from God's mouth when he bent over it! Nevertheless, the undertone of melancholy is unmistakable: a faint anticipation of the state of post-Adamic man! When God withdraws his breath (Ps. 104.29 f.; Job 34.14 f.), man reverts to dead corporeity.

The combination of both designations for God, "Yahweh-Elohim" (a construct relation?), is enigmatic, both syntactically (it is scarcely translatable) and with respect to its usage; for in Genesis it is used only in the story of Paradise and the Fall, but there consistently. (Outside Genesis it occurs only once in the Pentateuch!) Perhaps its use here is traceable to the redactor: originally Yahweh was used, but in order to assure the identity of this Yahweh with the Elohim of ch. 1, Elohim was added. Liturgical reasons could also be at work.

[8] God plants a garden for man in Eden, which we must think of as a park of trees (Ezek. 31.8). The cultivation of vegetable gardens was widely practiced in the ancient Orient, less frequently that of parks, which were laid out only by great kings. Here is a glimmer of the older conception of Yahweh as owner of the park. Accordingly, the narrative clearly regards this tree garden as a *holy* region, enclosing God's presence and therefore guarded by cherubim (cf. at ch. 3.24). Eden is here the proper name of a land in the distant east. What concrete tradition underlies the name or whether it can really be connected with similar-sounding place designations from historical times has not been explained (II Kings 19.12; Isa. 37.12). Is it because of our imperfect knowledge of the historical and geographical milieu of Israel that we do not see more clearly here? Did the Israelite of the kingdom attach no concrete historical or geographical conceptions to the word *'ēden*? The narrative speaks in rather an imprecise way of a "garden in Eden" (v. 8) (here Eden would be the name of a country), then of the "garden of Eden" (here Eden would be the name of the garden) (2.15; 3.23 f.), and once just of "Eden" (4.16). More important is the fact that this proper name certainly called to mind his own word *'ēden* ("bliss"). Eden occurs with this coloring even in the prophets as a quite definite term of mythically theological illustration, namely, almost as a synonym of Paradise (Isa. 51.3; Ezek. 28.13; 31.9). It must be stressed, however, that in our narrative the mythical is almost completely stripped away. (The allusions in Ezekiel are quite different!) The garden may not be called the garden of God at all, in the narrower sense, much less the "dwelling of God"! The garden was planned only for man and is to be understood as a gift of God's gracious care for the man he created.

[9] Verse 9 reports the origin of the garden again and is certainly a doublet of v. 8. (Man's transfer to the garden is also repeated in v. 15.) Here the description of the pleasures of the garden is somewhat more lively: a great multiplicity of trees (ch. 3.7 mentions the fig tree; Ezek. 31.8 f., cedars, cypresses, and plane trees) and in the midst the tree of life and the tree of the knowledge of good and evil. The myths of many peoples tell about the existence of a tree of life whose fruits (with continued eating) grant immortality. The occurrence of this idea in the Old Testament, which is so nonmythological, is almost startling. Apart from Genesis, only the book of Proverbs refers to a tree of life, but there only in a pale figure of speech (Prov. 11.30; 13.12; 15.4). The tree of knowledge, whose fruit gives omniscience, is mentioned nowhere else in the Old Testament. The suspicion can scarcely be suppressed that the duality of trees in the midst of the garden is only the result of a subsequent combination of two traditions. In what follows too there is only *one* tree that plays any role, the tree of knowledge. Only at the conclusion (ch. 3.24) do we hear again of the tree of life. To this material fact a syntactic one must be added. The mention of the tree of knowledge is obviously unsatisfactory after the prepositional phrase *bᵉtōk haggān*, "in the midst of the garden" (which refers back to the tree of life!). The attribute of the tree of knowledge ("of good and evil") is a separate question. Here, and primarily in God's admonition in v. 17a, it is perhaps an anticipation of the subsequent disclosure by a later commentator; furthermore, the syntactic combination here of the substantival infinitive *hadda'at* ("the knowing of . . .") with an object is stylistically difficult. Therefore in vs. 9b and 17a the *ṭōb wārā'* ("of good and evil") is to be considered a subsequent addition. At this point followed originally God's installation of man in the garden, vs. 16 f. Now there intervenes:

THE PASSAGE ABOUT THE RIVERS IN PARADISE

[10–14] This passage has no significance for the unfolding action, nor are its elements mentioned elsewhere. In fact, it is at variance with one declaration of the narrative (v. 8). It must therefore be considered as originally an independent element which was attracted to the story of Paradise but without being able to undergo complete inner assimilation. One river waters Paradise and then divides into four branches. Now suddenly we find ourselves in our historical and geographical world! The author projects a picture of the great river system that surrounded the world he knew, for the number "four" circumscribes the entire world (cf. the four horns as the kingdoms of the world, Zech. 2.1 ff.). The first river was the most difficult to describe. A series of notes from cultural history assist the vague notion. Does it refer to the ocean surrounding the Arabian peninsula or even to the distant Indus? The second river cannot be the Nile, more probably the Nubian Nile, south of the first cararact, which the Egyptians also distinguished from their own Nile. Or does Cush not refer to Ethiopia, but to *kuššū*, the land of the Cossaeans in the West Iranian hill country? The details in the table of nations (10.4) would support this. Here, as in the section generally, account must be taken of the vague notions the entire ancient world had about the origin and course of the great rivers. Even much later geographers of antiquity still had some rather fantastic conceptions in this respect. The third river is the Tigris, the fourth the Euphrates. This interpretation seems to presuppose that Eden and Paradise lay somewhere in the north, high in the (Armenian?) mountains, from whence the great rivers come. (Cf. the tradition of God's mountain in the north, Isa. 14.13; Ps. 48.2.) What an inexpressible amount of water was in

Paradise, if the river, after having watered the garden, could still enclose the entire world with four arms and fructify it! All the water outside Paradise, which supplies all civilizations, is, so to speak, only a remainder or residue from the water of Paradise! This strangely profound section strives without doubt to sketch the real geographical world. It projects an extremely archaic map of the world, although, it is true, this is only with regard to the waters of the inhabited world. But one must remember that in the Orient water is absolutely the basis of all civilized life. Here we find what we missed above (see at v. 8): a connection between the earth and the garden on the one hand and the historical world of man on the other. The entire passage probably owes its interpolation to this fact. It means to emphasize, for its part, the topical significance of Eden for men outside Paradise by the reference to that unbroken stream of water from Paradise. (Verses 10 ff. contain nominal sentences, i.e., statements of fact!)

[15] After this digression we are at v. 15 again in the actual Paradise story. The verse is obviously parallel to v. 8b, but in addition it indicates man's purpose in being in the garden: he is to work it and preserve it from all damage, a destiny that contrasts decidedly with the commonly accepted fantastic ideas of "Paradise." Our word "Paradise" as the proper name (which the Old Testament text does not know) for a state *sui generis* contains a mythical objectification and goes beyond the strict reticence of the biblical narrative.

There is "nothing here about abundant wonders of fertility and sensual enjoyment" (Fr.), but work was man's sober destiny even in his original state. That man was transferred to the garden to guard it indicates that he was called to a state of service and had to prove himself in a realm that was not his own possession (Jac.). **[16–17]** In the ensuing divine address the misunderstanding of the garden as an Elysium for sensual enjoyment is completely destroyed. God begins with a great release, which again reveals the abundance of his fatherly care, but also shows the greatness of the realm in which man can move, quite freely and untempted, limited by no restraint. Only *one* tree is singled out from the many. (How grievous then, when man nevertheless found no satisfaction and wished to assert himself precisely at this point!) Therefore, even though God's prohibition was not at all oppressive, since all other trees were unreservedly declared free, it nevertheless placed before man decision and the serious question of obedience. To seek a purpose in the divine prohibition, as exegetes have often done, is in our opinion not permissible; the question cannot be discussed. Nothing is said to indicate that God combined pedagogical intentions with this prohibition (in the sense of a "moral" development of man). On the contrary, one destroys the essential part of the story with such rationalistic explanations. Man in his original state was completely *subject* to God's command, and the question, "Who will say to him, What doest thou?" (Job 9.12; Dan. 4.35b) was equally out of place in Paradise. The snake (Gen. 3.1) was first to open discussion about the prohibition. The most that we may derive from this is that the command was certainly well intentioned, again dictated by God's providence; for the forbidden fruit was not good for man, and taken by him in disobedience, it necessarily would work destructively upon him. How simple and sober is our narrative, compared to the sensual myths of the nations, in letting the meaning of life in Paradise consist completely in the question of obedience to God and not in pleasure and freedom from suffering, etc.

The lack of agreement between the threat of death (the text does not say, "You will become mortal," but rather, "You shall die"!) and the actual punishment will be discussed at ch. 3.19. Further it must be admitted that God's mention of the "tree of the knowledge of good and evil" causes a difficulty for us even here. Apart from the syntactic difficulty (see above at v. 9b) there is the further question, Does man already know it as such? And if God here reveals the mystery, what sense has the snake's explanation (ch. 3.5)? The often suggested emendation "from the tree in the midst of the garden" (cf. BH) would agree exactly with what the woman gives as the wording of the prohibition (ch. 3.7). But one must consider whether the narrator does not expect much more of the reader and therefore in his explanation is much less bound to the law of psychological credibility. For the phrase about the knowledge of good and evil the Western reader must first of all learn from Old Testament usage that the pair of terms (good and evil) is not at all used only in the moral sense, not even especially in the moral sense. Knowledge of good and evil means, therefore, omniscience in the widest sense of the word. The exposition of the phrase in terms of the specific sexual experience ("what is pleasurable and sorrowful," H. Schmidt) is right in so far as the verb *yd'* ("to know") never signifies purely intellectual knowing, but rather an "experiencing',' a "becoming acquainted with" (cf. at Gen. 3.5). The old question whether the enjoyment of the tree of life was open to man—should we wish to ask it at all—will have to be answered affirmatively, primarily on the basis of the related ancient Oriental ideas (H. Th. Obbink, "The Tree of Life in Eden," ZAW, 1928, 105 ff.). Nevertheless, see the concluding notes.

[18] In the narrative as a whole, the prohibition (v. 17) is completely imbedded in the description of God's fatherly care for man. Previously the planting of the garden and its transfer to man was told; now follows the creation of the animals and the woman. Solitude "is not good"; man is created for sociability. God's kindliness sees that it would do man good if a helping creature were given to him "as his opposite," "a helper fit for him" (*k^{e}negdō*). "How much perception and experience of life as it is lived is concentrated in this statement" (Steck). Solitude is therefore defined here very realistically as helplessness (cf. Eccl. 4.9–11). From this point of view the wife receives quite an unromantic valuation that the Old Testament never forsakes, even in its most beautiful praises of a woman as wife (Prov. 31.10 ff.). The word *k^{e}negdō* ("fit for him") contains the notion of similarity as well as supplementation; but one may not here personify *'ēzer* ("helper") and translate it "helpmate" with reference to the later creation of the woman. The verse speaks in the first place only of an assistant, of one who is to be for man the embodiment of inner and outer encouragement. Thus the narrator speaks first of the animals. He sees them allotted by God to man for service and use. Truly they are "assistants" and encouragement for man in many ways, but not yet worthy assistants in the ultimate sense which God seeks. They are not yet beings like him, "as the mirror of himself, in which he recognizes himself" (Del.). **[19–20]** So God makes the animals (again quite simply and untheologically "God formed") and leads them to the man, and the man takes them and incorporates them into his life. That is what the remarkable passage about the naming of the animals means; we are not dependent for an explanation on the primitive view of the connection between a name and its bearer. Nor is the point here the name as a word, but rather the relation between word and fact, and this is much more complicated. "First every created thing is given a name from the language. Secondly, however, and here we go deeper, language itself is an originating, creative, interpretative something, in which arrangement, rearrangement, and regulation most properly occur." "Man attacks the confusion of the world; by probing, restricting and combining he brings together what belongs together. That which lies piled up in the confusion of the world does not at the start possess its own form; but rather, what is here distinguished with discrimination receives its own form only as it comes together in the analysis." (Jolles, *Einfache Formen*, 16, 21 f.)* This naming is thus both an act of copying and an act of appropriative ordering, by which man intellectually objectifies the creatures for himself. Thus one may say that something is said here about the origin and nature of language. The emphasis is placed not on the invention of words but on that inner appropriation by recognition and interpretation that takes place in language. Here, interestingly, language is seen not as a means of communication but as an intellectual capacity by means of which man brings conceptual order to his sphere of life. Concretely: when man says "ox" he has not simply discovered the word "ox," but rather understood this creature as ox and included it in his imagination and his life as a help to his life. Here, as in Gen. 1.24 f., one should note the creaturely proximity of man and beast to each other. The animal too is taken from the earth and is incorporated by man into his circle of life as the environment nearest him. Let us remind ourselves once more that name-giving in the ancient Orient was primarily an exercise of sovereignty, of command. This passage, therefore, stands close to v. 28b in spite of the completely different presentation of the material. Thus the passage about the creation and naming of the animals heightens suspense by impeding movement in the narrative. Within the context of the promise of a worthy assistant he lets a quite new part of man's environment be established and comprehended by man: the animal world. But rich and useful as this new environment is, and much as it has awakened in man the desire for a creature similar to himself, it is still not yet a worthy help. God has in mind a wonder greater yet than these!

*"Now release all the senses of man: let him see and taste and feel at once all beings which talk in his ear—heavens, what a classroom of ideas and language! Let no Mercury or Apollo be brought down as *deus ex machina* from the clouds—all nature, multisonous and divine, is language teacher and Muse! Then she will bring all creatures to him: each one bears its name upon its tongue and calls itself vassal and slave of this veiled, visible God. It delivers to him its cue for the book of his dominion, as a tribute in order that he may remember it by this name, call it in the future and enjoy it. . . . I ask whether this dry truth could ever have been said more nobly and beautifully in Oriental fashion that 'God led the animals to him to see what he would call them; and however he named them, that was their name!' Where in Oriental poetic fashion can it be said more definitely: man himself invented language! from tones of living Nature! as a mark of his ruling intellect!" (Herder, *Über den Ursprung der Sprache*, Sämtliche Werke V, 50 f.)

[21–23] A "deep sleep" falls upon man, a kind of magical sleep that completely extinguishes his consciousness. The narrator is moved by the thought that God's miraculous creating permits no watching. Man cannot perceive God "in the act," cannot observe his miracles in their genesis; he can revere God's creativity only as an actually accomplished fact. Thus even Abraham had to sink into fear and insensibility before God's coming (ch. 15.12), and Moses could not see God's face but only "God's back" (Ex. 33.18–23). The notion that God "built" woman from man's rib gives an ancient answer to the question of why ribs surround only the upper half of the human body rather than the entire body. It may be that the reference to the lower part of the body was connected with the special idea of the sexual community of man and woman. Regarding this passage as a whole, one must say that these notions are only remotely suggested, they are a kind of conclusion *a posteriori*; and that is a sign that this special aetiological question no longer raised lively interest at the time of the Yahwist. The Yahwist too wants to explain something, but something else, and as against that the question about the special constitution of the human body becomes nonessential (see at v. 24). Now God himself, like a father of the bride, leads the woman to the man. The man in supreme joy at once recognizes the new creature as one belonging completely to him, and he expresses his understanding immediately in the proper name that he gives the new creature. Here too (cf. v. 20) the naming is only the actual expression of a previous inward interpretative appropriation. The linguistic consonance (*'īš*, "man"; *'iššā*, "woman"), upon which much depends here, can be fairly represented in English. Man's joy in the first wifely "thou" (observe the threefold enraptured "this one") is quite elemental and knows nothing yet of the "supramundane facts (Eph., ch. 5), which are adumbrated in this mystery of marriage" (Del.).

[24–25] Much depends upon the right understanding of v. 24. First of all, the statement, "Therefore a man leaves his father and his mother" is not, of course, a continuation of the first man's speech, but rather a concluding, summarizing word of the narrator, a short epilogue, as it were, after the curtain has fallen. One must say, in fact, that in this statement the entire narrative so far arrives at the primary purpose toward which it was oriented from the beginning. This shows what is actually intended. The story is entirely aetiological, i.e., it was told to answer a quite definite question. A fact needs explanation, namely, the extremely powerful drive of the sexes to each other. Whence comes this love "strong as death" (S. of Sol. 8.6) and stronger than the tie to one's own parents, whence this inner clinging to each other, this drive toward each other which does not rest until it again becomes one flesh in the child? It comes from the fact that God took woman from man, and they actually were originally *one* flesh. Therefore they must come together again and thus by destiny they belong to each other. The recognition of this narrative as aetiological is theologically important. Its point of departure, the thing to be explained, is for the narrator something in existence, present, not something "paradisiacal" and thus lost!

Curiously, the statement about forsaking father and mother does not quite correspond to the patriarchal family customs of ancient Israel, for after the marriage the wife breaks loose from her family much more than the man does from his. Some scholars think that this tendentious statement preserves something from a time of matriarchal culture. One must emphasize, however, that our narrative is concerned not with a legal custom but with a natural drive (Pr.). So no recognition of monogamy should be read out of the word. The alliance of one sex to another is seen as a divine ordinance of creation. It is clearly evident that v. 24 is a conclusion, and that with it the end of a formerly independent and compact cluster of material has been reached. Chapter 3 begins something new, not only thematically, but also materially. Whether it was the Yahwist who first welded these differing traditions together by means of a unifying idea, we do not know. An important part in this coupling was assigned to v. 25 which points both backward and forward (cf. ch. 3.7) and in which the Yahwist obviously goes beyond the existing traditions to present something of his own. They "were ... naked, and were not ashamed." Shame is one of the most puzzling phenomena of our humanity. It can be judged from a great many aspects, but it always has to be seen as the signal of the loss of an inner unity, an unsurmountable contradiction at the basis of our existence.* That is not to deny that it can also appear as a noble protection. The closing sentence of the narrative speaks of it as a phenomenon that is inseparable from sexuality. In this aspect it is the sign of a disruption, the loss of a freedom appointed by God. (See further on ch. 3.7.)

*K. E. Løgstrup, in: *RGG* V, 1961[3], cols. 1383 ff.

4. THE STORY OF THE FALL. Ch. 3

3 [1]Now the serpent was more subtle than any other wild creature that the LORD God had made. He said to the woman, "Did God say, 'You shall not eat of any tree of the garden'?"* [2]And the woman said to the serpent, "We may eat of the fruit of the trees of the garden; [3]but God said, 'You shall not eat of the fruit of the tree which is in the midst of the garden, neither shall you touch it, lest you die.' " [4]But the serpent said to the woman, "You will not die. [5]For God knows that when you eat of it your eyes will be opened, and you will be like God, knowing good and evil." [6]So when the woman saw that the tree was good for food, and that it was a delight to the eyes, and that the tree was to be desired to make one wise, she took of its fruit and ate; and she also gave some to her husband, and he ate. [7]Then the eyes of both were opened, and they knew that they were naked; and they sewed fig leaves together and made themselves aprons.

8 And they heard the sound of the LORD God walking in the garden in the cool of the day, and the man and his wife hid themselves from the presence of the LORD God among the trees of the garden. [9]But the LORD God called to the man, and said to him, "Where are you?" [10]And he said, "I heard the sound of thee in the garden, and I was afraid, because I was naked; and I hid myself." [11]He said, "Who told you that you were naked? Have you eaten of the tree of which I commanded you not to eat?" [12]The man said, "The woman whom thou gavest to be with me, she gave me fruit of the tree, and I ate." [13]Then the LORD God said to the woman, "What is this that you have done?" The woman said, "The serpent beguiled me, and I ate." [14]The LORD God said to the serpent,

"Because you have done this,
cursed are you above all cattle,
and above all wild animals;
upon your belly you shall go,
and dust you shall eat
all the days of your life.
[15]I will put enmity between you and the woman,
and between your seed and her seed;
he shall bruise your head,
and you shall bruise his heel."

[16]To the woman he said,
"I will greatly multiply your pain in childbearing;
in pain you shall bring forth children,
yet your desire shall be for your husband,
and he shall rule over you."

[17]And to the man he said,
"Because you have listened to the voice of your wife,
and have eaten of the tree

*Luther: "I cannot translate the Hebrew either in German or in Latin; the serpent uses the word *aph-ki* as though to turn up its nose and jeer and scoff at one."

of which I commanded you,
'You shall not eat of it,'
cursed be the ground because of you;
in toil you shall eat of it all the days of your life;
[18]thorns and thistles it shall bring forth to you;
and you shall eat the plants of the field.
[19]In the sweat of your face
you shall eat bread
till you return to the ground,
for out of it you were taken;
you are dust,
and to dust you shall return."

20 The man called his wife's name Eve, because she was the mother
of all living. [21]And the LORD God made for the man and for his wife
garments of skins, and clothed them.

22 Then the LORD God said, "Behold, the man has become like one
of us, knowing good and evil; and now, lest he put forth his hand and
take also of the tree of life, and eat, and live for ever"—[23]therefore the
LORD God sent him forth from the garden of Eden, to till the ground
from which he was taken. [24]He drove out the man; and at the east of
the garden of Eden he placed the cherubim, and a flaming sword
which turned every way, to guard the way to the tree of life.

[1]The serpent which now enters the narrative is marked as one of God's created animals (ch. 2.19). In the narrator's mind, therefore, it is not the symbol of a "demonic" power and certainly not of Satan. What distinguishes it a little from the rest of the animals is exclusively its greater cleverness. On the basis of this characteristic alone the narrator initiates the following address. It would be well to withhold from this beginning of the narrative the great theological weight that the exposition of the church, almost without exception, has given it. The mention of the snake here is almost incidental; at any rate, in the "temptation" by it the concern is with a completely unmythical process, presented in such a way because the narrator is obviously anxious to shift the responsibility as little as possible from man. It is a question only of man and *his* guilt; therefore the narrator has carefully guarded against objectifying evil in any way, and therefore he has personified it as little as possible as a power coming from without. That he transferred the impulse to temptation outside man was almost more a necessity for the story than an attempt at making evil something existing outside man. "There is no aetiology of the origin of evil" (Westermann, *ad loc.*). Throughout the entire story this antagonist of man remains in a scarcely definable incognito, which is not cleared up. In the history of religions the snake indeed is the sinister, strange animal *par excellence* (v. d. Leeuw), and one can also assume that long before, a myth was once at the basis of our narrative. But as it now lies before us, transparent and lucid, it is anything but a myth.

We are not to be concerned with what the snake is but rather with what it says. It opens the conversation—a masterpiece of psychological shading!—in a cautious way, with an interested and quite general question (not mentioning the subtly introduced subject of the conversation, the tree of knowledge, which it leaves to the unsuspecting woman!). The serpent's question contains, it is true, a complete distortion, for God never said man should eat from *no* tree in the garden; but in just this way the serpent drew the woman into conversation. It gives her the opportunity first of all to be right and to defend herself for God's sake (Zi.). In the form of this question, however, the serpent has already made a deadly attack on the artlessness of obedience. **[2–3]** The woman is quite ingenuous with regard to this malice. She corrects the distortion but in so doing goes a bit too far in her zeal. God did withhold only *one* tree from man (this part of the narrative does not seem to know the tree of life), but God did not say that it should not even be touched. This additional word already shows a slight weakness in the woman's position. It is as though she wanted to set a law for herself by means of this exaggeration. **[4–5]** In any case the serpent can now drop the mask behind which it had pretended earnest concern for God's direction. No longer does it ask, but asserts with unusual stylistic emphasis that what God said was not true at all, and it gives reasons too. It asserts that it knows God better than the woman in her believing obedience does, and so it causes her to step out of the circle of obedience and to judge God and his command as though from a neutral position. It imputes grudging intentions to God. It uses the ancient and widespread idea of the god's envy to cast suspicion on God's good command. And man's ancient folly is in thinking he can understand God better from his freely assumed standpoint and from his notion of God than he can if he would subject himself to his Word. "Wherever man attacks the concrete Word of God with the weapon of a principle or an idea of God, there he has become the lord of God" (Bonhoeffer, *Creation and Fall*, 68). In what follows, the grammatical construction is uncertain. Is the *yōdᵉʻē ṭōb wārāʻ* appositionally connected to *'elōhīm* (meaning, "as divine begins *who* know good and evil")? It is more logical to understand *yōdᵉʻē ṭōb wārāʻ* as a second predicative designation (as God—or divine beings—*and* knowing good or evil). In the first instance the accent would be upon "like divine beings"; in the second, more on the knowledge of good and evil. *Elohim* can be understood as plural (LXX); the insinuation scarcely means that men could become like Yahweh, but rather that they could be divine, like gods. So far as knowledge of good and evil is concerned, one must remember that the Hebrew *yd'* ("to know") never signifies purely intellectual knowing, but in a much wider sense an "experiencing," a "becoming acquainted with," even an "ability." "To know in the ancient world is always to be able as well" (Wellhausen). "Knowledge of good" should not immediately suggest a capacity for distinction within the moral sphere in a narrower sense; it certainly does not indicate the knowledge of absolute moral standards or the confrontation of man with an objective idea. No objective element is involved. For the ancients, the good was not just an idea: the good was what had a good effect; as a result, in this context "good and evil" should be understood more as what is "beneficial" and "salutary" on the one hand and "detrimental," "damaging" on the other. So the serpent holds out less the prospect of an extension of the capacity for knowledge than the independence that enables a man to decide for himself what will help him or hinder him. This is something completely new in that as a result man leaves the protection of divine providence. God had provided what was good for man (2.18!), and had given him complete security. But now man will go beyond this, to decide for himself.* The question in mind is probably whether the coveted autonomy might not be the greatest burden of man's life. But who thinks of that now? The step to be taken is such a small one! The fascination of this statement is in its lack of restriction, its intangibleness; it is intentionally mysterious, and after it has brought the thoughts of man into a definite direction, it is again open on all sides and gives room to all whispering secret fantasies. What the serpent's insinuation means is the possibility of an extension of human existence beyond the limits set for it by God at creation, an increase of life not only in the sense of pure intellectual enrichment but also of familiarity with, and power over, mysteries that lie beyond man. That the narrative sees man's fall, his actual separation from God, occurring again and again in *this* area (and not, for example, as a plunge into moral evil, into the subhuman!), i.e., in

*H. Stoebe, "Gut und böse in der jahwistischen Quelle des Pentateuch", ZAW 1953, 188 ff.; O. H. Steck, *op. cit.*, 34 ff., etc.

what we call Titanism, man's *hubris*—this is truly one of its most significant affirmations.

The serpent neither lied nor told the truth. "With tiny shifts of accent, with half-truth and double meaning, it can bring the unsuspecting partner to the point when she joins in and acts of her own volition, which is precisely what it intended" (Steck). One should also observe that it speaks no summons; it simply gives men the great stimulus from which decision can be made quite freely. Here too we see the narrator's effort to transfer the matter and thus the question of guilt as little as possible outside of man.

[6] The speech is ended; the serpent for the time being departs completely from the reader's view; the woman is now alone. "Man is silent before the assertion that to transgress the prohibition will not bring him into death but rather into God's likeness. He lets himself be persuaded of this thesis." It begins to dawn on him that he is better off as an autocrat than in obedience to God. (E. Osterloh, *Ev. Theol.*, 1937, 439.) The narrator draws a wonderful picture in v. 6, a scene without words in which the woman stands before the tree reflecting and then decides. With it we rush through an entire scale of emotions. "Good for food," that is the coarsely sensual aspect; "a delight to the eyes," that is the finer, more aesthetic stimulus; and "desired to make one wise," that is the highest and decisive enticement (cf. I John 2.16, "the lust of the flesh and the lust of the eyes and the pride of life"). And then follows the plucking and eating. The narrator expresses no shock; he does not expect his reader to become indignant either. On the contrary, the unthinkable and terrible is described as simply and unsensationally as possible, completely without the hubbub of the extraordinary or of a dramatic break, so that it is represented from man's standpoint almost as something self-evident, inwardly consistent!

The one who has been led astray now becomes a temptress. That is meant to indicate that the woman confronts the obscure allurements and mysteries that beset our limited life more directly than the man does. In the history of Yahweh-religion it has always been the women who have shown an inclination for obscure astrological cults. What kind of fruit it was cannot be determined from the text; it was hardly the fig which is named later, but rather a unique, miraculous tree of Paradise. The tradition about the apple tree derives from Latin Christianity and may be occasioned by the association *malus* ("bad")—*malum* ("apple").

[7] "Then the eyes of both were opened." The words of the serpent are repeated. Something really new is disclosed to them; but they have not become like gods. They have not been able to take into their life what God withheld from them before. Scarcely was it grasped before it caused disruption to the very foundations of their creaturely existence ("stripped them of their glory," Del.). But they do not react to the loss of their innocence with a spiritual consciousness of guilt; rather, they are afraid of their nakedness. For the first time, in their shame they detect something like a rift that can be traced to the depths of their being. Shame always seeks to conceal, it is afraid of "nakedness," and to this degree it can also be given a positive evaluation. But the narrative sees it above all as the sign of a grievous disruption which governs the whole being of man from the lowest level of his corporeality.

[8–13] The deed becomes sin through the encounter with God which significantly follows at once. *Qōl* here does not mean voice but (as in II Sam. 5.24) the rustle of God's step; that is already enough to deprive man of all Titanism. "The anthropomorphic character of the event must not be entirely set to the account of the narrative; it corresponds with the paradisiac mode of God's intercourse with man. God does not come down from heaven, but dwells as yet on earth" (Del.).

Man cannot remain hidden from God; he admits that fear had driven him into flight from God. To appear naked before God was an abomination for ancient Israel. In the cult every form of bodily exposure was carefully guarded against (Ex. 20.26). If shame was the sign more of a disturbance in man's relation to other men, then fear before God was the sign of a disorder in his relation to his Creator. Fear and shame are henceforth the incurable stigmata of the Fall in man. This is the first thing of which the man speaks, of emotions, which exist objectively and not yet consciously completely beyond and before any rational reflection. In the second answer of the trial something new appears. Now (vs. 11 f.) begins the intellectual wrestle with guilt occasioned by God's question, and with its assistance man tries to clear himself of guilt and to place it, significantly, on God: "the woman whom thou gavest to be with me." This answer is first of all a reproof of God by which man, exonerating himself, wants to discern the ultimate cause of what has happened; but it is also the sign of the community of men with one another which has now been destroyed. This ultimate solidarity, the solidarity of sin, in which they are now united in God's sight, is not recognized by them. The man betrays the woman. The sin they committed in common did not unite men before God but isolated them. The woman too was unable to bear the responsibility before God: the serpent was the tempter! Significantly, a trial of the serpent, God's personal address to the serpent, is missing.

[14–15] The penalties go in reverse order to the trial proceedings. These penalties are all to be understood aetiologically; in them the narrator gives a reason for disturbing enigmas and necessities, he answers elementary questions about life. These are the real goal and climax toward which the narrative is directed in its present form. The *serpent*. Whence its marvellous physical constitution? In distinction from the other larger beasts it tortures itself by crawling along the ground on its belly. Whence this conduct? It appears to live from the dust in which it hisses (Isa. 65.25; Micah 7.17). Whence comes its special place among the beasts (it is cursed "above all wild animals")? Whence, above all, that bitter hostility between it and man, a hostility that is different from and deeper than that which otherwise may exist between man and beast, which is inherited, species against species, from generation to generation? That is not according to creation, but in this the serpent bears the curse of God, and this struggle with man is decreed by God because of its evil deed. One must, under all circumstances, proceed from the fact that the passage reflects quite realistically man's struggle with the real snake; but one must not stop there, for the things with which this passage deals are basic, and in illustrating them, the narrator uses not only the commonplace language of every day, but a language that also figuratively depicts the most intellectual matters. Thus by serpent he understands not only the zoological species (which in a Palestinian's life plays a quite different role from in ours), but at the same time, in a kind of spiritual clearheadedness, he sees in it an evil being that has assumed form, that is inexplicably present within our created world, and that has singled out man, lies in wait for him, and everywhere fights a battle with him for life and death. The serpent is an animal which, more than any other, embodies uncanny qualities that make it superior to man. The same thing applies to the forbidden fruit; one must guard against understanding it simply as symbolical, and yet no reader thinks of stopping with the realistic understanding. So too the serpent; a real serpent is meant; but at the same time, in it and its enigmatic relation to man, man's relation to the evil with which he has become involved becomes vivid. "The woman once opened the doors to the dark power, and now as a penalty the doors are always to remain open and man is daily to be exposed to attack by that power which he now knows makes him terribly wretched." (Fr.) So far as the struggle itself is concerned, it is completely hopeless. Wherever man and serpent meet, the meeting always involves life and death. The verb *šūp* in v. 15 has a primary meaning of "grind" and a secondary meaning (as a by-form of *šā'ap*) of "snap." But the passage does not mean that the same man who has trampled the serpent is always attacked by that very serpent. It is a struggle of the species ("between your seed and her seed"), and as such there is no foreseeable hope that a victory can be won by any kind of heroism. Just that is real doom! For the ancients, the curse was much more than an evil wish. By virtue of the effective power it was believed to possess, it brought about disastrous, irreparable situations (for instance, exclusion from communal relationships). The terrible point of this curse is the hopelessness of this struggle in which both will ruin each other. The exegesis of the early church which found a messianic prophecy here, a reference to a final victory of the woman's seed (Protevangelium), does not agree with the sense of the passage, quite apart from the fact that the word "seed" may not be construed personally but only quite generally with the meaning "posterity."

[16] The woman and the man are not cursed (it is unthinking to speak of their malediction!); but severe afflictions and terrible contradictions now break upon the woman's life. There are three facts which because they are related to one another in unresolved tension grind down the woman's life: (1) hardships of pregnancy, pains at birth, and (2) yet a profound desire for the man in whom she (3) still does not find fulfillment and rest (Ruth 1.9), but rather humiliating domination! "In the bondage of compulsive drive and yet most immediately involved in the wonder of creation; groaning in pain, cramped in travail, humiliated, overburdened, care-worn, and tear-stained . . ." (W. Vischer, *Christuszeugnis*, 80). Whence these sorrows, these contradictions, this degradation in the woman's life? It is not a small matter that our narrative absolves God's creation of this. Here a primeval offense receives its consequences, which faith recognizes as a punishment inflicted by God.

[17–19] As for the man, his punishment consists in the hardship and skimpiness of his livelihood, which he now must seek for himself. The woman's punishment struck at the deepest root of her being as wife and mother, the man's strikes at the innermost nerve of his life: his work, his activity, and provision for sustenance. Here again the curse is to be read as in the case of the serpent. It does not, however, strike the man himself, but goes, so to speak, through him. It goes more deeply to the lowest foundation of all human existence; it strikes the most elementary realm of male effectiveness, the earth. And here too is a cleft, a mutual recalcitrance that now breaks into creation as a profound disorder: Man was taken from the earth and so was directed to it; she was the material basis of his existence; a solidarity of creation existed between man and the ground. But a break occurred in this affectionate relationship, an alienation that expresses itself in a silent, dogged struggle between man and soil. Now it is as though a spell lay on the earth which makes her deny man the easy produce of subsistence.

Possibly the curse speaks clearly of two different forms of life outside Paradise:

A	B
vs. 17c, 19a, 19b	vs. 18, 19c
Cursed is the ground because of you; in toil you shall eat of it all the days of your life. . . . In the sweat of your face you shall eat bread till you return to the ground, for out of it you were taken.	Thorns and thistles it shall bring forth to you; and you shall eat the plants of the field. . . . You are dust, and to dust you shall return.

The one version (A) has in mind the life of the peasant (Fellah) and his unending trouble to exact a harvest from the soil; the other (B) the life of the Bedouin in the steppe. His existence is characterized less by the effort of preparing the ground than by the poverty and skimpiness of the livelihood accorded him. The misery, therefore, of both primary forms of life in Palestine is aetiologically established in this passage. (J. Begrich, ZAW, 1932, 102.) The fusion of the two passages, which at one time at an earlier stage were probably independent, makes the curse of the soil and therewith the misery of agricultural life thematically predominant, but because of this union the passage has become more comprehensive; it speaks not only of hardship but also of the wretchedness of human existence.

Must it be emphasized again that the passage does not consider work in itself a punishment and curse? Work was ordained for man even in Paradise (ch. 2.15). But that it makes life so wretched, that it is so threatened by failures and wastes of time and often enough comes to nothing, that its actual result usually has no relation to the effort expended—*that* the narrator designates as a dissonance in creation which is not accounted for by God's original ordinance. The passage touches on unfathomable relationships between man and earth; it does not attempt to explain more closely what it says about the disturbance which began with man and now has also brought the earth under the domination of misery. It only establishes the fact.

Both versions (A and B) conclude with the prospect of death as man's return to the earth. Thus in the present form of the passage this thought has become a threatening expression. Yet it is not easy to establish unambiguously the sense of the passage. Is death here a punishment ("the wages of sin")? One can object that the passage speaks of it only in secondary clauses. The curses do not speak of death as a primary issue, but rather of life, and they affirm that hardship and wretchedness will continue *until* man in death returns again to the earth. One cannot say that man lost a "germ of immortality" any more than one can say that a material modification occurred in him, as a consequence of which he must now fall prey to death; the narrator already said in ch. 2.7 that man was created of dust. The direct connection of this passage with the threat of death in ch. 2.17 is also difficult, for its meaning was not, "on that day you will become mortal," but rather, "you will die." But that did not happen at all. And one of the narrator's concerns may have been to show that God did not make good his terrible threat but had allowed grace to prevail. And yet with these considerations the matter is not settled. One fact first of all is that now the reality of death is the subject of the narrative. And *how* is it subject? As the melancholy end at which every living thing inevitably returns to dust and earth! That at least means that man now learns something of this end; it is forced into his consciousness, and he must let this knowledge overshadow his entire life. A second fact is that in the present plan of the whole narrative a threat of death precedes the deed, for one thing, and, for another, at its end is a terrible statement about actual death. This statement in its entire tone is overwhelming to man's ear. Whatever the case of man's mortality or immortality may otherwise have been, this statement would never have been addressed to man in such a way *before* his sinning, and therefore thematically it belongs with special emphasis to the penalty. We must in any case content ourselves with the fact that it cannot be made to agree absolutely with the threat of ch. 2.17, for men did not die after their deed, and the penalty itself is directed so intensively toward life that it must be considered as maintained and not basically forfeited (see Epilogue).

[20] With the penalties in ch. 3.14–19 which explain aetiologically in faith the severe dissonances and enigmas of human life, a high point, a kind of conclusion, has been reached. By continuing the narrative beyond this critical point, the author, who works altogether with preformed older traditions, could not avoid certain irregularities and breaks. The transition from v. 19 to v. 20 has long been considered one such noticeable fracture, and the naming of the woman (a second time, moreover, after ch. 2.23!) was not thought acceptable as the first echo, so to speak, to the penalty. "Mother of all living" is a name of honor; does it not presuppose, moreover, that she has already borne children? The Aramaic word too, *ḥēwyā* ("serpent"), has led to the supposition that at the basis of the narrative there is a very different older form, in which only two acting partners appear: man and a (chthonian?) serpent-deity. But nothing of that kind is evident now. Even though this verse may derive originally from another context and a seam be here recognizable, one must nevertheless seek to understand it in its present place. There can hardly be any doubt that the narrator connects *ḥawwā* (Eve) very closely with the Hebrew word *ḥay*, *ḥayyā*=life. One must see the man's naming of the woman as an act of faith, certainly not faith in promises that lie hidden, veiled in the penalties, but rather an embracing of life, which as a great miracle and mystery is maintained and carried by the motherhood of woman over hardship and death. We said above, at v. 19, that man could regard life in spite of all punishment as maintained and not basically forfeited. This life, which over and beyond the death of the individual is passed on by mothers, he now takes and blesses even though it is threatened by death. Who can express the pain, love, and defiance contained in these words?

[21] The statement that God made men "garments of skins" is in some tension with v. 7, and probably stems ultimately from another circle of tradition. One must have become familiar with our narrator's simple manner of presentation in order to understand the meaning of this statement. To be sure, God gives them only charity to take with them an "outfit for misery" (Gu.), and yet it is an act of marked significance. For the first time we see the Creator as the preserver!

"That means, he accepts men as those who are fallen. He does not compromise them in their nakedness before each other, but he himself covers them. God's activity keeps pace with man" (Bonhoeffer, *Creation and Fall*, 90).

[22] In v. 22 we come upon fresh difficulties. The verse concerns the tree of life, which is obviously strange to the context of vs. 1–19. We now hear more about man's expulsion from the garden, which is repeated immediately in v. 24. Here again seams are visible, but they do not release us from the duty of expounding the text in its present form in spite of the remarkably difficult anacoluthon. (Compare the "also" in v. 22b!) God's word that "the man has become like one of us" scarcely sounds predominantly ironic. A point of comparison between men and gods (the plural makes a comparison with Yahweh himself completely impossible) really exists: Man has stepped outside the state of dependence, he has refused obedience and willed to make himself independent. The guiding principle of his life is no longer obedience but his autonomous knowing and willing, and thus he has really ceased to understand himself as creature. One would scarcely grasp the fine style of the Yahwist, which accommodates so many thoughts at once, if one missed completely in this statement the ironic, perhaps sympathetic, undertone. Even God's withholding of the tree of life is a precaution not without a certain double meaning. Certainly it is first of all punishment and a new sealing of man's destined death, which, to be sure, does not quite agree with v. 19. Could man at all, after his sentencing, break through the ban of death? But we are not to ask such questions. Rather, we are to see that just the man, bowed so deeply by God's punishment, languishes unabatedly for immortality; and we are also to learn that the severe denial of eternal life also has a merciful reverse side, namely, the withholding of a good which for man would have been unbearable in his present condition.

[23–24] Verse 23 obviously belongs to vs. 17, 19a, the Fellah recension. Thus did man leave Paradise and become a farmer. Life in Paradise is not only lost, but with the guardians at the gate it is impossible to regain by defiance and one's own strength. The watch over Paradise is a double one. "Cherubim," according to the view of the ancient Orient, were winged, legendary creatures, half man and half beast, which accompanied the deity (Ps. 18.10) and had the duty, above all, of protecting sacred regions (I Kings 6.23 ff.; 8.6 f.). Along with them (not, therefore, in their hands) is mentioned the flame of the quivering sword, in which one must doubtless see a mythical objectification of lightning (cf. Jer. 47.6).

EPILOGUE TO THE STORY OF PARADISE AND THE FALL

To decide about the literary form of the story of Paradise and the Fall is very difficult. It is in this respect something unique. Ever since the victorious campaign of the science of the history of religions it has been clear that Gen., chs. 2 f., even though a direct Babylonian or other corresponding parallel has not yet been found, must be considered in connection with common Oriental myths of man's creation, the mountain of the gods, the tree of life, the water of life, cherubim, etc. This myth is also alluded to in another passage of the Old Testament (Ezek. 28.11–19). There the prophet applies it, "making it historical," in a lamentation for the king of Tyre. But the implied meaning in the context of a sinless original man whose wisdom was exemplary and whose beauty was perfect is clear enough. He lived in the Garden of Eden on the mountain of the gods; but he was cast out because of his arrogance. The relation of the material to Gen., ch. 3, is apparent, as is its origin from common Oriental, predominantly Mesopotamian conceptions. Nevertheless, it presents the matter to us in quite differentiated form. The Yahwist, who wrote in the period of the Solomonic enlightenment or shortly thereafter, when so much ancient sacred tradition had reached a crisis (see p. 18), was the last one to pass on a myth with archaic piety. Actually the didactic, clearly transparent manner which goes along so discreetly and far from all abstruse wonderfulness, has very little in common with a real myth. How much richer are the mythological colors even in Ezek. 28.11 ff., and how much "more modern" does the so much older Yahwist seem by contrast, if for no other reason than that he psychologically penetrates the events so incomparably! Genesis, chs. 2 f., is a sublime representation of the original state, which uses some mythological ideas freely. Its simplicity, however, is not archaic, but rather the highest command of every artistic means.

Scientific research has shown that behind the present form of this narrative are traditions of various kinds, traditions that only in small part were united with one another by the final hand of the Yahwist, but had already merged much earlier. This combination of older material is thus very close and organic. Along with the chief thought, which runs through the narrative from beginning to end and of which we shall speak later, there is, for example, also the *'ādām* (man)

—'^{a}*dāmā* (earth) motif, which now dominates and unites the whole (chs. 2.7, 19; 3.17, 23). Notwithstanding, one must admit many breaches, seams, and irregularities. The fate of the woman is not quite uniform: ch. 2.18, 23 sees her as help and wife, and though v. 24 significantly expresses the physical belonging of the sexes, ch. 3.7, 20 (and ch. 4.1) do so too. The context of the narrative ch. 3.1–7 obviously presupposes that man does not yet know the mystery of sex and learns it only after the Fall. Accordingly, the naming of the wife as *'iššā* ("woman") and *ḥawwā* ("Eve") is a doublet. Further, the two trees are cause for thought, for ch. 3.1 ff. knows only the tree of knowledge. The watering of the earth occurs both by means of the ground water (*'ēd*?) (ch. 2.6) and the streams of Paradise (ch. 2.10 ff.). Also, there is not complete clarity about the relation of the garden to the land of Eden. Possibly two traditions are discernible: according to one, Eden was Paradise; according to the other, the garden. Both are now drawn together in the expression "the garden of Eden" (chs. 2.15; 3.23 f.). The site of Paradise can be determined with just as little uniformity (ch. 2.8 points to the east; vs. 10 ff. to the north of Palestine). In an earlier, simpler version, perhaps the punishment of the man simply consisted in being driven from the garden. One can already understand the words of punishment in vs. 14–19 as a broad interpretation of this bare fact. The tension which now exists between the threat of death in ch. 2.17 and the word of punishment in ch. 3.19 has already been mentioned. Finally, mention must be made of the strange designation "Yahweh-Elohim." Perhaps this double form is also to be explained from the combination of two traditions.

The task of the commentary is not to make an exact demarcation of the supposed earlier form of the individual traditions which have merged in chs. 2 and 3. It is often assumed today that the stories of Paradise and the Fall have been made up of two narratives which at one time were quite independent of each other, a story about the creation of man (say in 2.4b–7, 18–24) and a story about the garden (say in 2.8–17; 3.1–24). The latter was then expanded in two directions: first by the theme of the tree of life (3.22) and then, principally, by the words of punishment (3.14–19). It is evident that in a much earlier version the punishment was single, and not twofold, and that means expulsion from the garden (3.23 f.). The words of punishment, which embrace the whole existence of man and woman, go far beyond what has preceded them in their scope.*

*For this analysis see W. H. Schmidt, *Die Schöpfungsgeschichte*, 1967², 194ff.

But any attempt to separate the individual traditions available to the present narrator quickly becomes hypothetical. Arguments could also be advanced for other views. It is a constant source of astonishment that the narrator succeeded in making a new entity from earlier material. The chief task of the narrator continues to be to comprehend the almost inexhaustible breadth of this narrative without either restricting it or being affected by "dogmatic" prejudice. It can be seen how the narrator was concerned to subordinate the older material to a much broader theme and to incorporate it into a new whole. It is impossible to miss a deeper caesura between ch. 2 and ch. 3, but a child can see the connection between the two parts. The serpent "which God had made" in ch. 3.1 points back to the creation of the animals in ch. 2.18. The theme of shame in ch. 3.7 ff. is taken up and attached (almost abruptly) to the narrative about the creation of man (2.25). Such connections make the careful reader think hard. But the unevennesses and fine seams should not simply be regarded as deficiencies which break the smooth course of the narrative. They are the things which in a special way constitute its richness and breadth. The creation narrative on the one hand and the story of the garden on the other, which originally had a one-sided aetiological purpose, have become more complete simply by their combination with each other. The narrator's only concern is no longer the aetiologies of chs. 2.24 and 3.14 ff., and one generally must guard against thinking that a story of such inner complexity can have only *one* meaning. It has occasionally perhaps lost some logical precision because of the heterogeneous character of its parts, but it has gained breadth of vision from the fact that everything is not fitted together quite so compactly. And precisely because here and there things do not fit and are not drawn together at the end, the narrative gains its unfathomable and inexhaustible character. Just because it does not sharply define all its statements, because it occasionally suggests instead of making tangibly clear what it is talking about—just this constitutes the mystery of its universality. Of course, these characteristics make special demands on the understanding and exegetical consideration of the reader. The things of which the narrative speaks are widely separated, and between them there is room for many questions and problems about which it does not speak and about which, therefore, it does not want to be asked, either.

The narrator does not reply to many impertinent questions because his own standpoint, of course, is not within Paradise but outside it, and he refrains from all fantasy and speculation about what existed before the Fall. In this respect the reticence, indeed soberness and calm, of the biblical story is especially noticeable in contrast to the arrogant and harsh colors in the myths of other peoples. The culmination of the story is not far away, in the past, but in life after the time of Paradise: the wife, father, mother, the animals, the soil, tribulation, childbirth. Nowhere does the narrator give way to describing an earlier mythological world, even in ch. 2; for what is said about the rivers of Paradise, the creation of man out of earth, the creation of the beasts, of the woman and her fate—all those things are creative acts and decrees that have the same validity for post-Paradise man. The narrator does not give a *direct*, positive description of conditions of life in Paradise. He limits himself to pointing out the great disorders of our present life—shame, fear, the dissonances in the life of the woman and the man—and ascribing them to human sin. And this, of course, is a chief concern of the entire narrative. One can well see in it "a theodicy of universal proportions" (Hempel), for it is concerned to acquit God and his creation of all the suffering and misery that has come into the world. If the Priestly story of creation showed how God separated the world from chaos, then the Yahwistic story of Paradise and the Fall intends to show how the chaos of troubled life which surrounds us today developed out of creation; and to this extent both texts have an important inner relationship. "The problem that the Yahwist investigates is the enigmatic fact that man does not adopt an unambiguous attitude toward his life, but faces it in extremely remarkable ambiguity. . . . The thought of death cripples the will to life; work, although recognized as the purport of life, becomes misery because of toil and failure; the happiness of motherhood, the highest fulfillment of a woman's life, is troubled by pain and sorrow. Only with broken bearing does man face his life; that is the enigmatic fact which the Yahwist contemplates and intends to explain by the narrative of Gen. chs. 2 f." (A. Weiser, *Deutsche Theologie*, 1937, 17). The manifold, profound troubles in human life have their root in the *one* trouble of man's relationship to God. Expressed more concisely, Gen., ch. 3, asserts that all sorrow comes from sin. But with such summaries one runs the danger of diminishing the vast content of the narrative. If we think only of how it shows man as the one who wants to be like God in knowledge and experience, we have before us a kind of Prometheus motif. With this knowledge, obtained in defiance, begins indeed a "higher development," but man pays for this progress by the loss of simple obedience; "it is a knowledge against God, which, therefore, does not bring us to Paradise, but on the contrary casts us into misery" (H. Gressmann, *Christl. Welt*, 1926, 846). Thus this narrative contains some serious criticism of culture too. All in all, it closes in profound sadness. Man was surrounded completely by God's providential goodness. But incomprehensibly he denied God obedience. Paradise is irreparably lost; what is left for a man is a life of trouble in the shadow of a crushing riddle, a life entangled in an unbounded and completely hopeless struggle with the power of evil and in the end unavoidably subject to the majesty of death.

The contents of Gen., ch. 2, and especially ch. 3 are conspicuously isolated in the Old Testament. No prophet, psalm, or narrator makes any recognizable reference to the story of the Fall. One actually does justice to the Yahwist only when one sees him in his isolation, facing the received tradition very freely and not even as the originator of a tradition or "school" either. But that must not mislead one into thinking of his witness to the primeval history of creation and the Fall as basically distinct from the witness to Yahweh's special act of covenant, and therefore into dismissing it. What enabled him to tell the story in this way was none other than the knowledge of Yahweh, the God of Israel. If the subjects of which Israel's faith tended to speak elsewhere through the mouth of her history-writers, priests and prophets seem to be rather far from those of this primeval history, nevertheless many important connecting lines run back and forth between the two. A reader is hardly in a position to take the narrative of Gen. 2–3 in complete isolation, because he cannot be content with what it says. He is not happy with it; he has to ask about the future. The Yahwist meets this need by keeping in mind the further history of this man with God and by going on to talk of Abraham and Moses. It is no chance that eschatology and, later, apocalyptic also took up on occasion the theme of the primal state (Paradise, primeval man, peace among the animals, abundance of water, etc.). In any case, behind both Old Testament protology and eschatology is the revelation of Yahweh, the God of Israel.

5. THE STORY OF CAIN AND ABEL. Ch. 4.1–16

4 1Now Adam knew Eve his wife, and she conceived and bore Cain,
saying, "I have gotten a man with the help of the Lord." 2And again,

she bore his brother Abel. Now Abel was a keeper of sheep, and Cain a
tiller of the ground. [3]In the course of time Cain brought to the LORD
an offering of the fruit of the ground, [4]and Abel brought of the firstlings
of his flock and of their fat portions. And the LORD had regard for Abel
and his offering, [5]but for Cain and his offering he had no regard. So
Cain was very angry, and his countenance fell. [6]The LORD said to Cain,
"Why are you angry, and why has your countenance fallen? [7]If you do
well, will you not be accepted? And if you do not do well, sin is couching at the door; its desire is for you, but you must master it."
8 Cain said to Abel his brother, "Let us go out to the field." And
when they were in the field, Cain rose up against his brother Abel, and
killed him. [9]Then the LORD said to Cain, "Where is Abel your brother?"
He said, "I do not know; am I my brother's keeper?" [10]And the LORD
said, "What have you done? The voice of your brother's blood is crying
to me from the ground. [11]And now you are cursed from the ground,
which has opened its mouth to receive your brother's blood from your
hand. [12]When you till the ground, it shall no longer yield to you its
strength; you shall be a fugitive and a wanderer on the Earth." [13]Cain
said to the LORD, "My punishment is greater than I can bear. [14]Behold,
thou hast driven me this day away from the ground; and from thy face
I shall be hidden; and I shall be a fugitive and a wanderer on the earth,
and whoever finds me will slay me." [15]Then the LORD said to him, "Not
so! If any one slays Cain, vengeance shall be taken on him sevenfold."
And the LORD put a mark on Cain, lest any who came upon him should
kill him. [16]Then Cain went away from the presence of the LORD, and
dwelt in the land of Nod, east of Eden.

[1–2] This new narrative is very closely tied in v. 1 to what has preceded. The man "knows" his wife, and she bears the first son. It is modesty of language which here and elsewhere uses the verb *yāda'* ("to know") to designate sexual intercourse. This verb, which means both "knowing intellectually" and "experiencing", "being acquainted" (see at chs. 2.16–17; 3.4–5), was especially suited to such a veiled manner of speaking.

Cain, the name of the first-born, means "spear" (II Sam. 21.16) and is also attested in early Arabic as a personal name. The etymology with which the mother justifies the name, however, is quite obscure. Every word of this little sentence is difficult: the verb *qānā* ("get," "acquire") is just as unusual for the birth of a child as is the use of *'îš* ("man") for a newborn boy. To apply the *'îš* ("man") to the husband is even less acceptable. But completely unexplainable is *'et-yhwh* (L: *mit dem Herrn*, "with the Lord"), which cannot be understood as accusative, but is still best taken prepositionally, even though one must remember that otherwise *'ēt* never means "with the help of."

The passage can no longer be clarified. The destination of man and woman to carnal community was a decree of creation made by God in Paradise. But a sensitive judgment of our narrator rests in the fact that he places the actual act of sexual intercourse outside Paradise.

Then Cain's brother is born who receives the name *hebel* ("Abel"). An explanation of this name is not given, but everyone who hears it thinks of the other Hebrew word *hebel* ("breath," "futility") and takes this connotation as a somber allusion to what follows. Abel was a shepherd, Cain a farmer. Thus begins the division of mankind, so fraught with grave consequences, into individual vocations with quite different attitudes toward life. The profoundness of this division, which leads to two altars and goes hand in hand with a real shattering of man's brotherhood, remains hidden for the time being. Verses 1 and 2 contain the exposition. The real action begins in v. 3.

[3–5] Both now offer sacrifice. Cultic interests do not move the narrator at all, and therefore he gives here a rather incidental report of the first sacrifice. One learns neither why it occurred (on the basis of what institution) nor what kind of sacrifice it was. But every reader must hear attentively what they sacrifice and that each one honors God separately from the other, and recognize therein disquieting signs. The shepherd sacrifices from his flock, the farmer from the produce of the earth—just as one would expect! And yet the difference in the life of both is not something external, but rather is so deep that it works itself out in distinctive acts of religious practice. Cult belongs intimately to culture, and every culture gives birth to its own peculiar cult. Thus there was more than one altar!

And now it is further stated that God did not honor both sacrifices, but only Abel's. Writers have looked diligently for the basis of this preference, but it lies neither in the ritual nor in Cain's attitude. Nothing of that kind is indicated. The only clue one can find in the narrative is that the sacrifice of blood was more pleasing to Yahweh. Obviously the narrator wants to remove the acceptance of the sacrifice from man and place it completely within God's free will. He refrains from making the decision for Abel and against Cain logically comprehensible ("I will be gracious to whom I will be gracious, and will show mercy on whom I will show mercy," Ex. 33.19). The narrative is so terse and keeps so tensely to the catastrophe that it leaves no room even for necessary explanatory accessories. Thus neither does one learn how Cain learned of this judgment of God. Since the entire ancient Orient learned about the acceptance or rejection of a sacrifice by examining the victim, one must suppose some such method here. But the point is not emphasized at all. To keep the reader from horror, some resting point is granted him in the divine word of v. 6. Hot resentment had risen in Cain, which had distorted even his body! He envies God's pleasure in his brother (Zi.). **[6–7]** God warns him about this change of his being and the danger of this sin seething in his heart. It is a fatherly address that wants to show the threatened man a way out before it is too late. (One sees that Cain was not completely rejected even though his sacrifice was not accepted.) Especially urgent is the appeal to Cain's acquiescence. "If you do well, you are able to lift it up." (RSV, "will you not be accepted?") God can still appeal to the better motives in the human heart. Unfortunately, the statement is in part really obscure. The *śᵉʾēt*, "lift up," in v. 7a can in our opinion be understood neither in the sense of forgiveness nor of the presentation or acceptance of the sacrifice; rather, one must relate it to *pānīm*, "face" (in contrast to the *nāpal*, "fall," in v. 6b): "If you do well, there is lifting up," i.e., you can freely lift up your face. In v. 7b the final *t* of *haṭṭāʾt* ("sin") is best taken as the initial letter of the following verb form and read *ḥēṭʾ tirbaṣ* ("sin lies in wait"); then one obtains the expected feminine form. The comparison of sin with a beast of prey lying before the door is strange, as is the purely figurative use of "door" (door of the heart?) in such an ancient narrative. One suspects that the meaning of the passage was once quite different. Now it can be understood only in this inner meaning. It is only a very short distance from the inner emotion to the act. The statement does not actually speak of an inner emotion, but it shows sin as an objective power which, as it were, is outside the man and over him, waiting eagerly to take possession of him. The man, however, ought to master it and curb it. Man's responsibility with regard to sin is not in the least annulled; on the contrary, this final imperative imposes on him the whole responsibility. (The final words at the end of v. 7 curiously correspond exactly to those of ch. 3.16b, where they are used in a quite different connection.)

[8–10] In v. 8 what Cain said to Abel is missing. A series of ancient text traditions contains the brief sentence: "Let us go out to the field!" This sounds like a subsequent addition. And now occurs the first murder, for God's sake! The statement is of lapidary brevity and detachment, but with it the narrator gives the only suitable expression to the awful fact. As in the story of the Fall, so here God is on the spot immediately after the deed. But now God's question to the man is not, "Where are you?" but rather, "Where is your brother?" Responsibility before God is responsibility for the brother. "God's question now appears as a social question." (W. Vischer, *Jahweh, der Gott Kains*, 1929, 45.) But Cain gets rid of this difficult question, which graciously offered him opportunity to confess his deed (Zi.), with an impertinent witticism: Shall I shepherd the shepherd? He lies impertinently directly to God's face, is therefore much more hardened than were the first human pair. A trial is impossible, but the narrator ventures it in the cry, "What have you done?" in order to express God's horror at this deed in the most human way. And then Cain learns something that he had not previously considered: the corpse was indeed covered over with earth, but the blood of the murdered man had raised a cry of complaint, and this cry of murder had come directly before God's throne. *Ṣāʿaq*, *ṣᵉʿāqā* ("cry," "outcry") is what ancient German law understands by *Zeterruf*, the *vox oppressorum*, the appeal to legal protection (Gen. 18.20; Deut. 22.24, 27; II Kings 8.3; Job 16.18 f.). According to the Old Testament view, blood and life belong to God alone; wherever a man commits murder he attacks God's very own right of possession. To destroy life goes far beyond man's proper sphere. Spilled blood cannot be shoveled underground; it cries aloud to heaven and complains directly to the Lord of life. In this statement that dismal, primitive feeling of shuddering before spilled blood is wonderfully combined with the most mature faith in God as the protector and guardian of all life.

[11–12] God's judgment on the fratricide is more terrible than the punishment in ch. 3. Something that could not be made good again, something that ancient man found much more terrible had happened: the earth, man's maternal basis of life, had drunk a brother's blood. At this point the punishment begins: Cain is banished from the soil (*ʾᵃdāmā*), the earth itself is to deny him its power of blessing. The punishment goes far beyond that inflicted in ch. 3.17 ff. The relation of the fratricide to the mother earth is disturbed much more deeply. It is so shattered, in fact, that the earth has no home for him. What remains for him is an unstable and fugitive life. As in the story of Paradise, so here there is throughout the story the *ʾᵃdāmā*-motif, the thought of the earth as the most basic foundation of all human existence. Cain had plowed the soil, offered the fruit of the soil, caused the soil to drink a brother's blood; but the blood complained against him from the soil, and therefore the soil denies him its fruit, and he is banned from the soil (Gu.). But this theme is completely sacred, for the story of Cain understands cultivated land as the realm of cult and blessing close to God. In this again it is very old. **[13–14]** Under the weight of this curse Cain goes to pieces, though not in remorse. The *'āwōn* of which Cain speaks and which he thinks himself unable to bear is the *punishment* for sin. It is a cry of horror at the prospect of such a life of unrest and harassment without peace. Cain sees immediately that a life far from God is a life that God no longer protects. Once God has withdrawn his hand from him, all others will fall upon him. **[15–16]** But the narrative surprisingly does not conclude with this picture of the condemned murderer. Indeed, one must say that only now does it reach its most important point: Cain does not have the last word in this story, but rather God, who now places Cain's forfeited life under strict protection. Yahweh obviously placed the sign on Cain's body; the narrator appears to be thinking of a tattoo or something similar. This sign, however, is not to disgrace him but to refer to that mysterious protective relationship in which Cain henceforth will be held by God. The conclusion of the story, according to which Cain then goes forth "away from the presence of the Lord," completely sharpens the riddle of his future existence: because of his murder he is cursed by separation from God and yet incomprehensibly guarded and supported by God's protection. Even his life belongs to God, and he does not abandon it. A land of Nod is geographically unknown to us; more important is the fact that the Hebrew recognized in the name his word *nad*, "fugitive" (v. 12). It is therefore the land of restlessness.

The historical background of the material of our narrative is very strange. It has long been supposed that Cain cannot be separated from the tribe of the Kenites often mentioned in the Old Testament. Cain is the embodiment or the ancestor of the Kenites, and therefore it is scarcely thinkable that the Yahwist, in whose time Kenites still existed, was not also thinking, in his story about Cain, of this tribe and its curious fate. But what, then, is the nature of our narrator's thoughts? For no proof is really needed that in the present story he is speaking to us not about the historically insignificant tribe of the Kenites but rather about the beginning of humanity. The Kenites were a difficult riddle to the Israelites. They too, like the Israelites, were worshippers of Yahweh, perhaps even before Israel. Their relatives, the Rechabites (II Kings 10.15 ff.; Jer., ch. 35; I Chron. 2.55), were even especially fanatic zealots of Yahweh. And in spite of this, the Kenites never belonged to the covenant community chosen by

Yahweh, nor were they heirs of the Promised Land. Coming themselves from the south they had indeed joined the desert wandering of the Israelites (Num. 10.29 ff.), but they never really achieved a sedentary life. Like Bedouins, they lived not from agriculture but wandered restlessly on the limits of the cultivated land, living from plunder too. Strange, this roving life on the other side of the soil that God had blessed! But even stranger Cain's enigmatic relation to Yahweh! Completely outside the covenants and still in a relationship to Yahweh (apparently the Kenites indicated this relationship to Yahweh by a tribal sign, a kind of tattoo, externally recognizable, cf. I Kings 20.41; Zech. 13.6; Ezek. 9.4)! But even though the Yahwist is not concerned in the present narrative with the Kenites or their ancestors, this much is certain: the Kenites, their weird, restless life at the edge of civilization, and, above all, the enigma of their relationship to Yahweh, may have given the Yahwist the colors for his narrative of primeval history. In the historical existence of the Kenites something primeval had become illustratively plain, something that is true in a wider and deeper sense for the existence and destiny of all men. In other words, the tribal saga, the original contours of which are quite clearly recognizable, is stripped of its historical contingencies in our Yahwistic narrative and enlarged to the original, the universal. Genesis 4.1–16 no longer relates the story of a tribe but rather a chapter out of the primeval history of humanity, and the story in its present form is thus linked as closely as possible with the preceding story of the Fall. The narrator shows what happened to mankind when once it had fallen from obedience to God. This is actually the first picture of man after he was expelled from Paradise, and the picture is a terrible one. Sin has grown like an avalanche. It has taken total possession of the man who associated with it, for this man outside Paradise is a fratricide from the beginning. The story expresses something of the essential nature of all mankind by condensing it into a picture of quite elemental power. The religious and historical background of the story of Cain has also been reconstructed in other ways. Thus, for example, the suggestion has often been made that originally the murder of Abel concerned human sacrifice (cf. Brock Utne, ZAW, 1936, 202 ff.).

This narrative too demands exegetical sensitiveness, for in the first place it thinks of man in a limited sphere of life, namely, the geographical and historical area of Palestine. Geographically, the narrative presupposes the two basic facts of this area, which are almost as determinative for all existence as life and death: tillable land and desert. And historically, the tribe of the Kenites, with its troubled existence on the edge of the desert and the riddle of its relationship to God, gave the basic character to this picture. But it is amazing how much the geographical and historical contingencies of the narrative recede into the background and how cogently it illustrates the universal, primeval, and original. The terribleness of Cain's sin lies in the fact that it does not catch him in a condition of separation from God, i.e., where he forgets himself in human life, but precisely at the point where he lifts his hands to God, at the altar.* God's judgment on the fratricide consists both in a wider, deeper disturbance of man's relationship to the life-giving soil and in a still more drastic banishment, for where Cain has to live is no cult of Yahweh. As the narrative itself says, Cain goes "away from the presence of the Lord." That he still is not abandoned by God but lives expressly in a protective relationship is the most enigmatic part of the narrative, for here God's ordering and protecting will is revealed. The spirit of murder which erupted in Cain, is not to spread into wider and wider circles (Di.), and the punishment that God inflicted on Cain is not to be the occasion for barbarism among men.

6. THE GENEALOGY OF THE KENITES. Ch. 4.17–26

4 17Cain knew his wife, and she conceived and bore Enoch; and he
built a city, and called the name of the city after the name of his son,
Enoch. 18To Enoch was born Irad; and Irad was the father of Me-
huja-el, and Me-huja-el the father of Me-thusha-el, and Methusha-
el the father of Lamech. 19And Lamech took two wives; the name of the
one was Adah, and the name of the other Zillah. 20Adah bore Jabal;
he was the father of those who dwell in tents and have cattle. 21His
brother's name was Jubal; he was the father of all those who play the
lyre and pipe. 22Zillah bore Tubal-cain; he was the forger of all instru-
ments of bronze and iron. The sister of Tubal-cain was Naamah.

23 Lamech said to his wives:
"Adah and Zillah, hear my voice;
  you wives of Lamech, hearken to what I say:
I have slain a man for wounding me,
  a young man for striking me.
24If Cain is avenged sevenfold,
  truly Lamech seventy-sevenfold."

*"In political anger there is still some trace of human nature . . . there is not such fury in political anger. Pharisaical rage is plainly diabolical rage"; Luther, WA, XLII, 193.

25 And Adam knew his wife again, and she bore a son and called his name Seth, for she said, "God has appointed for me another child instead of Abel, for Cain slew him." 26 To Seth also a son was born, and he called his name Enosh. At that time men began to call upon the name of the LORD.

A genealogy of eight members serves to let the narrator show the present development of man, his culture, and also something of his mental attitude. The word "serves" is intentional, for anyone who wants to probe the distinctive features and subtleties of the Yahwistic narrative must realize that it arose by a combination of several very distinct traditions. Who knows from what special conditions and for what special needs these ancient genealogies were originally produced? This genealogy is quite different in form from the narrative of Cain's crime and must therefore have a different origin. If each of these traditions had its own special character, then our narrator did not intend at all to orient them toward each other in all their details after welding them into the large work. Thus the Yahwist saw nothing strange in the fact that the genealogy speaks of Cain's wife, as though the reader had already heard of her. The conscientious reader must therefore always have some power of discrimination with this narrator, first for the peculiarities of each individual tradition, and secondly for the chief ideas that the narrator himself wants to express when he combines so many traditions into a whole. It is obvious, of course, that we must perceive our narrator's own contribution more in the composition as a whole than in its individual parts. And for the exposition, it is, of course, true that in the case of discrepancies between details in the accepted traditions the overlapping line of thought must have pre-eminence and the last word.

[17–22] The Kenite genealogy is evidently intended to answer elementary questions of cultural history: What is the origin of the first city? When did the division into various professions come about? Quite apart from the fact that the name Cain stands at the head of this genealogy, no other common features with the preceding narrative can be seen. It is not, of course, so certain whether the note about the founding of a city is in irreconcilable contradiction with the curse, which is to a life of wandering. It could be that, for example, Kenite smiths had also settled in cities and had even given such settlements a special character. I Sam. 30.29 also mentions Kenite cities. The list seems originally to have dealt with a group of professions which were practiced in the area between the cultivated land and the wilderness, predominantly by Kenites: smiths, tinkers, and musicians, who were either nomadic or had already settled to ply their trade. The tribe to which they belonged might well have been indicated by a tattoo. We still have no explanation for the striking similarity between the names in this genealogy and those in the Sethite genealogy in the Priestly document, nor do we know how these two genealogies are to be related to the ancient Mesopotamian kinglist (see above, p. 71). Tubal in v. 22 can, of course, only be understood as a personal name. In Isa. 66.19; Ezek. 27.13 it is the name of a people, the Tibarenes, south-east of the Black Sea and known from their copperware. Here, too, any connections that there may be are quite obscure.

If this genealogy does not fit quite smoothly into the previous narrative context, it cannot be linked without a break to the events that follow, either. In introducing the link between certain professions and the Kenites, it evidently does not reckon with the Flood and the annihilation of all living beings. Nevertheless, the text is an important part of the great structure of the Yahwistic primeval history. It shows man's cultural progress: the city arises, and smiths emerge alongside shepherds. They and the musicians also represent the beginnings of human art. For the Yahwist these now generalized details are enough to indicate something of the development of human culture. He gives us the most important fact in the "Song of the Sword" attached to the end of the genealogy. **[23–24]** This song must have been a very ancient song of revenge which our narrator found. Here, incorporated into his great work, it serves to make visible something of the other side of that advance, something of the change in the human attitude which goes hand in hand with that higher development. It is the spirit of a growing irreconcilableness and fierce self-assertiveness, by which human community is more and more profoundly ruptured. Lamech is not satisfied with the protection that God promised to his ancestor, Cain; he takes upon himself the execution of vengeance and takes his revenge recklessly. (Compare here a Corsican song of vengeance: "Twelve lives are still too few to avenge this fallen boot.") The song was once understood, of course, quite primitively as in praise of one's own self-affirmation ("boasting song"). Now, incorporated into the context of the Yahwistic primeval history, it speaks for itself. A sign of the working method of the Yahwist, who lets the text itself speak and reckons with attentive readers!

The Song of Lamech is the third section of the primeval history which the narrator emphasizes. It is a story of the increase in sin and the more and more profound disturbance of the original orders of life with which it goes hand in hand. First the Fall, then fratricide, and now the execution of vengeance (which God has reserved for himself!) is claimed by man. It becomes wanton, and in addition man boasts of it. One man for one wound, one boy for one stripe, and seventy-sevenfold vengeance. That is a spirit of brutality in contrast to which what the first man did and the way he did it appear almost trivial; for Lamech's defiant demand reaches into Yahweh's own domain. Did Jesus frame his statement in Matt. 18.22 about forgiving seventy times seven with conscious reference to this passage? (Fr.)

[25–26] The Yahwistic Sethite list is only a fragment. In the great final redaction of the sources it had to give way to the Priestly Sethite list (ch. 5). Thus only its beginning is left and a bit of the end in ch. 5.29. The church has thought a great deal about the two ancestral genealogies of the Kenites and Sethites; it found in the latter the beginning of a new human lineage and thus something like a prefiguration of the church and its relationship to the world. It is difficult, however, to determine here the correct meaning of the narrator. On the one hand the parallelism of the two genealogies is striking; both open into a trinity: one begins with the forefather's departure from God's presence and ends with a song of fiercest rebellion; the other tells at its beginning about the origin of the Yahweh cult and gives at its end—so far as we can see—a statement of profound prostration and great yearning for salvation. And yet such thoughts seem to be suggested to the text too, though they are not expressly stated. No major style has been followed, so that one cannot say that this idea of a double original lineage belongs to the special concern of our narrator. Even in the next section of his primeval history, the one about the angel marriages, and less than ever in the story of the Flood, no further trace of this idea can be discovered. The narrator needed the story and genealogy of Cain in order to show the increase of sin, and he needed the Sethite genealogy because it brought him down in the history of tradition directly to Noah and the Flood.

In v. 25 one sees clearly the way the Yahwist telescopes the traditions. The name, Seth (cf. Num. 24.17) is perhaps to be connected with the Guti, Aramean nomads, who, according to Egyptian and cuneiform sources, afflicted the civilizations west and north of the Arabian desert in the second millennium (E. Meyer, G. A. II/1, 93, 343, 474). Then Seth would be understood as an Aramean tribal hero, in contrast to the North Arabian Cain (Pr.). The notice about the beginning of the Yahweh cult is strange and can scarcely be rightly explained. This reference to an original revelation cannot easily be reconciled with the dominant primary tradition of the Old Testament (Ex. 3.14; 6.3).* This view appears to have been peculiar to the tradition taken over by the Yahwist; it not only considers the Yahweh cult as much older than Moses, but finds its origin in primeval history. Even though the Old Testament is unanimous in asserting that for Israel the name Yahweh was first revealed at the time of Moses, nevertheless the Yahweh cult can have roots which in the history of religions go back much farther (among the Kenites?). Our notice does not intend to answer the question about the pre-Mosaic worship of Yahweh in detail, but rather to indicate generally Yahweh-worship as the primeval religion of mankind in general.

7. THE ANGEL MARRIAGES. Ch. 6.1–4

6 [1]When men began to multiply on the face of the ground, and
daughters were born to them, [2]the sons of God saw that the daughters
of men were fair; and they took to wife such of them as they chose.
[3]Then the LORD said, "My spirit shall not abide in man for ever, for
he is flesh, but his days shall be a hundred and twenty years." [4]The
Nephilim were on the earth in those days, and also afterward, when the
sons of God came in to the daughters of men, and they bore children to
them. These were the mighty men that were of old, the men of renown.

[1–4] A completely new section of the Yahwistic primeval history begins here. Previously a way was shown that led from the first refusal of obedience to fratricide and from there to a defiant self-affirmation that despised all unfamiliar life (Song of Lamech). Can the narrator still pursue and intensify this account of the continuous increase of sin? The beginning of the new story is quite general in its chronology and without special connection with what precedes. The reader, therefore, who has learned to pay attention to such artless transitions, detects that he is being introduced into a previously quite independent narrative context, which seems like a "cracked erratic boulder" (Pr.). The only thing said is that the event occurred at a time when there were many men. (The twofold list of Kenites–Sethites is apparently not considered here.) The actual actors, however, are not these men but the upper inhabitants of heaven, who inhabit the heavenly world, according to the view of the ancients. They appear at the divine councils and are occasionally sent by God

*F. Horst, "Die Notiz vom Anfang des Jahwekultes in Gen. 4.26", *Festschrift Delekat*, 1957, 68 ff., attempts an explanation.

to carry out definite commands (Gen. 28.12; I Kings 22.19–22; Job 1.6 ff.). But even though frequent and candid reference is made to this popular conception in the Old Testament (Ps. 29.1; 89.7; 82.6; Job 38.7), still one notices how little significance these intermediary beings had for the life of faith; for Yahweh's action in nature and history was so pervasive and direct that scarcely any room was left for the activity of other heavenly beings. The question, which has been asked from the time of the early church down to our own day, whether, namely, the "sons of God" are to be understood as angelic beings or as men, i.e., as members of "the superior human race of Seth," can be considered as finally settled. The *b^{e}nē hā '^{e}lōhīm*, here, by the way, clearly contrasted to the daughters of men, are beings of the upper heavenly world. The *bēn* ("son") describes them, however, as sons of God, not in the physical, genealogical sense, i.e., mythologically, but generally as belonging to the world of the Elohim (cf. also *b^{e}nē hann^{e}bī'īm*, *disciples* of the prophets, II Kings 2.3, 5, 7). These angelic beings let themselves be enticed by the beauty of human women to grievous sin; they fall from their ranks and mix with them in wild licentiousness. Here too, as in the stories of the Fall and Cain, God is immediately on the spot with his word of judgment. The verb *yādōn* (L: *strafen*, "to punish") in v. 3a is to be derived from a word *dūn*, "be mighty," "rule" (BL, 398). Because of the union of these heavenly beings with earthly women, God's spirit and life-giving power entered mankind far beyond the original design at creation. *Rūaḥ* ("spirit") is not a *charisma*, i.e., an additional gift of the spirit, as it is in predominant Old Testament usage, but rather the habitual physical life-potency in man (so too Ps. 104.29). God, however, will not permit this superhuman power of life to grow powerful in man, because man in spite of this "demonic" invasion of his realm remains essentially flesh, i.e., of the earth and mortal. Therefore God sets a maximum age beyond which man, who has increased his vital power in such an antigodly manner, cannot go. The difficult *b^{e}šaggām* (L: *denn*, "for") in v. 3 is better not derived from *šāgag* ("in their wandering"), because then the suffix would have no antecedent; but one understands it best as a combination of the relative particle *še* with the preposition *b^{e}* and the particle *gām* ("also"), with the meaning "because" (BL, 264). This divine penalty lacks strict relation to what precedes. It is applied to man in general, and not only to the actual evildoers and their bastards. The impression that here older material could have been radically revised subsequently is now strengthened because of the remarkable position of v. 4 in the narrative context. The statement that when the heavenly beings went in to the human women, giants were on the earth, those illustrious warriors of antiquity—this statement is expected much earlier, namely, immediately after v. 2 and not only after the penalty, where it now seems only an archaeological notice, a general indication of date almost outside the context of the narrative. And in the earlier form of the narrative this statement undoubtedly once came after v. 2 for these giants were, of course, the children of that marriage of heavenly beings with human women. Indeed, the original purpose of this story was precisely this, to account aetiologically for the origin of heroes from such marriages. One still detects it in the primary importance and pathos of v. 4, which in addition interprets the apparently rare word *n*ᵉ*pīlīm* (L: *Gewaltige*, "mighty ones") as the "strong ones," the "heroes" (LXX: *gigantes*). The word occurs elsewhere only in Num. 13.33 and there too is explained to the reader. (Concerning giants, cf. Deut. 2.20 f.; 3.11; Ezek. 32.21, 27; Amos 2.9.) Possibly in the ancient myth even the widespread motif of a god's envy played a role. Nevertheless, no matter how clearly distinguishable this derivation of the giants from angel marriages may be in the original form of our narrative, it still is not mentioned at all in the present text. Our narrator cut the old intellectual context in three places. First, no longer is it said that the heroes were offspring of this union which is contrary to creation. Secondly, the *rūaḥ* ("spirit"), that power of life, is now designated as *Yahweh's* spirit. (To speak of a *rūaḥ* ["spirit"] of the Elohim would not fit into Old Testament tradition at all!) And again the *rūaḥ* ("spirit") is the spirit in man, not only in the heroes. Thirdly, the reduction of the life span no longer refers to the bastards born of those marriages. It is clear that the special aetiological concern of the ancient myth cannot move forward after that "demythologization." The Yahwist wanted to show man's general corruption. He wanted to represent the mixing of superhuman spiritual powers with man, a kind of "demonic" invasion, and thus point out a further disturbance caused by sin; and what is more, a more profound disturbance, for these were not only evidences of dissolution within the human community (Cain, Lamech); but in the rise of a super humanity (Jac.), overlapping decrees were broken, decrees by which God had separated the upper realm of the heavenly spiritual world from that of man. There had occurred a deterioration of all of creation, which cannot be more frightfully conceived. And from this rampant spread of sin God does draw a corresponding conclusion, about which our narrator now gives a full report.

8. THE PROLOGUE TO THE FLOOD. Ch. 6.5–8

6 [5]The LORD saw that the wickedness of man was great in the earth,
and that every imagination of the thoughts of his heart was only evil
continually. [6]And the LORD was sorry that he had made man on the
earth, and it grieved him to his heart. [7]So the LORD said, "I will blot
out man whom I have created from the face of the ground, man and
beast and creeping things and birds of the air, for I am sorry that I
have made them." [8]But Noah found favor in the eyes of the LORD.

[5–8] These four verses form an especially important and curious part of the Yahwistic primeval history. Before we expound their content, a word about their formal character and origin is in order. Up to this point our narrator has been bound almost completely to traditional material in the form it was given to him. In the story of Paradise and the Fall, in the story of Cain, the genealogy of the Kenites, the story of the angel marriages—in all of them, there were extant older traditions which he put together as building stones, occasionally refashioned quite independently, for his primeval history of mankind. A glance at these verses and their content shows that here the case is different. We read a communication about God's judgment on man and hear of a decision in the divine heart. These words of the narrator do not as such derive from an older literary tradition; they contain neither an actual story nor a compilation in the form of a list. It is quite obvious that the last-mentioned tradition revised by our narrator was the story of the angel marriages; the next is the Flood story. Between these clearly distinct and compact narratives are those statements which to us are so important because here for the first time the narrator himself speaks completely on his own. Until now he has spoken to us through the medium of ancient traditions or in the quite special way he has combined them. We have also seen that the ancient contents of the traditions sometimes did not quite coincide with the concern of the narrator; because of its great original dead weight, all the material could not be incorporated into the theological structure of the Yahwist without contradition. Chapter 6.5–8 is thus important to us because at this point the narrator for once speaks quite freely and without dependence on older material. These words, therefore, have for us programmatic significance, not only for the understanding of the Flood story but also for the entire Yahwistic primeval history. They show something of its literary technique (see the epilogue to the Yahwistic primeval history, pp. 152 ff.).

In substance, these verses contain a reflection about the extent of sin which has overtaken man. While the narrator up to this point simply described the fact of rapidly spreading sin, without giving any particular evaluation, now we hear a reflection about its universality, and, what is more, from the mouth of God himself. It is elicited by the preceding story of the disorder resulting from angel marriages, but beginning there, it refers to the eruption of sin into the world of men as a whole. (The link with the immediately preceding story is not quite smooth, for in vs. 1–4, Yahweh has already decided upon the measures he will take regarding the degeneration of his creation.) From the first Fall sin had grown like an avalanche; here at a special climax the narrator pauses and interrupts the regular progress of the account. He takes us from the world of complete disorderliness to God and dares to look into God's grieving heart. The judgment on man, about which we hear in this manner, is extremely sharp: "Every imagination of the thoughts of his heart was only evil continually!" The "heart," according to the Old Testament view, is the seat not only of the emotion, but also of the understanding and the will. The statement comprises, therefore, the entire inner life of man. "The thoughts of his heart"—the imagery of the expression is vivid! It means even the reflections of fantasy, the rising and freely formed movements of the will, were "only evil continually." In daring contrast to what is said about the human heart there follows a word about what takes place in God's heart: grief, affliction, and disappointment in man. Precisely in this way, by reference to the Creator's bewilderment, he has communicated something of the incomprehensibility of this incursion of sin. For the people of the old covenant, Yahweh was completely personal, a will most vital and lively. So far as the human description of God is concerned (in terms of pleasure, anger, aversion, zeal, love, etc.), the Old Testament (especially the prophets) reveals scarcely any attempt to "spiritualize" the picture of God. It was apparently easier in Old Testament faith to tolerate the danger of lessening God's greatness and "absoluteness" by human description than to run the risk of giving up anything of God's lively personalness and his vital participation in everything earthly.* Thus the Old Testament can say almost in one breath, Yahweh "repented," and then, "[God] is not a man that he should repent" (I Sam. 15.11, 29). The verb used can also be translated "let himself be sorry." Either way, the strong emotion of God indicates that God did not make the decision to destroy all life in unconcerned, cold indifference (Del.); and at the same time it intimates the real motive for Noah's reprieve. The expression for "destroy" ("wash away") is very hard; perhaps it already indicates the destruction by water (Jac.). To the reader of the Yahwistic work Noah is known only by name (ch. 5.29), i.e., not in such a way that God's choice could be made comprehensible. That choice finds its explanation only in God's gracious will, who even before the frightful judgment has chosen the man in whom someday his work of salvation can again be resumed.

9. THE FLOOD. (J) Chs. 7.1–5, 7, 16b, 8–10, 12, 17b, 22–23; 8.6a, 2b, 3a, 6b, 8–12, 13b, 20

7 1Then the LORD said to Noah, "Go into the ark, you and all your
household, for I have seen that you are righteous before me in this
generation. 2Take with you seven pairs of all clean animals, the male
and his mate; and a pair of the animals that are not clean, the male
and his mate; 3and seven pairs of the birds of the air also, male and
female, to keep their kind alive upon the face of all the earth. 4For in
seven days I will send rain upon the earth forty days and forty nights;
and every living thing that I have made I will blot out from the face of
the ground." 5And Noah did all that the LORD had commanded him. . . .
7And Noah and his sons and his wife and his sons' wives with him
went into the ark, to escape the waters of the flood. . . . 16bAnd the
Lord shut him in. . . . 8Of clean animals, and of animals that are not
clean, and of birds, and of everything that creeps on the ground, 9two
and two, male and female, went into the ark with Noah, as God had
commanded Noah. 10And after seven days the waters of the flood came
upon the earth. . .. .

12 And rain fell upon the earth forty days and forty nights. . . .
17bAnd the waters increased, and bore up the ark, and it rose high
above the earth. . . . 22Everything on the dry land in whose nostrils

*The meaning of the many human descriptions of God in the Old Testament "is not to bring God from afar to a level like that of man. The human likeness is not a humanization. And these descriptions were never thought of that way except in unfair polemic. Rather they are to make God accessible to man. . . . They present God as a person. They avoid the error of making God a static, unconcerned, abstract idea, or an inflexible principle. God is person, full of will, to be found in active discussion, prepared for his communication, open to the impact of human sin and supplication of human prayer and the weeping over human guilt; in a word, God is a living God." (L. Köhler, *Theologie des A.T.*, 6.)

was the breath of life died. [23]He blotted out every living thing that was upon the face of the ground, man and animals and creeping things and birds of the air; they were blotted out from the earth. Only Noah was left, and those that were with him in the ark. . . .

8 [6a]At the end of forty days . . . [2b]the rain from the heavens was restrained, [3a]and the waters receded from the earth continually. . . . [6b]Noah opened the window of the ark which he had made. [8]Then he sent forth the dove from him, to see if the waters had subsided from the face of the ground; [9]but the dove found no place to set her foot, and she returned to him to the ark, for the waters were still on the face of the whole earth. So he put forth his hand and took her and brought her into the ark with him. [10]He waited another seven days, and again he sent forth the dove out of the ark; [11]and the dove came back to him in the evening, and lo, in her mouth a freshly plucked olive leaf; so Noah knew that the waters had subsided from the earth. [12]Then he waited another seven days, and sent forth the dove; and she did not return to him any more. . . . [13b]And Noah removed the covering of the ark, and looked, and behold, the face of the ground was dry. [20]Then Noah built an altar to the Lord, and took of every clean animal and of every clean bird, and offered burnt offerings on the altar.

The biblical story of the Flood as it now exists is an ingenious interweaving of the two sources J and P. The redactor has wonderfully worked both texts together in such a way that both Flood stories have remained almost intact. Since the Priestly story of the Flood was larger, even externally, and since in addition it is also literarily younger, it became essentially definitive for the form and content of the final redaction. To understand the narrative as a whole one must, of course, refer to it (see pp. 125 f.). But to penetrate the thought more precisely, one cannot dispense with a separation of the texts. Only a knowledge of the characteristics of both traditions makes possible the correct understanding of the narrative in its present form.

The only major loss of text of which we have to complain concerns the Yahwistic source: In it the command to enter the ark could not have followed the "prologue" (ch. 6.5–8). This command must have been preceded by an order to Noah to build the ark and further by a short report about the building of the structure itself. This part, which in the concise manner of our narrator may have comprised only a few statements, was sacrificed to the more extensive account of the Priestly document, ch. 6.13–22 (ten verses!). But it is significant that only immediately before his final entry into the ark did Noah learn of God's plan to destroy mankind by a flood. Of course, only by this communication could the meaning of the ark and its purpose become clear to him. Therefore, Noah completed the entire structure without knowing God's intentions; he had only the command which drove him to blind obedience. But that was just Yahweh's intention —to test Noah. To Noah the command must have seemed strange and incomprehensible. A ship on dry land! (Gu.) That was a test of his obedience and faith. But he passed the test, just as Abraham later followed God's command implicitly (ch. 12.4 ff., J). "By faith Noah being warned by God concerning events as yet unseen, took heed and constructed an ark for the saving of his household." (Heb. 11.7.) When one sees that the Yahwist here tells of a test of faith that was passed then one also understands the judgment which Noah now learns from God's mouth (i.e., after the command to build and his completion of the building). The Yahwist did not simply assert Noah's "righteousness" as P did, but he described it! Unfortunately, we have no satisfactory English word for the theologically significant word *ṣaddīq* ("righteous"). According to the Old Testament the *ṣaddīq* ("righteous person") does justice to a relationship in which he stands. If God abides by his covenant, acts according to the covenant, then he is "righteous," i.e., gracious. If man stands in right relation to God, i.e., believes, trusts God, then he is "righteous." Righteousness in this sense is not a juridical term of relation, but rather a theological one (see also at Gen. 15.6).

From the clean beasts Noah is to take seven (pairs?) of each, from the unclean one pair of each, into the ark with him. The sacral depreciation of certain animals resulted from the defensive struggle of the Yahweh faith against strange, older cults or other magical practices in which one made use of these animals. Many animals considered unclean in Israel were highly valued for sacred use elsewhere or in older Palestinian cults. That Yahweh himself shut up the ark behind Noah is again one of those surprising statements of the Yahwist, almost hybrid in its combination of near-childlike simplicity and theological profundity.

According to the Yahwistic narrative the Flood was caused by a forty-day rain and lasted sixty-one days. (According to the Priestly tradition the extent of the catastrophe was much greater in every respect, see p. 128.) The Yahwistic description of the water's increase and the destruction of every living thing is obviously preserved completely. It lies before us in vs. 12, 17b, 22 f., which the redactor cleverly inserted each at its proper place in the Priestly narrative. In a similar way we obtain the likewise obviously unbroken account of the water's decrease and Noah's exit from the ark.

In a minor detail, unimportant in itself, the narrator subtly lets us witness the waiting and hoping of those enclosed in the ark, namely, in the sending out of the doves. Birds were frequently used by mariners in ancient times for such services. Thus this small insertion is to make perceptible something of Noah's wisdom, who knew what to do in such pressing circumstances. (Ancient reports about the use of birds as a compass are given by Gunkel.) The first dispatch was without success; the bird had to return. This return is described with great affection; the narrator's eye lingers on every movement: Noah puts forth his hand, he takes the bird and brings it back into the ark. The next dispatch appears to have proceeded in the same way, this dove too returns (disappointment!); "and lo," it has a fresh olive leaf in its bill. It still could not remain outside all night, but it did bring to those who were waiting a sign of the angry judgment's approaching end and of imminent release. After another seven days the attempt was successful; the dispatched bird did not again return. Noah takes that as a sign that the earth is again habitable. (Obviously the hatchway is to be thought of as on the roof and not on the side.) From this insertion one can see something of the great variety of both Flood narratives. The motif for both sources came from the older tradition; the Yahwist worked out the scenes with greater sympathy and finer art; for the Priestly document, which was concentrated exclusively on the theology, the subject was uninteresting. It is described awkwardly and without vividness (see at ch. 8.7). After his exit from the ark, Noah, before doing anything else, sacrifices whole offerings. The first human work that the liberated earth, which is again restored to man, sees is an altar for God the Lord. The usual distinctly noncultic theology of the Yahwist attributes great importance to this sacrifice, as the following verses show. It has the character of a sacrifice of reconciliation (v. 21). Here too, as in the entire Flood story, Noah is completely silent.

10. THE EPILOGUE TO THE FLOOD. Ch. 8.21–22

8 21And when the LORD smelled the pleasing odor, the LORD said in
his heart, "I will never again regard the ground as cursed because of
man, for the imagination of man's heart is evil from his youth; neither
will I ever again destroy every living creature as I have done. 22While
the earth remains, seedtime and harvest, cold and heat, summer and
winter, day and night, shall not cease."

[21–22] The Yahwistic story of the Flood is planned very skillfully. It began with the narrator's letting us share in the reflections about God's grieving heart and letting us learn directly from God's mouth the resolve of judgment. At the end of the narrative the Yahwist again takes us up into the immediacy of the thoughts in God's heart. And as in the prologue, so here we are faced with the Yahwist's very own words. Here the Flood story ends, and the Yahwist certainly found no precedent in the tradition for what he gives as Yahweh's word. Only the saying about the duration of the natural orders (v. 22) could be ancient material. (We learn, therefore, in these words of the prologue and epilogue the narrator's special concern and are thereby assisted in the proper understanding of the entire composition.)

That God "smelled" the pleasing odor of the sacrifice is a striking and daring statement, even for Old Testament anthropomorphism. We know today from the Gilgamesh Epic that this expression was apparently a firm part of the ancient tradition, and the Yahwist was not troubled enough by it to erase it. He had all the less reason for doing so since he could allude to the name, Noah (*nōaḥ*), with the expression *rēah hannīḥōaḥ*. In itself the term, which is especially frequent in later Priestly literature, would be translated by "odor of appeasement." That Noah, once again on the earth that has been freed from the waters of judgment, first of all offers sacrifice, would seem only natural to ancient man. The Yahwist, who is relatively uninterested in cultic ordinances, hardly understands this sacrifice as the sign of a new relationship between God and man. The inner connection between Yahweh's reflections which bring the flood story to an end and the sacrifice that has been offered is quite loose. Yahweh has resolved to guarantee that this relationship to the earth will be a beneficial one. The verb *qillēl* used here does not mean "curse," "lay a curse on," but probably "regard (and therefore treat) as cursed." Evidently the statement refers to the curse that Yahweh laid on the earth in ch. 3.17. Lamech had already interpreted the name of his descendant Noah prophetically in saying that it would be a consolation for all time (ch. 5.29). Now one can see clearly that this consolation will consist in an annulment of the curse that Yahweh laid on the earth.* This saying of Yahweh without doubt designates a profound turning point in the Yahwistic primeval history, in so far as it expresses with surprising directness a will for salvation directed

*R. Rendtorff, "Gen. 8.21 und die Urgeschichte des Jahwisten", in: *Kerygma und Dogma*, 1961, 69 ff.

towards the whole of Noachite humanity, "although" (the Hebrew particle can be translated in this way) "the imagination of man's heart is evil from his youth." So far as that is concerned—Calvin says in his exposition of the passage—God would have to punish man with daily floods. In its hard paradox this v. 21 is one of the most remarkable theological statements in the Old Testament: it shows the pointed and concentrated way in which the Yahwist can express himself at decisive points. The same condition which in the prologue is the basis for God's judgment in the epilogue reveals God's grace and providence. The contrast between God's punishing anger and his supporting grace, which pervades the whole Bible, is here presented almost inappropriately, almost as indulgence, an adjustment by God towards man's sinfulness.

The guarantee in v. 22 concerns the elemental temporal rhythm in which all creaturely life is involved. The ordinances which the saying guarantees correspond climatically to our narrator's world. It names the two chief seasons that influence life in Palestine—the completely dry summer and the rainy winter. Spring and autumn do not have the same significance because of the abrupt seasonal transition.

Thus this story concludes surprisingly with a statement about God's supporting patience. This grace is known in the incomprehensible duration of the natural orders in spite of continuing human sin. It is not yet, therefore, that grace which forgives sin, about which both the Old and New Covenants know, but a gracious will that is above all mankind and is effective and recognizable in the changeless duration of nature's orders. The testimony at the end of the Priestly story of the Flood is quite similar (see pp. 133 f.).

The inner motivation of the Yahwistic story of the Flood within the great complex of the primeval history is superior, in contrast to the Priestly document, which abruptly mentions man's corruption simply as a fact. For our narrator, the Flood is the Last Judgment, but one in which God checks sin's spread on the earth; a judgment, to be sure, which at its end reveals more strongly than the stories of the Fall and Cain a wonderful saving will of God.

Today, forty years after the height of the Babel-Bibel controversy, the dossier on the relation of the biblical tradition to the Babylonian story of the Flood as it is in the Gilgamesh Epic (AOT, 175 ff.; ANET, 72 ff.) is more or less closed. A material relationship between both versions exists, of course, but a direct dependence of the biblical tradition on the Babylonian is no longer assumed. Both versions are independent arrangements of a still older tradition, which itself stemmed perhaps from the Sumerian. Israel met with a Flood tradition in Canaan at the time of her immigration and assimilated it into her religious ideas. Her version, therefore, with all the material relationships here and there, is as different from the whole story as possible. The Babylonian version, along with many poetic merits, shows a very crude polytheistic conception of God. The decision of the council of the gods to destroy the city Shurrupak is revealed by the god Ea to Utnapishtim, the hero of the Flood. Utnapishtim, in a ship, survives the Flood, at the dreadfulness of which the gods "cower like watchdogs" and the goddess of heaven, Ishtar, "screams as one in travail." After the catastrophe, Utnapishtim makes a sacrifice. When the gods "smell the savor" (cf. ch. 8.21), "they swarm as flies around the sacrificer." Utnapishtim at the end is enrolled among the gods. Our exposition of the Yahwistic and Priestly accounts makes a comparison of the biblical tradition with the Babylonian unnecessary (AOT, 198 ff.). (Only one detail ought to be mentioned: the god Ea did not reveal the coming of the Flood to Utnapishtim directly, because of fear of the other gods, but only in a dream did he order him to build a ship. The same motif—construction of a ship without knowing why—was conceived by the Yahwist as a test of faith and obedience.) But more important than a neutral, historical, and religious comparison or an elaboration of a relative superiority which is easily established is the recognition that the biblical story of the Flood has been made a witness to the judgment and grace of living God.

As for the natural and historical aspect of the Flood problem, theology is not competent to express an independent opinion. It may be said, however, that even natural scientists have not considered the prevailing explanation—that the numerous Flood stories in the world arose from local catastrophes—to be sufficient (e.g., E. Dacqué). On the one hand the distribution of the saga (among Indians, Persians, Africans, Melanesians, and Australians, among the Eskimos, the Kamchatkans, Indians of the Americas, etc.), on the other hand its remarkable uniformity (flood caused by rain), require the assumption of an actual cosmic experience and a primitive recollection which, to be sure, is often clouded and in part often brought to new life and revised only later by local floods.

A redactor at a later time interwove the Priestly story of the Flood with the Yahwistic story which we have just interpreted. The separation of the two versions, which can be done easily by means of simple source analysis, is indispensable for more precise understanding of the details.

In the Priestly primeval history, the story of the Flood followed the genealogy of the Sethites (see at Gen., ch. 5) directly. Thus P surveyed the period from Adam to Noah simply by a genealogy without any description.

11. THE FLOOD. (P) Chs. 6.9–22; 7.6, 11, 13–16a, 17a, 18–21, 24; 8.1–2a, 3b, 4–5, 7, 13a, 15–19

6 9 *These are the generations of Noah. Noah was a righteous man, blameless*
in his generation; Noah walked with God. 10 *And Noah had three sons, Shem,*
Ham, and Japheth.

11 *Now the earth was corrupt in God's sight, and the earth was filled with*
violence. 12 *And God saw the earth, and behold, it was corrupt; for all flesh had*
corrupted their way upon the earth. 13 *And God said to Noah, "I have determined*
to make an end of all flesh; for the earth is filled with violence through them;
behold I will destroy them with the earth. 14 *Make yourself an ark of gopher wood;*
make rooms in the ark, and cover it inside and out with pitch. 15 *This is how you*
are to make it: the length of the ark three hundred cubits, its breadth fifty cubits,
and its height thirty cubits. 16 *Make a roof for the ark, and finish it to a cubit above;*
and set the door of the ark in its side; make it with lower, second, and third decks.
17 *For behold, I will bring a flood of waters upon the earth, to destroy all flesh in which*
is the breath of life from under heaven; everything that is on the earth shall die.
18 *But I will establish my covenant with you; and you shall come into the ark, you,*
your sons, your wife, and your sons' wives with you. 19 *And of every living thing of*
all flesh, you shall bring two of every sort into the ark, to keep them alive with you;
they shall be male and female. 20 *Of the birds according to their kinds, and of the*
animals according to their kinds, of every creeping thing of the ground according to
its kind, two of every sort shall come in to you, to keep them alive. 21 *Also take*
with you every sort of food that is eaten, and store it up; and it shall serve as food
for you and for them." 22 *Noah did this; he did all that God commanded him. . . .*

7 6 *Noah was six hundred years old when the flood of waters came upon the*
earth. . . .

11 *In the six hundredth year of Noah's life, in the second month, on the*
seventeenth day of the month, on that day all the fountains of the great deep burst
forth, and the windows of the heavens were opened. . . . 13 *On the very same day*
Noah and his sons, Shem and Ham and Japheth, and Noah's wife and the three
wives of his sons with them entered the ark, 14 *they and every beast according to its*
kind, and all the cattle according to their kinds, and every creeping thing that
creeps on the earth according to its kind, and every bird according to its kind, every
bird of every sort. 15 *They went into the ark with Noah, two and two of all flesh in*
which there was the breath of life. 16 *And they that entered, male and female of all*
flesh, went in as God had commanded him. . . .

17a *The flood continued forty days upon the earth. . . .* 18 *The waters pre-*
vailed and increased greatly upon the earth; and the ark floated on the face of the
waters. 19 *And the waters prevailed so mightily upon the earth that all the high*

mountains under the whole heaven were covered; 20 *the waters prevailed above the*
mountains, covering them fifteen cubits deep. 21 *And all flesh died that moved upon*
the earth, birds, cattle, beasts, all swarming creatures that swarm upon the earth,
and every man. . . . 24 *And the waters prevailed upon the earth a hundred and*
fifty days. . . .

8 1 *But God remembered Noah and all the beasts and all the cattle that were*
with him in the ark. And God made a wind blow over the earth, and the waters
subsided; 2a *the fountains of the deep and the windows of the heavens were*
closed. . . . 3b *At the end of a hundred and fifty days the waters had abated; and*
in the seventh month, on the seventeenth day of the month, the ark came to rest upon
the mountains of Ararat. 5 *And the waters continued to abate until the tenth*
month; in the tenth month, on the first day of the month, the tops of the mountains
were seen. . . .

7 *And he sent forth a raven; and it went to and fro until the waters were dried up*
from the earth. . . .

13a *In the six hundred and first year, in the first month, the first day of the month,*
the waters were dried from the earth. . . . 15 *Then God said to Noah,* 16 *"Go*
forth from the ark, you and your wife, and your sons and your sons' wives with you.
17 *Bring forth with you every living thing that is with you of all flesh—birds and*
animals and every creeping thing that creeps on the earth—that they may breed
abundantly on the earth, and be fruitful and multiply upon the earth." 18 *So Noah*
went forth, and his sons and his wife and his sons' wives with him. 19 *And every*
beast, every creeping thing, and every bird, everything that moves upon the earth,
went forth by families out of the ark.

The toledoth book, consisting only of genealogies, which we must probably consider as the original framework for the Priestly narrative (see p. 63), is in the case of Noah expanded by the unusual incorporation of the Flood tradition in such a way that the title, "this is the generation," almost loses its original meaning. Noah's righteousness and piety are soberly recorded as realities to which God's subsequent free act will be related. The designation *ṣaddīq*, "righteous" (see p. 120), *tāmīm* ("blameless"), does not mean "perfect" in an absolute (i.e., moral) sense; it is a term of sacred usage, and means the condition of a man (or a sacrifice) which conforms to the cult and is thereby pleasing to God. Our word "pious" corresponds only imperfectly. While the terms "righteous" and "pious" are leading theological words throughout the Old Testament, the statement about "walking with God" is quite isolated. Noah, as the last member of the first aeon and the beginner of a new age, is the last one of whom such a thing can be said theologically. Abraham could only walk *before* God (ch. 17.1).

The Priestly story of the Flood begins in ch. 6.11 with a statement about the totality of human corruption. The concentration upon the purely theological is here particularly striking in contrast with the Yahwist, who presents both the divine movements and the *humanum* before God. What the Yahwist exhibits in a series of pictures of unrivaled graphic power and realism, i.e., the increase of sin on the earth, is here disposed of very succinctly with a reference to the simple, accomplished reality. There is only one word about the nature of this total corruption: "violence" is the new word in the Priestly primeval history. It is a word, moreover, in which the whole weight of the disturbance receives expression, for *ḥāmās* (L: *Frevel*, "wantonness") designates arbitrary oppression, the culpable breach of a legal ordinance. According to both Priestly and prophetic judgment such violent highhandedness is the most serious sin against Yahweh and means a profanation of the "very good" earth. Here both the Priestly and Yahwistic narratives (ch. 4) agree almost exactly.

God's announcement to Noah of judgment is brief but very solemn. The judgment is "an end of all flesh." The word "end" (*qēṣ*) had become a weighty term in the language of prophetic eschatology (Amos 8.2; Hab. 2.3; Lam. 4.18; Ezek. 21.25, 29). We are not yet clear about the relation of our Priestly theology to the broad stream of these (approximately contemporaneous!) eschatological expectations. With this statement to Noah, P bears witness very simply to God's power and freedom in allowing even an entire age to be engulfed in judgment.

Behind the strange precision in the directions for building the ark, and later in the actual Flood account, behind the precise dates and measurements, there is both certainty of the absolute concreteness and reality of God's activity and an effort to depict God's activity, his commands, and movements with as much theological objectivity as possible.

Noah receives the command to build of cypress an "ark," an enormous houseboat by ancient standards (ca. 489 feet long, 81 feet wide, 49 feet high). Under the "roof" (the best translation of *ṣōhar*, L: *Fenster*, "window," in v. 16, the meaning of which is not certain) were three stories with separate cabins ("nests"). In the rooms of this strangest of all ships are to find shelter those whom God will save from the world judgment by a "covenant": Noah and his family and one pair of every kind of animal. (On the covenant, see pp. 133 f.)

In Noah's six hundredth year, on the seventeenth day of the second month, this remnant of the life of an entire age entered the ark; then on this same day the judgment of the great Flood began to come.

An understanding of the Priestly story of the Flood depends materially on the correct translation of the word *mabbūl*. *Mabbūl* does not mean "flood," "inundation," or even "destruction," but it is a technical term for a part of the world structure, namely, the heavenly ocean.* This heavenly sea, which is above the firmament (*rāqīa'*), empties downward through latticed windows (II Kings 7.2, 19). Here we have the same realistic and cosmological ideas as in Gen., ch. 1. According to the Priestly representation we must understand the Flood, therefore, as a catastrophe involving the entire cosmos. When the heavenly ocean breaks forth upon the earth below, and the primeval sea beneath the earth, which is restrained by God,† now freed from its bonds, gushes up through yawning chasms onto the earth, then there is a destruction of the entire cosmic system according to biblical cosmogony. The two halves of the chaotic primeval sea, separated—the one up, the other below—by God's creative government (ch. 1.7–9), are again united; creation begins to sink again into chaos. Here the catastrophe, therefore, concerns not only men and beasts as in the Yahwistic account but the earth (chs. 6.13; 9.11)—indeed, the entire cosmos. Accordingly, it lasts much longer: not sixty-one days, but a year and ten days. The Priestly account wastes no words about the unthinkable frightfulness of this world catastrophe; even Noah's faith is not the subject of its interest. With matchless concentration it directs attention to the divine occurrence alone. (In this respect the Yahwistic story of the Flood is quite different.)

But "God remembered Noah." God has not finished completely with the world. The bold anthropomorphism makes the freedom of the divine resolve for salvation especially impressive. A turn toward salvation has occurred, and it can be founded only on the fact that God remembered Noah. God checked the chaotic powers by which the entire earth was already engulfed, before they also brought Noah and those with him to destruction. Precisely at the first receding of the chaos-flood, at the first outgrowth of God's "remembering," the ark again receives a firm resting place on the earth. The importance of this event is emphasized in the text by a pun on the verb *nūaḥ*, "rest," which is the root of Noah's name. If the water stood fifteen ells above the highest mountains, and the ark (itself thirty ells in height) drew fifteen ells of water, then the text obviously reflects that

*J. Begrich, *Zeitschrift fur Semitistik*, VI, 1928, 135 ff.
†Cf. Job 7.12 (chs. 3.8; 41.1).

at the highest stand of the water it could float just over the mountain-tops; at the first receding of the water, however, it would come to rest upon the highest mountain. Between the time of the ark's first landing on the highest mountain of the world—that is certainly what Mount Ararat signifies to the narrator—and the disappearance of the water many months elapse. Ararat is here the name of a land (cf. II Kings 19.37; Jer. 51.27) in the vicinity of present-day Armenia. After the mountain peak became visible, Noah sent out a raven. The passage, received from tradition by the Priestly document, is without charm and is inserted into the narrative without proper vividness. Is the meaning of the statement really that the raven did not return to the ark? How different is the Yahwist at this point (see p. 121)!

Only after a wait of many months is the earth dry. The data in ch. 8.13a and 14 are scarcely consistent and are derived from different literary traditions. Now God's detailed command to leave the ark is issued to all its inhabitants. Human arbitrariness, therefore, could not seize the fresh earth, newly liberated from chaos; God himself liberated the earth for the survivors. After the judgment of the Flood, man on his own could not say as a matter of course that the earth was man's domain. It was, therefore, an important matter for the faith of those who came later, a matter about which they had to be sure, that the entrance into the new time, on to the new earth, did not arise from human initiative but from God's express will. The next chapter reports that God did not abandon man to himself, that he gave fixed orders for life upon the renewed earth.

The story of the Flood, less familiar to present-day theological thought than other facts of the primeval history, testifies first of all simply to God's power and freedom, which allowed his created world to be engulfed by chaos. It shows God as the one who judges sin, and it stands at the beginning of the Bible as the eternally valid word about God's deadly anger over sin. Thus it protects every succeeding word of grace from any kind of innocuousness (*Verharmlosung*); it undergirds the understanding of God's will for salvation as a pure miracle. Every one of the progressive revelations of salvation springs from God's heart, with whose radical anger over sin man can reckon, and not with the whim of an idol. Such a miracle is the choice of Noah and thus the preservation by divine patience of the whole Noachic aeon. Thus the story of the Flood—and this is theologically the most important fact—shows an eschatological world judgment, which becomes visible from the standpoint of preservation, i.e., in retrospect. Peter connected the water of baptism with the waters of the Flood, as a water of judgment beyond which is a life from the grace of the living God (I Peter 3.20 f.). Negatively stated, the Flood story formulates a statement of faith of fundamental importance: the man of the Noachic aeon has no further direct relation to the world of the first splendor of creation. The world judgment of the Flood hangs like an iron curtain between this world age and that of the first splendor of creation.

12. GOD'S COVENANT WITH NOAH. Ch. 9.1–17

9 1 *And God blessed Noah and his sons, and said to them, "Be fruitful and*
multiply, and fill the earth. 2 *The fear of you and the dread of you shall be upon*
every beast of the earth, and upon every bird of the air, upon everything that creeps
on the ground and all the fish of the sea; into your hand they are delivered. 3 *Every*
moving thing that lives shall be food for you; and as I gave you the green plants,
I give you everything. 4 *Only you shall not eat flesh with its life, that is, its blood.*
5 *For your lifeblood I will surely require a reckoning; of every beast I will require*
it and of man; of every man's brother I will require the life of man. 6 *Whoever*
sheds the blood of man, by man shall his blood be shed; for God made man in his
own image. 7 *And you, be fruitful and multiply, bring forth abundantly on the*
earth and multiply in it."

8 *Then God said to Noah and to his sons with him,* 9 *"Behold, I establish my*
covenant with you and your descendants after you, 10 *and with every living creature*
that is with you, the birds, the cattle, and every beast of the earth with you, as many
as came out of the ark. 11 *I establish my covenant with you, that never again shall all*
flesh be cut off by the waters of a flood, and never again shall there be a flood to
destroy the earth." 12 *And God said, "This is the sign of the covenant which I make*
between me and you and every living creature that is with you, for all future
generations: 13 *I set my bow in the cloud, and it shall be a sign of the covenant*
between men and the earth. 14 *When I bring clouds over the earth and the bow is seen*
in the clouds, 15 *I will remember my covenant which is between me and you and*
every living creature of all flesh; and the waters shall never again become a flood
to destroy all flesh. 16 *When the bow is in the clouds, I will look upon it and*
remember the everlasting covenant between God and every living creature of all
flesh that is upon the earth." 17 *God said to Noah, "This is the sign of the covenant*
which I have established between me and all flesh that is upon the earth."

A new, momentous chapter begins with ch. 9. P sketches with precision and theological subtlety the Noachic world age, which has newly begun in the story of God with man. It is fundamentally important to understand that P is not speaking of distant primeval things, but is answering definite elemental questions which had topical significance for the faith of later Israel. For the section speaks of our world age. What God's address takes simply for granted is a severe disruption and degeneration of creation, which came forth from God's hand as "very good." Violence and reciprocal killing characterize the communal life of the creatures; there is no peace among the creatures. This raised theological questions which ch. 9 answers. For Israel the answers were the result of a thorough reflection from every angle about its own faith, and from theological consequences which were drawn from it. Here too we are confronted with theological doctrine, i.e., with materials with which in such a form only the priests were concerned.

[1] First question: Under these altered conditions, did the first command of creation (ch. 1.28), "be fruitful," still hold? Did the creature which had fallen from God's first estate still have God's will on its side but only in its most elementary life function, namely, in its procreation and its taking of the earth, or had it become highhanded in this too? Answer: No. God, in spite of everything, has renewed this command for this generation too. After the great judgment the creature had not propagated itself over the earth again simply from its own initiative, which would not have been a good beginning; but it pleased God to speak as his first word a word of blessing on the new aeon. God still wills procreation and increase of humanity. (For the close relation of blessing to procreative power, see p. 56.) This question was the most basic.

[2–4] Second question: Which orders are to be observed in the degenerated relation of the creatures to one another, which was caused by violence; and above all, how was the violence exercised on earth and the killing to be reconciled with God's absolute sovereign right over all creatures? The relationship of man to the animals no longer resembles that which was decreed in ch. 1. The animal world lives in fear and terror of man. Obviously ch. 9.1 assumes that until then the condition of paradisiacal peace had ruled among the creatures. Now man begins to eat flesh (cf. ch. 1.29). "The sighing of the creatures begins." (Pr.) Answer: Just as God renewed for Noachic man the command to procreate, so he also renewed man's sovereign right over the animals. What is new, however, is that God will also allow man deadly intervention; he may eat flesh as long as he does not touch the blood, which the ancients considered to be the special seat of life. The Old Testament cultic laws speak in different ways about the abstention from eating blood. Originally blood was thought of in some way as the most important share of the divinity at a sacrifice or slaughter (still recognizable in Lev. 7.27 f.). With the strict distinction in Deuteronomy between sacrifice on the one hand and profane slaughter on the other, there resulted in the case of the latter the necessity for another regulation. Blood could not be eaten even at profane slaughter. It was to be poured out "like water" (Deut. 12.16, 24; 15.23). Even though a sacral character in the narrower sense was unambiguously denied the rite ("like water"), there still remained for the act a general testimonial character. The ordinance in v. 4 apparently assumes this "secularizing" of the ancient usage and it is thus shown to be historically a late reflection. But the new thing is that the command is shifted completely from Israel's cult to the universally human, and in its present interpretation becomes the lowest common denominator, so to speak: the usage is here legitimated quite uncultically on the basis of God's right of dominion over all life. Here, therefore, it is not an isolated "dietary law" at all (what would be the meaning of a rite without an existing cult?) but an ordinance for all mankind. Even when man slaughters and kills, he is to know that he is touching something, which, because it is life, is in a special manner God's property; and as a sign of this he is to keep his hands off the blood. This regulation of man's relation to the animal world could be designated a regulation of necessity. **[5–7]** But the establishment of the divine sovereign right over human life is expressed apodictically and unconditionally. It is absolutely inviolable and, moreover, not for man's sake because of some law of humanity, or "reverence for life," but because man is God's possession and was created in God's image. The saying in v. 6 is extremely ancient and forceful, masterfully pregnant both in form (exact correspondence of the words in both halves of the statement; talion!), as well as in content. It is not an independent formulation by P, but it appears to be an old statement from sacred legal terminology. It could be that it once legally prescribed and limited the exercise of blood vengeance: In the event of a murder the blood vengeance could not be reckless (cf. ch. 4.23); only the murderer (he, and no substitute!) atones with death. On the other hand, the demand could not be satisfied by ransom either (cf. Num. 35.31). Whatever is Yahweh's possession—and every *nepeš* ("life") belongs to Yahweh, Ezek. 18.4!—may not be dealt out as in business, cannot be taken under human management at all. But this saying is exactly like the prohibition against eating blood in v. 4. It too in its present context is estranged from its old *Sitz im Leben*. Formerly it may have been firmly anchored somehow institutionally with regard to its sacred legality; now it appears in the form of a theological reflection and it comprises two fundamental statements that are in strange tension with each other: (1) the inviolable holiness of human life (murder is punished by death) *and* (2) man's responsibility for the punishment of this crime. The phrase "by man" answers the very important question about whether man is at all justified in killing another man or whether God has reserved this for himself. The saying contains, therefore, both a negative and a positive aspect: God himself will not avenge murder, and that means a loss of immediacy *vis-à-vis* God which must now be recorded. But he empowers man to do it. The human community, executor of the direct divine will, of divine punishment—that is indeed a constitutive ordinance of the greatest significance and far-reaching consequence, for "that is the first feature in the institution of the authorities as the executors of the demands of moral world order and thus as God's representatives" (Del.). Primarily, therefore, God's word to this new aeon is a word of divine return. In spite of profound disturbance, mankind may know in the continuance of its reproducing generations that God has not withdrawn himself, but that it has a right, which is not theologically self-evident, even in this condition to continue to multiply. The right of dominion over the animals is also reconfirmed; indeed, by permitting deadly intervention God has even relinquished to man a part of his right possession. The Noachic aeon, therefore, is an aeon of divine forbearance (Rom. 3.25). But certainly the other aspect is equally clear. Even though a profound disorder has occurred in the world with the incursion of the violent struggle for existence, nevertheless God does not retreat from it, nor withdraw his demands on it; God does not abandon his sovereign claim over all creatures. He watches over all life in the world. That is the strong legal tone accompanying the gracious Noachic dispensation.

[8–17] Going beyond the Yahwist's representation, the Priestly document now speaks of a *covenant*, which God made with Noah and his descendants. In addition to the word of promise he also gave a sign and thus vivified his promise and guaranteed it in the visible realm. The passage is full of doublets (covenant promise, v. 9 and v. 11; covenant sign, v. 12 and v. 17; God sees the bow and remembers the covenant: v. 14 and v. 16, etc.), so that two complete recensions can be distinguished without effort.

A covenant is meant to clarify an intricate or opaque legal situation between two groups or individuals, in that it puts the relationship of the partners on a new legal basis. A covenant of God with Noah is not mentioned elsewhere in the Old Testament. This covenant with Noah differs from that with Abraham, the covenant on Sinai and all other covenants in that in the latter instances the individual or the nation was called quite personally into a relation of fellowship with God and thereby faced with the question of affirming this ordinance. Here the sign of the covenant with Noah, absolutely without any confessing appropriation by the earthly partner, is high above man, between heaven and earth, as pledge of a true *gratia praeveniens* (grace coming before the will)! God's gracious will is made visible to give mankind, terrified by the chaotic elements, renewed assurance that God will support this aeon and to guarantee the duration of his ordinances. The Hebrew word that we translate "rainbow" usually means in the Old Testament "the bow of war." The beauty of the ancient conception thus becomes apparent: God shows the world that he has put aside his bow. Man knows of the blessing of this new gracious relationship in the stability of the orders of nature, i.e., first of all in the sphere of the impersonal elements only.

In conclusion, one properly understands this chapter of Priestly theology only when one perceives its aetiological overtones. How does one explain the stability of nature and its orders, the continued blessing of mankind in spite of increasing human violence and barbarism? Answer: Here a divine will of healing forbearance is at work; indeed, faith even knows of a solemn guarantee of the cosmic orders which were disturbed by the temporary invasion of chaos. But that was only the beginning for this theology: the preservation and support of an aeon, which would be lost without the word of blessing which the Highest God spoke to it. The *natural* orders, fixed by God's word, mysteriously guarantee a world in which in his own time God's *historical* saving activity will begin.

From the powerful chapter about God's covenant with Noah the Priestly primeval history moved out into the vast international world (see at Gen., ch. 10). We must leave this originally firmly welded tradition, however, and turn our attention to a part of the Yahwistic primeval history that now occurs between the covenant with Noah and the table of nations.

13. NOAH'S CURSE AND BLESSING. Ch. 9.18–29

9 [18]The sons of Noah who went forth from the ark were Shem, Ham,
and Japheth (and Ham, the father of Canaan). [19]These three were the
sons of Noah; and from these the whole earth was peopled.

20 Noah was the first tiller of the soil. He planted a vineyard; [21]and
he drank of the wine, and became drunk, and lay uncovered in his tent.

22And (Ham the father of) Canaan saw the nakedness of his father, and
told his two brothers outside. 23Then Shem and Japheth took a garment,
laid it upon both their shoulders, and walked backward and covered the
nakedness of their father; their faces were turned away, and they did
not see their father's nakedness. 24When Noah awoke from his wine and
knew what his youngest son had done to him, 25he said,

"Cursed be Canaan;
a slave of slaves shall he be to his brothers."

26He also said,

"Blessed by the LORD my God be Shem;
and let Canaan be his slave.
27God enlarge Japheth,
and let him dwell in the tents of Shem;
and let Canaan be his slave."

28 After the flood Noah lived three hundred and fifty years. 29All
the days of Noah were nine hundred and fifty years; and he died.

[18–19] This narrative about Noah and his sons was placed in the Yahwistic primeval history between the Flood and the table of nations. It is, however, somewhat more loosely inserted in the large, teleological, Yahwistic narrative context of the primeval history than the other traditions (see below). It is filled with difficulties and obscurities for which the final explanatory word has not yet been spoken. This first picture after the Flood shows us a new world. Before the Flood the theme of the primeval history was man and his concerns; now it is the world of nations, but still man embodied in nations and marked by national characteristics. This international world has a uniform origin, according to the representation of the Yahwist and the Priestly narratives. Moreover, it is not something originally given by creation, but something that happened primevally.

One difficulty of the narrative is that because of a subsequent revision the notion of the three families of nations has become disunified. To begin with (v. 18), one reads the well-known trinity Shem, Ham, and Japheth. But one sees very soon that the actual narrative is talking, not about this *ecumenical* scheme of nations, but about a much older and more limited *Palestinian* one: Shem, Japheth, and Canaan. A redactor attempted to remove the inconsistency by making Ham, and not Canaan, appear in the story. He did this by inserting in v. 18 and v. 22 the words *ḥām hū’ ’*^{a}*bī* ("Ham, the father of") before the name "Canaan." But this correction only brought the narrative into external agreement with that ecumenical scheme; its inner orientation toward Canaan and the Palestinian sphere remained (cf. v. 24, "his youngest son"). Shem is here the people of Yahweh and not the Shem of Gen. 10.22; on the other hand, the insertion of Ham is obviously supposed to bring our story into harmony with the scheme of ch. 10. Thus the text has a hybrid form which makes the exposition of its climax especially difficult. Another difficulty results from the combination of our narrative with the story of the Flood. In the latter, the sons of Noah are married. Here, on the other hand, they are living unmarried in the tent with their father. Should one therefore place the event chronologically before the Flood? Then Canaan, the accursed, would have been included in the ark, which is scarcely thinkable. In spite of such discrepancies (cf. the derivation of present-day vocations from special ancestors, ch. 4.20 ff.) one may not conclude the presence of a secondary strand running parallel to the Yahwistic primary narrative. The traditions that the Yahwist united to form a great composition were complex, and he had much less need to reconcile them absolutely with one another from within.

[20–23] Noah was a tiller of the soil. With this statement recurs the *'ªdāmā*-motif which is of such great importance in the Yahwistic primeval history (cf. pp. 94, 106). Likewise, after the Flood man is referred completely to the earth and is dependent for his existence upon the soil which supports him. But—and this is what the beginning of our story means—he no longer has quite the same relation to the earth as antediluvian man had, for it was destroyed by a curse. In ch. 5.29 (see p. 72) we read a melancholy statement of suffering, spoken by Noah's father about the hardship of this curse, but at the same time of a hope for comforting amelioration that would come with Noah. The fulfillment of this hope is now reported in v. 20: Noah, although also a peasant, began to cultivate the grape and thereby brought comfort to the earth. From Noah's time is dated an amelioration of the severe curse; through Noah, God gave man the vine, which, according to the Old Testament view, is the noblest of all natural growth (Ps. 104.15). "To possess a vineyard, to enjoy its noble fruit and to rest in the peace of its shade, was for the Israelite bliss and messianic longing" (Jac.; Gen. 49.11 f.; I Kings 4.25; II Kings 18.31; Hos. 2.15; Micah 4.4; Amos 9.13). But the narrative is also an "inventor-saga." Noah must be the first to learn the mystery of the new discovery; indeed, he is completely overpowered by the unsuspected power of this fruit. The reader, therefore, must on no account morally condemn this drunkenness. The story describes vividly what happened during his drunkenness. How Shem and Japheth took the garment, which served also as a blanket (Ex. 22.26), and laid it over their father again is described in detail; and the immodesty of the younger son (Canaan in the older version) is to be sharply distinguished from their carefulness. Possibly the narrator suppressed something even more repulsive than mere looking (cf. v. 24, "what his youngest son had done to him").

[24–27] After awaking, Noah utters prophetic sayings about his sons. Today one looks for the origin of such maxims of curse and blessing on nations in the cult. Here in the sacred realm, perhaps at special feasts, they are proclaimed by specially authorized persons (cult prophets?) and supported by the faith of the community. The passage ch. 9.25–27 makes Shem, Japheth, and Canaan appear clearly as these great persons, who were obviously sharply distinguished from one another in the ancient Palestinian region. Nevertheless, they do not place the three brothers in the same rank next to each other, but Shem and Japheth are each related to Canaan as master to slave. There is little to say about v. 25. Canaan is cursed because of his immodesty; therefore the people is sunk in profound weakness and slavery. The Old Testament indicates in many places the amazement and abhorrence with which the newly arrived Israel encountered the sexual depravity of the Canaanites (cultic prostitution). In this, they saw aetiologically the true reason for the defeat of Canaan before the invading Israelites (cf. especially Lev. 18.24 ff.). A refinement of the second statement is that over against this depreciation of Canaan it does not set praise of Shem. Shem's *God* is praised. What Shem is and the advantage he has over others does not consist in special human merits, but Shem's portion is Yahweh! (But it is true that the use of the name Shem as a designation for Israel is unusual, indeed singular in the Old Testament. Perhaps the name Shem had the same fate as the name of the Habiru, that nomadic people of the steppe who, possessing nothing of their own, pushed into the civilized lands of the ancient Orient, and who later in ancient Israel became "the Hebrews." This supposition is probable because, according to Gen. 10.21, Shem is the father of the *eber*-people.) Chapter 9.27 is filled with questions: The pun *yapt *ᵉ*lōhīm, l*ᵉ*yepet* is still most safely translated "God give Japheth ample room" (so the ancient translators). The "ample room" was considered a special proof of Yahweh's grace (Gen. 26.22; Ps. 4.1; 18.19; 31.8; Job 12.23). Other exegetes have proceeded from the verb *pātā*, "allure," but it is used in the Old Testament in a bad sense and is not construed with the preposition *l*ᵉ—"May he dwell," i.e., Japheth and not God, as is usually agreed.

But who is Japheth? According to this saying he is apparently a nation that tented in close contact, even intermingled, with Israel (regarding dwelling in another's tents, cf. I Chron. 5.10) and that enslaved Canaan together with Israel. Japheth, therefore, is used here in a different, more limited sense than in the table of nations. Procksch connects this Japheth with the nations of Asia Minor, a few of whose former nobles were still to be found in the cities during the Israelite period. (The "Hittites," whom one would most naturally consider here, are connected by the table of nations with Ham-Canaan, Gen. 10.18.) Eduard Meyer would like to connect Japheth with the *Kafti* (the Egyptian designation for the Cretans).* From Greek mythology we know of a *Iapetos*, the father of Prometheus, but we see no clear connection with the biblical use of the name. Now if the table of nations (P) classifies under Japheth the predominantly Indo-European nations that had established themselves in the realm of the former Hittite kingdom (see at Gen., ch. 10), then our saying does not seem to know this broad term of Japheth. But one must keep to the general relationship of the nations. That is, the Japheth who together with Israel enslaved Canaan could really have meant only the Philistines, who settled in the southwestern plains of Palestine directly after the immigration of Israel, and with whom Israel had to share the possession of the Promised Land. If E. Meyer's interpretation is correct, then the ring would be closed, for the Old Testament on occasion connects the Philistines with the Cretans (e.g., Amos 9.7; Jer. 47.3 f.). That Israel alone did not possess the Land of Canaan, as it expected to do according to the promises, was certainly a disquieting question with which other texts of the Old Testament also struggled (cf. the various solutions in Judg. 2.20 to 3.2). On the other hand, in the "system of tribal boundaries" (cf. A. Alt, *Sellin Festschrift*, 1927, 16 ff.) how resolutely is Judah's border drawn on the west as far as the sea, thereby claiming theoretically the Philistine territory (Josh. 15.11; cf. 13.2 f.)! Did Yahweh not have enough power, then, to accomplish his plans completely? Did other events, which were not foreseen by him, occur in the meantime? No! Our saying makes it aetiologically clear that it was God's will from the beginning, that it was so arranged according to a plan of history prepared long in advance. Noah had already prophesied it. The saying is not a messianic prophecy. If one wants to learn its ancient meaning, one must forget about "Shem's religion" in which Japheth

*E. Meyer, *Geschichte des Altertums*, II, 1, 1953^3, 182 f.

one day will share, for such a spiritual interpretation of the "dwelling in tents" certainly was far from the ancients. What is at stake is a common territory, the promised gift of the land, and to this extent a great riddle in God's guidance of history. Japheth in the tents of Shem! That is like a breach made by God himself in the exclusive possession of Canaan. Israel is not alone in the Promised Land! But that is only a mute sign; the mystery is not revealed, and God's intention remains hidden. But is it conceivable that the Yahwist found our narrative as a *Noah* tradition? It is much more likely, as in the story of Cain (see above), that older ethnological narrative material is stripped of its specific ethnological character and expanded into something primevally historical and human. And what *then* is the meaning the Yahwist combined with v. 27? The origin of the Noah tradition is still completely obscure. The hero of the ancient Babylonian flood tradition is called Utnapishtim and not Noah. Nevertheless, there is much to be said for the assumption that the tradition about Noah goes back to pre-Israelite times. But where may it have been fostered and handed down in Israel?

[28] With that the story of Noah is ended. Now there follows the Priestly genealogical scheme of Noah, which (as the last member of the Sethite family tree) has remained open since ch. 5.32.

Now we take up again the Priestly thread, which we left at the chapter about God's covenant with Noah (ch. 9.1–17).

14. THE TABLE OF NATIONS. (P) Ch. 10.1a, 2–7, 20, 22, 23, 31, 32

10 [1a]*These are the generations of the sons of Noah, Shem, Ham, and Japheth. . . .*

2 *The sons of Japheth: Gomer, Magog, Madai, Javan, Tubal, Meshech,*
and Tiras. [3]*The sons of Gomer: Ashkenaz, Riphath, and Togarmah.* [4]*The*
sons of Javan: Elishah, Tarshish, Kittim, and Dodanim. [5]*From these the coast-*
land peoples spread. These are the sons of Japheth in their lands, each with his own language, by their families, in their nations.

6 *The sons of Ham: Cush, Egypt, Put, and Canaan.* [7]*The sons of Cush:*
Seba, Havilah, Sabtah, Raamah, and Sabteca. The sons of Raamah: Sheba and Dedan. . . .

20 *These are the sons of Ham, by their families, their languages, their lands, and their nations. . . .*

22 *The sons of Shem: Elam, Asshur, Arpachshad, Lud, and Aram.* [23]*The*
sons of Aram: Uz, Hul, Gether, and Mash. . . . [31]*These are the sons of Shem,*
by their families, their languages, their lands, and their nations.

32 *These are the families of the sons of Noah, according to their genealogies, in their nations; and from these the nations spread abroad on the earth after the flood.*

The present text of the table of nations belongs for the most part to the Priestly narrative. The fragments of the older Yahwistic version can be separated with relative ease from the very regularly constructed Priestly scheme by which the great register of nations is arranged. We will consider the Yahwistic version separately on p. 145.

The reader must not come to this text with erroneous presuppositions. The table of nations does not reveal humanity either according to race or according to language. Rather, these are the nations that were politically and historically distinct from one another or related to one another. Since, therefore, a definite phase of important and very complicated ancient Oriental history is mirrored in the Priestly table of nations, we must present the exposition in the form of a brief historical excursus.

In the second millennium B.C. two great kingdoms especially determined the history of the Near East: Egypt in the south and the Hittites in the north. Egypt reached the height of its power under the Pharaoh Thutmose III (1490–1436), who undertook seventeen expeditions against "Asia," i.e., Palestine and Syria, in order to establish Egyptian hegemony over these provinces. Under his successors the Egyptian dominion over Syria was lost (Amarna Age) and in Palestine the authority was at times only nominal. But Pharaohs of the nineteenth dynasty (1300–1200) again appeared with large armies in Palestine and actively enforced the old Egyptian claims to this important land bridge. Thus it is historically quite justifiable for the table of nations in v. 6 to include Canaan in the Egyptian circle (Cush is Nubia, Put is Libya).

The Hittites in Asia Minor, North Syria, and northern Mesopotamia, rising to power in about 1900, stood at the height of their power about 1390 after a long period of reverses. Syria was, of course, the bone of contention between the two powers. After the Hittites had been able to extend their political sphere of influence deep into Syria, thanks to the above-mentioned decline of Egyptian supremacy, there occurred, with the strengthening of the Egyptians under Rameses II, the unavoidable clash at Kadesh on the Orontes ca. 1295. The battle was indecisive, and a few years later both powers came to terms in a famous treaty. The treaty was exchanged in approximately verbatim versions and has now come to light again from the ashes of the royal archives. But the ancient Oriental world could not long rejoice in this peace. About 1200 the great kingdom of the Hittites was completely broken under the storm of the Aegean "sea peoples." That was "a large-scale migration similar to the expeditions of the Celts into the Balkans or those of the Mongols."* It was brought on by the incursions of the Illyrians into the Balkan peninsula; from there the push was partly toward Greece (end of the Mycenaean epoch) and partly toward Asia Minor, where the Phrygians from Thrace had settled. But the migration went farther: the Philistines pushed forward into Palestine and Egypt. Here the movement came to a halt with the victories of Merneptah in 1227 and Rameses III in 1192, and thus the southern coast of Palestine became the new homeland of the Philistines. This invasion sharply altered the power politics of the Near East.

If we return from this survey to our table of nations, we shall see at once that this great Hittite kingdom no longer exists; it has disappeared from the stage of world history and its territory contains instead a colorful society of peoples of the most diverse origin and way of life. These are the names that the table of nations links together under the name of Japheth. Politically, the table of nations shows the situation in the ancient East that arose because of the Aegean invasion (which had also set in motion many long-established tribes). The table lists such "seafaring" people (Tiras = Tyrseni = Etruscans?).† It lists the Ionians, who had by this time advanced to the coast of Asia Minor (Javan, v. 2, cf. Ezek. 27.13; Isa. 66.19; Joel 3.6); it lists long-established peoples of Asia Minor (Tibarenes, Meshech, Togarmah, v. 3); it also lists the Cimmerians and Medes (v. 2) who appeared farther eastward and much later in the eighth and seventh centuries. The *Scythians* were of special interest to the Palestinians. They participated in Assur's defeat; indeed, if we may believe Herodotus, they even advanced to Palestine and were halted only at the borders of Egypt. *Elishah* is doubtless the Alasia of the Amarna letters and probably equivalent to Cyprus. *Tarshish* is Tartessos of the Greeks in the extreme southwestern part of Spain. Since the table of nations does not relate it to the Phoenicians, who belong to Shem, but rather to Javan, it appears to be thinking of a colonization by the Ionian Phocaeans (Herodotus I. 163). Tarshish was well known in Israel (e.g., Ezek. 27.12; 38.13), often only as a term for a distant area (Jonah 1.3; Ps. 72.10; Isa. 60.9).

In the foreground of the southern Hamitic circle of nations are *Cush* (Ethiopia) and *Mizraim* (Egypt). *Put* is Libya, as the LXX

*E. Meyer, *Geschichte des Altertums*, II, 2, 1953^2, 587.

†Most recently on the Tyrseni (Tartessos!): A. Schulten, *Klio*, 1940, 1, 2.

correctly translated Jer. 46.9 (MT), etc. That the table of nations connects *Canaan* with Ham shows the extent to which it represents national connections from the political-historical viewpoint. For Canaan, peopled predominantly by Semites, was still nominally under Egyptian control when it was settled by Israel. And even the Hittites are reckoned as Canaanites! But that corresponds to the way in which the Old Testament often speaks of them. Apparently every source for that empire of the second millennium has disappeared; one includes under this term, which has now become very tangled, simply a part of the pre-Israelite population of Palestine (see at Gen. 23.3 f.). The southwest Arabian "nations" are derived from Cush.

Anyone who has noted the simple picture of power politics played by those two empires of the second half of the second millennium will be surprised by the mention of a third group, namely, the Semites. Such a power, which could have been put on a par in rank and significance with the Hittites and the Egyptians, was something new in the area where the Egyptians and Hittites rivaled each other. But by this time the Semites from the east, migrating in waves, had pushed between the two empires. Semites had, of course, previously pushed into Palestine (the Canaanites already in the third millennium); but now territorial formations occurred in Palestine and Syria only after the Semitic Aramean invasion (between 1500–1200), in association with which the Israelites entered the land.* The youngest member of that Semitic family of nations is significantly *Aram*, the last named in v. 22; and it was to some extent the point of the wedge that pushed into the Syrian-Palestinian area (see p. 157). In the historical view of the Priestly document, which arose at a much later time, this Aramean migration accounted for a state of affairs that had existed for centuries. Thus it happens that these Arameans in our table are given the same status as many older "Semitic" nations. They are the people who were making history at the time when Israel had learned to see the events on the great political stage of the Near East. The *Elamites*, the southeastern neighbors of the Assyrians, north of the Persian Gulf, already known as a people in the third millennium, often rivals or allies of Babylon, were not Semites at all; they lost their status as a power forever under Asshurbanapal (conquest of Susa 640). Most curious is the inclusion of the *Lydians* of Asia Minor among the Semites, which is perhaps related to an alliance of King Gyges with Asshurbanapal

*A. Alt, *Völker und Staaten Syriens im frühen Altertum* (Der Alte Orient, Bd.34, Heft 4, 1936).

against the Cimmerians ca. 660. *Asshur*, already a great power for a time during the second millennium, climbed step by step from the ninth century to the pinnacle of its historical greatness. The Assyrian kings invaded Phoenicia, Syria, Palestine (Samaria was conquered 722; Jerusalem surrendered 701), even Egypt (conquest of Thebes 666). In 612 this empire fell before the attack of the Medes and Neo-Babylonians. Puzzling that Babylon is not named in the list! (Is the interpretation, often given since Josephus, which connects Arpachshad with the Chaldeans correct at least in saying that the last inexplicable consonants of the word, *ksd*, equal *kasdim*?) One also expects more familiar names in the Aramean genealogy. (Is Arpachshad Arrapha of the Zagros?) Abraham was descended from Arpachshad and his offspring (ch. 11.10 ff.).

EPILOGUE TO THE PRIESTLY TABLE OF NATIONS

The table of nations is Priestly doctrine in the strict sense of the word; it is part of the sacred world picture as it was transmitted and taught in the sanctuaries, and as such it is a document of amazing theoretical power. "Nowhere is there a survey of international relations comparable to the biblical table of nations, so universal in its breadth of view and so comprehensive in its purpose." (Del.) A comparison with the lists of conquered cities or lands in which Oriental kings gloried is out of the question, because, to begin with, the table of nations does not belong to the genre of court-political literature, but rather to sacred literature. The broad range of vision is amazing for an inland people like Israel. It extends northward to the Black Sea, eastward to the Iranian plateau, southward to Nubia and westward to the Mediterranean coast of Spain. It is hard to imagine that there was not an actual map corresponding to this literary scheme. (The final form of this Priestly table may be contemporaneous with Anaximander's map of the world. Cf. especially the Neo-Babylonian world map, which is, of course, in no way comparable to the ancient Israelite table of nations. B. Meissner, *Babylonien u. Assyrien*, II, 377 ff.). In any case, considerable work preceded it, and we may assume that Israel did only part of it and made use of the knowledge of other nations (the Phoenicians).

As to the time of composition, one must remember that tradition played an important part in such documents, and that new international constellations were not necessarily entered immediately. Thus the omission of the Persians, who appeared on the scene in the sixth century, does not really mean much. After all, the recognizable signs point more to the historical picture of the seventh century.

The significance for biblical theology of the Priestly table of nations consists, first of all, in the fact that it shows the fulfillment, the execution of God's command to Noah and his sons: "Be fruitful and multiply" (ch. 9.1). God had "blessed" Noah and his sons (ch. 9.1). Blessing in the Old Testament is widely used to mean the bestowal of vitality; it means, first of all, an increase in life simply in the physical sense (Fr. Horst, *Ev. Th.*, 1947, 29 ff.). Now when the Priestly document in the table of nations reviews intellectually the fullness of the nations according to the ancient world view, there is hidden solemnity behind this barren enumeration, astonishment and reverence at the riches of God's majestic creativity. Paul expressed the same thing in his speech on Mars' Hill, "[God] made from one every nation of men to live on all the face of the earth, having determined allotted periods and the boundaries of their habitation" (Acts 17.26). In Gen., ch. 10, the extremely complex reality in which Israel found herself is represented from the historical viewpoint (as in Gen., ch. 1, from the natural) as God's creation. That is the real testimony of the table of nations. The (older) interpretations that relate these nations to God's gracious will which had been revealed in Israel, be it as "unredeemed," be it as "future beneficiaries of the same salvation," do not correspond with the Priestly text if we take it as it is. To speak of the "invisible verdure of hope which winds through the barren branches of this register of nations, the hope, namely, that the widely separated ways of the nations will meet at last at a goal set by the God of revelation" (Del.)—that is justifiable for theology only when it brings our chapter together with other (prophetic) witnesses and then, above all, with Acts, ch. 2.

If we consider the dramatic excitement of history during the centuries when the table of nations was formed, we must be astonished at the political dispassionateness of this document. Considering its exalted aloofness, what reader thinks of the oracle of nations in Isaiah, Jeremiah, or Ezekiel, and of the tense political situation during these centuries with which the purview in the table of nations was approximately contemporaneous? Here the nations are represented for once without any regard for the deadly threat they posed for Israel. Indeed, where is Israel in the table? The omission of Israel appears to us as one of its most striking characteristics; so striking that one could make the impossible assumption that here a view of history and the world belonging to a nation other than Israel was adopted. In any case, here Israel is not the center of the nations (Ezek. 5.5), the "world navel," a notion that occurs so frequently in the *polis* religions. Israel is represented in the table of nations by a name that is completely neutral for her faith and for sacred history—Arpachshad! That means Israel did not simply draw a direct line in time from the primeval myth to herself. This lineal connection with the myth is the essence of polis religion, where the specific political community can take only itself seriously. (The list of old Babylonian primeval kings begins: "When kingship came down from heaven the kingdom was in Eridu . . ." AOT, 147; ANET, 165.) Genesis is quite different. The line from primeval time does not lead lineally from Noah to Abraham, but it first opens into the universe of the international world. When Israel looked backward from Abraham, there was a decisive break in the line to the primeval beginning, the table of nations. That is to say, Israel looked at herself in the midst of the international world without illusion and quite unmythically. What Israel learns and experiences of Yahweh occurs exclusively within the realm of history. For biblical theology the inclusion of the table of nations means a radical break with myth.

15. FRAGMENTS OF THE YAHWISTIC TABLE OF NATIONS. Ch. 10.1b, 8–19, 21, 24–30

10 [1b](Shem, Ham, and Japheth), sons were born to them after the
flood. . . .
8 Cush became the father of Nimrod; he was the first on earth to be
a mighty man. [9]He was a mighty hunter before the LORD; therefore it
is said, "Like Nimrod a mighty hunter before the LORD." [10]The beginning of his kingdom was Babel, Erech, and Accad, all of them in the
land of Shinar. [11]From that land he went into Assyria, and built
Nineveh, Rehoboth-Ir, Calah, and [12]Resen between Nineveh and
Calah; that is the great city. [13]Egypt became the father of Ludim,
Anamim, Lehabim, Naph-tuhim, [14]Pathrusim, Casluhim (whence
came the Philistines), and Caphtorim.
15 Canaan became the father of Sidon his first-born, and Heth,
[16]and the Jebusites, the Amorites, the Girgashites, [17]the Hivites, the
Arkites, the Sinites, [18]the Arvadites, the Zemarites, and the Ha-
mathites. Afterward the families of the Canaanites spread abroad.
[19]And the territory of the Canaanites extended from Sidon, in the
direction of Gerar, as far as Gaza, and in the direction of Sodom,
Gomorrah, Admah, and Zeboiim, as far as Lasha. . . .
21 To Shem also, the father of all the children of Eber, the elder
brother of Japheth, children were born. . . . [24]Arpachshad became

the father of Shelah; and Shelah became the father of Eber. [25]To Eber were born two sons: the name of the one was Pelag, for in his days the earth was divided, and his brother's name was Joktan. [26]Joktan became the father of Almodad, Sheleph, Hazarmaveth, Jerah, [27]Hadoram, Uzal, Diklah, [28]Obal, Abima-el, Sheba, [29]Ophor, Havilah, and Jobab; all these were the sons of Joktan. [30]The territory in which they lived extended from Mesha in the direction of Sephar to the hill country of the east.

We have put the Priestly table of nations by itself for the sake of its unity and great compactness, and we have interpreted it as a document of the mature Priestly world view. This list, however, is based on the fragments of a much older Yahwistic table of nations, which the final redactor worked into the Priestly text only in part.

Of *Japheth* nothing has remained. J too divides *Ham* into Cush (Ethiopia), Mizraim (Egypt), and Canaan (about Canaan's belonging to Ham, see p. 142). From Cush, Nimrod is descended, about whom the list relates a variety of remarkable things. The statements are so general, and connected to one another so loosely, that one senses how remote and legendary the information about Nimrod was even in the ancient Israelite period; only particular recollections have been preserved. Our list considers Nimrod as the first wielder of power on earth, the first ruler of historical significance, the first in the series of those great men whose will become determinative for the fate of entire nations. At the same time he is said to have been a proverbial hunter; "before the Lord" is here equivalent to "on the earth" (cf. Jonah 3.3). Whence the saying? It need not be a proverb; it could as well be a citation from an epic or something of that kind (Num. 21.14). But how is one to understand the statements about his Babylonian dominion? Nimrod is a Cushite; is he not therefore a Hamite? Indeed, if one may take *rēʾšīt* ("beginning") in v. 10a as meaning "pinnacle" in the sense of high point, the exposition would be considerably easier! The subject of v. 11a, however, must be Asshur and not Nimrod. The question about which historical ruler these recollections refer to has not yet been answered satisfactorily. Sethe's suggestion of Amenhotep III (1411–1375) is attractive; he was called *neb ma re*, a name that recurs in the Amarna letters as Nimmuris. As a matter of fact, Amenhotep boasts that he extended his rule to the Euphrates and also tells of great hunts for lions and wild beasts.* But other interpretations are also possible. (A widely

* *Encyclopedia of Religion and Ethics*, Vol. VI, 650.

accepted suggestion is that the passage refers to the Babylonian god Ninurta, who was the god of the chase and about whom epic traditions existed. The difficulty with this, however, is his firm position in the genealogy of Ham.) Nimrod can have been a legendary figure who attracted to himself varied elements of tradition. Important among the sons of Mizraim are the Caphtorians (Cretans), with whom the Philistines are connected (see ch. 9.27). But what shall we make of their coming from the enigmatic Casluhim? The emendation suggested by many commentators is advisable. (Compare BH, "Egypt became the father of . . . Pathrusim, Casluhim, and Caphtorim, whence came the Philistines.") As to the origin of the Philistines from Caphtor-Crete, cf. Amos 9.7; Jer. 47.4. To Canaan are reckoned "nations" for some of whom only the name has been preserved. The Amorites are often mentioned in the Old Testament (Gen. 15.16; 48.22; etc.), but without any clear historical conception. What is meant is the pre-Israelite inhabitants of Palestine, or part of them. The boundaries of Canaan are defined in the northwest by Sidon, in the south by Gerar (between Gaza and Beer-sheba), and in the southeast by Sodom (southern Dead Sea).

The "nations" that are introduced under *Shem's* name are perhaps exclusively tribes from Arabia. The geographical horizon is thus much narrower than in P. For the identification and significance of the names, where it is possible (Ophir, I Kings 10.11; 22.48), cf. Guthe, *Bibelatlas*, plate 6; *Westminster Historical Atlas to the Bible*, plate II.

16. THE STORY OF THE TOWER OF BABEL AND THE CONFUSION OF LANGUAGE. Ch. 11.1–9

11 [1]Now the whole earth had one language and few words. [2]And as
men migrated from the east,* they found a plain in the land of Shinar and
settled there. [3]And they said to one another, "Come, let us make bricks,
and burn them thoroughly." And they had brick for stone, and bitumen
for mortar. [4]Then they said, "Come, let us build ourselves a city, and a
tower with its top in the heavens, and let us make a name for ourselves,
lest we be scattered abroad upon the face of the whole earth." [5]And the
LORD came down to see the city and the tower, which the sons of men
had built. [6]And the LORD said, "Behold, they are one people, and they
have all one language; and this is only the beginning of what they will
do; and nothing that they propose to do will now be impossible for them.
[7]Come, let us go down, and there confuse their language, that they may

*Or, "toward the East." (O. E. Raun, ZDMG 1937, 354; also, Jac. at this place.) Cf. Gen. 13.11.

not understand one another's speech." [8]So the LORD scattered them abroad from there over the face of all the earth, and they left off building the city. [9]Therefore its name was called Babel, because there the LORD confused the language of all the earth; and from there the LORD scattered them abroad over the face of all the earth.

This is the last of the great narratives of the Yahwistic primeval history; therefore it has special significance in the context of the whole (see, in this regard, the Epilogue). It too consists of older material which had first to be boldly hewn and recast; but even then it is incorporated into the Yahwistic primeval history, not in detail, but rather in its primary ideas. The beginning of ch. 11 does not quite agree with what one learned in the table of nations about the branching out of Noah's house into many nations, because it presupposes once again the unity and linguistic uniformity of mankind. Yet one may not draw literary conclusions from such irregularities (as, for example, the presence of a secondary source to J); our narrator has freely welded single traditions into a primeval history, and in doing it, he paid much more attention to the inner theological orientation of the whole than to a precise harmonizing of the details.

[1–4] Originally all of humanity had one language and one vocabulary. But they began to wander—from where is not said—and found a large plain which tempted them to become sedentary. (On Shinar for Babylon, cf. Gen. 10.10 and especially ch. 14.1, 9.) Obviously, with this beginning, we have entered into an originally independent narrative complex. There is no external connection with the preceding table of nations, which has already spoken of several nations and has even mentioned the historical Babylon (ch. 10.10). This beginning betrays an acute historical observation: nationalities tend to emerge from great migrations. Large bands for some unknown reason find themselves on the move; suddenly they step out of the obscurity of their previous unhistorical existence into the light of history and climb to cultural power. Accordingly, sedentariness takes on special forms. So it happened here. They did not settle down as they were before; rather, they were interested in a strong alliance and in fame. Thus, in building a great city and a tower, they began a monumental architectural work. Great zeal, the vital optimism of a young nation, animates them in this gigantic work of civilization (cf. the double summons in vs. 3 f.). Thus the city arises as a sign of their valiant self-reliance, the tower as a sign of their will to fame. Their joy in their inventiveness—they use asphalt as mortar—is shown in the Hebrew text by appropriate puns. "The effect is superb, and the language which appears only to have been waiting for it confirms it" (Jac.). The building material they use is that used in Mesopotamia. Our narrator, for whom the use of stone for larger buildings was a matter of course, has a special purpose in mentioning it: the material that men used for their gigantic undertaking was perishable and unsatisfactory! The statement that the tower should reach to heaven must not be pressed; it is only an expression for the special height of the building (cf. Deut. 1.28). That men wanted to storm heaven, God's dwelling place (cf., however, Isa. 14.13), is not said. Rather, one will observe a subtlety of the narrative in the fact that it does not give anything unprecedented as the motive for this building, but rather something that lies within the realm of human possibility, namely, a combination of their energies on the one hand, and on the other the winning of fame, i.e., a naïve desire to be great. Jacob points also to the underlying motive of anxiety. These are therefore the basic forces of what we call culture. But in them, in the penetrating judgment of our narrator, is rebellion against God, a concealed Titanism, or at least, as v. 6 will show, the first step in that direction.

[5–7] "And the Lord came down!" We should not apologetically weaken this very ancient way of speaking, when the Yahwist without embarrassment has let it stand. The God of the whole world and of mankind is meant here. On the Yahwistic idiom, Procksch comments correctly: "Yahweh must draw near, not because he is nearsighted, but because he dwells at such tremendous height and their work is so tiny. God's movement must therefore be understood as a remarkable satire on man's doing." God's eye already sees the end of the road upon which mankind entered with this deed, the possibilities and temptations which such a massing of forces holds. A humanity that can think only of its own confederation is at liberty for anything, i.e., for every extravagance. Therefore God resolves upon a punitive, but at the same time preventive, act, so that he will not have to punish man more severely as his degeneration surely progresses. The men said, "Come, let us"; God too says, "Come, let us." The "we" in God's mouth presupposes the idea at one time of a pantheon, a council of the gods. In Israel this idea was a meeting of the council of the Heavenly King, the notion of God which was perhaps most popular in the Old Testament (cf. especially I Kings 22.19 f.; Job 1.6). Now God breaks up the unity of mankind; he confuses their language so that men, who no longer understand one another, have to separate. **[8–9]** Thus mankind is "scattered," i.e., broken up into a great number of individual nations. Even today one infers from the city's name a reminder of that primeval judgment of God. This explanation of the word "Babel" ("medley," from *bālal,* "stir up, mix up") is of course etymologically irrelevant; it was popularly invented, for Babel means "gate of God."

In form the narrative is possibly woven together from two variants that are quite similar to each other, a recension about the building of a tower (mankind builds a tower in order to make a name for itself) and a recension about the building of a city (mankind builds a city in order not to be scattered; accordingly, God confuses their language and scatters them upon the earth). But this has recently been contested again and the unity of the narrative asserted. In content we shall designate it first of all as an aetiological saga; it seeks to explain why there are so many nations and languages; it also intends to explain the name Babel. This double aetiological point shows that the Yahwist took over the narrative in a comparatively late and complicated version. These aetiologies certainly do not stem from him (concerning his aetiology, see pp. 153 f.). In the epilogue to the primeval history we shall see that he did not remove this inner orientation from the story but gave it a special more comprehensive meaning within the context of the entire primeval history.

The saga about the confusion of language is concerned with a historical phenomenon that was made concrete in the cosmopolitan city of Babylon; but the story certainly does not originate from Babylon; rather, it shows ideas that were strange to Babylon. Babylon in ancient times, especially in the second millennium B.C., was the heart of the ancient world and its center of power (Hammurabi, 1728–1686), and the rays of its culture went out far into neighbouring lands. Thus even in Palestine there was legendary knowledge of its gigantic cultural achievements, especially of the mighty stepped towers in which the united civilized will of this strong nation had created an enduring monument. They were cult buildings of gigantic proportions (stylized mountains of God?); their remains are found today in the vicinity of various sanctuaries of the land, and on the basis of Akkadian data and a report of Herodotus (I. 178 ff.) their original form can be reconstructed with reasonable certainty. See E. Unger's attempt (not uncontested, it is true) ZAW, 1928, 162 ff.; cf. also AOB², No. 473. Such a ziggurat (Etemenanki) also stood in Babylon, a marvel of colored, glazed tiles, over 297 feet high, often renovated (founded "on the breast of the underworld," "its pinnacle shall reach to heaven"); our biblical narrative is probably to be distantly connected with it. The matter would be somewhat different if the *migdāl* in vs. 4 f. were to be translated not "tower" but "fortress," "acropolis" (O. E. Raun, ZDMG, 1937, 352 ff.), which is also frequently attested in the Old Testament (Judg. 8.9; 9.46 f.; Isa. 2.15; II Chron. 14.6; etc. Mesha stone, line 22). For fortifications "up to heaven," see Deut. 1.28; 9.1. This interpretation is debatable, for the saga contains no data whatever about the actual purpose of the building (profane building? religious building?). The meaning would then have more to do with mankind's transition to a collective ability to bear arms. But then one would also have to assume that the saga was related to remote knowledge about a gigantic building in Babylon, and that was particularly the ziggurat Etemenanki. In any case, the saga views such a development of power as something against God, rebellion against the Most High, as Babylon in many passages of the Old Testament is mentioned as the embodiment of sinful arrogance (Isa. 13.14; 14.13; Jer. 51.6 ff.). It appears indeed that the oldest version of the narrative represented the building of the tower precisely as a danger and threat to the gods. The Yahwistic revision removed this feature. Now, on the contrary, a touch of superior divine irony has been added to the whole: "He who sits in the heavens laughs" (Ps. 2.4). To be sure, the consequence of this revision of the old material is that now the narrative does not make clear what man's sin actually was, and thus Yahweh's interference has a preventive character. The story in its present form must be understood primarily from the great primeval context into which the Yahwist has placed it. Basically it no longer concerns Babylon and the impressions this world city made on men. As in the saga of Cain (Kenites), here too the story touches upon what is historical and conditioned by its time, and the old material of the saga is expanded into the universal and the primeval. What the narrative portrays is something thoroughly primeval; it shows how men in their striving for fame, alliance, and political development set themselves against God. But a punishment befell them: they who were so concerned with unity and alliance now live scattered in a disorder in which they can no longer understand one another. This is therefore a bit of human cultural history (here Babylon is thought of as the original seat of all culture); but it is not cultural history for its own sake but cultural history in which man's rebellion against God becomes evident and in which God's judgment took place.

We have said already that the inner connection of this narrative to the preceding table of nations is very loose. This story of mankind's dispersion into many nations actually begins once again where the table of nations began and is to some extent parallel with it; for it too seeks to explain humanity's division into many nations. The chapters must be read together, because they are intentionally placed next to each other in spite of their antagonism. The multitude of nations indicates not only the manifold quality of God's creative power but also a judgment, for the disorder in the international world, which our narrative regards as the sad conclusion, was not willed by God but is punishment for the sinful rebellion against God. In this conclusion, of course, the story about the confusion of language goes far beyond the picture drawn in the table of nations.

EPILOGUE TO THE YAHWISTIC PRIMEVAL HISTORY

The story about the building of the Babylonian tower is generally seen as the keystone to the Yahwistic primeval history. So we must look back briefly over the way along which this narrator has brought us. But this deliberation is all the more important because the Yahwist's outline has given to the canonical primeval history the character that was later combined with the Priestly document. The Yahwistic narrator has told the story of God and man from the time mankind began, and this story is characterized on the human side by an increase in sin to avalanche proportions. The sins of Adam and Eve, Cain, Lamech, the angel marriages, the Tower of Babel—these are stages along that way which has separated man farther and farther from God. This succession of narratives, therefore, points out a continually widening chasm between man and God. But God reacts to these outbreaks of human sin with severe judgments. The punishment of Adam and Eve was severe; severer still was Cain's. Then followed the Flood, and the final judgment was the Dispersion, the dissolution of mankind's unity. Thus at the end of the primeval history a difficult question is raised: God's future relationship to his rebellious humanity, which is now scattered in fragments. Is the catastrophe of ch. 11.1–9 final? We shall postpone an answer for the moment. The Yahwistic narrator shows something else along with the consequences of divine judgment. Adam and Eve remained alive in spite of the threat of death (ch. 2.17); indeed, God had clothed them. Thus, in all the hardship of punishment, God's activity of succor and preservation was revealed. Cain was cursed by God, to be sure, and his relationship to the earth was profoundly disturbed; but the story ends with the establishment of a mysterious protective relationship between God and Cain. He who went forth from Yahweh's presence was not abandoned by him but watched over and protected against being slain by a barbarous humanity. At the conclusion of the Flood story, God's will to preserve mankind becomes especially clear. God begins with man anew. As we saw, it was almost as though God had given in; at any rate, God transferred man, in spite of his unchanged corruption (ch. 8.21), to a newly ordered world, whose natural order was solemnly guaranteed to endure. We see, therefore (already in primeval history!), that each time, in and after the judgment, God's preserving, forgiving will to save is revealed, and "where sin increased, grace abounded all the more" (Rom. 5.20). None of that, of course, is theologically formulated in so many words; we look in vain for terms like "salvation," "grace," "forgiveness." The narrator tells only facts that, because of words of divine forbearance, did occur.

What is described, therefore, is a story of God with man, the story of continuously new punishment and at the same time gracious preservation, the story, to be sure, of a way that is distinguished by progressive divine judgment, but that, nevertheless, man could never have traveled without continued divine preservation. This consoling preservation, that revelation of God's hidden gracious will, is missing, however, at one place, namely, at the end of the primeval history. The story about the Tower of Babel concludes with God's judgment on mankind; there is no word of grace. The whole primeval history, therefore, seems to break off in shrill dissonance, and the question we formulated above now arises even more urgently: Is God's relationship to the nations now finally broken; is God's gracious forbearance now exhausted; has God rejected the nations in wrath forever? That is the burdensome question which no thoughtful reader of ch. 11 can avoid; indeed, one can say that our narrator intended by means of the whole plan of his primeval history to raise precisely this question and to pose it in all its severity. Only then is the reader properly prepared to take up the strangely new thing that now follows the comfortless story about the building of the tower: the election and blessing of Abraham. We stand here, therefore, at the point where primeval history and sacred history dovetail, and thus at one of the most important places in the entire Old Testament. Primeval history had shown an increasing disturbance in the relationship between humanity and God and had culminated in God's judgment on the nations. The question about God's salvation for all nations remains open and unanswerable in *primeval* history. But our narrator *does* give an answer, namely, at the point where sacred history begins. Here in the promise that is given concerning Abraham something is again said about God's saving will and indeed about a salvation extending far beyond the limits of the covenant people to "all the families of the earth" (ch. 12.3). The transition from primeval history to sacred history occurs abruptly and surprisingly in vs. 1–3. All at once and precipitously the universal field of vision narrows; world and humanity, the entire ecumenical fullness, are submerged, and all interest is concentrated upon a single man. Previously the narrative concerned humanity as a whole, man's creation and essential character, woman, sin, suffering, humanity, nations, all of them universal themes. In v. 1, as though after a break, the particularism of election begins.

From the multitude of nations God chooses a man, looses him from tribal ties, and makes him the beginner of a new nation and the recipient of great promises of salvation. What is promised to Abraham reaches far beyond Israel; indeed, it has universal meaning for all generations on earth. Thus that difficult question about God's relationship to the nations is answered, and precisely where one least expects it. At the beginning of the way into an emphatically exclusive covenant-relation there is already a word about the end of this way, namely, an allusion to a final, universal unchaining of the salvation promised to Abraham. Truly flesh and blood did not inspire this view beyond Israel and its saving relation to God! With this firm linking of primeval history and sacred history the Yahwist indicates something of the final meaning and purpose of the saving relation that God has vouchsafed to Israel. It is therefore not wholly apt to find in ch. 11 that conclusion to the primeval history, as is usually done; for then the primeval history has a much too independent and isolated importance. Rather, its real conclusion, indeed its key, is ch. 12.1–3, for only from there does the theological significance of this universal preface to saving history become understandable.

It is astonishing how the Yahwist succeeded in giving such vivid expression to the course traversed by humanity through his compilation of a relatively small number of different narratives. But this conception of the primeval history of mankind is not to be ascribed to the Yahwist, as was previously assumed. The outline of creation—

primeval time—Flood—new beginning to human history can already be found in Sumerian, i.e., in ancient Mesopotamian texts.* How this teaching, which was fixed at the latest about 2000 B.C., came to Israel and to the knowledge of the Yahwist, and who brought it, we do not know. However, in Israel the theological accents were placed in quite a different way. The old outline knew nothing of the Fall, of Cain's fratricide or the building of the tower. On the other hand, we can now understand better the great turning point at 8.21 f. (see above, pp. 122 f.), for the end of the Flood story at one time represented the beginning of the history of mankind, and that is still true of the Yahwistic primeval history. Of course, the history that interested the Yahwist did not begin with the beginning of human history, but with an event which took place within human history, and that was the call of Abraham.

The external genealogical link between primeval history (Shem) and the beginner of sacred history (Abraham) now exists only in the Priestly version (ch. 11.10–27). Presumably the Yahwist too had drawn a connecting line from the table of nations down to Terah and Abraham; it may have been very brief, and since materially it probably agreed somewhat with the names of the Priestly genealogy, the redactor gave preference to P's table of Semites, which was better developed with respect to form. The thread of Yahwistic narrative begins again in vs. 28–30.

17. THE FATHERS FROM SHEM TO ABRAHAM. (P)
Ch. 11.10–27, 31, 32

11 [10]*These are the descendants of Shem. When Shem was a hundred years old,*
he became the father of Arpachshad two years after the flood; [11]*and Shem lived*
after the birth of Arpachshad five hundred years, and had other sons and
daughters.

12 *When Arpachshad had lived thirty-five years he became the father of*
Shelah; [13]*and Arpachshad lived after the birth of Shelah four hundred and three*
years, and had other sons and daughters.

14 *When Shelah had lived thirty years, he became the father of Eber;* [15]*and*
Shelah lived after the birth of Eber four hundred and three years, and had other
sons and daughters.

16 *When Eber had lived thirty-four years, he became the father of Peleg;*
[17]*and Eber lived after the birth of Peleg four hundred and thirty years, and had*
other sons and daughters.

18 *When Peleg had lived thirty years, he became the father of Reu;* [19]*and*

*H. Gese, "The Idea of History in the Ancient Near East and the Old Testament," *Journal for Theology and the Church*, 1, 1965, 49 ff.

Peleg lived after the birth of Reu two hundred and nine years, and had other sons and daughters.

20 *When Reu had lived thirty-two years, he became the father of Serug;*
21*and Reu lived after the birth of Serug two hundred and seven years, and had other sons and daughters.*

22 *When Serug had lived thirty years, he became the father of Nahor;* 23*and Serug lived after the birth of Nahor two hundred years, and had other sons and daughters.*

24 *When Nahor had lived twenty-nine years, he became the father of Terah;*
25*and Nahor lived after the birth of Terah a hundred and nineteen years, and had other sons and daughters.*

26 *When Terah had lived seventy years, he became the father of Abram, Nahor, and Haran.*

27 *Now these are the descendants of Terah. Terah was the father of Abram, Nahor, and Haran; and Haran was the father of Lot.*

31 *Terah took Abram his son and Lot the son of Haran, his grandson, and Sarai his daughter-in-law, his son Abram's wife, and they went forth together from Ur of the Chaldeans to go into the land of Canaan; but when they came to*
Haran, they settled there. 32*The days of Terah were two hundred and five years; and Terah died in Haran.*

[10–27] This section is from the toledoth book, which is probably the oldest framework of the Priestly document. This genealogy, like the list of Sethites (ch. 5.32), also ends with three heads: Abram, Nahor, Haran (ch. 11.27). Yet the toledoth genealogies are not uniformly constructed with respect to their outer form (here, e.g., there is no mention of the total length of life, which was regularly given in the Sethite list), an indication that these genealogies were each independent traditions and only secondarily were coupled to one another in the toledoth book. Our gradually increasing knowledge of the political conditions in Syria and western Mesopotamia during the second millennium confirm the impression of the great age of this tradition. Though many questions are still unanswered precisely with respect to the backgrounds of this list, this much at least is clear; this tradition takes us to northwestern Mesopotamia and northern Syria. A few names can be confirmed as place names (Serug is Sarug, west of Haran; Nahor is Til-nahiri, likewise near Haran; Terach is Til-a-turahi on the Balikh; Peleg is Phaliga on the upper Euphrates); Haran as seat of the ancient moon cult has long been known. This points to an area into which the Arameans entered toward the end of the second millennium. (The cities themselves were, of course, not Aramean settlements, but were much older.) Even Ur, on the lower Euphrates, which can be shown to have been a cultural center as far back as the fourth pre-Christian millennium (C. L. Woolley, *Ur of the*

Chaldees, 1929), was later Arameanized by this wave of "Chaldeans." It was closely connected with this Semitic wave on which the Israelites came to Palestine. Thus this list handles very concrete prehistorical contingencies when it connects Israel's ancestors with the Arameans (cf. also Deut. 26.5; Gen. 28 f.).

There is an inconsistency between the data in ch. 5.32 and ch. 7.11 on the one hand and ch. 11.10 on the other wich has not yet been satisfactorily solved, if one decides against simply deleting the words "two years after the flood," for at this time Shem was not a hundred years old but one hundred and two.

Terah (like Noah) had three sons: Abraham, Nahor, and Haran. Haran's son was Lot. Abraham's wife was called Sarai. The name of the first-born was at first, until ch. 17.5, Ab (i) ram, "my father [the god] is exalted"; that of his wife Sarai, "princess." There is nothing special about either name, and both correspond completely to the convention of name-giving in ancient Israel and the Orient.

[31–32] Compared with Gen., ch. 5, this generation shows a further shortening of the life span; the procreative years also are earlier. This indicates the progressive decline of man's original state according to creation and at the same time prepares the reader for the miracle of Isaac's conception (ch. 21.5, P). (Here too it is true the figures of the LXX and Samaritan Pentateuch differ considerably.)

A great deal is expected of the theological reader, who in the fullness of the nations (ch. 10) has just perceived God's creative wealth, when this *one* genealogical line alone receives exclusive interest and is pursued farther. One can say, of course, that P was Abraham's descendant and therefore only this line was of interest to him. But what led him, then, to burden his sketch with the table of nations? He could very simply have constructed the genealogy from Adam directly to Abraham. The rigor with which he first traces all the nations back through Noah to Adam and only then describes a particular line down to Abraham shows that he knew about the riddle of divine election and wanted to make its harshness theologically vivid in his history.

According to the Priestly conception, Terah set out with Abraham, Sarai, and Lot on the way from Ur Chasdim to Canaan. Strangely enough, no motive is given for the departure on this peculiar trip. P too seems to see the really decisive thing in Abraham's journey from Haran (see below). The data about Ur as the starting place, that ancient cultural center at the mouth of the Euphrates, cannot be made to agree properly with the older (JE) account, in accordance with which Haran was the home of Abraham and his tribe (chs. 24.4 ff.; 29.4 f.). Did Terah, in order to migrate to Canaan, first go so far to the northwest? The long interruption of the journey at Haran holds still another riddle. There Terah dies at the age of two hundred and five. Now when it is said further (ch. 12.4) that Abraham moved from Haran farther toward Canaan in his seventy-fifth year (he was born in Terah's seventieth year, ch. 11.26), then Abraham left Haran sixty years *before* Terah's death! The conjecture that inconsistencies in the text arose when several traditions were worked into one is not really satisfying, for the "inconsistency" must also have been noticed by the redactor. Perhaps precisely the unnaturalness of Abraham's departure "from his father's house" was to become clear in the chronology?

18. ABRAHAM'S ORIGIN AND CALL. (J)
Chs. 11.28–30; 12.1–3

11 28Haran died before his father Terah in the land of his birth, in
Ur of the Chaldeans. 29And Abram and Nahor took wives; the name of
Abram's wife was Sarai, and the name of Nahor's wife, Milcah, the
daughter of Haran the father of Milcah and Iscah. 30Now Sarai was
barren; she had no child.

12 1Now the LORD said to Abram, "Go from your country and your
kindred and your father's house to the land that I will show you. 2And
I will make of you a great nation, and I will bless you, and make your
name great, so that you will be a blessing. 3I will bless those who bless
you, and him who curses you I will curse; and by you all the families of
the earth will bless themselves."

[11.28–30] Here, after a short break, the narrative thread of the Yahwist continues. Haran, the youngest of Terah's three sons, dies during his father's lifetime (that is the meaning of the *'al p^e^nē teraḥ*). Many exegetes consider "in Ur Chasdim" as a harmonizing gloss to reconcile the Yahwistic tradition with that of P. Actually J does know only Haran as the home of Abraham and his kinsmen. (Concerning Ur Chasdim, see at ch. 11.31.) Abraham and Nahor take wives. Strange that Milcah's father is named but not the father of the much more important Sarai! Perhaps the Yahwist too knew her as Abraham's sister (cf. ch. 20.12, E), but does not want to state it. Milcah's niece is Rebecca (ch. 24.15). Sarai's barrenness is mentioned in passing. The narrator had to do that not only to prepare the reader for the event that is conditioned by this fact, but, above all, to make him conscious of the paradox of God's initial speech to Abraham.

[12.1] And now follows the new point of departure in the divine revelation of salvation: an address to a man amidst the multitude of existing nations, a constraining of this one man for God and his plan of history by virtue of a free act of choice. Why God's choice did not fall upon Ham or Japheth, but rather upon Shem, and within Shem upon Arpachshad, and within the descendants of Arpachshad upon Abraham, the narrator does not explain. Yahweh is the subject of the first verb at the beginning of the first statement and thus the subject of the entire subsequent sacred history. The divine address begins with the command to abandon radically all natural roots. The most general tie, that with the "land," is named first, then follow, narrowing step by step, the bonds of the clan, i.e., the more distant relatives, and the immediate family. These three terms indicate that God knows the difficulties of these separations; Abraham is simply to leave everything behind and entrust himself to God's guidance. The goal of the migration is "a land," about which Abraham knows only that God will show it to him. Even though, as we indicated above, this tells an actual fact about Israel's beginning, yet it is doubtful that the narrator's interest here and in what follows is solely the representation of past events. In this call and this road which was taken, Israel saw not only an event in her earliest history, but also a basic characteristic of her whole existence before God. Taken from the community of nations (cf. Num. 23.9) and never truly rooted in Canaan, but even there a stranger (cf. Lev. 25.23; Ps. 39.12), Israel saw herself being led on a special road whose plan and goal lay completely in Yahweh's hand.

[2–3] In v. 2 begins the actual promise to Abraham. Its essential word, which is varied not less than five times, is the word "blessing." This blessing concerns Abraham first of all; but it also concerns those on the outside who adopt a definite attitude toward this blessing. One does not approach the substance of the Old Testament ideas about blessing if one proceeds primarily from the notion of a magically effective manistic "strength of mind" which is poured out like a fluid. This idea is *pre*-Israelitic in spite of some rudiments retained especially in the cultic vocabulary. *Yahweh* in freedom gives or withholds blessing; for men the effectiveness of this blessing depends strictly on their transmission of the creative divine word of blessing. The substance of Yahweh's blessing in the Old Testament is predominantly a material increase in life, especially in the sense of physical fruitfulness (cf. Gen. 1.22). The promise of innumerable descendants is a primary ingredient in the promise to the patriarchs (Gen. 13.16; 15.5; 17.5 f.; 18.18; 22.17; 26.4, 24; 28.14; 35.11). In the "name" that Yahweh will "make great" (i.e., famous) has been seen correctly a hidden allusion to the story of the Tower of Babel (Pr., Jac.): Yahweh now intends to give what men attempted to secure arbitrarily. (For the somewhat different tradition about the substance of the promise in the Priestly document, see at ch. 17.1 ff.)

The promise given to Abraham has significance, however, far beyond Abraham and his seed. God now brings salvation and judgment into history, and man's judgment and salvation will be determined by the attitude he adopts toward this work which God intends to do in history. The thought of judgment, however, is here almost overarched by the words of blessing (notice the singular "him who curses you" in contrast to the plural "those who bless you"). Our narrator does not yet consider what God begins here primarily as "a sign that is spoken against" (Luke 2.34) but as a source of universal blessing.

The question has been raised at vs. 2b and 3b whether the meaning is only that Abraham is to become a formula for blessing, that his blessing is to become far and wide proverbial (cf. Gen. 48.20). In favor of this conception (which reckons with a remnant of the magical-dynamic notion of blessing) one can refer to Zech. 8.13. It is, however, hermeneutically wrong to limit such a programmatic saying, circulating in such exalted style, to only *one* meaning (restrictively). In Isa. 19.24, for example, this conception is no longer applicable. In Gen. 12.1–3 its effect is trivial in God's address which is solemnly augmented—completely so in the final strophe! The accepted interpretation must therefore remain. It is like "a command to history" (Jac.). Abraham is assigned the role of a mediator of blessing in God's saving plan, for "all the families of the earth." The extent of the promise now becomes equal to that of the unhappy international world (Pr.), an idea that occurs more than once in the Old Testament. Both Isaiah (ch. 2.2–4) and Deutero-Isaiah have prophesied about this universal destiny of Israel. The unusual *nibrᵉkū*, to which the Yahwist gives preference against the *hithpael* for this promise, can be translated reflexively ("bless oneself"); but the passive is also possible.

This prophecy in ch. 12.3b reaches far out toward the goal of God's plan for history, but still it refuses any description of this final end.

It is enough that the goal is given as such and that with it is suggested the meaning of the road that God has taken by calling Abraham. This prophecy, which points to a fulfillment lying beyond the old covenant, was especially important to the retrospective glance of the New Testament witnesses. We find it cited in Acts 3.25 f.; Rom. 4.13; Gal. 3.8, 16. For the meaning of Gen. 12.1–3 as the conclusion to the primeval history, see p. 154.

19. ABRAHAM'S DEPARTURE. (J) Ch. 12.4–9

12 4So Abram went, as the LORD had told him; and Lot went with
him. Abram was seventy-five years old when he departed from Haran.
5And Abram took Sarai his wife, and Lot his brother's son, and all
their possessions which they had gathered, and the persons that they
had gotten in Haran; and they set forth to go to the land of Canaan.
When they had come to the land of Canaan, 6Abram passed through
the land to the place at Shechem, to the oak of Moreh. At that time the
Canaanites were in the land. 7Then the LORD appeared to Abram, and
said, "To your descendants I will give this land." So he built there an
altar to the LORD, who had appeared to him. 8Thence he removed to
the mountain on the east of Bethel, and pitched his tent, with Bethel on
the west and Ai on the east; and there he built an altar to the LORD and
called on the name of the Lord. 9And Abram journeyed on, still going
toward the Negeb.

[4–5] The account of Abraham's departure belongs to the Yahwistic source. There is included in it a brief remark from the Priestly document about the same subject (vs. 4b–5).

Abraham obeys blindly and without objection. The one word *wayyēlek* ("and he set out") is more effective than any psychological description could be, and in its majestic simplicity does greater justice to the importance of this event. Abraham remains dumb, "a wonderful trait of absolute obedience when compared with a promise the full importance of which he could scarcely surmise" (Pr.). Here is one of the passages where Abraham becomes a kind of model. Throughout the entire story one must always remember that to leave home and to break ancestral bonds was to expect of ancient men almost the impossible. It is the reader himself who has to say that this departure also represented a "change of faith." The religious aspect of the matter is stressed remarkably little by the Yahwist. Evidently he was not very interested in the religious and cultic differences which distinguished Israelite worship of God from that of her neighbours. It was only at a very late stage that attempts were made to give a psychological motivation to the departure, in terms of Abraham's criticism of the religion of his fathers (Apocalypse of Abraham, chs. 1 ff.; so, too, in a very sophisticated way in Thomas Mann's Joseph trilogy). But the Yahwist understands Abraham here merely as the object of a divine command. Earlier interpreters have wondered about the taking of Lot, whether it was done perhaps against God's will. But the narrator scarcely wants to inspire such thoughts. He knew something about the relationship to Israel of Lot's descendants, the Ammonites and Moabites, who also had entered Palestine in connection with that "Aramean migration" (see p. 142), and he wanted to prepare the way for chs. 13 and 19.

[6–7] Shechem, where Abraham made his first stop, was one of the oldest Canaanite cities, probably mentioned by Pharaoh Sesostris III (1887–1849) (for Shechem, cf. ch. 34). The "terebinth of Moreh" as a sacred tree was the focus of a Canaanite cultic center and still important in Israelite times (Gen. 35.4; Deut. 11.30; Josh. 24.26; Judg. 9.37). How unfree and unsuitable the land was for Abraham is emphasized in v. 6b. All the more strange, therefore, is Yahweh's address that this is the land which would be given to Abraham's descendants (not to him!). At best, says Calvin, does he not have to consider *se haberi ludibrio* to believe this *verbum nudum*? But Abraham builds an altar, the first in the Holy Land, and this altar, not far from the pagan cultic center, was a sign at first still silent, still noncombative, of infinite significance.

[8–9] Moving farther south, Abraham comes to the highland of Benjamin and Judah. Between Bethel and Ai, again two ancient Canaanite settlements (for Bethel, cf. ch. 28), he once more builds an altar and calls "on the name of" Yahweh. That does not mean, as the ancients and even Luther thought, that he preached to the heathen, but rather that in the cult he called on the God who was revealed with his name. Then he moved farther toward the Negeb, i.e., the southern highland, sloping southward between Hebron and Beer-sheba. So Abraham has arrived at his future home.

Strange that the actual destination of the migration is not named! (Even the narrative, ch. 12.10 ff., begins as though with a blank!) The narrator, of course, did not want to anticipate ch. 13.18; but one also sees in this lack of precision regarding local details that ch. 12.1–9 is not derived from an originally independent narrative that was centered in a place, as is almost always the case in the subsequent patriarchal stories. The narrative has too little action and is not concrete enough for that (Gu.). It was, rather, created *ad hoc* by the Yahwist as a transition from the primeval history to the new series of actual Abraham narratives. But just for this reason it is especially important for the exegete because in it the great collector of patriarchal narratives expresses himself programmatically. If one now remembers that Abraham's path up to this point is almost lost in insignificance after the great display of divine promissory words—what great thing did Abraham find in Shechem or later in the south? —then it will once again be clear that this special insertion by the Yahwist does not have meaning in itself but must be related programmatically to the entire composition of Abraham narratives. Indeed, the fulfillment of this promise lies beyond Abraham's own life, and it is scarcely thinkable that the Yahwist considered it as fulfilled in his day (Gu.). (On Gen. 12.1–9, see also pp. 165 f.)

III

THE BIBLICAL PATRIARCHAL HISTORY

THE ANCIENT CREDO of sacred history (see p. 14) touched upon the patriarchal period in only one statement: "A wandering Aramean was my father" (Deut. 26.5). And how powerfully this one statement is unfolded in Gen., chs. 12 to 25! In fact, the story of each patriarch (with the exception of Isaac) is itself filled with suspense because of a great display of divine promises and fulfillments. This expansion of the patriarchal stories into such a surcharged narrative is the product of long work at collecting and even more of superior art in theological composition. One should not think that the many individual traditions about the patriarchal period in circulation came together by themselves into such an artistic and theologically deliberate composition.

This simple fact that the biblical patriarchal history is a deliberate composition made up of many originally independent individual narratives means that the expositor's task is from now on a double one. First he must attempt to explain each individual narrative for itself, because each one contains a relatively compact meaning. But, in addition, he must also occasionally make some remarks about a presumably older form of the narrative in question and comment on its earlier purpose, because that will clarify certain characteristics of its present form. But in this composition the separation of ancient tradition from what was recast by the great collectors (Yahwist, Elohist) is not always possible. In general, one must exercise restraint and not ascribe certain prominent opinions or ideas too readily to the Yahwist. We have reason to suppose that these collectors handled their material very conservatively; we overestimate their freedom in the actual development and accentuation of the old material (see p. 37). So far as we can tell, the narratives came through the ages often with very decisive internal changes in meaning (cf. p. 19) but with surprisingly little external change. Formerly, when they were still cult sagas, was the external form of the narratives Gen. 22.1 ff.; 28.10 ff.; 32.23 ff., different, i.e., with regard to the number of sentences or the vocabulary used, from their present form?

The other task is to understand each narrative as a part of a great thread, and here the exegete comes up against the collector's work. We are not to think of this collecting as an event that was done all at once; here too, numerous previous states must be reckoned with.* But the arrangement which the Yahwist has given the material is so remarkable that we must consider his molding of the transmitted mass of material as a decisive literary event, which claims our whole theological interest (see pp. 16 ff.). For in this matter the collectors were much freer than they were in molding each individual narrative. The sequence they give the narratives, the focuses and climaxes, or the obstructions and even decelerations they give to events of the patriarchal stories have given the entire composition a theological theme, whose quality one must understand each time, because it determines anew the exposition of the individual narrative.

Of special interest are the few narrative paragraphs in which the collector does not give an existing older tradition, but which he creates to unite larger narrative sections to one another. These "transitional paragraphs" serve primarily, of course, to provide a transition and connection between larger cycles of material; but they are much more than external ties, for they give the collector opportunity to articulate theologically programmatic material, which is significant far beyond the scope of the individual verses for understanding the larger whole. One such transitional paragraph is in the prologue to the Flood, ch. 6.5–8 (the last tradition we met with there was Gen. 6.1–4, the next begins with vs. 9 ff.). But the section ch. 12.1–9 must also be considered transitional, for it is easy to see that these verses do not contain an old traditional narrative that had been previously polished. (Every story contains some kind of exciting event for which a number of characters—above all, conflict and solution—are required; this conflict then also becomes somewhat dramatically vivid.) If in this respect the paragraph is conspicuously poor, it is all the richer in programmatic theological substance. For ch. 18.17–33, see pp. 213 ff.

[12.1–9] God's promise to Abraham in vs. 1–3 extends through the

*Noth, *Überlieferungsgeschichte des Pentateuch.*

patriarchal stories like a red line, for it is renewed for every patriarch (cf. chs. 13.14–16; 15.5, 7, 18; 18.10; 22.17; 26.24; 28.3 f., 13–15; 32.12; 35.9–12; 48.16); but never again does the Yahwist let it be pronounced in such full discharge as here. The single formulations certainly derive from the oldest traditions (for the God of the fathers, see pp. 189 f.). Now, however, they are greatly varied by the Yahwist spiritually. Here blessing and curse are no longer a matter for cult and ritual as they were in ancient times; they are meant, rather, in the most general sense as God's gracious, beneficial, or destructive act in the control of history. In the associations of Israel's ancestors with the eastern Aramean neighbors the Yahwist preserves an ancient recollection (cf. Deut. 26.5). But one would greatly misunderstand the substance of ch. 12.1–9 if one were to take it only as the echo of a popular recollection. Rather, we shall grasp the narrator's intention when we consider what signs accompanied the migration which was set in motion by God's command.

The two promises of great posterity and landed property, which are usually coupled in the patriarchal stories, are curiously separated in our paragraph into two temporally distinct events. Apparently the narrator intends to represent Abraham's departure as a paradigmatic test of faith. Abraham started out in complete uncertainty ("for a land that Yahweh would show him"), to learn at his destination—but not before!—that precisely this way into uncertainty was the movement toward a great saving good (v. 7)! But the gates of salvation do not swing open at all with the solemn disclosure that God would give this land to Abraham. Rather, this promise is strangely contiguous to the statement that at that time the Canaanites were dwelling in the land. Abraham is therefore brought by God into a completely unexplained relationship with the Canaanites, and Yahweh does not hurry about solving and explaining this opaque status of ownership as one expects the director of history to do. On the contrary, this relationship derives its point from the altar which is erected within sight of the heathen cultic center. (What manifold political and cultic exigencies of later Israel are already implicit in this contiguity!) There is thus a strange contrast between the superlative promise at the beginning and Abraham's outwardly uneventful road into the south (literally, "wasteland"), because this road appears to lead the recipient of promise into a twilight that begins to limn difficult problems. Surely the Yahwist intends his programmatic transitional paragraph to be read with these thoughts in mind; for he himself in his whole patriarchal history articulates exigencies and temptations into which Abraham is led precisely in his position as the recipient of promise. With shrill dissonance he begins immediately in the first of his Abraham stories (ch. 12.10–20) with this theme.

1. ABRAHAM AND SARAH IN EGYPT. Chs. 12.10 to 13.1

12 [10]Now there was a famine in the land. So Abram went down to
Egypt to sojourn there, for the famine was severe in the land. [11]When he
was about to enter Egypt, he said to Sarai his wife, "I know that you
are a woman beautiful to behold; [12]and when the Egyptians see you,
they will say, 'This is his wife'; then they will kill me, but they will let
you live. [13]Say you are my sister, that it may go well with me because of
you, and that my life may be spared on your account." [14]When Abram
entered Egypt the Egyptians saw that the woman was very beautiful.
[15]And when the princes of Pharaoh saw her, they praised her to Pharaoh.
And the woman was taken into Pharaoh's house. [16]And for her sake he
dealt well with Abram; and he had sheep, oxen, he-asses, menservants,
maidservants, she-asses, and camels.

17 But the LORD afflicted Pharaoh and his house with great plagues
because of Sarai, Abram's wife. [18]So Pharaoh called Abram, and said,
"What is this you have done to me? Why did you not tell me that she
was your wife? [19]Why did you say, 'She is my sister,' so that I took her for
my wife? Now then, here is your wife, take her, and be gone." [20]And
Pharaoh gave men orders concerning him; and they set him on the way,
with his wife and all that he had.

13 [1]So Abram went up from Egypt, he and his wife, and all that he
had, and Lot with him, into the Negeb.

The composition of the Abraham stories begins with a narrative that is offensive and difficult to interpret. The narrative about the jeopardizing and saving of the ancestress occurs three times in the patriarchal tradition, each time, it is true, in a distinct setting (cf. chs. 20; 26). One can conclude from that that the same traditional material was connected with different figures of the past. But this would scarcely have happened, and the narrative would not have been preserved in these different forms if both narrator and reader had not ascribed to it a special significance. It has long been observed that in the context of the Abraham narratives the story is quite loosely rooted at this place. Abraham's road from the north to the south (ch. 12.4–9) and from there to Egypt (v. 10), from Egypt back to Bethel (ch. 13.1–4) and from there again into the south (v. 18), is strange enough. Actually an older, simpler, and clearer narrative sequence comes through faintly here, a sequence which knew nothing of Abraham's excursion into Egypt and in which ch. 13.2 ff. followed directly upon ch. 12.8. The Yahwist then must have had all the more reason for squeezing this block of material into the context here. The narrative itself, by the way, contrasts strangely with its relatively late insertion into the context, for among the three named variants its whole style of representation is by far the most ancient and difficult (cf. pp. 225 f.).

[10] The first event to be reported after the proclamation of the promise and the report of Abraham's journey to Canaan is the incidence of a deadly threat. Famine has again and again in their history forced the inhabitants of Palestine, that is, of its southern region, into the much more fruitful Egypt (cf. chs. 26; 41.54 ff.; 43; 47.4). The Egyptian representation of admittance to begging "Asiatics" who did not know how "they should keep alive" is known from the period ca. 1350 (AOB, XXXIX, 87; AOT, 93 f.). Abraham too "went down" (the narrative, in contrast to what precedes and follows, does not seem to know Lot). **[11–13]** But for all that he is worried, as his engaging remarks to his wife show; for he is afraid that the beauty of his wife (whom we must imagine as still young in contrast to the Priestly chronology, chs. 12.4; 17.1–7) could be his undoing. The husband of so beautiful a woman is in far greater danger abroad than her brother would be. When he persuades Sarah to pass as his sister, we must assume that our narrator also knew the tradition according to which Sarah was Abraham's half sister (ch. 20.12, E). **[14–20]** The narrative vividly describes how accurate Abraham's forecast was. Everything develops as one would expect until God intervenes, not to punish Abraham for his lie and betrayal, but to save Sarah. Abraham is severely reprimanded without the possibility of denial and is whisked out of Egypt under military escort. The swiftness with which the narrative ends after the denouement in v. 17 is striking. How did Pharaoh connect his malady with Sarah's presence in his harem? Did the malady then leave him? The narrative gives no answer to these and other more difficult questions. Apparently all details became unimportant after God's intervention. Thus the story, which began so humanly and understandably, brings us at its end terribly face to face with the darkness and mystery of Yahweh's power, for which no explanation is adequate.

In three respects and in exemplary fashion our narrative teaches the interpreter a lesson. First of all, it provides an extreme example of how little suggestion most of the patriarchal stories give the reader for any authoritative explanation and assessment of any occurrence. One will agree that Abraham's embarrassed silence shows that the author really recognizes Pharaoh's relative right (Gu.), and it is possible that one may detect the narrator's sarcasm, particularly in Abraham's speech in v. 12 (Pr.). But that is little enough. The event can be interpreted either very trivially or very profoundly. How does the interpreter proceed? Some have thought that the narrative makes few claims on its hearers; it extols the beauty of the ancestress and the sagacity of the ancestor who knew how to extricate himself so successfully from so precarious a situation with the help of his God (Gu.). The possibility of this interpretation cannot be dismissed out of hand, when we think of a much older version than the one we have here. Gunkel has already emphasized the fact that the cheerful, almost droll mood of the narrative is softened greatly by its connection with the pious statement about departure. One must, indeed, say that this spirit is now gone from it because of its combination with the composition as a whole. Thus the narrative is an example in the second place of how the collectors occasionally give meaning to a narrative from the overlapping whole. They do not see merely single stories which contain their own meaning, but they see a great divine event with the patriarchs, and there, if anywhere, is where one finds their interpretation. If the great promise, ch. 12.1–3, deserves the programmatic significance that we see in it, then these words overarch the story too! One must remember that the jeopardizing of the ancestress called into question everything that Yahweh had promised to do for Abraham. But Yahweh does not allow his work to miscarry right at the start; he rescues it and preserves it beyond all human failure. The narrative is thus, in the third place, an example of the fact that one must always discern the chief thing in God's action. Here the narrative is one-sidedly concentrated on that, and we have difficulty in following it because the moral problem of Abraham's guilt worries us. Was the departure from Canaan already an act of unbelief in the sense of the narrative? Perhaps so. But what concerns us most is the betrayal of the ancestress, and one must not exactly restrain one's thoughts if they recognize in the bearer of promise himself the greatest enemy of the promise; for its greatest threat comes from him. But though the narrative provokes these or similar reflections, they remain relatively secondary in the presence of Yahweh's activity. And our determination to understand is limited by Yahweh's power and mystery. The interpreter has to know about this limitation. Whoever said that everything here must or could be satisfactorily explained? The fact of the event is incomparably more important to our narrator than its manner of occurrence and all its possible interpretations. That this material is varied in three forms in the patriarchal history shows that Israel reflected on this saving intervention by God with special interest. If Yahweh did not go astray in his work of sacred history because of the failure and guilt of the recipient of promise, then his word was really to be believed. (A comparison of our narrative with that of Gen., ch. 20, is instructive; cf. pp. 225 ff.)

2. THE SEPARATION FROM LOT. Ch. 13.2–18

13 [2]Now Abram was very rich in cattle, in silver, and in gold. [3]And
he journeyed on from the Negeb as far as Bethel, to the place where his
tent had been at the beginning, between Bethel and Ai, [4]to the place
where he had made an altar; and there Abram called on the name of
the LORD. [5]And Lot, who went with Abram, also had flocks and herds
and tents, [6]*so that the land could not support both of them dwelling together; for
their possessions were so great that they could not dwell together*, [7]and there was
strife between the herdsmen of Abram's cattle and the herdsmen of Lot's
cattle. At that time the Canaanites and the Perizzites dwelt in the land.
8 Then Abram said to Lot, "Let there be no strife between you and
me, and between your herdsmen and my herdsmen; for we are kinsmen.
[9]Is not the whole land before you? Separate yourself from me. If
you take the left hand, then I will go to the right; or if you take the right
hand, then I will go to the left." [10]And Lot lifted up his eyes, and saw
that the Jordan valley was well watered everywhere like the garden of
the LORD, like the land of Egypt in the direction of Zoar; this was
before the LORD destroyed Sodom and Gomorrah. [11]So Lot chose for
himself all the Jordan valley, and Lot journeyed east; *thus they separated
from each other*. [12]*Abram dwelt in the land of Canaan, while Lot dwelt among the
cities of the valley* and moved his tent as far as Sodom. [13]Now the men of
Sodom were wicked, great sinners against the LORD.
14 The LORD said to Abram, after Lot had separated from him,
"Lift up your eyes, and look from the place where you are, northward
and southward and eastward and westward; [15]for all the land which
you see I will give to you and to your descendants for ever. [16]I will make
your descendants as the dust of the earth; so that if one can count the
dust of the earth, your descendants also can be counted. [17]Arise, walk
through the length and the breadth of the land, for I will give it to you."
[18]So Abram moved his tent, and came and dwelt by the oaks of Mamre,
which are at Hebron; and there he built an altar to the LORD.

[2–7] Abraham has returned to the region of Bethel. (Regarding the hypothesis that the narrative ch. 12.10–20 was only later incorporated into the Abraham story and the complication of Abraham's route which thus came about, see above, pp. 167 f.) To understand the outward life and nature of the patriarchs it is extremely important that they not be delineated from the narratives as actual Bedouins, i.e., as nomads on camels like the Midianites or Amalekites, for example (Judg. 3.13; 6.3, 7, 33 ff.). They were, rather, nomads with small cattle, who regularly sought out tilled areas with absolutely peaceful intention in order to let their herds graze during the summer on the already harvested fields, according to amicable agreement with the permanent population. Their movements between the steppe and the sown, therefore, are determined by the law of the so-called "change of pasture." In contrast to the nomads on camels they are completely unwarlike, a feature which of course is conditioned by the slowness of their large flocks of goats and sheep. A degree of settledness is not at all incompatible with their nomadic existence. Cities do attract them, but not to settle in them by force, which would at once compel them to give up their nomadic life as shepherds; but they attract them rather because of their character as cultural centers—primarily therefore for reasons of commerce and connubium (cf. Gen., chs. 20; 26; 34; etc.).* The reader must connect Abraham's great wealth with the increase that he received in Egypt. The difficulties of keeping together two greatly increased herds are not hard to understand. For subsistence, one herd requires a rather large radius for movement in the harvested fields of the resident farmers in addition to being dependent on the few valuable watering places. The collision of interests in the mountainous region of Benjamin—in other districts other nomads with small cattle may have had their use of pasture—and the proposal to separate with reference to the pasture available is therefore quite true to life. **[8–13]** Abraham was the first to feel the unworthiness of such strife between men of the same clan, and, although he is the older, he intends to abide by Lot's prior choice. The narrative here shows Abraham in the best light. It is one of the few passages in the patriarchal history where the figure of the patriarch is also intended by the narrator to be exemplary (cf. also chs. 15.1–6; 22.1 ff.). The contrast which this picture of Abraham makes with that of the previous story is great, but the Yahwist was not acquainted with the demand for a unified psychological penetration, a psychologically credible portrayal. The traditions he used were varied in this respect and were not, of course, harmonized with one another. Verse 10

*A. Alt, "The Settlement of the Israelites in Palestine," *Essays in Old Testament History and Religion*, 1966, 133 ff.

depicts simply a wonderful scene. Lot has considered the proposal, and now he "lifts up his eyes" to the commanding view. (The narrator exposes the inner psychological process of reflection and decision completely in this outward attitude of gazing, where indeed it does take place.) From Bethel one sees the entire Jordan valley as far as the southern tip of the Dead Sea where Zoar lay (cf. ch. 19.20, 22). Here and there, especially in the vicinity of Jericho, it is still richly watered even today; but the narrator considers it all before the catastrophe of Sodom to have been "like the garden of the Lord." (The twofold comparison with Paradise and with Egypt sounds surprisingly worldly and enlightened. Compare pp. 17, 29.) Lot, therefore, chooses quickly. Striking for our usually reticent narrator are the strong superlatives used to describe the beauty of the land and the wickedness of its inhabitants, as well as the broad ceremoniousness with which the fascinating impression and then the making of the decision are painted (four verses!). But the narrator wants to make a strong impression here. The unheard of beauty of the land—a fruitful land is beautiful to Palestinians—and the unheard of depravity of its inhabitants! And how quickly and naturally the man on the heights of Bethel made his choice! And afterward—as though drawn by the city—how step by step he approached the city of profound depravity! "Jordan valley" is a technical geographical term (I Kings 7.46; Deut. 34.3, "the valley").

The narrative is the first of the Lot stories which are now significantly parallel to the Abraham stories. The intent to contrast the two in the juxtaposition of ch. 13.1–13 and vs. 14–18 is unmistakable. But at the same time our narrative serves as a kind of commentary on the following Lot stories (ch. 19.1–29). Lot escapes from Sodom; Lot settles in Zoar, moves from there into the mountains and begets Ammon and Moab (vs. 30–38). Though the units of ch. 19 are very old and were combined relatively late into a larger story, there is no original independent tradition behind ch. 13.1–10. The narrative is fictional and presupposes a connected story of Lot's fate. (For the story of Lot, cf. pp. 224 f.)

[14–17] Some exegetes, following Wellhausen, have considered the following paragraph, vs. 14–17, as a later addition. What is correct in this is only the observation that the Yahwist did not find this divine address to Abraham in the ancient tradition about Lot (see above), but that he here expanded the old traditional material according to this special theme. (Seams that occur in the coupling of different traditions are not always to be explained literarily as signs of various "authors." Compare p. 74.) There is no need for considering the contrast between vs. 1–13 and vs. 14–17 as the unwilled result of "one who put them together." Rather, here the narrative as a whole (vs. 1–17) reaches its climax. Abraham is now alone, but Yahweh comes to him; and while Lot took the land that pleased him, God now says, "I will give it to you." The summons in v. 17 originally belongs in the sphere of legal proceedings, as what is done is a symbolic legal act by which the occupation of land is recognized in law.* Abraham chooses the south and settles by the terebinths of Mamre. Mamre has been fairly well identified with modern Râmet el-Khalîl, somewhat north (two miles) of Hebron. The cultic area was excavated in 1926–1927 by P. Mader. Among the ruins were remains of a Christian basilica from the time of Constantine, surrounded by a massive rectangular wall (Temenos, 130 feet by 195 feet) of Roman stone, in which was an Arabian layout for a pool. Below that were Israelite sherds and traces of Bronze Age (thus pre-Israelite) settlement (*Oriens Christianus*, 1927, 333 ff.; 1928, 360 ff.). This shrine, therefore, because of its reputation and its immense sacred tradition has been a cultic attraction in Canaanite, Israelite, Roman, Byzantine, and Arab times. The shrine existed as such, according to the ancient cultic legend of Mamre, Gen., ch. 18 (see pp. 198 ff.), prior to the Israelite-Canaanite period, while later Israel believed it was founded by Abraham. Hebron, however, was Calebite in the Israelite period (Num. 13.22; Judg. 1.20) and lay outside the later kingdom of Judah. The name Mamre is possibly non-Semitic.

The church historian Sozomen, himself a Palestinian (fifth century), describes vividly how the shrine in the early Christian era attracted to its festivals a motley throng from the immediate vicinity: (Herodian) hewn stone, in which was an Arabian layout for a pool. Below that were Israelite sherds and traces of Bronze Age (thus pre-Israelite) settlements (*Oriens Christianus*, 1927, 333 ff.; 1928, 360 ff.). This shrine, therefore, because of its reputation and its immense sacred tradition has been a cultic attraction in Canaanite, Israelite, Roman, Byzantine, and Arab times. The shrine existed as such, according to the ancient cultic legend of Mamre, Gen., ch. 18 (see pp. 203 ff.), prior to the Israelite-Canaanite period, while later Israel believed it was founded by Abraham. Hebron, however, was Calebite in the Israelite period (Num. 13.22; Judg. 1.20) and lay outside the later kingdom of Judah. The name Mamre is possibly non-Semitic.

*H. Daube, *Studies in Biblical Law*, 1947, 37 f.

appeared there to a devout man. Each one reveres this spot according to his cult and his religion. This place is under the open sky."

The immediate continuation of our narrative was originally ch. 15. Chapter 14 was inserted into the composition by a later hand.

3. ABRAHAM'S VICTORY OVER THE EASTERN KINGS AND HIS ENCOUNTER WITH MELCHIZEDEK. Ch. 14

14 1 In the days of Amraphel king of Shinar, Arioch king of Ellasar,
Ched-or-laomer king of Elam, and Tidal king of Goiim, 2 these kings
made war with Beara king of Sodom, Birsha king of Gomorrah, Shinab
king of Admah, Shemeber king of Zeboiim, and the king of Bela (that
is, Zoar). 3 And all these joined forces in the valley of Siddim (that is,
the Salt Sea). 4 Twelve years they had served Ched-or-laomer, but in
the thirteenth year they rebelled. 5 In the fourteenth year Ched-or-
laomer and the kings who were with him came and subdued the
Rephaim in Ashteroth-karnaim, the Zuzim in Ham, the Emim in
Shaveh-kiriathaim, 6 and the Horites in their Mount Seir as far as
El-paran on the border of the wilderness; 7 then they turned back and
came to Enmishpat (that is, Kadesh), and subdued all the country of
the Amalekites, and also the Amorites who dwelt in Hazazon-tamar.
8 Then the king of Sodom, the king of Gomorrah, the king of Admah,
the king of Zeboiim, and the king of Bela (that is, Zoar) went out, and
they joined battle in the Valley of Siddim 9 with Ched-or-laomer king
of Elam, Tidal king of Goiim, Amraphel king of Shinar, and Arioch
king of Ellasar, four kinds against five. 10 Now the Valley of Siddim was
full of bitumen pits; and as the kings of Sodom and Gomorrah fled,
some fell into them, and the rest fled to the mountain. 11 So the enemy
took all the goods of Sodom and Gomorrah, and all their provisions,
and went their way; 12 they also took Lot, the son of Abram's brother,
who dwelt in Sodom, and his goods, and departed.

13 Then one who had escaped came, and told Abram the Hebrew,
who was living by the oaks of Mamre the Amorite, brother of Eshcol
and of Aner; these were allies of Abram. 14 When Abram heard that his
kinsman had been taken captive, he led forth his trained men, born in
his house, three hundred and eighteen of them, and went in pursuit as
far as Dan. 15 And he divided his forces against them by night, he and his
servants, and routed them and pursued them to Hobah, north of
Damascus. 16 Then he brought back all the goods, and also brought back
his kinsman Lot with his goods, and the women and the people.

17 After his return from the defeat of Ched-or-laomer and the kings
who were with him, the king of Sodom went out to meet him at the
Valley of Shaveh (that is, the King's Valley). 18 And Melchizedek king
of Salem brought out bread and wine; he was priest of God Most High.
19 And he blessed him and said,

"Blessed be Abram by God Most High,
maker of heaven and earth;

[20]and blessed be God Most High,
who has delivered your enemies into your hand!"
And Abram gave him a tenth of everything. [21]And the king of Sodom
said to Abram, "Give me the persons, but take the goods for yourself."
[22]But Abram said to the king of Sodom, "I have sworn to the LORD
God Most High, maker of heaven and earth, [23]that I would not take a
thread or a sandal-thong or anything that is yours, lest you should say,
'I have made Abram rich.' [24]I will take nothing but what the young
men have eaten, and the share of the men who went with me; let Aner,
Eshcol, and Mamre take their share."

This chapter contains some of the most difficult and most debated material in the patriarchal history, indeed, in the entire historical part of the Old Testament. First of all, its substance differs from that of all the patriarchal stories. It takes us out into world history, tells of a coalition of empires, a war against another coalition, and it involves Abraham in this international incident. The picture, accordingly, which it gives of Abraham as a "traveling prince of war" is quite different from that of the other Abraham narratives. But the tradition in ch. 14 must be estimated quite differently with respect to its form, i.e., "*gattungsgeschichtlich*." The events are not told with the usual vividness but are reported like a chronicle. Almost every sentence is full of antiquarian information, and nowhere in the patriarchal stories do we find such a mass of historical and geographical detail. Recent study of the ancient Near East has shown that much of this material must derive from very ancient tradition. On the other hand, however, it must be emphasized that none of the patriarchal stories contains so much that is fantastic, historically impossible, and miraculous. Gunkel's statement is as true today as it was fifty years ago: "The narrative contains in blatant contrast very credible and quite impossible material." We are dealing, therefore, with tradition which was quite separate from the rest of the patriarchal tradition. Chapter 14 is a "world in itself" (L. Köhler). No wonder that this chapter cannot be connected with one of the Hexateuchal sources! It is substantially, generically, and literarily completely isolated and was apparently first incorporated into its present context by a redactor (though this, of course, gives no indication of the age of the material). The exposition, therefore, is methodically directed to this chapter alone. Any hasty combination with the historical view or chronology of the other Hexateuchal sources can only cause great confusion. Space forbids a more extensive discussion of some of the difficult points.

[1-4] The syntactically circumstantial beginning in v. 1 corresponds to the style of ancient cuneiform chronicles (but cf. Isa., ch. 7; Esth. 1.1). The identification of Amraphel with the famous Babylonian king and lawgiver Hammurabi, an identification once popular, is philologically untenable. ("Shinar" in Old Testament usage, and Egyptian too, by the way, is simply a word for Babylonia. Chs. 10.10; 11.2.) A figure with this name is not known to us outside the Bible. On the other hand, the name Arioch, until recently very doubtful, has been connected with Arriwuku, a person known to us from the archive of the North Syrian city Mari (on the upper Euphrates). If this connection is correct, we should have to do with the son of Zimrilim, King of Mari and a contemporary of the great Hammurabi (1728–1686). But this identification is not at all conclusive, for the identification of Ellasar with the south Babylonian city Larsa would then have to be given up. The name Chedorlaomer is good Elamite ("slave of Lagamer," an Elamite divinity). There could well have been an Elamite king of this name. Nevertheless, the difficulties here are very great, for it seems impossible to imagine Elam, east of Babylon, north of the Persian Gulf, as powerful at that time, indeed, at the head of such a coalition (v. 5) and furthermore operating strategically in southern Palestine. Tidal cannot be disassociated from the Hittite Tudhalia, probably Tudhalia I (ca. 1730 B.C.). But why is he called "king of the nations"? Of the four chief kings, therefore, only two at best are identifiable. Accordingly, the event must be placed in the beginning of the seventeenth century at the latest. We have no possibility at all for identifying the names of the Canaanite city-kings. (The absence of the fifth king's name has been considered a sign of historical reliability, because an inventive narrator would not have been at a loss for a name here.) Their cities, according to the conception of the report, lay close together in the region of the modern Dead Sea (cf. Deut. 29.23). That the destruction of these cities is connected with the origin of the Dead Sea (as v. 3b indicates) is quite impossible geologically. Yet when one considers the great fluctuations in the water level of the Dead Sea, it is possible that agricultural land to the south of the sea might at one time have been considerably more extensive; for the southern part of the Dead Sea is very shallow even today. (Dalman, *Palästinajahrbuch*, 1908, 77 ff.) Moreover, the ancient history of Syria-Palestine is filled with reports of coalitions of small states and cities against the empires in the northeast. As against those, however, the report of a coalition in such a small district against enemies so far away, to whom in fact those cities are said to have been tributary, sounds quite legendary.

[5–7] The route of the Eastern kings on their punitive expedition is especially strange. It does not advance toward the rebels but goes to the extreme south of East Jordan, returning from there to Kadesh —sixty miles south of the Dead Sea! And then finally it moves in a direction from south to north to the region of the Dead Sea where the Canaanites had long expected them for battle. One can assume perhaps that the Eastern kings went forth not only to punish the city-kings (even though the story represents it that way), but also to see to the security of the highly important trade route to the Red Sea and thence to Egypt and South Arabia (Albright). Actually they are engaged first in the defeat of the eastern and southeastern Palestinian "peoples." So far as the names in vs. 5–6 are concerned, one must again be skeptical about whether the report presents here any that are historically reliable, rather than working vaguely with the traditional names of a quite legendary original population of Palestine. For the Rephaim, cf. Deut. 2.11, 20; 3.11, 13; for the Emim, cf. Deut. 2.10 f.; the Zuzim are perhaps to be identified with the Zamzummim. The Emim are a people who had settled in the south of East Jordan before the Moabites. Colonized originally in the west, they migrated eastward. Their script was related to one in use in Crete (Alt, *Palästinajahrbuch*, 1940, 29 ff.). The Horites were a Mesopotamian people of the second millennium, living on the upper Tigris. But a Horite ruling class had also invaded the Syria-Palestine area, and thus the name "Horite" became a general term in Israelite literature for the original population of Palestine. (See the parallel process for the designation "Hittites," ch. 23.) The cities mentioned in v. 5 have all been identified in the land east of the Jordan. The mention of Amalekites in the south is incontestable, but not so that of the Amorites, who are usually understood in the Old Testament to be much farther north (Num. 21.21 ff.; Judg. 1.34 f.). The multiplication of these names gives the impression of a learned necessity rather than of a direct literary expression of historical events. **[8–11]** Also the way in which the allied Canaanite cities permit the enemy attack without doing anything about it is extremely strange. "Four kings against five" (v. 9b) is a real international battle as the narrative presents it. The Canaanite defeat is particularly dramatic because of the unfavorable lay of the land, for those in flight fell into the asphalt pits which were everywhere about. One doubts, however, that this was reported with humor (Jac.). The austere style of the narrative would not allow for such relaxation.

[12–16] Here, finally, this great political event dovetails with the patriarchal history. The victorious kings, of course, plundered the cities of the defeated, and in this manner Lot, who lived in Sodom, was taken captive. Abraham goes after them with his warriors, overtakes them at Dan, and pursues them north of Damascus! This victory of 318 men against the allied armies of the Eastern kings is the most wonderful event in a story so filled with marvels. The Hebrew word for Abraham's men (*ḥānīk*) occurs only here, and the translation "he led forth" (*ryq*, *Hiph*, "to empty," the quiver?) is also uncertain. The use of the long-known place name (Mamre) as a personal name is surely the product of an erudition which dabbles in antiquities. The mention of Dan is, in addition, a crude anachronism, for the place was called Laish in pre-Israelite times (Judg. 18.29).

It took a curiously long time for the narrative finally to reach its chief character, Abraham. It does not mention him at the beginning, as all Abraham stories do, nor at the climax of the action, but at the end, when the Eastern kings, after their victory, are already moving through northern Palestine on their way home. A second curious fact is that after the narrative has mentioned Abraham it immediately presses toward a different climax, namely, the encounter with Melchizedek. This second part, as we will see at once, was originally to be understood aetiologically, and therefore as a narrative it has a quite different generic character and purpose from the preceding war story. This suggests that our chapter is composed of two parts quite distinct from each other as to origin and nature, and it becomes certain, in our opinion, when one examines closely the seam between v. 11 and v. 12. Verse 11 speaks of captured booty and the departure of the Eastern kings; v. 12, however, with its repeated "they took," returns to the plundering, after the preceding verse has already mentioned the departure, obviously in order to add Lot's abduction and so connect the occurrence with Abraham. Before v. 12, therefore, a break occurs at which the narratives separate. The first one about the war of the Eastern kings against the Canaanites was not previously an Abraham story. One can scarcely consider it as a historical document, strictly speaking. One should think of it rather as an ancient epic or a part of one, i.e., one should still consider it a tradition from the pre-Israelite period, which lay, perhaps in cuneiform, in the archives of a Palestinian city. That this epic (fragment) knew of and mentioned

Abraham is, as we said, not to be assumed. Only through its fusion with the Melchizedek story was Abraham incorporated into the first narrative, or better, into its margin. As the whole narrative now stands, in view of many traces of an artificially archaizing erudition, one must consider it a rather late literary product, in spite of the great antiquity of isolated traditional elements. One such artificial element is the designation of Abraham as a "Hebrew." "Hebrew" in ancient times was not a national designation, but rather a frequent designation in the second millennium in many lands for a lower class of society. In the Old Testament the expression is used by non-Israelites or Israelites for foreigners. It is used as a general designation for a people only here and in a likewise literarily late text (Jonah 1.9). For more on the problem of the "Hebrews" see p. 366.

[17–20] The conclusion and climax of the present total narrative is Abraham's encounter with Melchizedek. And yet this Melchizedek scene itself (vs. 18–20), as one can easily see, is again inserted into the narrative of Abraham's encounter with the king of Sodom (vs. 17, 21–24), so that the literary history of this chapter should probably be described as even more complicated. The place for both encounters is conjectured to be a valley near Jerusalem (II Sam. 18.18). The name "Melchizedek" occurs only once more in the Old Testament, in Ps. 110.4. "Salem" is, of course, equivalent to Jerusalem. One must assume, then, that the full name of the city was intentionally avoided because it was too closely associated with the specific ideas of faith of a later period. Salem too, therefore, is an artificial name. Jerome did think of a Salem south of Skythopolis (Beisān); others have mentioned a Salem east of Shechem. Since, however, Ps. 110 connects the Melchizedek tradition with the Davidic throne and since Ps. 76.2 uses the name Salem for Jerusalem, one must here hold to the identification with Jerusalem. The supposition of a pre-Israelite city-king of Jerusalem does not cause the least difficulty since the discovery of the correspondence between the Syro-Palestinian city-kings and the Pharaoh during the fourteenth century B.C. In it were discovered letters from a prince of Jerusalem. The name Melchizedek is certainly old-Canaanite (cf. Adonizedek, Josh. 10.1). The combination of both offices, priest and king, in one person was not unusual in the ancient Near East (e.g., in Phoenicia). The report of a cult of the "highest God" (*'ēl 'elyōn*) has been surprisingly confirmed from extra-biblical testimony. Indeed, there is some support for the view that the cult of this *'ēl 'elyōn* was practiced in ancient Canaanite Jerusalem, before Israelite times. The "highest God" was the monarchic head of a pantheon whose diversity we have only learned to know from the mythological texts found in Ras Shamra. What is most strange, however, is that our narrative perceived in the cult of this god something related to the cult of Yahweh. Melchizedek, in his veneration of "God Most High, maker of heaven and earth," came close to believing in the one God of the world, whom Israel alone knew. This is surely the sense of the passage. Indeed Abraham's oath, "to Yahweh, God Most High" (v. 22), seems to presuppose an identification of Yahweh with the "highest God." But precisely this "Yahweh" is significantly uncertain textually. The LXX does not have it; other texts have the more neutral and the theologically less risky "God" (*hā'ᵉlōhīm*). Such a positive, tolerant evaluation of a Canaanite cult outside Israel is unparalleled in the Old Testament. Above all, Abraham's homage to a heathen servant of the cult is quite unusual from the standpoint of the Old Testament faith in Yahweh. The initiative came from Melchizedek. He honors the returning victor with a meal and gives Abraham the benediction of his god. He considers, therefore, full of presentiments, that the "highest God" helped Abraham to victory; and he knows nothing about the plans and secrets of Israel's God. But Abraham submits to this benediction and gives Melchizedek a tenth, which implies the recognition of a proprietary claim, a sovereign right. (There is a minor inconsistency in the fact that in vs. 22 ff. Abraham denies any claim to the booty; it arose apparently by the coalescence of the varied materials.)

The Melchizedek incident has been variously interpreted. It appears simply as an event, but one must nevertheless assume that it is spoken with special purpose for future readers. If it were really an ancient tradition, one would have to consider it an explanation and legitimation of some ancient contractual relationship existing between Israel and a Canaanite city-king (cf. chs. 21.22 ff., 32; 26.26–33). But it is not at all certain, not even probable, that this part of the narrative derives from such early times. It is much more likely that it attempts to connect Abraham with the location of the Davidic throne, the existence of which the narrative takes for granted; for Melchizedek, according to the sacred courtly view, was the type, i.e., the prototype and precursor of the Davidic dynasty (Ps. 110). In the insistence of our narrative that Abraham gave him a tithe we see Abraham bowing before the one who is holding the place for the future anointed one. But one must assume that our paragraph has an even more relevant point. We know about the rift between Jerusalem, city of the court and the Temple, and the patriarchally faithful country population with whom Yahweh's anointed in Jerusalem did not ingratiate himself, and who were, moreover, very reserved because of the material burdens and taxes that originated with him (cf. I Sam. 8.11 f.). It is probable, therefore, that the narrative is directed to observant circles of the liberty-minded population in Judah, for whom it would be hard to submit to the king of once heathen Jerusalem, and who considered their patriarchal and tribal organization as ordained by God. Chapter 14 is against this attitude. Abraham, although he had not compromised himself with any stranger about anything, still bowed to Melchizedek and gave him a tithe. And this Melchizedek was close to the later Israelite faith in Yahweh. Therefore the later Israelites and Judeans have every reason to submit to Yahweh's anointed and to give him the tenth. However that may be, the most important thing is that Abraham received the blessing of the precursor to David and the Davidic dynasty, that even Abraham had recognized his duty toward Jerusalem and its king. Obviously our chapter, through Melchizedek's blessing and his own tithe, makes Abraham mysteriously open to that salvation which God would later unite with David's throne in Nathan's prophecy. Abraham bows only to Melchizedek, in a story so full of kings. It is true, Melchizedek steps out of a remarkable incognito like a stranger, and from his mouth come the only sacred words spoken at all in this narrative (Hellbardt). **[21–24]** The business with the king of Sodom, of course (is he still alive after v. 10?), contrasts most sharply with this solemnity. Abraham rejects with dignity the insinuation that he intended to grow rich on a stranger's property. But when he gives the overbearing king what he asks, this proud nobility is quite the opposite of his humble tithing.

4. GOD'S PROMISE AND COVENANT WITH ABRAHAM. Ch. 15

15 [1]After these things the word of the LORD came to Abram in a
vision, "Fear not, Abram, I am your shield; your reward shall be very
great." [2]But Abram said, "O Lord GOD, what wilt thou give me, for I
continue childless . . .?" [3]And Abram said, "Behold, thou hast given me
no offspring; and a slave born in my house will be my heir." [4]And behold, the word of the LORD came to him, "This man shall not be your

heir; your own son shall be your heir." 5And he brought him outside
and said, "Look toward heaven, and number the stars, if you are able
to number them." Then he said to him, "So shall your descendants be."
6And he believed the LORD; and he reckoned it to him as righteousness.
7 And he said to him, "I am the LORD who brought you from Ur of
the Chaldeans, to give you this land to possess." 8But he said, "O Lord
GOD, how am I to know that I shall possess it?" 9He said to him,
"Bring me a heifer three years old, a she-goat three years old, a ram
three years old, a turtledove, and a young pigeon." 10And he brought
him all these, cut them in two, and laid each half over against the other;
but he did not cut the birds in two. 11And when birds of prey came down
upon the carcasses, Abram drove them away.
12 As the sun was going down, a deep sleep fell on Abram; and lo, a
dread and great darkness fell upon him. 13Then the LORD said to
Abram, "Know of a surety that your descendants will be sojourners in
a land that is not theirs, and will be slaves there, and they will be op-
pressed for four hundred years; 14but I will bring judgment on the
nation which they serve, and afterward they shall come out with great
possessions. 15As for yourself, you shall go to your fathers in peace; you
shall be buried in a good old age. 16And they shall come back here in the
fourth generation; for the iniquity of the Amorites is not yet complete."
17 When the sun had gone down and it was dark, behold, a smoking
fire pot and a flaming torch passed between these pieces. 18On that day
the LORD made a covenant with Abram, saying, "To your descendants
I give this land, from the river of Egypt to the great river, the river
Euphrates, 19the land of the Kenites, the Kenizzites, the Kadmonites,
20the Hittites, the Perizzites, the Rephaim, 21the Amorites, the
Canaanites, the Girgashites and the Jebusites."

The source analysis of the text of this chapter is very difficult. It is only certain that the "chief joint" in a text filled with joints occurs between v. 6 and v. 7 (Wellhausen), for we have to do with two narratives. There are too many contradictions in the chapter for one to think of it as an organic narrative unit (v. 5, night, v. 12, evening, v. 6, Abraham's faith, v. 8, his doubt which God helps to dispel with a real guarantee, etc.). If one must designate the section vs. 7–18, except for the long interpolation vs. 13–16, as genuinely Yahwistic, the view of classical source criticism, that vs. 1–6 mark the beginning of the Elohist source document, becomes very uncertain. The narrative—which is lacking in events—is essentially built up from forms of discourse which unquestionably derive from the sphere of the cult (God's presentation of himself, the oracle of salvation, the declaration of righteousness).* But whether it was the Elohist who composed an

*O. Kaiser, "Traditionsgeschichtliche Untersuchung von Gen. 15," ZAW, 1958, 107–18.

Abraham narrative in so unusual a way is very questionable. Even within the first part of the narrative there are many strange doublets and breaks; evidently the text has been worked over (v. 3 is parallel to v. 2, v. 5 probably to v. 4). We have given the text in its present form (a satisfactory source analysis seems absolutely impossible); but the variations in the narratives before and after the chief joint will occupy us in the theology of our interpretation.

[1] The formula "the word of Yahweh came" is foreign to the Hexateuch and frequent in the prophetic literature. The narrator and the circle in which this tradition was alive could only imagine God's communication with Abraham as a kind of prophetic call, mediated by a "vision" and a prophetic experience of authorization (cf. ch. 20.7). Apart from Balaam's vision (Num. 24.4, 16) there is nothing in the Hexateuch otherwise about visions. (A magnificent description of a vision at night—for in view of v. 5 such a vision must be meant here—which was received in intensified wakefulness with attending psychical circumstances, occurs in Job 4.12–16.) A direct address from God like this meant far more to the ancients than modern piety can imagine; it was extremely alarming. Abraham, however, was not to yield to this primitive readiness to fright before God (cf. Gen. 21.17; 26.24; 46.2–3; etc.). The metaphor of God as "shield" derives from the language of cult (cf. Ps. 3.3; 28.7; 33.20). In the stock of patriarchal promises that occur again and again, this expression too occurs only here. The word that Luther translated "reward" usually means "profit", but it is used in later literature in the religious sense for God's free gift (Isa. 40.10; 62.11; Jer. 31.16). Alternatively it is to be understood as the obedience displayed in the departure of Abraham, but in the sense of a divine *quid pro quo*, for in the course of the narrative Abraham's testing comes first, on the heels of this promise which is uttered in superlatives but defies at first any concrete realization. The gift is not really God himself, as Luther translated freely, but first of all the innumerable posterity (v. 5). But the outspoken programmatic statement must have caused later readers to think of every act and good thing of salvation of which Israel was ever conscious.

[2–5] Abraham demurs resignedly. His despondent scepticism in the face of the assurance of divine protection and the exceptionally great divine gift borders almost on blasphemy; and yet it contains a timorous reference to the real subject of his anxiety, his childlessness. The conclusion to v. 2 is absolutely untranslatable (we do not know the meaning of *mšk*, and *dammeśek* cannot be translated "the Damascene"). Probably Abraham refers to his servant Eliezer (the name, however, occurs only here in this mutilated sentence), who will inherit him in default of his own son. Israel does not know a general rule like this for regulating the inheritance. But in the so-called Nuzi texts (fifteenth century B.C., east of the Tigris) there are several contracts, according to which in the event of childlessness slaves were adopted; their duty then was to give the testator proper burial. Abraham appears to have known of such a regulation or to think of it now (v. 3). Whether *hōlēk* in v. 2 can be translated "go forth" in the sense of dying is not quite certain, since the verb is used alone in Hebrew only in the sense of "going." If one now remembers that we have here the beginning of the Elohist's narrative, the suggestion is appealing that the place in the original version where this conversation took place was Mesopotamia. (An exact parallel to ch. 12.1–3!) The meaning of Abraham's objection would then be: I am setting out childless (Galling). Verse 3 repeats the same thought, apparently from another source (in the repetitious beginning of Abraham's speech). Abraham, who up until now has lain in his tent, is to go out into the open and look at the innumerable stars as an indication of his innumerable descendants. This demand of God's does not mean at all an amelioration or accommodation for the despondent Abraham (as, for example, the visibleness of the ceremony of covenant-making in vs. 9 ff. does). On the contrary! When God makes the intangible promise of v. 1b vivid and graphic, he only increases the paradox. At this exciting moment, strangely enough, the actual narrative breaks off. **[6]** The narrator leaves the stargazing man, so to speak, and turns to the reader, to whom he communicates theological opinions of great theological compactness, without describing the actual occurrence upon which these opinions are founded, either in the case of Abraham or in the case of Yahweh. When one attempts to comprehend in any way—psychologically, for example—what the narrator designates in sum as perfect "faith," the text refuses any concrete possibility. It appears to concern something that cannot be described. This belief is not described but only asserted. Approached from without, this concealed event of believing is rather negative; it is muteness —silent listening and looking.

Excursus. Three terms in v. 6 require brief discussion: "reckoned," "righteousness," and "believed." *Imputing* was originally, as Lev. 7.18; 17.4 or Num. 18.27 show, an important judging function of the priests, whereby they, as those authorized by God, had to approve the offering that was presented. In the Priestly document we have a large number of such declaratory formulas which express the result of such priestly judgment and in which findings were then communicated to the worshipper concerned (cf., e.g., Lev. 13.17, 23, 28, 37, 44, 46). *Righteousness* is not an ideal, absolute norm which is above men, but rather a term of relationship. Thus, a man is called righteous who conducts himself properly with reference to an existing communal relationship, who, therefore, does justice to the claims which this communal relationship makes on him. This communal relationship can be human. But the passages where righteousness refers, as it does here, to the relationship of communion between man and God are more important. God is righteous so long as he turns towards man (that is then his *iustitia salutifera*). Man is righteous so long as he affirms the regulations of this communal relationship established by God, say, the covenant and the commandments. The close connection between righteousness and the divine commandments is shown in Ezek. 18.5 ff., a series of commandments of a kind to be used in the confessional, followed by a qualifying statement of acquittal, "He is righteous" (it could also say, "It shall be reckoned to him as righteousness"). *Belief* (faith) is fixing oneself on Yahweh" and refers as a rule to God's future saving act. Belief is an act of trust, a consent to God's plans in history. From the viewpoint of man's attitude, belief is something rather passive, at least within the framework of God's governing. (See Isa. 7.4, 9; 28.16; 30.15.)

In our passage Abraham's righteousness is not communicated within the realm of the cult by a cult official; it is transferred to the realm of God's free and personal relationship to Abraham. But above all, his righteousness is not the result of any accomplishments, whether of sacrifice or acts of obedience. Rather, it is stated programmatically that belief alone has brought Abraham into a proper relationship to God. God has indicated his plan for history, namely, to make of Abraham a great people; Abraham "has firmly assented" to that, i.e., he took it seriously and adjusted to it. In so doing he adopted, according to God's judgment, the only correct relationship to God. Verse 6 certainly has the effect of a conclusion. With this solemn statement the exciting event of God's call to Abraham concludes. Even though ancient narrative material forms the basis of this paragraph, it can no longer be considered as "saga" in view of its unusual theological reflectiveness. Its climax in v. 6 almost has the quality of a general theological tenet (see p. 189, for more on vs. 1–6).

[7–8] On the one hand, it is clear that a new narrative context begins with v. 7, for the self-introduction of the divinity, according to all comparable passages (cf. Gen. 28.13; Ex. 3.6; 6.2), makes sense only at the beginning of the self-revelation. On the other hand, it is obvious that the redactor is attempting to unite the event about to be described closely to the one that has preceded; for a narrative cannot have begun with v. 7 only. Such self-introductions in which the divinity permits itself to be identified by man in a definite manner (in the Old Testament almost always in a well-known historical deed that has preceded) are much more than solemn phrases. A man's life, according to ancient belief, was surrounded on all sides by divine powers which influenced it. Ancient Israel also admitted a certain existence and effectiveness to these powers (cf., e.g., Judg. 11.24) (without thereby being untrue to the First Commandment). But this world of the numinous, which often threatened man, had many aspects and many voices, and it was therefore simply decisive for the man who was called that God stepped out of his incognito on his own, that he let himself and his will be known, and therefore voluntarily differed from those enticements or threats. The notion that Abraham came from Ur in "Chaldea" is represented only by the Priestly narrative; therefore, the place name here is considered a later harmonizing correction (see p. 158). The promise of land appears here like a repetition of ch. 12. A later excursus will show, however (see pp. 189 f.), that our passage is really original, even unprecedented.

[9–12] Until now the two narratives of the call, vs. 1–6 and vs. 7–18, have been rather parallel with respect to form; now, however, the second branches off sharply, for God gives no further explanations in answer to Abraham's doubting question. There follows an act, and therefore God commands that preparations be made for a mysterious ceremony. It concerns the ritual of covenant-making, which, in a similar form, was well known to many ancient peoples. The meaning of the custom, which the Old Testament indicates elsewhere (Jer. 34.17 ff.), can be determined only indirectly, as is so often the case. When the animals are halved and laid opposite each other, and when the partners to the covenant stride through the lane that has been thus formed, they express thereby a curse upon themselves in the event the covenant is broken. It is not certain whether the killing of the animals is to be understood as a sacrifice, but the fact that the pieces of meat were neither burned nor eaten but covered with earth as something accursed speaks against the notion of sacrifice. The surprising fact, which is also unique in the history of religions, is that God himself enters a communal relationship with Abraham under the forms which among men guarantee the greatest contractual security. (Further regarding the covenant idea, see ch. 17.2.) The swooping down of birds of prey could be understood as an evil omen (Vergil, *Aeneid*, III, 235 ff.). Or are they perhaps evil powers who intend at the last moment to thwart the conclusion of the covenant? It is possible that the mysterious incident points to hindrances that stand in the way of the realization of the promise (Di.). With few words the dread that extends over the scene in the tense expectation of what is to come is wonderfully described. The sun is going down, and Abraham in dread and insensibility sinks into a miraculous sleep. "*Tardēmā*" is a deep sleep in which the natural activities of spirit and mind are extinguished (see at Gen. 2.21), which, however, sometimes awakens a man to receive a revelation (Job 4.13; 33.15).

[13–16] God's word in vs. 13–16 has long been recognized as an insertion (from E?). The theophany certainly followed immediately after the description of the preparations, the sunset, and the sleep. But now God's extensive speech ruptures the description of the exciting preparatory events, and by introducing Yahweh in the act of speaking at this point anticipates something of what is to come. The paragraph refers to the dark stretch of history which is to be experienced by Abraham's descendants before the promise is fulfilled. The concern of these verses is clear, they are "aetiological," designed to clarify a riddle: Abraham had received the promise, but it was not fulfilled for many generations. The answer is not to be found in a deficiency of God's power. The entr'acte, the Egyptian bondage, so filled with suffering, was not something unforeseen; but Yahweh had provided for it all, "for the iniquity of the Amorites" (here in the sense of "Canaanite aborigines") "is not yet complete." God allots to the nations their times (Dan. 2.21). The "iniquity of the Amorites" is here to be understood as their sexual corruption (Lev. 18.24–28). How the time span in v. 13 is related to Ex. 12.40 is not clear. But that of v. 16 does not agree either, for a "generation" (*dōr*) elsewhere in the Old Testament is not a hundred years. Abraham is to be allowed to die in peace before that. The expression "to go to one's fathers" is to be understood from the viewpoint of the family grave; here, to be sure, it does not quite fit, for Abraham had broken with his family. To die "in a good old age," "as a shock of grain comes up to the threshing floor in its season" (Job 5.26), was considered in the Old Testament as a special grace of God (see at ch. 25.8).

The paragraph is distinguished considerably by its theoretical spirit from the rest of the context in which it is now included. One can designate it in fact as a cabinet piece of Old Testament theology of history. Characteristic is first the universal aspect: God rules over world history in the sense of a *providentia generalis*; secondly, in the course of time allotted to the nations they become ripe for the judgment immanent in history; thirdly, God follows a special plan in world history for his people, Israel. The way of sacred history leads first down into disappointment and apparent despair. Fourthly, Abraham and Israel are to know about these mysterious historical thoughts of God; they are not to think of history as a riddle but to understand it in faith (see at Gen. 18.17 ff.).

[17] The theophany, for which the narrative has prepared with so much increasing tension, is now described very realistically. And yet one can detect a certain reticence, for the narrator avoids simply identifying Yahweh with those strange phenomena; Yahweh's relationship to them is not discussed. What became apparent after the fall of complete darkness was something like a furnace and a firebrand which moved between the pieces of flesh as they were laid out. One must not inquire too much about the meaning of this strange phenomenon in itself. Since *tannūr* (actually an oven) had the shape of a hollow clay cylinder tapering toward the top (on whose outer and inner walls round, flat cakes of bread were fastened), it has been thought that this phenomenon could be understood as a mysterious preview of God's fiery mountain, and thus as a reference to the conclusion of a covenant with Moses on Sinai. One should beware, however, of treating as symbolic the intentional material aspect of the phenomenon. By subjecting it to a meaning that appears reasonable, one loses the meaning of the whole, which is simply the gift of quite a real guarantee. The ceremony proceeded completely without words and with the complete passivity of the human partner! **[18–21]** The narrator explains the event in v. 18, not with a reference to a deeper "meaning," but rather by stating the fact of the concluded covenant with almost juristical objectivity and then paraphrasing the substance of the guarantee given by Yahweh as though in the minutes. The size of the Promised Land corresponds to the extent of Solomon's kingdom at the period of its greatest extent (I Kings 4.21). The boundary to the south, however, is not the "river" of Egypt (Nile), but rather the so-called "Brook of Egypt" (cf. I Kings 8.65), i.e., the Wâdi

'Arîsh between Gaza and the eastern limit of the Nile valley; and the text should be emended accordingly. The enumeration of the nations in vs. 19–21 must be considered an addition; in it was collected everything that was known of ancient names (on the "Hittites," see ch. 23).

The narrative about God's making of the covenant (vs. 7–18) is probably one of the oldest narratives in the tradition about the patriarchs. To the difficult question about the pre-Mosaic religion of Israel's ancestors (i.e., the religion prior to belief in Yahweh) one must answer that it was a cult of the "God of the fathers." In these pre-Mosaic communities the names of men with whom this cult began and in whom God's promise and guidance had proved exemplary were transmitted with great care. Abraham, Isaac, and Jacob were the first such recipients of revelation and the founders of the cult of the God of the fathers. If the conception of a "covenant" concluded with Abraham goes back to this very early period (see p. 159), we might regard the content of this account as primitive material from the patriarchal tradition. This would be supported by the fact that the narrative is quite different in character from early Palestine sagas attached to places, like Gen., chs. 16; 18; 28; 32. But we cannot exclude the possibility that the conception of the covenant only appeared in Israel at a later date and that it was projected by the narrator back into the patriarchal period. We may take it as certain that the promise of the possession of cultivated land was an essential ingredient of the old religion of the fathers. One must assume, however, that the promise of land was originally to be thought of as quite direct and at hand, i.e., that it did not reckon with another departure from the land and a second immigration. Only after the inclusion into the Hexateuch of the patriarchal period (the period of promise) and the period of Moses and Joshua (the period of fulfillment), and especially after the insertion of vs. 13–16, did that peculiar interruption in the promise occur and find its way into ch. 15.

The inner diversity of the two sections now combined in ch. 15 is as great as possible. The latter is an actual narrative of real events; the former contains a minimum of action. The former representation began in the spiritual vein and ended with the statement of a surely spiritual occurrence on the part of Abraham first and Yahweh second (v. 6). In vs. 7 ff., on the other hand, the representation quickly departed from the initial conversation and proceeded to the making of the covenant. Accordingly, in the first part Abraham's inner nature engaged our attention to a maximum degree, for his faith is understood as a decision made in complete consciousness. In the second part, however, Abraham's consciousness with all sensual apprehension is completely extinguished, and God's coming as well as his act receive our sole attention. Without doubt the two parts are completely different as regards both their origin and their literary nature. Verses 1–6 are quite theologically reflective and derive from a period when matters of faith were a problem. Verses 7–18 are perhaps ancient tradition from the patriarchal period itself.

both parts, precisely in their dialectical contrast regarding the human attitude toward the proffered salvation, present in an exemplary and vivid fashion the activity and passivity of the person called?

5. HAGAR. ISHMAEL'S BIRTH. Ch. 16

16 1*Now Sarai, Abram's wife, bore him no children.* She had an Egyptian
maid whose name was Hagar; 2and Sarai said to Abram, "Behold now,
the LORD has prevented me from bearing children; go in to my maid;
it may be that I shall obtain children by her." And Abram hearkened
to the voice of Sarai. 3*So, after Abram had dwelt ten years in the land of
Canaan, Sarai, Abram's wife, took Hagar the Egyptian her maid, and gave her
to Abram her husband as a wife.* 4And he went in to Hagar, and she conceived; and when she saw that she had conceived, she looked with contempt on her mistress. 5And Sarai said to Abram, "May the wrong
done to me be on you! I gave my maid to your embrace, and when she
saw that she had conceived, she looked on me with contempt. May the
LORD judge between you and me!" 6But Abram said to Sarai, "Behold, your maid is in your power; do to her as you please." Then
Sarai dealt harshly with her, and she fled from her.

7 The angel of the LORD found her by a spring of water in the wilderness, the spring on the way to Shur. 8And he said, "Hagar, maid of
Sarai, where have you come from and where are you going?" She
said, "I am fleeing from my mistress Sarai." 9The angel of the LORD
said to her, "Return to your mistress, and submit to her." 10The angel
of the LORD also said to her, "I will so greatly multiply your descendants
that they cannot be numbered for multitude." 11And the angel of the
LORD said to her, "Behold, you are with child, and shall bear a son;
you shall call his name Ishmael; because the LORD has given heed to
your affliction. 12He shall be a wild ass of a man, his hand against every
man and every man's hand against him; and he shall dwell over against
all his kinsmen." 13So she called the name of the LORD who spoke to her,
"Thou art a God of seeing"; for she said, "Have I really seen God and
remained alive after seeing him?" 14Therefore the well was called Beer-
lahai-roi; it lies between Kadesh and Bered.

15 *And Hagar bore Abram a son; and Abram called the name of his son,
whom Hagar bore, Ishmael.* 16*Abram was eighty-six years old when Hagar
bore Ishmael to Abram.*

[1–3] The story of Hagar exists in two versions: ch. 16 (J) and ch. 21.8 ff. (E). Regarding the differences in both versions, see pp. 234 f. (In ch. 16, vs. 3, 15–16, are attributed to the Priestly document.) Verse 1 has the function of a very brief "exposition" in the whole narrative. It outlines the problem which the subsequent occurrence solves, and it introduces the reader to the chief actors, who contribute in very different ways to the complexity of the event. The narrator mentions only the prominent fact of childlessness, but the reader who has read chs. 12; 13; 15 perceives the real problem at once: the delay—indeed, the failure—of the promise proclaimed with such display. Sarah formulates this fact in all its paradoxical harshness: Yahweh himself has spoken and acted in this affair (for according to the Old Testament the gift or denial of life is Yahweh's prerogative alone, chs. 30.2; 33.5; Ps. 127.3). Was it not inevitable that Abraham and Sarah should fall into severe temptation? There was no greater sorrow for an Israelite or Oriental woman than childlessness. Even today among the Arabs the barren woman is exposed to disgrace and even grievous wrongs. These views, which derive from the human code of honor, and the customs to which they give birth also play a role in the patriarchal stories. For there was a legitimate way to avoid all these difficulties, the way that Sarah proposed to Abraham in v. 2b. To understand the conflict that now ensues, one must refer to legal customs that were apparently widespread at that time. The wife could bring to the marriage her own personal maid, who was not available to her husband as a concubine in the same way his own female slaves were. If she gave her personal maid to her husband, in the event of her own childlessness, then the child born of the maid was considered the wife's child: The slave was born "on the knees" of the wife, so that the child then came symbolically from the womb of the wife herself (cf. ch. 30.3, 9)! From the legal and moral standpoint, therefore, Sarah's proposal was completely according to custom. And yet the narrator probably sees a great delinquency precisely in this (see the end of the exposition). There occurs what had to happen: **[4–6]** Hagar conceived, but she did not think of disowning the blessing of her womb in favor of Sarah. Rather, she enjoys it as a triumph over Sarah. "The glory of nature comes forth from Hagar wildly and colorfully." (Pr.)

Sarah, whose legal status both as wife and as mistress of Hagar is now threatened, strikes back. That she does not call Hagar to

*A. Heitzer, "Hagar," *Breslauer kath. theol. Diss.*, 1934, 54, 61 ff.

account but turns to Abraham corresponds to the legal situation, according to which Hagar now belongs to Abraham. Moreover, the maintenance of justice in the house was the man's affair in any case. (The cry *ḥ^{a}māsī 'alēkā* cannot be translated, "My wrong be upon you," the meaning is rather, "The wrong that has happened to me is your responsibility," i.e., you are competent and responsible to restore my right. This was the customary legal formula of appeal for legal protection.) Sarah goes to the limit with her counterstroke: she appeals to the highest judge, who sees every secret thing. Her agitation and passion at seeing Hagar obviously already taking her place and becoming mother of the heir of promise does not win her the reader's sympathy, in spite of her subjective right. Abraham, as a result, severs his relationship with Hagar and thereby restores the old legal situation; that is the meaning of v. 6a. With that, Hagar lost her higher station; she is "abased." What that meant becomes clear from a paragraph of Hammurabi's code. In it the punishment for a serving maid who has a child by her master and is for that reason induced into putting herself on a par with her mistress is that she shall be again reduced to the status of a slave (paragraph 146). But in Israel too, according to Prov. 30.23, there seems to have been trouble in this respect. The events that are here related, therefore, occur within the framework of ancient legal regulations and are accordingly vindicated by them. But what happens—Sarah's outburst of anger, Abraham's surrender of Hagar to Sarah's reprisal—is in the narrator's opinion disagreeable. "Abraham plays rather an unhappy role between these two raw-boned women." (Gu.) In any event, in the fact that Hagar too goes to desperate lengths in her flight the reader sees that in this obvious legal offense there is a certain inner consistency by which the events had to develop into this catastrophe. But in its course the reader's interest is exceedingly heightened. How muddled the situation has become by the application of right and wrong! What will happen to Hagar, and what of Abraham's child? Will it perish? Will it become the heir of promise?

[7–8] Verse 7 finally gives a place name. (One must suppose the site for the events in vs. 1–7 to have been Mamre, according to ch. 13.18.) According to this, Hagar must have fled far to the south, for the oasis—well known, of course, to ancient readers—lay not far from the Egyptian northeast boundary. (For Shur, cf. chs. 20.1; 25.18; I Sam. 15.7; 27.8. The word is perhaps not a place name but a designation for the Egyptian frontier wall.) Here the angel of Yahweh encounters the runaway and addresses to the expectant mother in her desperate situation the difficult double question of her past and her future. It is not clear whether Hagar recognized him at once as a divine being. Such messengers of God, whom we must not imagine as winged, are often not recognized in the beginning at all; but the narrators omit the psychological process of recognition (cf. ch. 18.1 ff.; Judg. 6.11 ff.). So Hagar only slowly became aware of her visitor from his knowing words.

The angel of the Lord. "Angel" is misleading, as in the Old Testament the Hebrew word designates a human or divine "messenger," just as the Greek *angelos* in the New Testament does not mean "angel" only. (The Latin *angelus* was the first to become a fixed term for heavenly beings.) Intermediary beings who actively intrude in the affairs of men were rather little known in ancient Israel in contrast with other religions. Israel apparently found it difficult, in view of Yahweh's all-encompassing "zeal," his omnipotent guidance of history, to make room for the activity of angels. All the more striking are the passages that speak of the appearance of the "angel [messenger] of the Lord." He lives in the people's mind, strangely enough, not as a fearful being, but as a beneficent, at all times helpful, messenger of God, to whose penetrating wisdom one can leave everything with confidence. He smites Israel's enemies (II Kings 19.35), helps the prophets arise (I Kings 19.7), confronts the hostile sorcerer (Num. 22.22), protects and guides the nation (Ex. 14.19; 23.20). The angel of the Lord, therefore, according to these passages, appears as an instrument of Yahweh's gracious relationship to Israel; he is God's personified help for his people. Those passages, however, where he enters the human realm not to act but rather to speak and proclaim, i.e., in the patriarchal narratives, are very strange; for here there is no clear distinction between the angel of the Lord and Yahweh himself. The one who speaks, now Yahweh (cf. chs. 16.10, 13; 21.17, 19; 22.11), now the messenger (who then speaks of God in the third person), is obviously one and the same person. The angel of the Lord is therefore a form in which Yahweh appears (*eine Erscheinungsform Jahwes*). He is God himself in human form. This strange shift between a divine and a human subject (the ancients even spoke of a doctrine of two natures!) is the intended result of an apparently intensive inner revision of very old traditions. In these cases we have ancient traditions about sites and shrines, which in an older revision once told quite directly of extremely spectacular divine appearances at definite places. Those who came later, then, understood it in such a way that not Yahweh but Yahweh's angel appeared. Thus the introduction of the angel of the Lord into those old cult traditions presupposes a distinct theological reflection. The naïve immediacy of the relationship to God was broken somewhat by the introduction of this mediating figure, in such a way that nothing of the directness of the divine address to man and the divine saving activity for man was lost. The figure of the angel of the Lord has conspicuous Christological qualities. In ch. 48.16 he is designated as the one who has redeemed from all evil. He is a type, a "shadow" of Jesus Christ.

[9–14] Hagar answered the first question openly and defiantly; to the second she has nothing to say. Thereupon the angel takes up both her past and her future. Hagar must go back to Sarah; Yahweh will not condone the breach of legal regulations. (For v. 9, cf. the conclusion to this exposition.) The child to be born of her will be a boy whom she is to name Ishmael ("God heard") because of God's mercy which found her in the desert. He will be a real Bedouin, a "wild ass of a man" (*pere'*, zebra), i.e., free and wild (cf. Job 39.5–8), eagerly spending his life in a war of all against all—a worthy son of his rebellious and proud mother! In this description of Ishmael there is undoubtedly undisguised sympathy and admiration for the roving Bedouin who bends his neck to no yoke. The man here pictured is highly qualified in the opinion of Near Easterners, but there is not a word about the great promise to Abraham.

The names by which Hagar attempts to fix her recollection of this encounter with God are obscure. The God who was revealed to her she calls "God of seeing," which refers to the miracle of God's seeing Hagar and prophesying a great future for her child (Pr., "God who appeared"). But one thinks immediately she saw the one who saw her (for seeing subsequently, cf. Judg. 13.20 ff.; Ex. 33.18 ff.). The "for" in the statement is not quite logical; only because God permitted himself to be seen by her can she make any utterances about God.* What is concerned here is obviously an old place name with which a sacred tradition was connected. But one senses that the narrative has broken loose somewhat from its old point of reference, for the etymological variation of the ancient place name is really thoughtful

*It should be noted that many exegetes have adopted Wellhausen's emendation, according to which the difficult sentence would read: " . . . have I really seen 'Elohim' and am alive after my seeing?" (so BH).

playing with ancient tradition (cf. a similar example, ch. 22.14). The localities that are mentioned in this chapter, with the exception of Kadesh, the large, famous oasis about sixty miles south of Beer-sheba, can no longer be identified. But it is quite clear from the original aetiological intention of the narrative that it came from the deep south of Palestine; there it must have arisen and there it must first have been circulated. Only after its incorporation into the large composition of Abraham narratives was it shifted to the north in such a way that Hebron became the point of departure for Hagar's flight. But even the preliterary form of our narrative must be characterized as complicated, because two aetiologies are intertwined in it, one relating to the history of the tribe and one to the history of the cult. (What connection is there between the origin of the Ishmaelites and their name? How did the oasis Beer-lahai-roi become a sanctuary?) These two elements were once independent, and one sees from that how ancient the materials of our narrative really are.

[15–16] There is no conclusion to the present Yahwistic narrative. Formerly it certainly reported Ishmael's birth, and, moreover, in this southern region where Ishmael was actually at home. But since the Elohistic parallel narrative (ch. 21) was later included in the composition of the patriarchal stories, Hagar had first to return to Abraham's house. Verse 9 especially, a later addition, now provides the link between the two Hagar stories, which cannot be understood as two events separated from each other in time. The ancient unusable conclusion to the Yahwistic narrative is now replaced by two statements from the Priestly document (vs. 15–16). According to them, one must assume that Hagar had meantime returned to Abraham. (Verse 3 also comes from P.) One recognizes from these verses that P apparently told the story as briefly as possible.

Epilogue. In many respects ch. 16 is typical of the Yahwist's narrative style. The expositor's first impression is that here he is introduced to an occurrence of great compactness and vividness, but that he does not catch sight of the one who introduced him, that he looks about in vain for an interpretation, and that he is left alone in wide terrain. But whoever impatiently seeks a meaning in this story must first ask himself whether it is so certain that such a narrative has only *one* meaning. The narrative here is very spacious, so to speak, with much to be read between the lines. The narrator makes room for many thoughts and reflections and is in no hurry to prescribe one idea or one opinion for the reader. The emphasis is no longer on the aetiologies. One cannot really say that the narrative has the special intention of explaining how the shrine "Beer-lahai-roi" ("of the living one who sees me") arose. And the Ishmaelites? Were they so important to the narrator's contemporaries that people wished to know about their origin? Was there during Solomon's day or later still a separate tribe of Ishmaelites? The aetiology itself breaks down, by the way, when Ishmael is not born in his native desert region in the south. No, the exposition of the present narrative must proceed from the context into which it is incorporated; then its effect is to retard the action of the main narrative and to heighten the suspense. The reader who, with Abraham, is expecting the fulfillment of the great promise is put off; for Ishmael is not the heir of promise but a secondary descendant who retires from the line of promise. The reader, therefore, has experienced a very strange incident which contains a special significance. The question about why Ishmael is not the son of promise must be answered by the reader himself on the basis of what has gone before. Abraham had to assume and did assume (v. 1) that Sarah would be the mother of the heir of promise. But there is an obstacle which in human terms is insuperable. This hard fact sets free human activity; human discretion takes control of the matter; impatience helps and finds a way out. But how uncannily complicated the circumstances now become, ending finally in a cul-de-sac! Everything is now complicated, not least by the resort to legal regulations. The question of guilt is also complicated, for Abraham, Sarah, and Hagar. But the narrator's great reticence in this respect shows that he does not want the reader to judge or condemn but rather simply to see and hear. There can be no doubt that in such stories the original narrative has been enlarged by a kind of typical universality, i.e., situations, temptations, problems, decisions, are described in which the reader can discover himself and his relation to God. Chapter 12.10 ff. told of the jeopardy of the promise, a disregard of the kind that springs from unbelief; the story of Hagar shows us to some extent the opposite, a fainthearted faith that cannot leave things with God and believes it necessary to help things along. All persons of the drama appear in a bad light. The narrator seems to be most sympathetic toward Hagar, although she offended most obviously against right and custom. But the reader understands that a child so conceived in defiance or in little faith cannot be the heir of promise. He becomes what he must, free and rebellious, going forth to a battle of all against all. But a primary point in the narrative is that God follows the one who goes forth from Abraham's house too; and it is a great wonder that his eyes are also open to mankind, that he includes it in his plans for history and that he established oases in the desert for Hagar and Ishmael too. "O thou God who seest!" (Del.)

6. GOD'S COVENANT WITH ABRAHAM. INSTITUTION OF CIRCUMCISION. Ch. 17.1–14

17 [1]*When Abram was ninety-nine years old the* LORD *appeared to Abram,*
and said to him, "I am God Almighty; walk before me, and be blameless. [2]*And I*
will make my covenant between me and you, and will multiply you exceedingly."
[3]*Then Abram fell on his face; and God said to him,* [4]*"Behold, my covenant is*
with you, and you shall be the father of a multitude of nations. [5]*No longer shall*
your name be Abram, but your name shall be Abraham; for I have made you the
father of a multitude of nations. [6]*I will make you exceedingly fruitful; and I will*
make nations of you, and kings shall come forth from you. [7]*And I will establish my*
covenant between me and you and your descendants after you throughout their
generations for an everlasting covenant, to be God to you and to your descendants
after you. [8]*And I will give to you, and to your descendants after you, the land of*
your sojournings, all the land of Canaan, for an everlasting possession; and I will
be their God."
9 *And God said to Abraham, "As for you, you shall keep my covenant, you and*
your descendants after you throughout their generations. [10]*This is my covenant,*
which you shall keep, between me and you and your descendants after you: Every
male among you shall be circumcised. [11]*You shall be circumcised in the flesh of your*
foreskins, and it shall be a sign of the covenant between me and you. [12]*He that is*
eight days old among you shall be circumcised; every male throughout your genera-
tions, whether born in your house, or bought with your money from any foreigner
who is not of your offspring, [13]*both he that is born in your house and he that is*
bought with your money, shall be circumcised. So shall my covenant be in your
flesh an everlasting covenant. [14]*Any uncircumcised male who is not circumcised in*
flesh of his foreskin shall be cut off from his people; he has broken my covenant."

Chapter 17 belongs to the Priestly document. But it does not have a unified structure and continuity. A series of seams can be recognized, from which one may infer that various Priestly traditions about the covenant with Abraham have been combined into a large unit. In the first part (vs. 1–14) Abraham's call is essentially parallel to the Yahwistic report (ch. 15.7 ff.). But what a difference in the presentation of essentially the same material! The Yahwist set God's call in the midst of Abraham's human situation, which became psychologically clear in Abraham's answer and in the delineation of his fear. The Priestly document, on the other hand, reduces Abraham's call to the purely theological, i.e., it speaks in vs. 1–14 of God only. Not a single word is said about Abraham, only the gesture of reverence in v. 3. The actual call and promise in the Yahwist's representation required only a single verse (ch. 15.7). Here, on the other hand, we read a long, ponderous, and detailed speech by God in which the theological substance of the covenant with Abraham is defined, not without repetitions or variants. The making of the covenant, therefore, consists for this document only in God's address, which is severe and solemn, almost in a vacuum. How dramatically the Yahwist told of God's coming! Here "the Lord appeared" in v. 1 and the "God went up" in v. 22 are completely ungraphic.

[1] Of the Pentateuch sources only P has a chronological framework (cf. chs. 5; 11), and all other chronological dates in the Abraham story derive from P: chs. 12.4; 16.3, 16; 21.5; 23.1; 25.7, 20. Regarding God's self-introduction by name, see exposition of ch. 15.7. The meaning of the name *'ēl šaddai* has not yet been explained satisfactorily. Frequently (but not here), LXX translates it with "the Almighty." In the theology of our source, God's revelation as *'ēl šaddai* designates a definite and, moreover, temporary stage of God's revelation to the patriarchs (Ex. 6.3, "By my name Yahweh I did not make myself known to them"). Strangely enough, the Priestly document does not define the theological distinction between the older stage of revelation and the one that was final for Israel. It may be, then, that everything was already expressed in the revelation of the name Yahweh. But it is interesting to see that even the latest of the documentary sources knows about the difference between the patriarchal faith and the later belief in Yahweh. In fact, it is even more accurate in this respect in that it consciously takes account of this break in the history of the cult in its theological plan, whereas the Yahwist frankly calls Abraham's God Yahweh.

The actual address to Abraham contains two imperatives. P is more concerned than the Yahwist with the obligation which falls to Abraham in the moment of revelation. It is the constraint of his whole life which is henceforth to be lived in the presence of this revealed God (life is a "walk," a "walking about"). This change of prepositions marks the difference in the relationship to God from that of the first world epoch, for Enoch and Noah walked "with" God. (Chs. 5.22, 24; 6.9.) The word that one usually translates "devout" (*tāmīm*), following Luther, actually means "whole" or "perfect," not, to be sure, in the sense of moral perfection but rather in relationship to God. It signifies complete, unqualified surrender. The demand, shortened here, is more fully stated in Deut. 18.13, "Be whole with your God." Similarly, i.e., with reference to a communal relationship among men, this "whole" occurs in ch. 20.5 in the sense of "without ulterior motives," "unreserved."

[2–3a] And now God proceeds to announce the covenant he has established. A "covenant" among men or groups of men serves to order a legal situation between two parties, in some way unclarified, by the assumption of particular obligations. It changes what is dangerous and unexplained into a salutary communal relationship by means of a legal ordinance which binds the two members. There is not necessarily a relationship of parity between those who subscribe to the covenant; on the contrary, it often happens that the more powerful member extends the covenant relationship to the weaker (Josh. 9.6, 11; I Sam. 11.1; II Sam. 3.12; I Kings 20.34). The Hebrew word is more appropriately translated "obligation," "promise." This obligation can be taken up one-sidedly by one party toward another, but it can also be enjoined on one party by the other; finally, it can be adopted mutually by both parties. Here (and in Gen. 15.18) we have the first of the three possibilities. God binds himself; Abraham remains the dumb recipient of the promise. To enter into such a communal relationship a special ritual was customary, about which we learn something from Jer. 34.18 and Gen. 15.9 ff. But whereas the Yahwist thought that God too concluded his covenant with Abraham in such human forms, P gives no suggestion. Indeed, the verb that indicates the completion of the ceremony (*kārat*, "cut") is avoided; God "gives," "establishes," the covenant, and its completion is only in the word directed to Abraham.

[3b–6] One has the impression that a paragraph ends with v. 3a. The word of covenant has been given, and Abraham has expressed his submission by a silent gesture. The substance of God's address, which begins in v. 4, is parallel to the preceding; it describes the divine promise further by combining a change of name with the making of the covenant and explaining it with a somewhat artificial pun ("father of a multitude of nations"). Here P has certainly theologized a double tradition of the first patriarch's name, for the name "Abraham" is linguistically nothing else than a "lengthening" of the simpler "Abram," which means "my father [the god] is exalted." Originally only the Priestly tradition contained this change in the name. But in weaving together the sources, the redactor found it necessary to change every Jehovistic mention of "Abraham" before ch. 17 into "Abram." The promise of a great posterity is here supplemented by a double statement: Abraham will be the father of nations, and kings will come forth from him. One does not grasp the meaning of this promise if one thinks primarily of the Ishmaelites, Edomites, and sons of Keturah (ch. 25.1 ff.); for the descendants about whom these words speak are not to be sought among those who are outside God's covenant, even less since later the same promise is made to Sarah (v. 16). As the Yahwist shows, Abraham's call was connected with the hope of a universal extension of God's salvation beyond the limits of Israel (ch. 12.3). The Priestly document also contains this element of tradition; but even though it is formulated more programmatically (chs. 17.16; 28.3; 35.11), P's real theological interest is much more in the inner circle of Israel's cultic regulations. The almost prophetic element, therefore, because it was anchored in the tradition, is given by P conscientiously but as though under seal.

[7–8] In v. 7, a new paragraph begins with another covenant declaration. What is new is the express statement that the covenant is made not only with Abraham but also with all his descendants. It is therefore a reference to its timeless validity. But the saving gifts mentioned here are also changed, namely, the new relationship to God and the land. To exhibit the regulations of this relationship to God, to show its cult forms, will be later the chief task of the Priestly document. But as an element of tradition, this "I will be God to you" does not belong originally to the ancient patriarchal promise, but is, rather, an antedating of the substance of the covenant at Sinai, for the two really old patriarchal promises are posterity and land (cf. the epilogue to ch. 15). The Priestly document could not leave the curiously broken relation of the patriarchs to the saving gift of the land (it was promised to them but not yet their possession) undefined theologically or conceptually; it calls it "the land of your sojournings" (chs. 21.23; 28.4; 35.27; 37.1; cf. the epilogue to ch. 23).

[9–14] The sections vs. 1–3a, 3b–6, and 7–8 have communicated what God will "accomplish"; now vs. 9–14 turn to the human side, i.e., to the observance which now falls to Abraham with the inauguration of the communal relationship. This section is the logical continuation to one of the previous covenant declarations, probably to vs. 7–8 because of the continual inclusion of the "descendants." God "establishes" the covenant (v. 7), man "keeps" it (v. 10). Here, therefore, an attitude is demanded of Abraham toward God's act, an attitude which he is to make explicit by circumcising every male of his house. Human covenants also were accompanied by an external sign that obligated the parties to keep the agreement (cf. ch. 31.44 ff.). Thus, according to the sense of this passage, circumcision is only the act of appropriation, of witness to the revelation of God's salvation, and the sign of its acceptance. This distinguishes this covenant from the covenant with Noah; it is for a definite circle of men and demands their obedience. This obedience, however, does not consist in performing definite legal acts, but only in the recognition and affirmation of God's offer. To this extent Abraham and his seed are not free partners to the covenant. Whoever refuses the sign of this recognition is to be "cut off from his people." This scarcely means the death penalty, which is expressed by P in a different way, but rather exclusion from the sacred community, a kind of excommunication, which also meant ruin for the one concerned. This emphasis on the conscious attitude of the individual toward the covenant, which required of the individual Israelite personal decision and responsibility, appears only in a later phase in the history of the Old Testament cult; for all older rites were collective, and the individual participated in them only as a member of the group. This change must be related to Israel's situation in the Babylonian exile. Because of the abolition of the great cultic regulations, the feasts, sacrifice, etc., which were binding on the national community, the individual and the family were suddenly summoned to decision. Each family with all its members, each of them personally, was bound to Yahweh's offer, and since the Babylonians (like all eastern Semites) did not practice circumcision, the observance of this custom was a *status confessionis* for the exiles; i.e., it became a question of their witness of Yahweh and his guidance of history. The significance that circumcision thus received was unknown to ancient Israel. It was a rite which was practiced from earliest times, but it was not yet connected in such a way with the center of faith. It was felt to be a mark of distinction from the "uncircumcised" (i.e., the Philistines, I Sam. 14.6; 17.26, 36; etc.), but there were other ancient interpretations as well (e.g., Josh. 5.2 ff.). (The extremely old story in Ex. 4.24 ff. cannot be properly understood at all.) The idea of circumcision as an act of bodily purification and dedication must also have played a role at times, otherwise the spiritualizing demand for a "circumcision of the heart" could not have been made (Lev. 26.41; Deut. 10.16; Jer. 4.4; 9.25; Ezek. 44.7). But this conception is far from our text. Here circumcision is understood quite formally, i.e., without significant reference to the procedure itself, as a sign of the covenant, as an act of confession and an appropriation of the divine revealed will.

7. THE PROMISE OF A SON. Ch. 17.15–27

17 15 *And God said to Abraham, "As for Sarai your wife, you shall not call*
her name Sarai, but Sarah shall be her name. 16 *I will bless her, and moreover I*
will give you a son by her; I will bless her, and she shall be a mother of nations;
kings of peoples shall come from her." 17 *Then Abraham fell on his face and*
laughed, and said to himself, "Shall a child be born to a man who is a hundred
years old? Shall Sarah, who is ninety years old, bear a child?" 18 *And Abraham*
said to God, "Oh that Ishmael might live in thy sight!" 19 *God said, "No, but*
Sarah your wife shall bear you a son, and you shall call his name Isaac. I will
establish my covenant with him as an everlasting covenant for his descendants after
him. 20 *As for Ishmael, I have heard you; behold, I will bless him and make him*
fruitful and multiply him exceedingly; he shall be the father of twelve princes, and
I will make him a great nation. 21 *But I will establish my covenant with Isaac,*
whom Sarah shall bear to you at this season next year." 22 *When he had finished*
talking with him, God went up from Abraham.

23 *Then Abraham took Ishmael his son and all the slaves born in his house or*
bought with his money, every male among the men of Abraham's house, and he
circumcised the flesh of their foreskins that very day, as God had said to him.
24 *Abraham was ninety-nine years old when he was circumcised in the flesh of his*
foreskin. 25 *And Ishmael his son was thirteen years old when he was circumcised in*
the flesh of his foreskin. 26 *That very day Abraham and his son Ishmael were*
circumcised; 27 *and all the men of his house, those born in the house and those*
bought with money from a foreigner, were circumcised with him.

The paragraph vs. 15–22 again contains a divine promise, but it is not parallel to the preceding at all. The promise is now much more concrete. It consists succinctly in the prophecy of the birth of a son, and moreover, from Sarah, and in addition the announcement of the name the child will bear. The succession, therefore, of vs. 1–14 and vs. 15–22 shows the advance in sacred history that occurs for the Yahwist between chs. 15.7 ff. and 18.1 ff. And as a matter of fact, our section (vs. 15–22) corresponds basically (of course again after extreme reduction to the theological) to the substance of ch. 18 (Sarah, subject of God's address, promise of a son, the laugh, the unbelieving question, the time "next year").

[15–22] Sarah's name is also changed, with no explanation for this change. (Linguistically, "Sarai" is only an archaic form of the later formation "Sarah" and probably means "princess.") God's blessing here too effects the miracle of physical fertility, cf. ch. 1.22, 28. The motif of laughing at the promise is here connected with Abraham, in contrast to ch. 18.12. Chapter 21.6a and 6b shows how this motif varies throughout the narratives. But of all the variations, our Priestly variant is the strangest. It must not, of course, be weakened or made trivial ("he rejoiced"—Jac.; Del.), and there is even less cause to doubt the genuineness of the passage (cf. Pr.). One must not one-sidedly apply the standard of the most general psychological credibility to the Priestly document. Abraham's laugh brings us in any case to the outer limits of what is psychologically possible. Combined with the pathetic gesture of reverence is an almost horrible laugh, deadly earnest, not in fun, bringing belief and unbelief close together. The promise that Abraham received in reverent willingness (readiness) "was so paradoxical that he laughed involuntarily" (Del.). Abraham attempts to side-step what is incomprehensible to him and to direct God's interest (typically!) to what is already a certainty, i.e., to Ishmael. God, however, rejects this attempt, not without harshness. Ishmael too will be "blessed," i.e., become a great nation. But the covenant is only with Isaac and his descendants. From this contrast it becomes clear that the covenant granted by God guarantees something quite different from national greatness.

[23–27] The Priestly document now has only to report the circumcision itself, which took place on the same day. It reports it in detail (still without becoming graphic) and demonstrates thereby Abraham's obedience and that of his household. This section originally followed the giving of the covenant and the instruction for circumcision (vs. 1–15); after the combination of this block of material with God's address concerning Sarah and Isaac, however, it was transferred to the end of the whole narrative. Chapter 17, therefore, thus appears as a theological corollary of Priestly tradition regarding God's covenant and promise to Abraham.

8. GOD'S VISIT WITH ABRAHAM. Ch. 18.1–16

18 1And the LORD appeared to him by the oaks of Mamre, as he sat
at the door of his tent in the heat of the day. 2He lifted up his eyes and
looked, and behold, three men stood in front of him. When he saw them,
he ran from the tent door to meet them, and bowed himself to the earth,
3and said, "My lord, if I have found favor in your sight, do not pass by
your servant. 4Let a little water be brought, and wash your feet, and rest
yourselves under the tree, 5while I fetch a morsel of bread, that you may
refresh yourselves, and after that you may pass on—since you have come
to your servant." So they said, "Do as you have said." 6And Abraham
hastened into the tent to Sarah, and said, "Make ready quickly three
measures of fine meal, knead it, and make cakes." 7And Abraham ran
to the herd, and took a calf, tender and good, and gave it to the servant,
who hastened to prepare it. 8Then he took curds, and milk, and the
calf which he had prepared, and set it before them; and he stood by
them under the tree while they ate.

9 They said to him, "Where is Sarah your wife?" And he said, "She
is in the tent." [10]He said, "I will surely return to you in the spring, and
Sarah your wife shall have a son." And Sarah was listening at the tent
door behind him. [11]Now Abraham and Sarah were old, advanced in
age; it had ceased to be with Sarah after the manner of women. [12]So
Sarah laughed to herself, saying, "After I have grown old, and my
husband is old, shall I have pleasure?" [13]The LORD said to Abraham,
"Why did Sarah laugh, and say, 'Shall I indeed bear a child, now that I
am old?' [14]Is anything too hard for the LORD? At the appointed time I
will return to you, in the spring, and Sarah shall have a son." [15]But
Sarah denied, saying, "I did not laugh"; for she was afraid. He said,
"No, but you did laugh."

16 Then the men set out from there, and they looked toward Sodom;
and Abraham went with them to set them on their way.

The narrative complex that begins with ch. 18 is Yahwistic and does not end until ch. 19.38. It is therefore relatively voluminous. Even though a critical survey reveals at once that in it many traditions are collected which were originally independent of one another, yet the inner unity here is such that the seams, which can still be recognized, seem to be integral paragraphs of the whole. This narrative unit is "an accomplished work of epic art" (Di.): it expects of the reader the willingness to be told a story, i.e., the open-mindedness which can share in the most incidental details and understand latent subtleties and intimations. (Gunkel's exposition is masterful in this kind of aesthetic exploitation.)

The only troublesome part of the narrative, ch. 18.1–16, is a certain lack of clarity regarding the visitors, i.e., the relationship of the "three men" to Yahweh. In v. 1, Yahweh appeared; in v. 2, Abraham sees "three men." The most obvious answer seems to be that Yahweh is one of the three men. This assumption would become certainty when in chs. 18.22 and 19.1, after Yahweh's departure, the "two messengers" come to Sodom. It is well, nevertheless, not to mix the section ch. 19.1 ff., which derives from a different tradition, with this. In the narrative ch. 18.1–16 the notion that Yahweh appeared with two messengers is not the only one possible; it is not even the most likely. That the three men accepted the invitation together, if we were to think of the two as only a guard of honor to Yahweh, would be just as strange as their common question about Sarah (v. 9). One is therefore rather inclined to think that Yahweh appeared in all three. This interpretation would coincide with the fact that where the text mentions Yahweh himself it is singular (vs. 10, 13), for Yahweh is one in spite of this form of his appearing. This way of appearing, to be sure, is so strange and singular in the Old Testament that it must belong to the peculiarity of this tradition and this tradition only. Actually we have here one of those narratives, widespread throughout the world, which tells of the visit of divine creatures to men.

Aye, and the gods in the guise of strangers from afar put on all manner of shapes, and visit the cities, beholding the violence and the righteousness of men.

(*Odyssey*, XVII, 485–487, tr. by A. T. Murray, 1924)

Especially related to our narrative is the Greek saga about the visit of the three gods, Zeus, Poseidon, and Hermes, to the childless Hyrieus in Boeotia. After they have been served by him, they help him acquire the son he longed for, Orion, who then came to earth after ten months. Such similarity requires that one think of some connection, no longer distinguishable, with our narrative, or better, with one of its previous stages. (Further examples of such sagas are given by Gunkel.) Those times when hospitality was the only real virtue were the ones primarily concerned with such narratives. (Gu.)* Accordingly, all of them have the motif of a test, a question about the preservation of strangers, who are unknown at least in the beginning; and this thought must also be considered in the exposition of our narrative. (Heb. 13.2.) Apparently Israel received such a narrative as this from the old inhabitants of the land. This sort of thing began to be told as an experience of the ancestor, Abraham, and thus the material was gradually included in the Yahweh religion. For the god who visited Abraham could for Israel only be Yahweh. The opening statement especially states the substantial significance of this theophany once for all. To be sure, there is a certain unclearness in Yahweh's relationship to the three. One must ask, however, whether this lack of precision is to be attributed only to a certain bondage to the oldest pre-Israelite tradition, or whether it did not rather lend itself to the narrator's intention by veiling Yahweh with incognito. And furthermore, in the sending of only two to Sodom (ch. 19.1 ff.), it gave the narrator the possibility of differentiating God's activity on earth. In view of the anthropomorphism, unusual even in the Old Testament (cf. the exposition in v. 8), the matter must have been of consequence to the Yahwist, who was very liberal in these matters.

*The right of a guest is the field in which the Oriental's religion speaks to men about love, not only for one's tribe, family, or fellow soldier, but also for one's neighbor. Hospitality is therefore the display and preservation before men of one's piety, simply of one's piety. (Fr., II, 97.)

The interpretation given by the early church that the trinity of visitors is a reference to the Trinity has been universally abandoned by recent exegesis. The understanding of the previous history of our narrative and especially the uniqueness of this kind of divine appearance in the other Old Testament witnesses led to this abandonment. To be sure, the narrator used this trinity which was transmitted to him to represent, as we said, God's singular, personally differentiated activity (cf. the exposition of v. 22).

[1–5] Even though the reader has already been informed by the opening sentences about the true subject of this strange visit, still he ought to view the newcomers who are described neutrally as the "three men," through the eyes of the unsuspecting Abraham. The place is Hebron, more accurately the terebinths of Mamre, a sanctuary that later became famous far and wide (see pp. 172 f.). Abraham is sitting at the door of his tent, which according to ancient as well as modern custom is usually somewhat out of the way. The event occurred at the hot midday, when one usually rests. Thus, in a single sentence, the Yahwist has given us a vivid picture of place and time with data for which we look vainly in the entire Priestly Abraham narrative (ch. 17). Gunkel observed correctly that the three men were suddenly there; Abraham did not see them coming. "Divine events are always so surprising." Abraham hastens to meet the men in order to bar their passage. But they have already indicated, by having stopped, that they desire to stay. His invitation is both respectful (he speaks in the third person, avoiding the use of "I") and urgent. The Masoretes considered his speech as an address to God and vocalized (*'ᵃdōnāy*, "Lord"); but how should Abraham have already recognized Yahweh? The better reading is therefore "my lord" (*'ᵃdōnī*). "If I have found favor" is surely "urbane courtesy" (Pr.), but for the reader who knows more than Abraham does, the words have a subtle double meaning. The brief, almost condescending answer contrasts noticeably with the wordy invitation.

[6–8] The preparations greatly exceed the modest offer ("a little water and a morsel of bread"). Abraham, with his haste, set all the inhabitants of the tent in motion. Grinding and baking is the women's affair; the men take care of the butchering. For this reason Abraham "runs" to the herd and then prepares drinks and trimmings for the meal. At the meal Abraham waits respectfully, and thus quiet again descends upon the scene. Ancient expositors were disturbed by the fact that Yahweh took food just as men do, that he complied with the request that he "refresh himself" (v. 5a, cf. Judg. 19.5); and it is indeed an unusual liberty of our narrator (cf., on the other hand, Judg. 13.16; Tobit 12.19). Josephus (*Ant.*, I, 122) and others say that heavenly beings only appeared to have eaten.

[9–16] Without much ado the guests go about their business. That they know Sarah's name and about her childlessness is strange; even more strange is the promise of a son. Sarah has become attentive inside the tent and listens (cf. ch. 27.5). The question whether in v. 10b the door of the tent was "behind him" (i.e., Yahweh) or Sarah was "behind it" (i.e., the door of the tent) is answered according to the former by the LXX, according to the latter by the Masoretes. What Sarah hears can only amuse her, and she rather bluntly dismisses the matter as absurd. Again the guests betray their divine knowledge by reproaching the thought of Sarah, whom they could neither see nor hear, as the narrator intentionally noted. It has been considered a special nicety that Sarah's reflection is unexpectedly stripped of its bluntness when repeated by God; the expressions *bālā*, for the "decay" of old clothes, and *'ednā*, "sensual pleasure," are not repeated. The narrative reaches its climax in the statement, "Is anything too hard for the Lord?" This word reposes in the story like a precious stone in a priceless setting, and its significance surpasses the cosy patriarchal milieu of the narrative; it is a heuristic witness to God's omnipotent saving will. The narrator works out the contrast very sharply: The unbelieving and perhaps somewhat evil laugh, and now this word which indignantly punishes the way of thinking that mistrusts Yahweh's omnipotence. Of course Sarah did not basically renounce Yahweh with conscious unbelief; her laugh is rather a psychologically understandable incident, just as unbelief so often expresses itself. But this masterful, psychologically correct observation does not bring the narrator to excuse Sarah completely for her ignorance of the guests' identity. Rather, the unquestionable, decisive fact both for narrator and reader is that a word of Yahweh was laughed at. In this the outlook of the narrative is quite ancient.

Sarah, who has been recognized by the guests in this way, now comes out of hiding to disavow it confusedly and rashly. The motivation for this audacious lie ("for she was afraid") is one of those subtle psychological characteristics which we find so often in the Yahwist (cf. ch. 3.3 ff.). "The contrast between the little woman, who has now slipped out of hiding in fear, trying to lie, and the abrupt, unfriendly 'No' of the Lord is an effective, serious conclusion to the scene."

(Pr.) The guests, who have preserved severe dignity from beginning to end, stand up and leave. The decisiveness of their departure already indicates something of the somber goal of their path.

Epilogue. On the one hand, as we have already indicated, our narrative leads straight to what follows. The name of Sodom has already been mentioned, and with it a new moment of great suspense has appeared in the conclusion of our text. The final course of the event, whose mid-point is Yahweh's appearance on earth, is not at all concluded. On the other hand, every reader feels that v. 16 is to some extent a conclusion; and we have seen how this segment fits into the previous history of the material which has now been interwoven to form an extensive composition. One must assume that at a much earlier stage, when our narrative existed by itself, the promise of a son was first given to Abraham. Then, however, the meaning of our narrative, precisely in this respect, has been greatly changed by its incorporation into the Abraham composition as a whole; for no one can read the promise in v. 10 without connecting it to chs. 12.2 and 13.16; 15.18. Contrasting with the repetition, indeed wonderful development, of the promise is Abraham's outward situation. After his immigration to Canaan the gates of fulfillment do not open up for him at all, but a famine overtakes him there. Knowledge of Sarah's barrenness seemed to exclude her from motherhood, and the detour through Hagar to the heir of promise was not acceptable to Yahweh. Finally Abraham's old age, humanly speaking, extinguished every hope. But then God appears and renews the promise precisely ("next year"). This outline of the narrative, which is somewhat disturbed, to be sure, by the presence of the preceding Priestly parallel narrative, ch. 17.15 ff., makes one great problem graphic: the delay of the promise almost to its apparently complete impossibility of fulfillment. Accordingly, the narratives show great interest in the human frame of mind and the temptations into which men were led precisely in their capacity as recipients of promise. In our narrative it is Sarah who because of her laugh stands out from the mutely attentive Abraham. (The woman as a negative figure of contrast was a favorite dramatic device, cf. Job 2.9; Tobit 2.14; 10.4 f.) Abraham's silence is beautiful; it gives the reader time for many thoughts. To what degree of certainty he arrives, after the first germinating suspicion, is not said; the narrative preserves a veil of mystery by allowing none of the persons involved to speak an actual identifying statement (as e.g., Judg. 6.22; 13.21 f.). The narrative intends to show that Abraham treated the strangers in an exemplary fashion. It is significant that the narrator, without letting the promise of a son cease to be a real gift ("*Gastgeschenk*," Gu.), prefaces it with a certain general test for the recipient of God's most elementary commands.

9. GOD'S SOLILOQUY. Ch. 18.17–19

18 [17]The LORD said, "Shall I hide from Abraham what I am about
to do, [18]seeing that Abraham shall become a great and mighty nation,
and all the nations of the earth shall bless themselves by him? [19]No, for
I have chosen him, that he may charge his children and his household after him to keep the way of the LORD by doing righteousness and justice; so that the LORD may bring to Abraham what he has promised him."

[17–19] Our statement (p. 207) that in v. 16 one can detect the end of an originally independent narrative leads naturally to the question about the beginning of the next unified narrative block. This short soliloquy can never have been an independent unit, for it presupposes what precedes and what follows. The same is true of the famous dialogue (vs. 20–33) which also cannot be considered a unified saga (cf. the exposition) because of its poverty of action and its concentration on abstract didactic material. That will be true, however, of the narrative in ch. 19.1–29 in every respect. We confront the fact therefore, that between the two great blocks of material, the Abraham-Mamre and the Lot-Sodom sagas, there are two shorter conversational segments, which do not derive from such ancient traditions. In them, therefore, we find our narrator's thoughts much more explicitly than in the large narratives where he was bound more or less to the wording of the tradition. One can suppose that the Yahwistic narrator here speaks on his own (cf. a similar case in ch. 6.5–8, pp. 116 f. and p. 165). Here, as there, the narrator ventures to give Yahweh's reflections before the judgment. In addition, the sections vs. 17–19 and 20–33 bear a strongly reflective character because of their conversational nature, and this strengthens their theologically programmatic significance. Since Wellhausen vs. 17–19 have been explained generally as a late padding, but Noth has shown that only v. 19 can be considered as a later addition (*Überlieferungsgeschichte des Pentateuch*, 259 n.). Actually it is filled with theological formulations which are quite foreign to the older narrators ("keep Yahweh's way," "doing righteousness and justice," "choose" instead of "know," *yd'*).

The paragraph is concerned with an important theological matter. God does not wish Abraham to learn of the frightful event at Sodom only, as it were, from without. God intends to tell him whom he, God, has called into a relationship of trust (*y^{e}daʿtīw*, "I have made him acquainted with me"), so that God's act outside, in history which otherwise is hidden from man, shall be revealed to him. He is to understand what will happen in Sodom! The reason for God's amazing intention is given particularly in v. 19: Abraham has the position of teacher for his descendants, and the event at Sodom will contain a special admonitory significance for all time (II Peter 2.6). Verse 17, however, in contrast to the preceding and succeeding verses, considers the judgment on Sodom as already fixed, indeed as already executed, whereas according to the context Yahweh is first going to test the city, which, to be sure, is already severely incriminated.

10. ABRAHAM'S DIALOGUE WITH GOD. Ch. 18.20–33

18 [20]Then the LORD said, "Because the outcry against Sodom and
Gomorrah is great and their sin is very grave, [21]I will go down to see
whether they have done altogether according to the outcry which has
come to me; and if not, I will know."

22 So the men turned from there, and went toward Sodom; but
Abraham still stood before the LORD. [23]Then Abraham drew near, and
said, "Wilt thou indeed destroy the righteous with the wicked? [24]Sup-
pose there are fifty righteous within the city; wilt thou then destroy the
place and not spare it for the fifty righteous who are in it? [25]Far be it
from thee to do such a thing, to slay the righteous with the wicked, so
that the righteous fare as the wicked! Far be that from thee! Shall not
the Judge of all the earth do right?" [26]And the LORD said, "If I find at
Sodom fifty righteous in the city, I will spare the whole place for their
sake." [27]Abraham answered, "Behold, I have taken upon myself to
speak to the Lord, I who am but dust and ashes. [28]Suppose five of the
fifty righteous are lacking? Wilt thou destroy the whole city for lack of
five?" And he said, "I will not destroy it if I find forty-five there."
[29]Again he spoke to him, and said, "Suppose forty are found there."
He answered, "For the sake of forty I will not do it." [30]Then he said,
"Oh let not the Lord be angry, and I will speak. Suppose thirty are
found there." He answered, "I will not do it, if I find thirty there."
[31]He said, "Behold, I have taken upon myself to speak to the Lord.
Suppose twenty are found there." He answered. "For the sake of twenty
I will not destroy it." [32]Then he said, "Oh let not the Lord be angry,
and I will speak again but this once. Suppose ten are found there."
He answered, "For the sake of ten I will not destroy it." [33]And the LORD
went his way, when he had finished speaking to Abraham; and Abraham returned to his place.

[20–21] The mystery surrounding the guests whom Abraham is here accompanying is now revealed. In the statement with which

Yahweh takes Abraham into his confidence he speaks quite openly as the protector of justice in all lands. That is not felt to be an unevenness in the narrative, for after the events at Mamre, Abraham could have no further doubt about the identity of his guests. Yahweh has received great complaints about Sodom and Gomorrah. The word "outcry" (*zeʿāqā*) is a technical legal term and designates the cry for help which one who suffers a great injustice screams. (We even know what the cry was, namely, "Foul play!" *ḥāmās*, Jer. 20.8; Hab. 1.2; Job 19.7.) With this cry for help (which corresponds to the old German "*Zeterruf*"), he appeals for the protection of the legal community. What it does not hear or grant, however, comes directly before Yahweh as the guardian of all right (cf. ch. 4.10). Yahweh, therefore, is not concerned with punishing Sodom but rather with an investigation of the case, which is serious, to be sure. The proceeding is hereby opened (Galling).

[22] But again we encounter the problem of Yahweh's relationship to the three. Actually one seems able to define it differently and more clearly than in ch. 18.1–16, for according to v. 22 two turn toward Sodom and one, Yahweh, remains behind (cf. v. 1). That is really connected with the fact that the narrator could express himself and move more freely with reference to this comparatively late material. But that does not explain the relationship at all in the sense of an exclusive two and one, for in ch. 19.13 the two speak as though they were Yahweh, and even more clearly in vs. 21 f. Besides, Yahweh himself has said that he will go down to Sodom (ch. 18.21), an intention that apparently was not abandoned or made impossible with his separation from the two men. One must not press, therefore, for a final rational clarification. Significant in any case is Yahweh's personal visitation of Abraham and his secret dealing with Sodom, i.e., mediately through messengers. In v. 22 occurs one of the very few arbitrary changes which the postexilic Jewish men of learning dared to make in the text (and which were of course precisely noted): That Yahweh remained standing, as though waiting for Abraham, appeared to them as unworthy of Yahweh. Therefore they changed the sentence so that Abraham remained standing before Yahweh. They sacrificed, therefore, Yahweh's gesture of lingering, which contained a silent demand to express itself, to their religious timidity. But the corrected text too has been defended as being in truth the original one.

[23–33] For the following conversation the reader may want to keep in mind the place where it occurred, namely, on one of the heights east of Hebron in view of the sinful city lying at a distance in the valley, the city which had no idea either of its judge or of its intercessor (cf. ch. 19.27 ff.). Abraham understood Yahweh's gesture and came close to him as one who wanted to say something both urgent and discreet. The conversation itself—subject both of great amazement and much derision—unfolds a serious problem of belief. Abraham is not especially concerned with saving Lot, not even with saving Sodom. Rather, Sodom becomes an extreme case of unparalleled validity for demonstrating the theological concern. Sodom is not considered here as a city expressly outside the covenant people, so that God would grant a different forgiveness for it than he would for Israel. On the contrary! Sodom is here for Israel the pattern of a human community toward which Yahweh's eyes turn in judgment. As in the case of every earthly judgment the question would first be, Is Sodom guilty ("godless," *rāšā*) or not guilty ("righteous," *ṣaddīq*)? The terms "righteous" and "godless" must not be understood here in the universal and summary sense of the later Jewish or Pauline doctrine of justification. No, the "sinner" is one who has been adjudged guilty in any judicial instance because of a definite transgression; the "righteous" is the one who has not been found guilty (cf. for this usage Deut. 25.1). This first question is, to be sure, so far as Sodom is concerned, as good as decided at the moment of our conversation. Both Yahweh and Abraham know what the result of the investigation will be and what the consequences will be for Sodom. But behind this first question is another more difficult, and this is where Abraham begins his pressing speech, vs. 23–25. What will happen if the result of the judicial investigation is not quite unambiguous, in that a majority of guilty men are nevertheless confronted by a minority of innocent men? This reflection is somewhat revolutionary, for Israel during its more ancient period was subject both in earthly judgment as in divine to the law of collective guilt. This proceeds from the deeply rooted solidarity of a community incriminated in any felony, a solidarity with fixed limits from which the individual could not simply be released. That is true of the blood ties of the family and tribe as well as of the city community, because the individual with his subjective responsibility is not actually free with respect to the community. (See Gen. 20.9; Josh. 7.24 ff.; esp. Deut. 21.1–9.) Now it would be a great misunderstanding to see in this conversation a protest against this ancient collective idea. Such individualism was often expressed in Israel from the seventh century on. (Deut. 24.16; II Kings 14.6; Ezek. 18.1 ff.) But one must not interpret this section from the viewpoint of this individualizing tendency, which was later present, for Sodom does not cease to be for Abraham a community that belongs together because of blood ties and destiny. Abraham is not concerned either with the release from the city of the guiltless nor with their special preservation. He is concerned with something quite different and much greater, namely, from beginning to end with Sodom as a whole! (Only v. 23, when loosed from the context, could be misunderstood individualistically: "Wilt thou indeed destroy the righteous with the wicked?") The meaning of his question then is: "What determines God's judgment on Sodom, the wickedness of the many or the innocence of the few?" This question shows that the conversation is doubtless the expression of very unyielding, penetrating, theological reflection; not one that forces its way from collectivism to individualism, but one that dares to replace old collective thinking with new. Should not a smaller number of guiltless men be so important before God that this minority could cause a reprieve for the whole community? "The law of guilt-transference has its counterpart in the law of substitution." (Pr.) Basically, Abraham is wrestling, as his appeal to the righteous Judge of the world clearly shows, with a new interpretation of the concept "the righteousness of God." Righteousness in Old Testament thought does not consist in the perfection of action, in the sense of approximation to an ideal, absolute norm. Rather, "righteous action" is always defined by a communal relationship which has been predetermined according to some form (cf. at ch. 15.7). Yahweh has a communal relationship with Sodom too. Is it now broken because of the sins of the majority of its inhabitants, and moreover inclusive of its few guiltless inhabitants? Or does Yahweh's "righteousness" with regard to Sodom not consist precisely in the fact that he will forgive the city for the sake of these innocent ones? Abraham does not ask that as a theological postulate, but rather most submissively and in great anguish of mind before God. Agitation gives him words. Obviously the command to fear God and the din of his problem of faith are struggling within him (cf. Jer. 12.1). Abraham knows, as modern man does not, that as "dust and ashes" (Job 30.19; 42.6) he has no right at all to reason (cf. Job 9.12; Dan. 4.32). But what is amazing is how his courage increases during conversation as Yahweh's grace is willing, how he stretches the capacity of God's gracious righteousness more and more audaciously until he arrives at the astonishing fact that even a very small number of innocent men is more important in God's sight than a majority of sinners and is sufficient to stem the judgment. So predominant is God's will to save over his will to punish! The discontinuance of the conversation at "ten innocent" has given rise to many reflections. But one must ask whether for the narrator it is a discontinuation of the conversation at "ten innocent" has given rise to many silence, i.e., his refusal to go on from the ten innocent to five and finally to one, raises many questions need not mean that the conversation ends with an open question. Apparently Abraham and the narrator, at Yahweh's answer in v. 32, reached a final limit, to ask beyond which did not occur to Abraham. Thereby, in our opinion, the narrative guards the uniqueness and marvel of the message about the one who brings salvation and reconciliation for the "many" (Isa. 53.5, 10); for this was not anything expected or inferred from men. Besides Isa., ch. 53, one should refer to Hos. 11.8–9 for the ultimate consequence not drawn in our conversation: God does not want to destroy, rather *his* heart "recoils"; he is as a holy one "in your midst" (cf. the word about the innocent "in its midst," v. 24b). The righteous one who redeems, the holy one is here not a man but God himself (K. Galling, *Deutsche Theologie*, 1939, 86 ff.).

The narrative of God's conversation with Abraham is thus heavily burdened with a problem of belief; it has a "theoretical spirit" (Pr.). But though one must struggle greatly for an accurate exposition of the dominant purpose of the whole, one may not assume that the conversation has only one meaning and one thesis toward which it is driving, like a modern philosophical treatise. Texts like this always have somewhat wide meshes; they are open toward many sides and have room for more than one single interpretation. It was not, of course, the primary intention of the text to extol Abraham as the paradigmatic, prophetic intercessor. But the narrator would scarcely feel himself badly misunderstood if we were to read this text from the viewpoint of intercession and its power. A different train of thought leads to the following narrative: after such willingness to forgive on God's part, everyone must consider the judgment on Sodom as really just.

The paragraph ch. 18.17–33, as one easily observes, goes back to no ancient saga, in contrast to most of the narratives presented by our narrator. We are dealing here, as also in ch. 12.1–9, for example, with an insertion which the Yahwist put between the ancient narratives. If these insertions do not come precisely from his pen, their whole intellectual stamp is still much closer to him than the actual ancient narratives are. For precisely these insertions are especially revealing to us for the exposition of the entire patriarchal history, because they show us something of the spirit in which the stories about the patriarchs were welded together and in which they are now to be read and understood. The extreme programmatic and theological character of these insertions gives us an important exegetical lead to the spirit in which the ancient narratives may also be expounded. Every expositor knows, of course, that many of them are subject both to a very primitive understanding and a theologically profound interpretation. But here we have a hermeneutic clue!

11. SODOM'S DESTRUCTION. LOT'S DELIVERANCE. Ch. 19.1–29

19 1The two angels came to Sodom in the evening; and Lot was
sitting in the gate of Sodom. When Lot saw them he rose to meet them,
and bowed himself with his face to the earth, 2and said, "My lords, turn
aside, I pray you, to your servant's house and spend the night, and
wash your feet; then you may rise up early and go on your way." They
said, "No; we will spend the night in the street." 3But he urged them
strongly; so they turned aside to him and entered his house; and he
made them a feast, and baked unleavened bread, and they ate. 4But
before they lay down, the men of the city, the men of Sodom, both
young and old, all the people to the last man, surrounded the house;
5and they called to Lot, "Where are the men who came to you tonight?
Bring them out to us, that we may know them." 6Lot went out of the
door to the men, shut the door after him, 7and said, "I beg you, my
brothers, do not act so wickedly. 8Behold, I have two daughters who
have not known man; let me bring them out to you, and do to them as you
please; only do nothing to these men, for they have come under the
shelter of my roof." 9But they said, "Stand back!" And they said,
"This fellow came to sojourn, and he would play the judge! Now we will
deal worse with you than with them." Then they pressed hard against
the man Lot, and drew near to break the door. 10But the men put forth
their hands and brought Lot into the house to them, and shut the door.
11And they struck with blindness the men who were at the door of the
house, both small and great, so that they wearied themselves groping
for the door.

12 Then the men said to Lot, "Have you any one else here? Sons-
in-law, sons, daughters, or any one you have in the city, bring them out
of the place; 13for we are about to destroy this place, because the outcry
against its people has become great before the LORD, and the LORD has
sent us to destroy it." 14So Lot went out and said to his sons-in-law, who
were to marry his daughters, "Up, get out of this place; for the LORD is
about to destroy the city." But he seemed to his sons-in-law to be jesting.

15 When morning dawned, the angels urged Lot, saying, "Arise,
take your wife and your two daughters who are here, lest you be consumed in the punishment of the city." [16]But he lingered; so the men
seized him and his wife and his two daughters by the hand, the LORD
being merciful to him, and they brought him forth and set him outside
the city. [17]And when they had brought them forth, they said, "Flee for
your life; do not look back or stop anywhere in the valley; flee to the
hills, lest you be consumed." [18]And Lot said to them, "Oh, no, my
lords; [19]behold, your servant has found favor in your sight, and you
have shown me great kindness in saving my life; but I cannot flee to the
hills, lest the disaster overtake me, and I die. [20]Behold, yonder city is
near enough to flee to, and it is a little one. Let me escape there—is it
not a little one?—and my life will be saved!" [21]He said to him, "Behold,
I grant you this favor also, that I will not overthrow the city of which
you have spoken. [22]Make haste, escape there; for I can do nothing till
you arrive there." Therefore the name of the city was called Zoar.
[23]The sun had risen on the earth when Lot came to Zoar.

24 Then the LORD rained on Sodom and Gomorrah brimstone and
fire from the LORD out of heaven; [25]and he overthrew those cities, and
all the valley, and all the inhabitants of the cities, and what grew on
the ground. [26]But Lot's wife behind him looked back, and she became
a pillar of salt. [27]And Abraham went early in the morning to the place
where he had stood before the LORD; [28]and he looked down toward
Sodom and Gomorrah and toward all the land of the valley, and be-
held, and lo, the smoke of the land went up like the smoke of a furnace.

29 *So it was that, when God destroyed the cities of the valley, God remembered
Abraham, and sent Lot out of the midst of the overthrow, when he overthrew the
cities in which Lot dwelt.*

It has long been known that the story of Sodom was originally an independent saga. Now, however, as its beginning and end show, it has been incorporated into the large Abraham story as a very striking occurrence. (Concerning the structure of the Abraham-Lot narratives, see the conclusion to the exposition, pp. 223 f.) A new element of suspense has been introduced into the story, of course, by the preceding story of Abraham's conversation with God: What will be the result of the exploratory visit of the messengers? (The older form of the saga reported only one judgment on Sodom, which came upon the city because of the unchastity which did not stop even with divine messengers. Now, however, the visit of the heavenly being is an act of judgment and at the same time a last chance to test Sodom.) On the other hand, Yahweh's previously described visit with Abraham demands further comparisons by the reader: here as there a visit by nondescript guests for a meal, here as there a visitation of God, here with judgment, there with salvation. Here too the representation is of unrivaled vitality and vividness. Yahweh's companions are now called "messengers" (*mal'ākīm*) and in this story appear definitely distinguished from Yahweh. But even here there is a conception of Yahweh himself as the actual subject of speaking and acting (vs. 17, 21; cf. the exposition of ch. 18.22). It is quite understandable that Yahweh visits Sodom in disguise, for it would have been unthinkable for Israel to allow even the possibility of Yahweh's coming into contact with the sin of Sodom. But it is characteristic for Israel's faith, which in every instance thinks ultimately only of Yahweh as the actor and not of some intermediate powers (Amos 3.6; Isa. 45.7), that at the climax of the event Yahweh appears speaking and acting directly, without any mediator (vs. 17, 21).

[1–5] The messengers arrived at Sodom with amazing speed. The preparation of the meal in Hebron began only at noon, and it would have been quite impossible for men to have arrived in Sodom the same evening (about forty miles of difficult road). Lot is now a townsman, a property owner, and already related by marriage to the native population. Corresponding to the milieu of the city, the visit is somewhat different from that in Hebron; and that gives the narrator opportunity to vary vivid incidents in the representation. Lot is sitting, when the strangers enter, right at the large thoroughfare through the fortified, tower gate where men were accustomed to gather in the evening. (For the tower at the gate, cf. II Sam. 18.24. During the day the place served as a court and a market, Ruth 4.1; II Kings 7.1.) Only he rises, goes to meet them, and respectfully invites them to his house. Here too the men are proud and terse, for, of course, they had not come to visit Lot (in contrast to their visit in Hebron with Abraham), but regarding another matter. But Lot's concern about the strangers is quite insistent, and they acquiesce to his invitation. Quickly unleavened bread is baked. Then, however, at bedtime, the Sodomites, both young and old, surround the house in order to lay hands on the guests. One must think of the heavenly messengers as young men in their prime, whose beauty particularly incited evil desire (Gu.). In Canaan, where civilization at that time was already old, sexual aberrations were quite in vogue. At any event the Canaanites seemed dissolute to the migrating Israelites, who were bound to strict patriarchal customs and commands. This was especially true of the Canaanite cult of the fertility gods Baal and Astarte, which was erotic and orgiastic at times. (Lev. 18.22 ff.; 20.13–23.) Sodom was always the example of greatest depravity that men could think of in Israel, but the notion about the particular nature of its sin was not always the same. Isaiah seems to have considered it the barbarity of their administration of justice (Isa. 1.10; 3.9); Ezekiel, however, thinks of "pride, surfeit of food, and prosperous ease" (Ezek. 16.49); and when Jeremiah speaks of adultery, lying, and unwillingness to repent (Jer. 23.14) he does not appear to be thinking directly of unnatural unchastity, which would have been expressed quite differently. It appears, therefore, that our narrative is somewhat distinct from the popular Israelite conception of Sodom's sin. This variation in the notion about Sodom is not particularly surprising over a long period of time, but one must ask even so whether the striking similarity of our narrative in this respect to that of the "infamy of Gibeah" does not point to a relationship, perhaps even a distant dependence of the one saga on the other (Judg., ch. 19). Perhaps an ancient narrative, well known in Israel, about a frightful violation of the law of hospitality was connected only secondarily with Sodom as the seat of all sin. (The clumsy phrase "the men of Sodom" in v. 4 might be explained in this sense as an addition.)

[6–8] The narrative now moves quickly to its climax. Lot goes courageously from the house, carefully shutting the door behind him (our narrator gives the most minute details where necessary), and does his best to avert the worst. The address "my brothers" must not be censured as "too mild." It is not the expression of a particularly friendly attitude but rather indicates a situation of legal equality, only on the basis of which Lot can deal with the men of Sodom at all. But he expected too much. He is told that he is a stranger and his right to act as arbitrator is thus in dispute (*šāpaṭ* is here as often better translated with "arbitrate"). Lot's speech is stirring and poetic ("shelter of my roof," v. 8b), as it had to be for the ancient Oriental in a critical situation. The surprising offer of his daughters must not be judged simply by our Western ideas. That Lot intends under no circumstances to violate his hospitality, that his guests were for him more untouchable than his own daughters, must have gripped the ancient reader, who knew whom Lot intended to protect in this way. But on the other hand, this procedure to which Lot resorted scarcely suited the sensibility of the ancient Israelite. Our narrator would be misunderstood if we did not give him credit for expecting his readers to judge a very complicated situation. Lot did attempt to preserve the sacredness of hospitality by means of an extreme measure, but was it not a compromise? ("In reality the visit of the men of God only revealed the ambiguity in which he had lived the whole time." Fr.) Actually, the narrator with great artistry draws a picture of Lot which awakens our sympathy, but it is a picture of a man whose decisions and acts are only half formed. And is not the subsequent narrative in vs. 30 ff. to be understood as a nemesis which Lot's daughters bring on him? (Jac.) **[9–14]** It is therefore a bit comical when this heroic gesture quickly collapses and the one who intended to protect the heavenly beings is himself protected when they quickly draw him back into the house and strike his assailants with a miraculous blindness. The word in question, which has not yet been etymologically explained, apparently does not mean complete blinding, but rather to be dazzled, to "see falsely" (Jac.), cf. II Kings 6.18. With the men outside groping about helplessly and finally having to leave comes a certain relaxation in the tension. The narrator brings us back into the house where the strangers now reveal their incognito, for in order to save Lot and his family they must make themselves known as messengers of God. Sodom's sin is now established, the outcry over the injustice of the Sodomites (see at ch. 18.20) is fully confirmed. The preliminary inquiry into the case is concluded, the preparation for punishment begins. Lot believed the heavenly beings, but that is only indirectly discernible in the rush of events when Lot goes to his sons-in-law that same night to warn them. (One can translate v. 14 "who had come [to marry]" or also "who wanted to take." But since the daughters were still living in the father's house, the futuristic conception is decisively better.) "But he seemed to them to be jesting." The narrative achieves a powerful effect with this statement of the completely negative result of this nocturnal conversation. The statement corresponds clearly in the inner structure of the narrative to Sarah's laugh (ch. 18.12). There a divine promise of grace was concerned, here judgment. But here as there the impression made was the same; the hearers were so unable to receive the message that it seemed even ridiculous to them.

[15–16] The events and conversations from the first rays of dawn until the occurrence of the catastrophe at sunrise are dramatically described: the messengers counseling greatest speed, Lot who hesitates and has lost his will, who with his family must be taken by hand and led from the city, and in the background the most terrible divine judgment which can break loose at any moment. The effectiveness of the Yahwistic narrative rests to a great extent on the fact that the reader is so intensively transported to the time of day in question.

Here it is the suspense of the imminent dawn, in ch. 18.1 it was noon, in ch. 15.7 ff. the approaching dusk (Pr.).

[17–22] It is probable that the section vs. 17–22 did not yet belong to an earlier version of the narrative. It has a certain independence because of its aetiological orientation, and is also striking in that Yahweh speaks and is spoken to directly. But now the passage belongs inalienably to the story, for the events of ch. 19.30–38, which belong to the chief narrative thread, are tied to it (v. 30). It transfers the emphasis of the whole from the judgment of Sodom more sharply toward Lot. Because of this addition Lot's deliverance and the circumstances attending it received thematically their ascendancy in the structure of meaning in the narrative over the description of the judgment on Sodom. Further, Yahweh's very personal speaking and acting emphasize the theological significance of the work of delivering Lot much more strongly. This change, which is unusual for our feeling for style, is not accidental. When a man is delivered from judgment, it is a matter for God only. Lot too speaks directly to God in the messengers (v. 19). The suspense has now reached its peak. Lot recoils at the demand that he flee into the mountains, i.e., the eastern Moabitic mountains. He asks, speaking much too much in his agitation, that he may flee to a small village in the vicinity. The narrative here plays etymologically with the name Zoar (*miṣʿār*, "a trifle"). The site of the place (southeast of the Dead Sea?) is not yet determined. The beginning of the catastrophe is described in vs. 23 f., in three statements which juxtapose three events as contemporaneous: sunrise, Lot's arrival in Zoar, and the fall of fire and brimstone. (They are so-called nominal sentences in which the subject appears first in the sentence for emphasis; in them one may notice the slackening narration.)

[23–25] It is quite possible that the tradition contains a distant recollection of an actual catastrophe. Perhaps a tectonic earthquake released gases (hydrogen sulphide) or opened up the way for asphalt and petroleum. If these minerals were ignited, "it would be easy for the entire mass of air over the opened chasm to be suddenly in flames" (Blankenhorn, *Zeitschr. des Deutschen Palästinavereins*, XIX, 1896, 1 ff.). As a matter of fact, the Dead Sea coastal area is today rich in deposits of asphalt and sulphur. This event, however, cannot be connected with the origin of the Dead Sea itself, for it belongs geologically to a much earlier period. On the other hand some have wondered whether the Dead Sea was later enlarged southward by a break in the land, and whether a catastrophe then came to an ancient civilized area. Our narrator, according to ch. 13.10, seems to assume that the entire "region" was agriculturally rich before the catastrophe of Sodom; and if our narrator here is not oriented precisely aetiologically in this sense, still it causes the reader tacitly to think of that death valley which was known to all. Thus Sodom was remembered by Israel as the example for all time of a complete divine judgment on a sinful community. (Deut. 29.23; Isa. 1.9 f.; 13.19; Jer. 49.18; 50.40; Ezek. 16.46 ff.; Hos. 11.8; Amos 4.11; Zeph. 2.9; Ps. 11.6; Lam. 4.6.) In these references Sodom and Gomorrah are always mentioned together as though identical. In contrast to them, it is striking that our narrative scarcely mentions Gomorrah and especially that it can give the reader not the least idea of this city and its conditions. It too was simply destroyed. But what were the findings here regarding the wicked and the blameless? The assumption, therefore, that the words "and Gomorrah" in chs. 18.20; 19.24 f., 28 are a later addition is justified. That too is a sign that the Sodom tradition (which is primarily prophetic) does not go back directly to our narrative (see at v. 5) but had somewhat different roots. Therefore, the name of the second city was added to harmonize the traditions. Also, the relation of the tradition about "Sodom and Gomorrah" to the quite similar one about "Admah and Zeboiim" (Deut. 29.23; Hos. 11.8) is not clear. Later writers simply add the cities (ch. 14.2). The book of the Wisdom of Solomon even speaks of a pentapolis (ch. 10.6), and therefore includes Zoar too.

[26] The narrative artist in the Old Testament is quite familiar with the difficulties of vividly presenting extensive events; he also knows that the description will be much more impressive if it can suggest the whole indirectly in detail. So our narrative ends with the description of two details from which the reader gains a glance at the terribleness of the whole, namely, with Lot's wife's backward look and Abraham's look at the wasted landscape. It is quite probable that an old aetiological motif is present in the strange death of Lot's wife, i.e., that a bizarre rock formation was the reason for this narrative. Because of severe erosion such pillars of salt can arise there very easily, but they also crumble again quickly. In ancient times such formations were pointed out and referred to as Lot's wife. Josephus (first century A.D.) saw one such formation. (*Antiquities*, I, 11, 4; cf. Wisd. of Sol. 10.7.) But beyond the aetiological motif, which is not directly suggested here, our narrator proposes another idea to his reader: where

God intervenes in a direct act on earth man cannot adopt the stance of a spectator (cf. at chs. 2.21; 15.12); and before divine judgment there is only the possibility of being smitten or of escaping, but no third alternative.

[27–28] The end of the story is very beautiful. What can the narrator say after all that and regarding it? He takes us back to Abraham to whom the conversation with God had not given an easy assurance. He hastens again in the morning to the place where the conversation had taken place so that he may look from there toward Sodom. The old man at the top of the mountain, bending over to peer below, who sees only a black cloud of smoke hovering in the valley over the place of the former abode—this quiet and silent picture is a marvelous conclusion to the dramatically moving story. With this concluding sentence the narratives of ch. 18 and ch. 19, which were originally quite foreign to each other, are welded together into a unit. If one considers the great difference in content in the two narratives and the simplicity with which they are closely united, one will become conscious of the masterly skill of this narrator.

[29] Verse 29 belongs to the Priestly source. It is clearly a summary condensation of the entire occurrence in one sentence and shows us how the Priestly document has cut the tradition down to the limit whenever it does not concern Israel's internal sacred regulations. It does not intend to tell a story (the statement presupposes a knowledge of the event) but only to note the divine facts as such. Accordingly, God is the subject of both the primary and the secondary clause. That God "remembered" Lot for Abraham's sake is a conception which is not emphasized in the Yahwistic narrative. Did P think of Abraham's conversation with God as intercession for Lot?

12. LOT'S DAUGHTERS. Ch. 19.30–38

19 30Now Lot went up out of Zoar, and dwelt in the hills with his
two daughters, for he was afraid to dwell in Zoar; so he dwelt in a cave
with his two daughters. 31And the first-born said to the younger, "Our
father is old, and there is not a man on earth to come in to us after the
manner of all the earth. 32Come, let us make our father drink wine, and
we will lie with him, that we may preserve offspring through our
father." 33So they made their father drink wine that night; and the
first-born went in, and lay with her father; he did not know when she
lay down or when she arose. 34And on the next day, the first-born said
to the younger, "Behold, I lay last night with my father; let us make him
drink wine tonight also; then you go in and lie with him, that we may
preserve offspring through our father." 35So they made their father

drink wine that night also; and the younger arose, and lay with him; and he did not know when she lay down or when she arose. [36]Thus both the daughters of Lot were with child by their father. [37]The first-born bore a son, and called his name Moab; he is the father of the Moabites to this day. [38]The younger also bore a son, and called his name Ben-ammi; he is the father of the Ammonites to this day.

[30–38] This event forms the keystone to the Lot story which the narrator has followed some distance since ch. 13 along with Abraham's story. From now on nothing further is said about Lot. As in the case of all these narratives, in spite of the coarse material, the emphases are always nicely put, and no judgment is expressed concerning the happenings. The reflective reader must make his own judgments. Thus the beginning provokes a rather decisive judgment: Lot has not remained in Zoar. Fear in the presence of the place of God's judgment has driven him farther east into the mountains of Moab. But was that a good journey, after Zoar was permitted to be the place of his abode by a special permission of divine grace? He did not feel safe there, and in his career of faintheartedness and temporization he is driven farther and farther from the ways which God had taken with him. Now we find him in "the" cave, a place apparently with which a particular tradition was connected which would have been familiar to the readers of that time. There, in the insensibility of his intoxication he becomes a tool, without any will of its own, of his two unmarried and childless daughters. Through incestuous intercourse with their own father they raise up descendants for the family which is threatened with extinction. The sons born of them are the tribal ancestors of the later Ammonites and Moabites. The explanations of the names are of course very free etymological allusions. They are wrong for Moab; for Ammon they accidentally correspond to the linguistic meaning of the name. (The word *'am* here has the ancient meaning of "uncle," "the closest male relative," "relations," which is quite common in Arabic but which has been only occasionally preserved in Hebrew.)

The question about the meaning of the story in its present context is easier to answer than the one about its nature in the history of saga. The material at the basis of the tradition has been considered to be a product of popular political wit by which Israel tried to repay her occasionally powerful enemies, the Moabites and Ammonites, for everything she had suffered at their hands, by such derogatory stories about their most disgraceful origin. A more probable assumption, however, is that the meaning of the tradition which is behind our present narrative was from the beginning serious. Accordingly, we should have to consider the section vs. 30–38 as an original Moabite tradition in which the wild determination of both ancestral mothers was glorified. The fact that Lot's daughters are in no wise ashamed of the origin of their children, but rather proclaim it openly and fix it forever in their son's names, leads to this interpretation. The sons who are born to such a bed, however, "proudly proclaim the heroism of their mother and the purity of their blood: they were not begotten from foreign seed, but from father and daughter, purest thoroughbreds" (Gu.). It has even been asked whether our story is not based on a very ancient myth about the origin of man. The statement of the daughters "There is not a man on earth to come in to us" (v. 31), it is said, shows that Lot and his daughters were the only men at all. Then the myth would have dealt with the begetting of men in the nuptials of primeval man and two primeval mothers (A. Lods, "La caverne de Lot," *Revue de l'histoire des religions*, 1927, 204–219). But the daughters' speech is explained more simply from the Oriental circumstance of that time and this, whereby a connubium was possible only within the framework of certain groups, and where it had to be regulated by a certain custom. Lot was loosed from his local group, and furthermore, the narrator presents the region to which he had gone as desolate.

Without doubt the narrative now contains indirectly a severe judgment on the incest in Lot's house, and Lot's life becomes inwardly and outwardly bankrupt. If one surveys the stages of his career, his succumbing to the attraction of the luxuriant Jordan valley, his inability to assert himself with his offer to the Sodomites, and his inability to make up his mind even before divine judgment or to entrust himself to the leadership of the messengers and Yahweh's protection, and finally his succumbing in drunkenness to vital forces, it will become clear that the narrator has drawn a very compact picture in spite of being bound to ancient traditions. Having been set on the way to a promise by Yahweh, just as Abraham was (ch. 12.4), he turned aside from this way (ch. 13), still supported by God's grace, and then finally slipped completely from God's hand, which directs history. Especially surprising is the similar psychological representation. We have here for once something actually like a "portrait"! And again, as in the Hagar story, the sympathetic interest of the narrator in the way of those who go out, i.e., those who leave Abraham's house and depart from his way, is striking. It is an interest in which we recognize the intellectually free and humanized atmosphere which our narrator breathed (cf. pp. 17, 29).

By comparison with the usual, perforce loosely connected string of ancient traditional units, the succession of narratives in chs. 18 and 19 is unusually compact. Chapter 13 is then also inseparable from it, for this chapter has no real conclusion in itself and never, indeed, existed for itself alone. It functions only as an exposition to chs. 18 f. The material of chs. 13; 18; 19, therefore, must already have been formed into a compactly connected event and so related before the Yahwist incorporated it into his work. This explains the unified psychological penetration which was much more difficult to accomplish in the composition of the great Abraham narrative, for example, which combines in itself so many different traditions. And this is quite apart from the fact that the ancients did not make such a strong demand for the psychological unity and credibility of a personality sketch at all.

13. ABRAHAM AND SARAH IN GERAR. Ch. 20

20 1From there Abraham journeyed toward the territory of the
Negeb, and dwelt between Kadesh and Shur; and he sojourned in Gerar.
2And Abraham said of Sarah his wife, "She is my sister." And Abimelech
king of Gerar sent and took Sarah. 3But God came to Abimelech in a
dream by night, and said to him, "Behold, you are a dead man, because
of the woman whom you have taken; for she is a man's wife." 4Now
Abimelech had not approached her; so he said, "Lord, wilt thou slay an
innocent people? 5Did he not himself say to me, 'She is my sister'? And
she herself said, 'He is my brother.' In the integrity of my heart and the
innocence of my hands I have done this." 6Then God said to him in the
dream, "Yes, I know that you have done this in the integrity of your
heart, and it was I who kept you from sinning against me; therefore I
did not let you touch her. 7Now then restore the man's wife; for he is
a prophet, and he will pray for you, and you shall live. But if you do not
restore her, know that you shall surely die, you, and all that are yours."

8 So Abimelech rose early in the morning, and called all his
servants, and told them all these things; and the men were very much
afraid. 9Then Abimelech called Abraham, and said to him, "What
have you done to us? And how have I sinned against you that you have
brought on me and my kingdom a great sin? You have done to me
things that ought not to be done." 10And Abimelech said to Abraham,
"What were you thinking of, that you did this thing?" 11Abraham said,
"I did it because I thought, There is no fear of God at all in this place,
and they will kill me because of my wife. 12Besides she is indeed my
sister, the daughter of my father but not the daughter of my mother;

and she became my wife. [13]And when God caused me to wander from my father's house, I said to her, 'This is the kindness you must do me: at every place to which we come, say of me, He is my brother.' " [14]Then Abimelech took sheep and oxen, and male and female slaves, and gave them to Abraham, and restored Sarah his wife to him. [15]And Abimelech said, "Behold, my land is before you; dwell where it pleases you." [16]To Sarah he said, "Behold, I have given your brother a thousand pieces of silver; it is your vindication in the eyes of all who are with you; and before every one you are righted." [17]Then Abraham prayed to God; and God healed Abimelech, and also healed his wife and female slaves so that they bore children. [18]For the LORD had closed all the wombs of the house of Abimelech because of Sarah, Abraham's wife.

The narrative vs. 1–17 (18) is unanimously ascribed to the Elohist, wherever one reckons with the existence of this document at all. It corresponds materially in detail to the Yahwist's pericope about the endangering of the ancestress (Gen. 12.10–20). The exposition of this earlier section must, therefore, be referred to because only a comparison of both theologically different conceptions will make clear the peculiarities of each. Our Elohistic narrative gives much more consideration to the requirements of a reflective, indeed sensitive, and theologically refined readership. Accordingly, it is strongly concentrated on the psychological, i.e., on psychological motivation. In this version of the narrative much is said, explained, and substantiated. The whole objective enigma of the occurrence itself, which was suggested to the reader in Gen. 12.10–20, does not come into its own here because of the many speeches; it is somewhat displaced by the explanations and motivations that the narrator felt important for his readers. On the other hand, there are here some ancient characteristics that are missing in the Yahwistic account. For a further comparison of the two versions, see the end of the exposition.

[1] To what the "from there" referred in the original Elohistic context can no longer be determined. (It certainly referred to a stage which is to be put shortly after Abraham's immigration to Canaan.) In any event, the story about the "jeopardizing of the ancestress" belonged, for E too, directly after the hearing of the promise. Now, that is, after the combination with the Yahwistic narrative, one must connect the data about place in v. 1 with Mamre. Whether it occurred immediately after the event at Sodom, so that Abraham also was impelled to move (cf. ch. 19.30) is difficult to say. The idea that

Abraham moved away from the vicinity of the horrible place seems quite reasonable to the reader. Actually, the narrator had to undertake this change of place because in what follows a whole series of Beer-sheba traditions is brought together. In itself we have in our narrative a good example of that "change of pasture" which has remained the law of life for nomads with small cattle from the patriarchal period down to the present day (see p. 170). Characteristic of it is also a certain symbiosis with the cities, into which those seminomads were necessarily led. Shechem exercised a very similar attraction for commerce and even for connubium according to Gen. 33.18 f.; 34.1 ff. (Gerar lay near Gaza; the place is probably identical with the modern Tell-es-Seria, southeast of Gaza.) It is one of those numerous dynastic centers and city-states which, together with its meadowland, were so characteristic for the political picture of pre-Israelite Palestine, especially in the plains.

Obviously the narrator imagines Sarah to be much younger; the inclusion of our story in the Yahwistic composition and its later combination with P (cf. chs. 18.12; 17.17) caused an inconsistency that the redactors could not remove. And the narrator states quite generally and briefly that Abraham passed Sarah off as his sister. Actually the matter seems less offensive, when presented so tersely, than it did in the conversation on the road, with its almost cynical utilitarian consideration (ch. 12.11 f.). Furthermore, the way Sarah found herself in the king's harem is reported much more briefly than in ch. 12.14 f. And finally, the affair is somewhat ameliorated when in the opinion of our narrator Sarah really was Abraham's half sister. Marriage with one's half sister was forbidden by later law (Lev. 18.9, 11; 20.17) but was still possible at the time of David (II Sam. 13.13). This notation (Gen. 20.12) must therefore be ancient tradition. (Did the Yahwist forgo mentioning it so as not to exonerate Abraham?) Actually, the continuation shows that our narrator knows exactly the captiousness of this half-truth. **[4–6]** For now, in the representation of the actual conflict, our source becomes very voluble. The particularly complicated question about guilt is the center of interest, and thus the emphasis is shifted to another level. In the Yahwistic version the concern, with strange exclusiveness, was with Yahweh's dealing with Abraham, Sarah, and the foreign king without any serious consideration of the guilt question. Our narrator is at least just as interested in the human aspect of the affair, in the guilty-innocent Abimelech and his deliverance and in Abraham's strange role as the guilty mediator. One could almost say that our story has two faces, an ancient and a modern. Ancient is the emphasis on Abimelech's guilt: the king infringed on another's marriage which was absolutely protected by the divinity. This is an objective fact, quite apart from premeditation or ignorance, which severely incriminates him. And not only him, for all his subjects collectively are caught with him in very great danger, liable to be drawn with him into a catastrophe (v. 9b)! Possibly the punishment that here threatened the "kingdom" is not to be understood in the sense of collective liability but rather as "the punishment of the sovereign" by which a king is deprived of his possessions (cf. II Sam. 24.15 ff., D. Daube, *Studies in Biblical Law*, 1947, 174 ff.). But even so, the matter is very ancient. In contrast to that is the advanced reflection over the subjective ignorance that caused Abimelech to act in good faith. Indeed, the personal blamelessness of the heathen king is delineated by the narrator to the profound humiliation of Abraham. It is audacious of our narrator to consider the heathen worthy of an address, indeed, a personal conversation with Yahweh. That Abimelech had actually violated Abraham's marriage was not questioned by the ancients. Therefore the divine address begins with a reference to the state of affairs and its fatal consequences for Abimelech. But God also knows that Abimelech did not act purposefully; God preserved him from the extreme limit and he shows him a way of deliverance through Abraham's intercession. Our narrator thinks of Abraham as the bearer of an office of mediator and prophet by virtue of which he has special access to God. Abraham apparently has authority for this effective intercession for the objectively guilty, subjectively innocent Abimelech without any regard for his own large share in the guilt. How complicated are the theological ideas that the narrative thus suggests!

[7] The designation of Abraham as a "prophet" (*nābī'*) must be explained from the viewpoint of the origin of our text, for the E source is presumably close to prophetic circles as they are described for us in II Kings, chs. 2 to 4. This was a phase in which this movement was connected much more closely to the sanctuary and cult than at the time of the major prophets. Their office at that time was less the proclamation of eschatological messages than of authorized intercession. The question in our narrative, therefore, concerns an anachronistic transposition of a cultic designation to the early period of Israel. Later periods naturally thought of Abraham by analogy with their own contemporary charismatic officials. The preference of this source for revelation in dreams is well known; it corresponds to a theologically refined notion of the process of revelation itself (see pp. 26f.).

[8–18] The divine disclosure of the strange and dangerous situation into which Abimelech had entered staggers the king. Also, the result of an immediate assembling of his council of state was only great fear. The way the narrator refrains from diminishing the subjective justice of the king and reveals in him and his court what Abraham had not thought he could count on, namely, the fear of God, is well done. Only the conversation and discussion with Abraham himself further clarifies this mysterious matter for Abimelech. It is humiliating for Abraham to have to be surpassed by the heathen in the fear of God. With that our narrator expresses recognition of an important fact that may not have been easy for the pride of Israel's faith to take. The "fear of God" must be understood here in the general ancient sense as reverence and regard of the most elementary moral norms, whose severe guardian was everywhere considered to be the divinity. The term is therefore not so much psychological as simply a word for "obedience" (see at Gen. 22.12; 42.18). Abraham's excuse, which gave as the motivation for his action the uncertainty of his nomadic life, is rather lame when contrasted with the loyalty of the foreign king, and completely so in view of the many honors and favors that Abimelech pours on Abraham and Sarah: the flocks and servants, the invitation to settle in his land, and especially the "covering of eyes"* for Sarah. The strange expression is probably a legal term. The gift means that the critical eyes of others will be covered so that they will be unable to discover anything shocking in Sarah. Also the fact that he calls Abraham Sarah's "brother" is apparently spoken legally and officially. In this way he avoids compromising Abraham. Abimelech does everything to demonstrate Abraham's and Sarah's honorableness, for no one can give gifts of honor to disgraced people without discrediting himself. (Notice how much more humiliating for Abraham the gifts in Gen. 12.16 were!) On the strength of Abraham's intercession the spell of sterility, which had fallen on the women of the court, was broken (v. 18 is considered by many a later addition). The gift of effective intercession, according to an older conception, was what made a man a real prophet (Num. 12.13; 21.7; Deut. 9.26; I Sam. 12.19–23). Regarding the ambiguous role

*Von Rad translates Hebrew *keṣut ʿeynayim* with "*Augendecke*," which corresponds to RSV, "vindication in the eyes of. . . ."

of a guilty prophet who was nevertheless authorized by God, see I Kings 13.11 ff.

Epilogue. There is scarcely another patriarchal story whose content is so complicated and full of problems. It is complicated because the archaic material was revised by a narrator who himself, without sacrificing the ancient tradition, lived in an atmosphere of more mature theological ideas and concerns and wrote for a considerably refined readership. The Yahwist left open all the possibilities for what might have happened to Sarah with the king; the Elohist painfully excludes the thought that Sarah could have been touched by Abimelech. What is new is, above all, the positive interest in Abimelech, in the problem of his guilt, his whole relationship to God (his fear of God). One can ask whether this extremely reflective impulse, which moves the reader to reflection, only benefits the primary concern of the narrative. The enigmatic and marvelous nature of the objective divine event, the preservation of the future mother of the heir of promise, is no longer so dominant as in ch. 12.10–20, where this free divine activity is represented as far removed from all human ideas and doubts. But now the narrator has to consider "problems." This loss is, of course, compensated for by the addition of new characteristics to the narrative. The question of whether and how the heathen king could be freed of his guilt introduces to the story a completely new theological concern.

14. ISAAC'S BIRTH. ISHMAEL'S EXPULSION. Ch. 21.1–21

21 [1]The LORD visited Sarah as he had said, and the LORD did to
Sarah as he had promised. [2]And Sarah conceived, and bore Abraham
a son in his old age at the time of which God had spoken to him.
[3]*Abraham called the name of his son who was born to him, whom Sarah bore him,*
Isaac. [4]*And Abraham circumcised his son Isaac when he was eight days old, as*
God had commanded him. [5]*Abraham was a hundred years old when his son Isaac*
was born to him. [6]And Sarah said, "God has made laughter for me; every
one who hears will laugh over me." [7]And she said, "Who would have
said to Abraham that Sarah would suckle children? Yet I have borne
him a son in his old age."

8 And the child grew, and was weaned; and Abraham made a great
feast on the day that Isaac was weaned. [9]But Sarah saw the son of
Hagar the Egyptian, whom she had borne to Abraham, playing with
her son Isaac. [10]So she said to Abraham, "Cast out this slave woman
with her son; for the son of this slave woman shall not be heir with my
son Isaac." [11]And the thing was very displeasing to Abraham on account
of his son. [12]But God said to Abraham, "Be not displeased because of the
lad and because of your slave woman; whatever Sarah says to you, do as

she tells you, for through Isaac shall your descendants be named.[13] And
I will make a nation of the son of the slave woman also, because he is
your offspring." [14]So Abraham rose early in the morning, and took
bread and a skin of water, and gave it to Hagar, putting it on her
shoulder,*along with the child, and sent her away. And she departed,
and wandered in the wilderness of Beer-sheba.

15 When the water in the skin was gone, she cast the child under one
of the bushes. [16]Then she went, and sat down over against him a good
way off, about the distance of a bowshot; for she said, "Let me not look
upon the death of the child." And as she sat over against him, the child
lifted up his voice and wept. [17]And God heard the voice of the lad; and
the angel of God called to Hagar from heaven, and said to her, "What
troubles you, Hagar? Fear not; for God has heard the voice of the lad
where he is. [18]Arise, lift up the lad, and hold him fast with your hand;
for I will make him a great nation." [19]Then God opened her eyes, and
she saw a well of water; and she went, and filled the skin with water,
and gave the lad a drink. [20]And God was with the lad, and he grew up;
he lived in the wilderness, and became an expert with the bow. [21]He
lived in the wilderness of Paran; and his mother took a wife for him
from the land of Egypt.

[1–7] All sources told of Isaac's birth, of course, and thus this section really lost its own literary unity in the final redaction of the Hexateuch, for obviously parts of all three documents are brought together here. P is the most detailed (vs. 2a–5) and refers to ch. 17. Abraham names and circumcises the child (cf. pp. 195 f.). The name Isaac, like the great majority of Hebrew personal names, is a statement (unshortened it is *yiṣḥāq'ēl*) and means "may the divinity smile (on the child)." But the root of this name (*ṣāḥaq*, "laugh") has become a dominant motif for the story, far beyond its etymological meaning. The narrators play with it by varying its meaning freely according to one or the other meaning (chs. 18.12; 17.17; 21.6a, 6b). The way in which Sarah seizes upon this leading word makes it probable that originally in the older sources the mother named the child, for both statements apparently accompanied and explained the name. In v. 6, however, there are two very different statements. The first speaks in the sense of devout thanksgiving of a laugh of joy which God gave to the sterile woman (I Sam. 2.5; Ps. 113.9). The other (v. 6b), apparently with reference to ch. 18.12, thinks in embarrassment of the laughter and talk that will now take place among the neighbors. It contains, therefore, no "religious" ideas, but precisely in its sober realism it shows how completely in-

*See BH. Present text: "gave it to Hagar, placing it upon her shoulder, and the boy . . ."

comprehensible this act of God was for all human intellect. One can derive these rather contrasting reactions of Sarah from two sources, but the narrators usually venture in the same statement to give several explanations in etymological plays of this kind (cf. chs. 16.13; 22.14).

The locale of this and the following narratives is the land south of Beer-sheba in which Abraham is still moving about according to the needs of his flocks for pasture. Only after about three years were children weaned in ancient Israel (I Sam. 1.23 f.; II Macc. 7.27), and this date was cause for a great family celebration. **[8–11]** From then on began a new period in the child's life, and the narrator accurately describes how the mother anticipates the first steps of her child into life. She sees "the son of Hagar the Egyptian" (the narrator emphasizes in her thought Ishmael's inferior rank), she sees him playing with her child; and unpleasant thoughts occur to the calculating woman. Whether the verb (*ṣāḥaq*, again an allusion to the name Isaac) here means simply "playing" or "behaving wantonly with someone" can no longer be decided. What Ishmael did need not be anything evil at all. The picture of the two boys playing with each other on an equal footing is quite sufficient to bring the jealous mother to a firm conclusion: Ishmael must go! Every year he, the older one, becomes a stronger rival for Isaac, and at last he will even divide the inheritance with him. So she brings in Abraham, speaking scornfully of "this slave woman" without calling her by name. The terse style of these narratives makes one suppose a lengthy and difficult discussion between husband and wife in v. 10, for Abraham felt himself bound to Ishmael and Hagar.

[12–13] Now, however, our story deviates from the parallel Yahwistic version in ch. 16. There Abraham was passive and without any opinion of his own up to the limit of his dignity; here the Elohist insists that Abraham resisted this demand and yielded to it only upon God's express directive. His compliance here was not the result of weakness but of obedience to God's plan for history. This plan, to be sure, only appears to coincide with Sarah's thought.* Even though

*Luther defended Sarah's offense, scarcely in accordance with the narrator's intention. "His wife's counsel displeased Abraham greatly, for he loved his son like any other man. But he was not regarding the promise so assiduously as Sarah was, for his paternal heart hindered him. Sarah made specific distinctions between the servant's son and her own; she does not speak according to her feminine feelings but by the Holy Spirit, and she supports herself by the certain promise she had heard about her son." (Oskar Ziegner, *Luther und die Erzväter*, Berlin, 1952, 97.)

the mother thought far ahead into the future, God's plans are made for much greater historical distances. One could call vs. 12 f. the "tense moment" in the structure of the narrative, for the reader has not expected that God would be on Sarah's side, but rather on Abraham's. But precisely this is what the patriarchal stories like to show, that God pursues his great historical purposes in, with, and under all headstrong acts of men.

[14–16] The description of Hagar's expulsion comes from a man who knew how to handle all the means of narrative representation superbly. He lets the reader participate in all the external work of the early morning preparations for departure. He sees the completely inadequate food supply but learns nothing of Abraham's or Hagar's feelings. But this silence amidst the bustle is all the more powerful. Then the representation becomes dramatic. The mother wandering in the wilderness, the child parched with thirst, the sight of whom is too much for the mother but whom she cannot bear to leave—here the narrator lets the persons speak and express themselves, he lets them cry and thereby intends to grip and move the reader. Doubtless the narrator considered Ishmael a small child whom Hagar had to carry, then put down, etc. By Priestly computation, however, Ishmael must have been sixteen or seventeen years old at this time (chs. 16.16; 21.5, P). At the price of a very difficult sentence stylistically the redactor altered the text of v. 14 without thereby removing the inconsistency.

[17–21] The conclusion of the human tragedy is very simple: "God heard the voice of the lad." Here the narrator alludes to the name, Ishmael ("God has heard"). Here too the angel of God is nothing else than a form of God's own appearing, by which Yahweh's "I" addresses man (cf. v. 18b, "I will make him"). It is noteworthy, however, that just because of that relationship of identity the Elohist no longer dares to let the angel of Yahweh walk on earth as a man. Rather he lets him be known to man only with his voice "from heaven" (cf. ch. 22.11). (Concerning the angel of Yahweh, see pp. 192 f.) Hagar is not to give up the child (literally, "keep your hand firmly on him"), for God intends great things for Ishmael. Again the narrator ventures an unbelievable paradox to the honor of his God. The child, parched with thirst and given up even by its own mother, will become "a great people" (Isa. 49.15). Compared with the promise to Abraham this statement seems like a pale reflection of that salvation which was promised to Abraham's sons who were to come from a sterile mother's womb. The promise of land and the call into a special relationship to God (ch. 17.7) are here missing. (This difference will become even more pronounced in the blessings of chs. 27.28 f. and 27.39 f.) Now Hagar by virtue of divine assistance sees a well of water which saves her life and the life of the child. (Apparently the well was previously there; it seems that the narrator avoided speaking of an external natural wonder in this affair; cf. also ch. 22.13.) Also God's protecting hand will be over Ishmael from now on. But his way of life became different from that of the patriarchs. He became a bowman, i.e., he lived by hunting and plunder. Expressed in modern terms, he became the ancestor of the Bedouins, the camel-nomads (see p. 170). His dwelling place in the almost sterile steppe between Palestine and Egypt determined his way of life. Also, the fact that he married an Egyptian woman indicates how far he had gone from the regulations of his father's house. (See chs. 24.3–4; 26.34; 27.46.)

Epilogue. That this narrative once had an aetiological purpose, that it answered the question about why the Ishmaelites, who were related to Israel, tent in the south beyond civilization (cf. p. 195), can no longer be noticed in our Elohistic version, in contrast to ch. 16. The name Ishmael has been completely deleted from it, apparently to lift the event even more than it was in J into the realm of the universally human, since the narrator's age no longer knew any Ishmaelites. The name Ishmael is barely suggested in a pun (v. 17), but genuine aetiologies were not satisfied with such subtle allusions. And the recollection that the place of appearing was a holy place has disappeared completely, again in contrast to J (ch. 16.13 f.). It is interesting to see how the materials of this narrative slowly strip off the external historical circumstances not to volatilize into timeless truths but to represent a divine act of typical validity. This narrative too is concerned with that strange theme in sacred history, namely, the departure from Abraham's house, the origin of a by-way of sacred history. This enterprise is not deprived of Yahweh's protection and blessing, but it will not be accompanied by the blessings of salvation which were promised to Abraham's legitimate offspring (cf. p. 193). Paul in Gal. 4.28 ff. follows an even more radical tradition. He sees in Ishmael the enemy of the heir of promise.

A comparison of the two versions chs. 16 and 21 is fascinating. We repeat the essence of what Gunkel wrote (pp. 231 ff.): "The actors are the same: the jealous Sarah, the peaceable Abraham, the

Egyptian servant Hagar." How Abraham's role was changed in our version was shown in the exposition. But Hagar too is described differently. In ch. 16 she is courageous and proud, in ch. 21 she finds herself in a miserable, pitiable situation. In ch. 16 she was partly to blame for her fate, here she is innocent. Thus ch. 16 is obviously the more original version in every respect, while ch. 21 can describe things movingly and is apparently designed for a much more sensitive readership. The redactor of the sources who had to reckon with both narratives made it possible by verses 9–10 in ch. 16 (the exile, Hagar's return to Abraham's house) to understand the two versions as two temporally distinct events. But this harmonization is not quite adequate, for Abraham in ch. 21 obviously does not know that Yahweh has quite different ideas for Isaac and Ishmael. With the combination of the sources JE and P, a further difficulty arose, for one must now assume that in ch. 17 Ishmael is about seventeen years old (chs. 16.16; 21.5), which was certainly not the opinion of the narrator (see at ch. 21.15).

15. ABRAHAM AND ABIMELECH OF GERAR. Ch. 21.22–34

21 [22]At that time Abimelech and Phicol the commander of his
army said to Abraham, "God is with you in all that you do; [23]now therefore swear to me here by God that you will not deal falsely with me or
with my offspring or with my posterity, but as I have dealt loyally with
you, you will deal with me and with the land where you have sojourned." [24]And Abraham said, "I will swear."
25 When Abraham complained to Abimelech about a well of water
which Abimelech's servants had seized, [26]Abimelech said, "I do not
know who has done this thing; you did not tell me, and I have not
heard of it until today." [27]So Abraham took sheep and oxen and gave
them to Abimelech, and the two men made a covenant. [28]Abraham set
seven ewe lambs of the flock apart. [29]And Abimelech said to Abraham,
"What is the meaning of these seven ewe lambs which you have set
apart?" [30]He said, "These seven ewe lambs you will take from my hand,
that you may be a witness for me that I dug this well." [31]Therefore that
place was called Beer-sheba; because there both of them swore an
oath. [32]So they made a covenant at Beer-sheba. Then Abimelech and
Phicol the commander of his army rose up and returned to the land of
the Philistines. [33]Abraham planted a tamarisk tree in Beer-sheba, and
called there on the name of the LORD, the Everlasting God. [34]And
Abraham sojourned many days in the land of the Philistines.

The most conspicuous difficulty of this brief narrative is its lack of uniformity. The attentive reader notices immediately (especially in the apparently unmotivated break, the leap in thought between v. 24 and v. 25) that in the agreement between Abimelech and Abraham two things are being handled which lie on quite different legal planes. **[22–24]** First it is concerned with an agreement between the two, in which the initiative was taken by Abimelech. **[27, 31]** The presuppositions to this demand are the events in ch. 20. Abimelech is still filled with misgiving, he is not yet sure of Abraham's loyalty (*ḥesed*) to him. Above all, he knows that Abraham is under the protection and blessing of his very powerful God, which makes him completely sinister to Abimelech, the one on the outside. The narrative presupposes, therefore, that Abraham's existence as the bearer of promise has qualities which even a heathen must derive from a special relationship to God. In order not to be subject to further vagaries, Abimelech pushes Abraham to an agreement which will put their relationship to each other on a stable, just basis. He never wants to have Abraham as an enemy and therefore wants to know that the loyalty he has shown him is rewarded. The concession that Abimelech makes does not seem large, but it does contain the unreserved recognition of the divine mystery which for him, the heathen, surrounds Abraham. Abraham agrees. The immediate continuation of v. 24 is in vs. 27 and 31. Abraham affirms his willingness with a gift, and the covenant is made. The well (*beʾēr*) where this oath was taken (*nišbāʿ*) received thenceforth the name Beer-sheba.

[25–26, 28–30, 32] In this narrative another agreement is treated, one about the arbitration of a dispute concerning a well. Here the initiative is taken by Abraham. In the first instance the narrative was concerned with matters which were hard to formulate, the calculation of uncertain possibilities behind which in the last analysis was God. Here the concern is a very real and immediate quarrel, about the rights to a well. Abimelech answers evasively. But Abraham makes him recognize his ownership of the well in the acceptance of seven specially separated lambs. (What occurs here is an ancient custom: the acceptance of a gift apparently included recognition of the just claim of the giver.) The name of the place became Beer-sheba because of these seven (*šebaʿ*) lambs which Abimelech accepted from Abraham.

The double aetiology of the name Beer-sheba as "well of seven" and "well of an oath," and the double making of a covenant in v. 27 and v. 32, remove all doubts that here two originally independent local traditions were combined. And yet the older view that there were here parts of two documents (J and E) was out of place. The two parts were not joined subsequently by a redactor but were actually meant to be a story in the E source. In the forefront of this narrative is the Abimelech-Abraham "concordat," while the business about the well now seems only "like an additional paragraph of the covenant" (Del.). The legal question which was raised by Abraham contains, of course, a clear criticism of that loyalty about which Abimelech had spoken so complacently (v. 23). The mention of the Philistines is a gross anachronism (cf. ch. 26.8). But v. 34 is perhaps an addition because it makes Abraham tent directly in the territory of the city-state of Gerar, to which Beer-sheba certainly no longer belonged.

[33] The notice about the cult of "the Everlasting God" (to "call on the name of a god" means to practice the cult) contains a very old tradition. In the pre-Israelite period an "everlasting god" was worshiped in Beer-sheba. (The Hebrew word *'ōlām* is often translated with "eternal," "eternity," but it does not contain the conception of timelessness or otherworldly time but rather of time which extends forward and backward without end.) Israel's ancestors then combined their "God of the fathers" with this cult (see pp. 188 f.) and thus the name "Everlasting God" finally became an epithet of Yahweh (Ps. 102.25, 28). Concerning the procreation of an "everlasting sun god" in a recently discovered Phoenician inscription, cf. A. Alt, *Theol. Lit. Zeitung*, 1950, 520 ff.

16. THE GREAT TEMPTATION. Ch. 22.1–19

22 [1]After these events God tested Abraham, and said to him,
"Abraham!" And he said, "Here am I." [2]He said, "Take your son,
your only son Isaac, whom you love, and go to the land of Moriah and
offer him there as a burnt offering upon one of the mountains of which
I shall tell you." [3]So Abraham rose early in the morning, saddled his
ass, and took two of his young men with him, and his son Isaac; and he
cut the wood for the burnt offering, and arose and went to the place of
which God had told him. [4]On the third day Abraham lifted up his eyes
and saw the place afar off. [5]Then Abraham said to his young men,
"Stay here with the ass; I and the lad will go yonder and worship, and
come again to you." [6]And Abraham took the wood of the burnt offering, and laid it on Isaac his son; and he took in his hand the fire and
the knife. So they went both of them together. [7]And Isaac said to his
father Abraham, "My father!" And he said, "Here am I, my son." He
said, "Behold, the fire and the wood; but where is the lamb for a burnt
offering?" [8]Abraham said, "God will provide himself the lamb for a
burnt offering, my son." So they went both of them together.

9 When they came to the place of which God had told him, Abraham
built an altar there, and laid the wood in order, and bound Isaac his
son, and laid him on the altar, upon the wood. [10]Then Abraham put
forth his hand, and took the knife to slay his son. [11]But the angel of the
LORD called to him from heaven, and said, "Abraham, Abraham!"
And he said, "Here am I." [12]He said, "Do not lay your hand on the lad
or do anything to him; for now I know that you fear God, seeing you
have not withheld your son, your only son, from me." [13]And Abraham
lifted up his eyes and looked, and behold, behind him was a ram, caught
in a thicket by his horns; and Abraham went and took the ram, and
offered it up as a burnt offering instead of his son. [14]So Abraham called
the name of that place The LORD will provide; as it is said to this day,
"On the mount of the LORD it shall be provided."

15 And the angel of the LORD called to Abraham a second time from
heaven, [16]and said, "By myself I have sworn, says the LORD, because
you have done this, and have not withheld your son, your only son,
[17]I will indeed bless you, and I will multiply your descendants as the
stars of heaven and as the sand which is on the seashore. And your
descendants shall possess the gate of their enemies, [18]and by your
descendants shall all the nations of the earth bless themselves, because
you have obeyed my voice." [19]So Abraham returned to his young men,
and they arose and went together to Beer-sheba; and Abraham dwelt at
Beer-sheba.

This narrative too, the most perfectly formed and polished of all the patriarchal stories, has only a very loose connection with the preceding. One can recognize from this that it existed a long time independently before it found its place in the Elohist's great narrative work. The expositor, therefore, here faces the complicated twofold task, first of discovering the meaning of the old independent narrative, and then, of course, of doing justice to its combination with a whole complex of Abraham stories which occurred relatively early. No direct information is given about the time that elapsed between Isaac's weaning and this narrative. One can see, however, that Isaac is no longer a baby (he knows what appertains to sacrifice and can carry a load of wood). The place where Abraham starts and to which he returns is Beer-sheba (v. 19).

[1–2] It is decisive for a proper understanding of what follows that one leave to the statement in v. 1 its entire weight (the word "God" is particularly emphasized in the syntax), and that one does not try to resolve it by a psychologizing explanation (e.g., by the assumption that Israel was here speaking her mind regarding her relation to Canaanite child sacrifice; she had come to grief over the greatness of this sacrifice and in this story answered the question whether she could justify her smaller sacrifice before God at all). One must indeed speak of a temptation (*Anfechtung*) which came upon Abraham but only in the definite sense that it came from God only, the God of Israel. The reader is told in advance, however, that the story concerns a temptation given by God, a demand which God did not intend to take seriously. But for Abraham the command that was directed to him was deadly serious. This twofold viewpoint for the story, which is about to unfold (one sees it through Abraham's eyes and at the same time from a higher level), unmasks the extraordinary narrator. He has not caused his reader any premature excitement regarding a horrible experience. The subject that now engages excited interest is rather Abraham's (and Isaac's) demeanor. For Abraham, God's command is completely incomprehensible: the child, given by God after long delay, the only link that can lead to the promised greatness of Abraham's seed (ch. 15.4 f.) is to be given back to God in sacrifice. Abraham had to cut himself off from his whole past in ch. 12.1 f.; now he must give up his whole future (Jac.). Because the entire previous, suspense-filled Yahwistic story of Isaac's birth (chs. 12.1 ff.; 16.1 ff.; 18.1 ff.) precedes our narrative (through the final reaction of the sources), God's demand becomes even more monstrous. And when one discovers in the address to Abraham that God is fully aware of the greatness of this sacrifice ("your only son Isaac, whom you love"), the impression is not diminished but rather sharpened.

Temptation. The idea of temptation, i.e., of a pedagogical test which God permits men to endure in order to probe their faith and faithfulness, is not really new in the patriarchal stories. The report about God's promise and conduct of Abraham from Mesopotamia (chs. 12.1 ff.; 15.1 ff.) contained a temptation motif. The outbreak of famine must also be understood as a test which Abraham did not pass (ch. 12.10 ff.). And finally, the visit of the three heavenly beings was a test for Abraham (see at ch. 18.1 ff.). What is here new, however, is the programmatic appearance of the idea of testing in the very first verse of the story as well as its destructive harshness. The idea of an act of testing arranged for man by God leads ultimately to the realm of the cult. In the ritual of the ordeal, God is seeking to bring to light guilt or innocence. (In earliest times Kadesh was such a place, Ex. 15.25b; but ordeals were also conducted in the Temple, I Kings 8.31 f. See Weiser, *The Psalms* at Ps. 7 or Ps. 26.) On the other hand, the application of the idea of temptation or testing to the paradoxes of God's historical leading is to be understood as a suppression of the ritual and an exit from the cultic realm, i.e., with respect to the history of faith, as a sign of positive maturity. Incidentally, the application of the notion of temptation to the history of all Israel (e.g., Deut. 13.3; Judg. 2.22) is comparatively older than the notion of tests to which God subjects the individual in his personal career.

The name "the land of Moriah" presents difficulties. The only passage where Moriah (with minor orthographic difference) is mentioned again, II Chron. 3.1, refers without doubt to the mountain on which the Temple stood. But our narrator means a land of Moriah about which we know nothing at all. Furthermore, it is striking that the passage in Chronicles defines the place where the angel appeared to David and not the place of our story, which would, of course, have given the place a much more ancient consecration. The name Moriah was perhaps inserted into our story from II Chron. 3.1 only subsequently in order to claim it as an ancient tradition of Jerusalem (perhaps only with a slight change in the vocalization of an ancient name). The ancient name, later suppressed, could be preserved in the Syriac translation of the Old Testament. It reads, instead of "Moriah," "the Amorites." The LXX reads something again different. It would be understandable for subsequent sanctuaries to compete for the honor of being the traditional place of this event.

[3–8] Here too the narrator refrains from giving us an insight into Abraham's inner self (cf. at ch. 21.14). He reports only how Abraham acted in accordance with the command which he had apparently received during the night. He was on the way three days, and one already sees from that that his obedience was firm and not simply a brief effervescence. Abraham says that he intends to go with Isaac onto a mountain to pray, which was customary at that time on journeys. Thus he separates from the servants, for he can do what he must only when he is completely alone with the child. From this point on, the tempo of the narrative slows down noticeably. The representation seems to drag and is circumstantial, letting the reader sense something of the agonies of this pathway. Our narrator exercises a chaste reticence on the emotional side and manages to use that indirect method in the presentation or suggestion of inner emotional circumstances with great skill. Thus he shows us, for example, Abraham's attentive love for the child in the division of the burdens. He himself carries the dangerous objects with which the boy could hurt himself, the torch and the knife. The words "they went both of them together" lets one suspect that the boy may have broken the oppressive silence only after a while. And after the conversation the statement is repeated. One sees that the final part of the way was traversed in silence. But the conversation itself is, above all, "a true picture of the soul"* (Pr.) in spite of its outward brevity. The old man's answer to the child's intelligent question is at first simply evasive. It is given with "tender love," to be sure, but not with "intuitive hope" (Del.), which would deprive the narrative of some of its most important substance. Actually the answer is ambiguous, but it contains a truth of which Abraham himself is not yet aware. "It comes close to the solution, only then to break off and leave both again to their thoughts." "Again profound silence descends until they arrive, and there too nothing more is said, but only done." (Jac.) Expositors like to compare the description of this walk with that of Elijah's last walk with Elisha (II Kings 2.1–6).

[9–14] The narrative is again slowed down by the preparations on the mountain. The details are noted with frightful accuracy: Abraham builds the altar, stacks the wood on it, binds Isaac, places him on top of it (now even the single movements!), stretches forth his hand, takes the knife. Here too the angel of God calls from heaven (cf. ch. 21.17, and pp. 192 f.), and here too the angel of God is only the form in which God makes himself known to man. In fact, the distinction here between the angel and Yahweh seems to be almost completely removed, for in everything it is God's voice that comes to Abraham and solemnly tells him he "fears God."

The fear of God. It has often been said that "the fear of God" replaces and more or less paraphrases the term "religion," which is not found in the Old Testament. But this statement must be limited, for the phrase "fear of God" says almost nothing directly about a special disposition of the soul, a special feeling for God. It must not be considered as a special emotional reaction to the reality of God which is experienced as *mysterium tremendum.* That the Old Testament is familiar with such a thing cannot be disputed, but where the phrases "fear of God" and "fearing God" occur in the Old Testament, they refer not to a particular form of strong emotions but rather to their consequence, i.e., to obedience (Gen. 20.11; 42.18; II Kings 4.1;

*"A subject on which all great poets of world literature from Aeschylus to Shakespeare and Goethe might write in competition would be, What did Abraham and Isaac say to each other as they went together to the place where the father was to sacrifice the son? . . . Here is the simplest and perfect solution of the problem." (Steinthal, according to B. Jacob, *Genesis,* 1934, 496.)

Isa. 11.2; Prov. 1.7; Job 1.1, 8). It would be more correct to interpret the phrase "fear of God" simply as a term for obedience to the divine commands. But the Old Testament rarely uses this predicatively. This passage, to be sure, and Job give exemplary proof of such obedient fear of God (Job 1.1, 8).

It is doubtful that the narrator considered the existence of the ram, caught in a thicket, as a miracle (see at ch. 21.19). A more likely assumption is that of a definite mitigation of the miraculous, i.e., that Abraham now sees the ram which perhaps was already there before and that it is thus obviously available to Abraham. "Not a sound of rejoicing is audible, in keeping with the ancient magnificence of the passage, from which every sentimental characteristic is far removed." (Pr.) The naming of the place, which Abraham now does, was an important matter for the ancients; for a place where God had appeared in so special a fashion was consecrated for all future generations. Here God will receive the sacrifices and prayers of coming generations, i.e., the place becomes a cultic center. It is strange, to be sure, that the narrator is unable to supply the name of a better-known cultic center. He gives no place name at all, but only a pun which at one time undoubtedly explained a place name. But the name of the place has disappeared from the narrative; only the pun is left, and it now lends itself all the more to a subtle playful change of the supposedly basic word "see" from active to passive (God sees, God is seen, i.e., he appears). The thoughts are not precise (What does God see? Abraham's obedience? Or does he "look with favor on the true sacrifice"? Or in general, does he see the man and what benefits him?). The reader is here to be summoned to give free reign to his thoughts. (See at ch. 16.13 f.)

[15–19] It is clearly noticeable that the narrative once concluded with v. 14. Its inner structure and former cultic purpose found their conclusion in God's appearing, the offering of the sacrifice, and the naming of the place. God's voice comes "a second time." This second speech of God is certainly an addition to the ancient cultic legend, though scarcely a later one, for the primary concern here is to link our narrative with the motif of promise, that motif which now thematically unites all Abraham narratives. Stylistically too there is a great difference here from the distinctly restrained representation of the narrative. This finale ends powerfully and celebrates the victor from Moriah in highest superlatives as greater than the victor from Dan (Del.). The development is almost excessive. That God "swears by himself" does not occur any more in the parallel passages; that his own words in direct address should be designated "says the Lord" (*n*^{e}'*um YHWH*) is stylistically somewhat difficult, and the promise that Abraham's seed "will possess the gate of their enemies" is an idea still foreign to the basis of the promises. (Cf. chs. 12.1–3, 7; 13.14–16; 15.7, 18; 24.7; 26.3–4, 24. Chapter 24.60 is not a divine promise.) A late Jewish tradition reports that Sarah uttered six cries and died when Abraham returned and told her what had happened (H. L. Strack and P. Billerbeck, *Kommentar zum Neuen Testament aus Talmud und Midrasch*, IV, 181 f.).

Epilogue. It may have become clear that the supposedly oldest version of the narrative was a cult saga of a sanctuary and as such legitimized the redemption of child sacrifice, actually demanded by God, with the sacrifice of an animal.* This idea is quite foreign to the present narrative. One sees it most clearly in the loss of the name of the cultic center. When the narrative lost its connection with its ancient cultic point of contact, any particular interest in its name also disappeared. What was once the most important point has now become an accessory to the narrative in the form of a pun. Perhaps the ancient name was lost because of the later combination of the narrative with the "land of Moriah." So much for the antecedents! But what about the meaning?

In the case of a narrative like this one, which obviously went through many stages of internal revision, whose material was, so to speak, in motion up to the end, one must from the first renounce any attempt to discover one basic idea as *the* meaning of the whole. There are many levels of meaning, and whoever thinks he has discovered virgin soil must discover at once that there are many more layers below that. Such a mature narrator as this one has no intention of paraphrasing exactly the meaning of such an event and stating it for the reader. On the contrary, a story like this is basically open to interpretation and to whatever thoughts the reader is inspired. The narrator does not intend to hinder him; he is reporting an event, not giving doctrine. Thus there is only one limitation for the expositor, but it is absolutely valid: the narrative must not be interpreted as the representation of a general unhistorical religious truth. It has been considered the protest of an awakening humanitarianism against

*Punic steles from the Roman period reveal the custom of redeeming a child, who was due the god because of an oath, by the sacrifice of a sheep. (O. Eissfeldt, *Molk als Opferbegriff*, 1935, 1 ff.)

child sacrifice; it has even been designated as a monument in human history of religion, and ideas have been found expressed in it like the one in Uhland's poem *Ver Sacrum*: God does not will death, he wills life. But just as it is difficult to impute to a narrative like this any prejudice or polemic, so it is impossible to suspect it of so theoretical an occupation with the phenomenon of child sacrifice as such or to imagine it capable of such a religious programmatic character. For it describes an event that took place in the sacred history which began with Abraham's call and whose enigmatic character is qualified only by this realm.

The exposition is much more accurate when it discovers in the narrative above all the idea of a radical test of obedience. That God, who has revealed himself to Israel, is completely free to give and to take, and that no one may ask, "What doest thou?" (Job 9.12; Dan. 4.32), is without doubt basic to our narrative. But one must be careful not to interpret the story in a general sense as a question about Abraham's willingness to obey and accordingly to direct all interest to Abraham's trial (as a "showdown for Abraham's religion," Pr.). Above all, one must consider Isaac, who is much more than simply a "foil" for Abraham, i.e., a more or less accidental object on which his obedience is to be proved. Isaac is the child of the promise. In him every saving thing that God has promised to do is invested and guaranteed. The point here is not a natural gift, not even the highest, but rather the disappearance from Abraham's life of the whole promise. Therefore, unfortunately, one can only answer all plaintive scruples about this narrative by saying that it concerns something much more frightful than child sacrifice. It has to do with a road out into Godforsakenness, a road on which Abraham does not know that God is only testing him. There is thus considerable religious experience behind these nineteen verses: that Yahweh often seems to contradict himself, that he appears to want to remove the salvation begun by himself from history. But in this way Yahweh tests faith and obedience! One further thing may be mentioned: in this test God confronts Abraham with the question whether he could give up God's gift of promise. He had to be able (and he was able), for it is not a good that may be retained by virtue of any legal title or with the help of a human demand. God therefore poses before Abraham the question whether he really understands the gift of promise as a pure gift (cf. the comparable disputing of a legal claim, ch. 48.8–14). Finally, when Israel read and related this story in later times it could only see itself represented by Isaac, i.e., laid on Yahweh's altar, given back to him, then given life again by him alone. That is to say, it could base its existence in history not on its own legal titles as other nations did, but only on the will of him who in the freedom of his will in history permitted Isaac to live. Is it too much to expect that the one who could tell such a story did not also make rather lofty demands on the thought of his hearers?

17. NAHOR'S DESCENDANTS. Ch. 22.20–24

22 [20]Now after these things it was told Abraham, "Behold, Milcah
also has borne children to your brother Nahor: [21]Uz the first-born, Buz
his brother, Kemuel the father of Aram, [22]Chesed, Hazo, Pildash,
Jidlaph, and Bethuel." [23]Bethuel became the father of Rebekah.
These eight Milcah bore to Nahor, Abraham's brother. [24]Moreover,
his concubine, whose name was Reumah, bore Tebah, Gaham, Tahash
and Maacah.

[20–24] The section is told as an event in Abraham's life (v. 20). But one can see immediately that an Aramean genealogy exists here, which is incorporated clumsily into the biographical context of the narrative. Accordingly, one must distinguish between the actual list on the one hand and on the other hand the literary links and other brief citations which owe their existence to the incorporation into and combination with the patriarchal history. The genealogy in itself shows us an Aramean band of twelve whose home territory is in the area northeast of the Jordan and to whom Nahor belongs as a summarizing title (Noth, *Überlief. des Pent.*, 235). Such a list of twelve also existed for Ishmael (ch. 25.13–16) and not least (also with two ancestral mothers) for Israel. The names of the Aramean tribes are attested in part from the Old Testament, in part from cuneiform sources. There is a certain inconsistency, however, regarding Rebekah's father. Here and in ch. 24 he is called Bethuel. But when in ch. 24.24 (and similarly in v. 27) Abraham's servant says he found Rebekah "in the house of his master's brother," one must consider Nahor as her father. Chapter 29.5 leads one to the same conclusion. Laban, usually Rebekah's brother, is designated as Nahor's son.

18. SARAH'S DEATH AND THE PURCHASE OF THE BURIAL PLOT. Ch. 23

23 [1]*Sarah lived a hundred and twenty-seven years; these were the years of the
life of Sarah.* [2]*And Sarah died at Kiriath-arba (that is, Hebron) in the land of
Canaan; and Abraham went in to mourn for Sarah and to weep for her.* [3]*And*

Abraham rose up from before his dead, and said to the Hittites, [4]*"I am a stranger and a sojourner among you; give me property among you for a burying place, that I may bury my dead out of my sight."* [5]*The Hittites answered Abraham,* [6]*"Hear us, my lord; you are a mighty prince among us. Bury your dead in the choicest of our sepulchres; none of us will withhold from you his sepulchre, or hinder you from burying your dead."* [7]*Abraham rose and bowed to the Hittites, the people of the land.*
[8]*And he said to them, "If you are willing that I should bury my dead out of my sight, hear me, and entreat for me Ephron the son of Zohar,* [9]*that he may give me the cave of Machpelah, which he owns; it is at the end of his field. For the full price let him give it to me in your presence as a possession for a burying place."*
[10]*Now Ephron was sitting among the Hittites; and Ephron the Hittite answered Abraham in the hearing of the Hittites, of all who went in at the gate of his city,*
[11]*"No, my lord, hear me; I give you the field, and I give you the cave that is in it; in the presence of the sons of my people I give it to you; bury your dead."* [12]*Then Abraham bowed down before the people of the land.* [13]*And he said to Ephron in the hearing of the people of the land, "But if you will, hear me; I will give the price of the field; accept it from me, that I may bury my dead there."* [14]*Ephron answered Abraham,* [15]*"My lord, listen to me; a piece of land worth four hundred shekels of silver, what is that between you and me? Bury your dead."* [16]*Abraham agreed with Ephron; and Abraham weighed out for Ephron the silver which he had named in the hearing of the Hittites, four hundred shekels of silver, according to the weights current among the merchants.*

17 *So the field of Ephron in Machpelah, which was to the east of Mamre, the field with the cave which was in it and all the trees that were in the field, throughout its whole area, was made over* [18]*to Abraham as a possession in the presence of the Hittites, before all who went in at the gate of his city.* [19]*After this, Abraham buried Sarah his wife in the cave of the field of Machpelah east of Mamre (that is, Hebron) in the land of Canaan.* [20]*The field and the cave that is in it were made over to Abraham as a possession for a burying place by the Hittites.*

The narrative about Abraham's sacrifice was the climax of the Elohistic source and the end of the Abraham narratives. In the final redaction of the Hexateuch it also became that for the whole group of Abraham stories. With it was concluded the theme of the reception of the promise and all the strange temptations that befell Abraham concerning the birth of the heir of promise. It had dominated the narrative of all the documents from ch. 12 on. From now on in the story of Abraham there are "final experiences, testamentary steps and procedures" (Del.).

The narrative about the purchase of the family vault belongs to the source P. But in the context of these severe traditions which are immovably concentrated on theology it surprises one with narrative graphicness and humorous freshness. If it is somewhat puzzling to us because of this aspect of the history of tradition (see Epilogue to this section), it still has throughout Priestly characteristics which remove all doubt that it belongs to this source. Such a characteristic is, for example, the precise chronology, which only this source has. (In the combination of all the sources, this chronology became decisive for the entire patriarchal history. But it caused many inconsistencies: according to it, Sarah would have been over ninety years old in the story ch. 20.1 ff. and Ishmael in ch. 21.9 ff. would have been nearly seventeen. Compare at ch. 21.14.)

[1–3] The site of the following event is Hebron, whose older name is also given here. (Compare Josh. 14.15; 15.13, where *'arba'* is considered legendarily as a personal name. *Kiriath Arba* means "city of four quarters," a strange old notation about the time of Hebron's founding, Num. 13.22.) The lamentation for the dead was caused less in those times by the depths of personal grief than by ceremony which was regulated by old custom and rites, for which one could also hire professional wailing women (Jer. 9.17 f.). Thereafter the question where the corpse could be buried had to be answered. Abraham was living near Hebron as a foreigner without property and was in this case absolutely dependent upon the consent of the native population for settlement of this matter. He had to consult quite officially with them, and the only way open to him was to negotiate with the elders at the city gate (cf. at ch. 19.1). It may appear to be a flaw in the narrative when the site of the following conversation is not mentioned until v. 10; for the ancients it may have been matter of course. When the inhabitants of the place are called "Hittites" they are not, of course, to be thought of as belonging to that famous people of Asia Minor in the second millennium (see p. 140). Already in the second millennium there were Hittite rulers in Syria and Palestine, some of whom had migrated far to the south. For the Israelites who came much later the name "Hittite" was reduced to a designation for the Canaanite aborigines (Gen. 15.20 and often). The negotiation, which was legal rather than commercial in character, moves within the framework of worldly politeness. It is a delightful miniature of adroit Oriental conversation!

Abraham begins by describing objectively his legal situation. He is not a full citizen, but a stranger within the city and its "environs" and of course not propertied. Thus his situation (and that of the inhabitants) would be significantly changed if he were now to possess a piece of ground, even though quite small. Probably the consent of the entire population was necessary. **[4–6]** Abraham knows from the beginning, of course, what he wants; but he first formulates his wish quite generally (v. 4b) in order to sound out the inclination of the people of Hebron. They then answer him with polite respectfulness by weakening Abraham's modest self-designation. They see in him the princely dignity of one who comes from God. They know nothing, of course, about God's particular plans for Abraham, but they have heard something (from without, as it were) about his position of trust before God and the protective relationship in which he stands. The designation "prince of God" thus contains a double meaning. In the mouth of the Hebronites it is little more than urbane politeness, for Israel's ears, however, a lofty title of honor with which faith revered Abraham (cf. "Yahweh's friend," Isa. 41.8). But so far as Abraham's actual business is concerned their answer, of course, contains nothing concrete. In so far as they have not politely denied his request they have avoided it, for the answer that any one of them would make a sepulcher available to him ignores Abraham's request for the granting of his own property (v. 4b). **[7–15]** Abraham thanks them politely for their willingness and refers to it by ignoring the evasiveness. His proposal is now precise: he tells what he wants, namely, the Cave of Machpelah, and that he will "pay good money" for it. But even with this indirect address to Ephron he does not make much progress. Most sincerely Ephron assures Abraham that he will give him field and cave (more than Abraham had wished!). Even today the seller avoids the coarse word "sell," which one feels to be an insult for the honored buyer. He wants to "give it," "bestow it," and thus obligates the buyer even more with such generosity. Abraham already knows from this noble gesture that he will have to pay a great deal. But first, after he has turned once again to Ephron with an especially urgent statement (v. 13), Ephron mentions the price in passing as though it were the least of his concerns. A conversion of this sum into our currency is impossible because of the completely different standards of value. Further, we do not know the size of the piece of ground. If, however, one compares this price with what Omri paid for the whole area of the later city Samaria (two talents, or six thousand shekels, I Kings 16.24), one can see that it was very high. In those times when business and commerce were carried on both in money and in kind, the merchants were the actual supporters of the monetary system. (Much less so the native farmers!) Silver was the customary means of payment. This explains the curious expression in v. 16b "silver, according to the weights current among the merchants" (*sḥr*, "travel about"). **[16–20]** Without entering into further negotiations Abraham agreed.

The narrator intentionally emphasizes this gentlemanly trait of character. In vs. 17–18 the story of how Abraham purchased the piece of ground in the presence of witnesses is precisely recapitulated; even the trees are noted. This conclusion reads, therefore, like the final contract of sale (Gu.). The affair is legally described in the terminology of the land register (Jac.). This Cave of Machpelah is usually identified with the cave under the mosque at Hebron. It is known that in early Christian times a Christian basilica once stood here (from the period of Justinian). Above all, the immense squares of Herodian hewn stone shows that the site was already a Jewish sanctuary in pre-Christian times. The sacred area (Arab., *ḥaram*) is particularly esteemed today by the Moslems; it is carefully guarded and opened to no archaeological examination. The site of ancient Hebron has not yet been determined beyond doubt. (The grave sanctuary was certainly outside the city.) Regarding the sacred grove of Mamre, situated about two miles north of modern Hebron, see pp. 172 f.

Epilogue. How little ancient Israel's faith was satisfied with the blessings of a spiritual relationship to God, how continually it was concerned with real, this-worldly saving benefits which to us are surprising, becomes clear especially in the detailed realism of land purchases in the Old Testament (cf. Ruth, ch. 4; Jer., ch. 32). The complete absence of a religious atmosphere and of pious words which makes our narrative seem so "worldly" must not hide the fact that here a fact central to Israel's faith is being described. But what interest can the source P have had in the pedantic and almost comic report of this sale? It appears that P here incorporated an older narrative pretty much unmodified into his narrative (against his usual practice); for this freshness and vitality of speech and answer is unique in this source. There seems to have been no actual sacred aetiology here. How should a grave, even that of a patriarch, have had a particular sacred dignity, when Israel denied so decisively any sacred character to the dead and the grave? Even rites and customs that seem harmless were forbidden to Israel, and the cult of the dead was stifled at the outset in the official Yahweh faith. None of the reports of burials in Genesis has any sacred character. On the contrary, they are emphatically sober and worldly. The assumption, therefore, that here an aetiology of a sacred grave was given is eliminated. This is not, of course, meant to dispute the fact that the narrative actually intends to describe and explain how the cave near Hebron, which the whole world certainly knew about, became a patriarchal grave. But what theological interest (it can be only theological) gave it such a favored place in the Priestly document? Abraham could not derive a claim to possess the entire land (as has been suggested) on the basis of the first property he acquired. How could such legal claims be based on the possession of a grave? Israel actually never did that either. Further, the explanation that the purchase must have meant an attachment (emotional) to the Land of Canaan is not satisfactory (Jac.). Hebron, by the way, was already outside Jewish territory in the exilic and postexilic period and was Edomite (Noth, *History of Israel*).

One must begin with an expression which plays a definite role in the Priestly stories of the patriarchs. Possession of the land of Canaan was promised to the patriarchs. They themselves were already living in the land, to be sure, but were not yet in possession of it, i.e., the promise was not yet fulfilled. This strangely broken relationship to the promised saving benefit, namely, the land—this promise, which was a fundamental characteristic of the patriarchal period, could not remain conceptually unformulated for so precise a theologian as P. Thus he says frequently, the patriarchs built "in the land of their sojourning" (*'ereṣ m^{e}gūrīm*, chs. 17.8; 28.4; 36.7; 37.1; 47.9). But this raised a question: Did the patriarchs who forsook everything for the sake of the promise go unrewarded? No, answers our narrative. In death they were heirs and no longer "strangers." A very small part of the Promised Land—the grave—belonged to them; therefore they did not have to rest in "Hittite earth" or in the grave of a Hittite (cf. v. 6), which Israel would have considered a hardship difficult to bear. In this story an indirect prophetic moment is especially clear, as it is in all patriarchal stories, namely, the foreshadowing of future benefits of salvation (Heb. 10.1). The chapter contains a preview of our relationship to the saving benefit promised to us, the new life in Christ into which we also bear.

In addition to Sarah, Abraham (ch. 25.9), Isaac (ch. 35.29), Rebekah, Leah (ch. 49.31), and Jacob (ch. 50.13) were also later buried here.

19. THE MATCHMAKING. Ch. 24

24 [1]Now Abraham was old, well advanced in years and the LORD,
had blessed Abraham in all things. [2]And Abraham said to his servant
the oldest of his house, who had charge of all that he had, "Put your
hand under my thigh, [3]and I will make you swear by the LORD, the
God of heaven and of the earth, that you will not take a wife for my son
from the daughters of the Canaanites, among whom I dwell, [4]but will

go to my country and to my kindred, and take a wife for my son Isaac."
[5]The servant said to him, "Perhaps the woman may not be willing to
follow me to this land; must I then take your son back to the land from
which you came?" [6]Abraham said to him, "See to it that you do not
take my son back there. [7]The LORD, the God of heaven, who took me
from my father's house and from the land of my birth, and who spoke
to me and swore to me, 'To your descendants I will give this land,' he
will send his angel before you, and you shall take a wife for my son from
there. [8]But if the woman is not willing to follow you, then you will be
free from this oath of mine; only you must not take my son back there."
[9]So the servant put his hand under the thigh of Abraham his master,
and swore to him concerning this matter.

10 Then the servant took ten of his master's camels and departed,
taking all sorts of choice gifts from his master; and he arose, and went to
Mesopotamia, to the city of Nahor. [11]And he made the camels kneel
down outside the city by the well of water at the time of evening, the
time when women go out to draw water. [12]And he said, "O LORD, God
of my master Abraham, grant me success today, I pray thee, and show
steadfast love to my master Abraham. [13]Behold, I am standing by the
spring of water, and the daughters of the men of the city are coming
out to draw water. [14]Let the maiden to whom I shall say, 'Pray let down
your jar that I may drink,' and who shall say, 'Drink, and I will water
your camels'—let her be the one whom thou hast appointed for thy
servant Isaac. By this I shall know that thou hast shown steadfast love
to my master."

15 Before he had done speaking, behold, Rebekah, who was born to
Bethuel the son of Milcah, the wife of Nahor, Abraham's brother, came
out with her water jar upon her shoulder. [16]The maiden was very fair to
look upon, a virgin, whom no man had known. She went down to the
spring, and filled her jar, and came up. [17]Then the servant ran to meet
her, and said, "Pray give me a little water to drink from your jar." [18]She
said, "Drink, my lord"; and she quickly let down her jar upon her hand
and gave him a drink. [19]When she had finished giving him a drink, she
said, "I will draw for your camels also, until they have done drinking."
[20]So she quickly emptied her jar into the trough and ran again to the
well to draw, and she drew for all his camels. [21]The man gazed at her in
silence to learn whether the LORD had prospered his journey or not.

22 When the camels had done drinking, the man took a gold ring
weighing a half shekel, and two bracelets for her arms weighing ten
gold shekels, [23]and said, "Tell me whose daughter you are. Is there room
in your father's house for us to lodge in?" [24]She said to him, "I am
the daughter of Bethuel the son of Milcah, whom she bore to Nahor."
[25]She said to him, "We have straw and provender enough, and room to
lodge in." [26]The man bowed his head and worshiped the LORD, [27]and
said, "Blessed be the LORD, the God of my master Abraham, who has
not forsaken his steadfast love and his faithfulness toward my master.
As for me, the LORD has led me in the way to the house of my master's
kinsmen."

28 Then the maiden ran and told her mother's household about
these things. [29]Rebekah had a brother whose name was Laban; and
Laban ran out to the man, to the spring. [30]When he saw the ring, and
the bracelets on his sister's arms, and when he heard the words of
Rebekah his sister, "Thus the man spoke to me," he went to the man;
and behold, he was standing by the camels at the spring.* [31]He said,
"Come in, O blessed of the LORD; why do you stand outside? For I
have prepared the house and a place for the camels." [32]So the man
came into the house; and Laban ungirded the camels, and gave him
straw and provender for the camels, and water to wash his feet and the
feet of the men who were with him. [33]Then food was set before him to
eat; but he said, "I will not eat until I have told my errand." He said,
"Speak on."†

34 So he said, "I am Abraham's servant. [35]The LORD has greatly
blessed my master, and he has become great; he has given him flocks
and herds, silver and gold, menservants and maidservants, camels and
asses. [36]And Sarah my master's wife bore a son to my master when she
was old; and to him he has given all that he has. [37]My master made me
swear, saying, 'You shall not take a wife for my son from the daughters
of the Canaanites, in whose land I dwell; [38]but you shall go to my
father's house and to my kindred, and take a wife for my son.' [39]I said
to my master, 'Perhaps the woman will not follow me.' [40]But he said
to me, 'The LORD, before whom I walk, will send his angel with you
and prosper your way; and you shall take a wife for my son from my
kindred and from my father's house; [41]then you will be free from my
oath, when you come to my kindred; and if they will not give her to
you, you will be free from my oath.'

42 "I came today to the spring, and said, 'O LORD the God of my
master Abraham, if now thou wilt prosper the way which I go, [43]behold
I am standing by the spring of water; let the young woman who comes
out to draw, to whom I shall say, "Pray give me a little water from your
jar to drink," [44]and who will say to me, "Drink, and I will draw for
your camels also," let her be the woman whom the LORD has appointed
for my master's son.'

45 "Before I had done speaking in my heart, behold, Rebekah came
out with her water jar on her shoulder; and she went down to the spring,
and drew. I said to her, 'Pray let me drink.' [46]She quickly let down her
jar from her shoulder, and said, 'Drink, and I will give your camels
drink also.' So I drank, and she gave the camels drink also. [47]Then I
asked her, 'Whose daughter are you?' She said, 'The daughter of
Bethuel, Nahor's son, whom Milcah bore to him.' So I put the ring on
her nose, and the bracelets on her arms. [48]Then I bowed my head and
worshiped the LORD, and blessed the LORD, the God of my master

*Von Rad rearranges the statements following the suggestion of BH: "Rebekah had a brother whose name was Laban. When Laban saw . . . he ran out to the man at the spring and came to the man who was still standing by the camels at the spring."

†Von Rad translates, again following the suggestion of BH: "They said, 'Speak'."

Abraham, who had led me by the right way to take the daughter of my
master's kinsman for his son. 49 Now then, if you will deal loyally and
truly with my master, tell me; and if not, tell me; that I may turn to the
right hand or to the left."

50 Then Laban and Bethuel answered, "The thing comes from the
LORD; we cannot speak to you bad or good. 51 Behold, Rebekah is before
you, take her and go, and let her be the wife of your master's son, as the
LORD has spoken."

52 When Abraham's servant heard their words, he bowed himself to
the earth before the LORD. 53 And the servant brought forth jewelry of
silver and of gold, and raiment, and gave them to Rebekah; he also
gave to her brother and to her mother costly ornaments. 54 And he and
the men who were with him ate and drank, and they spent the night
there. When they arose in the morning, he said, "Send me back to my
master." 55 Her brother and her mother said, "Let the maiden remain
with us a while, at least ten days; after that she may go." 56 But he said
to them, "Do not delay me, since the LORD has prospered my way; let
me go that I may go to my master." 57 They said, "We will call the
maiden, and ask her." 58 And they called Rebekah, and said to her,
"Will you go with this man?" She said, "I will go." 59 So they sent away
Rebekah their sister and her nurse and Abraham's servant and his men.
60 And they blessed Rebekah, and said to her, "Our sister, be the mother
of thousands of ten thousands; and may your descendants possess the
gate of those who hate them!" 61 Then Rebekah and her maids arose,
and rode upon the camels and followed the man; thus the servant took
Rebekah, and went his way.

62 Now Isaac had come from Beer-lahai-roi, and was dwelling in
the Negeb. 63 And Isaac went out to meditate in the field in the evening;
and he lifted up his eyes and looked, and behold, there were camels
coming. 64 And Rebekah lifted up her eyes, and when she saw Isaac, she
alighted from the camel, 65 and said to the servant, "Who is the man
yonder, walking in the field to meet us?" The servant said, "It is my
master." So she took her veil and covered herself. 66 And the servant told
Isaac all the things that he had done. 67 Then Isaac brought her into the
tent, and took Rebekah, and she became his wife; and he loved her. So
Isaac was comforted after his mother's death.

This Yahwistic narrative is the most pleasant and charming of all the patriarchal stories. In form it exceeds the length of Genesis narratives (about ten to twenty verses) more than three times and ought to be called a *Novelle*. Furthermore, the large space given here to artificial speeches distinguishes it from those narratives which have as their subject primarily events and actions. The older critical school (Dillmann, Wellhausen, Kuenen, among others) considered the chapter a unity and ascribed it to the Yahwist. Later, minor and major inconsistencies were noticed and a trace of another source was dis-

covered (J^1? E^2?) (Procksch went farthest in this regard). But the widely differing results of source criticism show that one here runs the risk of becoming lost in overrefined analyses. The number of discrepancies is not very small, to be sure. But even when we designate them as such they are far from being shown as traces of a second narrative variant. The same narrator, perhaps, did not report that the servant gave the girl such an expensive gift twice (vs. 22, 53). Verses 23–25 are also very uneven, for the prayer of thanksgiving in v. 26 obviously refers to the disclosure in v. 24, and the girl's brief answer in vs. 24 f. is suspiciously interrupted by a repeated "she said to him" (v. 25). The exposition will refer to others; but nowhere is there anything substantial.
undertakes a priori to deny such irregularities will not lack here possible explanations.

[1–9] The place to which the narrative transports us at its beginning is not mentioned. One must think of Hebron (ch. 23), and that is also the place where the Yahwistic narrative had left Abraham (chs. 18 f.). In spite of that, v. 1 is a short exposition. Abraham has grown very old and cannot postpone any longer the marriage of his son, which according to the custom of that time he had to manage. Indeed, he has to fear, as his commission to his servant suggests, that he will not live to see his servant's return. The narrative describes with relish the prosperity that enables him to manage this affair completely according to his status and desire. The story is therefore a good picture of a cherished custom and way of life that was to be found only in families so privileged by birth and resources. The "servant" who was entrusted with the delicate commission has no name; we call him Eliezer, according to ch. 15.2b, which is textually uncertain. The word that we translate by "servant" means much more than that. It can designate that degree and rank of service when the person concerned is vocationally dependent (the "king's servants" are his ministers and generals). In addition, the word goes beyond our English word "servant" to indicate a relationship of confidence (cf. the "servant" of Second Isaiah). Here, then, we must think of a kind of steward (Pr., "seneschal") who then carries out his commission with emphatic dignity and distinction.

Abraham charges his servant with the matter urgently and in the form of a very earnest obligation under oath. Swearing by the genital organ, cf. ch. 47.29, is a very ancient custom. It presupposes a special sanctity of this part of the body, which was no longer alive in the

Israelite period. Actually one swore by Yahweh, the God of heaven and earth (i.e., "the world"). This emphatically universal epithet for Yahweh is otherwise foreign to the patriarchal stories and is one of the signs of the relatively late origin of the story (see p. 258). The commission has several parts: (1) In the event of Abraham's early death, Isaac is not to marry a Canaanite from the neighborhood. Therefore (2) Eliezer is to look around in Abraham's country. (3) Under no circumstances, however, is that to be an excuse for Isaac to go back there. (4) If the girl refuses to make the long journey, then the servant is released from his oath. Two motifs underlie this complicated commission: (1) aversion to mixing with the Canaanites, which is to be explained to the wider circle of the clans as not for reasons of "keeping the blood pure" but because of the economic struggle of holding together the estate. But since this viewpoint is out of the question here because of spatial separation, one must think of the risk of mixing religions (cf. Ex. 34.15 f.; Deut. 7.3). The other care (2) concerns union with the Aramean relatives. Under no circumstances is the marriage to result in a reversal of the divine way of salvation on which God has led Abraham. Regarding the prohibition of retracting God's saving plan arbitrarily, cf. Deut. 17.16; 28.68. But on the other hand these careful safeguards (the servant also safeguards himself, v. 5) become almost unfounded because of the assurance by faith that Yahweh will show his faithful guidance here too. With this word of faith (v. 7) especially, the reader's attention is directed to the actual theme of the story (see pp. 258 f.). Those are the final words, by the way, to be given from Abraham's mouth (Jac.). It appears very much that in an older version of our story this was meant as the bequest of a dying man, indeed that formerly Abraham's death was related after v. 9 (or after v. 61). Why then the great care in obligating the servant with regard to the Canaanite women (v. 3b) if Abraham could still reckon with experiencing the outcome of the matchmaking? Moreover, v. 36 already mentions that Abraham had given his possessions to his son, and finally the servant calls Isaac "my master" in v. 65, which surely indicates that Abraham was no longer alive. Through the fusion of this story with the Priestly story of Abraham's death (ch. 25.7 ff.), this presupposition was removed from our narrative.

[10–11] Laden with many valuables, with a considerable caravan of ten camels, the servant departs and arrives at Haran in Mesopotamia. Haran lies on the Balîkh, a tributary of the upper Euphrates, and according to chs. 11.31; 27.43 was the home of Nahor and his clan.* The question about the tribal background of this derivation of Israel's ancestors from upper Mesopotamia is very difficult. The tenacity with which such traditions of tribal history tend to be preserved makes it quite possible that recollections reaching back to a very distant period are here preserved. On the other hand, we know that the historical circumstances in such tribal genealogies tend to be reflected only in a simplification and abbreviation of the actual conditions, which are much more complicated. One must also reckon with the fact that the old traditions were revived and revised under the pressure of much later historical encounters (in this case with the Arameans with whom Israel knew itself to be tribally related).

[12–14] Here Eliezer toward evening has reached the goal of his journey and therefore allows his caravan first to kneel at the well outside the city. Now, thinks the reader, he will do something! But he does not take the initiative at all; he prays, and in this prayer he places everything in Yahweh's hand. He prays for a sign, not as generally for strengthening of his faith, but for knowledge of God's will. The servant knows that the women will now begin coming to the well. But he will recognize the maiden whom God has "appointed" for him (*hōkīaḥ*, vs. 14 and 44) by the readiness with which she complies with his request for water for men and beasts. That is not the kind of "sign" which ancient, i.e., sacred, piety which believed in miracles was accustomed to obtain. These signs were minor miracles of nature which were obtained for any sphere which often had no connection with the matter in question. (Compare the sign requested by Gideon, Judg. 6.17 ff., 36 ff.; and Isa. 7.11.) Here, however, there is a very close connection between the sign and the servant's desire, for truly the servant subjects the girl to a very calculating test in which she has to show a woman's readiness to help, kindness of heart, and an understanding for animals. Further, the miracle here requested is no longer on the plane of externally material miracles. "Here childlike trust in God is combined with worldly-wise calculation in a most charming manner." (Gu.) **[15–27]** In the same moment, i.e., as the narrative understands it, God's answer to the prayer follows like a miracle; indeed, the compliance goes beyond the request. The servant could not really expect that the girl would be directly from Nahor's house (v. 24), and that in addition to all of her excellent qualities she would also be beautiful!

*A city Nahur is mentioned several times in the non-Biblical Mari texts.

The narrative is not clear about Rebekah's father (the name cannot be explained with certainty). In v. 15 and v. 24 he is called Bethuel; but aside from the fact that he plays no role in the story and makes way completely for the actual actor, Laban, there is the further fact that in ch. 29.5, Rebekah's brother Laban is called Nahor's son and in v. 48 the old servant says that in Rebekah he found the daughter "of his master's brother." In v. 50, Bethuel's name is noteworthy after Laban's (he should very well have been mentioned first), and in v. 53 and v. 55 it is absent. Bethuel was probably added later in order to harmonize the narrative superficially with the Priestly genealogy (ch. 25.20).

In sketching the scene at the well, the narrator is very detailed: the approach of the beautiful girl with the pitcher on her shoulder, the descent to the water, the filling of the jar, the ascent from the well—and then the servant "ran" to meet her. The reader must visualize this and everything that follows exactly. The well itself must be imagined as a large, deep hole in the earth with steps leading down to the water (spring water); above is a watering trough. In order to water ten camels the girl must of course carry up many jars of water. But without reflection she volunteered to do it, although the servant had asked water for only himself. The servant watches with great inner agitation, but silently, so as not to disturb the sign, for now he sees his prayer being fulfilled—an unforgettable picture! Here for the first time the narrator uses an expression for the central concern of the whole story, an expression which, because it is used four times, must almost be considered the motif for the narrative. It was namely the question "whether Yahweh had prospered his journey or not" (*hiṣlīaḥ darkō*, vs. 21, 40, 42, 56). The expression, like the "grant me success" in v. 12, is profane and belongs in no way to the traditional, pious vocabulary. (Luther's "grant grace" is much too spiritual.) And yet the servant is only at the beginning of his knowledge about miraculous leading. **[28–33]** But solemn and realistic commonplace occurrences are closely related for our narrator. While the servant is still praying the girl runs to her mother. Laban, scarcely having looked at the costly ornaments, hastens to the well so as not to neglect the well-to-do stranger and to invite him into the house. The rather awkward sequence of statements in vs. 28–30 has long since been smoothed out by transposing v. 29b between v. 30a and 30b. The old man seems to have been speechless; he silently follows his triumphant, hastening guide (Jac.). At the house the servant permits only the most necessary needs to be attended to. The animals are cared for, the guest's feet washed, but then before any further familiarity he requests attention to the solemn discharge of his commission. **[34–49]** The following detailed speech, which tells the reader nothing new, can be considered long only by Western standards. The ancients had a quite different feeling. To be able to speak worthily in decisive situations was considered a sign of special cultivation and training. One paid attention not only to material but also to method. The reader considered such speeches (cf. ch. 44.18 ff.; or II Sam. 17.7 ff.) as climaxes, if he did not go so far as to enjoy them with all their nuances as literary titbits. Thus here, for example, the servant tactfully says nothing of Abraham's refusal to allow Isaac to return under any circumstances, since that would be insulting to Nahor's clan. But, above all, the purpose of the long speech is to impress Rebekah's relatives with God's visible guidance, without passing over in silence the material benefits, and thereby to force them to the only possible conclusion.

[50–61] Actually, Laban's confession of Yahweh's guidance is the decisive turning point, and for Eliezer the other place is where he recognizes and reveres Yahweh's guiding hand (v. 26). For "cannot speak bad or good" in v. 50 see below, p. 307. The recognition of the divine guidance prevents the family from taking its own initiative. The girl's agreement was naturally included with that of the time in v. 55—literally "days or ten"—is often emended.) Here the narrator has created an especially good opportunity of referring once again to the serious background of the whole event. Rebekah's relatives have indeed perceived the divine guidance, but they have thought they could also satisfy their own wishes in addition. The servant, however, takes the matter very seriously and will not permit any delay where God is so visibly at work. Since the girl is also agreed to the rapid departure, her relatives comply. The wishes that accompanied her correspond to Oriental custom (cf. Ruth 4.11; Tobit 7.15). They know nothing of Yahweh's special plans and promises. They are quite worldly minded. May she be the mother of a great, martial tribe!

[62–67] Unfortunately, the conclusion contains difficulties that cannot be clarified. Above all, the situation that the mangled v. 62

*"We are admonished thereby that we should never hesitate or tarry in God's work but should clear away everything which could detain us from the work he has begun. . . . Whoever does not set out the hour or the moment the Holy Spirit calls will never apprehend him, for once he has gone he will never return." (Luther, WA, XLIII, 348 f.)

intends to describe is unclear, and thus the geographical end of the journey is also unclear. (Regarding the well of the "living one who sees me," cf. ch. 16.13 f.) Also strange is the fact that Abraham, to whom first of all the servant was bound to return, is not mentioned (see above at vs. 3–8). And finally, Isaac's activity in v. 63 immediately prior to the meeting is not clear; the verb is not translatable. ("To meditate" is guesswork and not even probable.) Verse 67 has also been corrected a great deal. Actually, stylistically it is remarkably clumsy, but the reconstructions are nothing more than suppositions. The first meeting of the future married couple is another moment which the narrator describes vividly. The series "he took Rebekah, she became his wife, and he loved her" is not the one familiar to us from novels (Jac.). With that the story has reached its goal: there is now another ancestress for Abraham's seed. Precisely because of this goal the mention of Sarah's tent is important.

Epilogue. The narrator has arranged the extensive mass of material clearly into four scenes: vs. 1–9, Eliezer and Abraham; vs. 11–27, Eliezer and Rebekah; vs. 32–60, Eliezer at Laban's house; vs. 62–67, Rebekah and Isaac. The transitions are made by very short narrative connections. If one compares the material as a whole with other patriarchal stories (e.g., chs. 16; 18; 19; 22), one sees that it can derive from no such ancient tradition. That becomes especially clear from the fact that the narrative is not connected at all with a place. (The starting place and the ending point of the journey are indistinct and can only be guessed from the surrounding narratives.) Further, the remarkable space which speech and conversation occupy here speak against a great age. Indeed, one can say that the actual "occurrence" is set in the speeches and thus in the hearts of the people concerned. Our chapter, therefore, must be considered from the viewpoint of the history of tradition as a "connecting piece," i.e., as a narrative whose origin presupposes an existing composition of patriarchal stories (Noth, *Uberlief. des Pent.*, 11). This special character of our narrative becomes clear above all, however, in its unmistakable theological nature. The usual commanding theme of the promise to the fathers (increase to a nation, possession of land) is quite secondary. In its place is the description of express divine guidance, which we find nowhere else (with exception of the Joseph story). Characteristic is the dispensing with external miracles. The story does not say, "God smote Pharaoh," "he opened Hagar's eyes," "he visited Abraham," "rained fire from heaven," "called to Abraham from heaven," etc. Here no causal connection is broken, but the miracle takes place in a concealed, quite unsensational management of the events. For in our narrative the actual field of activity for this guidance is less the external, spatial world of things, but rather the inner realm of the human heart in which God works, mysteriously directing, evening, and removing resistance. This was true of Rebekah's volunteering at the well and also of the surprising agreement of her relatives. We noticed at v. 21 the remarkable profaneness of the expressions which the narrator uses for this guidance ("grant success," "prosper the way"). They had to be profane, for at that time faith had no traditional forms of expression for such concealed all-pervasive management by Yahweh. In contrast to the notion that Yahweh acted primarily in miracles, in the charisma of a leader, or in a cultic event, this conception of faith was something quite new. It appears to have become vital only in the period of the Solomonic enlightenment (see pp. 30 f.). It would be wrong, to be sure, if one were to consider our story as only a witness to God's general control of human destiny, i.e., as only an example of what old dogmaticians called *providentia generalis*. The union of the narrative with the other Abraham stories which are so thoroughly molded thematically by the patriarchal promise makes the goal of this divine leading completely clear as sacred history in the narrower sense.

20. KETURAH'S SONS. ABRAHAM'S DEATH. ISHMAEL'S DESCENDANTS. Ch. 25.1–18

25 [1]Abraham took another wife, whose name was Keturah. [2]She
bore him Zimran, Jokshan, Medan, Midian, Ishbak, and Shuah.
[3]Jokshan was the father of Sheba and Dedan. The sons of Dedan were
Asshurim, Letushim, and Leummim. [4]The sons of Midian were
Ephah, Epher, Hanoch, Abida, and Eldaah. All these were the
children of Keturah. [5]Abraham gave all he had to Isaac. [6]But to the
sons of his concubines Abraham gave gifts, and while he was still living
he sent them away from his son Isaac, eastward to the east country.

7 *These are the days of the years of Abraham's life, a hundred and seventy-five
years.* [8]*Abraham breathed his last and died in a good old age, an old man and full
of years, and was gathered to his people.* [9]*Isaac and Ishmael his sons buried him
in the cave of Machpelah, in the field of Ephron the son of Zohar the Hittite,
east of Mamre,* [10]*the field which Abraham purchased from the Hittites. There
Abraham was buried, with Sarah his wife.* [11]After the death of Abraham
God blessed Isaac his son. And Isaac dwelt at Beer-lahai-roi.

12 *These are the descendants of Ishmael, Abraham's son, whom Hagar the
Egyptian, Sarah's maid, bore to Abraham.* [13]*These are the names of the sons of
Ishmael, named in their order of the birth: Nebaioth, the first-born of Ishmael;*

and Kedar, Adbeel, Mibsam, [14]*Mishma, Dumah, Massa,* [15]*Hadad, Tema, Jetur,*
Naphish, and Kedemah. [16]*These are the sons of Ishmael and these are their names,*
by their villages and by their encampments, twelve princes according to their tribes.
[17]*(These are the years of the life of Ishmael, a hundred and thirty-seven years; he*
breathed his last and died, and was gathered to his kindred.) [18]*They dwelt from*
Havilah to Shur, which is opposite Egypt in the direction of Assyria; he settled
over against all his people.

[1–6] The remark about Abraham's marriage to Keturah and the genealogy connected with it do not easily follow the previous narrative context by our standards. To be sure, one cannot understand the verses otherwise than that this marriage followed the one with Sarah. But then we are disturbed by the thought that forty years previously, Abraham no longer thought it possible to beget a son (chs. 17.17; 18). Actually this section does detract somewhat from the uniqueness and extraordinariness of Isaac's procreation and birth. But one must understand that in redacting the traditions contained in the sources, the ancients had much less need to present a consistent biography than to let the existing traditions speak as completely as possible for themselves. Thus the tolerably concluded Jehovistic block of narratives (J + E) was combined only superficially with the Priestly block of material. In other words, the redactor's interest is not directed primarily to the biographical circumstances of Abraham's life, but to the "Abraham tradition," which had to be collected and organized more or less organically as completely as possible and at the price of much absence of continuity. Our section was especially difficult to incorporate and has more the character of a postscript. It is not a narrative but a genealogical, ethnological list, which is connected in v. 1 and vs. 5 f. very loosely with Abraham's biography. The tribal names in the list take us to South Palestine and Northwest Arabia; but it is better to suppose that this genealogy is a subsequent learned compilation of individual ancient tribal names than that it directly reflects ancient historical conditions. Best known are the Midianites (cf. Ex. chs. 3; 18.1; Judg., chs. 6 to 8). Saba and Dedan are mentioned in another genealogical context in the table of nations (ch. 10.7). The Sabaeans were an Arab merchant people on the coast of the Red Sea; their rich caravans were known far and wide (I Kings, ch. 10; Jer. 6.20; Ezek. 27.22 ff.). The Dedanites are often mentioned in ancient Oriental sources as nomadic traders (Gen. 10.7; Isa. 21.13; Ezek. 27.20; etc.). The Asshurim mentioned in v. 3 are not the Assyrians, of course, but, according to ch. 25.18, an Arabian tribe living close to the Ishmaelites.

The list must be reckoned as belonging to the Yahwistic strand. Its peculiar "secular" interest in the secondary tribes which are lost in profane history corresponds well to the Yahwist's, which we have encountered often. (See epilogue to ch. 19.20–28.) One sees here that the history of Israel's ancestors was not limited to the chosen line but, with all knowledge of the promise and the sacred history begun by it, was still open to profane historical continuities. Abraham was for the Yahwist not only the recipient of the promise but also the starting point of rather complicated new formations in profane history. Verse 6 indicates the answer to the obvious question about Abraham's inheritance.

[7–11] The report about Abraham's death comes from the Priestly source and is accordingly limited to communicating the important objective facts, setting aside everything that a Yahwist could have presented in addition. Abraham died exactly one hundred years after his entrance into the Land of Canaan (ch. 12.4b). The report of Abraham's death does in fact anticipate the events, for at this time Jacob and Esau were already fourteen years old. But the story of Abraham was apparently here rounded off to a conclusion. His death was peaceful. Abraham had completed what God had marked out for his life. The expression "old man and full of years" shows that in ancient Israel one accepted life not with a defiant claim to endlessness but from the start in resignation, as something limited, something assigned to man, in which then the state of satiation was to be reached (cf. ch. 35.29; Job 42.17; I Chron. 23.1; 29.28; II Chron. 24.15). The expression reveals that one felt only an early or an "evil" death as a judgment from God. "Old and full of years" is the fulfillment of what was planned by God for the life in question, and a death without fear concludes such a fulfilled life. The expression "he was gathered to his people" is not correct here, to be sure, and is apparently used with a decidedly hackneyed meaning, for it presupposes the notion of an ancestral family grave. Peacefully Isaac and Ishmael bury the old man. Did P not know the tradition of Ishmael's ejection (ch. 21), or did he consciously ignore it? Or does he suppose that Ishmael was present at Abraham's death? (The case is quite similar, by the way, for Jacob and Esau, ch. 35.29.) Now the promise given to Abraham's seed is represented by Isaac alone.

[12–18] This is a section from the toledoth book consisting originally of genealogies, which is literarily closely connected with the source P (see pp. 70 f.). In contrast to the Keturah list (ch. 25.1 ff.), the Ishmaelite tribes seem to be a closer alliance. The list mentions twelve tribes and speaks of twelve "princes" (*nᵉśī'im*, v. 16); so the Ishmaelites too may have formed some kind of sacred unit of twelve tribes, for "prince," as we know from the Old Testament, is the title of the religio-political dignitary and chief who represents the tribe in the college of the chiefs of clan for the whole unit (Num. 1.5–15; 10.14–26; 13.4–15; Ex. 22.27; Noth, *History*; further suggestions of such units of twelve occur in chs. 22.20–24; 36.1–14). The home territory of these Ishmaelite Bedouin tribes is extremely spacious, corresponding to their nomadic way of life, namely, the entire wilderness of Northwest Arabia. It touches the Aramean twelve-tribe unit of whom we spoke above ("Nahor," ch. 22.20–24) only in the north. Its (cultic?) center could have been the famous oasis Tema (Isa. 21.14; Jer. 25.23; Job 6.19). The Old Testament gives information about some of these Ishmaelite tribes elsewhere. Kedar and Nebaioth are also mentioned together, e.g., in Isa. 60.7 (Isa. 21.16 ff.; Jer. 49.28 ff.). Yet one must remember that not all Old Testament references always combine the same historical ideas with the names. One must reckon with strongly universalized usage, especially in poetic utterances. The note about Ishmael's love of disputes is reminiscent of ch. 16.12. As it has not been copied from there, it could be a general way of speaking.

* * * *

The next large section in the history of the patriarchs, assembled by collectors from the received tradition, contains a very complicated series of events in the foreground of which is the opposition of Jacob and Esau. Obviously, with ch. 25.19 a large narrative complex begins, which is concluded in ch. 35 with Benjamin's birth, i.e., when the number of Jacob's sons has reached twelve. It has often been called "the Jacob story," but one must ask if the title is correct, for Isaac would then be almost ignored in the series of narratives. Actually the number of real Isaac stories is very small (see pp. 268 f.). But since our block of Jacob narratives is titled "these are the descendants of Isaac," and since this narrative complex ends with the report of Isaac's death (ch. 35.29), it is much better to think of the whole as an Isaac story intended by the collector. One must then, of course, be consistent and recognize in our so-called Joseph story a Jacob story. But that is supported by the fact that this large narrative complex also begins quite similarly with "This is the history of the family of Jacob" (ch. 37.2), and concludes with the report of Jacob's death and the bringing of his corpse to Canaan (ch. 50). Nothing more is said about the long period that lies between this event and Joseph's death. See further the excursus on the composition and theology of the Jacob narrative (pp. 313 ff.).

21. THE BIRTH OF ESAU AND JACOB. THE SALE OF THE BIRTHRIGHT. Ch. 25.19–34

25 19 *These are the descendants of Isaac, Abraham's son: Abraham was the*
father of Isaac, 20 *and Isaac was forty years old when he took to wife Rebekah, the*
daughter of Bethuel the Aramean of Paddan-aram, the sister of Laban the Ara-
mean. 21 And Isaac prayed to the LORD for his wife, because she was
barren; and the LORD granted his prayer, and Rebekah his wife conceived. 22 The children struggled together within her; and she said, "If
it is thus, why do I live?" So she went to inquire of the LORD. 23 And the
LORD said to her,

"Two nations are in your womb,
  and two peoples, born of you, shall be divided;
the one shall be stronger than the other,
  the elder shall serve the younger."

24 When her days to be delivered were fulfilled, behold, there were twins
in her womb. 25 The first came forth red, all his body like a hairy mantle;
so they called his name Esau. 26 Afterward his brother came forth, and
his hand had taken hold of Esau's heel; so his name was called Jacob.
Isaac was sixty years old when she bore them.

27 When the boys grew up, Esau was a skilful hunter, a man of the
field, while Jacob was a quiet man, dwelling in tents. 28 Isaac loved
Esau, because he ate of his game; but Rebekah loved Jacob.

29 Once when Jacob was boiling pottage, Esau came in from the
field, and he was famished. 30 And Esau said to Jacob, "Let me eat some
of that red pottage, for I am famished!" (Therefore his name was called
Edom.) 31 Jacob said, "First sell me your birthright." 32 Esau said, "I am
about to die; of what use is a birthright to me?" 33 Jacob said, "Swear to
me first." So he swore to him, and sold his birthright to Jacob. 34 Then
Jacob gave Esau bread and pottage of lentils, and he ate and drank,
and rose and went his way. Thus Esau despised his birthright.

[19–20, 26b] This Jacob story is introduced by a fragment from the Priestly toledoth book (see pp. 70 f.), from which v. 26b is also taken. It certainly must have contained a notice about the birth of Jacob and Esau, but it appears to have been omitted to make room for the more complete Yahwistic tradition of the birth of twins. According to this source, Isaac had to wait twenty years for the birth of children.

[21–26a] The Yahwistic report begins with v. 21. Judged as a narrative, however, this report is remarkably without vividness. The prayers to Yahweh in vs. 21 and 22b are simply asserted, but not related. The place is not named (there must have been a cultic center to which Rebekah "went"), nor are any details of this event described more closely. Only God's saying is given verbatim. It foretells at once great and enigmatic things. Rebekah will be the ancestral mother of two nations, but in the relationship of the two to each other something unsettling is intimated. Further, everything is left open, no word about the promise to the patriarchs or about any goal God has in mind. The saying is limited to a reference to the future external relationship of the brothers and is thus significant as an "exciting element" in the structure of the unfolding narrative. The entire section vs. 21–28 is not really a narrative and is not based on a compact older saga; rather, it is apparently intended as an expository preface to the whole, i.e., in the form of a rather loose string of statements it acquaints the reader with those facts which are important for understanding the following stories. This description, however, is very soberly realistic and does not idealize either Jacob or Esau, as sketches of national ancestors so often do. Indeed, the comic and ridiculous characteristics are emphasized. That is certainly true of the dark-skinned Esau (the Palestinians noticed the much darker color of the eastern and southern inhabitants of the desert), and besides, the child was so hairy that he seemed to have been given a fur coat by nature. The more civilized Israelites found their wilder neighbors rather scrubby. "These are neighborly kindnesses." (Gu.) But also what happened at Jacob's birth is scarcely more, to begin with, than a touch of popular joking: he already grasped his brother's heel in the mother's womb. Did he as a fetus attempt even then to dispute the birthright? One cannot understand the importance and real ramifications of this statement at this point in the narrative. It opens the way to all kinds of conjectures, none of which discover what happened then through human arbitrariness and still under divine providence. The statement derives the name, Jacob, from the word heel (*'āqēb*) in an audacious etymology and thus reveals an unusual self-irony. This interpretation almost amounts to bowdlerization, for it is not to be supposed that the real meaning of the originally theophoric name was forgotten at that time (*ya'ᵃqōb* probably means "may God protect").

[27–28] As they grew up, the boys lived completely separated from each other, for they personified two ways of life typical for

Palestine, which at that time was more wooded: that of the hunter and that of the shepherd. These two groups encountered each other particularly at the borders of civilization. From the viewpoint of cultural history the hunter is, of course, the older; the shepherd appeared only after a certain deforestation and working of the soil. But they lived for a long time contemporaneously and encountered each other especially on the borders of civilization in the East. They were unable to achieve a real symbiosis because of the profound difference in their needs. The relationship was in general rather tense. In any event the roving and more uncultured hunter was a sinister person for the settled shepherd living in more cultivated conditions. The evaluation of both ways of life, however, is not unprejudiced in our text, but is given from the standpoint of the established farmer. Jacob is "orderly," "respectable." The adjective (*tām*) means actually belonging to the solidarity of community life with its moral regulations, a solidarity that the hunter does not know because he is much more dependent on himself. Added to the concerns of these two ways of life is the partisanship of the parents. The basis of Isaac's preference for Esau, "because he ate of his game," is as soberly realistic as possible. Indeed, one must ask if such a statement can be considered only from the humorous viewpoint. So it went on and the men let themselves be driven by circumstances until the conflict came out into the open. The exposition goes to this point.

[29–34] The action which now begins is again robustly realistic. The hunter, in contrast to the shepherd with his much more economic and careful way of life, often does not have enough to eat. If he takes no prey, he goes hungry. This is the way we must imagine Esau's situation when he wearily bursts into Jacob's presence. He does not even know what Jacob is preparing; it is possible he never had seen its like before, or there may be another reason. He refers to it in a few clumsy words and unconsciously caricatures his own name (*'ādōm*, "red"—*'edōm*); he wants to "gulp it down." But the situation can be understood differently. Perhaps Esau did know the red pottage, i.e., he considered it a "blood soup" and is greatly deceived when he finds it to be only a dish of lentils (D. Daube, *Studies in Biblical Law*, 191 ff.). Esau's subsequent assertion that he was deceived by Jacob twice (ch. 27.36) supports this interpretation. Otherwise Esau's claim would not be understandable, for according to the usual interpretation one cannot really speak of deception in the sale of the birthright. Finally, one understands why Jacob demands confirmation with an oath, for without it the agreement could have been later rescinded. An oath, however, is absolutely binding on the partner in any case (cf. Josh. 9.19). The statement in which Esau makes light of the matter (v. 32) must not be understood in such a way that he considers the birthright nothing, since he must die anyway. That would be no argument at all, and would also depreciate Jacob's birthright. He says it, however, with respect to his present situation in which the birthright is not an equivalent worth discussing: "I am dying of hunger, after all." The conclusion contains the exposure, "It was lentils!" Possibly, however, Esau did not notice it at once. In any case he does not pay particular attention to it. The statement, "He ate and drank, and rose and went his way," caricatures once again his unpolished callousness.

This and the subsequent story of deception confront the expositor with difficult questions. It is clear that the modern reader must suppress all emotional judgments in the case of such an ancient narrative, which stems from strange cultural conditions and a different moral atmosphere. But even when we ask about the meaning of the story for its time and in the opinion of the ancient readers, the possibilities for interpretation are alarmingly numerous. These possibilities lie between the extremes of Gunkel on the one hand and Delitzsch or Frey on the other. The former finds in the narrative a cultural burlesque about which one ought to moralize as little as possible. The uncivilized hunter is outwitted by the shepherd who is culturally more advanced and also more calculating. Because of the combination of this story with the element of the promise to Abraham a "shrill dissonance" has occurred. Delitzsch considers Jacob's offensiveness but thinks it is the "basic orientation toward the promised salvation" which makes him "well-pleasing to God." Frey speaks similarly of his "passionate striving after God's gift." Now it is, of course, clear that the strange occurrence must be ultimately related to the great promise to the patriarchs; but the expositor must not overlook the fact that the narrator himself, i.e., on his own, gives the reader almost no clue for interpretation. The statement that Esau despised his birthright (v. 34b) contains the only judgment. But what is to be understood by the birthright is not sufficiently clear from the narrative. Besides, there is nothing in the oft-repeated promise to the patriarchs about each one binding himself always to the first-born alone. In its transmission from Jacob to his sons there is no further allusion to this obligation. In the question about the ultimate motive for Jacob's action, therefore, the expositor ought not to venture too far. Especially should he guard against psychological interpretations for which the narrative gives too few clues. How conscious the two were of the consequences of their agreement with reference to the divine promises is not revealed by the narrator. In the final analysis, only what God had already determined from the beginning (v. 23) comes to pass, not without the guilt of all concerned. Thus the divine promise is like a sign before and over all these individual narratives, and within this bracket, so to speak, there is much good and evil. Not everything can be interpreted spiritually point by point with reference to this sign. Least of all is the theological general theme of the patriarchal narratives to be considered a dictator for interpretation, as though this theme gave the reader a handy psychological key to all motives of the *dramatis personae.*

22. ISAAC STORIES. Ch. 26

26 [1]Now there was a famine in the land, besides the former famine
that was in the days of Abraham. And Isaac went to Gerar, to Abimelech king of the Philistines. [2]And the LORD appeared to him, and said,
"Do not go down to Egypt; dwell in the land of which I shall tell you.
[3]Sojourn in this land, and I will be with you, and will bless you; for to
you and to your descendants I will give all these lands, and I will fulfil
the oath which I swore to Abraham your father. [4]I will multiply your
descendants as the stars of heaven, and will give to your descendants
all these lands; and by your descendants all the nations of the earth
shall bless themselves: [5]because Abraham obeyed my voice and kept
my charge, my commandments, my statutes, and my laws."

6 So Isaac dwelt in Gerar. [7]When the men of the place asked him
about his wife, he said, "She is my sister"; for he feared to say, "My
wife," thinking, "lest the men of the place should kill me for the sake of
Rebekah"; because she was fair to look upon. [8]When he had been there
a long time, Abimelech king of the Philistines looked out of a window
and saw Isaac fondling Rebekah his wife. [9]So Abimelech called Isaac,
and said, "Behold, she is your wife; how then could you say, 'She is my
sister'?" Isaac said to him, "Because I thought, 'Lest I die because of
her.'" [10]Abimelech said, "What is this you have done to us? One of
the people might easily have lain with your wife, and you would have
brought guilt upon us." [11]So Abimelech warned all the people, saying,
"Whoever touches this man or his wife shall be put to death."

12 And Isaac sowed in that land, and reaped in the same year a
hundredfold. The LORD blessed him, [13]and the man became rich, and
gained more and more until he became very wealthy. [14]He had possessions of flocks and herds, and a great household, so that the Philistines
envied him. [15](Now the Philistines had stopped and filled with earth all
the wells which his father's servants had dug in the days of Abraham his

father.) [16]And Abimelech said to Isaac, "Go away from us; for you are
much mightier than we."
17 So Isaac departed from there, and encamped in the valley of
Gerar and dwelt there. [18]And Isaac dug again the wells of water which
had been dug in the days of Abraham his father; for the Philistines had
stopped them after the death of Abraham; and he gave them the names
which his father had given them. [19]But when Isaac's servants dug in the
valley and found there a well of springing water, [20]the herdsmen of
Gerar quarreled with Isaac's herdsmen, saying, "The water is ours."
So he called the name of the well Esek, because they contended with
him. [21]Then they dug another well, and they quarreled over that also;
so he called its name Sitnah. [22]And he moved from there and dug
another well, and over that they did not quarrel; so he called its name
Rehoboth, saying, "For now the LORD has made room for us, and we
shall be fruitful in the land."
23 From there he went up to Beer-sheba. [24]And the LORD appeared
to him the same night and said, "I am the God of Abraham your father;
fear not, for I am with you and will bless you and multiply your descendants for my servant Abraham's sake." [25]So he built an altar there and
called upon the name of the LORD, and pitched his tent there. And there
Isaac's servants dug a well.
26 Then Abimelech went to him from Gerar with Ahuzzath his
adviser and Phicol the commander of his army. [27]Isaac said to them,
"Why have you come to me, seeing that you hate me and have sent me
away from you?" [28]They said, "We see plainly that the LORD is with
you; so we say, let there be an oath between you and us, and let us
make a covenant with you, [29]that you will do us no harm, just as we
have not touched you and have done to you nothing but good and have
sent you away in peace. You are now the blessed of the LORD." [30]So he
made them a feast, and they ate and drank. [31]In the morning they rose
early and took oath with one another; and Isaac set them on their way,
and they departed from him in peace. [32]That same day Isaac's servants
came and told him about the well which they had dug, and said to him,
"We have found water." [33]He called it Shibah; therefore the name of the
city is Beer-sheba to this day.
34 *When Esau was forty years old, he took to wife Judith the daughter of*
Beeri the Hittite, and Basemath the daughter of Elon the Hittite; [35]*and they*
made life bitter for Isaac and Rebekah.

Whereas quite a considerable amount of traditional material concerning Abraham and Jacob was preserved up until the era of literary revision, the number of Isaac traditions is remarkably small by comparison. Only ch. 26 contains actual Isaac traditions, and it is not a narrative but a mosaic of Isaac stories. Only recent research, however, has grown aware of its great age, its originality, and its value as a source. (Compare Noth, *Überlief. des Pent.*, 114–118, 170 f., 208 f.) The question why this especially ancient trunk of tradition did not develop foliage and bloom like that of Jacob or Abraham cannot be easily answered. The chapter contains no less than seven traditional units: vs. 1–6, 7–11, 12–14, 15–17a, 17b–22, 23–33, 34–35. On the other hand, one can easily see that an attempt was made subsequently to weld these brief traditional units more or less into a compact continued event. With the exception of a few later additions (especially vs. 3b–5), the small literary complex belongs to the source J. Only vs. 34–35 are from the Priestly narrative. There is no reference to the Jacob-Esau tradition in chs. 25 and 27 in which this chapter is now imbedded. These Isaac traditions were written down essentially in their ancient version, without being harmonized with the subsequent large composition of the patriarchal stories.

For a better understanding of the individual parts (with the exception of vs. 34–35) a knowledge of the historical, cultural background against which these events take place is important. Isaac is here the type of nomad with small cattle who moves about according to the necessities of pasture (see p. 170). This basically unsettled way of life, however, was combined with some corn-growing, since these nomads, circumstances permitting, remained in one place for an extended period of time (cf. also ch. 37.7). Moreover, that the urban centers of culture exercised an attraction with a view to modest trading, or also perhaps protection, is plausible. The contact between two so different spheres of life naturally meant conflicts of all kinds. The nomads knew many unpleasant things about the sexual importunities of the cities and did not trust them out of sight in this respect (cf. chs. 19; 34). Also the valuable springs of water could easily be the subject of dispute, for the cities too had a stretch of meadowland, flocks that had to be watered, etc. It was only a step from this phase of nomadic life, which had begun regular tillage of the soil, to actual settlement.

[1–6] Famines occur in Palestine at times of insufficient rainfall. Conditions can then become desperate for the flocks. In such times the nomads are enticed by the distant but also much more fruitful Egypt (cf. ch. 12.10 ff.). Isaac, however, is surprisingly debarred from migrating by God, with whom every move rests. This notation at the beginning thus increases the suspense. How will Isaac be able to keep himself and his herds alive? The reader is told how in what follows. The divine word (v. 3a), which was given very briefly in the style of an oracle by the older document (J), is expanded stylistically into a mighty programmatic speech of promise by a very much later hand. It does contain the traditional elements of the promise (cf. chs. 12.1–3;

13.14–16; 15.5, 7, 18) but not without characteristic diffraction. That the promise, by virtue of Abraham's merit, must now pass to Isaac and approach its fulfillment is a quite new thought in the patriarchal stories. Not even the Priestly document has a special interest in describing Abraham from the viewpoint of exemplary obedience to all "commandments, ordinances, and instructions."

[7–11] The variations on the theme of the "jeopardy of the ancestress" in ch. 12.10–20 (J) and ch. 20 (E) must be compared with this narrative. Here too, in view of the great legal uncertainty, Isaac carefully passed off Rebekah as his sister, which, to be sure, assured his own safety, but not hers. Of the three versions of this strange narrative motif, ours here is the mildest and relatively least objectionable, for it shows only the danger in which Rebekah finds herself and only hints at the harm that could have been done if the city-king had not accidentally discovered the truth from his palace (cf. II Sam. 11.2). Details are left to the reader's imagination; the narrator veils it with an etymological allusion to Isaac's name (*yiṣḥaq—ṣāḥaq*), "jest." That the king is designated a Philistine is, of course, an anachronism (cf. ch. 21.32, 34). The narrator is speaking to the readers who knew the Philistines to be living in Gerar, although they moved to Palestine only about 1200. For the site of Gerar, see p. 226. Perhaps this version of the narrative really is the oldest of the three (Wellhausen, Noth); it would be conceivable that in the later tradition the danger to the ancestress was increased and that the story was thus expanded to an exemplary trial.

[12–14] The notation about the rich harvest now returns the reader to the famine mentioned at the beginning. According to Dalman a harvest of one hundredfold is not an exaggeration (*Arbeit und Sitte* II, 244). Verses 15 and 18 must be ascribed to a later hand which created a connection between the Abraham story (ch. 21.25) and what is related here. The verses hint at the toilsome adversities with which even the ancient ancestors who stood directly before God had to grapple. Even the wells of an Abraham were soon filled up again.

[15–22] The various well aetiologies, having to do with the watering places between Gerar and Beer-sheba, are obviously ancient traditions. They show the realism of ancient Yahweh faith, which is quite untouched by later theological reflection, a realism that accepted the most elemental goods of life directly from God's hand. Spring water is, of course, much more valuable than cistern water.

The verb "he found" speaks quite naturally about the spring as of an unhoped-for stroke of luck (Jac.). Characteristic of the nomadic feel for life is the desire for "room." The thought that God had made room lingered in Israel for a long time after this ancient period (Ps. 4.1; 31.8; 66.12; 118.5; cf. also Gen. 9.27). Here too the saga reckons candidly with the fact that such blessings from Yahweh were perceptible also to nonparticipants and could sometimes cause an unfriendly reaction (cf. at ch. 21.22 ff.). That Isaac yields to the unfriendly demand of the city-king relates more to the above-mentioned cultural and historical presuppositions than to a special trait of character. Older expositors have too often been influenced by ch. 22 and considered Isaac as a sufferer, but the clues given in the narrative do not permit this conclusion.

[23–25] In Beer-sheba, Isaac receives a revelation of "the God of the fathers." It is again remarkable that God does not represent himself as connected with one place, as a nature god where possible, but as the God of a definite group of men, and that accordingly God mentions the name of the first recipient of the revelation of this connection along with himself. Only after God's self-revelation is it possible for men to call on his name. (Luther translates wrongly "proclaim the name.") "For Abraham's sake" scarcely means "for the sake of Abraham's merit and obedience," but rather "for the sake of the promise given to Abraham." Our text understands the dedication of Beer-sheba as a cultic place as having occurred for the first time, of course. Actually, our tradition is much older and more original than the one in ch. 21.33, for in the history of the cult the Isaac tradition was bound to Beer-sheba, while that of Abraham moves from Mamre to Beer-sheba only later. (A. Alt, "The God of the Fathers," 50 ff.)

[26–33] The narrative about Abimelech's covenant with Isaac is, in the history of saga, a variant to ch. 21.22 f. (E). Here it forms an effective conclusion to the Isaac traditions; for Abimelech, who up until now has been very unfavorably inclined, must now solemnly confess that Isaac is "blessed by Yahweh." Indeed, the situation has so changed that he is the one who now feels insecure. The people of Gerar wish to ensure themselves against uncertainties on the part of a man whom so powerful a God has blessed. Isaac agrees and thus we have another etymology of the name Beer-sheba (cf. at ch. 21.22 ff.). It is quite understandable that the name of so famous a cultic place should have given rise to all kinds of aetiological interpretations.

Abimelech and Phicol, the commander of his troops, also appear in the parallel narrative, ch. 21.22 ff. But one can scarcely consider the two here and there identical, since a period of about eighty years lies between the two events.

[34–35] The Priestly notation about Esau's marriage certainly has nothing to do with those ancient Isaac traditions. It prepares the way for chs. 27.46 and 28.1–9. Behind these brief statements lies a completely different conception of the Jacob-Esau story and especially of the reason for Jacob's departure from his parents' house. (See at ch. 28.1 ff.)

23. THE CUNNING ACQUISITION OF THE BLESSING. Ch. 27.1–45

27 1When Isaac was old and his eyes were dim so that he could not
see, he called Esau his older son, and said to him, "My son"; and he
answered, "Here I am." 2He said, "Behold, I am old; I do not know the
day of my death. 3Now then, take your weapons, your quiver and your
bow, and go out to the field, and hunt game for me, 4and prepare for me
savory food, such as I love, and bring it to me that I may eat; that my
soul may bless you before I die."
bless you."]
5 Now Rebekah was listening when Isaac spoke to his son Esau. So
when Esau went to the field to hunt for game and bring it, 6Rebekah
said to her son Jacob, "I heard your father speak to your brother Esau,
7'Bring me game, and prepare for me savory food, that I may eat it, and
bless you before the Lord before I die.' 8Now therefore, my son, obey
my word as I command you. 9Go to the flock, and fetch me two good
kids, that I may prepare from them savory food for your father, such as
he loves; 10and you shall bring it to your father to eat, so that he may bless
you before he dies." 11But Jacob said to Rebekah his mother, "Behold,
my brother Esau is a hairy man, and I am a smooth man. 12Perhaps my
father will feel me, and I shall seem to be mocking him, and bring a
curse upon myself and not a blessing." 13His mother said to him, "Upon
me be your curse, my son; only obey my word, and go, fetch them to
me." 14So he went and took them and brought them to his mother; and
his mother prepared savory food, such as his father loved. 15Then
Rebekah took the best garments of Esau her older son, which were with
her in the house, and put them on Jacob her younger son; 16and the
skins of the kids she put upon his hands and upon the smooth part of
his neck; 17and she gave the savory food and the bread, which she had
prepared, into the hand of her son Jacob.
18 So he went in to his father, and said, "My father"; and he
said, "Here I am; who are you, my son?" 19Jacob said to his father,
"I am Esau your first-born. I have done as you told me; now sit up
and eat of my game, that you may bless me." 20But Isaac said to his
son, "How is it that you have found it so quickly, my son?" He

answered, "Because the LORD your God granted me success." Then
Isaac said to Jacob, 21"Come near, that I may feel you, my son, to know
whether you are really my son Esau or not." 22So Jacob went near to
Isaac his father, who felt him and said, "The voice is Jacob's voice, but
the hands are the hands of Esau." 23And he did not recognize him,
because his hands were hairy like his brother Esau's hands; so he blessed
him. 24He said, "Are you really my son Esau?" He answered, "I am."
25Then he said, "Bring it to me, that I may eat of my son's game and
bless you." So he brought it to him, and he ate; and he brought him
wine, and he drank. 26Then his father Isaac said to him, "Come near
and kiss me, my son." 27So he came near and kissed him; and he smelled
the smell of his garments, and blessed him, and said,

"See the smell of my son
  is as the smell of a field which the LORD has blessed!
28May God give you of the dew of heaven,
  and of the fatness of the earth,
  and plenty of grain and wine.
29Let peoples serve you,
  and nations bow down to you.
Be lord over your brothers,
  and may your mother's sons bow down to you.
Cursed be every one who curses you,
  and blessed be every one who blesses you!"

30 As soon as Isaac had finished blessing Jacob, when Jacob had
scarcely gone out from the presence of Isaac his father, Esau his brother
came in from his hunting. 31He also prepared savory food, and brought
it to his father. And he said to his father, "Let my father arise, and eat
of his son's game, that you may bless me." 32His father Isaac said to
him, "Who are you?" He answered, "I am your son, your first-born,
Esau." 33Then Isaac trembled violently, and said, "Who was it then
that hunted game and brought it to me, and I ate it all before you came,
and I have blessed him?—yes, and he shall be blessed." 34When Esau
heard the words of his father, he cried out with an exceedingly great and
bitter cry, and said to his father, "Bless me, even me also, O my father!"
35But he said, "Your brother came with guile, and he has taken away
your blessing." 36Esau said, "Is he not rightly named Jacob? For he
has supplanted me these two times. He took away my birthright; and
behold, now he has taken away my blessing." Then he said, "Have you
not reserved a blessing for me?" 37Isaac answered Esau, "Behold, I have
made him your lord, and all his brothers I have given to him for
servants, and with grain and wine I have sustained him. What then can
I do for you, my son?" 38Esau said to his father, "Have you but one
blessing, my father? Bless me, even me also, O my father." And Esau
lifted up his voice and wept.

39 Then Isaac his father answered him:

"Behold, away from the fatness of the earth shall your dwelling be,
  and away from the dew of heaven on high.

[40]By your sword you shall live,
and you shall serve your brother;
but when you break loose
you shall break his yoke from your neck."

41 Now Esau hated Jacob because of the blessing with which his
father had blessed him, and Esau said to himself, "The days of mourning
for my father are approaching; then I will kill my brother Jacob."
[42]But the words of Esau her older son were told to Rebekah; so she sent
and called Jacob her younger son, and said to him, "Behold, your
brother Esau comforts himself by planning to kill you. [43]Now therefore,
my son, obey my voice; arise, flee to Laban my brother in Haran,
[44]and stay with him a while, until your brother's fury turns away; [45]until
your brother's anger turns away, and he forgets what you have done to
him; then I will send, and fetch you from there. Why should I be bereft
of you both in one day?"

The period of time that has passed since the last event and the one here related is as usual only vaguely indicated. Nevertheless, with Isaac's blindness in his old age, an important fact for the understanding of what follows has been given, a fact that must be added to the exposition in ch. 25.21–28.

The picture of Esau which the Jacob story draws—a coarse, butchering, Edomite hunter—is, upon closer inspection, filled with tensions; and when we investigate the historical and traditional background of this picture, we raise questions that can be answered only conjecturally. The geographical area in which the Jacob stories formerly moved and in which they developed is defined approximately by the names Bethel, Shechem, and Peniel east of the Jordan. It is the central Palestinian mountain region, including a small sector east of the Jordan. Edom, however, is far to the south, i.e., south of the Dead Sea. Since the Jacob-Esau story thinks of both chief figures as ancestors of nations, it leads the expositor to interpret this narrative material first of all as the literary expression of tribal recollections, i.e., ethnologically and aetiologically. But how could the Israelites of central Palestine have had contact with the Edomites tenting in the south, and how could the two have rivaled each other? What was Edom looking for in Mahanaim, about a hundred miles from the southern tip of the Dead Sea? (ch. 32.3 ff., 8 ff.). It soon becomes apparent, however, that not all Jacob-Esau stories equate Esau with Edom, but that this identification is rooted in ch. 25. The Esau of ch. 27 and of ch. 33 belongs in East Jordan in the history of tradition. He is not the ancestor of a nation at all, but just that type of hunter which the people of Jacob, who were colonizing East Jordan, met and whom they as shepherds recognized (as we saw above) as having a different way of life from their own. Only after a subsequent transfer of this narrative complex into the Judean south did that connection with Edom occur, according to which the Judeans identified the figure of Esau with those neighbors who were their great rivals (Noth, *Überlief. des Pent.*, 103 ff., 210). Much attention has been given to the question whether Esau's name and person are to be connected with Οὔσωος, about whom Philo of Byblos (ca. A.D. 100) reports. Since this mythological figure was also imagined as a hunter clothed with a pelt, actual connections do appear to exist. We do not know at all what they are.

The narrative has been considered critically as a skillful fabric of two threads (J and E). According to one source, Jacob takes the pelt; according to the other, Esau's clothes. Accordingly, in the one the old man wants to touch the son; in the other, to smell him, etc. The question, however, as to which of the two sources is responsible for the one representation, and which for the other, has been answered quite differently. Wellhausen has already referred to the absence of really cogent criteria in this chapter, and more recently it has been proposed that the chapter, in spite of some unevenness, to which the above-mentioned "variants" do not belong, must be considered a unity (Noth). Yet a repetition as harsh as that in vs. 44 f. is suspicious ("until your brother's fury turns away; until your brother's anger turns away"). In its present form the narrative is excellently arranged. The dramatic event is divided into scenes that are sharply marked off from one another, so that the whole is clearly structured and any disturbing opacity is lacking: (1) Isaac and Esau, vs. 1–5; (2) Rebekah and Jacob, vs. 6–17; (3) Isaac and Jacob, vs. 18–29; (4) Isaac and Esau, vs. 30–40; (5) conclusion and transition to the subsequent events (vs. 41–45).

[1–5] The blind old man feels himself near death; therefore he wants to give his favorite son the paternal blessing, according to the context of the patriarchal blessings. Without question the effectiveness of this blessing, according to the conception of our narrative, does not rest with God only but requires active giving on man's part and a special will to give it to a younger man. Objective and subjective elements are here inseparably bound together. Thus the ancients ascribed to dying men the gift of prophecy (cf. Gen. 48.1 ff.; Deut. 33.1 ff.; II Sam. 23.1 ff.). But on the other hand, this gift of sight was not independent of the bodily condition of the one who blessed. Therefore Isaac wants to gain strength by means of a feast. The usage "that my soul may bless you" touches on primitive ideas where blessing is the transmission of an almost magically effective power of soul, an idea which, in any case, our narrator and his readers had long since outgrown.

[5–17] Rebekah, who had heard the conversation through the tent walls (cf. ch. 18.10), hastily makes her plan; and it becomes quite clear from Jacob's timorous objection that the mother had really thought of everything. In fact, she intends to take upon herself the expected curse in the event of exposure. It too was considered to be manipulable and could be intercepted ("the sign of a mother's passionate love," Pr.). One cannot deny that Rebekah's plan to substitute a kid for venison also has a comic aspect. Above all, the deception by means of a pelt on Jacob's arms and neck is rather ridiculous and is another coarse caricature of the unkempt brother. And yet when this story was told there can have been no nonchalant gaiety. Would the moral seriousness of Jacob's objection in v. 12 have not occurred either to the narrator or his listeners? And now in addition the frightful lie in v. 20b! To exploit a man's blindness was not only prohibited on grounds of humanity; God himself watched over dealings with the blind and the deaf (Lev. 19.14; Deut. 27.18). From the reticent silence of our narrator one may not conclude that for him morality and religion were not yet so closely connected (Gu.). The listeners, therefore, confronted Jacob's entrance before the helpless old man with very great suspense.

[18–29] In spite of the fact that our narrator has described Jacob's meeting with his father very sparingly, restraining again any opinion of his own, the listener must share all the detailed experience of this exceedingly insidious scene. Scarcely has Jacob entered and spoken the lie that will cost him twenty years of his life (Jac.), than he already confronts the first hurdle: his father has noticed his early return. Jacob saves himself from this plight by the worst of his lies (v. 20b). Isaac's questions show pathetically how the blind man cannot at first master a feeling of uncertainty, until finally in the close contact of mouth to mouth (painful moment for Jacob!) he becomes certain that he is dealing with Esau. It may be that Isaac's desire to kiss concealed the secret intention to smell in order to be quite sure (Gu.), for Orientals react strongly to smells. If in this scene the recensions of the two sources really are combined (Eissfeldt assigns vs. 18b–23 to J and vs. 24–28 to E), the reader even so does not feel a disturbing multiplication of detail or length in the narrative.* The way the blind man first yields to the earthy smell of Esau's clothes after the kiss and then in the spirit takes up the smell of the Promised Land blessed by God is wonderful. It is a wonderful testimony to the earthiness of Old Testament faith (cf. p. 248). The blessing is strangely independent of the otherwise rather uniformly formulated patriarchal promises (chs. 12.1–3; 13.14–16; 22.17; 26.24; 28.3 f., 13–15; etc.). It turns first to the land and its fertility, then to the son who is here viewed as a nation, to wish him a place of first rank. These words caused the contemporary readers to think of the obvious political superiority which Israel, dwelling in the center of agricultural land, enjoyed over against the much less favored Edom. Jacob leaves the father and at the same time Esau comes home from his hunt.

[30–40] The scene between Isaac and Esau reveals the monstrous crime and is accordingly the most dramatic. Here too the description of the process is masterful. The entrance and words of the unsuspecting Esau are represented with considerable restraint, but the narrator described the old man's shock by a superlative that we seldom hear from him in a narrative from Genesis. And still Isaac does not know that his own son has deceived him. He does not even know who is now before him. In this moment the unfortunate old man is completely bewildered. His expression of shock, however, is surpassed by the description that follows immediately on Esau's unrestrained wild cry. At this point the narrator forsakes somewhat his usually severe incognito; in any case, his style here reveals that he is relating much more than a burlesque. Esau in his anger misunderstands his brother's name etymologically by finding in the name, Jacob, the root *'qb* (originally the name probably meant "may God protect"). This realistic popular etymology of Jacob's name occurs again in Hosea (ch. 12.4) and Jeremiah (ch. 9.3). Regarding the charge that Jacob has now deceived for the second time, see p. 266. Esau too knows the irrevocability of the blessing once it has been given, but he asks his father if he cannot bless him in some other way. In this conversation

*The repetitions 18b, 21b, and 24a are not weaknesses of the narrative or signs of two sources, but rather very good art. The examination of the blind, mistrusting, correctly mistrusting father proceeds slowly; the hearer "enjoys" to the full the suspense, the torment of the wicked Jacob. The suspense reaches its height in the kiss, the hearer is ready to cry out. Now the father has to notice that Jacob's entire body is trembling at this paternal touch. The kiss is both a magnificent conclusion and a transition to the blessing. (P. Volz, *Der Elohist als Erzähler, ein Irrweg der Pentateuchkritik*, 68.)

too Esau is passionately urgent. The LXX reads in v. 38, "But Isaac was silent," which represents even more impressively the father's helplessness. Finally the father attempts once more to bless, but he no longer has the same powers. His second "blessing" is, to be sure, the opposite of what Jacob received. Its effect is especially bitter because it begins with almost the same words. The contrasting meaning is expressed only by the different syntactic use of one and the same preposition, which cannot be duplicated in English. (The *min* in v. 28 is partitive, i.e., in the sense of "a part of," that in v. 39, however, is privative, in the sense of "away from," "far from.") The stony Edomite mountain region can scarcely be cultivated. The sense of the saying is that a livelihood is possible there for the roving hunter almost alone of men. But Esau-Edom will be able to escape from the humiliating political bondage. Edom was subjected by David (II Sam. 8.12–14), but by Solomon's time it had again acquired some independence (I Kings 11.11–22, 25). The contemporary readers were reminded of both events by this saying. But the primary accent remains: Isaac could not indemnify his favorite son by any blessing anywhere near the equivalent of Jacob's; he had spent himself in blessing Jacob (Pr.). In these things there is only an either-or.

[41–45] Esau understood his blessing in this way, but quite in contrast to his more cunning brother, he makes no bones about his plans. Rebekah thinks she knows her wild son and does not reckon with a long period for his hate. First Jacob must leave the land, for if Jacob were slain, then Esau too would have to flee as a fratricide and Rebekah would have lost both sons—a sober maternal reckoning. But she had greatly underestimated the range of the mischief she had caused. Jacob's stay lasted not "a few days" (v. 44) but twenty years. Mother and son never saw each other after that (Pr.).

[46] Whereas our narrative is continued in ch. 28.10 ff., in v. 46 a statement from P has been inserted. It refers back to ch. 26.34 f. and reveals that in this later tradition Jacob's move to Haran was based upon quite different grounds. He is to seek a wife among his relatives.

Epilogue. In the recent history of the exegesis of this story of deception, Gunkel's conception was certainly a necessary counterstroke to the moral solemnity and stiff spirituality of almost all older interpretations. (Esau showed a "lack of theocratic faithful dedication," J. P. Lange.) Nevertheless, it is clear that the old master of saga interpretation has expressed himself badly by emphasizing the comic side of the narrative much too much.* Our interpretation intended to show that the whole style of the narrative is much more exalted and serious. The crime against the blind man, the blasphemy against Yahweh (especially v. 20), the outbreaks of terror in the scene between Isaac and Esau, and finally at the end the bankruptcy of the whole family—none of that would have caused an ancient reader to laugh. But how are we moderns to answer the obvious question about motives, especially those of Rebekah? Can it be answered at all according to the manner of the whole narrative? Did Rebekah really intend to further the divine plans which Isaac had culpably neglected? Doubtless Rebekah's deed has something magnanimous and militant about it (Pr.), but did it occur only because she kept her eye on the promise? Or ought one to speak of the greater worthiness of the younger son because of his character and way of life (Jac.)? The narrative says very little or nothing at all to that. Perhaps it does not completely exclude such motives, but it does not hasten to direct our thoughts in such a direction. And what if the motives of the actors were much more human and obvious? The narrator is convinced that ultimately in the human struggle for the blessing of the dying man divine plans are being worked out, and he intends to show it. And Isaac cannot retract the blessing because God himself has acted in and through him and has accomplished his will. The mysterious prophecy of ch. 25.23 was thus spoken truly. To what extent, however, Rebekah and Jacob know the ultimate consequence of their act is not answered because it is not so very interesting. The real question, therefore, is what circles and what ideas about faith those were for which our narrator is the spokesman. The story reckons with an act of God that sovereignly takes the most ambiguous human act and incorporates it into its plans. The guilty one becomes the bearer of the promise (Pr.)! To be sure, the narrator draws a powerful picture of the most extraordinarily entangled guilt, but his view of what God has decreed and accomplished keeps him from being ruffled before the question of the personal guilt and subjective motives of the individual persons. If one wants to ask the narrator what his thoughts are concerning these men who act in the story, his concern, in our opinion, will be this: he intends to awaken in the reader a feeling of

*The substance of this story is and remains that a deception ultimately has a happy ending: Jacob the knave really wins for himself the blessing; Esau draws the shorter one, without being morally guilty, and the hearers are the happy heirs of the deceiver. (Gu., 307.)

sympathetic suffering for those who are caught up mysteriously in such a monstrous act of God and are almost destroyed in it. For whether their subjective motives were worldly or spiritual, they go to pieces on the frightful incomprehensibility of the God who has made them the object of his saving will. And ultimately where did Jacob's great advantage over Esau become tangible? Jacob's life, as our narrator further describes it, reveals little enough of his prominence. And in our story he shows only how God, in pursuit of his plans which had to remain concealed from all relevant persons, broke into a family and how he seems to pass beyond its ruins.

24. JACOB'S DEPARTURE FOR ARAM.
Chs. 27.46 to 28.9

27 46 *Then Rebekah said to Isaac, "I am weary of my life because of the Hittite*
women. If Jacob marries one of the Hittite women such as these, one of the women of
the land, what good will my life be to me?" **28** 1 *Then Isaac called Jacob and blessed*
him, and charged him, "You shall not marry one of the Canaanite women. 2 *Arise, go*
to Paddan-aram to the house of Bethuel your mother's father; and take as wife
from there one of the daughters of Laban your mother's brother. 3 *God Almighty*
bless you and make you fruitful and multiply you, that you may become a company
of peoples. 4 *May he give the blessing of Abraham to you and to your descendants*
with you, that you take possession of the land of your sojournings which God gave
to Abraham!" 5 *Thus Isaac sent Jacob away; and he went to Paddan-aram to*
Laban, the son of Bethuel the Aramean, the brother of Rebekah, Jacob's and
Esau's mother.

6 *Now Esau saw that Isaac had blessed Jacob and sent him away to Paddan-*
aram to take a wife from there, and that as he blessed him he charged him, "You
shall not marry one of the Canaanite women," 7 *and that Jacob had obeyed his*
father and his mother and gone to Paddan-aram. 8 *So when Esau saw that the*
Canaanite women did not please Isaac his father, 9 *Esau went to Ishmael and took*
to wife, besides the wives he had, Mahalath the daughter of Ishmael Abraham's
son, the sister of Nebaioth.

[27.46 to 28.9] One must read this section first of all without relating it to the great story of deception. It will then become at once clear that here we have quite a different conception of the Jacob-Esau story. Here too the blessing of Jacob and his departure for Aram are reported. But the events are quite differently motivated. It is Esau's marriages to Canaanite women that greatly distress Rebekah and lead Isaac to a testamentary address to Jacob. Whereas according to ch. 27, Jacob flees in great haste (probably against Isaac's will), here he is sent to Laban by Isaac with great ceremony (vs. 5, 7). It is clear from every sentence that this tradition, which diverges so much from the Yahwist's, is to be attributed to P. For *El šaddai*, cf. ch. 17.1 and Ex. 6.3. For the expression "land of your sojournings," see p. 249. The expression "company of peoples" (*q^{e}hal 'ammīm*), v. 3, here occurs for the first time (but cf. chs. 35.11; 48.4, P), but it corresponds to the "multitude of nations" in ch. 17.4. Should one think of a universal eschatological cultic community of nations when reading this rather rudimentary prophecy (cf. at ch. 17)? The Hebrew word that we translate by "community" signifies primarily the cultic levy of men (Ex. 16.3; Num. 10.7; 14.5; 16.3; etc.).

Consciously or unconsciously, therefore, the old tradition was unmistakably purified of everything objectionable sometime between the Yahwist and exilic-postexilic period. Even Esau, whose annoying marriages P had to report, yields to the good (vs. 8 f.), except that he does not seek his wives among the mother's relatives but among the father's (Jac.). A later period was unable to view the ancient ancestors with so merciless a realism and pictured the relations as much more harmonious. Nevertheless, P is not concerned here simply with moral idealization. For this source only one thing in the ancient tradition was really interesting and important, namely, the question about the legitimate wife; and it is conceivable that the ancient tradition was transformed in the interest of a special problem of the time. Deuteronomy was still uninterested in the faith and cultic practice of the woman taken in marriage (Deut. 21.10–14), but in the early postexilic period the problem of mixed marriages became very important. For those who returned from the exile had to find their way to a home into which meanwhile some of the neighboring peoples had trickled (Ezra 9.1 f.; Neh. 13.23 ff.). The interest in the wife's origin, therefore, must be understood exclusively from the viewpoint of faith and not from a national or racial viewpoint. Thus P here speaks to his own time, regulating and showing the way. The usual assumption that P took his material from J or JE causes great difficulties in view of the great divergences. Hosea refers with his "Jacob fled" (ch. 12.13) to the older conception, of course; but see at Gen., ch. 32.

25. JACOB'S DREAM IN BETHEL. Ch. 28.10–22

28 [10]Jacob left Beer-sheba, and went toward Haran. [11]And he came
to a certain place, and stayed there that night, because the sun had set.
Taking one of the stones of the place, he put it under his head and lay
down in that place to sleep. [12]And he dreamed that there was a ladder
set up on the earth, and the top of it reached to heaven; and behold,
the angels of God were ascending and descending on it! [13]And behold,

the LORD stood above it and said, "I am the LORD, the God of Abraham
your father and the God of Isaac; the land on which you lie I will give
to you and to your descendants; [14]and your descendants shall be like the
dust of the earth, and you shall spread abroad to the west and to the
east and to the north and to the south; and by you and your descendants
shall all the families of the earth bless themselves. [15]Behold, I am with
you and will keep you wherever you go, and will bring you back to this
land; for I will not leave you until I have done that of which I have
spoken to you." [16]Then Jacob awoke from his sleep and said, "Surely
the LORD is in this place; and I did not know it." [17]And he was afraid,
and said, "How awesome is this place! This is none other than the house
of God, and this is the gate of heaven."

18 So Jacob rose early in the morning, and he took the stone which
he had put under his head and set it up for a pillar and poured oil on
the top of it. [19]He called the name of that place Bethel; but the name of
the city was Luz at the first. [20]Then Jacob made a vow, saying, "If God
will be with me, and will keep me in this way that I go, and will give me
bread to eat and clothing to wear, [21]so that I come again to my father's
house in peace, then the LORD shall be my God, [22]and this stone, which
I have set up for a pillar, shall be God's abode; and of all that thou
givest me I will give the tenth to thee."

The Bethel story (vs. 10–22) is joined to the story of the deception without a break, immediately following Rebekah's advice to flee (ch. 27.43–45). In spite of the magnificence of the present narrative as a whole, research has detected some breaks and irregularities in the outline, which show a combination of Yahwistic and Elohistic recensions. Apart from the change in the divine name, vs. 16 and 17 are obviously parallel, likewise vs. 19a and 22a, in the first of which Jacob recognizes the place as a house of God, and in the second of which he designates it as the place of a future house of God. It is also true that the oath does not quite fit God's great promise, or that the oath comes too late in the story. Thus one must recognize the Elohist's dominant role in the story in vs. 10–12 and 17–22 (except v. 19), the Yahwist's in vs. 13–16 and v. 19.

[10–12] The narrative begins by letting the lonely traveler rest at a place that has something emphatically coincidental about it. The sun had just gone down and had forced him to an improvised camp. Thus the reader is excitingly transferred to times long past, when the site of the later famous Bethel, where masses of pilgrims gathered at times of the great pilgrimages, was still quite waste, without settlement or cultic building.

The dream is now a masterful combination of originally two nocturnal revelations, namely, the "ladder to heaven" (v. 12) and the

Yahweh manifestation (vs. 13 ff.), a combination no longer perceptible to the unschooled reader of the Bible. Regarding the meaning of dreams in the Elohistic document, see pp. 26f. The dream first shows what Jacob later calls precisely "the gate of heaven" (v. 17b), i.e., that narrow place where according to the ancient world view all intercourse between earth and the upper divine world took place. "God's messengers" go back and forth here continually, not bearing prayers to God, but fulfilling divine commands or supervising the earth. Thus, for example, the accuser in the Job story is one of these divine messengers and in order to go "to and fro on the earth" had to pass the same place (Job 1.7). Zechariah in his first vision gives an especially beautiful picture of the evening return of mounted divine messengers, their arrival at the threshold and their formal report (Elliger, ATD, 25, 103 f.). When we think of the "ladder to heaven," however, we should not think of an actual ladder, for such a simultaneous mounting and descending of wingless divine messengers on it would not be easily conceivable. The Hebrew word (*sullām*, from *sālal*, "heap up") points to a ramp, or, in any case, a kind of stairlike pavement. To understand the whole, however, one must know that in the ancient Orient a rather general distinction was made between the earthly place of a god's appearing and his actual (heavenly) dwelling place. Thus on the gigantic Babylonian temple towers, the dwelling place of the god is symbolized by the uppermost chamber, while below on the earth there is a temple where the god appears; and from top to bottom, as the characteristic mark of this cultic building, there runs a long ramp. (Herodotus, in his detailed description, calls it a "staircase"; cf. also p. 150, and W. Andrae, *Das Gotteshaus und die Urformen des menschlichen Bauens*.) Thus Jacob too makes a basic distinction in this sense: this is a house of God, i.e., the place where God appears, which is to become a cultic center with a cultic building, "and this is the gate of heaven" (v. 17). Behind this conception, which now dominates the narrative, we can, however, recognize a much earlier one, in which the stone itself was understood as an "abode of God."

[13–15] The Elohist's version of the vision concluded with v. 12. It was therefore a very still and mute dream of great solemnity which the sleeper experienced, but it was sufficient to make Jacob certain that without knowing it he was precisely at the entrance into the heavenly world. The Yahwistic version thought of the event of this night as a theophany and a solemn address to Jacob. Here too, Yahweh is thought of as the "God of the fathers" (cf. at ch. 26.24).

The twofold promise of land and posterity shows us that here again we have met that ancient tradition from the pre-Mosaic faith of Israel's ancestors, for a share in tillable land and posterity was what was promised to those nomads by their god (cf. ch. 15.7 ff.). For the blessing that will go from there to "all the families of the earth," cf. ch. 12.3. If the divine address in vs. 13–14 contains the general substance of the patriarchal blessing, then in v. 15 it refers to the special situation of the emigrant Jacob, the dangers of which threaten him, and it guarantees him protection and a return. Israel always thought that Yahweh could be worshiped only in Canaan but that his sovereign realm also included all foreign lands. That is strange, because ancient Israel never considered the gods of the nations only as "nothings" but attributed to them too a relative sphere of power and cult (Judg. 11.24; I Sam. 26.19 f.). Our Genesis narrators, to be sure, show no further evidence of such ideas.

[16–17] The experience of this night was much more than an inner consolation for Jacob. Something had happened, a revelation of God had occurred that would affect the spatial and the material. Accordingly the two statements in which the weakened man reacts to what he has experienced are much more than an echo of his emotional experience. They are concerned, rather, with the realistic statement of an objective fact, namely, with the correct understanding of a place. The statement, "The Lord is in this place," here has a very definite and exclusive local meaning. The immediate effect of this bewildering experience is a feeling of pious shuddering. The narrator has preserved here a tone of original ancient piety, the effect of whose cogent simplicity is timeless.

[18–22] If Jacob erected the stone, which was mentioned quite incidentally at the beginning, as a memorial column, then he must have had colossal strength, for such massebahs, known from the entire Orient, were often nearly seven feet high. There are other references to Jacob's herculean strength in chs. 29.10; 32.25 f. But above all, the purpose of the narrative becomes clear in this verse: it intends to tell how Bethel, which was later so famous, came to be a cultic center and in what way the holiness of the place first became known. But there is more: it intends to explain what were the circumstances connected with the stone at Bethel. Jacob had erected it and dedicated it to God by pouring oil on it. (Anointing as a means of separating for and dedicating to the god, Ex. 30.26 ff.; Lev. 8.10 ff.; Gen. 31.13, was also practiced outside Israel.) Probably later the participants in the cult all anointed the stone. Certainly this was the case with the bringing of the tithe, for Amos also mentions that custom (Amos 4.4). It is characteristic, indeed, for all these cult legends to relate the first occurrence of such customs in order to demonstrate their general validity (see pp. 31 f.). When those who came later brought the tithe to Bethel, they shared somewhat in Jacob's vow. They identified themselves with him and held his promise as binding for all time. It will not do, of course, a priori, to cast suspicion on such a vow as a primitive religious barter. One can also attribute to it, as to so many pious customs, a lofty meaning. It contains here, first of all, because of its self-chosen purpose, a quite personal union of the individual with God, and an obligation to be thankful. Such a vow proceeds from the knowledge of the weakness and fickleness of the human heart, which requires the beneficent support of such a union. God's promise in vs. 13–15 contained a great offer. Jacob grasped the proffered hand and held drastically, i.e., he bound himself by a threefold vow to this saving act of God. The first vow ("then Yahweh shall be my God") reveals that the narrative wishes to be understood as Yahweh's first revelation to and call of Jacob; the second understands him as the founder of the later sanctuary; and the third, as the initiator of the tithe at that place.

The history of the sanctuary at Bethel is relatively clear to us. Its great period was certainly in the time after the reform of Jeroboam I, when it was a center for pilgrimage (926 B.C., I Kings 12.26–29), and our Genesis narrators are also close to this period. In fact, after the Assyrian occupation in 722, Bethel still had significance as a sanctuary of Yahweh, II Kings 17.28. It was then destroyed by Josiah and appears never to have recovered from this blow (II Kings 23.15). But Bethel must have been a widely known cultic center in pre-Israelite times as well; a god with the name "Bethel" was worshipped there. The Old Testament shows us that this god was still known to the Israelites, for "Bethel" is not always used as a place name only, but is occasionally used as a divine name as well (e.g., Amos 5.4 f.; Jer. 48.13). Already in the first half of the second millennium Israel's ancestors came in contact with this sanctuary, and here Jacob, as our narrative conceives it, received the revelation of his God. Actually, even in our relatively late tradition the revelation to Jacob is recognizable as that of the "God of the fathers" (v. 13). Archaeologically the oldest trace that excavators have found in Bethel goes back to the Middle Bronze Age (ca. 2000–1600 B.C.).

Epilogue. Our exposition had to treat the cultic center, Bethel, in detail because this sanctuary and its establishment is also important to our narrator. (Here, therefore, the case is quite different from that of the narrative in ch. 22, for example, which we recognized generically as also an ancient cultic aetiology. There, however, the recollection of the cultic center itself and the interest in it had completely faded, and the narrative had become an event in Abraham's life, which allowed for no special connection with the place.) This occurrence, therefore, left a deep impression upon the history and upon the area in which Israel lived, and the expositor of this narrative must give it due consideration. As for Jacob and his human nature, i.e., any worthiness that he may perhaps possess: no art of empathy can succeed in understanding the incomprehensible, namely, that the fleeing deceiver received such a word of grace. The narrative itself calmly disdains to explain it, to give the reason for it, or to interpret it. Rather, it reserves judgment on the fact and what did occur; and this reserve must be obligatory for any exposition. What would have become of these narratives if everyone had been permitted to make them amenable by his interpretation to his own understanding?*

26. JACOB'S ARRIVAL AT LABAN'S HOUSE. Ch. 29.1–14

29 [1]Then Jacob went on his journey, and came to the land of the
people of the east. [2]As he looked, he saw a well in the field, and lo,
three flocks of sheep lying beside it; for out of that well the flocks were
watered. The stone on the well's mouth was large, [3]and when all the
flocks were gathered there, the shepherds would roll the stone from the
mouth of the well, and water the sheep, and put the stone back in its
place upon the mouth of the well.

4 Jacob said to them, "My brothers, where do you come from?"
They said, "We are from Haran." [5]He said to them, "Do you know
Laban the son of Nahor?" They said, "We know him." [6]He said to
them, "Is it well with him?" They said, "It is well; and see, Rachel his
daughter is coming with the sheep!" [7]He said, "Behold, it is still high
day, it is not time for the animals to be gathered together; water the

*When Jacob is ready to leave the Promised Land, when everything is said and done, God reveals himself to him for the first time. There is no word of judgment on the human, all too human, behavior of the crafty man, and all that is given is the unbreakable assurance that the promise holds: the land is to become Israel's land, and this Jacob will grow to a nation so that all families of the earth may receive the blessing. For this simple purpose Jacob will not be forsaken by his God even in strange territory. (K. Elliger.)

sheep, and go, pasture them." [8]But they said, "We cannot until all the
flocks are gathered together, and the stone is rolled from the mouth of
the well; then we water the sheep."

9 While he was still speaking with them, Rachel came with her
father's sheep; for she kept them. [10]Now when Jacob saw Rachel the
daughter of Laban his mother's brother, and the sheep of Laban his
mother's brother, Jacob went up and rolled the stone from the well's
mouth, and watered the flock of Laban his mother's brother. [11]Then
Jacob kissed Rachel, and wept aloud. [12]And Jacob told Rachel that he
was her father's kinsman, and that he was Rebekah's son; and she ran
and told her father.

13 When Laban heard the tidings of Jacob his sister's son, he ran to
meet him, and embraced him and kissed him, and brought him to his
house. Jacob told Laban all these things, [14]and Laban said to him,
"Surely you are my bone and my flesh!" And he stayed with him a
month.

[1–14] The narrator tells nothing further of Jacob's long journey. He transfers us at once to the "people of the east." The expression is very general. It designates both the southeastern Arabian neighbors of Israel and the northeastern Aramean neighbors. But the narrative takes no pains at all to say anything special about the locale, i.e., about the cities there, etc. Conditions in that foreign place are the same as everywhere. This makes the interest in the human side of the scene all the greater. Jacob arrives at a well, without knowing exactly where he is, around which three flocks of sheep are waiting. The conversation between the eagerly questioning Jacob and the shepherds who are really too lazy to speak is delightfully sketched. It is natural that Jacob should first ask about the place, and then he learns that he is close to his goal. Indeed the shepherds point to Rachel, who is coming in the distance with her flocks, in order to direct him with his further questions to her (Pr.). Meanwhile, until Rachel has arrived with her slowly moving flocks, Jacob cannot restrain his amazement at the inactive waiting of the shepherds at the watering place. How does it happen that they spend so impractically their time, which they could use for their flocks if they would begin watering at once? Was that an attempt on Jacob's part to dismiss the shepherds so that he might be as alone as possible with Rachel (Jac.)? If so, this stratagem failed, for it was the custom to remove the stone cover to the cistern, to which several parties had equal rights, only when all were present, in order to avoid any mischief of individual partners. Verse 8, therefore, means "we are not permitted to" (Jac.). Furthermore, the stone was so heavy that it could be raised only by all of them together. As Rachel now had arrived, Jacob could no longer wait. He had to do something for the girl, and so he stormily broke the custom regarding the well and with gigantic strength lifted the stone from the opening by himself. After a likewise wearisome watering process (see ch. 24.20) he apparently fell on the girl's neck and broke into tears, before telling her who he was or whence he came.* Now Rachel becomes agitated. She hurries home, and at the news old Laban also comes out to greet Jacob most warmly.

The same narrator, who in the previous chapter provided a view into the upper world of God and into his rule of the world and also reported an event of utmost solemnity, here describes something quite "worldly," namely, the meeting of persons who are related and decreed for one another, and who have never seen one another—a moving familial story. The sensitive reader ought to enjoy all phases of this encounter. Especially effective is the contrast between the encounter with the idle shepherds and the subsequent more charming encounter with the girl and, finally, the one with Laban. They seem to be good people who have found one another, in any case people all three of whom show their best side at their first meeting. The narrator intentionally gives no hint of the knavery and conflict to which the companionship of these people will shortly give rise. It has been observed that our narrative is rather similar to the one in Ex. 2.15 ff. and also the one in Gen., ch. 24. But it is not surprising that the narrators prefer those places which were once focal points of life at that time.

27. JACOB'S MARRIAGE TO LEAH AND RACHEL. Ch. 29.15-30

29 [15]Then Laban said to Jacob, "Because you are my kinsman,
should you therefore serve me for nothing? Tell me, what shall your
wages be?" [16]Now Laban had two daughters; the name of the older
was Leah, and the name of the younger was Rachel. [17]Leah's eyes were
weak, but Rachel was beautiful and lovely. [18]Jacob loved Rachel; and
he said, "I will serve you seven years for your younger daughter Rachel."
[19]Laban said, "It is better that I give her to you than that I should give
her to any other man; stay with me." [20]So Jacob served seven years
for Rachel, and they seemed to him but a few days because of the love
he had for her.

[21]Then Jacob said to Laban, "Give me my wife that I may go in to

*That Jacob kissed the girl without having introduced himself previously is cited by Calvin as a mistake in Moses' redaction. (*Calvini Opera*, 23, 400.)

her, for my time is completed." 22So Laban gathered together all the
men of the place, and made a feast. 23But in the evening he took his
daughter Leah and brought her to Jacob; and he went in to her.
24(*Laban gave his maid Zilpah to his daughter Leah to be her maid.*) 25And in
the morning, behold, it was Leah; and Jacob said to Laban, "What is
this you have done to me? Did I not serve with you for Rachel? Why
then have you deceived me?" 26Laban said, "It is not so done in our
country, to give the younger before the first-born. 27Complete the week
of this one, and we will give you the other also in return for serving me
another seven years." 28Jacob did so, and completed her week; then
Laban gave him his daughter Rachel to wife. 29(*Laban gave his maid
Bilhah to his daughter Rachel to be her maid.*) 30So Jacob went in to Rachel
also, and he loved Rachel more than Leah, and served Laban for another seven years.

[15–20] The atmosphere of this narrative, the relationship of the two men to each other, is quite different from that in the preceding narrative. Laban, to be sure, begins quite loyally with a paraphrase of the rather unusual legal situation that was caused by Jacob's entry into his house. Slaves, as a rule strangers of land and blood, enjoyed maintenance and some bodily protection; but they worked on principle without remuneration. In addition, there were paid workers, as, for example, the shepherds. There were also domestic servants, who were paid (cf. Zech. 11.12). Jacob, however, was neither the one nor the other; he was a relative (*'āḥ*), which Laban mentions at the beginning of his speech. How then, in this special case, can he reward Jacob's service? Here Laban apparently is reckoning with Jacob's long stay, though in v. 14b perhaps a more ancient conception is evident, according to which Jacob remained only a short time with Laban. Jacob answers this question with the request for Rachel, whom he loves. Even though one cannot speak expressly of a "bought marriage" in Israel, still it was the common notion that daughters were a possession, an item of property that could be transferred from one owner to the other without further ado. Thus at the engagement a compensating sum was paid. (Luther wrongly translates the *mōhar* of Ex. 22.16 f. by "dowry," Hos. 3.2.) The same notion lies at the root of the "servant's marriage," widespread in cultural history, in which the man obligates himself to fulfill definite services; and this is the case here (cf. Josh. 15.16 f.; I Sam. 17.25; 18.17, 25). But the reader should be surprised that Jacob without hesitation offers so high a price. The commentaries have rightly interpreted the offer of a seven-year period of service as an extreme proposal, with which even Laban could agree; all the more so since Rachel would then still remain in the family—as important then as now. Laban, from whom Jacob's affection for Rachel could not remain concealed, must have suspected from the beginning that things would work out for him in this so desirable fashion. The sly old man's answer must have been understood by Jacob as a promise, though it leaves room for his silent reservation. The long period of service passes quickly for the unsuspecting lover. The name Leah probably means "cow"; Rachel, "ewe." It is not beyond question that the names preserve cultural and historical memories, for the Leah tribes were in Palestine longer and had already become cattlemen, while the Rachel tribes were still shepherds. The adjective by which Leah's eyes are described (*rak*) is usually translated "tender," "weak." What is meant is probably their paleness and lack of luster. The Oriental likes a woman's eyes to be lively, to glow, and therefore eye make-up was used from most ancient times.

[21–26] The narrator has also quickly skipped over the long period of waiting (v. 20), and transports us at once to the beginning of the wedding, the peculiar customs of which he, of course, assumes are known to the reader. He mentions only the invitation to a great feast, not, however, what is indispensable to an understanding, the evening escort of the heavily veiled bride to the groom's apartment. That Laban secretly gave the unloved Leah to the man in love was, to be sure, a monstrous blow, a masterpiece of shameless treachery, by which he for the time being far outmaneuvered Jacob, who was not exactly dubious either. It was certainly a move by which he won for himself far and wide the coarsest laughter. Jacob's anger in the morning could accomplish nothing. After this night he is legally bound to Leah, and therefore Laban does not need to exert himself in his explanation to Jacob. Laban's statement, however, that in his country one did not give the younger before the older, has a very serious aspect, in spite of the disregard with which it is thrown at Jacob. No one understood it better than Jacob, for he himself as the younger son had crossed the finishing line before his older brother. Thus the narrator shows how in this droll story of the coarsest kind a serious nemesis is at work. Even more, an even darker mystery is hidden in the event. It is ultimately God's decree against which Jacob's pent-up passion bounds (Fr.). Without Leah, Reuben, Levi, and Judah would not have been born, and neither Moses nor David would have appeared. God's work descended deeply into the lowest worldliness and there was hidden past recognition. The narrator leaves it at that and does not bring it into the open with pious words.

[27–30] Laban knows how to help the enraged Jacob to acquire Rachel. Jacob is to make the best of a bad bargain and keep the usual week of wedding festivities, which are observed in part in the Orient even today (for this custom, cf. Judg. 14.12; Tobit 11.18). Then Rachel will also be given to him, and, in fact, in advance if he will obligate himself to another seven-year period of service to Laban. Thus the master of deceit gained still another advantage. No one is amazed that the daughters seem to be wares sold by their father and complain bitterly at their treatment (ch. 31.14 f.). Laban's idea, however, was not that Jacob should receive Rachel only after another seven years' service; rather, in the space of a few weeks Jacob had received two wives. One can suppose nothing other than that the narrator and his contemporaries considered this double wedding as an exceptionally strange case. It is not certain whether they already knew the strict prohibition of a marriage to two sisters (Lev. 18.18).

The narrative is now disturbingly interrupted at v. 24 by the mention of the gift of Leah's handmaid, Zilpah. This statement, like the one about Rachel's handmaid, Bilhah (v. 29), has long been ascribed to the source P. These verses seem to stem from a Priestly report about Jacob's double wedding which was omitted at the final redaction. Both maids will play a role later (see at chs. 30.3 ff.; 35.22). Laban's gift of only one maid has been considered a sign of his greed. Rebekah received for her part her nurse and several servants (ch. 24.59, 61). Regarding the presuppositions in the history of the tribe for two mothers, Leah and Rachel, see p. 295.

28. THE BIRTH AND NAMING OF JACOB'S CHILDREN. Chs. 29.31 to 30.24

29 [31]When the Lord saw that Leah was hated, he opened her womb;
but Rachel was barren. [32]And Leah conceived and bore a son, and she
called his name Reuben; for she said, "Because the Lord has looked
upon my affliction; surely now my husband will love me." [33]She conceived again and bore a son, and said, "Because the Lord has heard
that I am hated, he has given me this son also"; and she called his name
Simeon. [34]Again she conceived and bore a son, and said, "Now this
time my husband will be joined to me, because I have borne him three
sons"; therefore his name was called Levi. [35]And she conceived again
and bore a son, and said, "This time I will praise the Lord"; therefore
she called his name Judah; then she ceased bearing.

30 [1]When Rachel saw that she bore Jacob no children, she envied her
sister; and she said to Jacob, "Give me children, or I shall die!" [2]Jacob's

anger was kindled against Rachel, and he said, "Am I in the place of
God, who has withheld from you the fruit of the womb?" 3Then she
said, "Here is my maid Bilhah; go in to her, that she may bear upon my
knees, and even I may have children through her." 4So she gave him
her maid Bilhah as a wife; and Jacob went in to her. 5And Bilhah conceived and bore Jacob a son. 6Then Rachel said, "God has judged me,
and has also heard my voice and given me a son"; therefore she called
his name Dan. 7Rachel's maid Bilhah conceived again and bore Jacob
a second son. 8Then Rachel said, "With mighty wrestlings I have
wrestled with my sister, and have prevailed"; so she called his name
Naphtali.

9 When Leah saw that she had ceased bearing children, she took her
maid Zilpah and gave her to Jacob as a wife. 10Then Leah's maid
Zilpah bore Jacob a son. 11And Leah said, "Good fortune!" so she
called his name Gad. 12Leah's maid Zilpah bore Jacob a second son.
13And Leah said, "Happy am I! For the women will call me happy";
so she called his name Asher.

14 In the days of wheat harvest Reuben went and found mandrakes
in the field, and brought them to his mother Leah. Then Rachel said to
Leah, "Give me, I pray, some of your son's mandrakes." 15But she said
to her, "Is it a small matter that you have taken away my husband?
Would you take away my son's mandrakes also?" Rachel said, "Then
he may lie with you tonight for your son's mandrakes." 16When Jacob
came from the field in the evening, Leah went out to meet him, and
said, "You must come in to me; for I have hired you with my son's
mandrakes." So he lay with her that night. 17And God hearkened to
Leah, and she conceived and bore Jacob a fifth son. 18Leah said, "God
has given me my hire because I gave my maid to my husband"; so she
called his name Issachar. 19And Leah conceived again, and she bore
Jacob a sixth son. 20Then Leah said, "God has endowed me with a good
dowry; now my husband will honor me, because I have borne him six
sons"; so she called his name Zebulun. 21Afterwards she bore a
daughter, and called her name Dinah. 22Then God remembered
Rachel, and God hearkened to her and opened her womb. 23She conceived and bore a son, and said, "God has taken away my reproach";
24and she called his name Joseph, saying, "May the LORD add to me
another son!"

It is almost impossible here to interpret this text to the reader in its ancient form. First of all, its extraordinary literary compositeness would have to be catalogued almost verse by verse. Here the remark must suffice that this piece is composed of small parts, in places very small fragments, of J and E. Even the unpracticed reader will himself discover considerable stylistic clumsiness and redundancy, e.g., in the explanation of the names of Issachar, Zebulun, and Joseph. The fourteen explanations of the names and their puns can only be understood altogether in the original and cannot be transferred into English. Above all, it is immediately obvious that this is not a formal narrative, but a number of small units without a context, which all conclude in the explanation of a name. In each case the accent lies on this explanation. Apparently there is here a very free etymological game in which the narrator sparkles, but which we cannot imitate. We must, however, imagine that not the least of the charms of this passage for the ancient reader consisted in the renewed suspense about how the next name (long familiar, of course) would be interpreted by the narrator. So these are not, therefore, etymologies in the strict sense of the word and do not claim to be. Rather, they are free allusions to which the narrator is inspired by the names and which the hearers receive as ingenious. Finally, one may consider the following: If the narrator could play so freely with the ancient names, their ancient, generally theophoric, meaning must have been very much in the background. The names are in part completely subjective, each one interpreted from the concrete family conditions, at the price of the pious substance which they had as testimonies to God as the giver and protector of life.

[29.31–35] After all the thoroughgoing worldliness of the previous story, God is again the subject of the event. He is the one who blesses and comforts the neglected wife. (The expression "was hated" comes from legal terminology, cf. Deut. 21.15 ff.) The interpretation of the name of her first-born is particularly hair-raising (Gu.). The narrator strangely bypasses the obvious explanation (*rᵉʾū bēn*, "Behold a son!") and speaks of looking upon affliction (*ʿonī*), in which one can find a distant suggestion of the consonants in the name Reuben. The name of the second is interpreted quite relevantly, for the ancient meaning of Simeon is "God has heard." Levi is not a personal name at all, but rather a tribal name. The word may not originally have been Hebrew. Here, then, the narrator had to improvise freely. (Regarding the tribe of Levi, see at ch. 49.) The same is true of the name Judah; it too is originally a tribal name and has not yet been satisfactorily interpreted.

[30.1–8] The section ch. 30.1–8 indicates a situation like the one related in ch. 16. It is certain that there was a legal procedure for childless women to acquire children by their handmaids *per adoptionem* (see p. 190). On the other hand, there seems to have been some criticism of the practice, for Jacob at first does not understand the suggestion of the despairing Rachel. Can one acquire children when the only Giver of Life denies them? But the passionate woman has her way and Bilhah bears "upon the knees" of Rachel, which is equivalent to Rachel's having borne Dan and Naphthali.

[14–24] The story that introduces Issachar's birth is not given like the others in a style of enumeration, but is actually a short narrative. The reason, however, is only that the etymological interpretation of the name Issachar in v. 16 was somewhat more complicated and necessitated a more detailed explanation of the situation from which it grew. Here, where the narrator goes beyond mere interpretation and vividly tells a story, the realism of the process (the struggle of the women for the man and the child, and, above all, the apparently complete lack of religious point of view) becomes again a disquieting question for the reader (see Epilogue to this section). From the viewpoint of the history of culture this is one of those rare traditions which pictures the patriarchs as also farmers. Nomads with small cattle did practice farming when they settled down for a time (see ch. 26). The fruits, which Reuben, who must be thought of as a child, found, come from the *mandragora officinarum*, the mandrake. The strange root, because of its remote resemblance to man, plays a great role in the superstition of many ages and peoples as a magical object. Its fruit, which smells strongly and looks like a tiny apple, was also known at all times as an aphrodisiac. Rachel, loved by Jacob but still childless, desires it because of this quality of increasing desire. For this wonderful fruit she will relinquish a night with Jacob in favor of Leah, and the result of this transaction between the rival women is Issachar's conception. As Leah greets Jacob, who is returning from the field, she already indicates the meaning of the name that the child to be born of her will bear (*śākar*, "to hire for wages"). We would call this derivation of the name from such a situation forced, but the ancients found this allusion to the well-known name in the improvised evening greeting very clever. The interpretation of the name in v. 18 goes in quite a different direction, however, and comes from another (the Elohistic) source. The magic fruit did not at first help Rachel at all, and when she finally did bear, it was not because of the mandrakes but because "Yahweh remembered" Rachel (v. 22). The name Zebulun is first connected, quite vaguely, with the (Aramaic) word for gift, to give (*zēbed*) (cf. the names Elsabad, Gabdiel, Zebadiah), then with a verb which was used as a technical term in Assyrian for marriage law (M. David, *Vetus Testamentum*, 1961, 59 f.). The mention of the daughter, Dinah, must be an afterthought. The statement is remarkable for the absence of an explanation of the name; further, none of the traditional lists of Jacob's children has this only daughter (see preface to ch. 34). Rachel's first child, born of her womb, is Joseph. One explanation of the name comes from the verb *'sp*, "gather, take away"; the other from *ysp*, "to add," and thus directs one's attention in advance to Rachel's other son, who will be born much later, to Benjamin (ch. 35.16 ff.).

Epilogue. There are many questions which this text about the birth of Jacob's sons raises. We shall discuss first the historical background and then ask about the meaning of the section in its present form. There is a series of enumerations of sons of Jacob in the Old Testament. If one compares them, one is struck by their great agreement, in spite of minor variations, for example, in the order. What is unassailably established, in spite of the quite different circles of tradition from which they come, is the number twelve. Is this the product of subsequent schematic reflection, i.e., with an artificial, "literary" structure, a theoretical genealogy in which the historical reality of the tribes and their relationship to each other is at best reflected only dimly? But this "system of twelve" which occurs so often in the Old Testament has an actual historical basis. In the period of the Judges, i.e., before the formation of the kingdom, the Israelite tribes formed a sacred tribal unit, i.e., a so-called amphictyony. This unity was rather politically loose, to be sure; but most important was the common worship of Yahweh and the submission to his revealed commands. From that came the commitment to a common sanctuary, and especially the participation in great pilgrimages. In the administration of the sanctuary the tribes were represented by the college of the twelve tribal princes (Num. 1.5–15). Here, therefore, the idea of the twelve fraternal tribes received its final form, and ultimately all the various traditions of Jacob's twelve sons go back to this cultic arrangement in the period of the Judges. Behind this system of twelve, which is, of course, a final conception, there are, to be sure, many rather complicated historical stages. An important indication of this is the tradition of the two ancestral mothers, Leah and Rachel. Probably the group of six sons of Leah represents an older confederation which united only later with the Rachel tribes. Also, the migration of the latter into Palestine took place in a later push. For details consult Noth, *History of Israel*, 74 ff. The figure of Jacob as a recipient of revelation and founder of cult was connected genealogically with this confederation of twelve only later, i.e., he was considered their ancestor. This connection appears from the fact that the ancestor bears the name Israel in the tradition.

Our text must be somewhat distinguished from the lists and enumerations of the twelve tribes mentioned above, for here the strict system is narratively quite loose. It would be wrong, therefore, if one were to consider this narrative about the birth of Jacob's twelve sons simply as a literarily disguised tribal history and accordingly were to explain it historically. On the contrary, it is not about tribes, even personified tribes, but about men. It tells of women and their struggle for husbands and for descendants. The interpretations of the names have no tribal or historical significance at all; every allusion to the political situation or any quality of any tribe is missing. Rather, they develop completely from the mother's personal, human situation and refer primarily to her relationship to Jacob. On the other hand, it is, of course, quite out of the question that the narrator could have forgotten even for a moment that this narrative concerns the two ancestral mothers of later Israel and the birth of the tribal ancestors. From this viewpoint the worldliness, indeed the occasional crass realism in the description is worth pondering. The birth of the tribal ancestors was just as human as that. But with this truly unedifying thicket of passions and naked human characteristics we are again face to face with the old problem of the interpretation of such texts. This narrative—completely without any helpful interpretation for the reader, without a religious framework, which presents religious ideas with the same reserve and the same daring objectivity as it does worldy ones—this narrative is nevertheless not profane in the last analysis. Here are the same narrators who told of Abraham's call and the renewal of the promise to Jacob. But these same narrators, who are occupied with the great words of God, are also able to give long descriptions of an event upon which they do not comment theologically.

29. JACOB'S WEALTH. Ch. 30.25–43

30 [25]When Rachel had borne Joseph, Jacob said to Laban, "Send
me away, that I may go to my own home and country. [26]Give me my
wives and my children for whom I have served you, and let me go; for
you know the service which I have given you." [27]But Laban said to him,
"If you will allow me to say so, I have learned by divination that the
Lord has blessed me because of you; [28]name your wages, and I will give
it." [29]Jacob said to him, "You yourself know how I have served you, and
how your cattle have fared with me. [30]For you had little before I came,
and it has increased abundantly; and the Lord has blessed you whereever I turned. But now when shall I provide for my own household
also?" [31]He said, "What shall I give you?" Jacob said, "You shall not

give me anything; if you will do this for me, I will again feed your flock
and keep it: 32let me pass through all your flock today, removing from
it every speckled and spotted sheep and every black lamb, and the
spotted and speckled among the goats; and such shall be my wages.
33So my honesty will answer for me later, when you come to look into
my wages with you. Every one that is not speckled and spotted among
the goats and black among the lambs, if found with me, shall be counted
stolen." 34Laban said, "Good! Let it be as you have said." 35But that
day Laban removed the he-goats that were striped and spotted, and all
the she-goats that were speckled and spotted, every one that had white
on it, and every lamb that was black, and put them in charge of his
sons; 36and he set a distance of three days' journey between himself and
Jacob; and Jacob fed the rest of Laban's flock.

37 Then Jacob took fresh rods of poplar and almond and plane, and
peeled white streaks in them, exposing the white of the rods. 38He set
the rods which he had peeled in front of the flocks in the runnels, that is,
the watering troughs, where the flocks came to drink. And since they
bred when they came to drink, 39the flocks bred in front of the rods and
so the flocks brought forth striped, speckled, and spotted. 40And Jacob
separated the lambs, and set the faces of the flocks toward the striped
and all the black in the flock of Laban; and he put his own droves apart,
and did not put them with Laban's flock. 41Whenever the stronger of
the flock were breeding Jacob laid the rods in the runnels before the eyes
of the flock, that they might breed among the rods, 42but for the feebler
of the flock he did not lay them there; so the feebler were Laban's, and
the stronger Jacob's. 43Thus the man grew exceedingly rich, and had
large flocks, maidservants and menservants, and camels and asses.

The connection of this strange narrative, difficult in many respects, with what precedes is very close. Almost without a break the narrator moves from the description of Jacob's many children to that of the increase in his flocks. As a whole the narrative is well arranged. In vs. 25–31a it shows broadly and in detail the preparatory conversation between Laban and Jacob. In vs. 31b–34 we experience the agreement. Then in vs. 35–42 the agreement is acted upon. Verse 43 notes briefly the huge success which Jacob could record. Even the unpracticed eye, however, will notice a certain compositeness of the text. The request to be allowed to return home is made to Laban in v. 25 and v. 26. Laban asks twice what he should give Jacob (v. 28 and v. 31), etc. More serious, however, are the factual obscurities that become obvious when one looks more closely at the narrative. How does Jacob's word "You shall not give me anything" (v. 31) fit with his immediate claim to the spotted animals? Above all, since Wellhausen, it has been recognized that in vs. 32–33 there is a different agreement from the one presupposed in the following narrative. The original meaning of vs. 32–34 is surely that Jacob may seek for the spotted animals in Laban's flocks and then submit his choice to Laban's inspection. Surprisingly, however, Laban separates the spotted animals in v. 35, and with that the representation begins, in which Jacob acquires spotted animals from the unicolored ones by breeding. Finally, v. 40 is very difficult. According to it, the animals that had already been separated by Laban (v. 35) still seem to be in Jacob's flocks. The representation in ch. 31.5b f. has correctly been adduced to reconstruct the conception which is now suppressed. According to it, Laban changed the terms of the agreement again and again ("ten times"). Once he promised the speckled animals to Jacob, once the striped ones. But however he turned, Jacob always had the advantage. This of course makes the matter even more complicated, for now a distinction is made between spotted and striped animals. In our narrative, however, striped (*ʿaquddīm*) animals are first mentioned at ch. 30.35; but here without any distinction between them and the spotted (*neqiddōt*) or the speckled (*telu'ōt*) (cf. v. 39). How difficult the text is in this respect becomes clear from the fact that it uses five different adjectives for the multicolored animals and that neither their precise meaning is stated (spotted? flecked? striped? speckled? mottled?) nor the reason for their alternating use. This is not the place for a more precise limitation of the various ideas or for determining which belongs to what source. Possibly one must reckon with the errors of later glossators who no longer completely understood the text or wanted the process to be understood differently at one point or another.

In spite of these irregularities and breaks in the context one cannot on the whole doubt the way in which the narrative should be understood. Therefore even the statements which seem to presuppose another context are to be interpreted from the present understanding.

[25–30] Jacob's request to be allowed to return home corresponds to his status of dependence on Laban. He requests a dissolution of his servant status. Above all, however, the legal question of taking with him his wives and children was not so simple as it might appear to modern thought. According to Hebrew law in the Book of the Covenant, the slave whose employer had given him a wife had to leave his wife and children with the master when he himself was released. If he does not wish to leave them, then he must remain a servant (Ex. 21.4–6). Now to be sure, Jacob had not been bought by Laban, but he was still a stranger without property and therefore not a free man, i.e., not a full member of the legal community but a dependent. Laban views the situation this way in ch. 31.43 ("The daughters are my daughters, the children are my children"). In this rather obscure legal situation, therefore, he attempts radically to force his conception and demand through. The case was further complicated by Jacob's close relation to Laban and on the other hand by the fact that Laban obviously had attained his wealth because of Jacob. The conversation between Jacob and Laban proceeds on the basis of this rather delicate legal situation—again a pattern of Oriental diplomatic courtesy and cunning (cf. ch. 23). It is the conversation of two men who are on their guard before each other, who know from the start exactly what they want, but who still slowly specify precisely their demands. At first Laban is dumbfounded. He found Jacob's demand, apparently, completely unexpected. The statement v. 27 shows how he struggles for words. To lose Jacob seems unbearable, for he has learned by divination (*nḥš*, cf. ch. 44.5)—a strange expression here—that the blessing he experienced was divine and had come from Jacob's God. This is one of the strangest confessions of Yahweh and his blessing in the Old Testament, a confession which even a Laban had arrived at by the dark process of his superstition!* Jacob, on the other hand, introduces the impending agreement by a general reminder of the length and fidelity of his service and of the blessing which Yahweh had given him "wherever I turned," of which Laban was the beneficiary. Now, however, it was time for Jacob to think of himself and his family.

[31–36] Jacob's answer to Laban's question about his demand is very surprising, in fact it is the "climactic moment" in the structure of the narrative. Every reader is expecting a very high price after this preliminary skirmish. Accordingly this statement "You shall not give me anything" increases the tension even more. And when Jacob proceeds to say that he would under certain conditions continue to be Laban's shepherd, it actually seems that he is ready to rescind his application for release in the event that these conditions are granted (Jac.). In any case, Jacob does not intend that Laban shall release him at once with the payment of a definite wage. To this point the negotiation appears to have taken a favorable turn for Laban. Laban hears first that he must give up none of his money or his flocks,

*In contrast to this usual interpretation, which was accepted by the LXX, another recent translation of the verb in question has been proposed: "I was bewitched, but Yahweh. . . ." (*Orientalistische Literaturzeitung*, 20, 10 ff.)

secondly, that Jacob will remain a shepherd in his service still longer, and thirdly, a condition to which he thinks he can agree without any risk. In order to understand what follows one must know that flocks of small cattle (*ṣō'n*) then, as today, consisted of sheep and goats which grazed together, further that the sheep are generally white, the goats generally dark brown or black, both, therefore, unicolored. Spotted or striped animals are much rarer. Jacob now proposes to Laban that he will separate these multicolored animals from the flocks, and then only the spotted offspring which are then born to the herds shall be his wages. Here Jacob seems to be playing a risky game, for every shepherd knows that unicolored female animals seldom give birth to striped or spotted offspring. Will not Jacob's share be minimal? The way Jacob, under such unfavorable conditions, performs a trick to arrive at enormous profit, the way he greatly outwits the clever Laban, seems like a burlesque farce and could be designated generically, when considered by itself, as only a humorous story. This is only the effect on the reader, however; for the men in question it is, of course, very earnest, almost solemn. Thus Jacob speaks in v. 33 solemnly of his "righteousness" (RSV, "honesty") before Laban. This is one of the few profane examples of that important biblical term which is so difficult to translate. Here too it presupposes an existing community relationship and refers to "loyalty" to an agreement equally binding on both partners. The term is then applied by Israel to Yahweh's relationship to Israel in exactly the same sense (see commentary on ch. 15.6). Laban can only perceive advantage for himself in this proposal, and he agrees, but not without first inserting a safety clause for himself. He himself (and not Jacob) separates all spotted and striped animals from the flocks which are now to be under Jacob's observation, and he makes them graze under the supervision of his sons at a distance of three days' travel from his own flocks, in order to exclude any deception or trickery on Jacob's part. This move shows the extreme caution with which Laban agreed to Jacob's proposal. But this caution will be of no avail whatever to him. He did make it impossible for Jacob to take any of the spotted animals, but Jacob does not need them. And furthermore by removing the flocks so far from each other Laban created a situation which soon worked to his disadvantage (ch. 31.22). Thus the cunning man was betrayed by his own caution.

[37–43] Now, when Jacob is alone with Laban's flocks, i.e., the majority of them, he acts. His plan is based on the ancient and widespread belief in the magical effect of certain visual impressions which in the case of human and animal mothers are transferred to their offspring and can decisively influence them. Jacob causes this "fright" of female animals, as it is popularly known, by peeling strips of bark from stakes so that they are striped and then placing them in the watering troughs. When the narrator mentions the "white" which is revealed in this way he plays with the word (*lābān*) with a sly glance at the name Laban. Less clear is why he mentions at once three different kinds of trees in describing a secondary circumstance. The procedure described in vs. 38–40 is clear and unambiguous: the bucks copulate with the female animals at the drinking troughs, and they conceive at that very moment when they have the stakes before their eyes. Jacob's hope for success lies in the coincidence of the two processes. By contrast, v. 40 is rather obscure. In addition to the reservation made above, this verse seems to indicate still another procedure Jacob used to increase his flocks. Even Delitzsch reckons with an insertion, but even so, must it not be explained? Since Jacob applies his procedure to the strong animals only, there is a further advantage which is at the same time a disadvantage for Laban, for there remains to him as the young brood of his already continually diminished flocks only the weak of the unicolored animals.

This is again, therefore, one of those narratives in which the narrator reveals not the slightest attempt to form his own opinion. One cannot say, of course, that the two confessions of Yahweh in Laban's mouth (v. 27) and Jacob's (v. 30)—and they are the only religious words in the story—are normative for understanding the whole. The Elohist is here much more intelligible and simple. He considers Jacob's increasing wealth as God's blessing (ch. 31.9 ff.). But it is not certain that the Yahwist also shares this view. He has not stated it, and that means that it is rather fruitless to attempt to wrest it from him in the form of any kind of supposition. Does he intend at all for the reader to judge, possibly to make a moral judgment—which seems so obvious to us? He knew the facts in the tradition about Jacob, and because they too belong to the chapter of the strangely circuitous path which Jacob followed in the shadow of God's promise, he preserved them for the memory of those who came later.

30. JACOB'S FLIGHT. HIS CONTRACT WITH LABAN. Ch. 31

31 [1]Now Jacob heard that the sons of Laban were saying, "Jacob has
taken all that was our father's; and from what was our father's he has
gained all this wealth." [2]And Jacob saw that Laban did not regard him
with favor as before. [3]Then the LORD said to Jacob, "Return to the land
of your fathers and to your kindred, and I will be with you." [4]So Jacob
sent and called Rachel and Leah into the field where his flock was, [5]and
said to them, "I see that your father does not regard me with favor as he
did before. But the God of my father has been with me. [6]You know that
I have served your father with all my strength; [7]yet your father has
cheated me and changed my wages ten times, but God did not permit
him to harm me. [8]If he said, 'The spotted shall be your wages,' then all
the flock bore spotted; and if he said, 'The striped shall be your wages,'
then all the flock bore striped. [9]Thus God has taken away the cattle of
your father, and given them to me. [10]In the mating season of the flock
I lifted up my eyes, and saw in a dream that the he-goats which leaped
upon the flock were striped, spotted, and mottled. [11]Then the angel of
God said to me in the dream, 'Jacob,' and I said, 'Here I am!' [12]And
he said, 'Lift up your eyes and see, all the goats that leap upon the
flock are striped, spotted, and mottled; for I have seen all that Laban is
doing to you. [13]I am the God of Bethel, where you anointed a pillar and
made a vow to me. Now arise, go forth from this land, and return to the
land of your birth.' " [14]Then Rachel and Leah answered him, "Is there
any portion of inheritance left to us in our father's house? [15]Are we not
regarded by him as foreigners? For he has sold us, and he has been using
up the money given for us. [16]All the property which God has taken away
from our father belongs to us and to our children; now then, whatever
God has said to you, do."

17 So Jacob arose, and set his sons and his wives on camels; [18]and he
drove away all his cattle, *all his livestock which he had gained, the cattle in his
possession which he had acquired in Paddan-aram, to go to the land of Canaan to
his father Isaac.* [19]Laban had gone to shear his sheep, and Rachel stole
her father's household gods. [20]And Jacob outwitted Laban the Aramean
in that he did not tell him that he intended to flee. [21]He fled with all
that he had, and arose and crossed the Euphrates, and set his face
toward the hill country of Gilead.

22 When it was told Laban on the third day that Jacob had fled,
[23]he took his kinsmen with him and pursued him for seven days and
followed close after him into the hill country of Gilead. [24]But God came
to Laban the Aramean in a dream by night, and said to him, "Take
heed that you say not a word to Jacob, either good or bad."

25 And Laban overtook Jacob. Now Jacob had pitched his tent in the
hill country, and Laban with his kinsmen encamped in the hill country
of Gilead. [26]And Laban said to Jacob, "What have you done, that you
have cheated me, and carried away my daughters like captives of the
sword? [27]Why did you flee secretly, and cheat me, and did not tell me,

so that I might have sent you away with mirth and songs, with tambourine and lyre? [28]And why did you not permit me to kiss my sons and
my daughters farewell? Now you have done foolishly. [29]It is in my
power to do you harm; but the God of your father spoke to me last
night, saying, 'Take heed that you speak to Jacob neither good nor bad.'
[30]And now you have gone away because you longed greatly for your
father's house, but why did you steal my gods?" [31]Jacob answered
Laban, "Because I was afraid, for I thought that you would take your
daughters from me by force. [32]Any one with whom you find your gods
shall not live. In the presence of our kinsmen point out what I have that is
yours, and take it." Now Jacob did not know that Rachel had stolen them.

33 So Laban went into Jacob's tent, and into Leah's tent, and into
the tent of the two maidservants, but he did not find them. And he
went out of Leah's tent, and entered Rachel's. [34]Now Rachel had taken
the household gods and put them in the camel's saddle, and sat upon
them. Laban felt all about the tent, but did not find them. [35]And she
said to her father, "Let not my lord be angry that I cannot rise before
you, for the way of women is upon me." So he searched, but did not
find the household gods.

36 Then Jacob became angry, and upbraided Laban; Jacob said to
Laban, "What is my offense? What is my sin, that you have hotly
pursued me? [37]Although you have felt through all my goods, what have
you found of all your household goods? Set it here before my kinsmen
and your kinsmen, that they may decide between us two. [38]These
twenty years I have been with you; your ewes and your she-goats have
not miscarried, and I have not eaten the rams of your flocks. [39]That
which was torn by wild beasts I did not bring to you; I bore the loss of
it myself; of my hand you required it, whether stolen by day or stolen
by night. [40]Thus I was; by day the heat consumed me, and the cold by
night, and my sleep fled from my eyes. [41]These twenty years I have been
in your house; I served you fourteen years for your two daughters, and
six years for your flock, and you have changed my wages ten times.
[42]If the God of my father, the God of Abraham and the Fear (?) of Isaac,
had not been on my side, surely now you would have sent me away
empty-handed. God saw my affliction and the labor of my hands, and
rebuked you last night."

43 Then Laban answered and said to Jacob, "The daughters are my
daughters, the children are my children, the flocks are my flocks, and
all that you see is mine. But what can I do this day to these my
daughters, or to their children whom they have borne? [44]Come now,
let us make a covenant, you and I; and let it be a witness between you
and me." [45]So Jacob took a stone, and set it up as a pillar. [46]And Jacob
said to his kinsmen, "Gather stones," and they took stones, and made a
heap; and they ate there by the heap. [47]Laban called it Jegar-sahadu-
tha: but Jacob called it Galeed. [48]Laban said, "This heap is a witness
between you and me today." Therefore he named it Galeed, [49]and the
pillar Mizpah, for he said, "The Lord watch between you and me, when
we are absent one from the other. [50]If you ill-treat my daughters, or if

you take wives besides my daughters, although no man is with us,
remember, God is witness between you and me."
51 Then Laban said to Jacob, "See this heap and the pillar, which
I have set between you and me. [52]This heap is a witness, and the pillar
is a witness, that I will not pass over this heap to you, and you will not
pass over this heap and this pillar to me, for harm. [53]The God of Abraham and the God of Nahor, the God of their father, judge between us."
So Jacob swore by the Fear of his father Isaac, [54]and Jacob offered a
sacrifice on the mountain and called his kinsmen to eat bread; and they
ate bread and tarried all night on the mountain.
55 Early in the morning Laban arose, and kissed his grandchildren and
his daughters and blessed them; then he departed and returned home.

This detailed narrative about Jacob's separation from Laban is also closely connected with what precedes. Hence one sees that the earlier individual narratives about Jacob and Laban, from which our narrative derives and which were certainly at one time much shorter, have now been merged in a long, compact and almost novellistic story about Jacob and Laban. It is made up of three parts: (1) the preparations for flight, vs. 1–16; (2) the flight, vs. 17–25; and (3) the contract with Laban, vs. 26–55, which ranges most widely. The greatest share of the narrative belongs to the Elohist (vs. 2, 4–18a, 19–24, 26, 28–45, 53–55). The Yahwistic parts do not always agree in their conception with what E relates. The interpretation will refer to the most important differences. Already at the beginning there is a difference in the representation of the procedure prior to Jacob's flight. The source J (vs. 1 and 3) had treated it quite briefly. There were two reasons which led Jacob to go home: unfavorable talk by Laban's sons and a saying of God, which latter reason was, of course, decisive. Whereas the Yahwist made Jacob's departure follow immediately (in v. 21bα), the source E narratively expanded what J had indicated only in a sketch. For E too Jacob's departure had a human cause (v. 2) and a divine cause (v. 13). But here in Jacob's conversation with his wives the narrator created an excellent means to show clearly Jacob's thoughts and moods, in order then to motivate his departure much better. Here, better than in J, one sees into the double situation where Jacob protests but is finally brought to a final separation from Laban by God and also by his wives. One perceives here that this narrator, again in contrast to the Yahwist, takes pains to exonerate Jacob's act and to justify his activity with regard to Laban (cf. Abraham's exoneration in the Elohistic Hagar story in contrast to his less reputable role in ch. 16).

[1–16] In E, Jacob discovers the changed situation (v. 2) by somewhat more hidden means than he does in J. Not unfriendly talk, but Laban's general attitude is what reveals to Jacob the state of affairs. He has Rachel and Leah summoned to meet him in the field, which he cannot leave, and delivers one of those speeches which the ancient Israelite narrator developed with such skill. To understand it one must be clear about Jacob's intention in speaking. He himself was not sure whether Leah and Rachel really would follow him to his distant homeland. They were, of course, Jacob's wives by marriage, but that did not make them cease belonging to Laban's great family, of which Jacob himself had also become part (vs. 32, 37). Actually this larger confederation felt itself affected by Jacob's flight and reacted accordingly (v. 23). This large family is called "father's house" (*bēt 'āb*) in the Old Testament and is so named here in v. 14b. It is the real owner of the land worked by individual families. To leave this confederation was something unusual, and when the husband did so his act was apparently not necessarily binding on his wives. One discerns here the woman's strong connection with property. Both are basically a possession which can be separated only with difficulty (cf. Ruth's tie to the land, Ruth 4.5, 10). The women's answer shows how much Jacob was encroaching on legal questions in his speech. Their answer does not express universal feelings, but, rather, it describes very realistically a legal situation as they see it (vs. 14–16). They are already excluded from sharing in the possession of the land. Their father has already used the bridal price (cf. ch. 29.18) for himself—which apparently was not the custom—and has thus actually "sold" his daughters. They are already excluded from the confederation; they do not need to separate from it any more. Perhaps they are also especially disappointed at the fact that Laban gave them no inheritance, for which they may have hoped in the event of an initial absence of male descendants. The statement that they are already considered "foreigners" (*nokriyyōt*) gave Jacob precisely the desired cue. Now Jacob can act.

But Jacob's speech had another purpose, namely, to reveal to the reader Jacob's entire inner and outer situation, and to clarify above all his attitude toward Laban and his decision to separate from him. The description of the events in vs. 5–13, however, cannot be interpreted step by step from the viewpoint of the Yahwistic narrative in ch. 31.29 ff. Then one would have to say that Jacob concealed essential facts from his wives (e.g., the trick with the stakes) and distorted others. But Jacob does not behave innocently here (so Pr.). Rather the source E tells a quite different story and has another conception of the proceedings. Apparently the material underwent a change in the Elohist's hands. The figure of Jacob is here almost without moral offense. He was not at fault if life with Laban became impossible. Laban had changed the agreement about Jacob's pay again and again (this characteristic too in v. 7a shows that E thought of the events differently). But above all, the whole thing has now become a pious story in which much is said about God and his relationship to Jacob. God has frustrated Laban's knavery (v. 7b), God was with Jacob (v. 5b), God has given Jacob Laban's flocks, and finally God has called him to leave Laban and go home. This amazing change from the Yahwistic narrative, especially the moral purification, the transfer of interest to the subjective aspect of the acting persons, apparently corresponds to the refined demands of a more sensitive group of readers which we have met elsewhere (see, e.g., pp. 233 f.). Only the substance of the dream in vs. 12–13 causes difficulties, for it deals with two directions which could not possibly have been given to Jacob at the same time. The one in v. 12 cannot be spoken immediately before the departure. That v. 12 is an inept insertion is clear furthermore from the fact that God's revelation, which always belongs to the beginning of the divine address (cf. ch. 15.7) is now removed from its place. The insertion, in which moreover it never becomes clear just what Jacob is directed to do, derives from one who wanted to derive Jacob's proceeding in the breeding of spotted animals from a direct divine order. (On the "God of Bethel," see at ch. 28.10–22.) The reference to the vow in Bethel shows that God remembers this pious deed and rewards it with blessing. This entire speech ends with an unspoken question to the women (Jac.). Actually they too are impressed with Jacob's right and God's guidance. This makes the situation ultimately clear for Jacob.

[17–24] Jacob's departure from Laban is mentioned three times. The most complete and therefore dominant description is here also Elohistic (vs. 17–18a, 19–21a, 21bβ–24). But in the final redaction of the sources the Yahwistic remark about the departure (v. 21bα) and even the unmistakable Priestly remark (v. 18) have been included without seriously disturbing the readability of the whole. If we stick to the Elohistic description, Jacob chose a very favorable moment, the time of the shearing. The spring shearing was considerable work but was also a feast (I Sam. 25.1 ff.; II Sam. 13.23 ff.). Then Laban and his people were busy with themselves and their concerns, and furthermore Laban had caused an unfavorable situation for himself in the separation of the flocks (cf. ch. 30.36). Thus Jacob could keep his complicated departure so secret that Laban first learned of this final complete disappointment on the third day (v. 20). Rachel's theft of course was a serious burden to this hurried departure. It is characteristic, however, of the attitude of our source that it studiously emphasizes Jacob's innocence. In the succeeding conflict he is really unsuspecting. Regarding the teraphim, we know only that they were small cultic objects. According to I Sam. 19.13 ff., they must have had the shape of a man or a human face. Recently cultic masks have been suggested. In any case they were used especially in obtaining oracles (Ezek. 21.21). That they appear in the Old Testament as household idols must not mean that they were that always and everywhere. Possibly they were crowded out by the exclusive Yahweh cult. In the late royal period there was still a struggle against such illegitimate private cults (II Kings 23.24). The other members of the family declare themselves affected with Laban, their "brother," and depart together to overtake Jacob. Thus a dangerous situation arises for Jacob, who must move very slowly because of his flocks. But here again our narrator reports of God's direct intervention: Laban is warned in a dream. (The expression "Say not a word . . . either good or bad"—translated freely above—is a common idiom; it does not of course mean that Laban is not to speak even good to Jacob, but is to be related to the matter in hand; he is not to influence it any direction.)

[25–35] The narrative calls the site of the encounter in v. 25b the "hill country of Gilead." (In v. 25a, a place name has surely disappeared after the word "hill country.") What is meant is the mountain area south of the Jabbok, north and northeast of the present city Es Salt. Here the name Gilead is still used in its original meaning as the name of mountains. Only after a slow, colonizing expansion of Israelites into the forested area of modern 'Ajlun did Gilead become the large stretch of land which the term designates in the later usage of the Old Testament. It is certainly impossible to reach this area from Haran in a seven-day journey. Yet it will become clear below that this tradition originally thought of a much nearer "Aramean." The discussion between Laban and Jacob that follows contains two elements which are thematically and traditionally quite different in nature and in origin and were added to this great scene only subsequently: the negotiation with Jacob regarding the stolen god, vs. 26–43, and the contract, vs. 44–55.

Laban's first statement surprises one by the moderation which Laban imposes upon himself. He also refers to his power, and he is in fact the superior man in the sense of external power because of the other members of the clan who had come with him. But the "God of your father" has placed his hand over Jacob and forbidden Laban to use any violence. Therefore Laban can only appear as the one injured by Jacob, who is anxious about his daughters and grandsons. The latter point is strongly emphasized, and here one must be just with Laban; for such a departure from the family confederation was an act of violence, and Jacob himself admitted that the plan to take the daughters would have caused resistance from Laban (v. 31). In a strange land his daughters had no legal protection. Who could give it to them in those circumstances if not the clan to which the women belonged? If Jacob had departed at least after an amicable agreement, the matter would not have become so disquieting. Laban would have been ready to accompany his children and grandchildren "with mirth and songs, with tambourine and lyre" (v. 27)—a scene which one cannot imagine without smiling, for it is too incredible. (Such a festive leave-taking with songs appears in ch. 24.60.) With his action Jacob has "stolen the heart" of Laban (v. 26), i.e., he has defrauded him by breaking a trust. (This part of Laban's speech is a combination of Yahwistic and Elohistic parts; the Elohistic narrative, however, is dominant here and in what follows as far as v. 45.)

In the matter of Jacob's departure Laban limited himself to reproaches, but in the matter of the theft of his idols, which is apparently more important to him than the legal protection of his daughters, he goes all lengths. Every sympathetic reader had had to follow with interest the narrative of Laban's dramatic encounter with Jacob, but now the scene becomes completely sinister, for Jacob unwittingly pronounced the death penalty on Rachel (v. 32). On the other hand, the narrative cannot rise to really dramatic heights, for Laban, who is storming about his stolen god, who rummages through one tent after another in search of this treasure, makes a scene bordering on buffoonery. The narrator cannot have intended it to be heard without provoking laughter. Israel expressed herself frequently regarding the impotence, even ridiculousness, of idols and their images, most fully in the humorous caricature of idol manufacture in Isa. 44.9 ff. Much older is the story about the stolen idol which was then erected in Dan, Judg., chs. 17 f. Here, as in our narrative, the theft is a very serious matter, for the idol was considered an object of great worth to men, for which one was willing to risk a great deal.* The apocryphal narrative about Bel also belongs to this series. Nevertheless Jacob's situation, because of his oath and Laban's threatening attitude, was dangerous enough. It was rescued only by Rachel's presence of mind (v. 35). Thus a very sharp judgment is given concerning the unholiness and nothingness of this "god"; a woman sat upon it in her uncleanness (Lev. 15.19 ff.).

[36–54] Laban's lack of success caused the tables to be turned. Now Jacob is superior and can settle with Laban in a passionate speech (vs. 36–42). This long speech is also a little work of art which the ancient reader knew how to value. It is not routine speech, but as such situations demand, it proceeds solemnly and in exalted style. To understand its content correctly, one must remember that here the blameless Jacob, the Jacob of the Elohist, is speaking, the Jacob who was repeatedly wronged by Laban, whose honor has now been stained and who looks back with righteous indignation. We have here, among other things, an insight into all the privileges of the shepherds, which obviously correspond to actual custom (cf. Ex. 22.9–14). The shepherd who was sometimes left alone with his flocks months at a time, often in unfavorable terrain, subject to all kinds of weather, found his service actually trying. He was legally protected to some extent; he could take whatever he needed to eat from the flock, and he did not need to replace what was lost "by act of God." Nevertheless, one can imagine that he had to struggle continually with the demands of mistrusting owners who were concerned with the maintenance and increase of their flocks. Laban was not molested with such annoyances, Jacob reminds him. The animals eaten by wild beasts (what was lost at night was of course dealt with more lightly) were not reckoned against Laban, and Jacob had not taken a single, large, fat

*Among the excavated so-called Nuzi tablets (see above, p. 183) there is a contract which calls for a comparison with the discussions between Jacob and Laban. A man named Naswi, because he had no son of his own, adopted a certain Wullu. Since he then became Naswi's heir he had to care for him. If, however, a son should now be born to Naswi, Wullu would have to share the inheritance with him. But the gods (idols) which Wullu would have otherwise inherited would belong to the real son. (*Bulletin of the American Schools of Oriental Research*, no. 66, 1937.) That is not an exact parallel to the Jacob-Laban story, for the latter says nothing either about Jacob's adoption or about the subsequent birth of Laban's sons, which was decisive for the legal situation. It is conceivable only that the narrative once contained more special data regarding the legal situation, which were then weakened in the long process of being transmitted. For the struggle for the idol reminds one very much of a legal situation such as the contract presupposes.

ram. But Laban had always changed the manner of payment so that Jacob never knew where he stood. (What the narrator actually means by that we do not know, because the Yahwist tells of this point differently.) Jacob's reference to Yahweh, to whom alone he is indebted for his present possession, makes use of a term for God which is extremely old. It is usually translated "Fear of Isaac," and is understood to refer to the God whom Isaac fears and whom he worships in awe. Recently, however, the translation "kinsman of Isaac" has been thought to be more probable.* In either case, this will be the name of the God whom the pre-Mosaic people of Isaac worshipped, that seminomadic confederation which traced its cult back to a divine revelation to Isaac. (For belief in the God of the fathers, see p. 188.) Later this name became a byname for Yahweh. Laban's reply, in which he circumstantially, that is, in the form of a solemn legal claim, declares his daughters, his grandchildren, and the flocks as his possession, must probably be interpreted in the following manner: It appears that he is arguing on the basis of the so-called Sadika marriage, a custom according to which not the wife but the husband is released from his paternal confederation, while the wife remains in her father's family. An example of this form of marriage, which disappeared early in Israel, is Samson's marriage to the woman of Timnah who after the wedding ceremony remained in her father's house (Judg. 14.2 ff.; 15.1).

An ancient unsolved problem is how the births of Jacob's children can be provided for in the succession of years as it is sketched in vs. 31 and 41. If one combines these data with those of ch. 29.20 and 30.25 the result is the much too brief span of seven years (+ seven years' service for Rachel and six years' service for the flocks = twenty years). Attempts to solve the problem have included source analysis, emendations, transpositions of the text, and the information that in the case of such sagas, especially in such contexts which have arisen from a conflation of several sagas, one cannot check figures.

The narrative about Laban's contract with Jacob is based on an ancient aetiological tradition which once circulated by itself and was not connected from the beginning with the preceding and succeeding Jacob stories. One can still sense it in the rather abrupt and unmotivated transition from v. 43 to v. 44; for this contractual agreement is not exactly what we expect of the angry Laban. Nevertheless, this surprising turn of affairs has sufficient foundation in God's

*W. F. Albright, *From the Stone Age to Christianity*, 1940 (1957), 248.

warning to Laban (vs. 24, 29). The text here is suddenly very clumsy. Various doublets show that it is composed of two recensions. In v. 45 a landmark is erected as a sign of covenant, in v. 46 a heap of stones; v. 46 tells of a ceremonial covenant meal, v. 54 tells of another. Especially remarkable is the double significance that is ascribed to the covenant itself. According to v. 50, it obligated Jacob to loyal treatment of Laban's daughters; in v. 51 it sanctions a boundary that may not be transgressed with evil intent by any party to the contract. There can be no doubt that the latter "internationally legal" conception is much older than the one that views the proceeding only as a family matter. It apparently goes back to a very old boundary agreement, which was made between Israelites (settlers east of the Jordan) and an Aramean tribe "Laban," and it must derive from the time of the first fairly peaceful encounter with the Arameans in Gilead. It was, therefore, a harmless affair in contrast to the deadly Aramean wars in which Israel was involved in the ninth and eight centuries. Obviously it thinks of Laban as living much closer than he does in chs. 24.10 f.; 28.10; 29.4 (Haran). Perhaps one can go even a step farther in the interpretation and assume that the boundary dividing the two "nations" once was that line beyond which fugitives were exempt from punishment. Israel then connected this ancient agreement with Jacob, who here was first legally sure of his goods before Laban (Noth, *Überlief. des Pent.*, 101). In any case, here again after long fictional sections we finally come upon traditional material aetiologically anchored in the story. The later version too, probably Elohistic, is aetiological. That is to say, it too wants to explain a well-known landmark in Gilead east of the Jordan, a landmark which possibly would be connected with Mizpah, also east of the Jordan, for there is a brief allusion to this name in v. 49 (cf. Judg. 11.11, 29, 34). In this recension, however, the memory of the international significance has completely disappeared. The interpretation of the sign within the framework of Jacob's family history now dominates the idea of the contract. The concern of this agreement in v. 49 is known to us from many extant Oriental marriage contracts. In the polygamy existing at that time there was always an understandable anxiety that one wife might be supplanted in the course of years by another and so lose her position and conjugal rights. This dispossession of conjugal rights was called "humbling" (*'innā*). (See ch. 16.6b.) What is concerned here, therefore, is rather a one-sided obligation which Laban places upon Jacob and to the solemn acceptance of which he brings him. The covenantal meal documents the amicable settlement of the partners. It is, however, a sacred meal, i.e., the god who sanctions agreements takes part in it as an unseen guest. The narrative represents this god as Yahweh, the God of Abraham, the Fear of Isaac. Actually, however, such a sacred covenant brought with it a problematic overlapping of two cultic circles, since each of the partners called on his own god. That meant, of course, a certain recognition by each partner of the other partner's god. One assumed, of course, that the other was bound in the act because of his faith to an absolute norm, that his god would avenge his every transgression. Thus v. 53 actually does speak of two gods, the God of Abraham and the god of Nahor. They are the guardians of this covenant. The heap of stones (the landmark) is the corroborating earthly sign by which the partners to the covenant will be warned in the future much more durably than by something written. The ancient narrators told frankly that Laban erected this sign. But Laban's name in v. 46 was later replaced by Jacob's. Apparently they did not like the idea that Jacob should have been warned by a sign which Laban erected. The conclusion to the long narrative is Elohistic and conciliatory. Laban is appeased and calmed by Jacob's guarantee and can take leave of his daughters and grandchildren and return again to his place ("Nahor's city," ch. 24.10). This concludes a long period in Jacob's life.

31. THE ANGELS OF MAHANAIM. Ch. 32.1–2

32 [1]Jacob went on his way and the angels of God met him; [2]and
when Jacob saw them he said, "This is God's camp!" So he called the
name of that place Mahanaim.

[1–2] After his separation from Laban (the time is not given more precisely), Jacob had a strange encounter: "The angels of God met him." The affair is communicated in extreme brevity, four words in the Hebrew text. The narrator gives the reader not the slightest notion of the apparently completely silent appearance, to say nothing of the fact that he wastes no words about the significance of the event for Jacob. Here, then, an impassable barrier is placed for the interpreter. What justification has he then to speak of protecting angels, as is often done? The statement mentions only heavenly "messengers," i.e., functionaries of the divine world dominion who are hurrying through the world entrusted with definite commissions, and whom

Jacob encounters (cf. at ch. 28, pp. 282 f.). The word "camp" need not necessarily have a warlike significance. Every tribe, every nomadic confederation had its camp. But passages like Josh. 5.13 ff.; II Kings 6.17 suggest the armed host of heaven. There is no direct relation of this appearance to Jacob and his situation, so far as we can see. Thus one can only say that when Jacob approaches the Promised Land he also approaches God's realm again. Outside, in foreign territory with Laban, his life lacked such appearances almost completely. The section (Gunkel speaks of its abruptness) is only a tiny pebble in the Jacob tradition, again formerly an independent brief tradition about a place, a tradition which was aetiologically connected with the name of the city Mahanaim (*maḥ^{a}nē*, "camp"), which later was so important in Israel's history. Here Eshbaal, Saul's son, had his court, II Sam. 2.8 ff. Here Absalom's army was defeated (II Sam. 17.24 ff.). Here one of Solomon's officers was stationed (I Kings 4.14). Its site, south of the Jabbok, has not yet certainly been identified archaeologically.

If one surveys the single parts of which our present Jacob story is composed, one is amazed at the complexity of the traditions which have here found their place next to one another. At the beginning were a few Jacob-Esau stories which the exposition noted for their quite distinct original quality and purpose. Then followed an ancient cultic narrative (Gen. 28.10 ff.) about which no one can doubt that it once existed independently in the realm of the sanctuary at Bethel. We recognized a quite different circle of material in the Jacob-Laban narratives. They were remarkable for the almost complete absence of an ancient aetiological mooring which was so characteristic until then for the patriarchal narratives. We are apparently dealing with anecdotal material that once circulated freely among the people and is now worked out in a strongly novellistic manner. (Only the story of the contract, ch. 31.44 ff., emerged from this framework as narrative material connected with a place.) The beginning of ch. 32 signifies another deep cleavage in this large composition, to the extent that here is the transition from the block of Jacob-Laban narratives to another block of Jacob-Esau narratives. This second group of Jacob-Esau narratives, when one looks at it closely, also divides into diverse traditional elements; it too emerges in an ancient cult tradition, and it thereby receives a theological emphasis (ch. 32.22 ff.). A final block of material, again consisting of quite diverse individual traditions, describes Jacob's experiences in Canaan (chs. 33.18 to 35.22). Thus the material was quite diversified, and one must think of the process of collecting and amalgamating it as proceeding slowly. What is most astonishing is the result, i.e., the fact that such disparate traditional material could be rounded into a compact "biographical" picture. It is not, as it might have been, a loose collection of anecdotes about the ancestor, Jacob, which are more or less without connection to one another, but it is a connected story. Stages on a way become clear, a way that leads from Beer-sheba (ch. 28.10) to Bethel and then to Haran and from there back by way of Penuel to Shechem and Bethel and ends in Hebron (ch. 35.27). This uniformity in the story could only be achieved, of course, by a process of generalization, leveling, and subsequent assimilation of data which formerly had a much more specialized significance in the individual narratives. Thus, for example, traditions are collected under Esau's name, some of which derive from East Jordan (Esau) and some from southern Judea (Edom). (See pp. 274 f.) What was the power which bound all the numerous single parts into such a compact picture? Where was the magnet which could arrange and orient the many filings in this way? First of all, of course, one must reckon with the fact that many narratives and anecdotes were connected popularly or by traveling storytellers more or less unintentionally, simply following the law of narrative association. The form, however, in which the total picture of Jacob's story first becomes tangible, namely, the form given by the Yahwist, has without question a distinct theological character. It did not achieve this because the narrator consistently made God the originator and director of the events. In this respect one must establish the contrary, namely, that for long stretches in the narrative any reference to God and his revealed will seems to be dispensable, and that the autonomy of the things and the willfulness of the persons involved is amazingly unrestricted. And still no reader can overlook the fact that this story unfolds under a particular divine sign and that in it, in profound secrecy, of course, God's plan is being accomplished. This plan includes Jacob's paradoxical preservation and his being blessed with twelve sons, in which the full number of the tribes of later Israel is announced; and God's preservation of Jacob is in a wider sense the same preservation that Israel as a whole experienced. Where else could Israel have acquired so profound a knowledge except from its own history with God? And without this it could never have related the patriarchal stories as it did (see p. 40, and the Epilogue to ch. 32.22 ff.). For this strange theological note the Jacob story is indebted primarily to the incorporation of the two former cultic narratives, chs. 28.10 ff. and 32.22 ff. into the composition. The programmatic significance of these two stories for the whole of the Jacob narrative is obvious. Here Jacob is quite directly subject to God's revelation. This and the words spoken by Yahweh point far beyond the limits of the individual story and determine the interpretation of the entire Jacob narrative. Accordingly, we are dealing with a kind of storytelling which did not penetrate the entire mass of material with the same intellectual and thematic thoroughness as Homer did for his. It is bound much more conservatively to what has been handed down, even to its form; but occasionally it has inserted sections of such compactness that they themselves determine the significance of the whole. That is also true, by the way, of Jacob's prayer (see at ch. 32.9–12).

32. JACOB'S PREPARATIONS TO MEET ESAU. Ch. 32.3–21

32 3And Jacob sent messengers before him to Esau his brother in the
land of Seir, the country of Edom, 4instructing them, "Thus you shall
say to my lord Esau: Thus says your servant Jacob, 'I have sojourned
with Laban, and stayed until now; 5and I have oxen, asses, flocks,
menservants, and maidservants; and I have sent to tell my lord, in order
that I may find favor in your sight.' "

6 And the messengers returned to Jacob, saying, "We came to your
brother Esau, and he is coming to meet you, and four hundred men with
him." 7Then Jacob was greatly afraid and distressed; and he divided
the people that were with him, and the flocks and herds and camels,
into two companies, 8thinking, "If Esau comes to the one company and
destroys it, then the company which is left will escape."

9 And Jacob said, "O God of my father Abraham and God of my
father Isaac, O LORD who didst say to me, 'Return to your country and
to your kindred, and I will do you good,' 10I am not worthy of the least
of all the steadfast love and all the faithfulness which thou hast shown
to thy servant, for with only my staff I crossed this Jordan; and now I
have become two companies. 11Deliver me, I pray thee, from the hand
of my brother, from the hand of Esau, for I fear him, lest he come and
slay us all, the mothers with the children. 12But thou didst say, 'I will
do you good, and make your descendants as the sand of the sea, which
cannot be numbered for multitude.' "

13 So he lodged there that night, and took from what he had with
him a present for his brother Esau, 14two hundred she-goats and twenty
he-goats, two hundred ewes and twenty rams, 15thirty milch camels and
their colts, forty cows and ten bulls, twenty she-asses and ten he-asses.
16These he delivered into the hand of his servants, every drove by itself,
and said to his servants, "Pass on before me, and put a space between

> drove and drove." 17He instructed the foremost, "When Esau my
> brother meets you, and asks you, 'To whom do you belong? Where are
> you going? And whose are these before you?' 18then you shall say, 'They
> belong to your servant Jacob; they are a present sent to my lord Esau;
> and moreover he is behind us.' " 19He likewise instructed the second and
> the third and all who followed the droves, "You shall say the same
> thing to Esau when you meet him, 20and you shall say, 'Moreover your
> servant Jacob is behind us.' " For he thought, "I may appease him
> with the present that goes before me, and afterwards I shall see his face;
> perhaps he will accept me." 21So the present passed on before him; and
> he himself lodged that night in the camp.

This text tells about the meeting with Esau, or rather, about the preparation for the meeting, with great ceremoniousness and constant postponement of the denouement. Even though the present extent of this section is due primarily to the redactor's combination of the two recensions (J and E), still each narrator makes Jacob prepare minutely for the encounter. This shows that something very important has to be settled between the two brothers. In this section two proceedings are quite distinct: vs. 3–13a (Jacob divides his possessions into two "camps" in fear of Esau) and vs. 13b–21 (Jacob again and again sends gifts to appease Esau). The first version is Yahwistic, the second Elohistic. Both narratives allude aetiologically to the place name Mahanaim; the first in the word for the two camps (*maḥ^{a}nē*, "camp"), the second in the word for "gift" (*minḥā*). Since, however, the two versions are not mutually exclusive, they can be understood in the combination of the two sources without difficulty as successive.

[3–13a] The time has now come for Jacob, who has settled his affairs with Laban, to straighten things out with Esau. Jacob clearly feels that matters have not improved at all during his twenty-year absence. This is recognizable especially from the form in which he has Esau addressed as lord and designates himself as his servant who desires to find favor in Esau's eyes. (The form of the "messenger's speech," which gives the commissioned message in direct address, is well preserved here.) He passes over his experiences with Laban in a rather noncommittal statement. The mention of his prosperity, however, is to awaken the prospect of gifts (Jac.). The announcement of Esau's coming is surprising, but it leaves the purpose of his coming open to all possible interpretations. Jacob's conscience, however, tells him that Esau's coming is dangerous. The state of his anxiety is strongly emphasized, when judged by the usual reserve this writer shows regarding psychological processes. Jacob, to be sure, is still

Jacob. He still knows what to do and soberly tells himself that bitter as the loss of half of his possessions would be, it might save him from losing everything. No one who heard the story would have blamed him for this. Each one, however, would have considered Jacob's prayer the climax of this scene. This prayer is the free prayer of a layman, i.e., it is not cultic and not poetic in form (in the sense of parallelism and rhythm); it is to be understood at the moment for the needs of the moment. One looks in vain here for reminiscences of special, cultic idioms. At best one can recognize a cultic scheme in the outline. The prayer begins with a broadly stylized invocation, in which the one addressed is ceremoniously identified. Jacob is not concerned simply with "God," but rather with the God of his fathers. He means Yahweh, who had commanded Jacob to return and had promised to bless him further. There follows the thanksgiving for miraculous guidance hitherto, of which Jacob confesses himself to be wholly unworthy. When the prayer turns from the past to the future (vs. 11–12) Jacob's whole perplexity and anxiety breaks forth, clothed in a petition and another appeal to the promise God has given him. This pattern for a prayer (Gu.), composed in the purest Yahwistic language (Pr.), has been called by some critics a later insertion because it does not fit with the profaneness of the rest of the passage. But this is right only to the extent that the narrator was bound in transmitting ancient traditional material to the conventional and was not so free as he could be here with the interpolation of the prayer. This prayer, then, is extremely significant for the whole Jacob story, as the Yahwist wanted it to be understood. It is a sign that the narrator, in spite of all the intricacy of the transactions in which Jacob was constantly involved, still did not lose sight of Jacob's relationship to God. One will not be wrong if one interprets this prayer also as the expression of a purification taking place in Jacob. Since the night for which Jacob is preparing (v. 13a) is the last one before his meeting with Esau, one must assume that Jacob's messengers have already met Esau on the way.

[13b–21] The source E told about Jacob's preparations to meet Esau in another way. Here Jacob stakes everything on Esau's change of mood. To give an official gift of honor is a polite custom throughout the Orient (cf. ch. 43.11). The way, however, in which Jacob staggers his gifts, letting the bearer announce that he, Jacob, is himself coming behind, his sending of another gift and still another—this way in which Jacob hopes to appease Esau's anger by stages must cause every reader to smile, in spite of the seriousness of the situation. Jacob acts according to the wisdom of Prov. 17.14 (Jac.). Here Jacob speaks quite frankly about "reconciliation" with Esau, more precisely about covering his face. The word "face" (*pānīm*), used five times in vs. 20 and 21, is a prelude to the following Penuel story (*p*^{e}*nīʾēl*, "God's face"). The dominant term of this story, however, gift (*minḥā*), alludes to the place name Mahanaim. This narrative must not be designated exactly as an aetiological one, however, for those terms are only more or less playful niceties of the narrator which pleased the listeners.

33. JACOB'S STRUGGLE AT PENUEL. Ch. 32.22–32

32 [22]The same night he arose and took his two wives, his two maids,
and his eleven children, and crossed the ford of the Jabbok. [23]He took
them and sent them across the stream, and likewise everything that he
had. [24]And Jacob was left alone; and a man wrestled with him until the
breaking of the day. [25]When the man saw that he did not prevail against
Jacob, he touched the hollow of his thigh; and Jacob's thigh was put out
of joint as he wrestled with him. [26]Then he said, "Let me go, for the day
is breaking." But Jacob said, "I will not let you go, unless you bless me."
[27]And he said to him, "What is your name?" And he said, "Jacob."
[28]Then he said, "Your name shall no more be called Jacob, but Israel,
for you have striven with God and with men, and have prevailed."
[29]Then Jacob asked him, "Tell me, I pray, your name." But he said,
"Why is it that you ask my name?" And there he blessed him. [30]So
Jacob called the name of the place Peniel, saying, "For I have seen
God face to face, and yet my life is preserved." [31]The sun rose upon him
as he passed Penuel, limping because of his thigh. [32]Therefore to this
day the Israelites do not eat the sinew of the hip which is upon the hollow
of the thigh, because he touched the hollow of Jacob's thigh on the
sinew of the hip.

In this narrative more than in any other of the ancient patriarchal traditions something of the long process of formation to which this material was subjected in history becomes clear. Many generations formed and interpreted it. It was in motion for centuries until it finally crystallized in the final form which it now possesses. This knowledge about such a long history is not, however, only a concern of a special science, but it concerns everyone who wants to understand the story; for only then can the reader be preserved from false expectations of a hasty search for "the" meaning of this story. There are scarcely examples in Western literature of this kind of narrative, which combines such spaciousness in content with such stability in form. Many generations have worked on them, as in the case of an old house; much of the content has been adjusted in the course of time, much has again been dropped, but most has remained. One will not be surprised, therefore, that such a narrative is filled with breaks in its construction and that all of its individual parts do not form an organic whole or have an even connection with or relation to one another. The earlier assumption that the narrative is composed of two versions which once existed independently must be given up. With the exception of vs. 23 and 24a, there is no real doublet in the narrative. It must therefore be ascribed completely to the Yahwist.

The Penuel story strikingly interrupts the story of the impending meeting with Esau, and its present position is surely very important for understanding all the Jacob stories. Jacob had become numb at the thought of meeting Esau; this impending event had occupied all his thoughts. And then this other, quite different encounter had occurred, one much more dangerous for Jacob and one for which he was completely unprepared. If, with many expositors, one interprets the whole event as an answer to Jacob's prayer which was still unanswered (ch. 32.9 f.), then this nocturnal event, in its quality as an answer to prayer, is under an even stranger omen.

[22–28] The long transition from the preceding narrative to our story is somewhat awkward, for v. 23a is parallel to v. 22. Flocks and caravans often travel at night. To lead a large flock over the Jabbok, which flows through a deep gorge, the modern Nahr ez-Zerqā, was a difficult task. When all the others were across (our narrative does not know the daughter, Dinah, see at ch. 34) and Jacob as a precaution had remained behind as the last one to cross, the frightful experience occurred. The word "man" is open to all possible interpretations. It transports us to Jacob's situation, who perceives nothing but a male antagonist closing in upon him. The expression "until the breaking of the day" reveals that a long bout of wrestling occurred. Indeed, the struggle was indecisive for a long period, until the mysterious antagonist touched Jacob's hip, which was put out of joint by the touch, as though by a magical power. Here is a passage where a much older form of our saga is revealed. The words in v. 25 are so strangely unrelated that one might think at first, in view of the hopelessness of the fight, that Jacob had won the upper hand over his antagonist (by a trick of fighting?). This interpretation would best suit the continuation, in v. 26, where the antagonist asks Jacob to let him go, and then also the later statement that Jacob had prevailed

(v. 28b). This monstrous conception, however, that Jacob nearly defeated the heavenly being, is now concealed by the clear text of v. 25b and v. 32b. (This concealment is made, to be sure, at the price of a clear logical connection between v. 25 and v. 26, for the request to Jacob to be released is now poorly motivated, since Jacob is, after all, crippled.) But even in its present form the saga does not conceal the fact that Jacob fought with gigantic power against his opponent. Elsewhere the narrator shows Jacob's almost superhuman strength (ch. 29.10). How close our story is to all those sagas in which gods, spirits, or demons attack a man and in which then the man extorts something of their strength and their secret, is clearly revealed in the examples collected by Gunkel. Especially frequent in such sagas is the notion that the effectiveness of these beings is bound to the night-time; when morning breaks, they must disappear. Thus the antagonist's request to be released because of the coming of dawn is obviously an especially ancient element in our tradition. And it has remained in it unchanged and uncorrected, in spite of the fact that no Israelite would have remotely considered Yahweh's power or that of his messengers so limited as that of a ghost. How the Yahwist and his readers explained this characteristic, who can say? Probably they did not consider that detail in such a saga at all susceptible of interpretation. The late Jewish Midrash understands the demand to be released as follows: I must sing in the morning choir before God's throne (Jac.). Now one must assume that Jacob has discovered something of the divine nature of his opponent, for in an odd contrast to his previous defense, he struggles to wrest a blessing from him, viz. divine vitality. It is better not to explain this as an especially pious quality; it is more correct to consider this request as a primitive human reaction to an encounter with God. This clutching at God and his power of blessing is perhaps the most elemental reaction of man to the divine. The request of Jacob, however, is not granted at all. Rather, Jacob must first be asked who he is. In the entire section which follows one must bear in mind that the ancients did not consider a name as simply sound and smoke. On the contrary, for them the name was closely linked with its bearer in such a way that the name contained something of the character of the one who bore it. Thus, in giving his name, Jacob at the same time had to reveal his whole nature. The name Jacob (at least for the narrative) actually designates its bearer as a cheat (cf. chs. 25.26; 27.36). Now he is given a new name by the unknown antagonist, a name of honor, in which God will recognize and accept him. The name Israel, which will be given to Jacob once more (ch. 35.10), is here interpreted very freely and contrary to its original linguistic meaning ("May God rule") in such a way that God is not the subject but the object of Jacob's struggle. (Our translation "strive" is not quite assured.) What the addition "and with men" means here has long been asked. To relate it to the disputes with Laban or Esau seems to be the only possibility, though it is somewhat forced. Perhaps "God [gods] and men" is only a superlative, stirring idiom which may not be pressed (cf., e.g., Judg. 9.9, 13). The enigmatic word about Jacob's prevailing is one of those roomy, strangely floating statements, so characteristic for this story. It once referred quite realistically to that struggle with the demon whom Jacob took on and from whom he wrested a victory. This astonishment at such suicidal courage was certainly not diminished when this nocturnal assailant was later considered to be Yahweh himself, God of heaven and earth, at work with Jacob. To be sure, the subject of wonder then shifted, for now it lay more in the fact that God let himself be coerced in such a way by Jacob's violence.

[29] The transition to v. 29 also seems loose at first, for the giving of the name of honor and its interpretation has almost the effect of a conclusion, at least of a first climax; and yet the inner continuity is unmistakable. Jacob is now clear about the divinity of his assailant, and his question about his name now illuminates his human situation and his intentions almost more harshly than did his request for a blessing (v. 26b). There stirs in him the most elemental force that can stir in a man when he encounters the divinity. Ancient man in particular knew himself to be surrounded by divine powers which determined his life, to be sure, but from whom he could not by his own power free himself. If a numen, however, became visible, tangible in his own sphere of life, then the most basic question was about its name, i.e., its nature and its intent. In such a case the numen was to be held fast, for if one knew its name, one could summon it, one could obligate it (by sacrifice, for example), one could even arbitrarily manipulate it, i.e., conjure with the divine power of this name. (On the importunate question about the name, cf. Ex. 3.13; Judg. 13.17.) Thus, embedded in this most urgent of all human questions, this question about the name, is all man's need, all his boldness before God. One must perceive here especially the longing for God, and our narrative shows that there is no need which can smother this ancient human thirst to find God and to bind him to oneself. In fact, our narrative augments the need. But the unknown power extricates himself from Jacob's grip; he does not answer the question, for he does not permit his mystery and his freedom to be touched. But he shows his freedom by blessing Jacob, nevertheless. "Thus Jacob's stolen blessing becomes legitimate, the promise at Bethel confirmed, and the petition (ch. 32.11 f.) heard." (Elliger.) One must remember, above all, Jacob's request for blessing in v. 26, which at first was not granted. But how far removed from the petition itself is the final fulfillment, and what lies between this petition and its fulfillment (v. 29b)! Jacob first has to reveal his name and his nature, he has to receive a new name, and he has to give up the question about the unknown assailant's name. Thus it becomes clear again that our narrative is far removed from all those sagas which tell of the extortion of a divine nature by man and of the winning of a blessing.

[30–32] When Jacob has received the blessing his assailant retreats. He gives the place of this encounter a name which is to contain what in his own eyes was the greatest marvel of all—that God was face to face with him, and the encounter had not meant his death! For according to the common Israelite conception, to see God meant death (Ex. 33.20; Judg. 6.22 f.; 13.22). The two forms of the name, Penuel and Peniel, differ inessentially only in the archaic nominal ending; the latter is used in v. 30 because it makes the pun on the word for face (*pānīm*), which is used in the language of the narrator, clearer. This narrative was therefore once aetiological, i.e., it explained the name of the city east of the Jordan, which later became so important (Judg. 8.8 f.; I Kings 12.25, situated on the site of modern Tulûl edh-Dhahab). It may even have been the saga about the sanctuary at that cultic center, which derived its holiness from this very experience. Since Mahanaim most probably and the "Mount of Gilead" certainly were south of the Jabbok, one must consider that Jacob crossed the Jabbok from south to north after he had moved along the south side of the Jabbok on his journey from the east (Noth, *Überlief. des Pent.* 240).

Miraculously the end of the struggle and the retreat of the horror coincide with the dawn: "The sun rose upon him as he passed Penuel." The narrative notes further that Jacob retained an injury from this night, that he lost something in a very vital spot, and therefore in a certain sense emerged from this struggle broken. Whether this notation conceals an earlier aetiology of a cultic dance, e.g., a limping dance (cf. I Kings 18.26) can no longer be decided. It is further reported that the Israelites reverently remembered this crippling of their ancestor in a very curious cultic usage connected with their slaughter of animals. Of all the things which happened on that night when the name Israel was received, this crippling of the ancestor became the subject of an especially nurtured memory.

Epilogue. The narrative ends with two aetiologies (vs. 30a, 32). Yet no one will assert that the actual point of the story (at least in its present form) rests in them. All that is said is that two traces of that monstrous event are still alive at the time of the narrator: the place name Penuel, and the attention given to the sciatic nerve in slaughtering. It is agreed that the story goes back to a very ancient period, in this case to a pre-Israelite period. It seems likely that Israel found in Penuel such a narrative about the nocturnal attack of a god on a man and then related it to Jacob. It is therefore all the more amazing that later Israel found this ancient framework and imaginative material, which derived from the crude, heathen past, completely suitable to represent Yahweh's work with Israel's ancestor. For the narrator's opinion is under all circumstances that in and behind this "man," this nocturnal assailant, Yahweh himself was most directly at work with Jacob.* (A similar weird narrative about such a nocturnal attack occurs in Ex. 4.24–26. Unfortunately it can scarcely be interpreted any more.) But in view of the long history and modification of the inner substance of this story in the interpretation of many generations one must not insist on discovering only one meaning for the narrative. We said above that by the time of the Yahwist many interpretations of the story had been made and that it had become quite broken in the tradition. But precisely because of its breaks and joints it received its essential spaciousness; precisely the looseness in the inner connection of the statements to one another makes room for many ideas; for the individual proceedings and words in the event, as every expositor senses, are not precisely limited with respect to their meaning and their significance. And every exegete will likewise encounter something somewhere in this narrative which can no longer be interpreted.†

*Luther makes Jacob say: "*Num tu is es?* Oh thou Heavenly Father and Lord! *Ego putavi esse spectrum . . . tu ergo es benedictor.*" (WA, XLIV, 107, 21 f.)

†There are parts that cannot receive proper attention. We are confronted with difficulties that stem from the way the Biblical authors worked. They used traditional material without working through it completely and refashioning it anew. (F. Baumgärtel, *Vom Text zur Predigt*, *Wittenberger Reihe*, Heft 9/10, 12).

The interpretation of the story must proceed from its position in the entire Jacob narrative, for its relation to the story of deception is unmistakable. The blessing is again mentioned but in a quite different tone, and thus something is made up which could not remain unsettled before God. In this respect the abrupt interruption in Jacob's preparations for the meeting with Esau by the Penuel story is clear enough. God's work with Jacob reveals at first a mortal judgment in which the bearer of the promise is nearly destroyed. The God upon whom Jacob had previously called here comes. Jacob was victorious in the sense of the present narrative because it pleased God to heed his importunity, his *anaidia* (Luke 11.8), and to tie his plan for history to Jacob, Israel. If one wishes to speak here of Jacob's faith, this faith is closely related both to despair and to confidence in God. But it is exceedingly doubtful that the narrator intends to interest us in Jacob's inner experience. Perhaps the nocturnal event ought really to designate an inner purification in Jacob. But whether, after it, he was "as God wanted him" (Di.) is doubtful. Under no circumstances is it permissible in the exposition to rectify Jacob's moral honor in catharsis. The entire emphasis is on God's activity, his destructive attack and his justification.

We have recognized this narrative in its present form as the spacious work to the formation and completion of which many generations contributed. This means then that the Yahwist presents in it theologically a witness of great complexity. The content of the narrative is certainly not exhausted in the presentation and interpretation of a brief event in the life of the ancestor. Rather, it contains experiences of faith that extend from the most ancient period down to the time of the narrator; there is charged to it something of the result of the entire divine history into which Israel was drawn. This event did not simply occur at a definite biographical point in Jacob's life, but as it is now related it is clearly transparent as a type of that which Israel experienced from time to time with God. Israel has here presented its entire history with God almost prophetically as such a struggle until the breaking of the day. The narrative itself makes this extended interpretation probable by equating the names Jacob and Israel. This renaming itself is here strangely isolated, to be sure; the following narratives do not seem to know it. The prophet Hosea alludes to this event once. Whether he knew our version of the narrative or another cannot be determined for certain because of the briefness of his statements. But the paradox of the victor, weeping and pleading for grace, is even more strongly suggested by him (Hos. 12.4). "And so we have this noble chapter, in which you see the marvelous dealing of God with his saints for our comfort and example, so that we may daily ask ourselves if he is also at work with us and be prepared for it." (Luther.) The narrator, in what immediately follows, tells of a remarkable consequence which is related to the event of that night and therefore must be considered along with it.

34. JACOB'S MEETING WITH ESAU. Ch. 33

33 1 And Jacob lifted up his eyes and looked, and behold, Esau was
coming, and four hundred men with him. So he divided the children
among Leah and Rachel and the two maids. 2 And he put the maids
with their children in front, then Leah with her children, and Rachel
and Joseph last of all. 3 He himself went on before them, bowing himself to the ground seven times, until he came near to his brother.
4 But Esau ran to meet him, and embraced him, and fell on his neck
and kissed him, and they wept. 5 And when Esau raised his eyes and saw
the women and children, he said, "Who are these with you?" Jacob
said, "The children whom God has graciously given your servant."
6 Then the maids drew near, they and their children, and bowed down;
7 Leah likewise and her children drew near and bowed down; and last
Joseph and Rachel drew near, and they bowed down. 8 Esau said,
"What do you mean by all this company which I met?" Jacob answered, "To find favor in the sight of my lord." 9 But Esau said, "I have
enough, my brother; keep what you have for yourself." 10 Jacob said,
"No, I pray you, if I have found favor in your sight, then accept my
present from my hand; for truly to see your face is like seeing the face
of God, with such favor have you received me. 11 Accept, I pray you,
my gift that is brought to you, because God has dealt graciously with me,
and because I have enough." Thus he urged him, and he took it.
12 Then Esau said, "Let us journey on our way, and I will go before
you." 13 But Jacob said to him, "My lord knows that the children are
frail, and that the flocks and herds giving suck are a care to me; and if
they are overdriven for one day, all the flocks will die. 14 Let my lord pass
on before his servant, and I will lead on slowly, according to the pace of
the cattle which are before me and according to the pace of the children,
until I come to my lord in Seir."
15 So Esau said, "Let me leave with you some of the men who are
with me." But he said, "What need is there? Let me find favor in the
sight of my lord." 16 So Esau returned that day on his way to Seir.
17 But Jacob journeyed to Succoth, and built himself a house, and made
booths for his cattle; therefore the name of the place is called Succoth.
18 And Jacob came safely to the city of Shechem *which is in the land
of Canaan, on his way from Paddan-aram*; and he camped before the city.
19 And from the sons of Hamor, Shechem's father, he bought for a

hundred pieces of money the piece of land on which he had pitched his tent. [20]There he erected an altar and called it El-Elohe-Israel.

[1–11] The meeting with Esau occurred immediately at the conclusion of Jacob's encounter with the God of his fathers. Jacob has just given the place its name as he sees Esau coming in the distance. Esau, therefore, had already been on his way when Jacob sent his messengers to him. Jacob has only time to stagger his family in such a way that those less close to him, i.e., first Zilpah and Bilhah, and then Leah are the first to be met in an encounter about which Jacob still does not know whether it will be hostile or friendly. If worst came to worst, Rachel, at least, would have time to escape while Esau was attacking the firstcomers. Jacob goes first so that when Esau approaches he may begin with a courtly, subservient ceremony of greeting. We are familiar with the sevenfold bowing from the ceremony of minor city princes before Pharaoh contained in the Amarna letters (fourteenth century B.C.). Usually a single bow was sufficient to express great reverence (cf. chs. 18.2; 19.1). And now finally the tension, which has been mounting continually since Jacob's departure from Laban, relaxes. After all the serious wrong that was done to him, how will Esau meet Jacob? The narrator draws a noble picture of Esau, who is simply overcome with the joy of reunion. In clear contrast to the deliberate Jacob, Esau expresses himself quite impulsively at the meeting. Not a word is said about the past, the embrace expressed forgiveness clearly enough. The unfortunate disfiguration of the scene by a late Jewish Midrash which changed the words "he kissed him" to "he bit him" (Jac.) completely misses the narrator's conception. What can be discussed is the reason for such a change of heart in one who formerly had waited for an opportunity to kill his brother (ch. 27.41). In this matter, however, the narrator's silence leaves room for all interpretations. What fascinates the narrator in this event lies deeper than the level of psychological explanations. There is a mysterious correspondence in the brothers' meeting to Jacob's nocturnal encounter with God, both with respect to the mortal threat to Jacob and his anxiety and also with respect to his amazement at the kindness he received. This strange parallel becomes clearest in Jacob's daring statement that seeing Esau's face was like "seeing the face of God" (v. 10), which is precisely an allusion to Penuel. But one must remember here that the narrator barely touches on the correspondence of the two events. He does not explain the mystery of the inner relation of the two encounters, the direction of the threads which tie the two together. After his struggle with God, Jacob's relationship to his brother was settled.

Jacob's speech is completely subservient. He calls Esau his "lord" several times and himself "Esau's servant." He says that he has found favor (v. 10a) while Esau condescends to a "my brother" (v. 9). Esau's question in v. 8 refers to Jacob's measures which were reported in ch. 32.8 f. That Jacob designates this part as a gift for Esau shows his intellectual grasp of the new situation, for Jacob's possessions were not divided for this purpose. **[12–16]** One sees, however, how little confidence Jacob has in this turn of affairs for the good by his stubborn refusal of Esau's friendly offer to accompany him. That is the mistrust of one who himself has often deceived (Fr.). Esau then leaves and goes back to Seir-Edom. This narrative, therefore, thinks of Esau as living deep in the south. That he originally was connected with the land east of the Jordan, however, is revealed rather clearly in the Jacob-Esau narratives, and not least by this very narrative which sets Jacob's meeting with Esau in the territory east of the Jordan. Only after the subsequent combination of Esau with Edom did Esau have to undertake so long a journey to greet his brother, and then return again to his distant home. (See pp. 270 f. and Noth, *Überlief. des Pent.*, 104 f., 210.)

[17–20] Succoth, mentioned in v. 17, was probably situated directly north of the Jabbok and is mentioned elsewhere (Josh. 13.27; Judg. 8.5 ff.). The aetiological reminiscence in connection with the name of the place (*sukkōt*, "huts") is probably an old Jacob tradition connected with this place. The narrator gives it without suggesting any special opinion to the reader. Then Jacob crossed the Jordan and went first to Shechem. The Hebrew word which characterizes Jacob's coming to Shechem (*šālēm*) means guileless, loyal, the contrary of everything crafty. The word refers to the following narrative, especially to ch. 34.21, unless the text here is corrupt (cf. LXX), which is quite possible. Jacob had in fact acquired property at this place and had erected an altar. (Concerning Shechem, see at ch. 34.) The narrative derives mainly from J, but E also shares in it, at least vs. 5 and 11. The statement in v. 18b about the return from Paddan-aram comes either from P or from a redactor.

35. THE RAPE OF DINAH. Ch. 34

34 1 Now Dinah the daughter of Leah, whom she had borne to
Jacob, went out to visit the women of the land; 2 and when Shechem the
son of Hamor the Hivite, the prince of the land, saw her, he seized her
and lay with her and humbled her. 3 And his soul was drawn to Dinah
the daughter of Jacob; he loved the maiden and spoke tenderly to her.
4 So Shechem spoke to his father Hamor, saying, "Get me this maiden
for my wife." 5 Now Jacob heard that he had defiled his daughter Dinah;
but his sons were with his cattle in the field, so Jacob held his peace
until they came. 6 And Hamor the father of Shechem went out to Jacob
to speak with him. 7 The sons of Jacob came in from the field when they
heard of it; and the men were indignant and very angry, because he had
wrought folly in Israel by lying with Jacob's daughter, for such a thing
ought not to be done.

8 But Hamor spoke with them, saying, "The soul of my son Shechem
longs for your daughter; I pray you, give her to him in marriage.
9 Make marriages with us; give your daughters to us, and take our
daughters for yourselves. 10 You shall dwell with us; and the land shall
be open to you; dwell and trade in it, and get property in it." 11 Shechem
also said to her father and to her brothers, "Let me find favor in your
eyes, and whatever you say to me I will give. 12 Ask of me ever so much
as marriage present and gift, and I will give according as you say to me;
only give me the maiden to be my wife."

13 The sons of Jacob answered Shechem and his father Hamor
deceitfully, because he had defiled their sister Dinah. 14 They said to
them, "We cannot do this thing, to give our sister to one who is uncircumcised, for that would be a disgrace to us. 15 Only on this condition
will we consent to you: that you will become as we are and every male
of you be circumcised. 16 Then we will give our daughters to you, and
we will take your daughters to ourselves, and we will dwell with you and
become one people. 17 But if you will not listen to us and be circumcised,
then we will take our daughter, and we will be gone."

18 Their words pleased Hamor and Hamor's son Shechem. 19 And
the young man did not delay to do the thing, because he had delight
in Jacob's daughter. Now he was the most honored of all his family.
20 So Hamor and his son Shechem came to the gate of their city and
spoke to the men of their city, saying, 21 "These men are friendly with
us; let them dwell in the land and trade in it, for behold, the land is
large enough for them; let us take their daughters in marriage, and let
us give them our daughters. 22 Only on this condition will the men agree
to dwell with us, to become one people: that every male among us be
circumcised as they are circumcised. 23 Will not their cattle, their
property and all their beasts be ours? Only let us agree with them, and
they will dwell with us." 24 And all who went out of the gate of his city
hearkened to Hamor and his son Shechem; and every male was circumcised, all who went out of the gate of his city.

25 On the third day, when they were sore, two of the sons of Jacob,
Simeon and Levi, Dinah's brothers, took their swords and came upon

the city unawares, and killed all the males. [26]They slew Hamor and his
son Shechem with the sword, and took Dinah out of Shechem's house,
and went away. [27]And the sons of Jacob came upon the slain, and plundered the city, because their sister had been defiled; [28]they took their
flocks and their herds, their asses, and whatever was in the city and in
the field; [29]all their wealth, all their little ones and their wives, all that
was in the houses, they captured and made their prey. [30]Then Jacob
said to Simeon and Levi, "You have brought trouble on me by making
me odious to the inhabitants of the land, the Canaanites and the
Perizzites; my numbers are few, and if they gather themselves against
me and attack me, I shall be destroyed, both I and my household."
[31]But they said, "Should he treat our sister as a harlot?"

All modern expositors are agreed about the extraordinary difficulty of a literary analysis of this narrative, but there is no agreement on the means of arriving at a satisfying solution. Indeed, it seems that ultimate scientific clarification is no longer possible. There are two contrasting opinions today. One asserts that two sources can be distinguished, that is, one story is a combination of two variants of the narrative which are quite similar on the whole but clearly different in detail. The other reckons with additions and corrective interpolations. (A third conception, according to which the irregularities are to be explained less by additions than by mutilation, has not proved satisfactory.) Most striking is that in vs. 4, 6, 8–10 Hamor, Shechem's father, undertakes the suit of Dinah (v. 6 clearly cuts the continuity of v. 5 and v. 7), while in vs. 11 f. and 19 Shechem himself deals with the sons of Israel. A further difficulty is that the attack in v. 25 is led by Simeon and Levi and that after their departure (v. 26b) all Jacob's sons intervene (v. 27). Does it not appear that another variant told of an attack by all of Jacob's sons? Further, the acceptance by the Shechemites of the conditions is told twice (v. 19 and v. 24). The parts which must certainly be separated from the basic narrative (J) produce such a mass of text that in our opinion the assumption of an actual parallel variant to the narrative is more probable than the assumption of larger additions. (See Eissfeldt's penetrating analysis, *Hexateuchsynopse*, 23–26.)

[1–24] This is the only narrative concerned with Jacob's daughter, whose name appears nowhere again except in chs. 30.21 and 46.15. Apparently the main body of Jacob traditions knew nothing of a daughter along with the twelve sons. The ancient expositors were also bothered about the question of her age, for according to the facts in chs. 30.21 and 31.41 Dinah cannot here have been a mature girl.

According to the narrator's dates she must have been about six years old at Jacob's departure. It may be that one allows several years for Jacob's stay in Succoth (ch. 33.17). The same is true of the age of Simeon and Levi, who have now become capable of bearing arms. But we know that one cannot expect biographical exactitude from such compositions of various traditional materials. A much later Jewish report romantically considers Dinah as Job's second wife; another tells that Asenath, Joseph's wife, was Dinah's child (ch. 46.20).

Here too, in order to understand the beginning of the story, one must consider the power of attraction which urban settlements had for nomads with small cattle. It was quite possible for them at these centers of culture to sell the products of their flocks and engage in modest trade (see p. 269). But our story wishes to show that the next logical step, the step from commerce to connubium, could lead to serious complications. The story describes very realistically how Dinah once stepped outside the small circle allotted to the life of the ancient Israelite woman, how she looked around rather curiously at the "women of the land," i.e., at the settled Canaanite women, and how she thus loosened the stone which became a landslide. The name Shechem is here a personal name, in contrast to ch. 12.6; but it is prepared for in ch. 33.18 f., "the city of Shechem." The vestige of a second source is usually seen in the double statement of the rape in v. 2b. The verb which is usually translated "humble" (*'innā*) indicates the moral and social degrading and debasing by which a girl loses the expectancy of a fully valid marriage. The designation "Hivite" is here used as usual quite generally of the settled Canaanite population. One must certainly assume, however, that this name, like that of the Hittites, for example, with which it is often associated, once designated a historically and politically definable group, about which we can say nothing more definite (Ex. 3.8; 23.23; Josh. 11.3). The piling up of expressions in v. 3 has also been considered a sign of a combining of sources, but perhaps not rightly. In any case, the emphasis on the great love for the girl, which brooks no hindrance, receives the benefit of the narrative, and the figure of Shechem is made more human for the reader. Regarding the combination of two recensions in what follows, see p. 329. According to the variant which is unquestionably the older, Shechem took matters into his own hands; apparently he had already abducted Dinah (cf. "he seized her" in v. 2b and v. 26). But he meets with a rejection by her family which is much more impassioned than he can understand, and no one tells him the reason for the irritation, even though he is quite ready for any compensation which will enable him to marry Dinah. For the argument that marriage with an uncircumcised man is impossible touches what is really troubling the brothers only in part. The brothers' indignation has a religious and cultic background. The word for infamous deed (*nᵉbālā*) is an ancient expression for the most serious kind of sexual evil. The references—especially Judg. 19.23 f.; 20.6 (Ex. 22.2)—reveal that surrounding this word was the horror of a sacrilege which incriminated the whole cultic community before God. The statement that "such a thing ought not to be done" (in Israel) was also an ancient formula expressing a tie with inviolable divine norms (II Sam. 13.12). The formal character is also shown in the anachronistic use of the word "Israel." Israel thought very severely in these matters and knew herself to be uncompromisingly distinct from the Canaanites in the sexual realm (cf. Lev. 18.22 ff.; 20.13–23). What is remarkable in the story is Jacob's passive attitude (v. 5); up to the very end he cannot pull himself together, to form a clear opinion. It is actually possible that Jacob's strange position as outsider is to be explained by the fact that the older form of the narrative did not know the figure of Jacob at all. The only actors are now and always were Dinah's brothers (Noth, *Überlief. des Pent.*, 93 f.).

The two courting scenes are also different with respect to the temperament of the suitor. Shechem stormily presents his case, quite contrary to custom, without regard for the costs of buying the bride under such circumstances. Old Hamor's speech is much calmer and transfers the matter from the personal basis to the basis of principle. With him there is to begin a general connubium between the people of Jacob and the Shechemites. He also offers the people of Jacob the opportunity to settle in his territory, a great privilege, for which the poor nomads with small cattle strove at all times! The lack of circumcision, which is presented by Dinah's brothers as the great impediment to marriage, appears here simply as a custom to which the people of Jacob are obligated: the reader does not learn its actual significance. Israel gave various explanations of its origin (cf. Josh. 5.2 ff.; Gen. 17.10 ff.), but the custom goes back certainly into much earlier prehistoric times. Probably it was formerly a rite of puberty which only in the course of time was performed on newborn babies. Israel knew the rite only in this later form. Our obviously ancient tradition reveals that Israel knew itself even in very early times to be distinguished profoundly from many of its neighbors by circumcision. Only at a much later period, however, did it receive conscious theological significance as a sign of the covenant in the faith of the people (see p. 200). That circumcision here also included the acceptance of faith in the God of Abraham and Jacob is not suggested in the demand of Jacob's sons. Jacob's passive role in the story is never more remarkable than it is here, where after old Hamor's speech, not Jacob but his young sons take over the conversation and stipulate the conditions. The statement that the brothers spoke "deceitfully" is a surprising moral judgment, for most of the patriarchal narratives are extremely reticent in evaluating human words or deeds. (Verse 13 has long been noticed because of its stylistic unevenness, but there is no reason to consider the word "deceitfully" as an addition.) The universal conception about the deceit is that whereas the Shechemites were honest in their offer, Jacob's sons were not, but were already planning their revenge. Their final statement that if the Shechemites will not submit, they will then take Dinah back is a threat which suggests that they are anxious for the Shechemites to accept their conditions. Again the aggressive Shechem "who did not delay" is conspicuous. Verse 19 reveals that the "Shechem recension" of our narrative reported in those words the acceptance of the condition and the performance of the circumcision. Shechem, "the most honored" of his family, could himself make the decision and be the first. The Hamor recension differs from this. According to it a council was first called in Shechem, in which Hamor stated the offer of the people of Jacob and recommended its acceptance. (The words "and his son Shechem" in v. 20 and v.24 are an addition to harmonize the two accounts.) Here too the reader must pay special attention to Hamor's speech as a little diplomatic masterpiece. He presents the matter as a great economic advantage for the townspeople. He wraps the most critical point, the demand for circumcision, with enticements, especially with the prospects, exaggerated of course, of possessing the flocks and property of the people of Jacob. What he means is, of course, a certain joint right of possession which would occur when the two groups became one large family; for the large related confederation had a superior possessor's right to the individual family's property. Thus in v. 22 the word which is usually translated "people" (*'am*) we have translated "kinsfolk," because it is much closer to what is meant and because here we are not dealing with "peoples" as we usually think of the term. One confederation, however, when united to another by connubium, can become a large community of blood and possessions; a large confederation of this kind was called a "nation" by the ancients (cf. remarks on ch. 19.38, p. 222). The old man, however, said nothing of the real occasion which should have been discussed, namely, the unfortunate relationship of his son to Dinah.

[25–31] Everything happened as Jacob's sons had planned. Hamor himself helped to plunge himself and his city into misfortune. Simeon and Levi are Dinah's full brothers and therefore feel themselves called upon for vengeance more than the others. The third day, which they chose for the attack, is according to ancient reports the most unfavorable for the men feverish with their wound. The two brothers may have had some men with them, but for the rest the ancient saga says nothing about the technical possibility of such an attack on a city. (The word "unawares," *beṭaḥ*, can be referred syntactically to the city and its state of indifference. Perhaps it is better, however, to refer it to the brothers' unhindered entrance into the city, which was unwalled, like all cities of that time, and undefended.) The assault of all Jacob's sons in v. 27 is only a brutal sequel in the present narrative; in reality, however, it is a variant. Simeon and Levi only murdered, the other brothers plundered. Here the ancient variants of the narrative concluded at one time. Later narrators added a comfortable scene with Jacob's appearance, which gave them the possibility of putting some distance between the event on the one hand and themselves and the readers on the other. To be sure, Jacob's role here is weak. His censure is more a peevish complaint. By contrast the answer of the two sons is proud and implacable; and the ancient reader, who felt more than we do the burning shame done to the brothers in the rape of Dinah, will not have called them wrong.

Our narrative, in contrast to the majority of patriarchal stories, is not an aetiological saga at all. Its concern is not to explain a custom or a name but to announce an event. Accordingly, the relationship of this tradition to political history is much more direct and unbroken than in all other patriarchal stories in which the reflection and revision of later writers also played a large part. The narrative seems to go back to the time when Israelite tribes were not yet settled in Palestine but on their way thither in search of new pasture. Indeed, it must come from a time when the tribes of Simeon and Levi were still tenting in central Palestine, i.e., it pictures a historical situation which must be dated considerably before 1200 B.C., for after 1200 the "house of Joseph" (Ephraim and Manasseh) settled in central

Palestine, while Simeon tented south in Judea and Levi no longer possessed a fixed territory. If the event spoken of in ch. 49.5–7 can be connected with the event here reported—and one can scarcely doubt that it can—then we learn something more about the consequences of this assault for Simeon and Levi. By some catastrophe they were pushed out of the territory around Shechem and other tribes could settle there later. The essential intention of the narrative in its present form is to present this prehistoric conflict of Simeon and Levi. But like many sagas it has changed the political proceedings into a conflict of fewer single persons and accordingly illustrated it on the level of the personal and universally human. Shechem is not a city, but one who has fallen in love with the girl, Dinah. Simeon and Levi are not tribes but the brothers who seek to purify the honour of their violated sister at the cost of a morally ambiguous deed. But our narrative is similar to the others in showing "a tangled skein of good and evil" (Del.), which could perplex the reader if he did not know that this event also belongs to a course of history subject to God's special plans. The narrator is clearly concerned to do justice to the Shechemites. Their offers in vs. 8–10 and v. 12 are generous and without guile. This knowledge of a real conflict was lost in later recollection of the event (Judith 9.2 ff.).

36. JACOB'S RETURN TO BETHEL. Ch. 35.1–8, 14–15

35 [1]God said to Jacob, "Arise, go up to Bethel, and dwell there; and
make there an altar to the God who appeared to you when you fled from
your brother Esau." [2]So Jacob said to his household and to all who were
with him, "Put away the foreign gods that are among you, and purify
yourselves, and change your garments; [3]then let us arise and go up to
Bethel, that I may make there an altar to the God who answered me in
the day of my distress and has been with me wherever I have gone."
[4]So they gave to Jacob all the foreign gods that they had, and the rings
that were in their ears; and Jacob hid them under the oak which was
near Shechem.

5 And as they journeyed, a terror from God fell upon the cities that
were round about them, so that they did not pursue the sons of Jacob.
[6]*And Jacob came to Luz (that is, Bethel), which is in the land of Canaan,* he and
all the people who were with him, [7]and there he built an altar, and
called the place El-bethel, because there God had revealed himself to
him when he fled from his brother. [8]And Deborah, Rebekah's nurse,
died, and she was buried under an oak below Bethel; so the name of it
was called Allon-bacuth. . . .

14 And Jacob set up a pillar in the place where he had spoken with
him, a pillar of stone; and he poured out a drink offering on it, and
poured oil on it. [15]So Jacob called the name of the place where God had
spoken with him, Bethel.

[1–5] Jacob's stay at Shechem, one concludes from the preceding context, came to a sudden end because of the misdeed of Simeon and Levi. But the occasion for his departure was a direct order from God. The statement that God directed Jacob to build an altar to the God who had appeared to him in Bethel was for the ancients neither remarkable nor polytheistic. They did not think of one supreme being whom we generally call God. They spoke of God only when he entered their time and their space and obligated them, and accordingly they called him the "God of our father Abraham," "God of Bethel," etc. Jacob is to go up to the cultic center lying much higher in the mountains of Benjamin. Yet in the Old Testament the verb (*ʿālā*) often means "to go on a pilgrimage" (I Sam. 1.3; Ps. 122.4; etc.), and this move by Jacob to Bethel actually does have all the characteristics of a pilgrimage (Jac.). A pilgrimage is a cultic observance, and the participants must therefore free themselves as in every other cultic celebration of everything which is displeasing to God. This "renunciation" is followed by an act of purification, i.e., ritual washing and probably also the beginning of sexual asceticism. Changing clothes is in religion a widespread cultic, symbolical act by which man represents himself as renewed by the divinity. All of this means, expressed in the language of the ancient Israelite cult: Jacob and his family "sanctify themselves" (cf. Ex. 19.10; Josh. 7.13; I Sam. 16.5; etc.). Holiness in the Old Testament is least of all a special quality which can belong to men or things, but rather simply the state of belonging to God. This state is made possible at all only by God's preceding choice or call and therefore it requires of men a kind of confessional renunciation of everything "unholy" and a cultic, symbolic demonstration of his desire for purification and clarification of his relation to God. This pilgrimage from Shechem to Bethel was certainly a regular custom in ancient Israel. An especially important part was at the start the renunciation of everything which belonged at all to the cult of strange gods. It was a question of nothing but objects, of small images which one had concealed (Deut. 27.15), amulets, etc. Earrings were probably credited with a magical deterrent power. These objects reached Israel as imported goods. What is concerned here is something different from a syncretistic mixture of Yahweh-objects with Baal-objects, a syncretism that began in the royal period. The official Yahweh-cult in ancient times was still pure and unadulterated, but in practice there was much that was illegitimate and magical. Joshua 24.23 indicates that such a rite of renunciation occurred at Shechem. The custom of this pilgrimage in the form described here certainly belongs to the cult of Yahweh and not to the God of the fathers, for this sharp intolerance of everything connected with the worship of other gods is the characteristic sign of Yahweh's revelation and his "zeal." That is to say, we must place this pilgrimage at the time of the ancient Israelite amphictyony, i.e., the period of the Judges; it preserves for us an interesting insight into the cultic history of ancient Israel (A. Alt, "Die Wallfahrt von Sichem nach Bethel," *Kleine Schriften zur Geschichte des Volkes Israel*, I, 79 ff.). Another question is the one about its origin. It may be related to the transfer of the central sanctuary from Shechem (Josh. 24.1, 25) to Bethel (Judg. 20.26 f.). At that time the custom of this pilgrimage was traced back to Jacob as its initiator, and this notion is reflected by our narrator, who is interested in this case only in its first performance. In Jacob's mouth the command to renounce everything heathen is directed primarily at Rachel's teraphim and similar cases (Gen. 31.19). In v. 5 the ancient aetiological material of the tradition about the pilgrimage is linked with Jacob's special historical situation at Shechem. Against expectation Jacob could leave this region unmolested. There was no revenge on the part of the Canaanites identified with Shechem. The "terror from God" which hindered them is really an event that Israel knew from her holy wars, a sinister paralysis or panic in which enemies lost the simplest use of their senses and powers and in which they sometimes destroyed themselves (Ex. 23.27; Josh. 10.10; Judg. 4.15; 7.22; I Sam. 14.15, 20; etc.).

[6–8, 14–15] Thus Jacob finally returns again to Bethel after long wandering (our narrative is to be understood this way in the whole context of Jacob stories) and can fulfill his former vow (ch. 28.20 ff.). And yet it is clear that our narrative did not belong from the beginning to this ring of Jacob stories, but was combined with it only subsequently. One expects a closer relation to the vow than the one in the text and also a word about the tithe. And besides, if one considers vs. 14 f. as the natural conclusion to our narrative, a conclusion that was placed in the Priestly story of Bethel when JE was redactorily combined with P, then it is apparent that our narrative was parallel to the one in ch. 28.10 ff., for here another tradition was given of the erection and anointing of the landmark in Bethel and Jacob's naming of the place (v. 15 in our opinion belongs to E and not to P). Our text is not a real saga with several acting persons, with moments of suspense and their release, but rather a formerly independent tradition which arose in close connection with an ancient cultic custom and which was then later inserted as a part of the narrative before Jacob's departure from Laban. The brief notice about the death of Deborah, who is not mentioned before or after, gives one the impression that the narrator and his readers once knew more about her. One may not ask what Rebekah's old nurse, who belonged in Isaac's house, was doing on Jacob's wandering. A tradition about Deborah was early connected with a place not far from Bethel. According to Judg. 4.5, it may have been one about the prophetess Deborah, but then a different tradition knew of a nurse of Rebekah. Since Jacob has now arrived in the vicinity of Bethel, this brief traditional element has been attached to the narrative.

37. GOD'S APPEARANCE AT BETHEL. Ch. 35.9–13

35 [9]*God appeared to Jacob again, when he came from Paddan-aram, and blessed him.* [10]*And God said to him, "Your name is Jacob; no longer shall your name be called Jacob, but Israel shall be your name." So his name was called Israel.* [11]*And God said to him, "I am God Almighty: be fruitful and multiply; a nation and a company of nations shall come from you, and kings shall spring from you.* [12]*The land which I gave to Abraham and Isaac I will give to you, and I will give the land to your descendants after you."* [13]*Then God went up from him in the place where he had spoken with him.*

[9–13] These verses contain almost everything the Priestly document has to say about Jacob! One has to take the share of the patriarchal stories which belongs to P and read it by itself to recognize the completely different theological quality of this work. A comparison with the source J or E brings to light the absence of all the colorful narrative material which quantitatively far exceeds the size of the Priestly tradition. And yet the often expressed doubt that P is to be designated as a historical work is in fact wrong. P is not simply a collection of cultic, ritual materials, clothed of necessity in historical garb, but an actual historical work, in so far as it successively notes in the patriarchal stories God's word and act revealed to Abraham, Isaac, and Jacob. Its representation differs in being limited strictly to noting the divine words and ordinances, to what is theological in the narrowest sense of the word, while J and E relate all the profane occurrences in which God's plan is realized in profound concealment. In a certain sense, then, the *Deus revelatus* is the subject of the Priestly narrative, while JE follows the ways of the *Deus absconditus*. Thus our section limits itself to that which God revealed to Jacob by summarizing in essence what is theologically important from ch. 28.10 ff. (JE) and ch. 32.23 ff. (J), the promise of land and the change of name. (In the case of the latter, one misses the interpretation of the new name corresponding to that of ch. 17.5. It is likely that such an interpretation was suppressed by the redactor because it collided with the one in ch. 32.28.) For the rest, what is promised to Jacob is word for word the elements of the promise to Abraham, and therefore the exposition of ch. 17 must be referred to here (see pp. 198 f.). Apparently a primary concern of our text is to show that the promise to Abraham was renewed completely to Jacob. Indeed it is now expanded by the creative command "be fruitful and multiply"! Abraham's seed branches out for the first time in Jacob, and in this number of children, according to P's conception, a command to Jacob was obeyed. It is easy to see that our Priestly pericope disagrees in this point with the Jehovistic narrative in which it is now placed. The command to be fruitful certainly was given to Jacob, according to the conception of this text, when he was still childless. But now it is given to a man who awaits the birth of the last of his many children. Our section was in P the only divine address to Jacob, corresponding to the Elohistic one in ch. 28.10 ff. The word "again" in v. 9 is a redactorial addition, in view of the preceding Bethel story. In the Priestly document the enumeration of the sons (vs. 22b ff.) followed immediately after our section, but since this continuation of our text concluded with the notice of Isaac's death it was moved for the sake of the Yahwistic narrative which was included.

38. BENJAMIN'S BIRTH. JACOB'S SONS. ISAAC'S DEATH. Ch. 35.16–29

35 [16]Then they journeyed from Bethel; and when they were still
some distance from Ephrath, Rachel travailed, and she had hard labor.
[17]And when she was in her hard labor, the midwife said to her, "Fear
not; for now you will have another son." [18]And as her soul was depart-
ing (for she died), she called his name Ben-oni; but his father called his
name Benjamin. [19]So Rachel died, and she was buried on the way to
Ephrath (that is, Bethlehem), [20]and Jacob set up a pillar upon her
grave; it is the pillar of Rachel's tomb, which is there to this day.
[21]Israel journeyed on, and pitched his tent beyond the tower of Eder.

22 While Israel dwelt in that land Reuben went and lay with Bilhah
his father's concubine; and Israel heard of it.

Now the sons of Jacob were twelve. [23]*The sons of Leah: Reuben (Jacob's
first-born), Simeon, Levi, Judah, Issachar, and Zebulun.* [24]*The sons of Rachel:
Joseph and Benjamin.* [25]*The sons of Bilhah, Rachel's maid: Dan and Naphtali.*
[26]*The sons of Zilpah, Leah's maid: Gad and Asher. These were the sons of
Jacob who were born to him in Paddan-aram.*

27 *And Jacob came to his father Isaac at Mamre, or Kiriath-arba (that is, Hebron), where Abraham and Isaac had sojourned.* [28]*Now the days of Isaac were a hundred and eighty years.* [29]*And Isaac breathed his last; and he died and was gathered to his people, old and full of days; and his sons Esau and Jacob buried him.*

[16–18] For the conclusion to the composition of the Jacob story there were apparently no broadly developed narratives available, but only what may be called the rubble of smaller or very small single traditions, often quite fragmentary in character (cf. vs. 21 f.!). The last self-contained narrative was the story of Dinah in ch. 34; after that the course of the narrative about events surrounding Jacob becomes restless because of the great number of small units which have been strung together. In this text three units are to be distinguished: the narrative of Rachel's death (vs. 16–20), the one of Reuben's crime (vs. 21–22a), and a Priestly list of Jacob's sons (vs. 22b–29).

Jacob's way now leads from Bethel farther south to Ephrath, probably to be identified with the Benjaminite Ophrah mentioned in Josh. 18.23. The expression "length of the land" does not designate a definite distance but generally only short distance, as II Kings 5.19 also indicates. There has long been agreement that our narrative originally did not think of Bethlehem as the place of Rachel's grave and that the words in v. 19 (and in ch. 48.7) "that is, Bethlehem" are therefore a later gloss. Rachel is the mother of the tribes of Joseph and Benjamin, and traditions about Rachel must therefore be sought, according to all laws of the history of tradition, in the territory settled by these tribes. Our narrative is in accord with that, for with the tower of Eder it obviously does not yet intend to lead to the territory of Judean Bethlehem. Also in accord with that are the references to Rachel's grave in I Sam. 10.2; Jer. 31.15, for both of these references put Rachel's grave in Benjaminite territory, i.e., north of Jerusalem. Another question is how and when the tradition about the grave moved and could be fixed at a place near Bethlehem, designated today by a small Arab sanctuary. But the movement of holy places to correspond to the changed needs of new political or commercial conditions is a frequent occurrence in cultic history. In her death Rachel saw the fulfillment of her desire (cf. ch. 30.24). A mysterious relationship existed between the name and its bearer, according to the belief of the ancients. A name could bring with it a destiny (cf. I Sam. 4.21) and often place its bearer in the protective sphere of another God (Dan. 1.7). Thus v. 18 suggests a drama which unfolds in an intellectual dimension which to us is quite strange. Rachel, already in the throes of death, gives the newborn a name that records the early death of his mother and that would have placed the child for the rest of his life under the shadow of this grief. Jacob, however, snatches the child from that darkness which is about to determine its beginning life. He grants no existence to this evil name by changing its meaning. The word *jāmīn* in Benjamin's name indicates "quarter of heaven," which is on one's right as one faces east, i.e., the south side. Furthermore the right side was widely thought of as the fortunate side. This cannot be seen elsewhere in the Old Testament, but must have been a common notion, judging by our passage. The name of a tribe, Benjamin, in history ("People of the South," cf. Arabic *Yemen*) has recently been considerably discussed because of the surprising mention of Benjaminites in the Mari texts (eighteenth century B.C., North Syria). A historical connection between this great and warlike Bedouin tribe from the steppe south of Haran and the Israelite tribe of Benjamin can well be supposed. In this case one must consider the latter tribe as a smaller group of that large Bedouin confederation which migrated farther south.

[19–20] The reports about the death and burial of Israel's ancestors are emphatically sober and free of every kind of religious pathos. The landmark set up by Jacob did not have any sacred significance for our narrator and his hearers. It is simply the landmark which, as everyone knew, marked the grave of one ancestral mother. To erect landmarks at sanctuaries or graves was a widely practiced cultic custom in Palestine before the time of the Israelites. The divine nature or the spirit of the dead was considered to be present in the stone, and was honored by anointing the stone or by offerings to the dead. The outward custom of erecting such landmarks was preserved in Israel, but in a form strangely empty and secularized; for belief in Yahweh had waged an especially implacable battle against every form of funerary cult.

[21–22a] The name Migdal Eder, to which the note about Reuben's crime is attached, means "cattle tower" and designates a rough stone structure for shepherds. It became the proper name of a place whose site is not certain. The crime itself is condemned by the narrator, without the necessity for his expressly stating it. The note is so brief and fragmentary that one can form no opinion about what is told in vs. 21 f. The narrative cannot have concluded with v. 22; on the contrary, the decisive word or act of Jacob must have followed.

The information that the redactor here removed something in favor of Jacob's later curse (ch. 49.3 f.) does not help. The redactors did not take such parallels so seriously, as a quite similar instance shows: ch. 34.30 is parallel to 49.5–7. Random guesses are to no purpose. Something is missing here, and thus the transition to the following unit, the list of Jacob's sons, is more awkward than almost any other place in Genesis.

[22b–29] In the Priestly narrative the list of Jacob's sons followed the divine address in vs. 11 ff., and with it formed the actual Priestly corpus of the Jacob story. There is a whole series of lists of the tribes of Israel in the Old Testament, with certain differences in the sequence (ch. 49.1 ff.; Num. 26.5 ff.; Deut. 27.12 f.; 33.2 ff.; etc.). Behind this scheme of twelve tribes, which we meet first of all as a literary form, there is a complicated history of tradition which at the end leads to the realm of political history and cultic history. For it is there that this scheme has its *Sitz im Leben*: the two groups of Leah and Rachel tribes constituted after the conquest the sacred union of twelve tribes which bore the name Israel (see above p. 295). P reports the end of Jacob's wandering with great soberness and objectivity, his return to Isaac and Hebron. Here too the Jacob story preserves its peculiar cryptic character. Whoever hopes finally to learn anything like a "solution" or a "meaning" here at the end of Jacob's unheard-of wandering will be disappointed at the parsimonious severity of the Priestly statements. Thus Isaac too dies, who at God's command was placed on the altar by his father, and he seems to take the secret of his life into the grave.

39. EDOMITE LISTS. Chs. 36.1 to 37.1

36 [1]*These are the descendants of Esau (that is, Edom).* [2]*Esau took his wives*
from the Canaanites: Adah the daughter of Elon the Hittite, Oholobamah the
daughter of Amah the son of Zibeon the Hivite, [3]*and Basemath, Ishmael's*
daughter, and sister of Nebaioth. [4]*And Adah bore to Esau, Eliphaz; Basemeth*
bore Reuel; [5]*and Oholobamah bore Jeush, Jalam, and Korah. These are the*
sons of Esau who were born to him in the land of Canaan.

6 *Then Esau took his wives, his sons, his daughters, and all the members of*
his household, his cattle, all his beasts, and all his property which he had acquired
in the land of Canaan; and he went into a land away from his brother Jacob. [7]*For*
their possessions were too great for them to dwell together; the land of their sojourn-
ings could not support them because of their cattle. [8]*So Esau dwelt in the hill*
country of Seir; Esau is Edom.

9 *These are the descendants of Esau the father of the Edomites in the hill*
country of Seir. [10]*These are the names of Esau's sons: Eliphaz the son of Adah*
the wife of Esau, Reuel the son of Basemath the wife of Esau. [11]*The sons of*

Eliphaz were Teman, Omar, Zepho, Gatam, and Kenaz. [12]*(Timna was a con-*
cubine of Eliphaz, Esau's son; she bore Amalek to Eliphaz.) These are the
sons of Adah, Esau's wife. [13]*These are the sons of Reuel: Nahath, Zerah,*
Shammah, and Mizzah. These are the sons of Basemath, Esau's wife. [14]*These*
are the sons of Oholibamah the daughter of Anah the son of Zibeon, Esau's
wife: she bore to Esau Jeush, Jalam, and Korah.

15 *These are the chiefs of the sons of Esau. The sons of Eliphaz the first-born*
of Esau: the chiefs Teman, Omar, Zepho, Kenaz, [16]*Korah, Gatam, and Amalek;*
these are the chiefs of Eliphaz in the land of Edom; they are the sons of Adah.
[17]*These are the sons of Reuel, Esau's son: the chiefs Nahath, Zerah, Shammah,*
and Mizzah; these are the chiefs of Reuel in the land of Edom; they are the sons
of Basemath, Esau's wife. [18]*These are the sons of Oholibamah, Esau's wife:*
the chiefs Jeush, Jalam, and Korah; these are the chiefs born of Oholibamah the
daughter of Anah, Esau's wife. [19]*These are the sons of Esau (that is, Edom), and*
these are their chiefs.

20 These are the sons of Seir the Horite, the inhabitants of the land:
Lotan, Shobal, Zibeon, Anah, [21]Dishon, Ezer, and Dishan; these are
the chiefs of the Horites, the sons of Seir in the land of Edom. [22]The sons
of Lotan were Hori and Heman; and Lotan's sister was Timna. [23]These
are the sons of Shobal: Alvan, Manahath, Ebal, Shepho, and Onam.
[24]These are the sons of Zibeon: Aiah and Anah; he is the Anah who
found the hot springs in the wilderness, as he pastured the asses of
Zibeon his father. [25]These are the children of Anah: Dishon and
Oholibamah the daughter of Anah. [26]These are the sons of Dishon:
Hemdan, Eshban, Ithran, and Cheran. [27]These are the sons of Ezer:
Bilhan, Zaavan, and Akan. [28]These are the sons of Dishan: Uz and
Aran. [29]These are the chiefs of the Horites: the chiefs Lotan, Shobal,
Zibeon, Anah, [30]Dishon, Ezer, and Dishan; these are the chiefs of the
Horites, according to their clans in the land of Seir.

31 These are the kings who reigned in the land of Edom, before any
king reigned over the Israelites. [32]Bela the son of Beor reigned in Edom,
the name of his city being Dinhabah. [33]Bela died, and Jobab the son of
Zerah of Bozrah reigned in his stead. [34]Jobab died, and Husham of the
land of the Temanites reigned in his stead. [35]Husham died, and Hadad
the son of Bedad, who defeated Midian in the country of Moab,
reigned in his stead, the name of his city being Avith. [36]Hadad died, and
Samlah of Masrekah reigned in his stead. [37]Samlah died, and Shaul of
Rehoboth on the Euphrates reigned in his stead. [38]Shaul died, and
Baal-hanan the son of Achbor reigned in his stead. [39]Baal-hanan the
son of Achbor died, and Hadar reigned in his stead, the name of his city
being Pau; his wife's name was Mehetabel, the daughter of Matred,
daughter of Mezahab.

40 *These are the names of the chiefs of Esau, according to their families and*
their dwelling places, by their names: the chiefs Timna, Alvah, Jetheth,
[41]*Oholibamah, Elah, Pinon,* [42]*Kenaz, Teman, Mibzar,* [43]*Magdiel, and Iram;*
these are the chiefs of Edom (that is, Esau, the father of Edom), according to
their dwelling places in the land of their possession.

37 [1]*Jacob dwelt in the land of his father's sojournings, in the land of Canaan.*

"Chapter 36 comes at the right place. After Isaac's death his sons separate, and since henceforth only Jacob is mentioned, an orientation about what happened to Esau is completely in order at the end." (Wellhausen.) This Edomite chapter contains only six lists of names, namely, vs. 1–8, 9–14, 15–19, 20–30, 31–39, 40–43. To bring some order into this confusing material we must pay attention to the external form of these lists, which is certainly not insignificant. Ancient lists, with their peculiarities, are generally better preserved in tradition than are narrative pieces which invited revision of their ancient material. **[1–19]** Five of the six lists begin with the words "These are the . . ." Two have the special title, "This is the genealogy of Esau," vs. 1–8 and vs. 9–14. But the similarity of the two lists goes much farther, for both mention the same wives and the same sons of Esau. The two lists vs. 1–8 and vs. 9–14 are therefore two traditions about the direct descendants of Esau-Edom, which are almost completely parallel both in form and in content. There is a difference only at the beginning and at the end: vs. 1–8 identifies Esau with Edom (vs. 1, 8); vs. 9–14 on the other hand calls Esau the father of Edom (v. 9). In addition, the list vs. 9–14 goes farther on, namely, to Esau's grandchildren. Curiously, however, the additional names are mentioned in full in the third list (vs. 15–19) except that they are there listed as "chiefs of the sons of Esau." This third list again concludes with the words "that is, Edom" which we already saw at the beginning and end of the first list (vs. 1, 8). Thus with respect to the names the parallelism between the second list (vs. 9–14) on the one hand and the first and third lists on the other hand (vs. 1–8, 15–19) is complete. Finally a connection can be shown between the second list (vs. 9–14) and the sixth list (vs. 40–43), for this final list of chiefs is shown to belong to the second list in its concluding word which designates Esau as the "father of Edom." In the second list, by the way, we miss the mention of chiefs. These four lists obviously belonged to that toledoth book, that most original genealogical framework of the Priestly narrative which we have to suppose is the oldest form of this source. That a large genealogical list began to be interspersed with narrative notes and so was expanded to a comprehensive documentary work would not be surprising. The first list (vs. 1–8) makes this transition, from a list pure and simple to a list of historical worth, quite clear; for in its second half it has been extended by P to a report about Esau's separation from Jacob. What is surprising, however, is the twofold nature of the tradition in the lists.

The orthographic wording of the lists does not correspond exactly. Therefore, in spite of the fact that they present the same factual traditions, they must have had a certain independence and they seem to derive from the same source only indirectly. Actually, the Priestly narrative is not uniform as a whole; we meet doublets at every step, and this literary problem could be raised for the entire Priestly document, namely, in the books of Exodus and Numbers. That these lists were not composed *ad hoc* for the toledoth book, that they were only assembled in it and already existed apart from this work, can be concluded from the double title in vs. 9 and 10 or from the double conclusion in vs. 19a and 19b or in vs. 43bα and 43bβ.

A serious offense has long been the incompatibility of the data about Esau's wives in chs. 26.34 and 28.8 on the one hand and our notice in ch. 36.2 f. on the other. Wellhausen too with his source analysis which was done purely on the basis of literary criticism was here in difficulties, because he would have liked to ascribe all these data to the Priestly document, if they could have been included in one and the same document without causing such contradiction. But this approach depended too much on the notion of a Priestly document which was "composed" as a continuous unit. Lists, however, have and maintain their own life, even when they are incorporated into more comprehensive literary contexts, especially in the Orient where the traditions were collected much more from the viewpoint of completeness than from the viewpoint of the harmonic compactness of the historical picture. Nothing positive can be said about the historical reliability of this group of lists. Much may go back to ancient tradition, some may derive from learned theoretical combination. Of the many names mentioned here more than a few were also used as personal names in Israel. The few which here and there indicate the same person or the same tribe (Kenaz, Amalek, Teman) allow no special conclusion. On the identification of Esau with Edom, see p. 274.

[31–37] Our knowledge about Edom rests upon Israelite sources only. If this nation had not had a neighbor with such an attentive eye for all the movements of history, a neighbor who could, as these lists show, look with a lively interest at the politics and history of its environment, then hardly the name of Edom would have been preserved. The Edomites, along with the Ammonites, Moabites, and others, belong to that large invasion which pushed from the east into Palestine about 1200, which we call the Aramean invasion (see p. 142).

They were thus related to the Israelites, among whom a consciousness of this brotherhood was preserved in spite of many disappointing experiences (Deut. 23.7; Num. 20.14; Amos 1.11). Perhaps Israel took over features of their long-renowned wisdom (Jer. 49.7; Obad. 8). A comparison of the constitutional nature of the two peoples and some of their common characteristics has called attention to the king list (vs. 31–39). Apparently it must be considered an ancient trustworthy document, which records a series of kings who ruled before the time of the Israelite and Judean kings (v. 31). Accordingly, the Edomites reached statehood considerably earlier than did Israel, who existed for many generations after her migration and settlement without the form of a state. How far back this list goes can scarcely be determined. Numbers 20.14 mentions a king of Edom. It is further of interest that this Edomitic kingdom was not bound to a dynasty, but was an elective kingship and therefore corresponds in this regard to the original form of the Israelite kingdom (Saul, kings of the Northern Kingdom). Just as Saul remained in his native town after his coronation, so also our list mentions the ruling king and "his city." Bela the son of Beor, mentioned in v. 32, has often been identified with Balaam the son of Beor (Num., chs. 22 to 24).

[20–30] The list vs. 20–30 also gives the impression of being a reliable ancient tradition. A notice like the one in v. 24 bears the stamp of authenticity, and the same is true of v. 35. But in the case of this list we have no possibility of comparison or verification. The name "Horites" as a designation for the original population of this territory can be explained to some extent. The Hurrians migrated into Mesopotamia in the second millennium, and some of them migrated farther south into Syria and Palestine. This explains the fact that the Egyptians of the second millennium generally designated the population of Syria and Palestine with this name. We have here, therefore, a derived and entangled use of a national name which is similar to the Palestinian "Hittites" (see pp. 176, 246). Why the use of the name Horite was concentrated in the Israelite period and for Israel especially on the ancient Edomite territory is impossible to say (cf. ch. 14.6; Deut. 2.12, 22). These two last-mentioned lists do not belong to P, as we said; one must consider them part of the Yahwistic work.

The Priestly note about Jacob's stay in the Land of Canaan (ch. 37.1) is best understood as the conclusion to Esau's toledoth. It corresponds to the statement in ch. 36.8 and leads back again to the genealogy of the chosen ones, who, in contrast to Esau's descendants living on the southern steppe, were claimants to the Promised Land. For the expression "land of sojourning," see p. 249.

40. THE STORY OF JOSEPH

We begin with a brief word about the literary quality of the Joseph story as a whole. It is distinct from all previous narratives because of its unusual length, for it considerably exceeds the length of the longest of the patriarchal stories, the one about Eliezer's suit of Rebekah (ch. 24). Further, it has not attained this length by means of a gradual comprehensive composition of individual narrative units. It does not belong to an "epic cycle," but it is from beginning to end an organically constructed narrative, no single segment of which can have existed independently as a separate element of tradition. Therefore, the division of chapters in it must be judged quite differently. In the patriarchal traditions from chs. 12 to 36 the chapters coincide as a rule with the beginning and the end of a formerly independent unit. In the Joseph story, on the other hand, the chapters designate only relative segments, namely, the end and the beginning of individual scenes. Often, as, for example, in the transition from chs. 43 to 44, the chapter division is disturbing because it indicates a much more critical point than the narrative intends. The reader, therefore, should first ignore the chapter divisions and read the narrative without hacking too crassly at its construction. The most conspicuous technique of this narrative is its division of the mass of material into single scenes or "acts." Almost every one of these scenes has its own exposition which is followed by the action itself, and this action always has a climax and at the end a definite conclusion, which, to be sure, does not detract from the suspense of the narrative as a whole. It is only a temporary resting point for the action, and this alone gives relative legitimacy to the chapter divisions which do not always exactly correspond to the division into scenes. This mastery of the material by a clear succession of scenes, this division of the massive and very complex occurrence into individual eventful waves, shows without question a very superior artistry in representation. It is quite possible that this long narrative developed from an originally simpler form to its present size. With respect to such a process of growth, however, one cannot go beyond vague conjectures.

The story of Joseph, in the narrower sense, comprises chs. 37; 39

to 47; and 50. The text of these chapters, apart from unimportant sections from the Priestly source, is an artistic composition from the representations of the sources J and E. Apparently both documents contained a story of Joseph. The redactor combined them with each other in such a way that he inserted extensive sections of the Elohistic parallel version into the Yahwistic story of Joseph and thus created an even richer narrative. In any case, the gain from this combination of sources is incomparably greater than the loss. Vestiges and unimportant breaks that arose from this working over of the sources can be shown at every point. But a serious discrepancy in the narrative, which disturbs even the untrained reader, occurs only in the transition from chs. 42 and 43 (see the exposition). A peculiarity of the Yahwistic source is that it calls the father of the twelve brothers Israel rather than Jacob.

A. JOSEPH'S DREAMS AND SALE INTO EGYPT. CH. 37.2–36

37 2 *This is the history of the family of Jacob.*
Joseph, being seventeen years old, was shepherding the flock with his brothers—
he was a lad—with the sons of Bilhah and Zilpah, his father's wives; and Joseph
brought an ill report of them to their father. 3 Now Israel loved Joseph more
than any other of his children, because he was the son of his old age;
and he made him a long robe with sleeves. 4 But when his brothers saw
that their father loved him more than all his brothers, they hated him,
and could not speak peaceably to him.
5 Now Joseph had a dream, which he once told to his brothers (and
they only hated him more).* 6 He said to them, "Hear this dream which I
have dreamed: 7 behold, we were binding sheaves in the field, and lo, my
sheaf arose and stood upright; and behold, your sheaves gathered round
it, and bowed down to my sheaf." 8 His brothers said to him, "Are you
indeed to reign over us? Or are you indeed to have dominion over us?"
So they hated him yet more for his dreams and for his words. 9 Then he
dreamed another dream, and told it to his brothers, and said, "Behold,
I have dreamed another dream; and behold, the sun, the moon, and
eleven stars were bowing down to me." 10 But when he told it to his
father and to his brothers, his father rebuked him, and said to him,
"What is this dream that you have dreamed? Shall I and your mother
and your brothers indeed come to bow ourselves to the ground before
you?" 11 And his brothers were jealous of him, but his father kept the
saying in mind.
12 Now his brothers went to pasture their father's flock near Shechem.
13 And Israel said to Joseph, "Are not your brothers pasturing the
flock at Shechem? Come, I will send you to them." And he said to
him, "Here I am." 14 So he said to him, "Go now, see if it is well with
your brothers, and with the flock; and bring me word again." So he sent
him from the valley of Hebron, and he came to Shechem. 15 And a man

*Probably included in error from v.8.

found him wandering in the fields; and the man asked him, "What are you seeking?" [16]"I am seeking my brothers," he said, "tell me, I pray you, where they are pasturing the flock." [17]And the man said, "They have gone away, for I heard them say, 'Let us go to Dothan.' " So Joseph went after his brothers, and found them at Dothan. [18]They saw him afar off, and before he came near to them they conspired against him to kill him. [19]They said to one another, "Here comes this dreamer. [20]Come now, let us kill him and throw him into one of the pits; then we shall say that a wild beast has devoured him, and we shall see what will become of his dreams." [21]But when Reuben heard it, he delivered him out of their hands, saying, "Let us not take his life." [22]And Reuben said to them, "Shed no blood; cast him into this pit here in the wilderness, but lay no hand upon him"—that he might rescue him out of their hand, to restore him to his father. [23]So when Joseph came to his brothers, they stripped him of his robe, the long robe with sleeves that he wore; [24]and they took him and cast him into a pit. The pit was empty, there was no water in it.

25 Then they sat down to eat; and looking up they saw a caravan of Ishmaelites coming from Gilead, with their camels bearing gum, balm, and myrrh, on their way to carry it down to Egypt. [26]Then Judah said to his brothers, "What profit is it if we slay our brother and conceal his blood? [27]Come, let us sell him to the Ishmaelites, and let not our hand be upon him, for he is our brother, our own flesh." And his brothers heeded him. [28]Then Midianite traders passed by; and they drew Joseph up and lifted him out of the pit, and sold him to the Ishmaelites for twenty shekels of silver; and they took Joseph to Egypt.

29 When Reuben returned to the pit and saw that Joseph was not in the pit, he rent his clothes [30]and returned to his brothers, and said, "The lad is gone; and I, where shall I go?" [31]Then they took Joseph's robe, and killed a goat, and dipped the robe in the blood; [32]and they sent the long robe with sleeves and brought it to their father, and said, "This we have found; see now whether it is your son's robe or not." [33]And he recognized it, and said, "It is my son's robe; a wild beast has devoured him; Joseph is without doubt torn to pieces." [34]Then Jacob rent his garments, and put sackcloth upon his loins, and mourned for his son many days. [35]All his sons and all his daughters rose up to comfort him; but he refused to be comforted, and said, "No, I shall go down to Sheol to my son, mourning." Thus his father wept for him. [36]Meanwhile the Midianites had sold him in Egypt to Potiphar, an officer of Pharaoh, the captain of the guard.

[1–2] The text of the Joseph story, exactly like that of the Jacob story, is introduced by part of the Priestly toledoth book (see p. 70). The link of the Jehovistic patriarchal stories with the corresponding Priestly tradition gave the redactors little difficulty because of the terse brevity of the latter. In combining the sources the stereotyped formula of the toledoth book, "This is the generation of . . ."

commended itself as a title for the continuous narrative which follows. It has long been observed that in this combination of the narrative material the original meaning of the word *tōlᵉdōt*, which once meant "succession of generations" or more precisely "procreations" is now stretched, if not burst asunder. One must assume that precisely because of this the word has acquired the much more general meaning of "family history," "history of the generation." What is interesting about this redactorial process is that what we like to call the Joseph story is really conceived as a Jacob story, just as our "Jacob story" was designated actually as the history of the generations of Isaac (see p. 262). But that is not surprising, for each of the large narrative complexes is also actually concerned with events in Isaac's or Jacob's family. So long as the oldest member of the generation was alive, and Jacob dies only at the end of the "Joseph story" (ch. 49.33), the family and everything that occurred in it, along with the unmarried sons, went by his name.

Obviously P follows a different tradition about the origin of dissension between Joseph and his brothers. According to this source Joseph as a youth helped his older half brothers Dan, Naphtali, Gad, and Asher in shepherding the flocks, and by tale-bearing brought on himself his brothers' hate. It is not clear what he told his father. The whole affair is told very abruptly and is never referred to again in the following narrative. Verse 2 is indeed quite awkward in general, especially in the twofold mention of the brothers. Thus the note remains a torso. The half brothers may be mentioned in order to exclude Reuben, Levi, Judah, and the others.

[3–4] With v. 3 the predominantly Yahwistic narrative begins, which, without a noteworthy break, tells us about the long chain of events from the beginning of the brothers' hate onward. Every reader, however, must be struck by the fact that here too the brothers' hate derives from two causes which seem to be independent of each other: the father's preferential treatment and the dreams. Both times the hate which they caused is mentioned at the end (v. 4 and v. 11). But it is not certain whether this doubleness is the trace of two sources. One could prefer to consider this complex motivation, so true to life, as an indication of the successive, preliterary growth of the material in the Joseph story. Verse 3 was also thought to be in this sense the remnant of a much older version of the narrative, according to which Joseph, as the youngest of the brothers, after profound humiliation in a strange land, rose to legendary greatness (Gressmann). But a Joseph story without Benjamin, i.e., without a total of twelve brothers, is unthinkable. It is true only that the narrative here considers the difference between the ages of Joseph and his brothers as much greater than does ch. 30.23, for according to that representation of the sons' births Joseph is not the "son of his old age."

The garment given to Joseph by his father was a dress coat, i.e., not the cloaklike wrap that the man on the street wore. It was distinguished from the usual ones by its length, and the length of its sleeves; it was a luxury which only those who did not have to work could think of having (Gu.). The garment is once again mentioned, significantly, as the garb of royal princesses (II Sam. 13.18 f.). The LXX and its dependent Vulgate have interpreted the Hebrew word, whose meaning has not yet been satisfactorily explained, in the sense of "variegated," and the translation in the King James Version derives from that. Thus the picture of the spoiled and preferred figure Joseph is painted with very few strokes; he is the foil for the brothers who are contriving evil. Verse 4bβ cannot be translated for certain. If the text is in order, one can translate either "they did not endure his friendly speech" or "they were not able to speak peaceably to him."

[5–11] The dreams, which always appear in pairs in the Joseph story, contain no profound, possibly mythological, symbolism or anything of the sort. They must be considered quite as they are, and they say neither more nor less than what is openly expressed in them; they are quite simple, pictorial prefigurations of coming events and conditions. They present only silent pictures, without any explanatory word, to say nothing then of a divine address. This worldly character which is so pronounced in them is all the more remarkable when one considers that the narrator undoubtedly thinks of them as real prophecies given by God. How much more primitive do those revelations in dreams seem which contain direct addresses by God, as they were related in chs. 20.3; 26.24; or 28.13! This lack of theological directness, this reserved distance from anything actually religious, with which the dreams are informed makes it possible for one to understand them in two ways, either as real prophecies or as the notions of a vainglorious heart. Their prophetic substance is unmistakable, and yet Joseph is at the same time chided on their account. The two aspects are inseparably intertwined. One cannot lessen the paradox by the explanation that Joseph was censured only because he told the dreams everywhere. A vision was for the ancients so important and obligatory that a demand to keep it tactfully to oneself would not have occurred to them.

The vision of the sheaves is evidence for the agricultural practices of nomads with small cattle, just as ch. 26.12 was. One ought not to see in it a reference to Joseph's later policy of storage. In the vision of the stars one must not think of single stars but of constellations, for the number eleven must be connected with the ancient notion of the eleven signs of the zodiac. The mention of Joseph's mother does not agree very well with the previous mention of Rachel's death in ch. 35.18. It appears that according to our narrative Rachel was still alive. In the matter of kingship, that one is to go beyond Joseph's exaltation and think of the Northern Israelite Kingdom, as commentaries assert, is improbable, for the connection of the Joseph story with political history is quite loose (see the Epilogue, pp. 432 f.).

The narrator does not intend in the dreams to prepare for the much later history of Israel but rather for Joseph's exaltation in Egypt. The dreams were fulfilled in the narratives of chs. 42.6 and 50.18. The brothers' reaction to the dreams was rather negative, the father's completely negative. As we said above, it was not a rejection of a direct, divine prophecy, but rather the instinctive reaction against an unpleasant and unbelievable picture of the future from the mouth of a youth. The father's irritation at the dreams, whose real substance he cannot grasp, and his inability to put them easily from his mind constitute one of those masterful psychological statements of which the Joseph story is so full. The section vs. 3–11 contains what amounts to a model exposition of the whole Joseph story. But it brings before the reader not so much the external circumstances within the framework of which the story will move as the inward tensions which must be seen if what follows is to be understood rightly. Here is a sketch of an uncanny field of force of inner emotions, over which stand the two dream pictures, pointing to a dark future. The old man cannot get them out of his head. First, however, it is the key-word "hate" that dominates (the hatred and jealousy of the brothers is mentioned four times in the present text).

[12–17] The story is set in motion in v. 12. The connection with what precedes is not quite precise, for while formerly Joseph lived together with his brothers and father, here the brothers are several days' journey distant with their flocks. One is also surprised that Jacob so carelessly sent the defenseless youth to the camp of his brothers, whose hate, as just reported, had already reached such a menacing pitch. The way Joseph finally found his brothers after initial aimless wandering is told with strange minuteness, for in the continuation of the narrative it is quite a secondary matter. Perhaps the narrator wishes to show the dangers which beset Joseph from the beginning on this way. Dothan, known as an ancient Canaanite city in the Egyptian sources of the second millennium, is identical with modern Tell Dôthā north of Samaria.

[18–36] From v. 18 until the end of the chapter the brothers' action and speech is very restless and overcharged, and is therefore related unmethodically. Two brothers, Judah and Reuben, make proposals to restrain the others from extremes. (In v. 21 Judah is to be read instead of Reuben, if one will not ascribe the verse to another source.) Two caravans appear at once, one of Ishmaelites and one of Midianites (vs. 25, 28). Is one to interpret it in such a way that the Midianites sold Joseph to the Ishmaelites? It is much more obvious to assume a double thread in the narrative. According to one (J), Joseph was sold by his brothers to the Ishmaelites; according to the other (E), Joseph was stolen from the cistern in an unguarded moment by the Midianites, which thwarted Reuben's plan to save him (vs. 28a, 29–31). The brothers' hate in the story is motivated, to be sure, in the best possible way psychologically, but one must consider that there is more to it than annoyance at the preference given to Joseph. There is, to be exact, a dark knowledge about the irrevocableness of such prophetic dreams. Only when it is expressed, only when it is told, does the prophecy contained in the dream become potent. This was the reason the prophets were so violently persecuted, because the effectiveness and validity of their words was indissolubly connected with their personal existence. The brothers' hate is therefore a rebellion against the matter contained in the dreams, against the divine power itself, standing behind them, who had given the dreams. The expression usually translated by "the dreamer" means much more than our English word, namely, the one empowered to prophetic dreams (*ba'al haḥ^{a}lōmōt*).

Reuben is described as the one who wants to save Joseph. In order to do so he must gain time in a situation of danger for Joseph. Why precisely Reuben, the ancestor of the tribe that disappeared earliest, should receive this sympathetic role cannot be explained, at least not from historical tribal conditions. He is simply the oldest and the most sensible. But one should not condemn Judah's proposal with its motivation "for he is our brother" as simply hypocritical. According to the ancient notion, there was a long step between even a very serious crime against one's brother and actual murder, shed blood.

Bloodguilt is something quite incalculable, which one avoided if at all possible. Blood cannot be "concealed" (v. 26b); its cry is irresistible (cf. at ch. 4.10). The motivation, therefore, is that their guilt will be much too great. The brothers' behavior toward Joseph, the way they cast him into a cistern and then sit down to lunch, and especially their attitude toward their father, is described, to be sure, in crass abominableness. Cisterns were large holes in the earth, formed like bottles, to store the winter rain for the summer; and one could put a man in them quite easily (cf. Jer. 38.6). From earliest times down to the present day caravans traversed Palestine, mediating the exchange of valuable products of civilization between the lands of the East and the Egyptian south. Even their route has scarcely changed down to the present. It goes from Damascus to Gilead, crosses the Jordan, and south of Carmel makes connection with the easy coastal road to Egypt. It is therefore quite accurate for the narrator to have these caravans pass Dothan. He even tells us what they were carrying: tragacanth, a gummy exudate of the astragalus plant, highly prized in ancient times as a healing agent. Mastic and labdanum are resinous products and were used especially for medicinal purposes ("balm"). The appearance of Ishmaelites is certainly an anachronism on the part of the narrator, for the sons of Ishmael were Joseph's uncles according to the genealogy in Genesis (Gu.). According to Lev. 27.5 f., twenty silver shekels seems to have been the proper price for a man. Our narrative section comes to a dramatic conclusion when the narrator takes us back again to Jacob. Reuben's horror, as the oldest son whose was the chief responsibility, was already a strong human reaction to the monstrous crime. But the reader feels quite differently about the inconsolable father to whom in addition the sons disgracefully tell lies. The bringing of the blood-dipped robe is not simply a cynical evil trick on the part of the brothers. Rather, it has a legal aspect, for this vestige of Joseph was considered proof of his death (cf. Ex. 22.13). The father was therefore supposed to "confirm" Joseph's death solemnly and legally; the brothers would then be released from any further liability.

At moments of great agitation the Oriental speaks with pathos. Jacob will not remove his mourning clothes until his dying day. The conception of a great realm of the dead, Sheol, is also poetic. Every man knew that the dead would suffer decomposition in the family grave. It is significant, however, that even the thought of a reunion in death was not a comforting bright spot (cf. David's complaint, II Sam. 12.23). One must understand the "daughters" as Jacob's daughters-in-law (cf. Ruth 1.11).

Here is the first resting point in the great event. It is naturally intended by the narrator, for nothing further will now be said about Jacob for a long time. The timeless veil of sorrow sinks over his life for many years. Indeed, if the narrator had not introduced the Egyptian scene with his final sentence, the reader would expect no continuation at all. What was more obvious than for Joseph, like thousands of others, to come to grief and die as a slave in a foreign land? The name Potiphar is given more accurately in chs. 41.45 and 46.20 as "Potiphera." It means "the one Re [the god] has given"; the official designation is "the Eunuch of Pharaoh, the chief of his bodyguard." "Eunuch" is probably not to be taken literally here; the word designates a high court official.

"The beginning of Joseph's story is still under the shadow of Jacob-Israel's guilt, which had clung to the old man since his youth. Just as he once deceived his father and robbed his brother whom his father loved more than him, so he is now deceived by his sons who have shoved his favorite son to one side. . . . Looking ahead, the narrative is a clear exposition of the following drama. All the chief actors—Israel, Judah, and Joseph—appear." (Pr.) Like the Greek tragedy in the house of Atreus or Labdacus, so in Israel in the family of the patriarchs there was a chain of guilt and suffering at work. But in these conditions, as the Joseph story in particular reveals, there was much more than a nemesis, than merely a punitive rule of the god (see p. 437).

41. JUDAH AND TAMAR. Ch. 38

38 [1]It happened at that time that Judah went down from his brothers,
and turned in to a certain Adullamite, whose name was Hirah. [2]There
Judah saw the daughter of a certain Canaanite whose name was
Shua; he married her and went in to her, [3]and she conceived and bore
a son, and he called his name Er. [4]Again she conceived and bore a son,
and she called his name Onan. [5]Yet again she bore a son, and she
called his name Shelah. She was in Chezib when she bore him. [6]And
Judah took a wife for Er his first-born, and her name was Tamar.
[7]But Er, Judah's first-born, was wicked in the sight of the LORD; and
the LORD slew him. [8]Then Judah said to Onan, "Go in to your brother's
wife, and perform the duty of a brother-in-law to her, and raise up offspring for your brother." [9]But Onan knew that the offspring would not
be his; so when he went in to his brother's wife he spilled the semen on
the ground, lest he should give offspring to his brother. [10]And what he did
was displeasing in the sight of the LORD, and he slew him also. [11]Then
Judah said to Tamar his daughter-in-law, "Remain a widow in your
father's house, till Shelah my son grows up"—for he feared that he

would die, like his brothers. So Tamar went and dwelt in her father's
house.

12 In course of time the wife of Judah, Shua's daughter, died; and
when Judah was comforted, he went up to Timnah to his sheep-
shearers, he and his friend Hirah the Adullamite. [13]And when Tamar
was told, "Your father-in-law is going up to Timnah to shear his sheep,"
[14]she put off her widow's garments, and put on a veil, wrapping herself
up, and sat at the entrance to Enaim, which is on the road to Timnah;
for she saw that Shelah was grown up, and she had not been given to
him in marriage. [15]When Judah saw her, he thought her to be a harlot,
for she had covered her face. [16]He went over to her at the road side, and
said, "Come, let me come in to you," for he did not know that she was his
daughter-in-law. She said, "What will you give me, that you may come
in to me?" [17]He answered, "I will send you a kid from the flock." And
she said, "Will you give me a pledge, till you send it?" [18]He said,
"What pledge shall I give you?" She replied, "Your signet and your
cord, and your staff that is in your hand." So he gave them to her, and
went in to her, and she conceived by him. [19]Then she arose and went
away, and taking off her veil she put on the garments of her widowhood.

20 When Judah sent the kid by his friend the Adullamite, to receive
the pledge from the woman's hand, he could not find her. [21]And he
asked the men of the place, "Where is the harlot who was at Enaim by
the wayside?" And they said, "No harlot has been here." [22]So he
returned to Judah, and said, "I have not found her; and also the men
of the place said, 'No harlot has been here.' " [23]And Judah replied,
"Let her keep the things as her own, lest we be laughed at; you see, I
sent this kid, and you could not find her."

24 About three months later Judah was told, "Tamar your daughter-
in-law has played the harlot; and moreover she is with child by
harlotry." And Judah said, "Bring her out, and let her be burned."
[25]As she was being brought out, she sent word to her father-in-law,
"By the man to whom these belong, I am with child." And she said,
"Mark, I pray you, whose these are, the signet and the cord and the
staff." [26]Then Judah acknowledged them and said, "She is more
righteous than I, inasmuch as I did not give her to my son Shelah."
And he did not lie with her again.

27 When the time of her delivery came, there were twins in her
womb. [28]And when she was in labor, one put out a hand; and the midwife took and bound on his hand a scarlet thread, saying, "This came
out first." [29]But as he drew back his hand, behold, his brother came out;
and she said, "What a breach you have made for yourself!" Therefore
his name was called Perez. [30]Afterward his brother came out with the
scarlet thread upon his hand; and his name was called Zerah.

Every attentive reader can see that the story of Judah and Tamar has no connection at all with the strictly organized Joseph story at whose beginning it is now inserted. This compact narrative requires for its interpretation none of the other Patriarchal narratives, and therefore the Yahwist, who found the story in tradition, faced the question where to insert this piece into the succession of traditions. It has often been said that the narrative's present location immediately after the exciting introduction to the Joseph story was relatively favorable. It is really effective for Joseph to disappear from the reader completely for a time just as he disappeared from the father and the brothers. On the other hand, the unevenness that has occurred from the combination of our narrative with the Joseph story must not be overlooked. Thus, for example, the Joseph story knows nothing at all about Judah's separation from his brothers, which is here viewed as a decisive step for the entire subsequent history of the house of Judah. The biographical and genealogical difficulty also disturbed earlier exegetes, the difficulty, namely, that later (ch. 46.12) Judah came to Egypt with grandchildren, a fact that is incompatible with the chronology of the Joseph story (chs. 37.2; 41.46; 45.11). But the genealogical section in ch. 46.8–27 is itself a later insertion in the Joseph story (see p. 402).

[1–11] The real action in the Judah-Tamar story begins at vs. 12 ff. But for the reader to understand this extremely odd occurrence the narrator must first acquaint him with a few conditions, the coincidence of which prepared the ground for what occurred between Judah and his daughter-in-law. Verses 1 to 11 bear all the marks of an explanation that gives the reader the most necessary facts in a rather dry enumeration and without particular vividness. What is especially striking is that the narrator dispenses with all causes and motivations in this section and limits himself to giving the bare facts.

1. Judah has "turned aside." He has separated from his brothers and has apparently "gone down" to the Canaanite plain with his flocks. This note preserves the tribal memory of a Judean expansion westward, which then led to intermarriage with the Canaanites. The narrator, to be sure, gives neither a reason for this event nor any idea of the more precise circumstances. But he knows about Judah's exceptional territorial position in the south and about Judah's westward penetration. In reality, however, the tribe of Judah did not migrate to its territory from the north but rather from the south or southeast.

2. This migration of Judah resulted in friendly contact with the Canaanites, even in intermarriage. The Canaanites lived almost exclusively in the plains, and the territory which in the ancient period remained for the tribes of Israel was primarily the Judean-Ephraimite

hill country. The two places mentioned in our exposition, Adullam and Chezib (=Achzib, Josh. 15.44), were thus situated in the Judean-Philistine hill country southwest of Jerusalem, where the Judeans were living with the Canaanites as neighbors.

3. Judah gave to his first-born son, whom his Canaanite wife bore him, a Canaanite woman in marriage, namely, Tamar (="Palm"). The subsequent events in Judah's family are sketched with extreme conciseness. The first-born dies early without children. The narrator seems to conclude from this fact of his early death that he "displeased" Yahweh. According to the practice of levirate marriage, the second son took Tamar as his wife. This family regulation, widely practiced outside Israel, is regulated by law in Deut. 25.5 ff. and is presupposed in the Book of Ruth as binding; but its meaning and real purpose is not indicated anywhere in the Old Testament. If "offspring are raised up" for the dead man (v. 8), then the preservation of the dead man's family and name, even though by a fiction, will have played a role in the custom. The son begotten by the brother is then considered the son and heir of the deceased man, "that his name may not be blotted out of Israel" (Deut. 25.6). But the practice has also been explained in the interest of preserving the property. The wife is also a capital asset, but as a widow she would return to her father's family. Furthermore, the remaining property of the deceased (land, flocks, etc.) would go to someone with another name. Onan, however, only pretends to fulfill this fraternal duty. The narrative is silent about the motive for this offensive conduct, and expositors correctly designate it as uncharitableness. Therefore Yahweh let Onan die too.

4. Judah is now in a difficult dilemma because of the death of his two sons. According to the ancient regulation, he must now give Tamar to his youngest son. His paternal obligation to his deceased first-born also prescribes this act for him. But he has reason to fear for the life of his last remaining son, for in cases like this the ancients suspected that the wife herself was in some way responsible for the deaths (cf. Tobit 3.7 ff.; 8.9 f.). In this conflict Judah treats Tamar dishonestly. It is not clear whether the reference to Shelah's great youth was only a pretense. In any case, Judah could not send Tamar back to her father's house. This could be considered only a half measure, for only one who was really a widow returned to her father's family (Ruth 1.8 ff.; Lev. 22.13). Judah's wrong lay in considering this solution as really final for himself but in presenting it to Tamar as an interim solution.

[12–23] Against the background of this very complicated story the actual occurrence between Judah and Tamar takes place. It begins when Judah, who had meanwhile become a widower, comes to the sheepshearing in the vicinity of Tamar's native town, namely, to Timnah (ten miles west of Bethlehem). It is not that Timnah, therefore, where the friction between Samson and the Philistines, who had immigrated in the meanwhile, took place (Judg., chs. 14 f.). For sheepshearing, see Gen. 31.19; I Sam. 25.2 ff.

Tamar has now understood that Judah wanted to get rid of her permanently. Possibly the news of Shelah's maturity as well as Judah's behavior after the death of his wife made her certain of Judah's intentions. The duty of the levirate, as the story of Ruth shows, was not binding only on the brother-in-law; therefore Tamar can well have reckoned with Judah's taking her in marriage. In any case she takes the initiative, and from now on till the end this woman remains the center of interest, for the narrator closely follows every detail of what she does and leaves undone so that the reader is also entertained with interesting details of cultural history.

We do not know exactly what the widows' costume was like. Apparently they were unveiled, whereas the unmarried and married women were veiled in public (Gen. 24.65). To understand Tamar's act, the reader must resist comparing it with modern conditions and judging it accordingly, for the modern world has nothing that could be compared with it. In the ancient Orient, it was customary in many places for married women to give themselves to strangers because of some oath. Such sacrifices of chastity in the service of the goddess of love, Astarte, were, of course, different from ordinary prostitution even though they were repulsive to Israel.* They were strictly forbidden by law, and the teachers of wisdom warned urgently against this immoral custom, which was apparently at times fashionable even in Israel (Deut. 23.17; Num. 30.6; Hos. 4.13 ff.; Prov. 7.1–27. See G. Boström, *Proverbiastudien*, 1935, 103 ff.). At the borders between Israel and Canaan, where our whole story takes place, the appearance on the road of a "devoted one" was obviously nothing surprising. Tamar thus does not pretend to be a harlot as we think of

*Herodotus tells, generalizing of course, that among the Babylonians "every woman of the land once in her life has to sit in the Temple of Aphrodite and sleep with a strange man. . . . Most however do as follows: they sit in the sacred grove of Aphrodite . . . and the strange men go there and choose a woman. And once a woman sits here she may not go home before a stranger has cast money into her lap and slept with her outside the sanctuary." (I. 199.)

it, but rather a married woman who indulges in this practice, and Judah too thought of her in this way. It is characteristic that our narrative in vs. 21 and 22 also uses the expression "devoted one," *qᵉdēšā* (RSV, "harlot"), which recalls the sacred meaning of this practice. For the waiting on the road, cf. Jer. 3.2; Ezek. 16.25; for the compensation for the night with her, cf. Judg. 15.1. The narrator goes into especially great detail in the matter of the pledge, for it makes the matter extremely risky for the still unsuspecting man. The objective value of the two objects may have been small, and what could such a woman do with the signet of a strange man! But for Tamar the pledge was invaluable because it bound Judah quite personally to her. Here the reader must admire Tamar's keen presence of mind. Herodotus says, to be sure, that every Babylonian carried a signet ring and a skillfully carved staff (I. 195); in Israel it can only have been the sign of a well-to-do man, of a fine lord. The seal was a so-called cylinder seal, like those found in excavations, a small cylinder that one rolled over the soft clay documents and wore on a cord around one's neck.

Judah took pains, therefore, to send the woman her pay. But the disappearance of Tamar without a trace and then the fear of being talked about because of further search kept him from accomplishing his purpose. It is also noteworthy that he settles the rather delicate situation through an intermediary.

[24] Now the narrative proceeds quickly to its dramatic climax. If one examines the legal aspect of the case, its difficulty becomes apparent. On the basis of what fact was the complaint made at all? Because of a widow's prostitution or that of an engaged girl? Those who turned to Judah in this matter seem to assume the latter. Judah assumes competence as judge; he thus reckons Tamar as part of his family, though Tamar's act proceeded from the assumption that Judah had released her permanently from the family and gave no further consideration to a marriage with his third son. In no case was Tamar herself competent. As a wife, she was dependent, so that no legal proceeding took place at the gate, where such cases were tried when a complaint was made against a free citizen. It is very ancient for the word of the family head to be decisive with no appeal possible. (Deut. 21.18 ff. is similar but combined with a complaint before the legal community.) The entire legal community then takes part in the administration of the punishment, as always in the case of an execution. The punishment itself is certainly, in the narrator's opinion, the severest possible. The later law recognized burning only in an extreme case of prostitution (Lev. 21.9). The custom was death by stoning for such offenses (Deut. 22.23 ff.; Lev. 20.16).

[25–30] Tamar's courage carried the matter to the limit; only immediately before the execution did she play her trump, and her moral victory is thus all the greater. Judah's statement in which he acknowledges her right and his wrong is the climax of the narrative. From there it moves swiftly to its end. We are told that Judah did not touch her again, i.e., he again considered her as daughter-in-law. The conclusion to the narrative, however, is somewhat unsatisfactory. Is v. 30 its conclusion at all? Strangely it concludes without telling whose wife Tamar finally became. According to v. 26b, in any case, she was not Judah's. Was she then Shelah's? Should that not have been said? The narrative about the birth of her sons is furnished with aetiological motives that perhaps reflect a recollection of a rivalry between the two Judean lines Perez and Zerah.

Epilogue. It is quite clear from the conclusion to our story that it is concerned with tribal conditions and, in fact, more directly than the Joseph story, for example (see pp. 432 f.). The list in Num. 26.19 ff., which derives probably from the time before the formation of the state, also knows the Judean lines Shelah, Perez, and Zerah. Thus Er and Onan are, of course, also to be understood as names of lines, which died out or could not hold together as independent units. The ancient reader of this story, therefore, had no other possibility at all except that of connecting what is here related with historical tribal conditions of his time, i.e., of understanding it as aetiology, as previous history of internal Judean lines. And still the narrative is much more than a thinly disguised tribal or lineal history. It has been correctly said that such histories do not exist at all, that such narratives present only what has occurred, the state of affairs, but not the occurrence step by step and the history. That would mean that the tribal history is only one aspect of this many-sided narrative. It can be recognized at the beginning of the narrative and then again at the end. In the middle, however, it falls right into the background in favour of the development of a complicated human event. It would be barbarism to want to decipher the main point (vs. 1–11 is only exposition) in ethnological terms, as this would be to misunderstand something of its essence, namely, its wonderful openness to what is human —passions, guilt, paternal anxiety, love, honor, chivalry, all churning up the narrow circle of one family in labryinthine entanglement! Of course the narrative presumes readers whose perspicacity lets them be caught by the hopelessly complicated legal situation and who then rejoice in the solution because it respects both parties. For this narrative, however, in contrast to many others, we are in the fortunate position of knowing the narrator's own opinion of the event. The narrative is so constructed that there can be no doubt: Tamar, in spite of her action which borders on a crime, is the one justified in the end. Judah states it at the climax of the story, and only Tamar is unmistakably praised by the narrator. The dominating role of man and things human becomes clear from the fact that the actual narrative in vs. 12–30 does not speak at all of Yahweh's acting or speaking. There does not seem to be any specifically religious aspect of the obscure event. Nevertheless, here is a world in which the narrator clearly believes that Yahweh is present (vs. 7–10). He need not always be spoken of explicitly. Here the astonishing humanity of a woman has attracted the narrator's attention. Onan is the negatively contrasting figure to Tamar. She, the woman, accomplishes by an unbelievable detour what he, to whom the obvious way was open, refused. The question of whether she was motivated more by the desire for a child than by her widow's duty is not raised in the story. In any event, she accomplished what was in the mind of her husband and the line. It is very difficult for us, if at all possible, to measure her act by the moral ideas of her time in order thereby to determine the measure of her guilt. It is certain that she did something quite unusual and even repulsive for the ideas of her time. It is best, however, not to think of our notion of incest. Tamar could, of course, always hope that people would find her act pardonable with more precise knowledge of the facts and conditions. Without this assumption it would have been quite senseless. But for the sake of her goal she drags herself and Judah into serious guilt. Nevertheless, this path of hers through profound shame and guilt has something splendid about it. The narrator follows her in it and lets the death penalty fail because of her (Lev. 18.15). Judah publicly acknowledges her "righteousness" and Delitzsch calls her in fact "a saint by Old Testament standards." One can recognize the theological substance of this story only if one knows about the material character of the saving gifts toward which Israel's ancestors directed their life. In contrast to the majority of Abraham and Jacob narratives this story is not concerned with the Promised Land but with the blessing of great progeny (see pp. 160 f. for this twofold promise).

B. JOSEPH'S TEMPTATION. CH. 39

39 [1]Now Joseph was taken down to Egypt, and Potiphar, an officer
of Pharaoh, the captain of the guard, an Egyptian, bought him from
the Ishmaelites who had brought him down there. [2]The LORD was

with Joseph, and he became a successful man; and he was in the house of his master the Egyptian, [3]and his master saw that the Lord was with him, and that the Lord caused all that he did to prosper in his hands. [4]So Joseph found favor in his sight and attended him, and he made him overseer of his house and put him in charge of all that he had. [5]From the time that he made him overseer in his house and over all that he had the Lord blessed the Egyptian's house for Joseph's sake; the blessing of the Lord was upon all that he had, in house and field. [6]So he left all that he had in Joseph's charge; and having him he had no concern for anything but the food which he ate.

Now Joseph was handsome and good-looking. [7]And after a time his master's wife cast her eyes upon Joseph, and said, "Lie with me." [8]But he refused and said to his master's wife, "Lo, having me my master has no concern about anything in the house, and he has put everything that he has in my hand; [9]he is not greater in this house than I am; nor has he kept back anything from me except yourself, because you are his wife; how then can I do this great wickedness, and sin against God?" [10]And although she spoke to Joseph day after day, he would not listen to her, to lie with her or to be with her. [11]But one day, when he went into the house to do his work and none of the men of the house was there in the house, [12]she caught him by his garment, saying, "Lie with me." But he left his garment in her hand, and fled and got out of the house. [13]And when she saw that he had left his garment in her hand, and had fled out of the house, [14]she called to the men of her household and said to them, "See, he has brought among us a Hebrew to insult us; he came in to me to lie with me, and I cried out with a loud voice; [15]and when he heard that I lifted up my voice and cried, he left his garment with me, and fled and got out of the house." [16]Then she laid up his garment by her until his master came home, [17]and she told him the same story, saying, "The Hebrew servant, whom you have brought among us, came in to me to insult me; [18]but as soon as I lifted up my voice and cried, he left his garment with me, and fled out of the house."

19 When his master heard the words which his wife spoke to him, "This is the way your servant treated me," his anger was kindled. [20]And Joseph's master took him and put him into the prison, the place where the king's prisoners were confined, and he was there in prison. [21]But the Lord was with Joseph and showed him steadfast love, and gave him favor in the sight of the keeper of the prison. [22]And the keeper of the prison committed to Joseph's care all the prisoners who were in the prison; and whatever was done there, he was the doer of it; [23]the keeper of the prison paid no heed to anything that was in Joseph's care, because the Lord was with him; and whatever he did, the Lord made it prosper.

[1–6] This narrative brings the reader again into the Joseph story. The reader had last learned that the Midianites have brought Joseph to Egypt. Now the narrative begins with the statement that the Ishmaelites had brought Joseph to Egypt. This detail, unimportant in itself, shows the care with which the redactors worked. There were two texts about the transfer to Egypt, an Ishmaelite recension (J) and the Midianite recension (E) (see p. 352). The narrative in ch. 37 concluded with the latter, and the former was used to resume the thread of the story which was broken by the Tamar story. Accordingly, our narrative in ch. 39 is Yahwistic. (For the way in which the Elohist thought of Joseph's first experiences, see p. 352.) Real doublets cannot be demonstrated in it. Joseph thus came as a slave into a good house and there soon enjoyed a position of trust. The narrator is very expansive in unfolding this matter; several times he emphasizes the reason for this surprising preferred status, namely, Yahweh. This reference to Yahweh, however, has only mediate significance here. The narrator is much more concerned to draw a rather sharply defined picture of Joseph the man, the picture of a clever, pleasing, modest, industrious, and handsome young man with whom Yahweh was. The narrator of I Sam. 16.18 also draws a very similar ideal picture of such a young man of good standing and good upbringing, with whom Yahweh was. One can almost say that here is expressed the educational and cultivated ideal of definite exalted stations which are familiar to our narrator (cf. pp. 434 f.). Furthermore, a lofty goal is at stake, for such a young man must be able to do much and participate in much. But when the most important characteristic is added, which no one can give oneself, it is there or it is not there, namely, that Yahweh is with him, then he drives the man to do something (he is a *maṣlīaḥ*, a fortunate man, Pr.). Even more, a blessing goes from him to all with whom he comes in contact. Thus Joseph received the responsible position of house overseer, because his master recognized therein his own advantage. Verse 6b could mean simply that the man worried really about nothing any longer except his own food. But it could also be a reference as in ch. 43.32 to ritual separation: only in matters that affected his kitchen did he not permit Joseph to care for him.

These verses, 1–6, which first of all describe only the conditions that occurred after Joseph's transfer to Egypt, are the setting for the actual drama, which begins with v. 7. The final statement of the exposition (Joseph apparently inherited his mother's beauty, ch. 29.17) brings the narrative easily to the conflict.

[7–9] The story of the temptation consists to some extent of two acts which clearly increase the tension. An important statement by Joseph forms the climax to the first; an act leading to catastrophe forms the climax to the second. The well-known statement, really a short speech, confronts the woman with her wrong against her husband and her sin against God. But the speech is not a succession of two different viewpoints; if that were the case it would be wrong that the first is expressed in more detail than the second. Joseph's statements must rather be understood in the sense that a wrong against the husband would be a direct sin against God. The fear of God, i.e., awe before the strict commands of the deity, is what binds Joseph (cf. at ch. 20.11). Thus the conclusion, v. 9b, is really the most important part of the entire speech: the ethos is completely and consciously bound to God. It is, however, noteworthy that Joseph in addition uses the argument of universal human decency which is unwilling to break a trust. We recognize in the latter the expressly human characteristic which the ethos of our narrator's own time had accepted (see Epilogue, pp. 436 f.). With this statement the narrator gave Joseph a beautiful line which brings the first stage of the temptation to its stirring and solemn conclusion.

Adultery was at all times considered in Israel one of the most serious of crimes. Decalogue (Ex. 20.14), Holiness Code (Lev. 18.20), and Deuteronomy (Deut. 22.22) apodictically forbid it. Intercourse with an engaged person was also considered adultery and was punished accordingly (Deut. 22.23 ff.; cf. also Gen. 38.24). As atonement for this crime Israel knew only the death penalty. Ancient Israelite marriage was, it is true, not basically monogamous. The man could have intercourse with other women of his house in addition to his actual wife, with female slaves (cf. ch. 16.2) or prisoners of war (Deut. 21.10 ff.). In this sense, therefore, equality of the sexes was unknown, for the woman was bound to absolute fidelity; she could belong to only one man. Whoever broke the marriage, i.e., whoever had sexual relations with a married woman, had broken one of the most sacred commands of Israel's God. The matter was thus removed from the private sphere and made absolutely an affair of the community, which was interested in seeing that "the evil was purged from Israel" (Deut. 22.22). Other nations of the ancient Orient also considered marriage to be protected by the deity, but they considered adultery more a proprietary misdemeanor which was accordingly a matter more of private litigation between the insulted husband and the adulterer (W. Kornfeld, "L'Adultère dans l'Orient antique," *Revue biblique*, 1950, 92 ff.). It is true that for Israel too the notion of marriage as a proprietary relationship and of adultery as a crime against the property of another man was not completely foreign (cf.

Deut. 22.29. The compensatory payment was to be made at the time of engagement!).

[10–19] Between the first and second act of our temptation story a stubborn effort to win Joseph was taking place (v. 10) which finally resulted in a dramatic scene. The garment that Joseph had to leave in the woman's hands was actually the undergarment, a long shirt tied about the hips. It was not the coatlike cape, which men were not accustomed to wear indoors. This means that Joseph fled completely undressed, at once disgracefully and honorably. "Out of the house" need not mean onto the street; the living quarters of an ancient Oriental house surrounded a courtyard.

The sudden change from sexual desire to the hate in which the woman acts with great presence of mind is realistically described also in II Sam. 13.15. The narrators of these literary epochs know a great deal about the depths of the human psyche. The woman's situation was critical because of Joseph's refusal and flight. She saves herself by using the abandoned garment as evidence against Joseph and by making witnesses of the men of the house. Both to them and later to her husband when he came home she repeats her charge against Joseph. The verb "play" (RSV, "insult") in vs. 14, 17 (*ṣḥq*) to mean erotic play is used similarly in ch. 26.8 (RSV, "fondling"). For the insulting usage "a Hebrew," see pp. 366 f. The way the woman falsifies the matter by reproaching Joseph with her own importunity has a striking parallel in the well-known ancient Egyptian "Story of the Two Brothers" (AOT, 69 f.; ANET, 23 f.). Two brothers are living together. The younger serves the older who is married. During his absence his wife attempts to seduce the younger brother. But he "became as angry as a leopard because of the evil which she had suggested to him." She presents the matter to her husband when he comes home as though she had been harassed, by attributing to her brother-in-law her own seductive words and claiming for herself his disapproving reproaches. The younger succeeds, however, in persuading the older of his innocence, whereupon the older kills his wife. But in spite of the striking similarity in the treacherous activity of the woman in each instance one cannot speak of a direct dependence of our Joseph narrative on that tale. One can only see that a motif is also present in the Joseph story which obviously was widely known (cf. Gunkel for similar narratives).

[20–23] Ever since the Joseph story has been expounded, people have been surprised at the relatively mild punishment which the angry master of the house inflicted on Joseph. If a free citizen deserved death for violating another's marriage, how much more a slave who had violated a position of trust! There have been those, therefore, even today, who think that the man's anger (v. 19) was not directed basically against Joseph but against his wife. But if the man did not trust his wife's story and put Joseph away only "to save face," the narrator would surely have said so more clearly. And it is completely improbable that Potiphar would have transferred Joseph to another post only to remove him from persecution by his wife (Jac.). The other explanation that the man was too attached to Joseph is too psychological. The narrator would probably have explained the affair by saying that Yahweh was "with Joseph," which was everywhere the case in Joseph's new situation.

Joseph has now sunk one degree lower, but there too he is protected by God's care. Obviously the statement "Yahweh was with him" implies quite real protection and promotion in the matters of his external life, not, to be sure, protection from distress, but rather in the midst of distress. The narrator's theology is not so naïve. On the contrary, the way he combines emphatic belief in God's protection and presence with the "permission" of severe afflictions is amazing. Here too Joseph is presented as the example of a young man who is recommended to men both because of his breeding and because of the divine pleasure which attaches to him ("Yahweh showed him steadfast love"). Ancient wisdom is full of exhortations and instructions that train the young man for this goal, so far as it can be reached at all through education. (For more on this temptation story, see the Epilogue at p. 435.) For the question about why the slave, Joseph, was placed in the prison for royal prisoners see below, p. 369.

The word "Hebrew" occurs five times in the Joseph story: three times on the lips of foreigners (chs. 39.14, 17; 41.12), once on Joseph's lips with respect to foreigners (ch. 40.15), and once in the mouth of the narrator who contrasts the Hebrews with the Egyptians (ch. 43.32). It is a peculiarity of the use of this word in the Old Testament that it occurs in the narrative literature where foreigners speak of Israelites or where Israelites speak of themselves in contrast to foreigners. But in the broad field of narrative literature there are curiously only three places in which the word suddenly appears in profusion. First, in the Joseph story; second, in the first ten chapters of Exodus (Hebrews and Egyptians); and third, once again in the first half of the first book of Samuel (Hebrews and Philistines). Quite a new light first fell on the problem from excavated finds; then from letters, contracts, and other documents on clay tablets it became clear that there were "Hebrews" not only in Palestine but also among the Babylonians, Assyrians, Hittites, and even the Egyptians. This makes the older assumption that "Hebrew" was from the first the name of a people seem untenable. Hebrews seem rather to have been a fluctuating lower level of the population who, without possessions and perhaps also without any tribal affiliation, must have been a danger for those states.. "Hebrew" is thus a designation that originally said nothing about what national group a person belonged to, but rather told something about his social and legal status. The legal axiom in Ex. 21.1 ff. corresponds to this. According to it, the Hebrew apparently belonged to that lower, de-classed level of the population. The same is true of I Sam. 14.21, which is concerned with Hebrews who seek to free themselves from the status of servant. One is also reminded of I Sam. 22.2, even though the word "Hebrew" is here missing. In Israel, however, the word "Hebrew" in time became more and more a designation for the nation, for the people themselves, as the use in Jonah 1.9; Gen. 14.13 shows. But this change in meaning is evident in earlier texts, e.g., in the Elohistic Joseph story where the "land of the Hebrews" is mentioned (ch. 40.15), or in Deut. 15.12. For the Hebrew who sold himself into slavery to pay his debts was in a situation different from that in Ex. 21.1 ff.; he was free and owned property before he found himself forced to this step. Furthermore, the Deuteronomistic law designates the Hebrews as members of the community of God and as "brothers." As the Yahwist, doubtless theorizing, includes Eber (ch. 10.21, 25) among Shem's descendants, he too must have considered the Hebrews to be a national, political unit (ch. 10.25).

C. THE INTERPRETATIONS OF THE DREAMS IN PRISON. CH. 40

40 [1]Some time after this, the butler of the king of Egypt and his
baker offended their lord the king of Egypt. [2]And Pharaoh was angry
with his two officers, the chief butler and the chief baker, [3]and he put
them in custody in the house of the captain of the guard, in the prison
where Joseph was confined. [4]The captain of the guard charged Joseph
with them, and he waited on them; and they continued for some time in
custody. [5]And one night they both dreamed—the butler and the baker
of the king of Egypt, who were confined in the prison—each his own
dream, and each dream with its own meaning. [6]When Joseph came to
them in the morning and saw them, they were troubled. [7]So he asked
Pharaoh's officers who were with him in custody in his master's house,
"Why are your faces downcast today?" [8]They said to him, "We have

had dreams, and there is no one to interpret them." And Joseph said
to them, "Do not interpretations belong to God? Tell them to me,
I pray you."
9 So the chief butler told his dream to Joseph, and said to him, "In
my dream there was a vine before me, [10]and on the vine there were
three branches; as soon as it budded, its blossoms shot forth, and the
clusters ripened into grapes. [11]Pharaoh's cup was in my hand; and I
took the grapes and pressed them into Pharaoh's cup, and placed the
cup in Pharaoh's hand." [12]Then Joseph said to him, "This is its interpretation: the three branches are three days; [13]within three days Pharaoh
will lift up your head and restore you to your office; and you shall place
Pharaoh's cup in his hand as formerly, when you were his butler. [14]But
remember me, when it is well with you, and do me the kindness, I
pray you, to make mention of me to Pharaoh, and so get me out of this
house. [15]For I was indeed stolen out of the land of the Hebrews; and
here also I have done nothing that they should put me into the dungeon."
16 When the chief baker saw that the interpretation was favorable,
he said to Joseph, "I also had a dream: there were three cake baskets
on my head, [17]and in the uppermost basket there were all sorts of
baked food for Pharaoh, but the birds were eating it out of the basket
on my head." [18]And Joseph answered, "This is its interpretation: the
three baskets are three days; [19]within three days Pharaoh will lift up
your head—from you!—and hang you on a tree; and the birds will eat
the flesh from you."
20 On the third day, which was Pharaoh's birthday, he made a feast
for all his servants, and lifted up the head of the chief butler and the
head of the chief baker among his servants. [21]He restored the chief
butler to his butlership, and he placed the cup in Pharaoh's hand; [22]but
he hanged the chief baker, as Joseph had interpreted to them. [23]Yet the
chief butler did not remember Joseph, but forgot him.

The transition from the text of ch. 39 to that of ch. 40 is one of the few places where the combination of the two documents J and E has resulted in obvious rough spots. The text of ch. 39 was Yahwistic, as the free use of the name Yahweh showed. Joseph had been placed in prison, to be sure, but through the favor of the prison keeper he had been able to assume the position of a supervisor. This obvious position of trust which Joseph enjoyed agrees poorly with the statement that Joseph is now made the servant for two noble prisoners. There all prisoners were under "Joseph's care" (ch. 39.22), i.e., he was over them. Here he is subservient to two of them as an attendant slave. When one observes in addition that in our narrative Joseph says that he was stolen from the land of the Hebrews (ch. 40.15), one sees clearly that this narrative is connected with that report of Joseph's transfer to Egypt which told of a theft by the Midianites and not of a sale to the

Ishmaelites. (See pp. 352 f.) Chapter 40 is therefore Elohistic, an obvious fact when one considers the importance which prophetic dreams and interpretations of dreams here assume (see p. 26). We must suppose that the document E did not know of the episode of Joseph's temptation at all (ch. 39). According to it, Joseph was bought in Egypt by the captain of the guard (ch. 39.1b) who then made him the slave of the two prisoners. But how did J understand the event? If one attributes the statement ch. 39.1b to E, then Joseph was not sold by the Ishmaelites directly to Potiphar, but rather to a rich Egyptian. In favor of this conception reference has correctly been made to the strange fact that this high state official, Potiphar, is designated in ch. 39.1bα strangely as "an Egyptian." Actually this piling up of phrases occurred because of the joining of the sources. In E, Joseph was sold to Potiphar, an officer of Pharaoh; in J, Joseph was sold to "an Egyptian." According to E, Potiphar is the official under whose direction the prison was; the source J did not name the "keeper of the prison" (v. 22). In any case the narrative in ch. 39 did not identify him with Potiphar. If one accepts this conception of the combination of the Yahwistic with the Elohistic tradition, one must only reject the statement in ch. 39.20bα, according to which Joseph was placed in the state prison of the king's prisoners, as a connective addition to the original Yahwistic narrative.

[1–4] Here too the narrator, before he can present the matter itself, namely, the interpretations of the dreams, has to acquaint the reader with the external and internal situation, which is necessary for their understanding. The butler and the baker, as the titles in ch. 40.2 and v. 9 show, were very high officials. Ancient Egypt was a bureaucratic state. There, as in all courts with ancient tradition, there was also a complicated hierarchy of officials. Such serving positions in close proximity to the Pharaoh were both sought after and dangerous. Our narrative shows how far one could fall if the king's mood changed suddenly. But despotism is not especially emphasized here; the men seem actually to have been delinquent. This whole aspect of the occurrence does not interest the narrator. Joseph is given to them for all kinds of minor services which imprisonment at that time permitted. His position as the slave to prisoners was accordingly as low as possible.

[5–23] The narrator moves very nicely from quite an external observation to the matter itself. The observant slave is struck immediately by something in the faces of the two men. Hebrew narrators seldom describe inner emotional conditions directly. When it was necessary, they did it as here, indirectly. The situation of the two prisoners is as follows. They are sure that their dreams contain prophecies of their personal destiny. If they had been free, many possibilities would have been available to them for learning the meaning of the dreams. The interpretation of dreams was a science. There were men who had learned the technique of interpreting dreams, and there was a considerable literature on the subject. All of this is now inaccessible to them. For this reason "they were troubled." By contrast, Joseph's answer, "Interpretations belong to God," is completely polemic. It is again one of those splendid statements which our narrator loves and which go far beyond the situation in the programmatic, doctrinal form in which they are spoken (cf. at ch. 39.9). Spoken by a very lowly foreign slave, whom the two prisoners had not dreamed of questioning, the statement contains a sharp contrast. Joseph means to say that the interpretation of dreams is not a human art but a *charisma* which God can grant. In everything that concerned the interpretation of the future, ancient Israel's faith reacted very strongly. The events of the future lay in Yahweh's hand only, and only the one to whom it was revealed was empowered to interpret. One reads of a similar parrying of professional interpretation of dreams in Dan. 2.26 f. The dreams themselves, however, as they are related here, have little left of the "diffuse structure" and "asyntactic style" of really dreamed dreams (v. d. Leeuw, *Phänomenologie d. Religion*, 528). They are artificial dreams, i.e., what is seen in them has already been greatly stylized and raised to the dimension of the rational. In the butler's dream only the temporally widely separated events are brought closely together in stylistic abbreviation. The Pharaoh, of course, received wine to drink and not unfermented grape juice. The baker's dream is also quite simple and transparent in its pictorial content; as an occurrence in daily life it is palpable, and if it had not been a dream it would have required no special interpretation. So far as the process of interpretation is concerned, Joseph takes only a few parts of the dream. In taking the decisive elements and passing over the unimportant and insignificant parts, his charismatic power becomes evident. It also becomes evident in his explanation of the parts he chose. In this process of interpretation Joseph allegorizes somewhat freely. How he came to interpret the three branches and the three baskets as three days cannot be determined. This, like the choice of the explainable elements of the dream, is a factor of the freedom and mystery in which his divine power is exercised.

Both dreams show that the prisoners are still imprisoned pending trial and await Pharaoh's final decision. Thus after three days the butler's head "will be lifted up." This expression goes back ultimately to an actual custom in an audience: the petitioner stands or kneels with bowed head while the one on the throne takes him under the chin and raises his head (cf. II Kings 25.27; etc.). By using this manner of speaking, Joseph employs an ironical pun: someone will also "lift up" the baker's head, but "from you!" It is not quite certain whether one is to understand this to mean decapitation and subsequent hanging (as, e.g., Deut. 21.22). In any case the violation of the corpse is a special severity, especially for the Egyptians who took such great pains with the corpse. The concluding statement of our narrative section has a special function in the structure of the whole. Because of Joseph's request in v. 14 and the butler's restoration, the reader begins to have hope for Joseph; but he soon learns that help is still distant. On the other hand, the statement introduces what follows by passing over a long period during which Joseph remained forgotten in prison and thus anticipating the beginning of a new turn of events.

D. THE INTERPRETATION OF PHARAOH'S DREAM. JOSEPH'S ELEVATION TO POWER. CH. 41

41 [1]After two whole years, Pharaoh dreamed that he was standing by
the Nile, [2]and behold, there came up out of the Nile seven cows sleek
and fat, and they fed in the reed grass. [3]And behold, seven other cows,
gaunt and thin, came up out of the Nile after them, and stood by the
other cows on the bank of the Nile. [4]And the gaunt and thin cows ate
up the seven sleek and fat cows. And Pharaoh awoke. [5]And he fell asleep
and dreamed a second time; and behold, seven ears of grain, plump and
good, were growing on one stalk. [6]And behold, after them sprouted
seven ears, thin and blighted by the east wind. [7]And the thin ears
swallowed up the seven plump and full ears. And Pharaoh awoke, and
behold, it was a dream. [8]So in the morning his spirit was troubled; and
he sent and called for all the magicians of Egypt and all its wise men;
and Pharaoh told them his dream, but there was none who could interpret it to Pharaoh.

9 Then the chief butler said to Pharaoh, "I remember my faults
today. [10]When Pharaoh was angry with his servants, and put me and
the chief baker in custody in the house of the captain of the guard, [11]we
dreamed on the same night, he and I, each having a dream with its
own meaning. [12]A young Hebrew was there with us, a servant of the

captain of the guard; and when we told him, he interpreted our dreams
to us, giving an interpretation to each man according to his dream.
[13]And as he interpreted to us, so it came to pass; I was restored to my
office, and the baker was hanged."

14 Then Pharaoh sent and called Joseph, and they brought him
hastily out of the dungeon; and when he had shaved himself and
changed his clothes, he came in before Pharaoh. [15]And Pharaoh said to
Joseph, "I have had a dream, and there is no one who can interpret it;
and I have heard it said of you that when you hear a dream you can
interpret it." [16]Joseph answered Pharaoh, "It is not in me; God will
give Pharaoh a favorable answer." [17]Then Pharaoh said to Joseph,
"Behold, in my dream I was standing on the banks of the Nile; [18]and
seven cows, fat and sleek, came up out of the Nile and fed in the reed
grass; [19]and seven other cows came up after them, poor and very gaunt
and thin, such as I had never seen in all the land of Egypt. [20]And the
thin and gaunt cows ate up the first seven fat cows, [21]but when they had
eaten them no one would have known that they had eaten them, for
they were still as gaunt as at the beginning. Then I awoke. [22]I also saw
in my dream seven ears growing on one stalk, full and good; [23]and
seven ears, withered, thin, and blighted by the east wind, sprouted after
them, [24]and the thin ears swallowed up the seven good ears. And I told
it to the magicians, but there was no one who could explain it to me."

25 Then Joseph said to Pharaoh, "The dream of Pharaoh is one;
God has revealed to Pharaoh what he is about to do. [26]The seven good
cows are seven years, and the seven good ears are seven years; the dream
is one. [27]The seven lean and gaunt cows that came up after them are
seven years, and the seven empty ears blighted by the east wind are also
seven years of famine. [28]It is as I told Pharaoh, God has shown to
Pharaoh what he is about to do. [29]There will come seven years of great
plenty throughout all the land of Egypt, [30]but after them there will arise
seven years of famine, and all the plenty will be forgotten in the land of
Egypt; the famine will consume the land, [31]and the plenty will be unknown in the land by reason of that famine which will follow, for it will
be very grievous. [32]And the doubling of Pharaoh's dream means that
the thing is fixed by God, and God will shortly bring it to pass. [33]Now
therefore let Pharaoh select a man discreet and wise, and set him over
the land of Egypt. [34]Let Pharaoh proceed to appoint overseers over the
land, and take the fifth part of the produce of the land of Egypt during
the seven plenteous years. [35]And let them gather all the food of these
good years that are coming, and lay up grain under the authority of
Pharaoh for food in the cities, and let them keep it. [36]That food shall be
a reserve for the land against the seven years of famine which are to
befall the land of Egypt, so that the land may not perish through the
famine."

37 This proposal seemed good to Pharaoh and to all his servants.
[38]And Pharaoh said to his servants, "Can we find such a man as this, in
whom is the Spirit of God?" [39]So Pharaoh said to Joseph, "Since God
has shown you all this, there is none so discreet and wise as you are;

40you shall be over my house, and all my people shall order themselves
as you command; only as regards the throne will I be greater than you."
41And Pharaoh said to Joseph, "Behold, I have set you over all the land
of Egypt." 42Then Pharaoh took his signet ring from his hand and put it
on Joseph's hand, and arrayed him in garments of fine linen, and put
a gold chain about his neck; 43and he made him to ride in his second
chariot; and they cried before him, "Bow the knee!" Thus he set him
over all the land of Egypt. 44Moreover Pharaoh said to Joseph, "I am
Pharaoh, and without your consent no man shall lift up hand or foot in
all the land of Egypt." 45And Pharaoh called Joseph's name Zaphenath-
paneah; and he gave him in marriage Asenath, the daughter of
Potiphera priest of On. So Joseph went out over the land of Egypt.

46 *Joseph was thirty years old when he entered the service of Pharaoh king of
Egypt.* And Joseph went out from the presence of Pharaoh, and went
through all the land of Egypt. 47During the seven plenteous years the
earth brought forth abundantly, 48and he gathered up all the food of the
seven years when there was plenty in the land of Egypt, and stored up
food in the cities; he stored up in every city the food from the fields
around it. 49And Joseph stored up grain in great abundance, like the
sand of the sea, until he ceased to measure it, for it could not be
measured.

50 Before the year of famine came, Joseph had two sons, whom
Asenath, the daughter of Potiphera priest of On, bore to him. 51Joseph
called the name of the first-born Manasseh, "For," he said, "God has
made me forget all my hardship and all my father's house." 52The
name of the second he called Ephraim, "For God has made me fruitful
in the land of my affliction."

53 The seven years of plenty that prevailed in the land of Egypt
came to an end; 54and the seven years of famine began to come, as
Joseph had said. There was famine in all lands; but in all the land of
Egypt there was bread. 55When all the land of Egypt was famished, the
people cried to Pharaoh for bread; and Pharaoh said to all the Egyptians, "Go to Joseph; what he says to you, do." 56So when the famine
had spread over all the land, Joseph opened all the storehouses, and
sold to the Egyptians, for the famine was severe in the land of Egypt.
57Moreover, all the earth came to Egypt to Joseph to buy grain, because
the famine was severe over all the earth.

In contrast to the previous narrative sections the actual story here begins at v. 1. That was possible because all of ch. 40, apart from bringing the occurrence one step farther, is at the same time an exposition for ch. 41. The persons, Joseph, the butler, the baker, the Pharaoh, the captain of the guard, are all mentioned again; and the beginning of ch. 41 is based on the situation in ch. 40. But above all the interpretation of the dreams in prison anticipates the interpretation of the dreams at court; the parallel contrast in the two interpretations, on the one hand in the misery of prison and on the other in the splendor of the royal court, is extremely effective. The narrative is uniformly Elohistic at least up to v. 30; from there on doublets and irregularities show evidence of a mixture of sources.

The events themselves occur about two years later. The note that Joseph was thirty years old when he first appeared before Pharaoh is certainly a part of the Priestly Joseph story about whose content and style we know very little. According to it, thirteen years elapsed between Joseph's humiliation and his elevation (cf. ch. 37.2 f.).

[1–25] Regarding the dreams and their interpretation, one must refer to what was said at chs. 40.9 ff. and 37.5 ff. Here too it would be wrong to consider the details of the dreams symbolically (e.g., the cows as animals sacred to the goddess Hathor and as symbols of fertility). The exposition is not connected with these supposedly subtle allusions, but it goes its own way in freedom. We must apparently consider the cows which are coming up out of the water as water cows which have been raised in Egypt from the most ancient times down to the present. Cows that eat one another and ears that swallow one another belong to the fantastic world of dreams. Nevertheless, the Pharaoh saw the things so realistically that when he awoke he first had to adapt himself to reality: they were dreams (v. 7). But that was more alarming than ever (Pharaoh's spirit was "troubled"), for there could be no doubt that a dream of such clarity and uniformity, which had occurred twice, contained a reference to the future.

The narrator now vividly shows the wrong approach which the king used because he had the erroneous notion that knowledge of the future was open to human art and specially trained mantic skill. This error becomes especially touching in the address to Joseph who has been summoned. The Pharaoh first considers him a scientific specialist of this kind, but one who is quite superior who does not need to exert himself. Joseph decisively rejects this assumption (*bilʿādāy*, literally "not in me," i.e., I do not come in question). Again we have come to a place of programmatic theological significance. The difference between the vocational interpretation of the future which is destined to fail and a charismatic illumination which does not require any technique is emphasized strongly (see at ch. 40.8).

The butler's thankless forgetfulness is just as realistic as his awakening recollection at Pharaoh's question. In the statement "I remember my faults" (*mazkīr ḥaṭā'ay*) the butler probably refers to an actually existing office for bringing suit. An accuser seems to have belonged to the court (*mazkīr ʿāwōn*, cf. the allusions in I Kings 17.18; Ezek. 21.28; 29.16). The statement, therefore, means, "I must now be my own accuser." Furthermore, the statement refers nicely to ch. 40.14 where Joseph asked that the butler remember him; and now he must also remember his sin.

[25–36] Here too the interpretation itself is not given in esoteric twilight and mystery, but the process is rather very simple, clear, and sober. Everything stands and falls with the freedom, quite beyond control to be sure, in which Joseph explains the number of the cows and the ears as years, while in prison he had interpreted the three branches as days. One sees how sober this whole process is in the fact that Joseph proceeds from the actual interpretation of the future immediately to quite practical suggestions. But this second part of his long speech is also a part of the interpretation itself; it explains what the consumption of the cows and ears really means: the lean years will devour the reserves of the fat years. What is theologically noteworthy is the way in which the strong predestinarian content of the speech is combined with a strong summons to action. The fact that God has determined the matter, that God hastens to bring it to pass, is precisely the reason for responsible leaders to take measures!

We have here a good example of the goal toward which all training and education in Israel during the royal period directed a young man of good standing. He must be able to speak publicly and in significant situations and he must be able to give advice (Prov. 15.7; 16.23 f.; 18.21; 20.18; 25.11 f.). This counseling always occurred in political affairs and supported the one responsible, who had to make his decision on the basis of the quality of the counsel he received. (See especially II Sam. 17.1 ff.) The one who was reared in wisdom and found reliable was called especially to political activity both in Israel during the royal period and in ancient Egypt. Thus Joseph unconsciously gives evidence of just those gifts which he assumes to inhere in the one in the empire who now has to take measures against the imminent distress (v. 33). In Egypt the storing of grain in public granaries was a customary measure of the government (see AOB, no. 177 for the picture of one such silo, the upper opening of which could only be reached with a ladder). The narrator lets Joseph plan a large granary of this kind; such a building was unknown to the Hebrew readers and therefore was all the more interesting!

[37–45] The effect of Joseph's speech on the Pharaoh is telling. Both his interpretation of the dream and his counsel were convincing.

The criterion by which the Pharaoh tacitly tested the interpretation is not given by the narrator. He apparently assumes that there was a truth in it which was absolutely convincing, and another interpretation can no longer come into question. Joseph's counsel was just as convincing because of its lucid expedience.

A more precise discussion of the measures recommended by Joseph leads to the realm of source analysis. In v. 33 Joseph recommends the selection of a single official with a special commission, in v. 34 the appointment of a whole group of "overseers." While these are to take one fifth of the harvest in the land (v. 34b), v. 35 speaks of taking the entire harvest. These are inconsistencies which apparently derive from the different conceptions of the sources J and E regarding the process. Joseph's appointment to his high office is also clearly related twice, in v. 41 and in vs. 40 and 42 f. Joseph's first trip of inspection is told in vs. 46b and in 47 and finally the note about the coming of the famine is reported in vs. 54 and 55.

The narrator describes Joseph's installation by describing ceremonies, customs, and laws that were actually practiced in Egypt. The office given to Joseph is that of grand vizier, i.e., the authorized representative of the king himself. He is at the same time director of the palace and thus the most powerful man in the kingdom. Later, in Judea, there was also a director of the palace who in fact exercised the office of vizier (he is the *'al habbayit* of Isa. 22.20 ff.; II Kings 18.18, 37). David and Solomon do not appear to have introduced this office. Especially important was the handing over of the royal seal, which the vizier had to administer; with it he becomes the actual public executor of the royal decrees. The giving of a chain about the neck as a sign of honor is also attested in ancient Egyptian sources. The splendid chariots, like those, for instance, which were found in Tutankhamen's grave, were two-wheeled with a platform upon which the relevant dignitary stood next to the charioteer. The "second chariot" is apparently the vizier's chariot, which is also called simply the second (I Sam. 23.17; Esth. 10.3; II Chron. 28.7; cf. II Chron. 35.24). The cry of the guard who ran before the vizier has not yet been explained for certain. If the word is Egyptian, it could be interpreted in the sense of "look out!" But a derivation from Hebrew has also been suggested, "to your knees!" (A form of the verb "to kneel"? Less probable is the suggestion to connect the word with Babylonian *abarakku*, which designates a high military and court dignitary.)

In all these honors only one person in Egypt is to be over Joseph, the Pharaoh himself. The change of his name was also an important act of court ceremony; by it Joseph was drawn completely into the Egyptian court circle, and this did not happen, furthermore, without Joseph's being placed within the protective sphere of an Egyptian deity. The name is translated "the God speaks and he lives." The candid way in which Joseph's not quite unobjectionable inclusion into the Egyptian court is related is surprising in view of Israel's faith. There is reflected in it a period when Israel had not yet had any negative experiences of faith with the heathen world. In the Book of Daniel, which derives from a much more troubled situation, a change of name like this is made for Daniel as one of the serious measures of a heathen court (Dan. 1.7). The same thing is even more true of Joseph's marriage into the family of the high priest of On, i.e., Heliopolis, north of modern Cairo. But the older period did not object to marriages with women from foreign religious circles; up until the royal period they were rare, to be sure, but they did not affect the body of the cultic community at all. That changed only after the exile, especially because of Ezra and Nehemiah. The name of Joseph's father-in-law, apart from an orthographic difference, is like that of Joseph's previous master (chs. 37.36; 39.1). It would be rather surprising if the narrative had used only one name for two different persons. But since the source J, as we saw above, probably did not know Potiphar, the captain of the guard, each source could have known only one Potiphar, if v. 45 is Yahwistic.

[47–57] The fulfillment of the prophecy is described in the same detail as the preceding. But here too the great detail of the presentation is to be derived from a combination of the sources. That is true both of the description of the good years in vs. 47–49 and of the famine in vs. 53–57. In the latter case there appears to be a factual inconsistency, for on the one hand the way in which the distress came upon Egypt and the way the hungry people were then referred to Joseph and his granaries are described (vs. 55–56b); on the other hand, the emphasis is placed upon the fact that in a world famine only Egypt suffered no want and that people from other lands came to it for help (vs. 54b, 56a, 57).

The remark about the birth of two sons now completes the picture of the mighty turn of fate in Joseph's life: grand vizier of Egypt, married to the daughter of the highest priest in the land, and now two sons from this marriage! The statements in which Joseph interprets the names are accordingly an expression of his gratitude for the unsuspected turn of events and the fulfillment of his life according to such a completely new plan. By these new connections Joseph has become completely Egyptian. Even though the reader may not reproach him for that, in the narrator's opinion it is still certainly an intentional fine point of the story that immediately after Joseph has related this period to his previous life the narrator introduces those events which again bring Joseph into relationship with his father's house. The meaning, therefore, is not that Joseph has "forgotten" his father's house, in the strict sense of the word, perhaps with an overtone of bitterness; for the continuation of the story shows how attached to it he is. "Forget" does not mean here "not remember" but rather to have something no longer (cf. Job 39.17; 11.16. See, too, the Arabic proverb, "Whoever drinks water from the Nile forgets his fatherland if he is a foreigner"). The phrase refers, therefore, more to an objective external fact than to a subjective, psychological process. Regarding Manasseh and Ephraim, see at ch. 48.

E. THE BROTHERS' FIRST JOURNEY TO EGYPT. CH. 42

42 1When Jacob learned that there was grain in Egypt, he said to his
sons, "Why do you look at one another?" 2And he said, "Behold, I
have heard that there is grain in Egypt; go down and buy grain for us
there, that we may live, and not die." 3So ten of Joseph's brothers went
down to buy grain in Egypt. 4But Jacob did not send Benjamin, Joseph's
brother, with his brothers, for he feared that harm might befall him.
5Thus the sons of Israel came to buy among the others who came, for the
famine was in the land of Canaan.

6 Now Joseph was governor over the land; he it was who sold to all
the people of the land. And Joseph's brothers came, and bowed themselves before him with their faces to the ground. 7Joseph saw his
brothers, and knew them, but he treated them like strangers and spoke
roughly to them. "Where do you come from?" he said. They said,
"From the land of Canaan, to buy food." 8Thus Joseph knew his
brothers, but they did not know him. 9And Joseph remembered the
dreams which he had dreamed of them; and he said to them, "You are
spies, you have come to see the weakness of the land." 10They said to
him, "No, my lord, but to buy food have your servants come. 11We are
the sons of one man, we are honest men, your servants are not spies."
12He said to them, "No, it is the weakness of the land that you have
come to see." 13And they said, "We, your servants, are twelve brothers,
the sons of one man in the land of Canaan; and behold, the youngest is
this day with our father, and one is no more." 14But Joseph said to
them, "It is as I said to you, you are spies. 15By this you shall be tested:
by the life of Pharaoh, you shall not go from this place unless your
youngest brother comes here. 16Send one of you, and let him bring your

brother, while you remain in prison, that your words may be tested,
whether there is truth in you; or else, by the life of Pharaoh, surely you
are spies." [17]And he put them all together in prison for three days.

18 On the third day Joseph said to them, "Do this and you will live,
for I fear God: [19]if you are honest men, let one of your brothers remain
confined in your prison, and let the rest go and carry grain for the
famine of your households, [20]and bring your youngest brother to me;
so your words will be verified, and you shall not die." And they did so.
[21]Then they said to one another, "In truth we are guilty concerning our
brother, in that we saw the distress of his soul, when he besought us and
we would not listen; therefore is this distress come upon us." [22]And
Reuben answered them, "Did I not tell you not to sin against the lad?
But you would not listen. So now there comes a reckoning for his blood."
[23]They did not know that Joseph understood them, for there was an
interpreter between them. [24]Then he turned away from them and wept;
and he returned to them and spoke to them. And he took Simeon from
them and bound him before their eyes. [25]And Joseph gave orders to
fill their bags with grain, and to replace every man's money in his
sack, and to give them provisions for the journey. This was done for
them.

26 Then they loaded their asses with their grain, and departed.
[27]And as one of them opened his sack to give his ass provender at the
lodging place, he saw his money in the mouth of his sack; [28]and he said
to his brothers, "My money has been put back; here it is in the mouth
of my sack!" At this their hearts failed them, and they turned trembling
to one another, saying, "What is this that God has done to us?"

29 When they came to Jacob their father in the land of Canaan,
they told him all that had befallen them, saying, [30]"The man, the lord
of the land, spoke roughly to us, and took us to be spies of the land.
[31]But we said to him, 'We are honest men, we are not spies; [32]we are
twelve brothers, sons of our father; one is no more, and the youngest is
this day with our father in the land of Canaan.' [33]Then the man, the
lord of the land, said to us, 'By this I shall know that you are honest
men: leave one of your brothers with me, and take grain for the famine
of your households, and go your way. [34]Bring your youngest brother to
me; then I shall know that you are not spies but honest men, and I will
deliver to you your brother, and you shall trade in the land.' "

35 As they emptied their sacks, behold, every man's bundle of
money was in his sack; and when they and their father saw their bundles
of money, they were dismayed. [36]And Jacob their father said to them,
"You have bereaved me of my children: Joseph is no more, and Simeon
is no more, and now you would take Benjamin; all this has come upon
me." [37]Then Reuben said to his father, "Slay my two sons if I do not
bring him back to you; put him in my hands, and I will bring him back
to you." [38]But he said, "My son shall not go down with you, for his
brother is dead, and he only is left. If harm should befall him on the
journey that you are to make, you would bring down my gray hairs
with sorrow to Sheol."

Between chs. 41 and 42 there is a marked caesura. Up until the events of ch. 41, Joseph and what became of him was the narrator's subject. From the beginning up to the wholesome measures of the grand vizier the reader did not lose sight of Joseph. In ch. 42, this line is broken, and the narrator takes us back to Palestine to Jacob and his sons. This prepares the way for an inner thematic change in the story, for whereas previously Joseph's fate concerned the reader more than anything else, from now on his interest is transferred to something much more hidden, namely, Joseph's relationship to his brothers. The transition to this theme is made very easily, almost imperceptibly, by the motif of the famine which also had come upon the Land of Canaan. The narrative which begins here, especially if one also considers its continuation in ch. 43, shows, upon close inspection, obvious irregularities. If one begins with the sections vs. 13–26 and vs. 29–35, which are unified and whose content is decisive for the understanding of the chapter in its present form, then Joseph suspected the brothers of being spies. At first he wants to send only one of them back to bring Benjamin and thus prove the truth of their story (vs. 14–16), but in the end he imprisons only Simeon as a guarantor. The others go home and there to their astonishment find their money in the sacks of grain (vs. 35–37). The most obvious inconsistency concerns the discovery of the money in the sacks. According to v. 35, it occurred at the end of the journey; they did not have to open the sacks on the way because Joseph had given each of them rations for the journey (v. 25). According to vs. 27 f., however, the brothers found the money on the evening of their first day's journey when they were preparing to feed their animals. A much more profound inconsistency appears in the continuation of the narrative in ch. 43.1 ff. There every reader must notice that the brothers did not go back to Egypt at once, as one would expect them to do, to redeem the imprisoned Simeon, but that they remained quietly in the land until their supply of grain finally was consumed and their need forced them to a second buying trip. The sons reply to Jacob's request that they may appear before the vizier in Egypt only with their brother Benjamin. Two things are surprising here: was it necessary for them to inform their father in such detail (ch. 43.3–7) after they had told him the state of affairs immediately upon their return home (ch. 42.29–34)? One is especially surprised to find that in the second description of the brothers' meeting with Joseph in ch. 43.3–7 what was primary in ch. 42, namely, Simeon's detention, is not mentioned at all. Everything becomes clear if with Wellhausen one recognizes ch. 43.1 ff. as the representation of another source (J). It knows nothing at all of a detention of Simeon. Rather, according to it, Joseph only impressed his brothers with the fact that they could appear before him again only with their brother, Benjamin. This explains the waiting in ch. 43.2 which, given the facts of ch. 42, is so difficult to understand. It was the subsequent insertion of vs. 15 and 23b with their mention of Simeon which created the close connection between chs. 43 and 42.

This twofold character of the narrative can also be recognized elsewhere in ch. 42. The beginning, for example, has really two starts, vs. 1a and 1b. This double description is especially evident where Joseph recognizes his brothers but conceals himself from them (vs. 7 and 8 f.) and where he suspects the brothers of being spies (vs. 9b and 12). The essential fact is common to the two versions, namely, the conception of Joseph's intention which determines his strange behavior: he wants to force the bringing of his younger brother, Benjamin. The motive is moving and doubly gripping because the reader understands it at once while it confronts the brothers with an enigma.

[1–12] Egypt was always the land of wheat for Palestine, especially for its stony hill country, where it had to look in years of drought (cf. ch. 12.10 ff.). The narrator imagines that the brothers went to Egypt with many others, similar to the way in which "Asiatics who did not know from what they would live" are pictured on the famous ancient Egyptian grave relief as bowing before the general Haremhab ca. 1330 (AOB, no. 87), and that they met the powerful vizier at the wheat market. It is only natural for them not to have recognized him in the completely strange surroundings, for they certainly did not expect him at this place. On the other hand, it is much easier to imagine that Joseph was looking for them. But it is exciting for the reader when Joseph does not do what seems obvious but rather treats them as strangers (pun *wayyitnakkēr wayyakirēm* in v. 7). The narrator scarcely intends to say that Joseph disguised his face or his dress, as it is told, for example, in I Kings 14.5. What is meant is rather his conduct, and the Egyptian oath (v. 15) makes his mask even more impenetrable (Holzinger). The fear of a hostile infiltration of the land is a very genuine characteristic of ancient Egyptian life. The northeast frontier was one of the vulnerable places of the Egyptian empire, which they had sought to block by garrisons and even a wall. Joseph's suspicion is very offensive because of his metaphor of the "weakness (= shame) of the land"; for he insinuates that they are up to some very indecent mischief. The brothers' words are very subservient in form, and their profound humility makes Joseph consider that his dreams have now been fulfilled. Joseph's reference to his fear of God in v. 18 is to indicate his reliability. He cannot allow himself to break his word, but he is bound to absolute divine commands; the brothers can therefore trust him. Fear of God, therefore, is here, as in ch. 20.11 or ch. 22.12, a term for obedience to commands. With this reference Joseph touches on an affection for the brothers of which they suspect nothing yet.

[13–24]The way in which the conversation between the vizier and Jacob's sons slowly moves to the no longer present Joseph, and the way the dark shadow of the unforgotten Joseph strikes the brothers' emotions, while the one who is thought dead stands shaken before them, is extremely beautiful. Every reader, of course, wonders about Joseph's intention and motives in this scene. Clearly he does not intend to punish the brothers; rather, Joseph says twice in peculiar ambiguity that he wants to "test" them. He wants to learn first of all if they have told him the truth, whether they can prove their honesty to him. But this test goes much farther. It could be that the ancient evil still dominated them. Or had they changed? What Joseph does to them occurs not only to reveal their present character, but the suffering and crises into which he wants to lead them are to discipline the brothers further and more severely and to chasten them. In this he changes the plan which he had first told them (v. 16), probably because he had convinced himself that if he followed it he would overstrain the bow. To send only one of the brothers home would afflict the father too much and might thwart the return of this one with Benjamin. Thus Simeon was "bound before their eyes." This meant that they too were bound and obligated to return. In this distress the brothers say precisely what Joseph intended them to say, for the situation is in fact similar to the former one. Now again they have to appear before their father without one of their brothers, and what they once unsympathetically observed, the "distress of soul" of the one, they now find impossible to bear. The evil which they did long before has now arisen all of a sudden and has come upon the perpetrators; they immediately recognize the connection. Many commentators ask what Joseph was really weeping about, but the reader's own heart must answer that for him. To be sure, the actual worldly form in which these pangs of conscience are expressed is surprising. It is more the moral in man which reacts in the brothers than that very ancient terror before the avenging deity.

[25–38] Joseph's replacement of his brothers' money in their sacks is to show that they were his guests; it is a sign of his deeply veiled love which makes them so great a gift. But this, like everything about Joseph, must be enigmatic to them at first and frighten them. Regarding the discovery after the first day's ride (v. 27) and that after their return home (v. 35), see p. 380. Jacob is deeply dismayed. Again the shade of the lost Joseph appears (vs. 36, 38). Jacob speaks with pathos of his descent to Sheol, the realm of the dead. That was a rather poetic idea; for everyone knew that the dead lay in the family grave. But it was apparently considered to be especially bad to die in such sorrow and not "in a good old age" because it was then possible that the spirit of the dead would find no rest.

F. THE BROTHERS' SECOND JOURNEY TO EGYPT. CH. 43

43 [1]Now the famine was severe in the land. [2]And when they had
eaten the grain which they had brought from Egypt, their father said to
them, "Go again, buy us a little food." [3]But Judah said to him, "The
man solemnly warned us, saying, 'You shall not see my face, unless
your brother is with you.' [4]If you will send our brother with us, we will
go down and buy you food; [5]but if you will not send him, we will not go
down, for the man said to us, 'You shall not see my face, unless your
brother is with you.' " [6]Israel said, "Why did you treat me so ill as to
tell the man that you had another brother?" [7]They replied, "The man
questioned us carefully about ourselves and our kindred, saying, 'Is
your father still alive? Have you another brother?' What we told him
was in answer to these questions; could we in any way know that he
would say, 'Bring your brother down'?" [8]And Judah said to Israel his
father, "Send the lad with me, and we will arise and go, that we may live
and not die, both we and you and also our little ones. [9]I will be surety for
him; of my hand you shall require him. If I do not bring him back to
you and set him before you, then let me bear the blame for ever; [10]for if
we had not delayed, we would now have returned twice."

11 Then their father Israel said to them, "If it must be so then do
this: take some of the choice fruits of the land in your bags, and carry
down to the man a present, a little balm and a little honey, gum,
myrrh, pistachio nuts, and almonds. [12]Take double the money with you;
carry back with you the money that was returned in the mouth of your
sacks; perhaps it was an oversight. [13]Take also your brother, and arise,
go again to the man; [14]may God Almighty grant you mercy before the
man, that he may send back your other brother and Benjamin. If I am

bereaved of my children, I am bereaved." [15]So the men took the present, and they took double the money with them, and Benjamin; and they arose and went down to Egypt, and stood before Joseph.

16 When Joseph saw Benjamin with them, he said to the steward of his house, "Bring the men into the house, and slaughter an animal and make ready, for the men are to dine with me at noon." [17]The man did as Joseph bade him, and brought the men to Joseph's house. [18]And the men were afraid because they were brought to Joseph's house, and they said, "It is because of the money, which was replaced in our sacks the first time, that we are brought in, so that he may seek occasion against us and fall upon us, to make slaves of us and seize our asses." [19]So they went up to the steward of Joseph's house, and spoke with him at the door of the house, [20]and said, "Oh, my lord, we came down the first time to buy food; [21]and when we came to the lodging place we opened our sacks, and there was every man's money in the mouth of his sack, our money in full weight; so we have brought it again with us, [22]and we have brought other money down in our hand to buy food. We do not know who put our money in our sacks." [23]He replied, "Rest assured, do not be afraid; your God and the God of your father must have put treasure in your sacks for you; I received your money." Then he brought Simeon out to them. [24]And when the man had brought the men into Joseph's house, and given them water, and they had washed their feet, and when he had given their asses provender, [25]they made ready the present for Joseph's coming at noon, for they heard that they should eat bread there.

26 When Joseph came home, they brought into the house to him the present which they had with them, and bowed down to him to the ground. [27]And he inquired about their welfare, and said, "Is your father well, the old man of whom you spoke? Is he still alive?" [28]They said, "Your servant our father is well, he is still alive." And they bowed their heads and made obeisance. [29]And he lifted up his eyes, and saw his brother Benjamin, his mother's son, and said, "Is this your youngest brother, of whom you spoke to me? God be gracious to you, my son!" [30]Then Joseph made haste, for his heart yearned for his brother, and he sought a place to weep. And he entered his chamber and wept there. [31]Then he washed his face and came out; and controlling himself he said, "Let food be served." [32]They served him by himself, and them by themselves, and the Egyptians who ate with him by themselves, because the Egyptians might not eat bread with the Hebrews, for that is an abomination to the Egyptians. [33]And they sat before him, the first-born according to his birthright and the youngest according to his youth; and the men looked at one another in amazement. [34]Portions were taken to them from Joseph's table, but Benjamin's portion was five times as much as any of theirs. So they drank and were merry with him.

To understand the beginning of this chapter, especially, the reader must remember that here (and including ch. 44) we have the idea of the J document, an idea that diverges somewhat from what was narrated in ch. 42 (E). According to it, Joseph had released the brothers only on the condition that they bring Benjamin with them the next time. He was certain they would come again because he knew about the unusual duration of the famine. Furthermore, Joseph could assume that the will to live would break the father's obstinacy. (Our narrative harmonizes with the Elohistic narrative of ch. 42 only because of the insertion of vs. 14 and 23bβ.) This is where our first verse begins: the unusual duration of the famine actually did force another trip to Egypt. That this was the reason for the second trip and not the obligation toward Simeon; and that the brothers waited so long, is one of the few really disturbing irregularities in the Joseph story arising from the fusion of the source documents which do not quite agree.

[1–10] The father's summons to go again to Egypt raises the problem the unfolding and solution of which the narrator renders in the rather large space of twelve verses. Some expositors have noticed that the father is here told insistently about Joseph's condition, which he had already learned in ch. 42.38. They have therefore transposed this v. 38 to the conversation of ch. 43 after v. 2. But that is not necessary; it is quite possible that the obstinate old man considered this aspect of the matter settled by his earlier no. But Judah emphasizes the great definiteness with which "the man" had impressed upon them precisely this condition. (*Hē'īd* here means "warn, admonish," cf. I Kings 2.42.) Without Benjamin they would be unable to "see Joseph's face." That is an expression from the language of the court and it means to be permitted an audience. Thus the dilemma is presented which the reader himself is to experience: on the one hand is the famine which threatens all their lives; on the other hand it was not a small matter to send the favorite son on such a journey to a strange court, and it was especially sinister when there was such singular interest in him there. Benjamin's age in this phase of the occurrence can only be ascertained indirectly. Joseph, according to ch. 41.46, was at that time at least thirty-seven years old; Benjamin accordingly could have been only a few years younger, corresponding to the time span occurring between ch. 30.23 ff. and 35.16 ff. One has the impression, however, that the Joseph story has its own chronology, that it does not presuppose the later Priestly chronology of chs. 37.2; 41.46, and that it considers Benjamin as still a boy. Or is the word "the lad" (*na'ar*) in ch. 43.8 and later in ch. 44.22 really only the familiar, tender reference to one who has long since grown up?

The difficult conversation with the old man is conducted by Judah, with the other brothers agreeing. Its charm for the reader consists in the fact that it again follows the great mystery of the story and that the partners to the conversation have not the remotest idea of it. How curious that the man had asked so in detail about the family, about the father and the one absent brother! But the old man can see nothing at all promising in that; rather, he considers the brothers' answer as only an indiscretion which they might have spared him. It is possible that this narrator had a somewhat different conception of the brothers' first conversation with Joseph from the one in ch. 42.10 ff. For here Joseph on his own inquires into the family business to a perfidious extent, while there the brothers reveal everything at once in order to clear themselves of the suspicion of being spies. Judah's solemn decision to be surety for the younger brother marks the turning point in this struggle. His offer is nothing less than a secularly formulated curse upon himself in the event that Benjamin did not return. Every reader will consider Judah's unconditional tie of his life to that of his brother as something magnanimous and uplifting. Actually this solidarity and willingness to give themselves for one another on the brothers' part is a hidden desired result of the hard test to which Joseph had put them.

[11–15] Once Jacob has brought himself to send Benjamin he turns at once to the very practical necessities of this ticklish journey. Bringing gifts to a high official is still practiced in the Orient and is no more than a sign of good breeding. The fruits of the land (the strange expression in v. 11, *zimrat hā'āreṣ*, really means "strengths, powers of the land") are some delicacies and spices known elsewhere as wares for export (cf. at ch. 37.25). Mastic, labdanum and tragacanth are spices from the resin of certain shrubs or trees ("balsam"); pistachio nuts were eaten or used in preparing delicate foods. The honey is wild bees' honey which was used in the kitchen instead of sugar, which was unknown at that time; it is mentioned in Ezek. 27.17 as an article for export. The unfinished business about the money is also to be clarified. Jacob thinks of everything, for he alone is in charge. In the blessing in v. 14 only the unusual designation for God can be considered foreign to the verse (cf. at ch. 17.1). The melancholy conclusion in v. 14b shows the sad resignation of a man who has long resisted but who no longer wants to set his will against the course of events, and who still cannot bring himself to any real assurance.

Chapter 43 shows with special clarity that the narrator knows the dangers of a long, extended narrative. He therefore divides the material into individual scenes, each of which is rounded off to a certain extent, and he quickly skips over the events in between. The material of ch. 43, therefore, contains three scenes that one could call "scenes" in the sense of our theatrical productions: (1) Jacob and his sons, (2) the brothers and the master of ceremonies, (3) the brothers and Joseph. While the long journey to Egypt is referred to in a single statement (v. 15), the actual meeting with Joseph is preceded by an entire scene, which of course increases the suspense. In no less than ten verses the narrator describes for us the events and conversations of that morning which preceded Joseph's meal with his brothers (vs. 16–25).

[16–25] Joseph saw his brothers coming or learned that they were on the way; thus he could give the necessary instructions to the steward, a high palace official who was responsible for receiving visitors to the vizier. The steward may at first have been rather surprised at the invitation of the Palestinian shepherds to the vizier's table, but his statement to the brothers in v. 23 presupposes that Joseph had made him familiar with the facts regarding the strange guests. Joseph still has things to do; so the brothers are at first placed under the steward's care. The brothers here appear as humble people who are awkward and servile in strange and elegant surroundings. Once in the front door they begin to talk (Gu.). They must have been uneasy at the surprising invitation to the vizier's private apartment after they had received such rough handling the first time and then had had the strange experience with the money. Who knows all the knavery one might experience at a strange court? The brothers are expecting that a guard will appear from somewhere and "fall upon" them (*hitgōlēl*, v. 18). The brothers' verbose exculpations give a true emotional picture. The narrator is here quite concerned to reveal their inner anxiety; next to this all the graphic descriptions of the external events are only indirectly important to the extent that they make these emotional conditions comprehensible. The master of ceremonies' gracious answer is the jewel in this masterful scene. It is reassuring and intended to distract the upset men from the object of their fear; but its dark ambiguity touches the innermost mystery of the whole Joseph story: God's concealed guidance. God is at work in the events and therefore nothing is said now about money but rather about a "treasure" which God has placed for them in their sacks. This answer may at first have reassured the brothers somewhat, but they could only understand it later. The redactor has very cleverly inserted here in v. 23b Simeon's release and thus connected the somewhat different representation of events in ch. 42 with those of ch. 43 (see p. 381). The brothers pass the time still remaining to them by washing themselves for their reception, feeding the animals, and making ready their gifts in Joseph's house.

[26–34] The reader must look forward with great excitement to the new meeting with Joseph after all the preparations. In the previous scene the brothers' surprise and anxiety were particularly described; now Joseph himself is the center of attention. One can say that the narrator does not lose sight of the aristocratic man for a minute from the time of his return from the ministry until the relaxed gathering at wine. One hears him speak, one sees him overcome by inner emotion and follows him into one of his private apartments until his weeping is over, one sees him wash his face, control himself, and one sees him at the meal sitting somewhat apart with his retinue. In contrast to this very troubled picture the brothers remain uniformly respectful, even obsequious, becoming more relaxed only when wine was served.

It has long been noticed that Joseph does not wait for an answer to his second question, the one about Benjamin, in contrast to his first one in v. 27. Here too the words "my son" in v. 29 seem to assume that Benjamin was still very young (see p. 381).

Herodotus (cf. I. 2.41) and other Greeks wondered at the extremely exclusive ritual ideas of purity among the ancient Egyptians. Noble Egyptians at the time of the new kingdom sat for dinner on chairs at small tables. Regarding the particular portion of food, cf. I Sam. 1.5; 9.23. To get drunk on wine occasionally was not considered improper at all; it was part of a festive social gathering. This second meeting with Joseph was therefore quite different from the first one. For the brothers, who of course did not know who Joseph was, it was very enjoyable; for the reader, it almost led to their recognition of Joseph; and for both, the reversal which is now related comes as a severe disappointment.

G. THE FINAL TEST OF THE BROTHERS. CH. 44

44 [1]Then he commanded the steward of his house, "Fill the men's
sacks with food, as much as they can carry, *and put each man's money in the*
mouth of his sack, [2]and put my cup, the silver cup, in the mouth of the
sack of the youngest, *with his money for the grain*." And he did as Joseph

told him. [3]As soon as the morning was light, the men were sent away
with their asses. [4]When they had gone but a short distance from the city,
Joseph said to his steward, "Up, follow after the men; and when you
overtake them, say to them, 'Why have you returned evil for good?
Why have you stolen my silver cup? [5]Is it not from this that my lord
drinks, and by this that he divines? You have done wrong in so doing.' "

6 When he overtook them, he spoke to them these words. [7]They said
to him, "Why does my lord speak such words as these? Far be it from
your servants that they should do such a thing! [8]Behold, the money
which we found in the mouth of our sacks, we brought back to you from
the land of Canaan; how then should we steal silver or gold from your
lord's house? [9]With whomever of your servants it be found, let him die,
and we also will be my lord's slaves." [10]He said, "Let it be as you say:
he with whom it is found shall be my slave, and the rest of you shall be
blameless." [11]Then every man quickly lowered his sack to the ground,
and every man opened his sack. [12]And he searched, beginning with the
eldest and ending with the youngest; and the cup was found in Benjamin's
sack. [13]Then they rent their clothes, and every man loaded his ass, and
they returned to the city.

14 When Judah and his brothers came to Joseph's house, he was
still there; and they fell before him to the ground. [15]Joseph said to them,
"What deed is this that you have done? Do you not know that such a
man as I can indeed divine?" [16]And Judah said, "What shall we say to
my lord? What shall we speak? Or how can we clear ourselves? God has
found out the guilt of your servants; behold, we are my lord's slaves,
both we and he also in whose hand the cup has been found." [17]But he
said, "Far be it from me that I should do so! Only the man in whose
hand the cup was found shall be my slave; but as for you, go up in
peace to your father."

18 Then Judah went up to him and said, "O my lord, let your
servant, I pray you, speak a word in my lord's ears, and let not your
anger burn against your servant; for you are like Pharaoh himself.
[19]My lord asked his servants, saying, 'Have you a father, or a brother?'
[20]And we said to my lord, 'We have a father, an old man, and a young
brother, the child of his old age; and his brother is dead, and he alone is
left of his mother's children; and his father loves him.' [21]Then you said
to your servants, 'Bring him down to me, that I may set my eyes upon him.'
[22]We said to my lord, 'The lad cannot leave his father, for if he should
leave his father, his father would die.' [23]Then you said to your servants,
'Unless your youngest brother comes down with you, you shall see my
face no more.' [24]When we went back to your servant my father we told
him the words of my lord. [25]And when our father said, 'Go again, buy us a
little food,' [26]we said, 'We cannot go down. If our youngest brother goes
with us, then we will go down; for we cannot see the man's face unless
our youngest brother is with us.' [27]Then your servant my father said to
us, 'You know that my wife bore me two sons; [28]one left me, and I said,
Surely he has been torn to pieces; and I have never seen him since. [29]If
you take this one also from me, and harm befalls him, you will bring

down my gray hairs in sorrow to Sheol.' [30]Now therefore, when I come
to your servant my father, and the lad is not with us, then, as his life is
bound up in the lad's life, [31]when he sees that the lad is not with us, he
will die; and your servants will bring down the gray hairs of your
servant our father with sorrow to Sheol. [32]For your servant became
surety for the lad to my father, saying, 'If I do not bring him back to
you, then I shall bear the blame in the sight of my father all my life.'
[33]Now therefore, let your servant, I pray you, remain instead of the lad
as a slave to my lord; and let the lad go back with his brothers. [34]For
how can I go back to my father if the lad is not with me? I fear to see
the evil that would come upon my father."

The text of ch. 44 is the direct continuation of that of ch. 43. The chapter division is only relatively justified in that the scenes contained in this chapter belong closely together and their substance leads to the first climax of the whole Joseph story. Actually, the structure of the narrative in ch. 44 is exactly parallel to that of ch. 43.16 ff. At the beginning the "exciting element" is Joseph's command to the steward (vs. 1–5; cf. ch. 43.16); it is followed by a preparatory scene in which the brothers are busy with the steward (vs. 6–12, cf. ch. 43.17–24). This scene leads powerfully to the brothers' meeting and conversing with Joseph (vs. 15 ff., cf. ch. 43.26–34). The sequence of scenes in ch. 44 is more dramatic than that in ch. 49, and the narrator, again the Yahwist, here ranges much farther.

[1–2] During the night, Joseph gave his instructions to the steward. He is playing an insolent, almost wanton game with the brothers. The reader, of course, knows at this moment much more than the brothers. He knows who the powerful Egyptian vizier is, but what the vizier now has in mind for the brothers is also quite obscure to him. The fact that Joseph again had their money placed in their sacks is considered by some expositors as a somewhat unnecessary subsequent addition. Actually, nothing further is said about it in what follows (cf. v. 11!). While this fact because of its enigmatic character was decisive for the event the first time and troublesome for the brothers, the matter is here dropped by the narrator. Furthermore, the dramatic climax of the event which centers in Benjamin and which is the primary new thing in the story is disturbed by this fact. The words in parentheses in our translation (italics above) are the addition of a later hand who could not believe that Joseph really took the brothers' money this time.

The crime of which Benjamin is now suspected—the theft of a sacred object—is a very serious one. The Old Testament elsewhere shows us how seriously one considered it (cf. ch. 31.30 ff.; Judg. 18.17 ff. For the legal aspect of this matter, cf. D. Daube, *Studies in Biblical Law*, 235–257). Normally the penalty for such a crime was death. The cup (the Hebrew word also means flower cup) was certainly not irreplaceable so far as its intrinsic value was concerned, but it was an object that occasionally served mantic purposes and was therefore particularly sacred. Divining by means of a cup was a widespread practice in antiquity. Many ancient reports make the process rather clear. Small objects were placed in the cup so that one could then see concealed references to the future from the effect that was produced in the liquid. (The German pouring of molten lead into water on New Year's Eve is a final vestige of this custom.) We have here one of those not uncommon cases where our narrator reports something in passing without commenting upon it and without intending the reader to form any serious judgment. He is not to ask here whether what is said in passing about Joseph was theologically permitted, pardonable, or not permitted. It is, of course, not implied that Joseph had completely forsaken the faith of his fathers, though there is no doubt that Joseph had adopted more and more of the customs and habits of the Egyptians. The narrator is not very interested in Joseph's subjective attitude toward religion. One must assume, however, that the Yahwist considered this custom as harmless and as consonant with faith in Yahweh.

[3–17] The events succeed one another within a short time. The brothers set out very early, as was then and is now customary. Scarcely have they left the city before they are overtaken, and when they return to Joseph he is still at home, i.e., he had not gone to the ministry. Their conversation with the steward has a strong legal character; the scene is already that of the tribunal. The brothers refer, to their credit, to their honesty regarding the money in their sacks. Then, in their feeling of innocence before the search, they state the penalty: death for the thief and slavery for the brothers. They proceed, that is, from the notion of collective liability. This statement of the penalty is the rational, secular form of the curse on oneself which in ancient times occurred in such cases (Daube). It is strange and at first not quite understandable that the steward, who represents the interests of the wronged man, greatly limits the penalty by his almost binding answer even before the search. He changes the death penalty for the thief into slavery and he completely rejects slavery for the others. The words "he shall be my slave" is of course to be understood in the sense that the steward is speaking here completely as Joseph's representative.

After the cup has been found in Benjamin's sack, the brothers surrender. The modern reader asks here whether they now really consider themselves subjectively guilty or whether they only find themselves under the ban of a completely enigmatic evil with which they can cope no longer. But to pose these alternatives is to misconstrue the situation as the brothers experienced it. The discovery of the cup speaks so devastatingly against them that in this inescapable fact they see an objective verdict of guilt from God. Ancient Israel did not know our notion of objective right as an absolute norm. Rather, God decides what is right, and he is completely free to adjudge a man righteous or guilty. The brothers, therefore, accept this verdict, which has been passed regarding them, without being able to understand it. That is also apparently Judah's opinion in his speech (v. 16). Besides, Joseph himself had suggested to the brothers this religious interpretation of the event with his reference to his mantic gift, for the *charisma* of seeing the future came from God (cf. ch. 40.8). For the one who himself had started this insolent game to appeal to his divine gift as a seer in the presence of those in despair borders on blasphemy. It is nevertheless an important factor in the whole turn of events which begins here, that Joseph emphatically surrounds himself before his brothers with the mystery of supernatural knowledge. What is here surprising is that Joseph, as his steward previously had done, rejects the proposal of the collective liability of all the brothers. That the brothers themselves no longer demand the death penalty for the thief (cf. v. 9) is understandable enough after the positive circumstantial evidence. But what is behind Joseph's strict refusal in v. 17? Here is the most important part of the test which Joseph made his brothers endure: he wants to isolate them from Benjamin; he wants to prove them, to learn whether they will seize the opportunity to go free without Benjamin. Now they could again return to their father and announce to him the loss of a son; they could even justify themselves, for so far as they knew Benjamin alone was actually guilty and the balance of power was completely unfavorable to them. Joseph's test, therefore, was that he constructed a situation in which it had to become evident whether they would again act as they once had done or whether they had changed in the meantime.

[18–34] At this climax of the dramatic event, when the tension has reached its limits, Judah utters a speech into which he pours everything that could perhaps still alter the misery which has befallen the brothers and Jacob. It is one of the most beautiful examples of that lofty rhetorical culture which was in full blossom at the time of our narrator, i.e., in the early days of the kingdom. Doubtless this speech is to be evaluated for itself by the reader as a little work of art. A modern reader could be surprised that the narrator here inserts a long speech which in fact presents nothing at all new and whose powerful effect stems from the fact and the way that all these things are now expressed. Judah has stepped before Joseph. That was a liberty in this situation which could have been easily misunderstood. But his speech, restrained and at the same time pervaded by inner emotion (Jac.), is courtly in style and avoids anything defiant. Characteristic of that is the way Judah interprets the demand to bring Benjamin, which had caused the brothers and the father so much hardship, as a kindness on Joseph's part. The expression "to set one's eyes upon someone" derives from language of the court and means "to show someone favor" (Jer. 39.12; 40.4). Again, other matters, which were not now in order, remain unexpressed.

The speech has essentially two parts, a detailed review and the actual proposal. The first part is, of course, to justify from every angle the request which Judah directs to Joseph in the second. This request is simple and not unreasonable: Judah requests that he, instead of Benjamin, be allowed to bear the punishment of slavery, because he finds it absolutely impossible, after what has happened previously between himself and his father, to go back without Benjamin. Toward the end the speech becomes very urgent in describing the father's sorrow, and on the whole it strongly emphasizes the emotional aspect of the situation. Judah, of course, could not suspect how monstrous and almost unbearable would be the effect of this speech on Joseph. It is his brother, before whom he appeals on behalf of his father and wrestles for the sake of a brother (Jac.). And again, the way the shadow of Joseph, who no longer lives but is present, lies across the speech and is revealed more and more as the really troubling factor, is particularly moving. Because Joseph is gone, Jacob does not want to let Benjamin go; because Joseph is gone, the loss of the second favorite son would inevitably destroy the father. Again and again the thought returns to this one dark point (vs. 20, 28). Indeed, the statement "God has found out the guilt of your servants" doubtless has a double meaning intended by the narrator. It seems at first to refer only to the matter of the cup, but it is much more true of that guilt of which the brothers were really guilty. Judah's words have considerable significance in the structure of the Joseph story, as they show how the brothers have changed in their relationship to each other and above all in their relationship to their father. Judah now sees the danger completely from his father's viewpoint and is ready even to surrender his own life in order to protect that of Benjamin. It is now clear that the brothers have passed the great test which Joseph set them.

Step by step the narrator has described Joseph's rise from the depths to the splendor of the heights; no characteristic in this picture is superfluous, everything is closely interlocked. Now, after this skillful preparation, he brings the tension of all motives to its climax. One is astonished at the transparence of the plan for his narrative which now arrives at its denouement. With very few persons a tragic situation of great beauty is unfolded. After the steward has done his work, only Joseph, in terrifying power, and Judah, in purified devotion which compels him to speak, stand over against each other. But the picture is enlivened by the silent Benjamin, who stands by as an innocent victim of an unknown fate, and by the prospect of the grief of the old father, who is in danger of losing two sons of the wife of his youthful love. One can conceive of no scene simpler and more powerful (Pr.).

The confusion has reached its limit and the next moment must bring things to a head. Charmed, one's gaze is fixed on the speaker's lips and is only torn away to wander to the powerful man opposite, to read what is on his face. We know the outcome and still tremble—so great art knows how to make one forget! (Jac.)

H. THE RECOGNITION. CH. 45

45 1 Then Joseph could not control himself before all those who stood
by him; and he cried, "Make every one go out from me." So no one
stayed with him when Joseph made himself known to his brothers.
2 And he wept aloud, so that the Egyptians heard it, and the household
of Pharaoh heard it. 3 And Joseph said to his brothers, "I am Joseph; is
my father still alive?" But his brothers could not answer him, for they
were dismayed at his presence.
4 So Joseph said to his brothers, "Come near to me, I pray you."
And they came near. And he said, "I am your brother, Joseph, whom
you sold into Egypt. 5 And now do not be distressed, or angry with yourselves,
because you sold me here; for God sent me before you to preserve
life. 6 For the famine has been in the land these two years; and there are
yet five years in which there will be neither plowing nor harvest. 7 And
God sent me before you to preserve for you a remnant on earth, and to
keep alive for you many survivors. 8 So it was not you who sent me here,
but God; and he has made me a father to Pharaoh, and lord of all his

house and ruler over all the land of Egypt. [9]Make haste and go up to
my father and say to him, 'Thus says your son Joseph, God has made me
lord of all Egypt; come down to me, do not tarry; [10]you shall dwell in
the land of Goshen, and you shall be near me, you and your children
and your children's children, and your flocks, your herds, and all that you
have; [11]and there I will provide for you, for there are yet five years of
famine to come; lest you and your household, and all that you have,
come to poverty.' [12]And now your eyes see, and the eyes of my brother
Benjamin see, that it is my mouth that speaks to you. [13]You must tell my
father of all my splendor in Egypt, and of all that you have seen. Make
haste and bring my father down here." [14]Then he fell upon his brother
Benjamin's neck and wept; and Benjamin wept upon his neck. [15]And he
kissed all his brothers and wept upon them; and after that his brothers
talked with him.

16 When the report was heard in Pharaoh's house, "Joseph's brothers
have come," it pleased Pharaoh and his servants well. [17]And Pharaoh
said to Joseph, "Say to your brothers, 'Do this: load your beasts and go
back to the land of Canaan; [18]and take your father and your households, and come to me, and I will give you the best of the land of Egypt,
and you shall eat the fat of the land.' [19]Command them also, 'Do this:
take wagons from the land of Egypt for your little ones and for your
wives, and bring your father, and come. [20]Give no thought to your
goods, for the best of all the land of Egypt is yours.' "

21 The sons of Israel did so; and Joseph gave them wagons, according to the command of Pharaoh, and gave them provisions for the
journey. [22]To each and all of them he gave festal garments; but to
Benjamin he gave three hundred shekels of silver and five festal garments. [23]To his father he sent as follows: ten asses loaded with the good
things of Egypt, and ten she-asses loaded with grain, bread, and provision for his father on the journey. [24]Then he sent his brothers away,
and as they departed, he said to them, "Do not quarrel on the way."
[25]So they went up out of Egypt, and came to the land of Canaan to
their father Jacob. [26]And they told him, "Joseph is still alive, and he is
ruler over all the land of Egypt." And his heart fainted, for he did not
believe them. [27]But when they told him all the words of Joseph, which
he had said to them, and when he saw the wagons which Joseph had
sent to carry him, the spirit of their father Jacob revived; [28]And Israel
said, "It is enough; Joseph my son is still alive; I will go and see him
before I die."

The material contained in this chapter includes the scene of recognition, vs. 1–15; then a message from Pharaoh to the brothers, vs. 16–20; finally their return home and Jacob's notification, vs. 21–28. Even though the uncritical reader is accustomed to consider this text a unit, and even though certain doublets in the scene of recognition scarcely detract from the inner credibility of the story but rather increase it, still there can be no doubt that the text is not so smooth as that of ch. 44, but reveals obvious traces of a combination of sources. Joseph's revelation of himself twice to his brothers, namely, in vs. 3a and 5, is one of those doublets which one feels in the course of the narrative to be more of a psychological vivification, that is, an enrichment. Nevertheless the original texts of J and E were certainly simpler in this respect. One is accustomed to divide the text in such a way that vs. 1, 4, 5a are considered the Yahwistic scene of recognition and vs. 2, 3, 5b the Elohistic. The difference with respect to the summons to Jacob to emigrate is more serious. In vs. 9 ff. Joseph has his father summoned at once to Egypt. In vs. 16 ff. the same thing is told as a gracious offer from Pharaoh which he made later to Joseph after he had learned of the events in Joseph's family. It is possible, if need be, for one to understand the juxtaposition even though Pharaoh's offer really should have preceded Joseph's; but the continuation in chs. 46.31 to 47.5 shows that later Pharaoh must first be informed about the arrival of Joseph's relatives and that only then does he grant them permission to stay. The interlocking of the sources here, therefore, is rather complicated. Similarly, Joseph's summons to settle in Goshen (v. 9) clashes with Pharaoh's offer in vs. 18 and 20, for the latter offers the father and brothers any place in Egypt for settlement. Finally there seems to be a disorder respecting the means of transportation: v. 17 their own asses, v. 23 asses given by Joseph, vs. 19, 27 wagons. Verses 19–21 have therefore often been considered a later addition.

[1–7] Judah's speech in every respect brings the climax to the suspense, both with regard to the brothers' despair and to Joseph's inner emotion. Judah's description of the domestic proceedings, the picture of the father eaten by worries, and not least the gloom of seeing his own shadow troubling the whole family—all of this agitated Joseph profoundly. He reaches the limits of his capacity, he can no longer "control himself." But this seething of his emotion coincides precisely with the inner end of the test of the brothers, for Judah's words had shown that the brothers had changed. They obviously intend to treat Rachel's younger son, Benjamin, quite differently from the way in which they had formerly treated the elder son. The text of this wonderful scene scarcely requires the interpretative help of an expositor. The reader simply must remember that he has to do with a narrator who also takes pains with respect to inner emotional agitation which is extremely realistic psychologically. Twice, in vs. 3 f. and in vs. 26 f., he lets us experience the transition from the first dumbfounded astonishment to the slow, unbelievable realization ("and his heart fainted, for he did not believe them," v. 26). Joseph had all strangers leave the room, not primarily because he did not want to show himself before his retinue in such an emotional state, and not primarily so as not to embarrass his brothers before the Egyptians, but rather because something had to be done which concerned only him and his brothers for which they had to be quite alone. Joseph's conversation with his brothers shows, however, that this whole art of psychological representation is not an end in itself for the narrative. It belongs, of course, inseparably to the essence of this perfected style of narration, but the real concern of the whole narrative is by no means that of a complete, psychological, genuine experience. Here in the scene of recognition the narrator indicates clearly for the first time what is of paramount importance to him in the entire Joseph story: God's hand which directs all the confusion of human guilt ultimately toward a gracious goal. After so much has been said exclusively about men's actions, it is surprising for Joseph in two statements to mention God as the real subject of the whole occurrence; God, not the brothers, "sent" Joseph here. Joseph veils the actual event with this alleviating expression. But it would be wrong to see only distracting friendliness in Joseph's remarks; rather, Joseph wants to state an objective truth, in which, to be sure, the enigma mentioned above, the question of how this activity of God is related to the brothers' drastically described activity, remains an absolutely unsolved mystery. The matter must rest with the fact that ultimately it was not the brothers' hate but God who brought Joseph to Egypt and moreover "to preserve life." This sober statement, which is in no way a statement of the language of religion or a theological concept, corresponds completely to the secular style of our narrator. Still it is not possible to overlook the great theological and programmatic significance of these statements, for through this guidance that family was preserved which was the heir of the promise to the fathers (cf. ch. 50.24). The terms "remnant" (*š^{e}'ērīt*) and "survivor" (*p^{e}lēṭā*) in v. 7 allude to that motif of rescue which is so thematically important for the entire narrative composition of Genesis. The story of the Flood contains it: Noah is rescued from the universal catastrophe by divine providence and made the father of a new humanity. One must also think of Abraham's departure from his family confederation, his calling and blessing, as they contrast with the gloomy background of God's judgment on the nations (ch. 11.1 ff.). Above all, Lot's gracious rescue from

Sodom reveals this saving activity of God. Here again, Joseph interprets the confused event in this comprehensive sense as the mysterious realization of a divine act of rescue, for, as often in the Old Testament, "remnant" is a word of hope. In the remnant the whole group survives to new life. This idea of the remnant is different from the prophet Isaiah's idea (Isa. 6.13; 7.3; 10.20 f.; 14.32), for there it concerns the preservation of a remnant of God's people, but here the deliverance of the bearer of the promise from a universal catastrophe. This reference to the mystery of divine guidance is for Joseph combined with the fear that his sudden unveiling will be too much for the brothers, that they can be plunged into new conflicts by it. He knows about the passions which can burst into flame in new form (v. 24). But neither are they to be distressed (v. 5), for by God's guidance everything appears in a completely new light.

[8–28] The wonderfulness of this guidance confronts the brothers and the father first of all quite externally in Joseph's high position. Therefore Joseph unfolds in v. 8 the various functions of his office. "Father," here as in Isa. 22.21, is the title of a high court official. The vizier Ptahhotep, ca. 2350 B.C., was called among other names "Father of God," i.e., of the divine Pharaoh. "Lord of all his house" refers to his office as lord chamberlain, and as vizier he is "ruler over all the land of Egypt," who is authorized externally to the actual execution and carrying through of the royal dominion. The brothers are to take home the report of this position of honor. Benjamin especially is to be impressed, because he will have to confirm their report to their father. His testimony is still less suspicious than that of the half brothers. Regarding the two parallel summons to emigrate to Egypt and the assurances of sustenance for Jacob, once from Joseph, vs. 9–11, and then from Pharaoh, vs. 17–20, see p. 392. Verse 9 contains a good example of a runner's message.

The land of Goshen is identified with the modern Wâdī Tumilât, a narrow flat depression that transverses the strip of land between Port Said and Suez in an east-west direction.* Since, according to v. 10, Goshen was not far from the residence, the question arises here as to which of the lower Egyptian cities our narrator is thinking about. This question was important to many expositors because they

*An Egyptian source (Papyrus Anastasi VI, 4, 14) reports a similar proceeding. About 1220 the Pharaoh Merneptah permitted Edomite Bedouins to settle in the land Goshen "to keep themselves and their flocks alive in the territory of the king."

thought that by it they could arrive at a chronological incorporation of the Joseph story into the political history of Egypt; for in new kingdom Egypt the Pharaohs did not generally reside in Lower Egypt. The fact, however, that neither the Pharaoh nor his city of residence is named makes the whole story, in spite of its vividness, somewhat remote. It places it at the distance of the typical, at which the short story loves to keep things historical and geographical, and which would be unthinkable in an actual historical narrative or writing.

The gifts with which the men are laden as they return home are mentioned in detail. The specific meaning of the Hebrew word for "clothes" (*ḥ*^{a}*līpōt*) is not clear. Perhaps it concerns one of those words for style, the meaning of which tended to be lost very quickly. In Akkadian a noun of the same root means "garment." The silver coins must be thought of as pieces cut off a bar of coin, they were not stamped but weighed. The wagons were two-wheeled carts but still covered wagons for freight and men (cf. Num. 7.3). Thus the reader sees the brothers depart in pleasure with their wagons and many asses heavily laden and sees them bring the message to their father. There the brothers' confession must also have been made. Perhaps the narrator omitted it because in his view the guilty deed had been overtaken by the divine saving act and its consequences had come to an end (see p. 437 below).

I. JACOB'S REMOVAL TO EGYPT. CH. 46

46 1So Israel took his journey with all that he had, and came to
Beer-sheba, and offered sacrifices to the God of his father Isaac. 2And
God spoke to Israel in visions of the night, and said, "Jacob, Jacob."
And he said, "Here am I." 3Then he said, "I am God, the God of
your father; do not be afraid to go down to Egypt; for I will there
make of you a great nation. 4I will go down with you to Egypt, and I
will also bring you up again; and Joseph's hand shall close your eyes."
5Then Jacob set out from Beer-sheba; and the sons of Israel carried
Jacob their father, their little ones, and their wives, in the wagons which
Pharaoh had sent to carry him. 6*They also took their cattle and their goods,*
which they had gained in the land of Canaan, and came into Egypt, Jacob and all
his offspring with him, 7*his sons, and his sons' sons with him, his daughters, and*
his sons' daughters; all his offspring he brought with him into Egypt.

8 *Now these are the names of the descendants of Israel, who came into Egypt,*
Jacob and his sons. Reuben, Jacob's first-born, 9*and the sons of Reuben: Hanoch,*
Pallu, Hezron, and Carmi. 10*The sons of Simeon: Jemuel, Jamin, Ohad,*
Jachin, Zohar, and Shaul, the son of a Canaanitish woman. 11*The sons of Levi:*
Gershon, Kohath, and Merari. 12*The sons of Judah: Er, Onan, Shelah, Perez,*
and Zerah (but Er and Onan died in the land of Canaan); and the sons of Perez

were Hezron and Hamul. [13]The sons of Issachar: Tola, Puvah, Iob, and Shimron. [14]The sons of Zebulun: Sered, Elon, and Jahleel [15](these are the sons of Leah, whom she bore to Jacob in Paddan-aram, together with his daughter Dinah; altogether his sons and his daughters numbered thirty-three). [16]The sons of Gad: Ziphion, Haggi, Shuni, Ezbon, Eri, Arodi, and Areli. [17]The sons of Asher :Imnah, Ishvah, Ishvi, Beriah, with Serah their sister. And the sons of Beriah: Heber and Malchiel [18](these are the sons of Zilpah, whom Laban gave to Leah his daughter; and these she bore to Jacob—sixteen persons). [19]The sons of Rachel, Jacob's wife: Joseph and Benjamin. [20]And to Joseph in the land of Egypt were born Manasseh and Ephraim, whom Asenath, the daughter of Potiphera the priest of On, bore to him. [21]And the sons of Benjamin: Bela, Becher, Ashbel, Gera, Naaman, Ehi, Rosh, Muppim, Huppim, and Ard [22](these are the sons of Rachel, who were born to Jacob—fourteen persons in all). [23]The sons of Dan: Hushim. [24]The sons of Naphtali: Jahzeel, Guni, Jezer, and Shillem [25](these are the sons of Bilhah, whom Laban gave to Rachel his daughter, and these she bore to Jacob—seven persons in all). [26]All the persons belonging to Jacob who came into Egypt, who were his own offspring, not including Jacob's sons' wives, were sixty-six persons in all; [27]and the sons of Joseph, who were born to him in Egypt, were two; all the persons of the house of Jacob, that came into Egypt, were seventy.

28 He sent Judah before him to Joseph, to appear before him in Goshen; and they came into the land of Goshen. [29]Then Joseph made ready his chariot and went up to meet Israel his father in Goshen; and he presented himself to him, and fell on his neck, and wept on his neck a good while. [30]Israel said to Joseph, "Now let me die, since I have seen your face and know that you are still alive." [31]Joseph said to his brothers and to his father's household, "I will go up and tell Pharaoh, and will say to him, 'My brothers and my father's household, who were in the land of Canaan, have come to me; [32]and the men are shepherds, for they have been keepers of cattle; and they have brought their flocks, and their herds, and all that they have.' [33]When Pharaoh calls you, and says, 'What is your occupation?' [34]you shall say, 'Your servants have been keepers of cattle from our youth even until now, both we and our fathers,' in order that you may dwell in the land of Goshen; for every shepherd is an abomination to the Egyptians."

The textual unity of this section also is uneven. The non-Priestly narrative thread of vs. 1–5 continues, to be sure, in v. 28 and again in ch. 47. But it too is obviously not unified, especially at the beginning; for Jacob, who according to chs. 45.28; 46.1a decided at Hebron to set out for Egypt, receives instruction to follow the summons to Egypt without hesitation only in vs. 1b–5. That is to be explained from the fact that according to the Yahwistic representation Jacob made his decision at Hebron, according to the Elohistic he was encouraged by God himself to leave Beer-sheba, and that both conceptions are now combined in chs. 45.28 to 46.5. The section vs. 6–27 is Priestly tradition, but the long list which now gives it the preponderance of text is clearly itself a subsequent compilation.

[1–5] The dwelling place from which Jacob departed, according to chs. 45.28; 46.1, is Hebron, according to ch. 37.14. The Elohistic version does not explain the departure as occurring on Jacob's initiative. In this momentous matter it does not permit human impulse to decide, but rather divine instruction. The land was promised to Abraham and Isaac; might Jacob leave it? This source is concerned to show that this step, which was decisive for the subsequent history of the growing nation of Israel, did not proceed from human arbitrariness, even the most humanly comprehensible, but that God here directed the steps of Israel's ancestors by a command. Thus this narrator strongly emphasizes here the theme of overarching sacred history. He makes Jacob at the moment of his departure turn back to a certain extent and enter once more into the cult of his father Isaac. Beer-sheba had been Isaac's dwelling place and there the traditions about Isaac were centered (see p. 271). Accordingly, the style of God's self-revelation in vs. 2 f. corresponds completely to that cult of the God of the patriarchs, that cult which was connected with the family and the locale, which was the real religion of Israel's pre-Mosaic ancestors (see p. 188). The promise to bring Jacob back to Canaan scarcely refers to the return of his corpse, which is reported in ch. 50.4 ff., but rather to his return in his descendants. Ancient Israel considered the ancestors and the nation as connected closely with each other, in fact, it considered them both as a great living organism with a common destiny. That was one of the reasons Israel with relative tranquillity could dispense for so long with the hope of a personal life after death.

[6–27] In the older narrative, vs. 28 ff. followed v. 5 without a break, but the redactor has here cleverly inserted the Priestly report of Jacob's emigration to Egypt. The great rupture in the continuity of the narrative occurred only after the incorporation of the long list in vs. 8–27. One can see that it is a subsequent appendage from the minor inconsistency that v. 7 mentions daughters and granddaughters while the list itself mentions only one daughter and one granddaughter. And is one to suppose that P in Ex. 1.1–5 would have given so simple and summary a note about the number of Israel's sons in Egypt if so detailed a list had immediately preceded? Finally, it can be shown that our list has been made useful at its present place by means of a revision of its special purpose. Formerly it was a list of all the male descendants of Jacob, in which Er and Onan (cf. ch. 38.1 ff.) were included and Jacob and Dinah were excluded (33 sons of Leah, 16 sons of Rachel, 14 sons of Zilpah, and 7 sons of Bilhah = 70). Since, however, the list here is to report the family status at the time of Jacob's departure, Joseph and his sons Ephraim and Manasseh have to be left out, likewise Er and Onan who were at that time already dead. Dinah was included and that gave the total 66 (v. 26). The list arrives at the number 70 by reckoning Joseph, his two sons, and Jacob to the total (but cf. Ex. 1.5). The number 70 was prescribed for this computation; it was a fixed tradition, as Deut. 10.22 shows, and therefore had to be obtained in some manner. Originally this number was intended, of course, as a round figure, as an approximate, large number of men (cf. Ex. 24.9; Num. 11.16; Judg. 8.30). But our list pedantically considers it an exact figure. For Benjamin already to be the father of ten sons here does not fit into the narrative at all.

In distinction from the list in Num. 26.5 ff., for example, which must be considered a historically accurate statement of the generations from the period before the formation of the state, our list has to be thought of as the work of very late and theoretical erudition. It is the product of erudite occupation with ancient traditions and belongs, therefore, to a theological, Priestly literature of which there is much in the Old Testament (cf. Num., ch. 7), but the actual life and real purpose of which is only recognizable with difficulty behind the hard, dry shell with which it is covered.

[28–30] One sees how coarsely the list of vs. 8–27 broke the thread of the narrative when in v. 28 one must go back to the statements about Jacob in vs. 1–7 to find the reference of the verb with its indefinite subject "He sent . . . before him." Judah had been singled out elsewhere in the Yahwistic narrative as the brothers' spokesman (cf. chs. 43.3 ff.; 44.18 ff.). But what was the purpose in sending Judah? The Hebrew text says "to show the way before him in Goshen" (*l*^{e}*hōrōt*). It has long been suspected that the text is here corrupt, the more so since the LXX has a different verb, namely, "to appear before him" (*l·hiqqārōt*). To be sure, the LXX translation is made suspicious by the addition of the place name "at ʽΗρώων πόλιν."

The meeting between Joseph, believed dead twenty-two years, surrounded by a great retinue, and the father should move the reader profoundly. The expression that Joseph "appeared" to his father is also unusual, for it has been used by the same narrator hitherto only for God's appearing, for example, chs. 12.7; 18.1; etc. But the narrator does not intend this scene, as a modern reader might like, to be the climax to the whole story. The climax lies rather in ch. 50.20. The translation of v. 29b "and wept on his neck a good while" is only approximate. The construction of the Hebrew sentence cannot be literally reproduced; cf. Ruth 1.14. (Compare v. 30 with Luke 2.29 f.)

[31–34] The new situation now requires quite practical considerations. Above all, where will Jacob and his sons, his numerous servants, and his flocks settle? That depends on Pharaoh's decision, and therefore Joseph prepares his family for the unavoidable audience. If one reads vs. 31–34 impartially, one gets the impression that the Pharaoh is here (in contrast to ch. 45.16 ff.) to be informed for the first time about the coming of Joseph's relatives. The way in which Joseph prepares Pharaoh for this audience is a little masterpiece of court diplomacy, which dares, circumstances permitting, to exercise slight pressure on the Pharaoh's decision. Doubtless Joseph's apparently objective announcement contains a certain constraint. He would like to see to it that his relatives can settle in Goshen. But strangers from Palestine were always suspect to the Egyptians, and therefore they were scarcely inclined to settle those of whom they were suspicious in a border province where they would be difficult to supervise and could do harm. On the other hand, it was even less possible that the Pharaoh would arrange for their settlement anywhere in the center of the country, for "every shepherd is an abomination to the Egyptians." This sharp conception of the narrator cannot be substantiated from Egyptian sources. It is sufficient that he assumes this hindrance to exist and it is an important factor in Joseph's calculation. Joseph does not intend to express to the Pharaoh his desire that his relatives be settled in Goshen, but by strongly emphasizing the fact that his relatives are shepherds and instructing his brothers not to conceal their profession, he indicates that he knows in advance what Pharaoh's decision will be; and things actually turn out as the experienced minister had forseen.

K. JACOB BEFORE PHARAOH. JOSEPH'S AGRARIAN POLICY. CH. 47.1–27

47 [1]So Joseph went in and told Pharaoh, "My father and my
brothers, with their flocks and herds and all that they possess, have
come from the land of Canaan; they are now in the land of Goshen."
[2]And from among his brothers he took five men and presented them to
Pharaoh. [3]Pharaoh said to his brothers, "What is your occupation?"

And they said to Pharaoh, "Your servants are shepherds, as our fathers
were." [4]They said to Pharaoh, "We have come to sojourn in the land;
for there is no pasture for your servants' flocks, for the famine is severe
in the land of Canaan; and now, we pray you, let your servants dwell
in the land of Goshen." [5]Then Pharaoh said to Joseph, "*Your father and*
your brothers have come to you. [6]*The land of Egypt is before you; settle your*
father and your brothers in the best of the land; let them dwell in the land of
Goshen; and if you know any able men among them put them in charge of my
cattle."

7 *Then Joseph brought in Jacob his father, and set him before Pharaoh, and*
Jacob blessed Pharaoh. [8]*And Pharaoh said to Jacob, "How many are the days of*
the years of your life?" [9]*And Jacob said to Pharaoh, "The days of the years of my*
sojourning are a hundred and thirty years; few and evil have been the days of the
years of my life, and they have not attained to the days of the years of the life of my
fathers in the days of their sojourning." [10]*And Jacob blessed Pharaoh, and went*
out from the presence of Pharaoh. [11]*Then Joseph settled his father and his*
brothers, and gave them a possession in the land of Egypt, in the best of the land, in
the land of Rameses, as Pharaoh had commanded. [12]And Joseph provided his
father, his brothers, and all his father's household with food, according
to the number of their dependents.

13 Now there was no food in all the land; for the famine was very
severe, so that the land of Egypt and the land of Canaan languished by
reason of the famine. [14]And Joseph gathered up all the money that was
found in the land of Egypt and in the land of Canaan, for the grain
which they bought; and Joseph brought the money into Pharaoh's
house. [15]And when the money was all spent in the land of Egypt and in
the land of Canaan, all the Egyptians came to Joseph, and said, "Give
us food; why should we die before your eyes? For our money is gone."
[16]And Joseph answered, "Give your cattle, and I will give you food in
exchange for your cattle, if your money is gone." [17]So they brought
their flocks to Joseph and Joseph gave them bread for the horses and
for the flocks and for the herd, and for the asses; and he supplied them
this year with bread for all their flocks. [18]And when that year was
ended, they came to him the following year, and said to him, "We
will not hide from my lord that our money is all spent; and the herds of
cattle are my lord's; there is nothing left in the sight of my lord but our
bodies and our lands. [19]Why should we die before your eyes, both we
and our land? Buy us and our land for food, and we with our land will
be slaves to Pharaoh; and give us seed, that we may live, and not die,
and that the land may not be desolate."

20 So Joseph bought all the land of Egypt for Pharaoh; for all the
Egyptians sold their fields, because the famine was severe upon them.
The land became Pharaoh's; [21]and as for the people he made slaves of
them from one end of Egypt to the other. [22]Only the land of the priests
he did not buy; for the priests had a fixed allowance from Pharaoh, and

*Von Rad translates Gen. 47.17, "So they brought their flocks to Joseph and Joseph gave them bread for the horses and for the flocks and for the herd, and for the asses; and he led them this year with bread for all their flocks." But cf. p. 404.

lived on the allowance which Pharaoh gave them; therefore they did not sell their land. [23]Then Joseph said to the people, "Behold, I have this day bought you and your land for Pharaoh. Now here is seed for you, and you shall sow the land. [24]And at the harvests you shall give a fifth to Pharaoh, and four fifths shall be your own, as seed for the field and as food for yourselves and your households, and as food for your little ones." [25]And they said, "You have saved our lives; may it please my lord, we will be slaves to Pharaoh." [26]So Joseph made it a statute concerning the land of Egypt, and it stands to this day, that Pharaoh should have the fifth; the land of the priests alone did not become Pharaoh's.

27 Thus Israel dwelt in the land of Egypt, in the land of Goshen; *and they gained possessions in it, and were fruitful and multiplied exceedingly.*

The chapter division here breaks a continuous text. Verses 1–6 are the direct continuation of what has preceded. In vs. 5–6 the sequence of statements must be transposed according to the LXX and completed by a statement which has disappeared in the MT. This statement which is preserved by the Greek translation stands at the beginning of the parallel Priestly report of Jacob's removal to Egypt and introduces the description of the audience in vs. 7–11, which this source also tells. Apparently the harmonizing revision of this Priestly section to conform with the older representation was not yet firmly established at this point in the MT at a relatively late period. Regarding the literary problem of the section in vs. 13–26 see the exposition.

[1–12] The audience, prepared far ahead of time by the experienced court official, goes off according to plan. Joseph speaks first; he introduces the strangers to Pharaoh. Pharaoh then opens the conversation, as is proper at court, with the most universal of all royal questions, namely, the one about vocation and walk of life. From there the conversation turns quickly to the desired point. The word "Goshen" is spoken, but only in Joseph's mention of Goshen as the momentary abode of his relatives. The brothers admit in answer to Pharaoh's question that they are shepherds and request permission to settle in Goshen. Their speech ends with the same decisive word as Joseph's did (Jac.). It is a subtlety of the story that the Pharaoh not only grants their request but also leaves it to his minister to enroll the brothers as officials. If they are suited to it, they can be placed in charge of the flocks on the royal domains. This is again evidence for the unlimited favor which the once despised brother now enjoys with the Pharaoh.

The following non-Masoretic statement is preserved in the LXX:

"Jacob and his sons came to Joseph in Egypt, and when Pharaoh, the king of Egypt, heard about it he spoke to Joseph." If one follows the LXX and lets v. 5b and then v. 6a follow this statement, it becomes completely clear that the resulting text was originally a narrative parallel to vs. 1–4, 5a, 6b. Common to both is the audience with Pharaoh and the permission to the new arrivals to live in the land. But while there Pharaoh spoke with the brothers, here Jacob is the partner to the conversation. The allotted land, which there was Goshen, is here called the "land of Rameses"; what is meant is obviously here as there the same strip of land, the Wâdī Tumilât. The land of Rameses certainly derived its name from the city of Rameses mentioned in Ex. 1.11, and this was named for the Pharaoh, Rameses II (1290–1223 B.C.). The mention of the name is thus an anachronism. For the historical background, see "Epilogue to the Joseph Story," p. 433.

What is here surprising, however, is the unbelievable success of the audience, which goes far beyond our expectations: Joseph could settle the new arrivals "in the best of the land." The older narrative was here much closer to reality. It was concerned with permission to settle in the grazing land of a border province, and the permission was received as a great favor from the Pharaoh. It is evident that the report about the audience in vs. 5–12 stems from the source P both from the usage and the content of the conversation. In this conversation, which consists merely of a question and answer, the stiff and solemn style of the Priestly document has created a scene of extreme beauty: the patriarch before the king! The Pharaoh, obviously impressed by the outward appearance of the 130-year-old man, asks the old man his age. It is possible that this question was a rejoinder to the wish for long life with which one was accustomed to greet kings in the ancient Orient; cf. II Sam. 16.16; I Kings 1.31; Dan. 2.4; 5.10; 6.6 (Jac.). But Jacob demurs. In his answer he does not speak of age, as the Pharaoh had asked, but instead, of the years of his sojourning, thereby diverting attention from the number to the content of his years. But his complaint may not be understood from the viewpoint of the modern conflict between insatiable will to live and disillusion. Jacob does not here express universal resignation, but he makes rather a factually sober statement. Sojourning was indeed the characteristic of the entire road of life which God had pointed out to the patriarchs. Sojourning meant renunciation of settlement and land ownership; according to the theology of the Priestly document it meant a life which was oriented toward future fulfillment, namely, toward the promise of land which was often renewed to the patriarchs. Thus the patriarchs had lived in Canaan in a curiously ambiguous relationship to promise and fulfillment in the "land of their sojourning" (see p. 249). What Jacob means in his answer to Pharaoh's question is this: the circumstances of this life of sojourning became much more unfavorable in his generation. In comparison with his father's his life has been briefer and more difficult. He does not indicate the reason for this; obviously this narrator shares the idea of a continual worsening of the external conditions of life. Abraham lived 175 years; Isaac, 180 (chs. 25.7; 35.28). The shortening of the life span goes hand in hand with an inner complication and also an increase in the power of evil (cf. p. 69). It may also be observed that Daniel's vision of the image representing the kingdoms with metals whose value decreases, i.e., with its descending course of historical epochs (Dan. 2.31 f.) was probably contemporaneous with the early postexilic, final form of the Priestly document; it may be further observed that the periodization of the Priestly narrative into the primeval period, the Noahic age, patriarchal period, age of Moses, shows a certain kinship with that apocalyptic picture of history. Verse 12 is rather clumsy as to content. Perhaps the Priestly report of the audience and the settlement was concluded in v. 11, and v. 12 is still part of an older source. It is certain, however, that the Priestly narrative continues in vs. 27b–28, which already prepare for the subsequent events of the oppression.

[13–26] The question to which source the section vs. 13–26 belongs is disputed. It is usually attributed to the Yahwist, but one cannot be really sure about it. A certain stylistic stiffness and some awkward places raise objections to this assumption, although the explanation could be that the content is hard to describe. The real difficulty, however, is that this report about Joseph's administrative measures would at its present position disturb the structure of each of the three documents. It takes us back, as Wellhausen long ago pointed out, to the events narrated in ch. 41. Did the section really come after ch. 41 originally as its continuation (Di.)? And are verses 41.55 f. actually to be thought of as the exposition of this section (Gu.)? Or do we have to do rather with a subsequently added growth, i.e., with the elaboration of a culturally interesting detail? In any case, the reader now loses sight of everything that has previously occupied his attention: Joseph's relationship to his brothers, to Jacob, the question of their stay in Egypt, etc.

Verse 13 is the simple exposition for the narrative which now begins, the famine that burdened Egypt and Canaan and the exhaustion of the land. In the event that now unfolds, the narrator's interest is fixed rather exclusively on Joseph and his activity. His partner, the hungering and despairing people, is rather anonymously colorless and becomes concrete for the reader only in so far as it was necessary to clarify a new phase of Joseph's activity against this background. Indeed, the narrative is unmistakably schematic so far as these varied acts of Joseph are concerned. Joseph's diverse economic measures are sharply distinguished from one another; nothing overlaps. They each concern summarily the whole country and follow one another by stages and distinctly. In this respect the narrative betrays clearly a theoretical interest.

First phase: The people buy the grain, which Joseph has stored, with money. With this statement we find ourselves in accord with what was told in ch. 41.56. The first complication occurred when the people's reserves of money were exhausted and the hungering masses besieged Joseph.

Second phase: Joseph gives the people breadstuffs and takes their cattle in payment. This raises questions which cannot be answered directly from the rather schematic narrative. Does the narrator really think that the farmers handed over all their flocks, etc.? And what did Joseph do then with the innumerable flocks, which were uneconomically assembled at one place? This difficulty would disappear if we could assume that the farmers' "living inventory" was not handed over but assigned to Joseph as security, and so legally passed over into the possession of the Pharaoh but was used by the people (Jac.). But v. 17a, "so they brought their cattle," does not support this notion. The expression that Joseph "led the people with bread" (v. 17b) is very curious. The verb is usually used only for the leading of flocks. What it means, therefore, unless the text contains an ancient error, is that he carefully brought the hungering masses through.

Third phase: The famine continues and a serious crisis arises. The people come to Joseph to obtain bread, but they have no more movable possessions. This time the farmers themselves make the proposal: they will sell themselves and their land to the Pharaoh in order to obtain in exchange breadstuffs and seed corn. The mention of seed corn can be interpreted to mean that some tillage was continually attempted even in those years of famine. Or it can be understood to mean that the end of the period of need seems near and that the problem was thus raised for the farmers of how, when they were completely impoverished, they could begin a normal cultivation of the fields. This assumption is more obvious, for Joseph's decree that a fifth be given to Pharaoh seems to presuppose the advent of normal conditions and not the continuation of the harvest failures.*

Another question to which the narrative has not yet given a satisfactory answer is the one of chronology. How has the narrator calculated when he speaks in v. 18 of "the second year"? The assumption that it means simply "the following year" (RSV), i.e., the seventh year of the distressing period, is not satisfying. It has therefore been suggested that this narrative did not originally presuppose the idea of a seven-year famine, but rather that it reckoned with one of only two years.

What opinion is one to form of the strange narrative, a showpiece in the arsenal of anti-Semitic polemic against the Old Testament? One must seek to discover the "meaning" which the ancient narrator himself wanted to convey, toward the end of the story; and there it is stated clearly enough: the nation is grateful; it praises Joseph as its savior. Joseph, therefore, has accomplished the gigantic task of preserving the people throughout the period of distress. The narrative shows us Joseph's wisdom which is capable of mastering every new complication. It would be an insertion of a modern idea, in our opinion, if one were to derive from the narrative anything like a subtle ridicule of the all too submissive Egyptians who valued life more than freedom (Pr.; Jac.). Further, the expositor must resist as much as possible the question of the extent to which Joseph's measures stand the test of modern opinion. The ancient narrator is honestly amazed and wants the reader also to be amazed at the way an expedient was found to save the people from a gigantic catastrophe. In this respect there pervades the narrative a naïve pleasure in the possibilities of human wisdom which can conquer economic difficulties by a venturesome shift of values, money for bread, manpower and land for seed corn, etc. The narrator lived in an enlightened, awakened period, which was very interested in life in foreign lands. There is therefore nothing more behind this narrative than the intention of telling how such strange economic conditions

*In v. 21a the translation of the MT is debated, and its meaning is so strange that expositors have long preferred the sense of the LXX. What can it mean when Joseph "removed the people to (?) cities"? Instead of *heʿebīr leʿārīm*, one must read *heʿebīd laʿabādīm*, "he made slaves of them."

arose in a foreign land. There is no special reference to Israel, either as an ideal or an abomination, in the narrative. Even though the narrative errs in aetiologically deriving this economic absolutism of the state from Joseph its knowledge of conditions in Egypt is quite accurate. The decline of the free peasanty which owned its own land began in the so-called new kingdom, and only the Pharaoh was nominal owner and lord of all agricultural land. It is also well informed that the extensive temple lands were not included—formally at any rate—in this royal right of possession (Diodorus I. 73; Herodotus II. 168). Judged by conditions of that time, a tax of about 20 per cent must be considered normal. In private business transactions the interest rates were often considerably higher. In the Babylonian economy the interest rates for the purchase of seed corn went as high as 40 per cent; in the Jewish military colony at Elephantine in the fifth century B.C. they went even to 60 per cent. Nevertheless, it must be emphasized that the vocation of merchant was not followed in Israel, which had settled in Palestine, until the late postexilic period. The law forbade every form of usury (Ex. 22.25; Deut. 23.20 f.). It is significant that the term "Canaanite" became the word for "dealer" (Isa. 23.8; Zech. 14.21; Prov. 31.24). Only in the Diaspora did Judaism give up its ties with the vocation of agriculture.

L. THE BLESSING OF EPHRAIM AND MANASSEH. CHS. 47.28 TO 48.22

47 [28]*And Jacob lived in the land of Egypt seventeen years; so the days of*
Jacob, the years of his life, were a hundred and forty-seven years.
29 And when the time drew near that Israel must die, he called his
son Joseph and said to him, "If now I have found favor in your sight,
put your hand under my thigh, and promise to deal loyally and truly
with me. Do not bury me in Egypt, [30]but let me lie with my fathers;
carry me out of Egypt and bury me in their burying place." He answered, "I will do as you have said." [31]And he said, "Swear to me";
and he swore to him. Then Israel bowed himself upon the head of his
bed.

48 [1]After this Joseph was told, "Behold, your father is ill"; so he
took with him his two sons, Manasseh and Ephraim. [2]And it was told
to Jacob, "Your son Joseph has come to you"; then Israel summoned
his strength, and sat up in bed. [3]*And Jacob said to Joseph, "God Almighty*
appeared to me at Luz in the land of Canaan and blessed me, [4]*and said to me,*
'Behold I will make you fruitful, and multiply you, and I will make of you a
company of peoples, and will give this land to your descendants after you for an
everlasting possession.' [5]*And now your two sons, who were born to you in the land*
of Egypt before I came to you in Egypt, are mine; Ephraim and Manasseh shall

be mine, as Reuben and Simeon are. 6And the offspring born to you after them shall be yours; they shall be called by the name of their brothers in their inheritance. 7For when I came from Paddan, Rachel to my sorrow died in the land of Canaan on the way, when there was still some distance to go to Ephrath; and I buried her there on the way to Ephrath (that is, Bethlehem)."

8 When Israel saw Joseph's sons, he said, "Who are these?" 9Joseph said to his father, "They are my sons, whom God has given me here." And he said, "Bring them to me, I pray you, that I may bless them." 10Now the eyes of Israel were dim with age, so that he could not see. So Joseph brought them near him; and he kissed them and embraced them. 11And Israel said to Joseph, "I had not thought to see your face; and lo, God has let me see your children also." 12Then Joseph removed them from his knees, and he bowed himself with his face to the earth. 13And Joseph took them both, Ephraim in his right hand toward Israel's left hand, and Manasseh in his left hand toward Israel's right hand, and brought them near him. 14And Israel stretched out his right hand and laid it upon the head of Ephraim, who was the younger, and his left hand upon the head of Manasseh, crossing his hands, for Manasseh was the first-born. 15And he blessed Joseph, and said,

"The God before whom my fathers Abraham and Isaac walked,
the God who has led me all my life long to this day,
16the angel who has redeemed me from all evil, bless the lads;
and in them let my name be perpetuated, and the name of my fathers Abraham and Isaac;
and let them grow into a multitude in the midst of the earth."

17 When Joseph saw that his father laid his right hand upon the head of Ephraim, it displeased him; and he took his father's hand, to remove it from Ephraim's head to Manasseh's head. 18And Joseph said to his father, "Not so, my father; for this one is the first-born; put your right hand upon his head." 19But his father refused, and said, "I know, my son, I know; he also shall become a people, and he also shall be great; nevertheless his younger brother shall be greater than he, and his descendants shall become a multitude of nations." 20So he blessed them that day, saying,

"By you Israel will pronounce blessings, saying,
'God make you as Ephraim and as Manasseh' ";

and thus he put Ephraim before Manasseh. 21Then Israel said to Joseph, "Behold, I am about to die, but God will be with you, and will bring you again to the land of your fathers. 22Moreover I have given to you rather than to your brothers one mountain slope which I took from the hand of the Amorites with my sword and with my bow."

With the narratives about Jacob's legacy, death, and burial we come to the end of the Joseph story, which the final redactor, however, as is here evident, wished to be understood as a Jacob story. The text is here again and to the end very uneven because of the juxtaposition and union of narrative sections from various documents.

Wellhausen once said one could perceive the strata of the interlocking source documents in Genesis nowhere so palpably as at the end of ch. 47 and beginning of ch. 48. A report of Jacob's death begins at ch. 47.28; it is continued in ch. 48.3–6, and that is the Priestly report. In ch. 47.29–31 another, essentially more detailed narrative of Jacob's death obviously begins. Especially conspicuous is the break between this part of the narrative and the beginning of ch. 48: after Joseph has learned of the final arrangements at the dying man's bed, he learns in ch. 48.1 about the approaching death of his father. In the first the old man had him summoned (ch. 47.29); here anxiety brings him to his father's bed (ch. 48.1). In the first version (ch. 47.29–31) the Yahwistic narrative of Jacob's death begins, in the other (ch. 48.1–2a) the Elohistic. Even though the threads of J and E cannot be clearly distinguished from one another in what follows, still at the climax the double strand is again evident. The blessing is given twice, in v. 20 and in vs. 15–16, and even the unpracticed eye can see that the blessing of vs. 15–16 abruptly interrupts the context of vs. 13–14 on the one hand and vs. 17–19 on the other. All three versions (JEP) are variants of one and the same narrative, namely, the one about the blessing and adoption of Joseph's two sons by the dying Jacob, and about his request to be buried in Canaan after his death.

This is the only place in the Joseph story where the expositor has to consider tribal facts, because the ancient reader, when he heard of Manasseh and Ephraim, of Ephraim's preferential position, etc., was also reminded of the tribes represented by the two boys. We, however, have to reconstruct from the sources what the ancient reader actually knew about the two tribes. The leading part of the migration of the so-called Rachel tribes was the "house of Joseph" which settled on the Samaritan mountains in the central part of the land west of the Jordan. This house of Joseph seems still to have been split into the two tribes, Manasseh and Ephraim, at the period of the Judges (cf. Josh. 17.17; 18.5; Judg. 1.27, 29). The Song of Deborah already knows Ephraim as a separate tribe (Judg. 5.14), and the very ancient lists in Num. 26.5–51 and Num. 1.5–15 mention Joseph's two sons side by side, however with a very significant minor difference. In the first-mentioned and older list the order is Manasseh-Ephraim, in the others Ephraim-Manasseh. Obviously the more centrally located tribe of Ephraim had early politically surpassed the fraternal tribe Manasseh. Our narrative will also make mysterious allusions to that fact.

[28] According to P, Jacob lived in Egypt seventeen years. In J and E, one has the impression that Jacob died soon after his emigration and reunion. The Priestly representation of the adoption of the two grandsons is stiffly formal, as usual on such occasions, but not really vivid, and without all those little, external details which make this narrative so unforgettable in JE. Jacob's citation of the revelation he received at Bethel is his legal basis for his action regarding Joseph's sons. Jacob fulfills a divine purpose, which had promised numerous progeny and great possessions of land, when he accepts Ephraim and Manasseh as sons of Jacob, i.e., grants them the dignity of fully accredited tribal chiefs. We saw above that an ancient conflicting tradition was behind this representation. According to one scheme, only Joseph was numbered among Jacob's twelve sons (e.g., Gen., ch. 49); according to the other tradition Ephraim and Manasseh belonged to the twelve. Our narrative intends to clarify this inconsistency in the ancient tradition and to make an adjustment. Regarding El Shaddai, see p. 197. The continuation and conclusion of the Priestly narrative about Jacob's legacy and death is now widely removed. It comes in ch. 49.28b–33 and contains Jacob's request to be buried in Canaan after his death.

[29–31] In the older narrative the order is reversed. Here the dying man begins with the request for an oath that he will be buried with his fathers. The urgency of his words shows that he knows about the difficulties and costs which stand in the way of fulfilling this request. Later Joseph actually has humbly to request permission of the Pharaoh and ask for his own leave (ch. 50.4–6). We do not know whether the Yahwist thought of the Cave of Machpelah as the grave of the fathers. It is almost to be assumed from Jacob's statements. But in ch. 50.5 mention is made of a grave which Jacob himself dug, which again does not quite agree with our passage. Regarding the oath by the male genital, cf. ch. 24.2 and p. 249.

The meaning of the gesture described in ch. 47.31b is not quite clear. The LXX has a somewhat different text which is followed by Heb. 11.21 (*māṭṭē* instead of *miṭṭā*), but that only makes the matter much less clear. Since the verb (*šāḥā*) expresses not merely a general bodily movement but rather always a gesture of reverence or adoration, one must think of a solemn manifestation of gratitude.

[1–7] This clear context of the narrative is now interrupted first by the Elohistic beginning ch. 48.1–2 and second by the parallel Priestly report in ch. 48.3–6. The question about which context v. 7

belongs to cannot be answered. The reference to Rachel's death has no recognizable relation to what follows or precedes. **[8–13]** But from v. 8 on, the Yahwistic-Elohistic text, apart from the misplaced blessing in vs. 16–17, is rather even. The statement in v. 8 ("when Israel saw . . .") and the assertion of his blindness in his old age in v. 10 do not necessarily contradict each other. The verb "see" is often used in the Hebrew text in the general sense of "notice." But the text may refer to an ability to divine which is no longer clear. Obviously the old man is surprised to meet sons of his son already. Here again one must assume that this scene took place shortly after Jacob's arrival in Egypt and not seventeen years later. Furthermore, according to the computations of the Priestly chronology (ch. 47.28), Joseph's two sons would already be about twenty years old. In addition, the two presentations of the boys in v. 9 and v. 13, if they reveal the presence of two traditions, do not disturb the reader. Everything in this narrative is told in such a way that the reader sees palpably every detail, even the quite external proceedings and movements. There are really two proceedings. At the beginning there is the quite personal welcome and caress of the grandsons, behind which there appears to be something more official, namely, the so-called "placing upon the knees," i.e., a legal rite of adoption. (This would be completely clear if one were to translate *bērēk* in v. 9 with Procksch and others not by "bless" but by "take upon the knee.") Joseph's very solemn gesture also reveals that there was more to this scene than simply the grandfather's personal pleasure in his grandchildren. Joseph is apparently here the recipient too, for he expresses his gratitude in profound reverence. This concludes the first proceeding. Joseph takes the boys from Jacob's knees and lets them depart.

[13–14] For the ancients an act of blessing was a positive occurrence. They believed that by definite rites and gestures a blessing could be effectively and irrevocably bestowed upon another. **[17–19]** The narratives about blessings are therefore extremely interested in the spiritual content, i.e., in the words of blessing themselves. But just as important for them is the external event, i.e., the way in which the blessing was given. Both the narrative in ch. 27 and ours amaze us by their drastic realism. The one who actually blesses is, of course, God himself. The blessing in vs. 15 f. shows how such blessing is first of all simply an intercessory invocation to God. On the other hand, the human agent of blessing also plays a decisive role. He realizes that he is empowered by God to bestow or refuse the divine blessing. In the blessing uttered by God upon Abraham there was that authority for a human transmission from generation to generation. God's blessing is thus bound to the responsible decision of the one who bestows the blessing in a solemn moment. Our narrative shows an extreme example of the way this decision could under certain circumstances be very surprising and that a suspicion of arbitrariness or error could arise among the men concerned. Here, then, a dramatic scene is described in which one gazes in suspense at every movement of the chief actor. The way in which Joseph brings his sons to the old man is not, of course, particularly deliberate; he does what everyone in his situation would have done, for the privilege of the first-born was absolutely uncontested in the ancient Orient. Thus Manasseh is brought in by Joseph in such a way that the right hand of the man bestowing blessing can rest upon his head. When Jacob crossed his hands, the verb really means "plait" (*śkl*), Joseph was so dumbfounded that he interrupted the sacred act to call the old man's attention to what he could only consider an obvious error on the blind man's part. But Jacob is undisturbed: I know it, my son, I know it! What might the blind old man have known? Obviously this, that where God's blessing is bestowed every legal claim, even the most legitimate, must not be considered. Thus in this wonderful narrative, that which was actually a minor incident has become the primary affair. The narrative doubtless has an aetiological purpose as well. That the tribe of Ephraim politically surpassed the older brother, Manasseh, in history—let one remember that the prophet Hosea often calls the Northern Kingdom simply "Ephraim"—caused some reflection which is also active in our narrative. The narrative considers this historical event a characteristic sign of the rule of Israel's God. It is certain that no reader in the post-Solomonic era could hear this story without thinking at the same time of its actual background in tribal history; but it is wrong to think of the story as only a coded tribal history, so to speak. For what happens here in the realm of tribal history is only an example, a typical precedent for what happened again and again in Israel through God's guidance. It is a great mystery that this narrative, which is constructed from such obviously dated materials and notions (let one remind oneself of the ancient, primitive idea of the greater power of blessing with the right hand), also speaks so powerfully to us across the ages as the bearer of profound spirituality.

[15–16] In the present form of the story, Jacob gives the blessing itself in two sayings (vs. 15–16 and v. 20). Obviously the one who combined the two older forms of the narrative did not want to sacrifice either of them. Even though the first could not find a fortunate position, since it interrupts the context of the narrative (see p. 408), it still is decisively superior in content to the second. It begins solemnly with a wide-ranging, threefold invocation of God. Its style is that of a cultic hymn. Characteristic of it is the fact that God is spoken of in the third person and is not directly addressed as "Thou." But what are particularly important are the various theological predications which can be transferred into English only in relative clauses, "God, who . . . who . . . who . . ." (cf. Ps. 103.1–5 and Weiser, *The Psalms*, 53). These are expressed in Hebrew much more tersely by participial constructions.

This variation in the utterances of adoration is of course made in stirring, poetic style, but it is more than mere ornament. Behind this ancient cultic style is a very definite conception of God and all talk about God. These predications are intended to identify the divinity and define it exactly according to its revelation. For the believer can never speak generally and abstractly about God but only about definite revelations and experiences that exist in his own sphere of life. To this sphere belong, of course, the relationship to God of the fathers and forefathers, i.e., everything they learned of God which in the tradition of the cult has been handed down to the present as authentic knowledge.

Thus Jacob begins by first re-establishing connection with the worship of his father, whose life was also a walk before the revealed God. This God, the second statement continues, has "led" him continually. God as the shepherd of his faithful is also an element of cultic language (cf. Ps. 23.1; 28.9). The third statement, however, is the most important theologically. When Jacob here no longer speaks of God but rather of "the angel," that does not mean that he is here speaking of a being subordinated to God; on the contrary, his speech now prepares for its final and most concentrated statement about God's rule. The "angel of the Lord" is of course God himself as he appears on earth; in him Israel experienced Yahweh's special supporting and redeeming activity (see pp. 192 f.). Thus here too a statement about him is made which mentions the ultimate thing that Israel was authorized to say about Yahweh. Actually the term "redeemer" belongs to the profane realm of family law. If an Israelite were sold into slavery for his debts, a relative could "redeem" him

(Lev. 25.25 f.). In such cases the relative was actually obligated to redeem him. But in Israel one also spoke in a similar manner of God's "redeeming," and our verse is the oldest evidence for it. In his covenant Yahweh had offered himself as redeemer; he is the closest relative, prepared to redeem man (Pr.). The passage does not say exactly *what* is meant by this "redemption from all evil," but the statement is purposefully general and allows room for many ideas. The term recurs later, especially in Deutero-Isaiah, where it refers to the eschatological redemption of Israel (cf. Isa. 48.20; 41.14; 43.1; 44.22; etc.). The theological differentiation in the two statements about God, v. 15a and v. 16, is therefore very remarkable. While the former refers to the blessings of universal providence and divine preservation and guidance, i.e., to the substance of the first article of faith, the last predication is much more concerned with God's saving rule as Jacob has experienced it. This divine blessing, identified in this way, is what Jacob beseeches God for his grandson. The conception of blessing is again in terms of wonderful physical fertility (cf. Gen. 1.22; the verb used here, *dāgā*, probably refers to the swarming of fish). The emphatic neglect of Manasseh seems to lie quite outside the horizon of this word of blessing.

That the name of Jacob and his fathers are named "in them" means of course that these boys, born in Egypt of a foreign woman, shall be considered full descendants of the patriarchs (cf. the other possibility in the case of Ishmael, ch. 17.19 f., P, and 21.21, E).

[20–22] The second blessing (J?) seems to contain a difficulty. In it Jacob speaks personally to the recipients, but why in the singular? Probably the form of speech of a blessing was so fixed in cultic usage that it was also retained in the blessing of more than one (cf. Num. 6.22 f.: "Say to *them*, Yahweh bless *thee* . . ."). Here too the blessing signifies great physical increase. The two boys will be proverbial in this respect in Israel; they will be a formula for blessing in everyone's mouth. In Israel! Here, apart from the rather awkward and anachronistic mention in ch. 34.7, the nation Israel is mentioned for the first time. "The veil parts, the nation Israel appears before the breaking view of the old man." (Pr.)

In vs. 21 f. the assignment of a "shoulder-height" is very strange. The Hebrew word "shoulder" is also the name of the ancient Canaanite city Shechem in the heart of the Joseph group and is indeed a mysterious allusion to it. The prophets too in their prophecies like to avoid precise names of peoples and places. Apart from the abrupt new beginning in v. 21, however, Jacob's assertion that he conquered Shechem with the sword is remarkable. This cannot refer to what was narrated in ch. 34, for there Jacob complained about his sons' deed, while here he glories in it. And how could he promise to one of his sons what his sons had conquered? And further, how can Jacob, dying in Egypt, possess and bequeath Shechem? The assumption seems unavoidable that a tradition is contained in these verses, which does not place this whole proceeding in Egypt but in Palestine. Evidently we have a very ancient fragment of tradition concerning Jacob's death, which was only inserted subsequently into the context of Jacob's experiences in Egypt because of its combination with the Jacob tradition. So far as Shechem is concerned, this fragment seems to presuppose a tradition that differs considerably from that in ch. 34. Like ch. 38 it will have once been independent, but unlike ch. 38 it could be fitted in more easily. J and E found it already in the Joseph *Novelle*.

M. JACOB'S BLESSING. CH. 49.1–28a

49 1 *Then Jacob called his sons, and said*, "Gather yourselves together,
that I may tell you what shall befall you in days to come.

2 Assemble and hear, O sons of Jacob,
and hearken to Israel your father.

3 Reuben, you are my first-born,
my might, and the first fruits of my strength,
pre-eminent in pride and pre-eminent in power.
4 Unstable as water, you shall not have pre-eminence
because you went up to your father's bed;
then you defiled it—you went up to my couch!

5 Simeon and Levi are brothers;
weapons of violence are their counsels (?).
6 O my soul, come not into their council;
O my spirit, be not joined to their company;
for in their anger they slay men,
and in their wantonness they hamstring oxen.
7 Cursed be their anger, for it is fierce;
and their wrath, for it is cruel!
I will divide them in Jacob
and scatter them in Israel.

8 Judah, your brothers shall praise you;
your hand shall be on the neck of your enemies;
your father's sons shall bow down before you.
9 Judah is a lion's whelp;
from the prey, my son, you have gone up.

He stooped down, he couched as a lion,
  and as a lioness; who dares rouse him up?
10The scepter shall not depart from Judah,
  nor the ruler's staff from between his feet,
until he comes to whom it belongs;
  and to him shall be the obedience of the peoples.
11Binding his foal to the vine
  and his ass's colt to the choice vine,
he washes his garments in wine
  and his vesture in the blood of grapes;
12his eyes shall be red with wine,
  and his teeth white with milk.

13Zebulun shall dwell at the shore of the sea;
  he shall become a haven for ships,
  and his border shall be at Sidon.

14Issachar is a strong ass,
  crouching between the sheepfolds;
15he saw that a resting place was good,
  and that the land was pleasant;
so he bowed his shoulder to bear,
  and became a slave at forced labor.

16Dan shall judge his people
  as one of the tribes of Israel.
17Dan shall be a serpent in the way,
  a viper by the path,
that bites the horse's heels
  so that his rider falls backward.
18I wait for thy salvation, O LORD.

19Raiders shall raid Gad,
  but he shall raid at their heels.
20Asher's food shall be rich,
  and he shall yield royal dainties.

21Naphtali is a hind let loose,
  that bears comely fawns.

22Joseph is a fruitful vine,
  a fruitful vine by a spring;
  his branches run over the wall.
23The archers fiercely attacked him,
  shot at him, and harassed him sorely;
24yet his bow remained unmoved,
  his arms were made agile

by the hands of the Mighty One of Jacob
(by the name of the Shepherd, the Rock of Israel),
25by the God of your father who will help you,
by God Almighty who will bless you
with blessings of heaven above,
blessings of the deep that couches beneath,
blessings of the breasts and of the womb.
26The blessings of your father
are mighty beyond the blessings of the eternal mountains,
the bounties of the everlasting hills;
may they be on the head of Joseph,
and on the brow of him who was separate from his brothers.

27Benjamin is a ravenous wolf,
in the morning devouring the prey,
and at even dividing the spoil."

28 All these are the twelve tribes of Israel; and this is what their father said to them.

This collection of aphorisms is commonly called "Jacob's blessing." But this designation is not quite apposite, for the twelve are not really blessed; the aphorisms have no generally common feature at all. Some are prophecies of the future, some contain censure or curse regarding what has happened, some describe current affairs. It cannot be maintained at all, therefore, that these aphorisms regarding Jacob's sons are a single, compact poem, as Judg., ch. 5, is, for example. There is no general inner or outer uniformity, and furthermore, the aphorisms often speak quite directly about the tribes whose historical confederacy is assumed to be self-evident, and often about only their ancestors and their deeds. The picture at the beginning (vs. 1–2) of the ancestor surrounded by his sons is not consistently followed at all in the course of the sayings, but is often obviously broken. Finally, the age of the individual sayings is different, for the events described in them are not on approximately the same historical level. Between the event envisaged in the aphorism about Simeon and Levi and the one in the saying about Judah there are at least three hundred years. On the other hand, the chapter as a whole is not an indiscriminate collection of tribal aphorisms but a careful collection made with a view to completeness; and moreover, this collection arose at a relatively early time, in the period of the Yahwist at the latest, for the order of the tribes as they are given here points to an older phase in the development of the twelve-tribe system than the list in Num., ch. 26, or even the one in Deut., ch. 33. (See Noth, *System der zwölf Stämme Israels*, 7 ff.) This blessing of Jacob's is generally attributed to the source J. But to consider J the author is impossible, for J is not even the author of the prose narratives attributed to him; one must then think of him as the collector of the aphorisms. But there are no clear signs which lead one to connect J with this collection. The text is sometimes obviously damaged and scarcely understandable.

Theologically the document demands a great deal of the modern expositor because of the intensity and one-sidedness with which it concentrates on historical and political facts. Whoever is looking only for religious ideas, i.e., pious thoughts, will be betrayed into setting aside large sections of this text as "profane" if anything. But Israel's faith considered the movements of its history as a special "arrangement of God" (L. Köhler) with purposes and goals which were, to be sure, recognizable to only a few enlightened ones. But even more, the entire document is dominated by the conviction that all the various destinies of the tribes are to be understood only as the outcome of the prophetic statements of the ancestor. As later in the case of the prophets, so here Jacob created history by the authority of his creative word, either of blessing or of curse. This does not, of course, dispute the fact that this activity of God was concentrated especially in certain tribes. In this respect the two sayings about Judah and Joseph are clearly singled out from the others.

[1–2] The introduction in v. 2 is the work of the collector, but the opening sentence in prose in v. 1 obviously belongs to the Priestly narrative about Jacob's last blessing (vs. 28b–33) into which our collection of aphorisms has been inserted. This collector has understood the individual aphorisms as utterances about what "will befall" the tribes "in days to come." In fact, he uses a term here (*'aḥarīt hāyyāmīm*) which in prophetic literature signifies the last days ("*Endzeit*") (Isa. 2.2; Ezek. 38.16). But it is nevertheless questionable whether it must be understood here too in the sense of an eschatological end to history. It is sometimes also used in the more general sense of "in latter days" (Deut. 4.30; 31.29). This understanding of the aphorisms as single prophecies is applicable, as we said, to all the sayings only to a minor extent. The sayings about Zebulun, Issachar, Dan, Gad, Asher, Naphtali, Joseph, and Benjamin were not originally understood as prophecies of the future. This overlapping viewpoint was obviously taken from the saying about Judah, which actually predominates over all other sayings. It is thus quite an interesting example of the way in which one text in the Old Testament might become decisive for a quite definite theological understanding of a larger context.

[3–4] About no other tribe do we know so little as about *Reuben.* It disappeared as a tribe very early, in the period of the Judges. The Song of Deborah mentions it with censure (Judg. 5.15 f.); the blessing of Moses, which is to be dated later, already pictures it as dying (Deut. 33.6a). It scarcely would have maintained the dignity of the first-born if in a prehistoric period it had not had a position of power among the Leah tribes. Its domicile in historical times lay in the south of the land east of Jordan (Josh. 13.15 ff.). But in our aphorism the tribe of Reuben is mentioned only indirectly. If what is said in v. 4 about the ancestor contains some recollection of a severe crime committed by the tribe of Reuben, it is completely incomprehensible to us, for the mention in ch. 35.22 is only a fragment. This misdeed of the ancestor is now connected with the tribe's loss of position. The saying considers its fate a retribution which came upon it by virtue of the ancestor's saying. The tribe produced no significant man, no judge, no king, no prophet (Jac.).

[5–7] We are more certain about *Simeon* and *Levi*, thanks to the circumstance that they are spoken of as tribes and that we have in ch. 34 an ancient tradition which obviously refers to the same event as that in our saying, namely, the attack on Shechem. That our saying goes beyond what is reported in the prose narrative in one detail, namely, the crippling of oxen, cannot be surprising when one considers the independence of the two traditions from each other. What is meant is probably the "crippling" of the animals, that is, cutting the tendons in the hocks (cf. Josh. 11.6, 9, etc.). Here, as there, the deed is condemned as a serious disgrace, because of which the two are denied social association. This saying about the two is unusually severe, for exclusion from the community of the tribes could mean ruin for those concerned. Actually, the purpose of the aphorism is to establish aetiologically on the basis of this deed and the condemnation of it the dispersion of the two tribes which apparently really did occur. But who is the "I" speaking in the aphorism? Because of v. 7b it cannot be assumed that the saying in its oldest form was pronounced by Jacob. Could Jacob have said, "I will divide them in Jacob"? Perhaps one must think of a man of God who, in a situation similar to the summons of the tribes against Benjamin (Judg. 20.1 ff.), called a ban against the guilty. The "I" in v. 7b is

God himself, who punishes the crime by means of the decisive saying of his authorized agent. Whether the tribe of Simeon suffered a "catastrophe" in the vicinity of Shechem, as is often assumed, is beyond our knowledge. Guilt and its expiation are often widely separated, according to the Old Testament. Later the tribe lived in the south in the region of the tribe of Judah (Josh. 19.1 ff.). But it too, like Reuben, disappeared early. It is interesting that our saying and ch. 34 consider *Levi* to be a tribe like Simeon and the others; they probably do not yet know it in its exceptional position as a tribe of priests. This is an indication of the age of the passage. The tribal conditions which the passage has in mind are very early, i.e., long prior to the migration of the house of Joseph into central Palestine (cf. what is said in ch. 34, pp. 333 f.). However, we know almost nothing about the early history of the tribe of Levi. Even the evaluation of the saying is restricted because it refers to only one event, an event which involved not only Levi but also another tribe. So the saying raises more questions than it answers. Does it not speak of a curse on and a dissolution of the two tribes? In v. 6a, parallel to the word "soul" (actually "life") there is a word (*kābōd*) which should not be translated "honor." A few references in the Psalms (Ps. 7.5; 16.9; 30.12; 57.8; 108.1b) make it evident that the word, which probably originally meant "liver," sometimes also expresses something of the individuality itself and can therefore be used as an anthropological term.

[8–12] The saying for *Judah* is a series of statements that are in part extravagantly laudatory. This archaic, poetic pathos makes the statements somewhat indecisive if not downright obscure. Unfortunately, the most important word in the aphorism (*šīlō*), upon the understanding of which almost everything depends, has not yet been linguistically clarified. The first part (vs. 8 f.) is not difficult. Judah (here again the tribe is addressed) is strong, he has conquered his enemies, and therefore the brother tribes honor him. The picture of the young lion is also unreservedly laudatory. The statement about "prey" is not damaging either. The Hebrew word (*ṭerep*) refers only to the prey of animals and is therefore much more limited in meaning than the English word "plunder." More difficult is the question of how the statement about the scepter and ruler's staff is to be interpreted, for the two do not necessarily have to be understood as attributes of a king. They were also honorary symbols of tribal princes who, when they were seated in council, held them between their feet in front of them (Micah 7.14; Num. 21.18). But this assumption breaks down because of the understanding of the passage as a whole; for Judah achieved its pre-eminence among the tribes only because of the kingdom, by which it was brought quickly out of its isolated existence into the center of political life. This consideration is important because the "until he comes" does not then foretell David but an event after David. But who or what will come? The word *šīlō* in the Hebrew text could be the name of the well-known cultic center, but for what reason Judah would "come" to Shiloh in Ephraim and why that would be such an epochal event no one can say. This exhausts the possibilities for interpreting the passage without altering the Hebrew wording. The assumption that the Hebrew word has a special meaning no longer found in the Old Testament, e.g., "the prince," corresponding to the Arcadian *šelu*, is a scientific hypothesis for which, as for the numerous corrections of the existing letters, there is only a greater or lesser degree of probability. Among the interpretations that presuppose a somewhat altered wording, the best one, more because of its age than because of its greater probability, is the one in the LXX: "until that which belongs to him comes" (*šellō*, as in Ezek. 21.32, or even better, "until the one comes to whom—the scepter—belongs"). A more recent proposal is: "until the one he has requested comes" (*šeʾīlō*); more probable, however, is "his ruler" (*mōšlō*), which has been accepted by many more recent expositors. The obedience he will find could be that of the related tribes according to the statement, but since Judah already exults in the reverence of these tribes (v. 8b), one has to think of the nations. If v. 10b refers to the coming of some person, then it seems obvious to relate the utterances in vs. 11 f. to that person. If one assumes that the subject of vs. 11 f. is again Judah, then the conclusion of the saying would again revert to the statements before the climax in v. 10b, which is improbable.

No Judean would tie his ass to a vine, for it would be eaten up, of course. Anyone who can be so careless and who can wash his garment in wine, lives in paradisiacal abundance. Probably these statements intend to say just this in antiquated poetry—are they intentionally rhymed in Hebrew?—he who will come will live in an time of paradisiacal fertility.

Many interpreters regard v. 10 as a (fictitious) prophecy of David. The question is how "until" is to be interpreted. Does this refer to the period of the tribe of Judah, or to a series of Judean kings? Israel, too, associated the expectation of a paradisiacal fertility of the land with the enthronement of a king (Isa. 11.1–9; Ezek. 34.23–31; Amos 9.11–15; Ps. 72.16). Still, one must admit that our saying goes farthest in presenting the one to come as himself enjoying that superabundance. He is almost a Dionysiac figure.

[13] It is doubtful that the saying about *Zebulun* was from the beginning so short. The only thing that is said of him concerns the situation of his dwelling place. That, however, was something astonishing for the ancient Hebrews; one of the tribes by ships and the sea! Israel was an inland people because of its geographical situation. The coast for the most part was not suited to shipping, and the plains were in the hands of the Canaanites in the more ancient period. But Zebulun and Issachar were exceptions in this regard. Zebulun, however, did not have this exposed situation from the beginning. A source that is older than our saying makes one assume that Zebulun had previously tented on the western side of the Ephraimite hill country (cf. Judg. 12.11 f. "Aijalon in the land of Zebulun"). But in historical times the tribe migrated northward to the sea, in the vicinity of modern Haifa. That "his flanks" reached "toward Sidon" is, of course, an exaggeration. The author of the saying probably mentions Sidon to represent Phoenicia, which was very far away from him. That such tribal migrations occurred more frequently long after the conquest is shown by the saying for *Issachar*.

[14–15] This tribe too seems to have lived formerly inland in the mountains, according to Judg. 10.11 f.; later it pushed into the western plain. The move was a bad one, however, because the tribe thereby lost its political independence and became a vassal of the Canaanites, into whose sovereign territory it had entered. The saying is filled with the derision of the freemen toward those who had let themselves be enticed by the fertile plain and had thereby become humiliated as beasts of burden. It is the sadly comical picture of an ass which has knelt with its heavy saddle baskets and can no longer stand up. In contrast to this picture the Song of Deborah is full of praise for Issachar (Judg. 5.15).

[16–18] The aphorism about *Dan* begins with a pun (*dān jādīn*). "To judge" means to "help achieve justice," and it was a very respected act. Apparently this legal practice is to be praised in the tribe of Dan. Perhaps in II Sam. 20.18 (LXX!) there is a recollection of a widely known legal tradition about this place. Then the saying would know the tribe in its new home in the North, to which it came in the period of the Judges (Judg., ch. 18). "His people" is Dan's people, not the people of Israel. Since v. 17 begins once more with the proper name Dan, and also says something substantially different, this continuation has been often considered an original independent saying about Dan. The comparison with a snake certainly does not accuse the tribe of furtiveness; the image indicates rather the victorious struggle of the very small tribe against powerful enemies. What the inner connection of the short prayer with the saying itself is, no expositor has been able to say. Is it perhaps the marginal gloss of a later reader or copyist who was reminded of the saying about the serpent in ch. 3.14 f.?

[19–21] For *Gad*, *Asher*, and *Naphtali* each, Jacob can speak only a single line. Gad is from East Jordan south of the Jabbok, and at his outpost in the east he had to withstand the especially numerous attacks of plundering Bedouin hordes. Asher, in the western Galilean hill country, is extolled because of his rich produce, similarly to the way he is praised in Deut. 33.24. One must think of the "royal dainties" as delivered to the court in Jerusalem or Samaria (cf. I Kings 4.27). The saying about Naphtali can scarcely be interpreted by us any more. The abandoning of the imagery in the second half of the saying is not disturbing, according to the laws of poetry at that time, and in itself would not be cause for emendation. The wisdom teachers were preoccupied with "comely speech" (Prov. 15.26; 16.24). Was Naphtali known for that among the tribes? (Others interpret the word *šemer*, which only occurs here, to mean "tidings of victory.") Naphtali's territory lay along the western shore of the Lake of Genesaret and extended farther north.

[22–28] Jacob's statement for *Joseph* was certainly a saying in exalted poetic style. The text, however, is in bad condition and filled with questions that concern first of all the meaning of the words and their syntactic relation to one another. The exposition, therefore, must first proceed word by word. But since here we must proceed without this detailed work we can adhere only to the general lines which are recognizable in the still magnificent torso. The translation given above has been limited to the emendations proposed in BH*. Trees beside perennial water are rather rare on the Palestinian landscape. They are conspicuous at a great distance and were therefore a subject often used in poetry (Ps. 1.3; Jer. 17.8). To refer its branches ("daughters") allegorically to Ephraim and Manasseh was of course a mistake. Likewise one cannot derive any support for historical dating of the saying from the mention of an attack by archers. One may think of events like the Midianite attack in Judg., chs. 6 to 8, but the saying could refer to something quite different just as well.

*Von Rad's translation deviates only occasionally and slightly from text or notes of RSV.

Joseph defended himself and was helped by his fathers' God, who is here to be thought of as aiding in a holy war. From vs. 25b–26 we have before us without doubt the very ancient form of a blessing of fertility, characterized by the stereotyped new beginning with formula of blessing (cf. Deut. 28.3–6). The appeal to *t*^{e}*hōm* (RSV, "the deep"), i.e., the waters under the earth, for a blessing is, to be sure, a particular boldness. Here *t*^{e}*hōm* is not considered a neutral element, but is personified mythologically as "couching beneath."

Benjamin too is praised for courage and might. It is noteworthy that the ancient standards of value from the period of the desert dominate in these sayings. The virtues which these aphorisms praise occurred as a rule among the peaceful and sedentary peasant population of Israel only on rare occasions. But in poetry the ancient ideals are maintained through the ages.

N. JACOB'S DEATH AND BURIAL. JOSEPH'S FORGIVENESS. CHS. 49.28b TO 50.26

49 28b*And [RSV as] he blessed them, blessing each with the blessing suitable to him.*

29*Then he charged them, and said to them, "I am to be gathered to my people;*
bury me with my fathers in the cave that is in the field of Ephron the Hittite, 30*in*
the cave that is in the field at Machpeleh, to the east of Mamre, in the land of
Canaan, which Abraham bought with the field from Ephron the Hittite to possess
as a burying place. 31*There they buried Abraham and Sarah his wife; there they*
*buried Isaac and Rebekah his wife; and there I buried Leah—*32*the field and the*
cave that is in it were purchased from the Hittites." 33*When Jacob finished*
charging his sons, he drew up his feet into the bed, and breathed his last, and was
gathered to his people.

50 1Then Joseph fell on his father's face, and wept over him, and
kissed him. 2And Joseph commanded his servants the physicians to
embalm his father. So the physicians embalmed Israel; 3forty days were
required for it, for so many are required for embalming. And the Egyptians wept for him seventy days.

4 And when the days of weeping for him were past, Joseph spoke to
the household of Pharaoh, saying, "If now I have found favor in your
eyes, speak, I pray you, in the ears of Pharaoh, saying, 5My father made
me swear, saying, 'I am about to die: in my tomb which I hewed out
for myself in the land of Canaan, there shall you bury me.' Now therefore let me go up, I pray you, and bury my father; then I will return."
6And Pharaoh answered, "Go up, and bury your father, as he made you
swear." 7So Joseph went up to bury his father; and with him went up
all the servants of Pharaoh, the elders of his household, and all the
elders of the land of Egypt, 8as well as all the household of Joseph, his
brothers, and his father's household; only their children, their flocks,
and their herds were left in the land of Goshen. 9And there went up with

him both chariots and horsemen; it was a very great company. [10]When they came to the threshing floor of Atad, which is beyond the Jordan, they lamented there with a very great and sorrowful lamentation; and he made a mourning for his father seven days. [11]When the inhabitants of the land, the Canaanites, saw the mourning on the threshing floor of Atad, they said, "This is a grievous mourning to the Egyptians." Therefore the place was named Abel-mizraim; it is beyond the Jordan. [12]*Thus his sons did for him as he had commanded them;* [13]*for his sons carried him to the land of Canaan, and buried him in the cave of the field at Machpelah, to the east of Mamre, which Abraham bought with the field from Ephron the Hittite, to possess as a burying place.* [14]After he had buried his father, Joseph returned to Egypt with his brothers and all who had gone up with him to bury his father.

15 When Joseph's brothers saw that their father was dead, they said, "It may be that Joseph will hate us and pay us back for all the evil which we did to him." [16]So they sent a message to Joseph, saying, "Your father gave this command before he died, [17]'Say to Joseph, Forgive, I pray you, the transgression of your brothers and their sin, because they did evil to you.' And now, we pray you, forgive the transgression of the servants of the God of your father." Joseph wept when they spoke to him. [18]His brothers also came and fell down before him, and said, "Behold, we are your servants." [19]But Joseph said to them, "Fear not, for am I in the place of God? [20]As for you, you meant evil against me; but God meant it for good, to bring it about that many people should be kept alive, as they are today. [21]So do not fear; I will provide for you and your little ones." Thus he reassured them and comforted them.

22 So Joseph dwelt in Egypt, he and his father's house; and Joseph lived a hundred and ten years. [23]And Joseph saw Ephraim's children of the third generation; the children also of Machir the son of Manasseh were born upon Joseph's knees. [24]And Joseph said to his brothers, "I am about to die; but God will visit you, and bring you up out of this land to the land which he swore to Abraham, to Isaac, and to Jacob." [25]Then Joseph took an oath of the sons of Israel, saying, "God will visit you, and you shall carry up my bones from here." [26]So Joseph died, being a hundred and ten years old; and they embalmed him, and he was put in a coffin in Egypt.

[28b–33] The first section of our text belongs to the Priestly document, and v. 28b is, moreover, the precise continuation of ch. 49.1a; i.e., the narrative context is interrupted by the insertion of Jacob's blessing. If the section vs. 29–33 is uniform, it is very circumstantial, especially with regard to the numerous details about place. The narrative uses the expression "to be gathered to one's people" very freely. Compare at ch. 25.8 (the word *'am* is used here with the meaning "relatives," which is scarcely documented elsewhere in the Old

Testament; see at ch. 19). Since the narrator is referring to burial in the family grave, the expression seems to us to be in the wrong place at least at v. 33b. But probably we have here only a well-worn phrase, which was no longer understood in its original literal sense.

There is something very sober about the dying of the father of Israel. With respect to his own lot the dying man is neither especially sorrowful nor especially hopeful. There is no stirring gesture in the face of death, neither one of a man who by virtue of some mythology thinks to achieve life, nor one of a man who is dying. But precisely in this, these narratives about the deaths of the patriarchs show obedience to the reality of death (cf. at ch. 25.7–11).

The continuation and conclusion of this P narrative is in ch. 50.12 f., where the performance of Jacob's last will is communicated. Jacob is buried by his sons in the Cave at Machpelah.

In the older tradition (JE), two things are narrated at the end of the Joseph story: the transfer of Jacob's corpse and a conversation between Joseph and his brothers about the past and the future. These two concluding sections belong to the sources J and E. Verses 1–14, without vs. 12 f., are essentially Yahwistic; vs. 15–26, Elohistic. Several irregularities in vs. 1 ff. do not need to be discussed here. It is scarcely thinkable that the source E did not also tell about Jacob's transfer and burial.

[1–14] The narrator knew that in addition to the agitating and moving aspects of the story many attendant circumstances were to be told which would necessarily grip his readers. There was first of all the necessary embalming of the corpse for the long trip. In this respect one was best advised in Egypt, for there mummification had developed to a science. What a protracted process it must have been, and how expensive! The duration of the period of mourning was also protracted. Moses and Aaron were mourned thirty days, Saul only seven days (Deut. 34.8; Num. 20.29; I Sam. 31.13). Diodorus relates that mourning for the king lasted seventy-two days in Egypt. Jacob was thus mourned as a king. Mourning for the dead was formerly a very strict ritual affair; one wore a special garb of mourning, cut one's hair, and submitted to a mourning fast. When, of course, "the Egyptians" at Jacob's death held such a long period of mourning, it can have been only something much more conventional.

A difficult matter was Joseph's leave of absence. Did not Pharaoh have to fear that Joseph would not return again from his homeland and have therefore to deny his request? But why had not Joseph himself proposed it? He was the closest man to Pharaoh. Among the many reasons suggested the best one is that Joseph had to avoid the court during the mourning ceremony.

Finally the pomp of the funeral procession had to be described. In it, besides members of the family, high Egyptian officials took part, and it was even accompanied by a considerable military escort. Even the Canaanites were astonished at this funeral.

A difficulty that cannot be conclusively clarified is the fact that the two places, the "threshing floor of Atad" (v. 10) and the "river of Egypt" (RSV, "Abel-mizraim") (v. 11), are designated as being "beyond the Jordan." The road from Lower Egypt to Palestine has for ages followed the caravan route along the coast to Beer-sheba. Doubtless one must now assume that at that time the detour across the Sinai peninsula to the land east of Jordan was followed. That must be explained from the fact that our narrative is here tied to a very old tradition about a grave for Jacob in East Jordan. One must remember how freely and independently of one another the various place traditions circulated and how difficult it was for a summarizing literary representation to do justice as far as possible to all important traditions. The combination of this old tradition with the Priestly text of the burial of the corpse in the Cave of Machpelah (vs. 13 f.) made of the threshing floor of Atad the place of a temporary mourning ceremony. (The pun *'ēbel*, "mourning," *'ābēl*, "river bed," cannot be imitated in English.) But one can see that this older narrative had not yet considered the Cave of Machpelah in the fact that it speaks of a grave that Jacob himself had dug (v. 5).

Here, with the mention of Joseph's return with his brothers to Egypt, the Yahwistic Joseph story seems to have ended. Were we to read it without its interweaving with the Elohistic version, we would be struck by what is characteristic of all Yahwistic narratives, namely, the strict precedence given to naked event as against all reflection, i.e., as against all subtle hidden "meaning" or doctrine or any other attitude of the narrator to the events themselves. In this respect the Elohistic conclusion to the Joseph story is quite different.

[15–21] The father's death aroused great anxiety among the brothers, which is quite realistic psychologically. Perhaps Joseph has forgotten nothing and has only been waiting for this moment (cf. ch. 27.41). The end of the narrative thus reverts to what is not yet cleared up between Joseph and his brothers, namely, the question of guilt; and it shows that the brothers' conscience had been uneasy all along. This difficult matter is tackled and broached in two scenes. In the first the brothers do not dare to see Joseph but send him a message. Joseph's answer to that is only his weeping, which leaves a great deal open, to be sure, but does give them courage to appear before him in person. That the appeal to an order of Jacob relating to this should be considered a lie on the part of the brothers (v. 17) is an ancient but certainly quite false assumption. What is important, however, is its reference to the community of their faith. Real forgiveness is not a purely interpersonal matter, but it reaches deeply into the relationship of men before God. This becomes much clearer in the second scene.

When the brothers fall down before Joseph one must again remember Joseph's dreams (cf. ch. 44.14). Thus the end goes back to the beginning (Gu.). Joseph's answer to the brothers' self-surrender contains two important statements: in one he defines his relationship to God, in the other that of his brothers to God. A great deal depends on one's not interpreting Joseph's amazed question as a universal pious truth, i.e., as a humble declaration of noncompetence, as though not he but God alone had to judge in this matter. This would be poor comfort for the brothers if Joseph were merely moving the matter with this statement to a higher court. But Joseph's meaning here is that, in the remarkable conduct of the whole story, God himself has already spoken. He has included the guilt, the brothers' evil, in his saving activity; he has preserved for them the "great remnant" (45.7) and has thus justified them. Were Joseph to condemn them now, he would be setting a negative statement beside the one God had already spoken and would thus be putting himself "in the place of God." The statement about the brothers' evil plans and God's good plans now opens up the inmost mystery of the Joseph story. It is in every respect, along with the similar passage in ch. 45.5–7, the climax to the whole. Even where no man could imagine it, God had all the strings in his hand. But this guidance of God is only asserted; nothing more explicit is said about the way in which God incorporated man's evil into his saving activity. The two statements "you meant . . ." and "God meant . . ." are ultimately very unyielding side by side (see pp. 433 f.). Everything that Joseph says is very sober; nothing of what has happened is veiled in the exuberance of good feelings. One can even speak here of a downright didactic tendency in the narrative, if one only remembers that not timeless truths are being spoken, but that an opinion is being formed with regard to a very definite event which occurred at one time.

The Elohist has thus unrolled the moral and theological problem of the whole story; the Yahwist has apparently neglected to do so. But one cannot ascribe that to the higher moral level of the former. Rather, here we have two quite different conceptions of the task to which the two narrators set themselves.

[22–26] Verses 22–26 are the epilogue to the Joseph story, which give briefly a review of the rest of Joseph's life. In spite of his great age he was still the first of the brothers to die. In v. 20b Joseph spoke about God's plans in the past; in v. 24 he turns prophetically to the future and refers to the nation which will arise from Israel's sons. The promise of land to the patriarchs has long since been lost sight of in the Joseph story, and it was also originally foreign to this narrative. But the incorporation of this narrative into the composition of the patriarchal stories meant that it too, with all its confused happening, was oriented toward this ultimate goal of all patriarchal stories.

Joseph's corpse was then also embalmed and placed in one of those sarcophagi which are today in all our museums. There is, of course, no reference here to the Ark of the Covenant, which in Hebrew is also called a "chest." The further history of this coffin is told in Ex. 13.19 and Josh. 24.32.

EPILOGUE TO THE JOSEPH STORY

The Joseph story, considered as a literary document, i.e., as a literary genre, must be judged quite differently from the narrative complex of Abraham stories, for example. To be sure, it too is not homogeneous, and its form as we have it in J and E is scarcely original. To reconstruct supposedly earlier and simpler versions is a delicate business, and until now little that is certain has been discovered. The Joseph story is not a "wreath" of sagas, plaited from originally independent and compact narrative units, but it is an organically unified story from beginning to end. It is not a saga at all, but a *Novelle*. The difference becomes especially evident when we recall the characteristic quality of the saga: the patriarchal stories were mostly based on sagas which were originally connected with a place. They each adhered to a locality, and the narrative revolves about this ultimately historical core. These traditions about places are completely absent from the Joseph story, if we overlook the marginal one about the threshing floor of Atad in ch. 50.10. The result is just as meager if we look for recollections of historical tribal conditions in it. Certainly, the material in the narrative will derive in the last resort from central Palestine and from some historical precedence of the house of Joseph over other tribes. But it cannot be said that in the present narrative Joseph and his brothers are to be considered the representatives of their tribes, i.e., that their relationship to one another reflects the relations of the tribes to one another. This would not explain why only Reuben, Simeon, and Judah appear as spokesmen in the story. It is quite impossible, therefore, to interpret the Joseph story from the viewpoint of tribal history, for the ancestors of the tribes are already weakened in it to fictional figures. Only for Joseph himself can one assume that his towering role in the narrative is a direct reflex of the political predominance of the house of Joseph. (The narrative Gen. 48 was, as we saw, an independent passage; it is different from the tenor of the Joseph story in the directness of its reference to tribal history.)

It is just as unsuccessful, of course, to consider the Joseph story as a precise historical biography. Even though an actual historical event should underlie it, i.e., if it should have preserved the memory of the work of a vizier from Palestine (and that only would be debatable), still this "historical kernel" could never be precisely distinguished from the fiction with which it is entwined. And whoever wants to accept this whole narrative only according to the degree of its historical authenticity would overlook everything it was trying to say. How far this purpose is from the narrated events, and how little the narrative poses as a precise document, becomes especially clear from the fact that at no point can it name the Pharaoh who was involved in the action. (H. H. Rowley suggests Akhenaton-Amenhotep IV, *From Joseph to Joshua*, 115 f.) How different by contrast is the precision of real historical reports, e.g., I Kings 14.25; II Kings 23.29! The same is true of "the city" in Gen. 44.4, 13. The expositor does not need, therefore, to trouble himself at all with the question of whether a Pharaoh, during the period under consideration, had his residence in Lower Egypt. The Pharaohs of the new kingdom lived at Thebes (Upper Egypt); it was the Ramessides who transferred their residence to Lower Egypt (ca. 1300), at a time which under all circumstances is later than Joseph's, for Rameses II is probably the Pharaoh of Israel's oppression. A more probable assumption is that the narrator was thinking of the conditions of his own day with respect to the Pharaoh's residence. No one can deny that he has a good and very competent working knowledge of Egyptian conditions; but this is essentially the knowledge of his own day. In Solomon's day especially, there was lively commerce with Egypt, not only political but also in the realm of universal culture. Just as Solomon was interested in South Arabian wisdom (I Kings 10.1 ff.), so teachers of wisdom traveled between Palestine and Egypt exchanging their wisdom (Ecclus. 39.4). The Joseph story, as will be shown, is obviously related to the older teachings of wisdom. In fact, it has been thought that one can detect in the Joseph story joy in the opening of a large horizon. Gunkel noticed this enlightened interest in the customs and conditions of a great foreign nation: the splendid court, the installation of a vizier with whom one can speak only with the aid of an interpreter, the public storage of grain, the strange conditions regarding laws of land, the mummification of corpses, etc. This awakened interest in the exotic is the sign of an age mature and enlightened, intellectually and culturally. And Solomon's era must be characterized as just that.

Whoever wants to comprehend the inner substance of the Joseph story will do well not to ask the question about its notions of faith too quickly or one-sidedly. It is in itself such a wide-ranging work of art that it cannot be considered from one viewpoint only. It has already been said that the story does not disdain to entertain and educate its readers with all kinds of interesting cultural history. Joseph himself, who rose from deepest misery to highest honor, was an especially gripping figure for the ancient reader because of the strange situations in which he was placed and because in him problems were sketched which had especially topical interest in the age of the narrator. But here too the narrative is interested in something much more comprehensive than what we understand by "the religious," i.e., Joseph's inner purification, or his severity, or his kindness toward his brothers. Rather, in Joseph a picture is sketched of a youth and man of best education and upbringing, of faith and experience in worldly affairs, such as the teachers of wisdom had instructed their youths to be. Above all, we must remember one thing: Joseph is a court official. (What did the Israel of the period of the Judges know about the possibilities and problems of such an existence!) The most prominent task, indeed the art, of a court official was that of public speaking. He had to give addresses—and, what is more, in political matters—or be able to give "counsel" as one spoke of it at that time. One may read two beautiful examples of such skillful political addresses in II Sam. 17.1–13. The ancient teachers of wisdom were never weary of referring to the importance of proper speech and proper silence, for it was a coveted goal to stand in such manner before a king and be counted among his counselors ("Do you see a man skillful in his work? he will stand before kings" (Prov. 22.29); "Do not neglect the speech of the wise . . . for in it you will learn knowledge, so that you may stand before princes" (Ecclus. 8.8; cf. Prov. 10.21; 11.14; 12.8; 15.7; 16.23 f.; 18.21; 25.11 f.). In order to arrive at such a goal, however, a steep ladder had to be scaled. Such an office required great exercise in propriety and self-discipline. It is completely clear that the Joseph story is now and then interested in this educational ideal. One could document Joseph's conduct step by step with striking statements concerning wisdom—his skill in appropriate and cultivated speech, his self-control and his faith.

The narrative about Joseph and Potiphar's wife leads to the narrower field of morality, and with it we find ourselves again in very close proximity to an important subject of wisdom literature, namely, the warning against "strange women" (Prov. 2.16; 5.3, 20; 6.24; 22.14; 23.27 f.). Thus the temptation story in ch. 39 reads like a story composed *ad hoc* to illustrate these admonitions of wisdom. This narrative, however, is also important because it shows the absolute foundation upon which the whole educational ideal rests, namely, the "fear of God," i.e., obedience to his commands which is the basis of this art of life (Prov. 1.7; 15.33). Joseph also admits to this absolute obligation (Gen. 42.18). This touches on something essentially important. The older teachers of wisdom did not cultivate a man to seek God and his revelation, but rather they cultivated him on the basis of that revelation. Thus they prescribe training and education which is not standardized by an absolute ideal above them and does not intend to lead to an ideal image. This educational ideal is much less stable and axiomatic, less doctrinaire than most of the modern prescriptions. It lacks every kind of saving pathos especially, and in its concentration on the possible and attainable is much more realistic and even occasionally opportunistic. It also lacks every form of autonomy. Joseph, therefore, appears from beginning to end as a man who is not "in the place of God" (ch. 50.19).

Much later the image of a young man who rose to a high position is again drawn in Israel, namely, in the Daniel stories, especially in Dan., ch. 1. In many respects it is very similar to the Joseph story: the ease with which such a court office is accepted, the test of a genuine way of life based on fear of God, the interpretations of dreams, the counsel, a conflict that leads to a *status confessionis* (Dan. 1.8 ff.). But there are also considerable differences. In contrast to the Joseph story, the Daniel narratives emphasize again and again that Daniel remained loyal to the faith and sacred customs of the fathers. The absence of that in the Joseph story does not mean, of course, that the narrator has any doubt about Joseph's loyalty in this respect. It means rather the contrary, that he takes it for granted, as he understands it; it also means that the great problem of true preservation of faith in heathen surroundings did not yet trouble him. Thus, for example, the question about whether Joseph remained faithful to Yahweh in spite of what is related in Gen., chs. 41; 44.5 is not answered for the reader. All of this is related to the fact that Israel, in the epoch to which the Joseph story belongs, first noticed the great multiplicity and depth of human nature and that it at the same time discovered the possibilities of representing them literarily. One must therefore look at the masterful descriptions of complicated, psychological processes in some sense as a new literary attempt which these storytellers of the Solomonic and post-Solomonic era made. (Think of the "distress of soul," ch. 42.21; the dumb astonishment, ch. 45.3, 26; the mutual looks of fear, ch. 42.28; the agitations of conscience, ch. 43.18; or of Joseph's seething emotion, ch. 43.30.) In its day, of course, Joseph was a modern man and the story about him a modern book.

One does not, of course, attain such a model life as that shown by Joseph overnight. One must first learn it in the difficult school of humility. And that too is the teaching of the ancient wise men, that humility is before honor (*"anāwā*, Prov. 15.33; 22.4); and it is well illustrated in the first part of the Joseph story. But a man who is trained in this way by discipline and self-control radiates something edifying, a beneficent goodness. Of whom is the statement that "the long-suffering man stills enmity" more true than of Joseph? Joseph's abstention from retribution also has convincing parallels in ancient wisdom ("Do not say, 'I will do to him as he has done to me; I will pay the man back for what he has done,' " Prov. 24.29; "love covers all offenses," Prov. 10.12). But Joseph, in his relationship to his brothers, does not limit himself to passive tolerance and forgiveness. He deals with them, and moreover severely and boldly. Joseph exerts an authority that makes the reader anxious and afraid. But Joseph has it because he alone knows how to interpret the completely confused event in the light of God's purpose. This brings us to the actual theological substance of the narrative.

The Joseph story rarely speaks directly about God and matters of faith, considering the great extent of the narrative. But the indirectness with which it does so is striking. Many ancient sagas, as for example the Bethel story, reported a sacred event directly and thoroughly. One cannot speak of the Joseph story in this sense. The event is anything but sacred. Its characteristic is rather a downright realism without miracle, and the narrator himself does not speak about God, but leaves it to Joseph. (One looks in vain throughout the Joseph story for such a direct statement as "and God hearkened to Leah," ch. 30.17.)

Obviously the story recognizes a divine *charisma* in Joseph, that of dream interpretation; but how secular is the whole scene in which it operates (ch. 41.16 ff.)! It is true that the passages in which Joseph really speaks about God have programmatic significance for the interpretation of the narrative as a whole. And here an unmistakable doctrinal intention in the narrative becomes evident. The passages are chs. 45.5–7 and 50.20 f. What was most necessary to say about them was said in the exposition and will not be repeated here. Both texts point to God's saving rule, which is concealed in profound worldliness. This rule of God for the salvation of men continuously permeates all realms of life and includes even man's evil by making the plans of the human heart serve divine purposes, without hindering them or excusing them. The human heart is therefore the principal realm for God's providential and guiding activity. This again is a favorite theme of the wise man: "A man's steps are ordered by the Lord; how then can man understand his way?" (Prov. 20.24). This statement could entitle the whole Joseph story, for it is very similar to the statement in ch. 50.20. It is also related to Prov. 16.9, "A man's mind plans his way, but the Lord directs his steps." This all-sufficiency of divine sovereignty makes human action almost irrelevant (cf. Prov. 21.30). This is expressed in the Joseph story in the fact that with respect to the brothers' guilt there is no moral pathos, no passion to expose it or define it more precisely; and that is certainly noteworthy for guilt of such proportion. Retribution is, of course, clearly recognizable (ch. 42.21 f.), and Joseph does not excuse anything either (ch. 50.20). But in the statement that God has included this dusky terrain of human guilt and passion in his saving rule and that in all men's guilty action he has prepared "the great escape," the narrator believes that forgiveness, too, is implied.

The reader must remember, however, that Joseph's statement in ch. 50.20 expresses something extreme by its downright abrupt separation of divine and human activity. It relegates God's activity to a radical secrecy, distance, and impossibility of recognition. So long as the charismatic interpreter was there, as in the Joseph story, there was no danger. But what can happen when man is left alone with this radical knowledge as such is shown in the book of Ecclesiastes. There the question "How can a man understand his way?" already has an undertone of despair (Eccl. 3.11; 7.25; 8.17; 11.5). The skepticism of this book has roots which go very far back.

Finally, the Joseph story is closely related to wisdom literature in the fact that its statements of faith about God and his rule seem completely detached from covenant theology, from reference to Yahweh's special plans for Israel, in other words, from all sacred history. But precisely in this last matter there has been a further decisive change, for the great collector and shaper of the whole patriarchal history has finally included even the Joseph story in the theme of the promise to the patriarchs (see above, pp. 22f.). This subsequent anchoring of the Joseph *Novelle* in the great historical plan into which Yahweh drew the lives of Abraham, Isaac, and Jacob, is achieved above all in ch. 46.1–5. Any perceptive reader will recognize that the theme and mode of portrayal differs considerably from the bulk of the narrative. It is equally striking when, after the decisive theological point has been made (ch. 50.20), Joseph finally goes on to speak of the promise of the land which was given to the fathers (ch. 50.24), for here we have a circle of ideas which is far removed from the original narrative. But this incorporation of the Joseph story into the larger complex of the patriarchal stories (which we perhaps have to ascribe to the Yahwist) is of great theological significance, for the guidance of divine providence, which the Joseph story portrays in so many mysterious ways, is now part of the great historical plan which Yahweh drew up in order to call his people Israel into existence. The "great escape" which Yahweh brought about so marvellously (ch. 45.7) now means more than the saving of a whole family from famine, and the remark about the God who can turn evil devices to good (ch. 50.20) extends still further, for it touches on the whole mystery of the biblical saving event.

The interpretation of the Joseph story given here began from the presupposition, widely accepted today, that whole stretches of the Elohist have been incorporated into the main Yahwistic recension. It should not be forgotten, however, that voices are continually raised in support of the view that the source theory (apart from the undisputed contribution of the source P) is not applicable to this narrative complex (most recently D. B. Redford, *A Study of the Biblical Story of Joseph*, SVT XX, 1970; also O. H. Steck, *Die Paradieserzählung*, Biblische Studien 60, 120 ff.). Larger or smaller discrepancies are obvious. But they must be regarded as glosses, as subsequent interpolations or as constructions of whole narrative variants. By means of this explanation it is possible to argue for a single narrative complex. But the explanation fails in an analysis of all the Pentateuchal material, which both before and after leads to the assumption of the dualism of a Yahwistic and Elohistic recension. This is not, of course, an answer to the question whether the Joseph story also shares in this dualism. But the question cannot be answered on the basis of the Joseph story alone; it must come from a comprehensive new analysis of the Pentateuchal narrative material, which we urgently need.